D0723587

digital media

# net_condition
## art and global media

edited by

**Peter Weibel**
and
**Timothy Druckrey**

**steirischer herbst**
**Graz, Austria**

**ZKM**
**Center for Art and Media**
**Karlsruhe, Germany**

**The MIT Press**

**Cambridge, Massachusetts**
**London, England**

## Initial Conditions

## Social Conditions

## Media Conditions

## Community Conditions

700.1
NET
2001

## Ideological Conditions

## Critical Conditions

## Artistic Conditions

Artistic Conditions

## Urban Conditions

## Economic Conditions

## Power Conditions

## Working Conditions

*Logo: Ecke Bonk*

# The Project

Peter Weibel

## I (scope)

The *Art and global media*. An exhibition in the media space project took place over a period of approximately two years (October 1998 - February 2000) in a number of cities (Barcelona, Graz, Karlsruhe, Tokyo), in various media, and in collaboration with several partners. The project was launched in 1998 as part of the *steirischer herbst* festival in Graz, Austria, where it focused on the newspaper, poster, video, film and television media. The project was concluded in 1999-2000 at the Center for Art and Media (ZKM) in Karlsruhe, Germany, where the focus was shifted to the network medium. In addition to the *steirischer herbst* festival and the ZKM, the partners of the *Art and global media* project included the museum in progress in Vienna, Austria, the Schubert-Kino cinema and the KIZ-Kino im Augarten cinema in Graz, the Austrian daily newspaper *Der Standard*, Austrian television (ORF), the global newspaper combine World Media Network, the British art magazine *n.paradoxa*, the Media Centre d'Art i Disseny (MECAD) in Barcelona, Spain, and the Intercommunication Center (ICC) in Tokyo and their journal *InterCommunication*.

The *Art and global media* project was a networked, multimedia and multilocal event. The aim of the project was to make us aware of and visualise the way the media change and construct reality with the aid of a media project taking place primarily in the media space. Logically enough, the global network plays a key role in a project exploring the global conditions of art and media. The aim of holding an exhibition in the media space, from print media to electronic media, from television to the World Wide Web, is essentially to leave the traditional places and institutions of exhibitions such as museums, galleries, etc. Ideally, an exhibition focused on the social, economic and political consequences of the new media can only take place within these very media. In what is a kind of placelessness, an exhibition was organised mainly taking place in the new media themselves. In this case, the traditional material places and cultural institutions served as a basis for extending artistic activities from local physical spaces into the immaterial global information space. The media conditions were geared to the production and distribution conditions of the artistic projects. Poster actions took place, films were screened in cinemas, TV films shown on television, media installations featured in exhibition spaces, and net projects on the net.

The *Art and global media* project tended towards a form of realisation in the global media space, so it was not tied down to any particular venue or local time. The project left behind both the traditionally limited structures of space and time to which an exhibition is amenable and the restrictions in terms of media. The works produced by the artists in the media for the Internet, TV, cable television, radio, film, daily newspaper, magazine and poster media were published at specific points around the globe in these media. The international networking of the artistic contributions corresponded to an inter-media networking. Some of the contributions connected one medium to another and were acted out in several different media - one medium is reflected on in another medium. Television works analyse how news is constructed in newspapers (*Noam Chomsky Reads the New York Times*, Paper Tiger Television, 1985, 1986), or what cultural transformations the telephone brought about (*Avital Ronell, The Call*, GRENZ-film, Vienna, 1998). Media and media constructions of reality and media fictions are reflected on in the media. How is intimacy coded on the net? What kind of news do we see on television? What kind of politics do we read about in newspapers?

The way media construct society, history, memory, politics, market, economy and knowledge is the main focus of the *Art and global media* project. All over the globe we are seeing how the media have formed and taken over the traditional

**Art and Global Media**
Una mostra sui media, nei media, per la durata di
festival steirischer herbst – Graz / museum in p
Locations:
World Media Network
http://www.xspace.at

Initial Conditions

functions and operators involved in the construction of reality. To an ever increasing extent, the construction of the world is being dominated by the media. Society is increasingly becoming a media society. This is why media observation is increasingly taking the place of world observation in art. From law to financial markets, from leisure to the world of work, from eroticism to politics, there is no social sphere that isn't decisively shaped by individual and mass use of media. Thanks to the interplay of the global economy and global mass media, there are emerging new social structures, new classes and hierarchies, new forms of economic and political power. This project about media in the media was not only about portraying the representation of reality in the media, it was rather about a new approach, namely to shed light on the different methods with which reality is constructed in the various media.

## II (film)

A first major project in Graz in 1998 explored film as a medium of the representation and construction of reality. Retrospectives curated by Peter Weibel featuring the overall oeuvre of three outstanding representatives of three generations of critical documentary film, Joris Ivens, Chris Marker and Harun Farocki, provided some typical examples.

Joris Ivens (1898 – 1989), after formal movement studies *Études des mouvements* (1928), *De Brug* (1928) and above all *Regen* (1929), began his actual documentary work with *Wij Bouwen (We Are Building)* (1929), *Philips Radio* (1931), and *Misère au Borinage* (1933), which were protests against the conditions of the economic and social system that engendered so much misery. *Nieuwe Gronden* (1934) was his first collaboration with the composer Hanns Eisler. For many people, *Nieuwe Gronden* (1934) is Ivens' masterpiece. Afterwards, Ivens did not make any more films in Holland for more than 30 years, but rather worked in Moscow, Spain (*Spanish Earth*, 1937, with a commentary by Ernest Hemingway), in China (*The Four Hundred Million*, 1938), and from 1938 to 1945 in the USA. In 1946 he shot *Indonesia Calling* and in 1949 he depicted the constitution of the socialist societies of Czechoslovakia, Bul-

garia and Poland in *Pierwze Lata (The First Years)*. In Eastern Europe he also shot the famous film *Das Lied der Ströme* (1954) with music by Dimitri Shostakovich and texts by Bertold Brecht, a celebration of the world-wide labour movement with material from 32 nations. In 1956 Ivens settled in Paris where he remained until his death, apart from travel for his numerous works abroad. In 1963 he shot *...A Valparaiso* in Chile with a commentary by Chris Marker. In 1965 he made *Le ciel, la terre (The Threatening Sky)* in Vietnam.
In 1967 he began working with his later wife Marceline Loridan (*Le dix-septième parallèle*, 1968; the 12-hour film *Comment Yukong déplaça les montagnes*, 1973-76).

Chris Marker (1921, lives in Paris) wrote for André Bazin's magazine *Cahiers du Cinema*, from which the main representatives of the *Nouvelle Vague* emerged. In 1955 he visited Peking with Gatti and shot the film essay *Dimanche à Pekin*. In 1964 he made his only fiction film, the legendary science fiction film *La Jetée*, that consisted solely of still frames apart from the moment in which a sleeping girl opens her eyes.
*Si j'avais quatre dromadaires* (1966) is comprised of 800 photographs taken by Marker in 27 different countries over a period of ten years. In 1967 Marker initiated the collective film *Loin de Viêt-Nam* with contributions from Resnais, Godard, Ivens, Lelouch, Klein and Varda. After May 1968 Marker mainly worked for the film collective SLON, that was to become ISKRA in 1974 (Images, Sons, Kinescope, Réalisation Audiovisuelles in allusion to Lenin's newspaper *Iskra*). In 1974 Marker began filming under his own name again. In 1977 he analysed the hopes of international leftists in *Le Fond de l'air est rouge* in a very personal style. In the 1980s he shot *Sans Soleil* (1983) and a portrait of Akira Kurosawa *A.K.* (1985) in Japan. In the words of Michel Chion "Chris Marker has made one of the best documentaries ever filmed on the making of a film." Marker's interest in film as a medium of memory, both in terms of the private and collective, becomes increasingly evident. In *Level Five* (1996) he searches for the traces of memory in a video game database. After the death of Simone Signoret he created the documentary film *Mémoire de Simone*

*Helix* by eichinger oder knechtl, werkraum and virtual real estate (A) in the daily paper *La Stampa* (I), 6/27/1998 (Collaboration with World Media Network)

Peter Weibel

(1986). In *Sans Soleil* he says "I wonder how people who don't film, don't photograph, don't do video can remember, I wonder what humanity does to remember."

Harun Farocki (1944, lives in Berlin) attended the film academy in Berlin (in 1966) and made his first film, *Nicht löschbares Feuer* (1969), that focused on the war against Vietnam (1998 remake by Jill Godmilow in collaboration with Harun Farocki.) Afterwards he collaborated with Hartmut Bitomsky, *Die Teilung aller Tage* (1970) and *Eine Sache, die sich versteht* (1971). Since 1972 he has been an author and, from 1974-1984 , editor at *Filmkritik* magazine. Between 1972 and 1977 he mainly earned a living in television. In 1978 he made his film treatise *Zwischen zwei Kriegen* (1978) on the relation of economy and Fascism and followed that in 1982 with a film about the Vietnam war, *Etwas wird sichtbar* (1982). By the 1980s he was developing his own type of film with *Wie man sieht* (1986) and *Bilder der Welt und Inschrift des Krieges* (1988), a film about the different learnable role plays in life, life as a test: *Leben-BRD* (1990). At the end of the Ceausescu regime in Romania he made *Videogramme einer Revolution* (1992) together with Andrei Ujica. Since 1992 he has been guest lecturer at the University of California, Berkeley, and, with Kaja Silvermann, co-authored *Speaking about Godard* , a book in dialogue form (1998). His recent films are *Die Umschulung* (1994), *Schnittstelle* (1995), *Der Auftritt* (1996), *Stilleben* (1997).

What these representatives of three generations have in common is the fact that their work is woven around the big historical conflicts and political constellations of the twentieth century. The scenes of the anti-Fascist and anti-colonial wars and the great political transformations were their locations - the Spanish Civil War, battles in China and Russia, strikes and demonstrations in Australia and Chile, the Algerian War, the Vietnam War, the revolution of 68, etc. Ivens and Marker were cosmopolitans, tirelessly travelling to the world's flash points and taking a stand for the oppressed, the disenfranchised, and revolutionaries by means of their social documentaries. Their image stories were images of history. Joris Ivens in particular, but also Chris Marker, are film

artists operating at the forefront of the global revolutions. Whereas Joris Ivens, trained as he was by the formal mastery of Walther Ruttmann, Dziga Vertov, Jean Vigo, and by the visual anthropology of Robert Flaherty, was still a convinced humanist who saw film as an instrument of political struggle, Chris Marker had realised that the war of men was matched by a war of images and that there is a common logic in both. His films are personal comments rather than pamphlets in the name of collectives. Where Ivens married the register of perception and the register of the social sphere in a formally differentiated manner, in his film essays Chris Marker shows us how the images of history are constructed by the stories that images tell. A criticism of images begins to take shape in Marker's work. Harun Farocki focuses directly on the registers of the visual as instances of the social, presenting the "images of the world" as an "inscription of war" (1988). "Philosophy asks: what is man? I ask: what is an image? Images have too little importance in our culture." (Harun Farocki)

Chris Marker from political siding in Joris Ivens' pictures to political treatment of images in Harun Farocki's work articulates the transition with great precision. What we see is militant cinema that not only declares war on the political actors but also on the images themselves. The camera is not only found at the great scenes of dramatic historical events, but the cutting room, the cutting of the images, becomes the scene of analysis. Political action continues from the macrostructure of politics to the microstructure of images. Political education also takes effect in the images provided by the camera. Education about political, social and cultural contexts morphs into education about the conditions of production of images and social communication. Ivens', Marker's, and Farocki's film essays show how cutting images and sound already served to create or deconstruct constructions of reality in the classical medium of film.

In his films, Marker translated the political and social upheavals that were taking place around the world into an aesthetics that reconciles the subjectivism of Jean Vigo with the documentarism of Dziga Vertov. Marker, originally a writer, returns to the original media of memory, writing and images. Marker uses film as a form of writing, functioning as a medium of memory. His films are film writings that treat events, images and sounds as elements with which the author constructs his reflections. For Marker, culture is memory work. His films oppose the imperial interests of hegemonic political systems to forget and repress certain moments in history, certain utopias. He deploys his discursive images to counter the antidemocratic images of historical unawareness and a loss of experience as supplied by the daily routine of mass newspapers, TV pictures and Hollywood films. Language and images, more so than in the work of Ivens, a child of the silent film era, are united in Marker's films to create the characteristic (film) style of an author who interrupts the endless visual loops of global multimedia systems that destroy knowledge.

Farocki adopts this style of filming, this marriage of language and images, dealing directly with the conditions in which the visual is produced at the global front. He is particularly interested in the social and political conditions of image production. He not only distrusts the industry, but also the images themselves. Thus he analyses how we see, *Wie man sieht* (1986). In his film essays, following the work of Ivens and Marker, he investigates the conditions in which the world becomes images of the world. *Etwas wird sichtbar* (something becomes visible) is the title of one of Farocki's films dating from 1980-1982, a film that makes visible what matters to Farocki: to show how the world is portrayed, to show something of the world by showing how something becomes visible. By showing us the conditions in which the world transforms into a statement about the world, he rectifies the view of the world distorted by the public media and global media conglomerates: *Ihre Zeitungen* (1967), *Ein Bild* (1983), *Videogramme einer Revolution* (1991/92), *Die führende Rolle* (1994). Whereas Joris Ivens depicted civil wars, Farocki portrays wars of images.

But Marker and Farocki not only restricted their film style to the classical medium of film, but also transposed the cinematographic experience to other technical dispositives. Media installations that work with video, CD-ROM and com-

puter, for example *Schnittstelle* (1995) by Harun Farocki and *Zapping Zone. Proposals For An Imaginary Television* (1990/97) and *Immemory* (1997) by Chris Marker, amplify the discursive elements as a result of their intermediality, intertextuality and interactivity. They show us how reality is constructed with the aid of the media.

With their discursive films, Ivens, Marker and Farocki declare war on the "undeclared war" (David Puttnam, 1997) of the Hollywood film industry, a war for global control of image production and distribution. They oppose the industrial mechanisms of image construction and the related media mechanisms of the construction of reality. Their discursive films form artistic, productive and distributive models of independence in the bought-out, commercialised global public space. If film is the real art of the twentieth century, Ivens, Marker and Farocki count among the film artists who have added the language of images and sound to the work of writing and language. In 1977 Michel Foucault called for philosophers to "become more sensitive to events. Philosophers must become journalists." Ivens, Marker and Farocki are exactly this kind of critical philosophical journalist in the global media age. Their film essays provide standards for analysing the media conditions of the construction of the world.

## III (symposium)

One of information technology's fundamental effects on the world of today is that it allowed a global economy characterised by an almost instantaneous flow of information, capital and cultural communication. Advanced information technology and the process of globalisation cannot be divided. The outlines of the previous 'world order,' characterised by North-South relations and which resulted in a political landscape of three worlds, have undergone a fundamental transformation in the age of the information society and global media. We are seeing the dissolution of the three worlds theory 1) the Western world of the European/North American axis, 2) the now defunct Eastern bloc and, 3) the poor developing countries, witnessing the emergence of a "fourth world" (Manuel Castells) excluded from the global information flow and which, as such, can be found in certain places in both the First and Second worlds and in the Third World. The affluence of the industrialised nations of the First World hinges more than ever on exploitation of the Third World. Increasing the efficacy of exploitation is served by an information and economic network that is also linked with Asia, i.e. a global network. Globalisation is gaining the whole world as its marketplace, safeguarding the continuation of First World colonial hegemony in combination with Asian partners. This explains the trend of the so-called 'free market' towards globalisation. The megafusions of big telecommunications, IT companies, print media, electronic media, content providers and distribution providers (e.g. film companies and Internet firms), banks and insurance companies, are symptomatic of attempts to subdue the global market hegemonically. The global greed of the big media associations, capital conglomerates and industrial groups is expressed in cartel-style or monopolistic dominance of the world market. By means of the monopoly in a single service sector, e.g. software, the aim is to put the global market at the mercy of a single company, e.g. Microsoft. Global expansion means global monopoly.

The architecture of the global economy goes hand in hand with the development of media globalisation, a global network. The rise of a global media market in the late 1980s took place accordingly. The new missionaries of capital increasingly became aware of the significance of a global media culture for the liberal economic market. Global telecommunications systems and the world wide web thus do not serve the previous cultural, instructional purposes of public media companies, e.g. as with state-controlled European TV and radio stations, but rather - as can be seen by the example of private US media systems - we can recognise the negative consequences of media globalisation for the public sphere. The rise and triumph of global neoliberalism can only be seen and comprehended in context with the installation of global media conglomerates and transnational groups that take advantage of world-spanning communication technology, from the telephone to the Internet. The anti-democratic tendencies of neoliberal-

ism and the mass media reciprocally augment their power. Thus, it will be all the more important for us to be informed about the social construction mechanisms of media and the media construction mechanisms of society. This is why media critique and social critique can no longer be divided.

In a society in which civil rights are constantly being diminished by the media construction of the world, art has a historic opportunity to put communication technology in the hands of the individual and to wrest it from the dictates of capital, commercialism and the military. Art has a chance to contribute to recivilising global media technology.

At a symposium curated by Peter Weibel, which brought together a selection of the first social and media theorists to introduce into their writings the data, facts and theoretical concepts that allow a criticism of global media culture, the aim was to investigate and name the effects of the global media on culture and economy. Parallel to the real-world symposium in Graz (featuring Christa Blümlinger, Timothy Druckrey, Edward S. Herman, Diana Johnstone, Bruno Latour, Gerhard Johann Lischka, Robert W. McChesney, Vincent Mosco, Florian Rötzer, Dan Schiller, and Siegfried Zielinski) with the lectures printed in this book, a virtual symposium was also held in the print media and on the net, in which Pierre Bourdieu, Manuel Castells, Jürgen Habermas, Immanuel Wallerstein and Peter Weibel took part.

## IV (newsroom)

The film programme and symposium were accompanied and extended in a local material newsroom in Graz and in the multilocal immaterial newsroom of the media.
As a local indication of the exhibition project *Art and global media* taking place in the immaterial, global public media space of the print and electronic media, there was a physical, local public space, dubbed 'newsroom,' at the *steirischer herbst* organisers' building in Graz, in which visitors were able to inform themselves on site about this project or log in via the website http://www.xspace.at. In this room, visitors were not only able to regularly follow and read all the contributions continuously published in the print

media, but also view some of the video-graphically documented lectures of the participants in the symposium (Siegfried Zielinski, Bruno Latour), specific works by Paper Tiger Television and the essay film *Der Angriff der Gegenwart auf die übrige Zeit* (1985) by Alexander Kluge, etc. This video programme was supplemented by the STROBE trailer by TIV - True Image Vision, Vienna, and productions of the alternative cable TV producers XXkunstkabel, Graz, e.g. with Peter Fend speaking about the *Ocean Earth* and *News Room* projects. A comprehensive media-specific library on the subject of global media was also installed for visitors. Visitors to the newsroom were thus able to inform themselves in depth about the *Art and global media* project with the aid of books, newspapers, videos and the Internet.

In the public space of the print media, the Austrian daily newspaper *Der Standard* not only featured the contributions of the participants in the symposium, but also published contributions of the artists Martine Aballéa, Peter Fend and DeeDee Halleck & David Thorne. Alongside artist interventions and theoretical essays, *Der Standard* also featured a specific series of publications curated by Christian Muhr and Walter Pamminger entitled *Signs of Trouble* which focused on international positions in information design of the 1990s. A new generation of designers, developing aesthetic strategies for the age of global media and mobile information and the knowledge society, was presented: The Designers Republic (GB), Mevis & Van Deursen (NL), David Crow (GB), Michael Rock & Susan Sellers (USA), J. Abbott Miller (USA), Anne Burdick (USA), Cornel Windlin & M/M (CH/F), Tomato (GB) and Jonathan Barnbrook (GB). At the same time, it was also possible to place a visual logo developed by the team of architects eichinger oder knechtl, which served as a link to the http://www.xspace.at website of the project in Graz/*steirischer herbst*, allowing visitors to view all information on the *Art and global media* project globally; the logo appeared in international daily newspapers affiliated with the World Media Network: *Le Soir* (B), *Libération* (F), *La Stampa* (I), *To Vima* (GR) and *La Presse* (CAN).

In addition to artist contributions in daily newspapers, there were also artist contri-butions in art magazines. *n.paradoxa* Vol.3, 1999 (London), published works by Susan Hinnum (DK), *Copulo Ergo Sum;* Edda Strobl (A), *What they do;* Sonja Gangl (A), *REBEKA underwear;* and Lou Ann Greenwald (USA), *Untitled*, while *InterCommunications*, No.30, 1999 (ICC, Tokyo), featured works of Haim Steinbach (USA), *dirty dozen*, and *more or less,* and *Ontological Loneliness within the Alphabet* by Markus Huemer (A). Another public space constructed by the print media were the public billboards. A specially designed poster *Jardin Voyageur/ Travelling Garden* by Martine Aballéa, curated by Ulrich Obrist, was shown in collaboration with the museum in progress (Vienna) in the period of October/November 1998 in Graz and in November/December1998 and January 1999 in 23 European cities.

In addition to these discursive and artistic interventions in the classical media space, i.e. the public space constructed by the print media, there were also discursive and artistic interventions in the public space constructed by the new electronic media. In the electronic media space of television, in collaboration with the Austrian broadcasting company ORF, the *kunst-stücke* series featured existing films on the subject of global media: *Stilleben* (1997) by Harun Farocki, *Manufacturing Consent – Noam Chomsky and the Media* (1992) by Peter Wintonick and Mark Achbar and *Avital Ronell. The Call* (1998) by Susanne Granzer and Arno Böhler. On the other hand, specially produced programmes on the subject of *Art and global media* were also screened under the series title *STROBE* (with contributions by participants in the symposium and news correspondents around the world) by the alternative TV producers TIV - True Image Vision, Vienna, in *kunst-stücke* on ORF television.

# V (net condition)

Under the heading *net_condition. art/politics in the online universe*, the ZKM presented an exhibition that took place in the form of a multilocal networked event simultaneously in Karlsruhe (ZKM), Graz (*steirischer herbst*), Tokyo (*ICC* Intercommunication Center) and Barcelona (MECAD Media Centre d'Art i Disseny).

Peter Weibel

This exhibition, featuring some 100 works, aimed not only at providing a comprehensive overview of the current status of international net art, but above all, to introduce visitors to the political and economic ideas, social practices and artistic applications of on-line communication.

The title *net_condition* is meant at several levels to reflect the conditions introduced by the net, both artistic and social. There are social conditions that necessitate and promote the development of the net. The net, in turn, creates the possibilities and conditions with which the information society can continue to develop. The title is to be seen in this sense: as a social and technical condition. This exhibition is not called net.art, but rather, for the aforementioned reasons, *net_condition*, as it focuses on the social conditions forced into existence by the net, while at the same time exploring the conditions that the net itself imposes on society. In addition to these social conditions, the focus of the exhibition project is on investigating which new conditions the net imposes on the historical media and historical social forms of communication and art. Every new medium relinquishes several characteristics as compared to the previous media, but generally introduces a host of new characteristics that are superior to historical media in terms of certain aspects. Thus, the result of the emergence of new media is not the eradication of the old media, rather the new media subdue the old media to their conditions. "The Photographic Condition" (Rosalind Krauss) has changed painting, video has changed film, digital technology has changed film and video, etc. As a technical dispositive, the net changes music, visual culture and literature.

This is why, alongside net-based two-dimensional images and texts on screen, we see net-based installations that adequately widen the overly narrow definition of net art. Net-based installations are the latest stage of media art after the video-based sculpture of the 1980s and the computer-based, interactive installations of the 1990s. In net-based installations, the changes and advances of net art are particularly clearly demonstrated by two traits: firstly, the net forges a link between the local, physical, real and material space of the *hic et nunc* and the dislocated, virtual, immaterial space of

the information sphere. The net, then, consists of islands of non-locality. We are not driving as if in a car along a continuous space-time, as the information highway metaphor would erroneously have it, but rather we are jumping from one local time to another, from one location (locus) to another. The structure of the non-locality, introduced by the telephone and television, is amplified by the net. The arena of the action is enlarged from the image to the global information space.

For the first time, dislocation and non-locality allow communication beyond the local horizon. Up to now of course, the viewer and the image were in the same local horizon. Even in an interactive computer installation, the viewer and the image were in the same space at the same time. Interactive net art makes it possible for the image and the viewer to be at different places at different times. For the first time, images, texts and sounds are not tied to specific localities, to the viewer's locality. Secondly, the interaction is not unidirectional, monosensory and irreversible, as was previously the case. Even in computer installations the viewer's movements, e.g. touching a plant, triggered movements in the image, e.g. the simulated growth of artificial plants. The movement in virtual space, however, had no repercussion on real space, the growth of virtual plants had no effect on real plants. In a computer-based net installation, for the first time the relation between the image and the viewer is reversible, i.e. it takes place in two directions: the information flow passes from the viewer to the image, from real space to virtual space, and from the image back to the viewer, from virtual to real space. Net activity in virtual space controls the sequence of events in real space and the events in real space control the sequence of events in virtual net space. The reversible nature of the effect between real and virtual, between local and non-local, is the next stage of radicality after interactivity. The virtuality of storing information, the variability of the image content and the viability of image behaviour in the interactive computer image is followed by the reversibility of the effect and simulation of non-locality, two characteristics of the algorithmic artificial image that are perhaps even more radical than interactivity. Interactivity which is reversible and which dislocates, is the

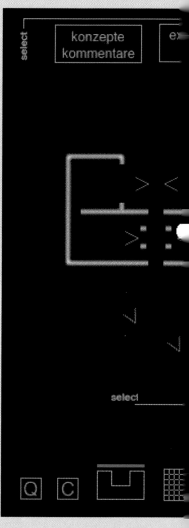

laut / dialekt  |  visuelle arbeiten  |  szenische arbeiten  |  übersicht

play movie ▶

Die Wiener Gruppe
(TheVienna Group), 1997

new characteristic of net-based computer installations.

Distributed virtual reality, shared cyberspace, non-local communication, multi-user environments, web TV and net games are thus the focal issues of this exhibition. In this context, the net_condition is not only explored in terms of image media, but also with regard to sound media. Net-based music and NetRadio are thus important aspects of the exhibition.

## VI (examples)

As artistic director of *Ars Electronica*, I already dedicated the festival to the net phenomenon in 1995, under the heading "Mythos Information. Welcome to the Wired World." As part of this festival I myself performed an Internet opera that took a critical look at the ideological conditions of the creation of Wagner's music: *Wagners Wahn oder das heilige Land des Kapitals. Cyberoper für Bühne und Inter-*

*net* (1995). (*Wagner's Mania or the Holy Land of Capital. A Cyberopera for Stage and Internet*) I also commissioned an Internet game, implemented by Orhan Kipcak from Graz, as an art game at the virtual Brucknerhaus (the base of the Ars Electronica festival). At the occasion of the *Biennale di Venezia* 1997 I also commissioned an internet presentation of *Die Wiener Gruppe (The Vienna Group)* by Orhan Kipcak.

### Internet project: *The Vienna Group, Biennale di Venezia 1997*

At the *Venice Biennial 1997*, a digital multimedia information system was introduced on the net that presented the history and works of the Austrian avant-garde group Die Wiener Gruppe from the 1950s and 1960s (H.C. Artmann, Friedrich Achleitner, Konrad Bayer, Gerhard Rühm, and Oswald Wiener). The work was commissioned by the Austrian Commissioner of the Biennial, Peter Weibel, who also played a substantial role in editing the contents of the project.

The version showed in Venice totalled 3 GB (hard drives were used as data storage media). The information system was installed on two terminals; a spin-off version in the form of a web database with a VRML interface, produced by adm, was accessible for one year on the net at http://wienergruppe.at.

A CD-ROM version of the project was completed in summer 1998 and added to the publisher's list in September 1998 as a digital supplement to the printed publication *Die Wiener Gruppe – ein Moment der Moderne* (Springer-Verlag, Vienna/New York). The CD shows key works of The Vienna Group, interviews with the protagonists and documents the exhibition situation at the Austrian pavilion. In order to give an impression of the size of the Biennial version, which could not be accommodated on this CD for technical reasons, we added the *Text-und Bildmatrix feature*. The application attempts to synchronise both diachronic and thematic access to the contents from a single interface.

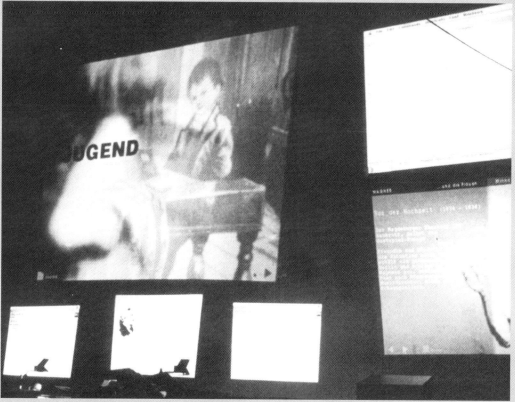

16

*Wagners Wahn oder das heilige Land des Kapitals. Cyberoper für Bühne und Internet, 1995 (Wagner's Mania or the Holy Land of Capital)*

**Internet Project: *Wagners Wahn oder das heilige Land des Kapitals. Cyberoper für Bühne und Internet***

During *Ars Electronica* 1995 (June 20–23) information about Richard Wagner was made availabe to the public via www. A worldwide online-discussion on the subject of *Wagners Wahn*, moderated and participated in by Peter Weibel, took place via IRC-server during the performance.

In the Foyer Brucknerhaus two multimedia-terminals were installed which gave visitor access to the Ars-Electronica-software *Wagners Wahn*. At the same time video-inserts from the Wagner-www-infopages, which had been especially set up for this event, were fed into the terminals along with inserts from the online-discussion via internet and the events on the stage. The paths of information that the users of the *Wagners Wahn* software

travelled became part of the performance in the auditorium. In the Brucknersaal (Bruckner Auditorium), during the performance of Wagner's *Wesendonck Lieder*, video projections of the *Wagners Wahn* CD-ROM (operated from the multimedia terminals in the foyer), web pages on the subject of Wagner and of the online discussion constituted a telematic, electronic stage set.

ARSDOOM, 1995
Orhan Kipcak/adm (concept, production design)
Reinhard Urban (scripting), Curd Duca (sounds), Helmut Blasch (connectivity) and others (a total of 16 individuals worked on implementing this project) The virtual exhibition was curated by Peter Weibel and Orhan Kipcak ARSDOOM was available free of charge via the Internet.

Another important internet project I commissioned at *Ars Electronica* 1995 was *ARSDOOM* by Orhan Kipcak.

*ARSDOOM*, an art adventure (1995) was the first digital, virtual exhibition to allow action and interaction at the technical level of computer games. *ARSDOOM* was presented at "Mythos Information" and was accessible via LAN and the Internet. The computer action game about art and artists showed the works of approx. 20 artists from Austria and the US.

A digital model of the Brucknerhaus (the venue of *Ars Electronica*) served as a virtual exhibition site. Based on the action/adventure game *DOOM*, there evolved a world of real-time 3D animation, texture mapping, and ray casting, populated by modernist artist icons. Virtual visitors and artists interact amidst digital objects and images. The visitor was able to slip into the stylistic signa-

tures and artistic techniques that turned the artists into trade-marks. The visitor roaming around the virtual exhibition at the Brucknerhaus was able to turn over every object and every work with the Baselitz tool, spray everything black with the Rainer gun, etc. However, visitors to this exhibition were also attacked by digital alter egos of the artists present, but they could also defend themselves.

The work was one of the attractions of *Ars Electronica* 95. *ARSDOOM* came to be the legendary precursor of numerous interactive 3D environments brought forth by media art in recent years.

The network capacity of *ARSDOOM* allowed up to four users to interact. In addition, it was possible to visit the virtual environment we had created from anywhere in the world via the Internet – *ARSDOOM* thus became an event in the space of information technology.

# VII (from DEW to DOCS)

The technological revolutions, to which the civil society at the close of the twentieth century owes its technical advance, are for the main part the results of mid-twentieth century military research or applied research in the service of the military. Control and communication technologies, e.g. the computer, which constitute the foundations of post-industrial information society, were developed particularly during World War II. The takeoff of the Russian *sputnik* on 4 October 1957 not only marked the advent of space travel and the manifest peak of the Cold War, but was also indirectly the beginning of the net age. The Department of Defense was so shocked by the Russian lead that they commissioned a defense system intended to identify and thwart air strikes early. The superiority or rather equal strength of the Russians in terms of atom bombs and long-range bombers was a cause of concern to the US government at a very early stage. Thus, in 1951, the US Air Force commissioned the Lincoln Laboratory at the military, industrial think-tank (MIT, Boston) to devise an air space defense system that could discover, identify and attack enemy aircraft. This system was dubbed DEW (Defense Early Warning). In 1951 the psychologist J. C. R. Licklider was also called to the Lincoln Lab, one of the founding fathers of cyberspace, for which he laid the first foundations with his "Man-Computer Symbiosis" paper in 1960. 'Symbiosis' was not only the first draft of interactive computing in real time, but also the first blueprint for a "computer network, connected to one another by leased-wire services." In 1962, J. C. R. Licklider published a first Internet concept, "Online Man Computer Communication," together with Walden Clark. The group at the Lincoln Lab began using computers very early on, withdrawing them from the Whirlwind project, another military MIT undertaking. Whirlwind was replaced at the Lincoln Lab by SemiAutomatic Ground Environment (SAGE), another defense project operating on the basis of room-sized storage systems and vacuum-tube computers. SAGE was the first computer network to span the United States and thus the basis for the computer and digital communication industry. IBM was the main contract partner for SAGE computers and went from being business machine spe-cialists to the world's biggest computer manufacturers. Two of SAGE's employees were Kenneth Olsen and Harlan Anderson, who could build computers cheaper and smaller than IBM. They founded the Digital Equipment Corporation (DEC). Another employee of the Lincoln Lab was Len Kleinrock, who published his seminal work on "Information Flow in Large Communication Nets" in 1961, that contains the sentence "The nets considered consist of nodes that receive, sort, store, and transmit messages entering and leaving by way of links." In 1964, Kleinrock published a doctoral thesis entitled *Communication Nets*. Internet technology is not only indebted to him for its theory, but also for "packet switching," the key invention behind the Internet. In 1962 Paul Baran at the Rand Corporation published his report "On Distributed Communication Networks."

After the Russians had launched a second sputnik, President Eisenhower founded the Advanced Research Projects Agency (ARPA) in 1958, whose aim was to cluster all space and strategic rocket research. ARPA began their hi-tech research in the field of information processing on an initial budget of 150 million dollars. The department of ARPA that was actually to supply the foundations for today's networked information society was originally called Command and Control Research, and as of 1965 Information Processing Techniques Office (IPTO), and its first director in 1962 was J. C. R. Licklider, the prophet of the "Intergalactic Computer Network" (1963). Licklider recruited Robert Taylor, manager at NASA, to his department at ARPA in 1962. Ivan Sutherland, inventor of Sketchpad, succeeded Licklider in 1965. Sutherland appointed Bob Taylor associate director of IPTO. Taylor took over from Sutherland in 1966. Taylor, in turn, hired Larry Roberts (from Lincoln Lab) to be a program manager for ARPA in 1966. Roberts was to become the primary architect of the ARPAnet. Roberts, a friend of Kleinrock's, performed the first network experiment to link two remote computers, the TX-2 at Lincoln and the Q-32 mainframe in Santa Monica, in 1965 by commission of Sutherland, Director of IPTO at ARPA. In 1966, Larry Roberts and Thomas Marill published a report on this network experiment "Toward a Cooperative of Time-Shared Computers."

The first original ARPAnet design paper was published in 1967 by Lawrence Roberts, "Multiple Computer Networks and Intercomputer Communication." ARPAnet first went public in 1969 in the form of computer installations (distributed computing) at UCLA and at Stanford Research Institute. There Doug Engelbart, the inventor of the mouse, headed the Augmented Human Intellect Research Center and at a famous lecture held at the Fall Joint Computer Conference in San Francisco in 1968 demonstrated networked computers, video conferencing, hypermedia and hypertext, windows, etc. Bob Taylor left ARPA in 1969 and Larry Roberts became the fourth director of IPTO. Bob Taylor founded the Computer Science Laboratory at the newly opened Xerox Parc in 1970. In 1970, Norm Abramson developed the Alohanet, while Bob Metcalfe from Xerox PARC developed the Ethernet in 1973. He had expanded the Alohanet packet radio concepts and applied them to cable technology. Robert Kahn and Vincent Cerf published "A Protocol for Packet Network Interconnection" in 1974. The first personal computers began to appear between 1975 and 1976, from the Altair 8800 to Apple. In 1980, Tim Berners-Lee wrote a program entitled 'Enquire Within,' a precursor of the WorldWideWeb from 1990. The CSNET (Computer Science N1ETwork) for universities and research facilities was also created in 1980. IBM announced its personal computer in 1981, while Microsoft, numbering 40 employees, created the DOS Operating System. In 1984 there were 1000 hosts on the Internet, and in 1989 there were already 100,000 hosts. In the 1960s Bob Taylor, Len Kleinrock, Frank Heart, Severo Ornstein, Larry Roberts, Wes Clark, Dave Walden, Bob Kahn and others began implementing the idea of computer networking with ARPA at the Pentagon, Washington, that was to change to world.

A new world is constructed. The world goes on-line. On-line communication creates new technical conditions for globalisation. A new global economy emerges, no longer primarily based on products, but rather on time. The net allows the economy to restructure: no longer do people pay for the product, but rather use of the product is billed on the basis of units of time. As a result, the key forces of economic development shift from the primary and secondary sphere of production to the tertiary sector of marketing, communication, information and other services. A net-based economy requires an unprecedented upheaval in our historical perceptions of society and the subject. Questions of the social and private sphere - from new forms of a community shaped by information technology to gender identity politics - are posed in new ways through the net. Society has attained a complex state of development in which a technological instrument such as the net has become necessary for it to work. Society invents the net in order to differentiate and distinguish itself as an information society. The global net is the driving force of a radical economic, social and cultural revolution at the beginning of the next millennium, whose contours are made visible for the first time at this exhibition.

Net art, from physical local installations to world-wide networked computer games, has become the forum in which many of the emancipatory hopes of the historical avant-gardes are being rephrased. Web art is a form of art to which the great political hopes are linked. The socio-revolutionary utopias of the historical avant-gardes and educational movements such as freedom of contract, equal opportunities and inter-cultural emancipation are now set to be redeemed by technology.

Modern art created the aesthetic object as a closed system as a reaction to the machine-based industrial revolution. Post-modernism created a form of art of open fields of signs and action as a reaction to the post-industrial revolution of the information society. At the moment, net art is the driving force most radically transforming the closed system of the aesthetic object of modernism into the open system of the fields of action of post-modernism (or Second Modernism). A Cold War military project, DEW (Defense Early Warning), evolved to become a global medium of communication, DOCS (Defense Of Civil Society).

The net has not only become a new medium for artistic practises but comparable to the revolution of plein air peinture, which led to Impressionism and modern art, artists for the first time operate with the net in a global medium beyond geopolitical borders.

SIMMS LIBRARY ALBUQUERQUE ACADEMY

Timothy Druckrey

To: weibel@zkm.de
From: Timothy Druckrey <druckrey@
Subject: [...]J8~.g#|\;NET.ART{–s1[...
cc:
bcc:
attachments:

Timothy Druckrey

I remember so well the comments you made at the *Transmediale 98* in Berlin where you proposed the phrase "the net condition" as a signifier of an emerging sphere in which increasingly contingent artistic events were creating a framework in which experience and information disputed the hierarchies of modernity, the rhetorical traps of postmodernity, and its incorporation within a nearly inevitable economic homogenization. In this context, there is both a long and short history of telecommunications media, technology, and art practice, histories that oscillate between resistance and assimilation. It is in this sphere that the histories of technical media and creative approaches to staging are so intricately discursive and potential.

In the particular case of the net, a differentiated arena has emerged, one that is catalyzed by practices that are transitional, unstable, event-driven, nomadic, or, in your term, a 'condition.' The term 'condition' is intriguing for number of reasons. A "state," "attribute," "disposition," "stipulation," is linked with some if its synonyms: "situation; circumstances; station; case; mode; plight; predicament;..." (according to Webster's) to suggest that this *noun* establishes itself in a context of referring, to behaviour, and emerges too in mathematics, logic, and particularly, in programming. "Conditional expressions are one of the most important components of programming languages because they enable a program to act differently each time it is executed, depending on the input."[1]

Yet the term 'net_condition' is also distinctly rooted, as you note, in Krauss' seminal essay "The Photographic Conditions of Surrealism" (that demonstrated the reciprocity between technology and representation ...) and is echoed in her recent book on Marcel Broodthaers, *A Voyage on the North Sea: Art in the Age of the Post-Medium Condition*. A reflection on the crumbling "specificity" and "formalism" of both the academy and theory, the term "medium" resounds with its art historical context and falters before the real condition of *media* culture. Indeed the conclusion of the extended essay reverberates with a characterization of "the international fashion of installation and intermedia work, in which art essentially finds itself complicit with a globaliza-

tion of the image in the service of capital."[2] A distinct over-simplification, this kind of diagnosis surely finds many adherents in the left-over aesthetics of a telephobic modernity still expecting to find legitimacy in the somehow uncompromised margins of the art world. Few, if any, of Krauss' generation (particularly the Americans) have extended their analysis into the realms of communication technologies and the public sphere. This is what so interestingly suggests that the phrase 'the net_condition' complicates the thinking of traditional art theory with a precise linking of its terms to evoke the cultural effect in which the media - and not the medium - constitute the broad terrain in which experiences are articulated, expressed, and distributed.

In this context it is interesting to find struggling discourses still attempting to frame, or de-frame modernism, notably in recent works by Bruno Latour and T.J. Clark, but also in assessments of the so-called 'second modern.' Latour's *We Have Never Been Modern* is filled with assessments of the struggle to find a coherent approach:

"... by multiplying the hybrids, half object and half subject, that we call machines and facts, collectives have changed their topography. Since this enlistment of new beings had enormous scaling effects by causing relations to vary from local to global, but we continue to think about them in terms of the old opposite categories of universal and contingent, we tend to transform the lengthened networks of Westerners into systematic and global totalities. To dispel this mystery, it suffices to follow the unaccustomed paths that allow the variation in scale, and to look at networks of facts and laws rather as one looks at gas lines and sewage pipes."[3]

For Latour modernity is either unfinished or unachievable while for T.J. Clark it is to be in the trial of art and expression. In *Farewell to an Idea: Episodes from a History of Modernism* he writes: "It is because the 'modernity' which modernism prophesized has finally arrived that the forms of representation it originally gave rise to are now unreadable (or readable only under some dismissive fantasy rubric - of 'purism,' 'opticality,' 'formalism,' 'elitism,' etc.) ... Modernism is unintelligible now

                          FNC Resolution:
                       Definition of "Internet"
                             10/24/95

--------------------------------------------------------------------

On October 24, 1995, the FNC unanimously passed a resolution defining the
term Internet. This definition was developed in consultation with the
leadership of the Internet and Intellectual Property Rights (IPR)
Communities.

--------------------------------------------------------------------


RESOLUTION:

  "The Federal Networking Council (FNC) agrees that the following
   language reflects our definition of the term "Internet".

   "Internet" refers to the global information system that --

   (i)     is logically linked together by a globally unique address
           space based on the Internet Protocol (IP) or its subsequent
           extensions/follow-ons;

   (ii)    is able to support communications using the Transmission
           Control Protocol/Internet Protocol (TCP/IP) suite or its
           subsequent extensions/follow-ons, and/or other IP-compatible
           protocols; and

   (iii)   provides, uses or makes accessible, either publicly or
           privately, high level services layered on the communications
           and related infrastructure described herein."

--------------------------------------------------------------------

                  Last modified on October 30, 1995

Questions or Systems problems should be reported to FNC_Webmaster@arpa.mil.
--------------------------------------------------------------------

because it had truck with a modernity not yet fully in place. Post-modernism mistakes the ruins of those previous representations, or the fact that from where we stand they seem ruinous, for the ruin of modernity itself - not seeing that we are living through modernity's triumph."[4]

In some ways Latour and Clark sustain the retroactive debate about modernity and its discontents with extraordinary clarity (perhaps hindsight is better), but with too little regard for the present as more than a repository for its cumulative symptoms. Though easily encompassed in a "recognition of the social reality of the sign," and equally "of turning the sign back to a bedrock of World/Nature/Sensation/Subjectivity," (as he thoughtfully suggests), the failure of modernity was in sustaining a decisive relationship with technologies and not merely subjectivities. Much of postmodern theory suffers the same overdetermination of subjectivity in the service of leveling the hierarchies in often tortured readings of a culture reeling in the effects of mass media but, more often than not, without unmasking the programming ideology embedded in the history of the so-called 'postmodern condition' - rightly characterized by Lyotard (and far less by his followers) as a situation in which computation "... is changing the way in which learning is acquired, classified, made available, and exploited. It is reasonable to suppose that the proliferation of information-processing machines is having, and will continue to have, as much of an effect on the circulation of learning as did advancements in human circulation (transportation systems) and later, in the circulation of sounds and visual images (the media)."[5] But as we understand in hindsight, the 'crisis of representation' was not merely a narrative issue, but one heading on a collision course with virtualization.

Rather than the 'rubrics' (tropes is more like it) of 'opticality,' 'purism,' etc., modernism was invested in centrality, the centrality of vision, the centrality of the body, the intellect, the institution, subject, authority, curatorship and the museum. Sustained in ideologies of focused distribution or dispersal, centralization maintained its power enveloped by the technologies of representation linking it with broadcast media.

Of course, there's little doubt that this 'unconditional' media of modernity (largely ignored in twentieth century art theory), and in particular the broad sweep of broadcast media, have been eclipsed in the model of a transnational distribution system represented by the netcast metaphor - centrality revived in databases and distributed systems. Even a cursory look at the history of the tele-communications industry can serve to signify that the metaphor of mergers and consolidations - done under the twin disguises of necessity and efficiency - is a not so subtle cover for centralization under the not so subtle 'rubric' of globalization, a shift that Armand Mattelart identifies as one from "economies of scale" to "economies of scope." Hence it is not insignificant that the implicit conflicts in this shift are finally crossing out of the aesthetic into the social spheres in forms signified by a willingness to expose the WTO and World Bank, Project Echelon, and the race to totalize an international wireless network, as signifiers of consolidation and hegemony outside any representative legal accountability. Indeed, the multinational, now they say planetary, corporation seems a suitable illusion for the reduction of difference in across-the-board homogenization and the marginalization of opposition. The 'second modern'? Thus, as the network has emerged, centralization comes to herd willing artists into located ideologies manageable by predictable notions of legitimation - particularly the legitimation of *technique*.

Like it or not, Benjamin's "one-way street" has been superseded by the 'superhighway.' But greater notions of creative mobility aside, this shift has not come without clear links between the scam of multi-nationalism, the incorporation of multi-culturalism, or the racket of multi-media. Deeply powered by government and corporate technologies, the net has well-established continuities with the trajectory of frenzied globalization, even while it is often marketed as 'revolutionary,' counter-cultural, and democratically empowering. This apparent contradiction has not escaped either the artists or theorists engaged in developing reasoned approaches to working in the electronic and new networked sphere.

Despite the marketing of the net as a 'global village' (with McLuhan as its cosmopolitan patron saint), the promotion of the web as the 'global brain,' the repository of 'collective intelligence,' the consolidation of the web as a vast database 'mined' for user-profiles or surveilled for incriminating communication, a remarkably flexible community has emerged whose concerns are deeply and critically engaged with a cultural sphere in which the 'condition' is understood as a 'state' in which permutations supplant resolutions, in which stability is merely a special condition of instability, where localization is not abandoned in faux globalization, or where creativity, critique, or communication is not relinquished to empty promises of a world without history, otherness, identity, opposition, discourse, or art.

The first World Wide Web Conference was held in CERN in 1994. This followed several dizzying years in which the first browser was written by Tim Berners Lee (not incidentally called "WorldWideWeb," and later Nexus) in 1990. By early 1993, Marc Andreessen's alpha version of Mosaic was released in collaboration with the NCSA. At this point the web traffic on the NSF backbone accounted for about 0.1% of net communications. The CERN conference even awarded an overall prize (drawn from 12 categories) for Best Overall Site. It went to NCSA! No art category in this list, but the availability of an easily installable, cross platform, and functional browser was the catalyst for a decade of explosive development whose reverberations continue to rattle every assumption about the stability and organization of culture! In this sense it comes as a slight shock that the FNC (the US Federal Networking Council, a division of ARPA) took until 1995 to draft a resolution defining the internet!

Within months (see Tilman Baumgärtel's text in this volume), the net generation, already working in the BBS systems gravitated (with some exceptions) to the then easily manageable coding of HTML. Already in 1993 one of the first net art symposia was held in Graz: "OnLine: Kunst im Netz" (organized by Robert Adrian X and Gerfried Stocker). This event, and the volume that accompanied it, brought together the generations of artists working in video and satellite work (Roy Ascott, *Electronic Café*, Richard Kriesche) and opened the net to theory (Florian Rötzer, Friedrich Kittler, Heidi Grundmann) and to an emerging generation that included Ponton (VGTV), Hilus, Armin Medosch, Eva Ursprung, and others. "The metaphors," wrote Robert Adrian X, "of machinery and processes are giving way to metaphors of circuitry and oscillation."[6] Indeed the range of materials in the proceedings shows persuasively that a critical and artistic generation had already mobilized to merge an already long history of electronic art with its most dramatic implementation.

Within a year, Peter Weibel, then artistic director of *Ars Electronica*, was conceptualizing "Mythos Information: Welcome to the Wired World" that opened in June 1995. "*Ars Electronica 95*," wrote Weibel, "gives critical and euphoric experts an opportunity to appraise this brave new net-worked world."[7] An extraordinary moment, the symposium and exhibitions brought together a dizzying array of artists, historians, and theorists whose names have become synonymous with the net.art, net.culture, and net.activist domains (Florian Rötzer, Pierre Levy, McKenzie Wark, John Perry Barlow, Geert Lovink, Saskia Sassen, Melita Zajc, Michael Bielicky, David Blair, Eva Grubinger, Markus Huemer, *Internationale Stadt*, Knowbotic Research, Public Netbase, The Thing, Stadtwerkstatt, amongst others). "Critical and euphoric" was apropos for an event that was the first to establish a formidable international discourse concerned with the formative phase of what would become net.art.

In many ways the watershed years of 1994 and 1995 also saw the establishment of the *Digital City* project in Amsterdam, artnetweb in NY, and the formation of the nettime and syndicate mailing lists (see Walter van der Cruijsen's essay in Working Conditions). "<nettime>," in a text from January 15, 1995 by Geert Lovink and Pit Schulz, "was born out of the immediatist 'Medien ZK' gatherings, a series of open, informal, international meetings centered around 'netculture and its discontents' in Spessart, Venice, Budapest and now Amsterdam. Herein, we discussed telecom policies, multiple personalities, the city metaphor, neo-vitalists, Californian Ideologies, *Wired*

critique, tribalism in the net and elsewhere, the tragic end of net.art, the
comeback of the Enemy (Telekom,
Scientology, Netscape)..." Over the past
five years nettime has indeed stood as
the focal point for the development of a
critical approach to net culture that has
included postings from every corner
of the world covering every aspect of
the debate about the dot.culture world.
The nettime mailing list, archive
>>www.nettime.org<< and its pivotal
readers, ZKP 1 - 5 (which is the published anthology README!), are indispensable for any reasoned understanding
of electronic culture. The first extended
discussion of net.art appeared in ZKP 4
with a special section with contributions
by Robert Adrian, Olia Lialina, Alexej
Shulgin, Josephine Bosma, Joachim
Blank, Mark Amerika, Jano Sugar,
Marina Grzinic and others. Indeed it
was a posting on nettime that coined
the term net.art. It came in this posting:


>>Date: Tue, 18 Mar 1997
>>From: easylife@hawk.glas.apc.org

>>Net.Art - the origin

>>I feel it's time now to give a
>>light on the origin of the
>>term - "net.art". Actually, it's a
>>readymade.

>>In December 1995 Vuk Cosic
>>got a message, sent via
>>anonymous mailer.
>>Because of incompatibility of
>>software, the opened text
>>appeared to be practically
>>unreadable ascii abracadabra.
>>The only fragment of it that
>>made any sense looked
>>something like:

>> [...] J8~g#|\;Net. Art{-^s1 [...]

>>Vuk was very much amased
>>and exited: the net itself gave
>>him a name for activity he was
>>involved in!
>>He immediately started to use
>>this term. After few months he
>>forwarded the mysterious message
>>to Igor Markovic, who managed
>>to correctly decode it. The text
>>appeared to be pretty controversal
>>and vague manifesto in which
>>it's author blamed traditional
>>art institutions in all possible

>>sins and declared freedom of
>>self-expression and independence
>>for an artist on the Internet.
>>The part of the text with above
>>mentioned fragment so strangely
>>converted by Vuk's software
>>was (quotation by memory):
>>"All this becomes possible
>>only with emergence of the
>>Net. Art as a notion becomes
>>obsolete...", etc.

>>So, the text was not so much
>>interesting. But the term it undirectly
>>brought to life was already in
>>use by that time. Sorry about
>>future net.art historians - we don't
>>have the manifesto any more.
>>It was lost with other precious
>>data after tragic crash of Igor's
>>hard disk last summer.

>>I like this weird story very
>>much, because it's a perfect
>>illustration to the fact that the
>>world we live in is much richer
>>than all our ideas about it.


The syndicate list emerged from
Rotterdam with an equal commitment
but a slightly different emphasis: "In the
autumn of 1995, V2_Organisation has
taken a new initiative, V2_East, which is
aimed at creating a network of people
and institutions who are involved with
or interested in media art in Eastern
Europe. More than sixty people in nine-
teen countries are connected to the
V2_East / 'Syndicate' mailing list where
they exchange information which is also
collected on a website,
(www.v2.nl/east/). V2_East wants to
create an infrastructure that will facilitate cooperations between partners in
East and West, and it will initiate collaborative media art projects." Working
with and helping to sustain open channels, the syndicate list widened the cir-
cumference and extended the discourse
of media and its art practices into the
nascent - but decidedly active - net
communities in Moscow, Sofia, Estonia,
Belgrade, St. Petersburg, Albania,
Sarajevo, Bulgaria, etc,. A small excerpt
from the excellent essay "Small Media
Normality for the East" by Inke Arns
and Andreas Broeckmann, from the
Deep Europe anthology, will suggest a
perspective:

"Throughout the Cold War, the public propaganda machines of the east and west told their great stories of the crime ridden system of exploitation and of the Evil Empire. At the same time, the readers and watchers in the east were better prepared for what was to follow and what now not only affects the pseudo-east, namely, learning how to live, as the Agentur Bilwet put it, in the society of the debacle."[8]

Within a short time the proliferation of mailing lists (7-11, rhizome, faces ... ), web initiatives (C-Theory, adaweb, the thing, public netbase, *kunstradio*, *Internationale Stadt*, the DIA center, *Telepolis*...), symposia, and books, dedicated to net culture, net.art, on-line communities, net critique, etc., grew as swiftly as did the diversity of on-line artistic projects and cautiously critical approaches to the 'euphoria' of the net. The issues that emerged in the rapid-fire art (as is well documented in this volume) and theory that surged in this setting set a rich agenda that has framed a discourse identified as *Media Archaeology* in which an assessment is being made of the distinct effects that technology has played across a number of disciplines including art, media, literature, philosophy, science, cinema, and sound. Already there are several generations who are affiliated with this approach. From Max Bense and Vilem Flusser through the work of Oswald Wiener, Otto Rössler, Gerhard Lischka, and into the works of Gilles Deleuze, Felix Guattari, Armand Mattelart, Regis Debray, Paul Virilio, joined by Peter Weibel, Friedrich Kittler, Siegfried Zielinski, Bernard Stiegler, Margaret Morse, Erkki Huhtamo, Heidi Grundmann, Florian Rötzer, and a newer generation of Geert Lovink, Pit Schulz, Lev Manovich, Andreas Broeckman, Josephine Bosma, Inke Arns, Kathy Huffman, Hans Ulrich Reck, and many, many others, a complex history is being realized in which the rethinking of modernity is set within the deep study of how the trajectory of culture and its representations have been enveloped in technologies - historical, theoretical, and speculative.

A few citations will help contextualize the range of concerns and commitments coming from these figures:

Vilem Flusser:
"Electronic memories can receive information more easily than brains can and they have a much larger storage capacity. They are better at preserving information and can recall individual items more easily. It is also not difficult to transmit information from one electronic memory to another. All these (and other) advantages mean that acquired information (data) will no longer be stored in brains but in electronic memories. As a consequence, brains will be free to adopt other functions. People will no longer have to memorize facts but learn how to store, recall and vary data expediently. They will no longer need to learn systems' repertoires but instead their structure. Data processing of this kind - which had been checked by the need to learn facts - is called "creativity"; hence, we can now reckon with a true burst of human creativity."[9]

Gerhard Lischka:
"We can speak of media art only if the artistic intent asserts itself within a certain medium: unlike the usual seedy eyewash. It makes no difference if the medium is used pure, mixed, or in new combinations. The emphasis will always be on passing on that spark to real life to intermediary action and performance."[10]

Armand Mattelart:
"Mass culture seizes on our attitudes... and packages them for our consumption...meanwhile - and this is the masterstroke - the interests which offer these products to the public...are able to claim as an alibi that all they have done is to encapsulate in the cultural product our free will and free choice...(1980) ..."
"What this eschatological belief in the 'information society' hides is the fact that, as the ideal of the universalism of values promoted by the great social utopias drifted into the corporate techno-utopia of globalization, the emancipatory dream of a project of world integration, characterized by the desire to abolish inequalities and injustices in the name of the imperative of social solidarity, was swept away by the cult of a project-less modernity that has submitted to a technological determinism in the guise of refounding the social bond. (2000)."[11a, b]

Regis Debray:
"Not 'where does this information come from and what does it mean?' but 'what

1. www.pcwebopaedia.com

2. Rosalind Krauss, *A Voyage on the North Sea: Art in the Age of the Post-Medium Condition* (Thames and Hudson, London, 1999) p.56.

3. Bruno Latour, *We Have Never Been Modern* (Harvard University Press, 1993) p.117.

4. T.J. Clark, *Farewell to an Idea: Episodes from a History of Modernism* (Yale University Press, 1999) p. 3/4.

5. Jean Francois Lyotard, *The Postmodern Condition: A Report on Knowledge* (University of Minnesota Press, 1985) p. 4.

6. Robert Adrian X, "Zero: The Art of Being Everywhere," in *On Line/Kunst im Netz* (Steirischer Kulturinitiative, 1993) unpaginated.

7. Peter Weibel, "The Noise of the Observer," in *Mythos Information: Welcome to the Wired World* (Springer Verlag, Wien/NY, 1995) p.22.

has this new information transformed in the mental space of this collective and its devices of authority'?"[12]

**Paul Virilio:**
"Thus, after the development of the transport networks in the nineteenth and twentieth centuries, with the network of networks, the Internet, comes the imminent establishment of *real networks of transmission of the vision of the world*, the audiovisual information superhighways of those on-line cameras which will contribute, in the twenty-first century, to developing the *panoptical* (and permanent) tele-surveillance of planetary sites and activities, which will very probably end in the implementation of networks of virtual reality. This is a *cyberoptics* which will leave intact neither the old *aesthetics* that was a product of European modernity, nor the *ethics* of the Western democracies."[13]

**Gilles Deleuze and Felix Guattari:**
"The depths of shame were plumbed when computing, marketing, design, advertising, all the communications disciplines, seized upon the word 'concept' itself, as if to say: this is our business, we are the creative people, we are conceptual! It is profoundly depressing to learn that 'concept' now designates a service and computer engineering society."[14]

**Peter Weibel:**
"In this zone of electronic feudalism, media art would have the task of liberating itself from its slavish function towards the industry and to transform the media into an instrument of the citizens in this age of media, emancipating itself from a mechanical art and evolving to become free art. In the techno-industrial complex, what is involved is a new dynamics between art, culture, and technology, between society and technology, a mapping of this dynamic of the art work itself. In this age of global displacements, the role of the mass media is to create a network to strengthen historical forms of rule by restructuring them. In view of the fact that the big companies themselves are becoming the driving force of global displacements, art, specifically media art - if it can recall its original function at all - will have the task of analyzing this displacement and its causes within the global network so as to create the conditions for a resistance to the new feudalisms and the new vertical structures of mediacracy.'"[15]

**Siegfried Zielinski:**
"Thinking further along the lines traced by others, Georges Bataille for example, I attempt to think and write about the previous technical and aesthetic and theoretical richness of the development of artefacts of media articulation heterologically. In this concept both re-construction and the conception of possible future developments rub together. Against the enormously growing trend toward the universalization and standardization of aesthetic expression, particularly in the expanding telematic nets, the only strategies and tactics that will be of help are those that will strengthen local forms of expression and differentiation of artistic action, that will create vigourously heterogenous energy fields with individual and specific intentions, operations, and access in going beyond the limits that we term mediatization."[16]

**Friedrich Kittler:**
"The project of modernity had essentially been one of arms and media technology... all the better that it was shrouded in a petty phraseology of democracy and the communication of consensus."[17]

**Pit Schulz:**
"... an interface is not an image. it can be a plug, the ringing of a telephone, some push buttons, or the parameters of a program. it is not a one-to-one simulacrum, but a one-to-one-to-another-one transmission of parallel streams, a process of translation between different levels of code. the interface limits a system as a 'membrane' for transitional elements. it has nothing to do with a TV screen. it is constitutive for the definition of systems and works not for 'humans' only but also between and within machinic aggregates. it does not have to end in visuality or a neo-baroque garden of an expensive art installation. Visuality can become an ideology of enlightenment. Trying to expose the mysterious under light is where we speak about the hidden in terms of optical media. I see therefore I understand. the net has no given visuality but it produces a lot of narratives and works as a universal plane of projection. like the Ocean in Stanislav Lem's *Solaris* it functions as a 'cathartic interface' (Perry Hoberman). more a gigantic group ther-

apy then an athenic agora but fundamentally based on the interconnected subjectivity of its users which leads to the questions of social network architecture, cultural groupware and a redefinition of urban life."[18]

Andreas Broeckman:
"The theory of network creativity, and of the creative use of digital media in general, has emphasised the fact that this technology empowers every user of a computer to become a creator and to participate in the 'global concert' of online artists. Even if digital media theoretically offer this possibility, what we can see now is that the same network environments might be of exclusive interest for those people who actually want to become producers. Participation becomes not only an option, but a condition. If this is true it means that the Brechtian utopia of a community of media producers could fail once again, in part because commercial interest prevents strong uploading channels, but in part also because large sections of the prospective producer-receivers would make no use of the tools and the bandwidth, even if they were available."[19]

Kathy Rae Huffman:
"The question about how to personalize one's identity, one's persona is important. There is relative ease in the sending and receiving of e-mail, it can be quite spontaneous, so how we emote our feelings or reactions with words alone - and with symbols - furnishes all the underlying enthusiasm for the ideas, and the direction of the communication. CYBERSPACE provides a place for the body without boundaries, and the interconnection of individuals with machines is an essential element of CYBER theory. This discussion is being articulated by many theoreticians, artists and scientists, who seek answers for survival and understanding of our human position, and relationships in the future. Many ask the rhetorical question, that as more and more high technology surrounds us - is the need greater for more human touch?"[20]

Slavoj Zizek:
"Agents also 'mediatize' us. Since my cyberspace agent is an external program which acts on my behalf, it is easy to imagine the paranoiac possibility of another computer program controlling and directing my agent unbe-

knownst to me - if this happens, I am, as it were, dominated from within..."[21]

"Freedom exists only where intelligence and courage succeed in cutting into inevitability."[22]

The international developments in the field of media no longer reside in the mega-cities that seem to be proliferating in the media world. This is spectacle. In spite of the ever more breath-taking mergers between portals and so-called 'content,' much of the mania in the field of telecommunications seems headed towards foreclosure rather than extension. Indeed, the focus of so much of the hype for 'new' media often comes at the expense or the severing of any reasoned relationship with experiences in the now glibly prosaic 'real' world. Little attention is given to reflection, history, or consequences of a mediasphere whose development traverses the entire history of modern culture. Of course every technological transformation has emerged under the sign of revolution and collapses under the weight of domination. And in the culture of speed we are, in the words of Eric Kluitenberg, facing a "fatal acceleration towards the immediate."[23] In the instability, uncertainty of this endophysical morass, we are yet promised that technology will become ever more friendly, ubiquitous, embedded, powerful, and subtle, that technoscience has found the code and will program a debugged genetic future.

The spheres of the public, as is abundantly clear from the events of the past decade, are caught between the gleaming infosphere, the economic sphere, and the political sphere But between the clean rooms of the infosphere, the speculative economy of virtualized riches, and the potential of electronic repressive tolerance in the political sphere (just think of Echelon or the incorporation of the Life Sciences), is a social sphere in which the socialization of cybernetics comes with significant resistance. To slip into mystification or universalization behind the veil of benevolent globalization, 'neoliberal' capitalism, or systems integration is as much self-deception as it is cowardice. We cannot deceive ourselves with the modest symptoms of satisfaction that come from an uncritical relationship as beta-testers of cultural software systems, nor can we congratu-

8. Inke Arns and Andreas Broeckmann, "Small Media Normality for the East" in *Deep Europe* (Syndicate Publication Series, Rotterdam, 1997) p. 8.

9. Vilem Flusser, "Electronic Memories" in Timothy Druckrey & *Ars Electronica* (eds), *Ars Electronica: Facing the Future* (MIT Press, Cambridge, 1999) p. 203.

10. Gerhard Johann Lischka, "Media Art" in Timothy Druckrey & *Ars Electronica* (eds), *Ars Electronica: Facing the Future* (MIT Press, Cambridge, 1999) p. 187.

11.a: Armand Mattelart, *Mass Media, Ideology and the Revolutionary Movement* (Harvester Press, Brighton, 1980) p. 19
b: Armand Mattelart, — *Networking the World: 1794-2000* (University of Minnesota Press, 2000) p. 120.

12. Regis Debray, *Media Manifestos* (Verso, New York, 1996) p. 7-8.

13. Paul Virilio, *The Information Bomb* (Verso, New York 2000) p. 121.

14. Gilles Deleuze and Felix Guattari quoted in Armand Mattelart, *Networking the World: 1794-2000* (University of Minnesota Press, 2000) p. 119.

15. Peter Weibel, "On the functional transformation of electronic media art in the nineties" (distributed at the "Media and Ethics" conference, Helsinki, September 1996 and published on nettime.

16. Siegfried Zielinski, "Media Archaeology," (published on *C-Theory*, 1995) Unpaginated.

17. Friedrich Kittler, "The History of Communication Media" in *On Line/Kunst im Netz* (Steirischer Kulturinitiative, 1993) p. 71.

18. Pit Schulz, posting to nettime (Date: Fri, 04 Apr 1997 , 23:12:28 +0200)

19. Andreas Broeckman, "Are You On-Line?" in Timothy Druckrey & Ars Electronica (eds), *Ars Electronica: Facing the Future* (MIT Press, Cambridge, 1999) p. 441.

20. Kathy Rae Huffman, Interview, published on nettime.

21. Slavoj Zizek, "Cyberspace, or, The Unbearable Closure of Being," *The Plague of Fantasies*, Verso, New York, 1997, p.42.

22. From the corresponden- ce between Roger Caillois and Victoria Ocampo, Paris- Buenos Aires, 1956, quoted in Armand Mattelart, "Against Global Inevitability" in *Key Issues in Global Communications*, 2.99. unpaginated.

23. Eric Kluitenberg, "The Politics of Cultural Memory," in Stephen Kovats (ed) *Ost- West Internet: Media Revolution* (Campus Verlag, Frankfurt/NY, 1999) p. 201.

24. Siegfried Zielinski [for *Paris Revue Virtuelle*] (1995), published on http://www.khm.uni- koeln.de/~mem_brane/

late ourselves for posing alternative operating systems, or appease our responsibilities for being 'outside' the system. As Critical Art Ensemble write it, "The profit machine is on...."

Our responsibility is perhaps not so much to turn the machine off, as it is to reprogram it, break the assumption that creativity in the media, net, or web is the brainchild of the computer, soft- ware, or telecommunications industry. Nor can we continue to extend our assessments back into an art world that continues to endorse the endless 'legiti- mation crises' of art as a symptom of modernist culture's endless errors, on recklessly tottering assumptions that 'new media' is merely the logical off- shoot of video, performance, or installa- tion art, or on already wearisome sup- positions that the world wide web represents the only artistic frontier. The web is an array of relations. It can be merely functional. But it can also be truly "connective, tactical, tendential, operative" (to use the words of Christian Huebler of Knowbotic Research), it can be a zone of discourse, of transforma- tion, it can figure a set of relationships beyond the predicted performance of its protocols, and can still pose a dynamic strategy to constitute a community un- imagined by the engineers of on-line commerce.

The *net_condition* is brazen, impertinent, reflective, and not limited to the symp- tomatic *mise en scène* of closed systems. The works emerging are often open ended, invoke critiques of the central- izing effects of illusory communities (as opposed to imaginary ones), interrogate technology itself as self-justifying, and deconstruct the presumptions of univer- sality or authority that have come to mystify cyberspace. Without acceding to inevitability, the net sphere and its art will have to find its way past its initial condition and prompt a reconsideration of the compelling interdependence bet- ween technology, communication, and creativity. As Siegfried Zielinski writes:

"What we need are models of working toward, models of intervention, of oper- ation (opis = fortune, riches). This is what taking action at the boundary, that which I call subjective, targets: strong, dynamic, nervous, definitely processual aesthetic constructions ... not in order to assume a virtual identity

there that can then be retrieved in this or that state, but to demonstrate the impossibility of constructing identity through the exchange of pure symbols. The deficits that these constructions exhibit, namely that, quasi reeling, they have lost their connection to the real, is that which needs to be developed as their strength: they produce new, auto- nomous realities ... at the boundary bet- ween art, politics and natural science - that, daydream-like, develop beside our experiences and our experience into constructs of the mind, visionary models, precipitating meaningful inter- ference with order, turbulence but also inertia, they irritate, they help to make greater complexity imaginable."[24]

# The Net and
## Working notes for a
# informational

# the Self
# critical theory of the
# Society

A process of structural transformation is underway in most societies. It stems from the combined impact of a major technological revolution based around information technologies, the emergence of an informational/global economy, and a process of cultural change whose main manifestations are the transformation of women's position in society and the rise of ecological consciousness. The new world disorder, the demise of Communism and of Marxist-Leninist ideology, are also fundamental trends of a new historical epoch. Indeed, I will argue that the collapse of the Soviet Empire is partly the consequence of its inability to manage the transition to the informational society. A number of social theories are trying to grasp the meaning of this structural transformation without indulging in futurology, while resisting the temptation of technological determinism (Barglow, 1994; Beniger, 1986; Bourdieu and Coleman, 1991; Giddens, 1991; Harvey, 1990; Imai, 1990; Ito, 1991; Lash and Urry, 1994; Lyon, 1998; Martin, 1998; Miles et al., 1998; Monk, 1989; Salvaggio, 1989; Touraine, 1992; Williams, 1988, among others). They generally agree on the centrality of knowledge, information processing, and symbol manipulation in generating wealth and power in our societies. This is why I call this society 'information-al', to indicate that social attributes of information generation and processing go beyond the impact of information technologies, just as the industrial society could not be reduced to the diffusion of industrial machinery. This article intends to contribute to a growing stream of research and thinking that aims to provide a theoretical compass to navigate uncharted courses in new historical waters. In so doing, it seems useful to start by assessing classical theories of post-industrialism that still provide, implicitly or explicitly, the framework to analyze processes of transition towards a new social structure.

## Theories of post-industrialism

It is a striking paradox that the theory of post-industrial society was formulated, in its essential nucleus, in the late 1960s and early 1970s (Bell, 1973; Touraine, 1969), just before the blossoming of the information technology revolution. Yet today's social theorizing of structural transformation is still dominated by these harbingers of a broader set of social and economic interpretations elaborated around that time (Fuchs, 1968; Machlup, 1962, 1980; Porat, 1977; Richta, 1969). These theories, while being highly diverse, concurred on the idea that the industrial society (not capitalism) was historically superseded in its logic and structure. The fact that the theory anticipated the major technological discoveries to come (e.g. the microprocessor in 1971; recombinant of DNA, 1973; personal computer, 1974-76; formation and diffusion of the Internet in the 1970s and 1980s, etc.), shows that information technologies are an essential component of current processes of transformation, but not their single determining factor. Technologies are induced by social and institutional demands for the tasks they can perform, and they are shaped by the social characteristics of these demands. In turn, they become sources of basic transformations in the way we produce, consume, manage, live and die.

In its essence, the theory of post-industrialism starts from a major empirical observation: productivity and economic growth organize societies around their own logic, both in the work process and in the distribution of the wealth thus generated. In this sense, the theory is in line with the Marxian tradition. Furthermore, the engine for the transition to post-industrialism is the process of innovation that transforms productive forces, emphasizing the role of science and technology as sources of productivity growth. However, a further elaboration of this statement complicates the issue. Technology is not just science and machines: it is social and organizational technology as well. Technological change implies the simultaneous change of productive forces and social relationships. Thus, in the econo-

metric analyses used in support of post-industrial theory (Kendrick, 1961; Solow, 1957), it was argued that productivity growth was essentially dependent on the combination of production factors (capital and labor) rather than coming from adding more capital or more labor. These analyses showed that productivity growth resulted mainly from a mysterious, unidentified 'statistical residual' in the equations characterizing the aggregate production function. It was hypothesized that such a 'residual' was the empirical expression of science, technology and management.

Because science, technology and social technology were considered to be critical forces in inducing productivity growth, and thus sustained economic growth, social processes and institutions were to be deeply involved in the productive forces. In this view, the various dimensions of society become more interdependent, economy and technology were more than ever under the influence of government, and therefore largely conditioned by political processes. Post-industrial societies, organized around social choices, are more directly political than either agricultural societies (organized around survival in a hostile Nature) or industrial societies (organized around processes of economic accumulation).

Under such new productive conditions the occupational structure becomes more diversified. The expansion of 'services' means an ever-growing extension of human work beyond the sphere of direct, material production. Post-industrial societies were characterized, and even defined, by the employment shift from goods-producing to service-handling activities. The demise of agriculture and manufacturing to the benefit of 'service activities' is the hard empirical trend repeatedly used by social theorists as evidence of post-industrialism. The concomitant transformation of occupational structure features the rise of higher-educated social strata, such as managers, professionals and technicians. The substantial growth of scientists and managers, both in absolute numbers and in their share of total employment, is of critical importance in post-industrial theory. They occupy the strategic position in the new social organization.

Social change is not limited to changes in the social structure. It also relates to a new social dynamics, structurally opposing certain interests, and creating new centers of conflict and power-making (the *situses*, in Bell's terminology). The theory offers two different, but not mutually exclusive, hypotheses on what are the central social conflicts in the new society.

First, control over knowledge and information decides who holds power in society. Technocrats are the dominant class, regardless of the fact that political power is exercised by politicians controlling the state. Who are the 'dominated' classes? The answer of post-industrial theory on this point becomes more tenuous. In any case, they are not the workers, but the 'citizens', 'consumers', 'communities', the 'non-participant population'. But they are also those professionals and experts who, while being a part of the productivity establishment are not part of its power system. As Touraine argues, the agents of change may be the professionals leading the alienated citizens, opposing the professionals/technocrats. The environmental movement could be a good example of the new kind of social movements in the informational society: scientists and experts mobilizing consumers and citizens via the mass media, on the basis of processing and communicating information about health, safety and the conservation of Nature.

Second, the analysis of new social dynamics becomes easier if we define the structural logic behind opposing interests. The dominant interests are those of scientific-technological rationality and economic growth. The alienated (rather than dominated) interests are those of specific social identities. In Touraine's words the fundamental opposition is between productivity and private life; or, in Bell's words, between meritocratic technical elites and the communal society. The mass media is the crucial site for the playing out of the socio-cultural battle, while the major social institutions expressing the orientations of society as a whole (education and health) are the privileged situses for power 'games.'

Theories of post-industrialism emphasize (and this point is crucial) that they place the defining structural principle of the new (post-industrial) society on a different axis than the one opposing capitalism to statism (or collectivism). Their distinction concerns the technical relations of production, not the social (property-based) relations of production. Both axes must be considered when trying to understand any specific society.

In assessing theories of post-industrial society a quarter of a century after their original, path-breaking formulation, several questions have to be dealt with in order to understand our societies, and, by extension, societies of the 21st century.

(1) Although all theories reject ethnocentrism and proclaim the diversity of national and cultural expressions of post-industrialism, their formulation in fact refers exclusively to the American and Western European experience. This is particularly embarrassing in the 1990s, when one of the most economically and technologically advanced societies, Japan, has to be taken into the picture. Indeed, it was Japanese writers who, in the mid-1960s, first elaborated the concept of information society (*Johoka Shakai*) (Hayashi, 1987; Ito, 1991). And yet, post-industrial theory has not taken into consideration the original Japanese path of socio-technical transformation, nor has it truly engaged in a dialogue with Japanese scholars (Shoji, 1990), except under the form of futurology for ideological consumption (Masuda, 1990). It is essential to incorporate in the theory of the new social structure not only the experience of transformation of Japan and other countries, if we are to correct the 'Western' (actually Anglo-Saxon, with a French touch) interpretation of informationalism.

(2) The relationship between manufacturing and services, the internal differentiation of service activities, the specification of information processing and knowledge generation activities, are questions still open to empirical research. Japan and Germany, arguably the informational economies with the highest gains in productivity and competitiveness in the last two decades, are also those with the higher proportion of manufacturing employment, and with the slowest long-term decline of manufacturing activity. Linkages between manufacturing and

services are complex, and have been transformed by technological change, thus excluding a simple opposition between 'secondary' and 'tertiary' sectors: Colin Clark's taxonomy must be buried at last, with all due respect (Castells and Aoyama, 1994).

(3) Although the theory has not been invalidated by the blossoming and diffusion of the revolution in information technologies since the mid-1970s, the historical experience of the last two decades allows for a full assessment of original hypotheses in the light of the actual transformation of the technological paradigm. For instance, Bell's emphasis on 'new intellectual technology' (such as simulation models), has been much less relevant than he forecasted, while the penetration of microelectronics at the work place has truly revolutionized work, organization, productivity and competitiveness. Biology, not physics, is the decisive science of the 21st century. Computers have induced decentralized networks, rather than centralized institutions. And universities do not seem to have emerged as the central institutions of the post-industrial society: corporations and their ancillary networks, hospitals/health-care organizations, school systems and the media, are such central institutions, deeply transformed by the use of new information technologies.

(4) Theories of post-industrialism generally overlooked the importance and specificity of women in the social structure, and the transformation of the women's condition in advanced societies, with the exception of Bell's addition (in the foreword to the 1976 edition) on expanded opportunities of employment for women in post-industrial society. Yet the experience of the last two decades, and general theoretical reasons, suggest that specific analysis of women's roles and practices is not only a cornerstone of any social theory, but is particularly relevant to the understanding of the informational society (Calhoun, 1994).

(5) Another fundamental difficulty with post-industrial analyses is that they refer to economic growth as the overarching value of our societies. It is not necessarily

so. Power, sheer power, has been all through human history as fundamental a goal for society as the generation of wealth – and still is in the new, emerging society. Thus, the stimulation and appropriation of science and technology as a means of military power, have been as influential as the knowledge basis of productivity in re-shaping our societies during and after the Second World War. Bell shares Herman Kanh's view that 'military technology' is the new mode of production. But this is quite an ambiguous formulation and this fundamental point is not fed back into the theory. Furthermore, extended power through symbol manipulation in electronic multimedia - setting aside their potential interactivity - is the new frontier of technological innovation. Thus, it would seem that economic, military and symbolic systems of power-making under the new technological paradigm must all be included in the analysis as dominant instances of social organization, breaking with the implicit economicist view of post-industrialism.

(6) Post-industrial theory, both in its classical and contemporary versions, does not pay attention to a fundamental feature of our societies: we live in an interdependent, global economy whose internal linkages, particularly in the organization and circulation of capital, have closely connected economic systems and cultural traditions across national boundaries (Carnoy et al., 1993). To be sure, societies are not reducible to their economies. But it seems to be intellectually unacceptable that social structures could be analyzed independently of what happens at the level of the economic structure. This point could be accepted by post-industrial theories as far as it refers only to the North, namely OECD countries, as Bell explicitly mentioned the issue in his book. But what about the rest of the world? Bell, again, identifies the problem, but declares it to be 'the outer limit of our trajectory – a problem for the twenty-first century' (1976:486).

As for Touraine, over the years, he has extensively and thoroughly analyzed the contemporary dynamics of dependent societies (Touraine, 1988). However, in both cases (and, a fortiori, in less elaborated formulations of post-industrialism), the new social structure is analyzed as specific to dominant, Western societies. With some rare exceptions (Dordick and Wang, 1993; Katz, 1998) less advanced societies are considered to be external to the system. Neither their effects on post-industrial societies or those of post-industrial societies on developing societies are taken into consideration. This approach reduces the explanatory power of any theory, not only because it leaves most of the planet out of its scope, but because it misses essential points concerning the dynamics of most advanced capitalist societies. Critical examples that justify this assertion are the following: the crisis and eventual demise of the Soviet Empire cannot be understood without considering the internal contradictions generated in the Soviet economy and in the Soviet military machine by the inability of statism to assimilate the information technology revolution and its social implications (Castells and Kiselyova, 1995); the growing internal differentiation of the former Third World between newly industrializing countries (e.g. in the Asian Pacific), relatively self-sustaining societies (India, China) and decomposing societies (much of sub-Saharan Africa), has much to do with the different degrees of integration and adaptation to the processes of the informational economy (Carnoy et al., 1993); immigration from the South to OECD countries is the consequence of a pattern of asymmetrical integration of labor in different levels and areas of an interdependent system (Portes and Rumbalut, 1990); the explosion in the production, traffic and consumption of drugs (a fundamental feature of our economies and societies) is related both to the new infrastructure of communications, to new (criminal and speculative) financial networks, and to the social/psychological demands specific to informational societies in contradiction with old moral and religious structures (Laserna, 1995). In sum: a theory of the informational society that does not place global economic interdependence at its heart will be of limited value in understanding the actual structure and processes of our societies, be they advanced, developing or stagnant. It is certainly easier to theorize advanced capitalist societies by considering them strictly from the point of view of their internal logic, but such an 'easy' intellectual foundation ignores a key point about their historical specificity.

These are issues to be addressed in shifting our attention from the theories of post-industrialism to a preliminary theorization of the informational society.

## On the truly revolutionary nature of new information technologies in their interaction with the social structure

Technological determinism is in essence the negation of social theory (Smith and Marx, 1994). Thus, we must reject from the outset any attempt to consider technological change as the exclusive source of historical change. Yet it is just as important to acknowledge the extraordinary social change represented by new information technologies. In an obvious historical parallel the steam engine did not create the industrial society by itself. But without the steam there would not have been an industrial society (Mokyr, 1990). Without the microprocessor, without computer networking, and without the recombinant of DNA, there would not be an informational society.

It is now generally accepted that in the last quarter of the 20th century a technological revolution of historic proportions has taken shape. Two basic features characterize the current technological revolution:

(a) It is focused on process, as are all major technological revolutions, although it also spurs the continuous innovation of products. Because it is process oriented (as was the industrial revolution) its effects are pervasive, and cut across all spheres of human activity.

(b) Its fundamental raw material, as well as its principal outcome, is *information*, as the stuff of which the industrial revolution was made was energy. In this, the information technology revolution is distinctive from preceding technological revolutions. While information and knowledge were always essential elements in any process of scientific discovery and technical change, this is the first time in history in which the new knowledge applies primarily to generation of knowledge and information processing. Information technologies are not limited to micro-electronics based technologies. We must also include as a fundamental component of information technologies genetic engineering, since it deals with the decoding and eventual reprogramming of information codes contained in living matter. Indeed, the interaction between micro-electronics based information technologies, and genetically based information technologies will be the most fundamental frontier of science and technology in the 21st century (Kelly, 1994).

How does this technology revolution affect society? To be sure, there is an interactive relationship between technology and society. Indeed, from the perspective of social theory, technology is a component, and an essential one, of society. The origins and trajectory of major technological changes are social. The application of technology is socially determined, so is the feedback on technology of the social consequences of its applications. Having granted all these crucial points, I still think it is important to focus upon the specific effects of this specific technological revolution on the social structure to understand the new, emerging social system.

The first distinctive feature is that because information and knowledge are deeply embedded in the culture of societies, culture and symbol processing become direct productive forces in the new society. This blurs the traditional distinction between production and consumption, as well as superseding the metaphysical debate about productive and unproductive labor.

If symbol manipulation by a highly skilled, creative and increasingly autonomous labor force becomes the fundamental source of productivity and competitiveness, all factors that contribute directly to the enhancement of such a capacity are forces of production. The mental capacity of labor is certainly linked to education and training, but in an open, complex society, it also depends on a variety of cultural and institutional conditions: health, communication, leisure, housing and environmental conditions, cultural recreation, travel, access to the natural environment, sociability, etc. Thus the processes of production and consumption, and beyond them the spheres of economic and social life, become increasingly intertwined.

A number of important institutional consequences follow from this observation. For instance, the welfare state cannot be seen simply as an unproductive, redistributive institution. By improving conditions of social life and cultural capacity, the welfare state, in its broadest sense, can be a decisive productive force in the informational society. The major distinction to be made from the economic point of view will be between the different types of welfare state institutions, depending upon their role: enhancing social life for the majority of the population versus bureaucratic redistribution and stigma-prone charity. By bringing down the secular distinction between production and consumption in the social system, the new technological paradigm forces theory to analyze societies in terms of social relations cutting across various institutional spheres of social action.

A second major effect of new information technologies is that they link up processes of production, distribution and management across organizations and across types of activities. Thus, manufacturing or agriculture can no longer be conceived independently of the information and service activities that are embedded into the production of goods (Cohen and Zysman, 1987). The evolution of employment and occupational structure cannot be expected to follow the linear, historical succession from primary to secondary sectors, then to tertiary activities. Instead, there is a fundamental change from a techno-organizational division of labor to a complex matrix of linkages of productive and management activities that command the logic of the entire occupational system. To test this analysis I have studied, with Yuko Aoyama, the evolution of employment and occupational structure of the G-7 countries between 1920 and 1990 (Castells and Aoyama, 1994). The findings unveil some surprises for post-industrialist dogma: Japan and Germany, while being among the most competitive and technologically advanced economies, display a much higher level of manufacturing employment than the US or the UK, and a smaller informational workforce. It does not follow that information is not important. What appears to happen is that the linkage between information processing and material production takes different organizational forms in different institutional and managerial structures (e.g. Japanese and German manufacturing firms internalize a higher proportion of their own services; also Japan and Germany offshore a much lower proportion of their industrial production than the US does, etc.). In sum, information technologies allow different types of activities to link up according to the organizational form that best suits the strategy of the firm or the history of the institution. The flexibility of new technologies allows for a diversity of organizational arrangements, that make it possible for people to work together in different firms, and/or in different locations, and/or in different sectors of activity. This results in the blurring of the fundamental traditional distinction between agriculture and services, or between manufacturing and services in the production process, as well as the enormous diversity of 'service activities' to the point where the notion of 'service' no longer makes sense.

Furthermore, new information technologies allow for the constitution of a production and management system spread all over the world, yet working on real time and working as a unit through the combination of telecommunications, fast transportation, and computerized flexible production systems. This worldwide production system is not confined to the multinational corporations. Networks of firms and the ancillary networks of suppliers and distributors also gravitate around the global production/management flows (Gereffi and Wyman, 1990; Harrison, 1994). The process is most obvious in the case of the global financial markets (Chesnais, 1994).

Three critical concepts emerge from such a fundamental transformation in the way the new production system operates:
- linkages between activities;
- networks made up of organizations;
- flows of production factors and of commodities.

Together, they form the actual basis of the new economy and will force the redefinition of the occupational structure, and thus of the class system, of the new society.

The same logic applies to the fundamental process of organizational change underway, a third major distinctive effect of information technologies. As complexity and uncertainty become essential characteristics of the new environment in which organizations must operate, the fundamental needs for the management of organizations are those of flexibility and adaptability (Benveniste, 1994): flexibility to gear the external system of the organization toward the demands of a rapidly changing world; adaptability to modify the internal system of the organization in accordance with each new pattern of strategic guidance. The demands for such organizational changes have existed for some time in the market place. But it was only with the spread of affordable information technologies that firms and institutions were able to decentralize and become flexible without undermining their control and guidance systems. Thus, small and medium-sized firms were able to link up among themselves, relate to a broader market, and become suppliers to a variety of large firms, adding substantial flexibility to the system as a whole (Piore and Sabel, 1984). Multinational corporations decentralized their units to the point of forming constellations of quasi independent entities. Major firms formed strategic alliances, joint ventures and partnerships in different product lines and in different markets and functions, often becoming competitors against their own allies in specific areas of action. While the concentration of wealth and power in major conglomerates has continued in most countries and at the world level, the structure of the economy, and the structure of social institutions at large, has become increasingly decentralized and diversified, with a growing number of hierarchies, alliances and competitions (Harrison, 1994). Overall, and as a general trend, multidirectional networks are substituting for vertical bureaucracies as the most efficient, and increasingly powerful information/communication technologies (Ernst, 1994).

The direct impact on the media, and thus on the formation of images, representations and public opinion in our societies, is a direct, obvious impact of the new communication technologies. This has been the object of endless studies and interpretations, to the point that it seems hardly necessary to further elaborate on the issue. And yet, new communication technologies have made obsolete the 'classic television' era, forcing a reconsideration of the new interaction between communication and communication technologies. What is new in the new media, as they have been affected by direct satellite broadcasting, cable, VCRs, portable communication devices, and the emergence of interactive multimedia, is the simultaneous tendency toward globalization and individualization of image/sound-making and broadcasting, inducing what Japanese researchers call the 'Segmented Society' (*Bunshyu Shakai*), under the impact of customized messages (Ito, 1991). On the one hand, the whole planet is (unevenly) connected in global networks of information and images that travel throughout the world instantly (Doyle, 1992). On the other hand, the media are less and less mass oriented. Markets and audiences (ultimately the same) have been segmented and specifically targeted (Sabbah, 1985). The emergence of specialized networks, through cable television or satellite transmission, depending on societies, is not only a challenge to traditional TV networks: it is a new form of image distribution and reception. Together with specialized radio stations they are forming a new media system that looks for specific audiences or specific moods and tastes of general audiences (Rogers, 1986). VCRs are also becoming powerful instruments of individualization, since they are decreasingly used to rent films, and increasingly used for videotaping films and events, thus selecting available images while preserving the time and conditions of image consumption (Alvarado, 1988). The walkman device (that will shortly have its video equivalent, beyond the current primitive wrist-TV sets) reaches the ultimate individualization for the reception of messages, moving from the mass media to the individual consumption, and segmented distribution of a flexible, global production of audiovisual messages. To some extent, now the message is the medium, since it is the message that determines the medium to be used, as well as the how, where, when, and for whom it is to be used.

In a related development, the rapid diffusion of 'virtual reality' representation in the computer networks, and the potential of multimedia, create the possibility of individualized, self programmable image representation and perception, that will increasingly disconnect individuals from the mass media, while connecting the individualized communication expres-

sions to the individuals' mental world. As Negroponte likes to say, in the new media system 'prime time is my time' (Negroponte, 1995).

The social consequence of such technological developments is the growing tension between globalization and individualization in the audiovisual universe, bringing about the danger of the breakdown of the patterns of social communication between world information flows and the pulse of personal experiences (Moran, 1993).

Last but not least, the strategic character of information technologies in the productivity of the economy and in the efficiency of social institutions changes the sources of power in society, and among societies. The mastery of science and technology of information technologies becomes a source of power in itself. Granted, the state, because it holds the institutional monopoly of violence, remains the source of power in society. But a state incapable of keeping up with the rapid, endless process of technological change, will become a weak state both internally (its economic basis will deteriorate) and externally (the coercive means of its institutional monopoly of violence will become technologically obsolete). This is a fundamental development, because the ability to foster technological change under the new conditions of the information technology revolution is directly related to the ability of a society to diffuse and exchange information, and to relate to the rest of the world. On both counts, secluded, military empires cannot compete with open societies and market economies in the fostering of new technologies. Nuclear power is in fact the last, most destructive technology of the industrial era. Communication technologies can indeed be used for purposes of war, destruction and police control. But the potential of an institutional system to develop communication technologies depends on a number of social conditions that found serious obstacles in closed societies and military-oriented apparatuses (Guile, 1987). The surprising collapse of the Soviet Empire is the most striking evidence supporting this hypothesis: the inability of the Soviet system to compete with the West and Japan in information technologies decisively undermined its military power, opening the way for a last-ditch attempt at reforming the system that eventually precipitated its demise (for an empirical analysis of this process see Castells and Kiselyova, 1995).

## The transformation of the women's condition and the social redefinition of family, sexuality and personality

A fundamental feature of the new society is the transformation of women's condition, at least in the most developed countries. At the roots of this transformation, that has taken place at an accelerated pace since the 1960s, there are two inter-related phenomena: the massive entry of women into the labor market in most advanced economies; and the social movements based on the defense of identity that nurtured the development of the women's movement and of feminism at large. Both structural change and social mobilization are important to understand the transformation of women's roles and values in society. But because feminist and/or women's movements had already taken place in earlier historical periods, I am inclined to attribute the greatest weight in the process of change to the transformation of the labor market and to the access of women to paid jobs, even under conditions of structural discrimination. Thus, the informational economy is directly related to the change in women's position in society.

Whatever the causes, women seeing themselves as life-long members of the workforce, found themselves in a better bargaining position at home, while the social division of labor between the breadwinner and the housekeeper lost its basis of cultural legitimization. At the same time the fact of having to cope simultaneously with four tasks (working for a living, housekeeping, rearing the children and managing the husband) stressed women to the limit in their everyday life in a context where society was not matching the incorporation of women in work with the provision of services to assist in the functioning of the household. The result was a great receptiveness among women for the feminist values debated in the media following the initiatives of social movements and ideologists. Thus, while most women in most

societies would not call themselves feminists, a dramatic change in the values of society, and particularly in the values of women, took place in just one generation. Equal rights became an institutional goal for most women. But more importantly, the overwhelming majority of women in advanced countries in the 1990s do not accept the values underlying the social institution of the patriarchal family. Gender discrimination is still a fact in all societies, and the true sharing of housework is still the practice of a small fraction of the population. But the structure of legitimation of patriarchalism has been fundamentally shaken. By and large, most women do not accept men's authority any longer. The power game has to be played out now on an interpersonal basis. The institutions of society have greater difficulty than in the past in coming to the rescue of patriarchalism. The penetration of women's demands in the media, and widespread political mobilization of women, have made substantial inroads in the structure of power of all societies, signaling unmistakably the historical trend toward gender equality. Granted, thousands of years of patriarchalism will not disappear easily. The ingrained reflexes of gender domination will remain alive for generations, transmitted by some of the most fundamental cultural values of any society. Yet, the economic need to incorporate women into the labor force, the political interest in appealing to women's votes, and the pressures of a powerful, albeit diffused and divided, feminist movement, combine to create a new historical ground that has already had a fundamental impact on society.

The first and most important aspect has been the impact on the family. The patriarchal family has been called into question. A period of institutional crisis has followed, as in all historical transitions. Women's demands in their partnerships find strong resistance on the part of men who see their interests threatened and their values challenged. Separatism between genders has been on the rise, with the rate of divorce going up in most societies and the number of single households exploding. In the 1990s, in the United States, for instance, over 50 percent of marriages end in a divorce, and in France about one-third. Also, the traditional family, formed by a married couple with children, is today the exception in the United States: only 25 percent of the households fit that model. Single-parent families are the fastest growing category, followed by singles, then by couples without children. Although patriarchal nuclear families survive better in Western Europe (and still thrive in Japan), the trends toward the disintegration of the patriarchal model are similar in all advanced capitalist societies.

For couples who stay together there is a fundamental transformation of the roles in the family. Dual-career households become the norm and there are constant negotiations to accommodate the requirements that each member of the family has to respond to in his/her professional life.

Because society continues to consider it a non-essential service to provide child-care for the whole working population, caring for the children has become a fundamental element around which family life revolves. Different societies adapt differently to the child-care crisis. In Western Europe extended family relationships play a certain role in cushioning the crisis, with grandparents doing their share of family work, which, interestingly enough, leads to the revitalization of extended family relationships. In the United States, in what I would expect to be the general norm as other societies reach the same high rate of women's participation in the labor force, there are two principal modes of child-care, depending on social class. Professional middle-class women subcontract their child-care to domestic workers, mainly from Third World countries while working-class women rely on support networks that socialize child-care on the basis of the neighborhood. In both cases, the patterns of socialization of children are fundamentally affected. In addition, while men still hardly participate in domestic work, they do take more care of the children, because of the emotional rewards involved in the task. The net result is that the new generations are being socialized out of the traditional pattern of the patriarchal family, and being exposed from an early age to the need to cope with different worlds and different adult roles. In sociological terms, the new process of socialization to some extent downplays the role of the patriarchal family and diversifies the roles within the family world. The results we would expect to be

more complex personalities, less secure, yet more capable of adapting to changing roles and social contexts (see Hage and Powers, 1992, on this subject).

The increasing individualization of relationships within the family tends to emphasize the importance of personal demands beyond the rules of the institution. Thus, to some extent sexuality becomes, at the level of social values, a personal need that does not necessarily have to be channeled and institutionalized within the family. With the majority of the adult population living outside the boundaries of the traditional nuclear family, the expression of sexuality is acted out in interpersonal relationships, and becomes an open dimension of the new self. The socialization of teenagers under these new cultural patterns leads to a dramatically higher degree of sexual freedom in comparison to that of preceding generations. This is why even the fatal threat of the AIDS epidemic has not been able to reduce promiscuity among teenagers.

The open expression of sexuality, and the slow but growing acceptance of sexuality by society, has allowed the expression of homosexuality, fostered by powerful gay and lesbian movements that have become major agents of cultural change. Indeed, the gay movement, at least according to the findings of my own study on San Francisco's gay community, is not only a movement for the defense of gay rights, but a movement for the legitimation of sexuality in society, without boundaries or controls relative to the kind of sexuality (Castells, 1983).

Thus, the revolt of women against their condition at home, induced and allowed by their massive entry into the informational labor force, has called into question the patriarchal nuclear family. The crisis of the traditional family has taken the form of the increasing separation between the different dimensions that were previously held together in the same institution:
- interpersonal relationships between the two members of the couple;
- the professional life of each member of the household;
- the economic association of the members of the household;
- the distribution of domestic work;

- the raising of the children;
- sexuality.

The difficulty of coping with all these roles at the same time, once they are no longer fixed in a given, formal structure such as the patriarchal family, explains the difficulty of maintaining stable social relationships within the family-based household. It is obvious that for families to survive, new institutionalized forms of social relationships, in accordance with the new social roles and functions of women, will have to emerge (for a discussion on the transformation of sexuality/gender relationships, see Giddens, 1992).

At the same time, technological change in reproductive techniques has made it possible to disassociate the reproduction function from the social and personal functions of the family. The possibilities of in vitro fertilization, of surrogate mothers and of laboratory-produced babies, open up a whole new area of social experimentation that society will try to control and repress as much as possible because of the threat it poses to our moral and legal foundations. Yet the fact that women can have children on their own without having to even know the father, or that men can use surrogate mothers to have their children, even after they die, break down the fundamental relationship between biology and society in the reproduction of the human species, thus separating socialization from parenting. Under these historical conditions, families are being redefined in terms which are still unclear.

Because family and sexuality are fundamental determinants of personality systems, the calling into question of known family structures and the coming into the open of sexuality bring about the possibility of new types of personality that we are just starting to perceive. My hypothesis combines the views of Hage and Powers (1992) with a more adventurous speculation. I agree with them that the key ability to respond to current changes in society at the individual level is the ability to engage in 'role redefinition', what they consider to be the 'pivotal micro process' of post-industrial society. While this is a fundamental statement, it is too general and does not allow us to specify the social dynamics emerging in the new historical context. Let us try a complementary

approach to their analysis of new, emerging personality systems.

If we dare to introduce some elements of psychoanalytical theory into this excursus we could say that the open recognition of individual desire would lead to such an aberration as the institutionalization of desire. Because desire is, by definition, constant transgression, the recognition of sexuality outside the family would lead to extreme social stress. This is because as long as the transgression consisted merely in expressing sexuality outside the family boundaries, society could easily cope with it, channeling it through coded situations and organized contexts (e.g. prostitution, tolerated sexual harassment, etc.). If the patriarchal family is not there any more to be betrayed, however, the transgression will have to become an individual act against society. The buffering function of the family is lost. This opens the way to the expression of desire in the form of irrational, random violence. The breaking down of the patriarchal family (the only form that has existed in historical societies, until now) is indeed giving way to the normalization of sexuality (porno movies in prime time network television in Spain, France or Italy), and to the spread of senseless violence in society through the back alleys of uncontrolled desire. The liberation of the family confronts the self with its own inflicted oppression. The escape to freedom in the open, informational society may lead to individual anxiety and social violence until new forms of control are found that bring together men, women and children in a reconstructed family structure better suited to reconcile liberated women and uncertain men.

## The global economy, the informational society and the interdependence of social structure across the world

We live in a global economy. This is not the same as a world economy, a reality that has existed since the 16th century, as we were taught long ago by Fernand Braudel and Immanuel Wallerstein. A global economy is an economy where the strategic, dominant functions in all processes work as a unit in real time throughout the planet. That is, an economy in which the dominant segments of

## References

Alvarado, Manuel (ed.) (1988) *Video Worldwide*. London and Paris: John Libbey.

Barglow, Raymond (1994) *The Crisis of the Self in the Age of Information. Computers, Dolphins, and Dreams*. London: Routledge.

Bell, Daniel (1973) *The Coming of Post-Industrial Society. A Venture in Social Forecasting*. New York: Basic Books, cited in the 1976 paperback edition.

Beniger, James R. (1986) *The Control Revolution: Technological and Economic Origins of the Information Society*. Cambridge, MA: Harvard University Press.

Benveniste, Guy (1994) *The Twenty-First Century Organization*. San Francisco: Jossey-Bass.

Bourdieu, Pierre and James S. Coleman (eds.) (1991) *Social Theory for a Changing Society*. Boulder, CO: Westview; New York; Russell Sage Foundation.

Bradford, Colin (ed.) (1994) *The New Paradigm of Systemic Competitiveness: Toward More Integrated Policies in Latin America*. Paris: OECD Development Centre.

Calhoun, Craig (ed.) (1994) *Social Theory and the Politics of Identity*. Oxford: Blacwell.

capital flows, labor markets, markets, production, management, information and technology operate simultaneously at the world level. This is not to say that nations and nation-states disappear. In fact, states become major players in the global economy on the basis of the defense of the specific national interests they represent. But the economic unit of operation (and of analysis) is the global system of interactions: such a system shapes national economies and national economic policies. These policies become nationally based strategies operating in a global system differentiated and articulated across and between national boundaries.

There is a close connection between the globalization and informationalization of the economy, and the structure and dynamics of the new, global economy (Carnoy et al., 1993). Without being able to develop the analysis of the new economy within the limits of this text, I will emphasize the consequence of such a new economy for the theory of the information society.

If economies are linked throughout the planet, how can societies be analyzed independently? Unless we assert that economies and societies are entirely autonomous systems, if there is a global economy, there must be a structural relationship among the societies integrated into such an economy. Thus, the theory of the informational society cannot concentrate exclusively on the most advanced societies. It must also account for the structure of dependent societies and for the interactive effects between social structures asymmetrically located along the networks of the global economy. To be sure, information technologies spread throughout the whole world and the information workforce has increased in all countries. However, the study by Katz (1988), one of the few existing analyses of the informational society in an international perspective, has shown that the meaning of the information workforce in 'developing countries' is very different from that in advanced countries; its expansion is mainly linked to government employment, concentrated on generally unproductive activities. Also, he shows a limited diffusion of information technologies in most 'developing countries', and generally under government

supervision (Katz, 1988). The evaluation of the role of information technology industries in Third World development that I conducted with Laura Tyson in 1988 shows the gigantic gap between most countries on this planet and the OECD area (Castells and Tyson, 1988). On the other hand, the work by Dieter Ernst and David O'Connor on the electronics industries in the Asian Pacific Rim shows that the ability of new industrializing countries to adapt, produce and diffuse new information technologies has become the critical factor for their development (Ernst and O'Connor, 1992).

Thus, there is no single essential path toward the informational society that all countries must follow. But there is a comprehensive global structure based on the rules of the informational society that affects all countries in one way or the other. Let us look more precisely in which ways. First of all, the ability to use (and to some extent produce) information technologies has become a fundamental tool of development. It is the historical equivalent to electrification during the industrialization stage. But we know that the use of information technologies is not only a matter of hardware. Without the informational capacity of society, that is without informational labor, organizations and institutions, there would be little chance for developing countries to develop. Technological dependency, in the broadest sense of the notion, becomes the fundamental obstacle to development in our world (Castells and Laserna, 1989). Second, the whole world becomes interconnected in its economic functions through information and communication flows. Access to these flows becomes critical for any economy, and thus for any society. Being switched off the network is the equivalent of not existing in the global economy. The position in the network, that is the function obtained in the new international division of labor, becomes an essential element in defining each country's or region's material conditions of existence.

Third, the informational economy, while connecting the whole planet in a series of networks of flows, does so selectively. Because productivity and competitiveness rely less and less on primary resources, and more and more on knowledge and information, cheap, unskilled labor and

Carnoy Martin, Manuel Castells, Stephen Cohen and Fernando Henrique Cardoso (1993)
*The New Global Economy in the Information Age.* University Park, PA: Penn State University Press.

Castells, Manuel (1983)
*The City and the Grassroots.* Berkeley: University of California Press.

Castells, Manuel and Yuko Aoyama (1994)
"Paths Toward the Informational Society: Employment Structure in G-7 Countries, 1920-1990," *International Labor Review* 133 (1): 5-33.

Castells, Manuel and Emma Kiselyova (1995)
*The Collapse of Soviet Communism: The View from the Information Society.* Berkeley: University of California, International and Area Studies Book Series.

Castells, Manuel and Roberto Laserna (1989)
"The New Dependency: Technological Change and Socio-economic Restructuring in Latin America," *Sociological Forum* 4

Castells, Manuel and Laura d'Andrea Tyson (1988)
"High Technology Choices Ahead: Restructuring Interdependence," in John W. Sewell and Stuart Tucker (eds.) *Growth, Exports, and Jobs in a Changing World Economy.* New Brunswick, JJ: Transaction Books.

Chesnais, Francois (1994)
*La Mondialisation du capital.* Paris: Syros.

Cohen, Stephen and John Zysman (1987)
*Manufacturing Matters.* New York: Basic Books.

Dordick, Herbert S. and
Georgette Wang (1993)
*The Information Society.
A Retrospective View.*
Newbury Park: Sage.

Doyle, Marc (1992)
*The Future of Television.
A Global Overview of Pro-
gramming, Advertising,
Technology and Growth.*
Lincolnwood, IL: NTC Busi-
ness Books.

Ernst, Dieter (1994)
"Inter-firms Networks and
Market Structure Driving
Forces, Barriers and Patterns
of Control," Berkeley: Berke-
ley Roundtable on the Interna-
tional Economy, Working
Paper.

Ernst, Dieter and David
O'Connor (1992)
*Competing in the Electronics
Industry: The Experience of
Newly Industrializing Coun-
tries.* Paris: OECD, Develop-
ment Centre.

Fuchs, Victor (1968)
*The Service Economy.*
New York: National Bureau
of Economic Research.

Gereffi, Gary and Daniel
Wyman (eds.) (1990)
*Manufacturing Miracles:
Paths of Industrialization in
Latin America and East Asia.*
Princeton: Princeton
University Press.

Giddens, Anthony (1991)
*Modernity and Self-Identity.*
Stanford, CA: Stanford
University Press.

Giddens, Anthony (1992)
*The Transformation of Inti-
macy. Sexuality, Love and
Eroticism in Modern
Societies.* Stanford, CA:
Stanford University Press.

raw materials cease to be strategic inputs in the new economy. There is ample evidence of the increasing irrelevance for the global, informational economy of large areas of the world (Bradford, 1994; Rodgers et al., 1995). Exploitation of labor or natural resources becomes too costly in relation to the actual benefit obtained from it. As the economy evolves toward higher value-added, information-based products, the accumulation of capital increasingly proceeds at the core, not at the periphery: the economic theories of imperialism are now doomed. In the new economy, markets, skilled labor, capital and technology are increasingly concen-trated in the OECD countries, with the addition of a few newly industrializing economies, and the fundamental addition of China as a potential economic super-power. Beyond that, the incorporation of Eastern Europe and Russia into the core system will provide, in the future, mar-kets and the required natural resources (drawn from Siberia) for informational capitalism to thrive for a long time – except if it is challenged from the inside, by social movements opposing its short-sighted profit-seeking logic.

The consequence of this new economic configuration is that many countries, and many regions of many countries are being bypassed by the expansion of the global, informational economy. National, local and regional societies are shifting from a position of dependent exploitation to structural irrelevance in the new econ-omy. Such development is triggering sev-eral processes that are all part of the new social structure characteristic of the infor-mational society:
- increasing dualization of dependent societies, with a few segments incorpo-rated into the global economy and cul-ture, with marginality spreading in a variable, but substantial proportion of the population;
- a desperate attempt by excluded soci-eties to reject the rules of the game by affirming their cultural identity in funda-mentalist terms, opening the way for a variety of jihads and crusades against the infidels of the dominant order;
- efforts by marginalized countries to establish what I have called 'the perverse connection' to the global economy, spe-cializing in criminal trade: drugs, weapons, money laundering, traffic of human beings (women to prostitute, babies to adopt, human organs to be transplanted, etc.);
- reconstructing the unity of the world by mass migrations to the core countries in flows of people that could only be stopped by massive police measures that will fundamentally affect the character of democracy in advanced countries.
The separation between the dynamic of the global economy and the structure of the informational society is transforming the social fabric of both advanced and dependent countries in a fundamental way. The reintegration of both processes in an articulated historical practice requires a concerted body of institutional action that does not exist today.

The process of historical transition to the informational economy is likely to be dominated by the fundamental disjunc-tion between, on the one hand, a global economy and a worldwide information network, and, on the other, nationalistic civil societies, communal structures and increasingly powerless states.

## The networks society

After more than 20 years of speculation and attempts to describe, analyze and theorize the 'new society' there is still a great deal of uncertainty about what this society is. The reconstruction of a theoreti-cal paradigm suitable for the new social processes we are observing must start from a critical observation that should have become apparent in the preceding pages of this paper: our societies are fun-damentally made of flows exchanged through networks of organizations and institutions. By 'flows' I understand pur-poseful, repetitive, programmable sequences of exchange and interaction between physically disjointed positions held by social actors in organizations and institutions of society. The convergence of social evolution and information tech-nologies has created a new material basis for the performance through the social system. This material basis is so his-torically specific that it imposes its inher-ent logic on most social processes, thus essentially conditioning the structure of society.

The determining effects of these networks of flows on the social structure operates at least at four different levels:

-Networks organize the position of actors, organizations and institutions in societies and economies. The social relevance of any social unit is thus conditioned by its presence or absence in specific networks. Absence of a dominant network leads to structural irrelevance. Only life in the net amounts to social existence in accordance with the structurally dominant values and interests. Because networks shape in an uneven way: societies, segments of society, social groups and individuals, the most fundamental social distinction refers to the position in a given network. Examples of such presence/absence logic are the position of countries or regions in the global economy (some areas become structurally irrelevant, including their population in their irrelevance, while others become nodal), or the position of individuals of different educational level in the new organizational structure (information holders and generators of knowledge are critical to the organization, while information processing executants are periodically displaced by automation);

-There are also important differences within networks and between networks in terms of the structural importance of the flows generated in such networks (or in some network's position) for a given system's goals. The structural hierarchy between networks and the hierarchy between positions within a network's flows largely determines the ability to influence the overall social logic from a particular position. However, such a hierarchy is unstable and may constantly change depending on the transformation of social conditions. The critical question concerning the dynamic of society is that of the relationship between the changes in the hierarchy of flows and the changes in the allocation of individuals to the positions in these flows. For instance, a region may increase or decrease its competitiveness in the world economy, thus reflecting these changes in the economic conditions of its residents. But it is crucial to know if when there is decline, the region's residents suffer the decline of their position in the economic networks, whereas when there is prosperity it is a labor force of outsiders that is brought in because they better fit the requirements of the worldwide networks for the region's revival;

-Within networks, there are important asymmetries between different positions: the CEOs of major financial institutions have a dominant position vis-a-vis borrowers; the reviewers of scientific journals control the innovation efforts of young researchers; the news editors of TV networks shape the content of information for the viewers; the shopfloor manager of a factory organizes the team work that leads to specific production procedures, etc. Whoever sends the message and shapes the channel of transmission of the flow largely conditions the social effects of the communication, be it an order, an investment, an instruction or a self-serving image. Yet, the networks of flows tend to become largely autonomous of the power-holders that control the nodes of the network. The flows of power are easily transformed into the power of flows: this is a fundamental characteristic of the new society. An obvious example is that of financial markets: once a 'speculative' movement is triggered in the international market, the reserves of the Central Banks of the wealthiest nations may be gobbled up in a few days trying to go against the flow. Who are these 'speculators'? Many and nobody. There are certainly organizations (actually networks) living off the turmoil in the financial markets. But they have no real power by themselves. Their role is to trigger a dynamic sequence of flows that surpasses by far the wealth and power of any organization (or group of organizations). In some cases, the computers themselves, by random effect of their programs, have been triggered at the same time in preventive buying or selling and are themselves the 'speculators'. Similar, although less powerful examples, may be found in the world of political images, or intellectual fashion or of pop music. In all cases, extremely important social, economic and cultural consequences follow the formation of 'turbulences' in the space of flows. I am not arguing that social action becomes random. I am arguing that a structural logic dominated by largely uncontrollable flows within and between networks creates the conditions for the unpredictability of the consequences of human action through the reflection of such action in an unseen, uncharted space of flows;

- The logic of flows in our societies is universal but not comprehensive. Selective networks cover through their flows all spheres of society and all areas of the planet. But they segment countries and people according to the specific goals of

Guile, Bruce (ed.) (1987) *Information Technologies and Social Transformation.* Washington, DC: National Academy Press.

Hage, Jerald and Charles Powers (1992) *Post-Industrial Lives. Roles and Relationships in the 21st Century.* London: Sage Publications.

Harrison, Bennett (1994) *Lean and Mean. The Changing Landscape of Corporate Power.* New York: Basic Books.

Harvey, David (1990) *The Condition of Postmodernity.* Oxford: Blackwell.

Hayashi, S. (1987) *Nihon gata no joho shakai (The Japanese Model for Information Society).* Tokyo: University of Tokyo Press.

Imai, Ken'ichi (1990) *Joho netto waku shakai no tenbo (The Information Network Society).* Tokyo: Chikuma Shobo.

Ito, Youichi (1991) "Birth of Joho Shakai and Johoka Concepts in Japan and their Diffusion outside Japan," *Keio Communication Review* 13:3-12.

Katz, Raul Luciano (1988) *The Information Society. An International Perspective.* New York: Praeger.

Kelly, Kevin (1994) *Out of Control. The Rise of Neo-biological Civilization.* San Francisco: Addison-Wesley.

Kendrick, John (1961) *Productivity Trends in the United States.* Princeton, NJ: Princeton University Press.

Laserna, Roberto (1995)
"Regional Development and
Coca Production in
Cochabamba, Bolivia,"
unpublished Ph. D. Disserta-
tion. University of California,
Berkeley.

Lash, Scott, and John Urry
(1994)
*Economies of Signs and
Space.* London: Sage.

Lyon, David (1988)
*The Information Society:
Issues and Illusions.* Cam-
bridge: Polity Press.

Machlup, Fred (1962)
*The Production and Distribu-
tion of Knowledge in the
United States.* Princeton:
Princeton University Press.

Machlup, Fred (1980)
*Knowledge: its Creation, Dis-
tribution, and Economic Significance. Volume I: Knowledge and Knowledge
Production.* Princeton: Princeton University Press.

Martin, William (1988)
*The Information Society.*
London: Aslib.

Masuda, Yoneji (1990)
*Managing in the Information
Society. Releasing Synergy
Japanese Style.* Oxford: Basil
Blackwell. (Orig. Published
as *The Information Society as
Post-Industrial Society.* Tokyo:
Institute for the Information
Society, 1980.)

Miles, Ian et al. (1988)
*Information Horizons: The
Long-Term Implications of
New Information technolo-
gies.* Cheltenham, UK:
Edward Elgar.

Mokyr, Joel (1990)
*The Lever of Riches. Techno-
logical Creativity and Economic Progress.* New York:
Oxford University Press.

each network and according to the specific characteristics of people and countries. This results in an extremely uneven
social geography, where the structural
meaning for each locale, for each group,
for each person, is deconstructed from its
experience and reconstructed in the flows
of the network. The reaction against such
restructuration takes the form of affirming basic, cultural, historical or biological
identities as fundamental principles of
existence. The society of flows is also a
society of primary ascription communities
where the affirmation of the being (ethnic
identity, territorial identity, gender identity, religious identity, historic/national
identity) becomes the organizing principle
for a system-in-itself that becomes a sys-
tem-for-itself.

Under such conditions we could predict a
tendency toward the breakdown of the
communication pattern between the dominant institutions of society, working
along ahistorical, abstract networks of
functional flows, and the dominated communities, defending their existence
around the principle of irreducible, fundamental, non-shared identity. A society
made up of the juxtaposition of flows and
tribes ceases to be a society. The structural
logic of the informational age bears the
seeds of a new barbarianism, made out
of the fundamental opposition between
the *net* and the *self*.

The structural domination of the organizational logic of networks and of the relational logic of flows has substantial consequences for the social structure, all of
which are often considered as indicators
of the new, informational society. In fact,
they are manifestations of a deeper
trend: the emergence of flows as the stuff
from which our societies are made. I will
hypothesize the main consequences of
such a fundamental historical trend:
(a) The ability to generate new knowledge and to gather strategic information
depends on access to the flows of such
knowledge or information, be it flows
between major research centers or
insider knowledge in Wall Street trading.
It follows that the power of organizations
and the fortunes of individuals depend on
their positioning vis-a-vis such sources of
knowledge and on their capacity to actually understand and process such knowledge. It is in this fundamental sense that
we live in a knowledge-based, informa-

tional society. But the key point to keep in
mind is that there is no single, privileged
source of science or information. Knowledge is also a flow. No researcher, or
research center can survive in isolation in
modern science. No financial investment
can be made without specialized information on the market, that is on a flow of
transactions.

(b) The productivity and competitiveness
of the economic system, a fundamental
subsystem in our society, depends on the
position of economic units in the networks
of the global economy. These units may
be firms, cities, regions, countries or economic areas (such as the EU). They all
depend on their positioning in a network
of economic exchanges. This network
does not solely consist of the market. It is
a market subject to government intervention, to technological change, to privileged business information, to firms'
strategies and to global flows of capital,
labor and raw materials. So the actual
operational network is made up of a networking of networks, making the structures of flows so complex that successful
positioning ultimately depends on an
advantageous relationship of the economic unit to a flow that happens to be
strategic: e.g. the relationship of firms in
Silicon Valley to high technology firms
around the nationalist project; Airbus'
connection to the last stand of French
grandeur, etc. Thus, economic dominance
ultimately depends on relative position
vis-a-vis a flow in the overall system of
networks. Relative positions can indeed
be changed by the ability to maneuver
economic flows through flows of information (better management, better marketing strategy, more educated labor, better
access to suppliers' networks, better technology, etc.).

(c) The flows of images/sounds/mes-
sages created by the new media are fundamental elements in shaping the representation and communication patterns of
our societies. We have left the Gutenberg
Galaxy a long time ago, and we live now,
as I briefly mentioned above, in a collection of related constellations, made up of
specialized audiovisual universes living
off the bridges formed by worldwide networks of information and entertainment.

(d) The political system is now fundamentally dependent upon the skilled manipu-

lation of messages and symbols. The media are the fundamental battleground for political control, at least in the democratic systems. 'Reality' is increasingly mediated by the media, because they are indeed the real virtuality of the majority of the population.

Politics that do not exist in the media, particularly in television, simply do not exist in today's democratic politics. To the extent that other forms of political expression are relevant, they are also based on networks of a different kind: local networks or organizational networks, linked to a strong, historically rooted political basis, such as local chapters of a party or such as labor union organizations under direct party influence. Indeed the only political parties that still have a relevant function as parties, different from mere electoral machines, are those with widespread grassroots organizations that provide an adequate ground for a targeted deployment of a media-oriented political strategy (e.g. cheering, crowded political rallies have as their major function to portray the image of popular support for the candidate's personality and ideas). Personalization of politics is a fundamental trend in all societies. Because the candidates are symbols their personalities are scrutinized in the media, and the result of such scrutiny is often decisive for their political fate. Thus, flows of images and information are the critical ingredients of political power in our societies. Power no longer lies in the barrel of the gun, but on the editing programs of the television networks' computers.

(e) Because the materiality of our existence is made up of flows and/or from community-based resistance to such flows, representations of values and interests in our societies are no longer structured on the basis of work. They are either expressed in terms of a symbolic message or in terms of the defense of primary identities of self-identified communities. Thus, collective action is often expressed as a rejection of the logic of flows on behalf of ethnic communities, local communities, gender communities or culturally/biologically defined communities (disabled, gays, etc.). Sometimes the rejection is addressed to other communities similarly identified in terms of primary ascription: this is the frequent basis for racism and xenophobia.

Collective action that breaks through ascribed social conditions is constructed around messages and symbols that strike a chord with a diverse and unpredictable constituency, from an indignant reaction against political corruption, to saving whales. These messages are usually generated, or at least transmitted, in the world of the media, therefore in a world of flows of images and representations. Their appeal often cuts across a broad segment of the population, although it generally mobilizes the better educated groups more easily. This symbol-trigged mobilization can be the result of deliberate action, as is often the case with the environmental movement. But more often than not its success depends on random circumstances. If my hypothesis is correct, then we have lost the direct linkage between the structure of social organization in terms of identifiable material interests and the logic of social mobilization. Processes of change occur according to a symbolic logic located in the processes of representation of the space of flows. Such tendencies lead to the demise of forms of collective action that are neither rooted in primary identities nor triggered by a powerful symbol. This is for instance the case of the labor movement, that becomes in our societies a professionalized organization specializing in articulating and negotiating grievances of various interest groups.

(f) At the level of personal interaction, Hage and Powers (1992) have brilliantly hypothesized that what characterizes the new society is the endless construction of the self by people engaging in the interaction process, instead of representing themselves in everyday life. This is because the constant changes of roles and situations in a society defined by innovation, flexibility and unpredictability in all spheres, requires people to constantly redefine themselves in their roles at work, in the family, with their friends. Therefore, the restructuring of the personality to adequately fulfill the new functions demanded by society requires bringing together all the new codes and messages from the different networks relating to the various dimensions of people's lives. The construction/reconstruction of the self is tantamount to managing the changing set of flows and codes that people are confronted with in their daily experience.

Monk, Peter (1989)
*Technological Change in the Information Economy.* London: Pinter.

Moran, Rosalyn (1993)
*The Electronic Home. Social and Spatial Aspects. A Scoping Report.* Dublin: European Foundation for the Improvement of the Living and Working Conditions.

Negroponte, Nicholas (1995)
*Being Digital.* New York: Alfred Knopf.

Piore, Michael and Charles Sabel (1984)
*The Second Industrial Divide.* New York: Basic Books.

Porat, Marc (1977)
*The Information Economy.* Washington, DC: Department of Commerce, Office of Telecommunications.

Portes, Alejandro, and G. Rumbault (1990)
*Immigrant America.* Berkeley: University of California Press.

Richta, Radovan (1969)
*La Civilisation au carrefour.* Paris: Anthropos.

Rodgers, Gerry, Charles Gore and Jose B. Figueiredo (eds.) (1995)
*Social Exclusion: Rethoric, Reality, Responses.* Geneva: International Institute of Labour Studies.

Rogers, Everett (1986)
*Communication Technology: The New Media in Society.* New York: Free Press.

Sabbah, Françoise (1985)
"The New Media," in
Manuel Castells (ed.) *High
Technology, Space, and Soci-
ety*. Beverly Hills, CA: Sage.

Salvaggio, Jerry L. (ed.)
(1989)
*The Information Society:
Economic, Social, and Struc-
tural Issues*. Hillsdale, NJ:
Eribaum.

Shoji, Kokichi (1990)
"Le Nipponisme comme
méthode sociologique,"
Tokyo: Tokyo University,
Department of Sociology,
unpublished paper.

Smith, Merrit Roe and Leo
Marx (eds.) (1994)
*Does Technology Drive His-
tory? The Dilemma of Technological Determinism*. Cambridge, MA: MIT Press.

Solow, Robert M. (1957)
"Technical Change and the
Aggregate Production Function," *Review of Economics
and Statistics* 39:214-31.

Touraine, Alain (1969)
*La Société post-industrielle*.
Paris: Denoel.

Touraine, Alain (1988)
*La Parole et le sang. Politique
et société en Amérique
Latine*. Paris: Odile Jacob.

Touraine, Alain (1992) *Critique de la modernité*. Paris:
Fayard.

Williams Frederick (ed.)
(1988) *Measuring the Information Society*. Beverly Hills,
CA: Sage.

Thus, the materiality of networks and flows creates a new social structure at all levels of society. It is this social structure that actually constitutes the new informational society, a society that could be more properly named as the society of flows, since flows are made up not only of information but of all materials of human activity (capital, labor, commodities, images, travelers, changing roles in personal interaction, etc.).

In a broader historical perspective, the network society represents a qualitative change in the human experience. If we refer to an old sociological tradition according to which social action at the most fundamental level can be understood as the changing pattern of relationships between Nature and Culture, we are indeed in a new era of the human experience.

The first model of the relationship between the two fundamental poles of our existence was characterized for millennia by the domination of Nature over Culture. The codes of social organization almost directly expressed the struggle for survival under the uncontrolled harshness of Nature, as structural anthropology has taught us by tracing the codes of social life back to the roots of our biological entity.

The second pattern of the relationship, established at the origins of the Modern Age and associated with the industrial revolution and the triumph of Reason, saw the domination of Nature by Culture, making society out of the process of work by which humankind found both its liberation from natural forces and its submission to its own abysses of oppression and exploitation.

We are just entering a new stage in which Culture refers to Culture, having superseded Nature to the point that Nature is artificially revived ('preserved') as a cultural form: this is in fact the meaning of the environmental movement, to reconstruct Nature as an ideal cultural form. Because of the convergence of historical evolution and technological change we have entered a purely cultural pattern of social interaction and social organization. This is why information is the key ingredient of our social organization and why flows of messages and images between networks constitute the basic thread of our social structure. This is not to say that history has ended in a happy reconciliation of humankind with itself. It is in fact quite the opposite: history is just beginning, if by history we understand the moment when, after millennia of a prehistoric battle with Nature, first to survive, then to conquer it, our species has reached the level of knowledge and social organization that will allow us to live in a predominantly social world. It is the beginning of a new existence, and indeed the beginning of a new society, marked by the full autonomy of culture vis-a-vis the material bases of our existence. But it is not necessarily an exhilarating moment. Because, alone at last in our human world, we will have to look at ourselves in the mirror of historical reality. And we may not like the vision.

Note
I wish to acknowledge the thorough comments to the draft of this text by Ida Susser, Loic Wacquant, Claude Fischer, Fernando Calderon, Vicente Navarro, Shujiro Yazawa, Jesus Leal and Alain Touraine. The article is based on the paper delivered as 1994 Distinguished Interlocutor of Anthropology at the joint session of the Society of Urban Anthropology and the Society for Anthropology of North America at the Annual Meeting of the American Anthropological Association, Atlanta, 30 November 1994.

# From a Culture-Debating to a Culture-Consuming Public

## Developmental Pathways in the Disintegration of the Bourgeois Public Sphere

Along the path from a public critically reflecting on its culture to one that merely consumes it, the public sphere in the world of letters, which at one point could still be distinguished from that in the political realm, has lost its specific character. For the "culture" propagated by the mass media is a culture of integration. It not only integrates information with critical debate and the journalistic format with the literary forms of the psychological novel into a combination of entertainment and "advice" governed by the principle of "human interest;" at the same time it is flexible enough to assimilate elements of advertising, indeed, to serve itself as a kind of super slogan that, if it did not already exist, could have been invented for the purpose of public relations serving the cause of the status quo. The public sphere assumes advertising functions. The more it can be deployed as a vehicle for political and economic propaganda, the more it becomes unpolitical as a whole and pseudo-privatized.

The model of the bourgeois public sphere presupposed strict separation of the public from the private realm in such a way that the public sphere, made up of private people gathered together as a public and articulating the needs of society with the state, was itself considered part of the private realm. To the extent that the public and private became intermeshed realms, this model became inapplicable. That is to say, a repoliticized social sphere originated that could not be subsumed under the categories of public and private from either a sociological or a legal perspective. In this intermediate sphere the sectors of society that had been absorbed by the state and the sectors of the state that had been taken over by society inter-

meshed without involving any rational-critical political debate on the part of private people.

The public was largely relieved of this task by other institutions: on the one hand by associations in which collectively organized private interests directly attempted to take on the form of political agency; on the other hand by parties which, fused with the organs of public authority, established themselves, as it were, above the public whose instruments they once were.

The process of the politically relevant exercise and equilibration of power now takes place directly between the private bureaucracies, special-interest associations, parties, and public administration. The public as such is included only sporadically in this circuit of power, and even then it is brought in only to contribute its acclamation. In so far as they are wage or salary earners and entitled to services, private people are forced to have their publicly relevant claims advocated collectively. But the decisions left for them to make individually as consumers and voters come under the influence of economic and political agencies to the same degree that any public relevance can be attributed to them.

To the extent that social reproduction still depends on consumption decisions and the exercise of political power on voting decisions made by private citizens there exists an interest in influencing them – in the case of the former, with the aim of increasing sales; in the case of the latter, of increasing formally this or that party's share of voters or, informally, to give greater weight to the pressure of specific organizations. The social latitude for private decisions is, of course, predetermined by objective factors like buying power and group membership and by socioeconomic status generally. Yet the more the original relationship between the intimate sphere and the public sphere in the world of letters is reversed and permits an undermining of the private sphere through publicity, the more decisions within this latitude can be influenced. In this fashion the consumption of culture also enters the service of economic and political propaganda.

Originally publicity guaranteed the connection between rational-critical public debate and the legislative foundation of domination, including the critical supervision of its exercise. Now it makes possible the peculiar ambivalence of a domination exercised through the domination of nonpublic opinion: it serves the manipulation of the public as much as legitimation before it. Critical publicity is supplanted by manipulative publicity. How the idea as well as the reality of a public operating in the political realm were transformed simultaneously with the principle of publicity is demonstrated by the dissolution and obsolescence of the link - still pretended to by liberalism - between public discussion and legal norm.

Since the separation of state and society was overcome and the government intervened in the social order through advance planning, distribution, and administration, the generality of the norm could no longer be maintained as a principle. In the same degree to which this kind of mutual penetration of state and society dissolved a private sphere whose independent existence made possible the generality of the laws, the foundation for a relatively homogeneous public composed of private citizens engaged in rational-critical debate was also shaken. Competition between organized private interests invaded the public sphere. If the particular interests that as privatized interests were neutralized in the common denominator of class interest once permitted public discussion to attain a certain rationality and even effectiveness, it remains that today the display of competing interests has taken the place of such discussion. The consensus developed in rational-critical public debate has yielded to compromise fought out or simply imposed non-

publicly. The laws that come into existence in this way can no longer be vindicated as regards their elements of "truth," even though in many cases the element of universality is preserved in them; for even the parliamentary public sphere - the place in which "truth" would have to present its credentials - has collapsed.

The original connection between the public sphere in the political realm and the rule of law, so clearly formulated by Kant, is captured by neither of these conceptions of law. The altered structure of the law brings out the fact that the task of

providing a rational justification for political domination can no longer be expected from the principle of publicity. To be sure, within an immensely expanded sphere of publicity the mediatized public is called upon more frequently and in incomparably more diverse ways for the purposes of public acclamation; at the same time it is so remote from the processes of the exercise and equilibration of power that their rational justification can scarcely be demanded, let alone be accomplished any longer, by the principle of publicity.

What in this way only intimates itself in the daily press has progressed further in the newer media. The integration of the once separate domains of journalism and literature, that is to say, of information and rational-critical argument on the one side and of *belles lettres* on the other, brings about a peculiar shifting of reality – even a conflation of different levels of reality.

Under the common denominator of so-called human interest emerges the *mixtum compositum* of a pleasant and at the same time convenient subject for entertainment that, instead of doing justice to reality, has a tendency to present a substitute more palatable for consumption and more likely to give rise to an impersonal indulgence in stimulating relaxation than to a public use of reason. Radio, film, and television by degrees reduce to a minimum the distance that a reader is forced to maintain toward the printed letter – a distance that required the privacy of the appropriation as much as it made possible the publicity of a rational-critical exchange about what had been read.

With the arrival of the new media the form of communication as such has changed; they have had an impact, therefore, more penetrating (in the strict sense of the word) than was ever possible for the press. Under the pressure of the "Don't talk back!" the conduct of the public assumes a different form. In comparison with printed communications the programs sent by the new media curtail the reactions of their recipients in a peculiar way. They draw the eyes and ears of the public under their spell but at the same time, by taking away its distance, place it under "tutelage."

The critical discussion of a reading public tends to give way to "exchanges about tastes and preferences" between consumers – even the talk about what is consumed, "the examination of tastes," becomes a part of consumption itself. The world fashioned by the mass media is a public sphere in appearance only. By the same token the integrity of the private sphere which they promise to their consumers is also an illusion.

In the course of the eighteenth century, the bourgeois reading public was able to cultivate in the intimate exchange of letters (as well as in the reading of the literature of psychological novels and novellas engendered by it) a subjectivity capable of relating to literature and oriented toward a public sphere. In this form private people interpreted their new form of existence which was indeed based on the liberal relationship between public and private spheres. The experience of privacy made possible literary experimentation with the psychology of the humanity common to all, with the abstract individuality of the natural person.

Inasmuch as the mass media today strip away the literary husks from that kind of bourgeois self-interpretation and utilize them as marketable forms for the public services provided in a culture of consumers, the original meaning is reversed. On the one hand, the socialized patterns of eighteenth-century literature that are used to serve up twentieth-century affairs for human interest and the biographical note transfer the illusion of an untouched private sphere and intact private autonomy to conditions which have long since removed the basis for both.

On the other hand, they are also imposed on political matters of fact to such an extent that the public sphere itself becomes privatized in the consciousness of the consuming public; indeed, the public sphere becomes the sphere for the publicizing of private biographies, so that the accidental fate of the so-called man in the street or that of systematically managed stars attain publicity, while publicly relevant developments and decisions are garbed in private dress and through personalization distorted to the point of unrecognizability.

This phenomenon once more sums up the disintegration of the public sphere in the world of letters. The sounding board of an educated stratum tutored in the public use of reason has been shattered; the public is split apart into minorities of specialists who put their reason to use non-publicly and the great mass of consumers whose receptiveness is public but uncritical. Consequently, it completely lacks the form of communication specific to a public.

Excerpts from: Jürgen Habermas: *The Structural Transformation of the Public Sphere. An Inquiry into a Category of Bourgeois Society*, MIT Press, Cambridge, Mass. 1999

# All Technologies To The People

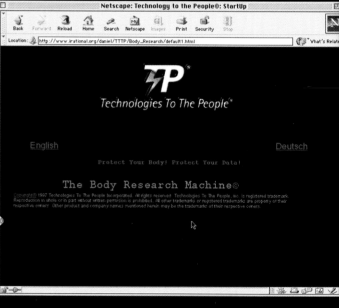

### Technologies To The People®
is both a metaphor for the use of technologies and a public provocation. I have created a virtual company that exists only as an artist project operating, really, for the rest of society.

### Technologies To The People®
works with the media infrastructure of corporate companies and sponsors art events in its representation policies.
Daniel Andujar, 1996

### Technologies To The People®
is aimed at people in the so-called Third World as well as the homeless, orphaned, expatriated or unemployed, at fringe groups, runaways, immigrants, alcoholics, drug addicts, people suffering from mental dysfunctions and any other categories of 'undesirables', at all those without social ties and unable to find a safe place to live, at all those who have to beg in order to survive.

Technologies To The People®
is for people denied access to
the new information society and
new technologies, for all those
living in the confines of new and
alien borders.

Technologies To The People®
wants to facilitate your access
to the information society.

Technologies To The People®
wants more people to be networked.

Technologies To The People®
has developed and manufactured
the Street Access Machine®
specifically for the fringe
groups named above. The machine
can be used 24 hours-a-day with
all credit cards (cybercash).
With the Street Access Machine®,
credit cards are now welcome
everywhere - including the
street. All you need to do is
install a Street Access Machine®
and problems with begging will be
a thing of the past.

Those wishing to donate money to
the needy simply present a credit
card and stipulate the sum they
are willing to part with. The
destitute can withdraw the money
from a cash dispenser using their
Recovery Card® in conjunction
with a personal password. Simple
to use and interest-free. All-
round credit card service for one
and for all.

# A Correcti

Niek van de Steeg

http://www.tgad.com

54

Social Conditions

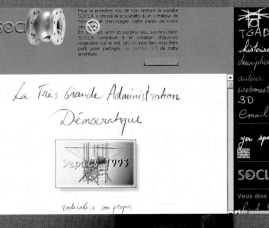

A Correction Structure invites the user to browse the internet, to print out pages, and subsequently to paste these onto the paper ceiling covering the room-like installation space. Soon the pictures, motifs and structures combine to form a new ceiling. The title of the work refers to the structures which are necessary to add mistakes to and carry out repairs on already existing architectures. In arranging textual and pictorial information from the internet to form a purely decorative collage the work refers to the often manipulative use of the material contained in the information architecture of the World Wide Web.

Is it time to stop caring? Wohin gehen die geträumten Dinge?

'The Berkeley Oracle' is the second internet-based artwork –
after the 'Plural Sculpture,' 1995 – by the renowned German
conceptual artist Jochen Gerz.
The internet is well-suited for Gerz's ephemeral,
public and interactive mode of art-making.
'The Berkeley Oracle' was launched as an interactive, internet-
based art-work on August 1, 1997. Designed by Gerz with the
assistance of Richard Rinehart, it includes texts and images
concerning the fundamental value of the spirit of questioning

Wohin gehen
die geträumten Dinge?

in our society. Visitors to the web site are asked to submit their questions
to the Oracle and may then view the questions that others throughout the
world have submitted. The Oracle is available in English, French, German,
and Spanish versions.
Recalling the paradoxically responsive Greek Oracle at
Delphi, which gave answers in the form of riddles, Gerz's
Oracle gives no answers at all.

# net·s

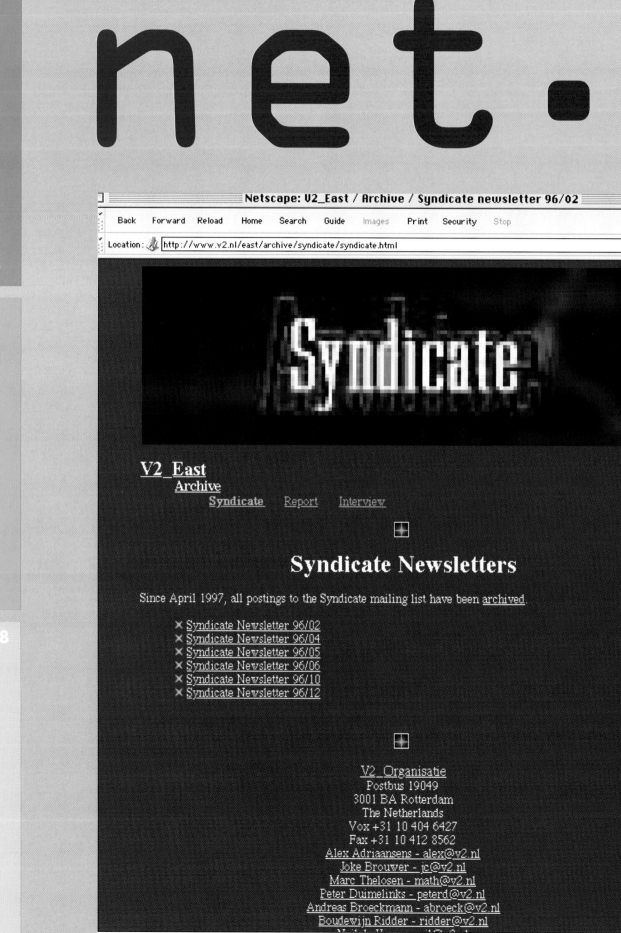

Netscape: V2_East / Archive / Syndicate newsletter 96/02

Back   Forward   Reload   Home   Search   Guide   Images   Print   Security   Stop

Location: http://www.v2.nl/east/archive/syndicate/syndicate.html

## V2_East
### Archive
Syndicate   Report   Interview

## Syndicate Newsletters

Since April 1997, all postings to the Syndicate mailing list have been archived.

- Syndicate Newsletter 96/02
- Syndicate Newsletter 96/04
- Syndicate Newsletter 96/05
- Syndicate Newsletter 96/06
- Syndicate Newsletter 96/10
- Syndicate Newsletter 96/12

V2_Organisatie
Postbus 19049
3001 BA Rotterdam
The Netherlands
Vox +31 10 404 6427
Fax +31 10 412 8562
Alex Adriaansens - alex@v2.nl
Joke Brouwer - jc@v2.nl
Marc Thelosen - math@v2.nl
Peter Duimelinks - peterd@v2.nl
Andreas Broeckmann - abroeck@v2.nl
Boudewijn Ridder - ridder@v2.nl

# hop #2

The Syndicate mailing list was set up in 1996 as a translocal communication network above all between artists, curators and critics based in Eastern Europe who work with New Media. Precisely because the situation of the art scenes in these countries was comparable, it seemed to make sense to communicate and collaborate regularly with each other and to forge a strategic alliance. Meanwhile, Syndicate has become a means of acting as a platform for an 'extended Europe' in the media-art landscape. A revised structure of the dialogue is given in the readers, of which the fourth issue is presented in theLounge.

# On Television

So I would like to analyze a series of mechanisms that allow television to wield a particularly pernicious form of symbolic violence. Symbolic violence is violence wielded with tacit complicity between its victims and its agents, insofar as both remain unconscious of submitting to or wielding it. The function of sociology, as of every science, is to reveal that which is hidden. In so doing, it can help minimize the symbolic violence within social relations and, in particular, within the relations of communication.

Let's start with an easy example - sensational news. This has always been the favorite food of the tabloids. Blood, sex, melodrama and crime have always been big sellers. In the early days of television, a sense of respectability modeled on the printed press kept these attention-grabbers under wraps, but the race for audience share inevitably brings it to the headlines and to the beginning of the television news. Sensationalism attracts notice, and it also diverts it, like magicians whose basic operating principle is to direct attention to something other than what they are doing. Part of the symbolic functioning of television, in the case of the news, for example, is to call attention to those elements which will engage everybody - which offer something for everyone. These are things that won't shock anyone, where nothing is at stake, that don't divide, are generally agreed on, and interest everybody, without touching on anything important. These items are basic ingredients of news because they interest everyone, and because they take up time - time that could be used to say something else.

And time, on television, is an extremely rare commodity. When you use up precious time to say banal things, to the extent that they cover up precious things, these banalities become in fact very important. If I stress this point, it's because everyone knows that a very high proportion of the population reads no newspaper at all and is dependent on television as their sole source of news.

Television enjoys a de facto monopoly on what goes on in the heads of a significant part of the population and what they think. So much emphasis on headlines and so much filling up of precious time with empty air - with nothing or almost nothing - shunts aside relevant news, that is, the information that all citizens ought to have in order to exercise their democratic rights. (p.17)

The world of journalism in itself is a field, but one that is subject to greater pressure from the economic field via audience ratings. This very heteronomous field, which is structurally very strongly subordinated to market pressures, in turn applies pressure to all the other fields. (p.54)

I think that all fields of cultural production today are subject to structural pressure from the journalistic field, and not from any one journalist or network executive, who are themselves subject to control by the field. This pressure exercises equivalent and systematic effects in every field. In other words, this journalistic field, which is more and more dominated by the market model, imposes its pressures more and more on other fields through pressure from audience ratings. Economic forces weigh on television, and through its effects on journalism, television weighs on newspapers and magazines, even the "purest" among them. The weight then falls on individual journalists, who little by little let themselves be drawn into television's orbit. In this way, through the weight exerted by the journalistic field, the economy weighs on all fields of cultural production. (p.56)

Audience ratings - Nielsen ratings in the US - measure the audience share won by each network. It is now possible to pinpoint the audience by the quarter hour and even - a new development - by social group. So we know very precisely who's watching what, and who not. Even in the most independent sectors of journalism, ratings have become the journalist's Last Judgment: everyone is fixated on ratings. In editorial rooms,

# (excerpts)

**51**

*dungen sind wichtig, was ist von Bedeutung fürs eigene Leben? Fahrrad-Taxter und chüsseln im indonesischen Sarabayo.* Foto: Gaval/AFP

## DER QUOTEN

*es kämpfen und sich von seinem Bann lösen soll*

*„Aufgabe der Soziologie wie aller Wissenschaften ist es, Verborgenes zu enthüllen": Pierre Bourdieu.* Foto: Demaczyr

Contribution in the newspaper
*DER STANDARD*,
Pierre Bourdieu,
11/6/1998

---

publishing houses, and similar venues, a "rating mindset" reigns. Wherever you look, people are thinking in terms of market success.

Only thirty years ago, and since the middle of the nineteenth century - since Baudelaire and Flaubert and others in avant-garde milieu of writers' writers acknowledged by other writers or even artists acknowledged by other artists - immediate market success was suspect. It was taken as a sign of compromise with the times, with money ... Today, on the contrary, the market is accepted more and more as a legitimate means of legitimation. You can see this in another recent institution, the best-seller list. Just this morning on the radio list I heard an announcer, obviously very sure of himself, run through the latest best-seller list and decree that "philosophy is hot this year, since *Le Monde de Sophie* sold eight hundred thousand copies." For him this verdict was absolute, like a final decree, provable by a number of copies sold. Audience ratings impose the sales model on cultural products.

But it is important to know that historically, all of the cultural productions that I consider (and I am not alone here, at least I hope not) the highest human products - math, poetry, literature, philosophy - were all produced against market imperatives. (p.27)

The audience rating system can and should be contested in the name of democracy (this is a favorite argument of advertisers, which has been picked up by certain sociologists, not to mention essayists who've run out of ideas and are happy to turn any criticism of opinion polls - and audience ratings - into a criticism of universal suffrage). You must, they declare, leave people free to judge and to choose for themselves ("all those elitist intellectual prejudices of yours make you turn your nose up at all this"). The audience rating system is the sanction of the market and the economy, that of an external and purely market law.

Submission to the requirements of this marketing instrument is the exact equivalent for culture of what poll-based demagogy is for politics. Enslaved by audience ratings, television imposes market pressures on the supposedly free and enlightened consumer. These pressures have nothing to do with the democratic expression of enlightened collective opinion or public rationality, despite what certain commentators would have us believe. (p. 66)

From the choices made by French writers in the occupation can be derived a more general law: The more a cultural producer is autonomous, rich in specific capital from a given field and exclusively integrated into the restricted market in which the only audience is competitors, the greater the inclination to resist. Conversely, the more producers aim for the mass market (like some essayists, writer-journalists, and popular novelists), the more likely they are to collaborate with the powers that be - State, Church, or Party, and, today, journalism and television - and to yield to their demands or their orders. (p.62)

It is not a pure world, free of concessions to politics or the economy. But its image of purity produces absolutely real social effects, first of all, on the very individuals whose job it is to declare the law. But what would happen to judges, understood as more or less sincere incarnations of a collective hypocrisy, if it became widely accepted that, far from obeying transcendent, universal verities and values, they are thoroughly subject, like all other social actors, to constraints such as those placed on them, irrespective of judicial procedures and hierarchies, by the pressure of economic necessity or the seduction of media success?

excerpts from:
**Pierre Bourdieu:**
*On Television*
(New Press, NY, 1999)

# Event/Transformation/Information:

"We must be able to pass on to the coming generations - if not as the legacy of these times then as a kind of message in a bottle - what computer technology meant to the first generation it affected." (Friedrich Kittler)

The signs are everywhere about looming crisis. The crisis of art, the crisis of the economy, the crisis of information, the crisis of the image, the crisis of the millennium, the crisis of identity, the crisis of mega-mergers, the crisis of confidence, the crisis of the Middle East, Asia, Africa, the crisis of health, the crisis of modernity, the crisis of post-modernity, the crisis of cyber-modernity, the list goes on and on and on. For us in the field of media archeology, the crisis is signified in many ways. The Fall line-up of festivals was itself a dizzying array of crisis esthetics. *Ars Electronica*'s "Infowar," *ISEA*'s "Revolution and Terror," the "Art and Global Media" symposium, the upcoming *DEAF98* festival "The Art of the Accident." And here we are in an emerging environment in which the siege of representation is taking place amid stunning conflicts and mergers in every field. Just in the past week the formation of the world's biggest financial institution (Deutsche Bank and Banker's Trust), the world's biggest energy company (Exxon and Mobil), the world's biggest internet portal (as AOL buys Netscape). This while the world's biggest software manufacturer is in the midst of significant anti-trust litigation in Washington, this while the Russian economy is propped up by the World Bank. All these shocking reminders that the stability of our relationship with history, memory, politics, identity, and technology is itself under siege.

On the recent flight, there was an article in the *International Herald Tribune* about the misrepresentation of scientists in Hollywood. It said, in part, "Science is out of reach as perceived by the vast, vast, vast majority of people." It continued, "From Dr Frankenstein to Dr Strangelove, from the grave robbers of yesteryear to the cloners of today, scientists in movies are almost invariably mad, evil, antisocial, clumsy, or eccentric." The article reminded me of a remark made in a fascinating symposium in New York last year called "Technology and the Rest of Culture." Of the many aging luminaries on the panel (Langdon Winner, Leo Marx,

Peter Galison and others), there was a rambling talk by the great poobah of Artificial Intelligence, Marvin Minsky. His unintentionally erratic (actually more incoherent than erratic) presentation was filled with zealous exaggerations. The most glaring was an almost passing characterization of the relationship between science and culture that still makes me wince with anxiety. In the midst of his talk he paused for a moment and said: "Culture ... is just bad science." It was a shocking sound bite that revealed the scope of a crisis that haunts the discourse between the allegedly unscientific disciplines of philosophy, sociology, or art. It was diagnostic - and hence a sort of revelation - in the most insidiously grandiose way. Yet Minsky's reckless (one assumes) comment comes while the 'triumphs of reason' that come with technoculture are again in the forefront of cultural studies. For Minsky culture is failure, failure to heed the legitimations of scientific method, of technical mastery masquerading as social logic, a kind of systems-ideology that is predominating the end of the millennium debates about the role of technology as integrated not just into every single transaction we have in the world but in the speculative technologies that will enact the willed - should one say programmed - realities that will come in the near future.

The same *Herald* article cited a remark by Oxford geneticist Richard Dawkins, patron saint of the memetic frenzy that attempts to socialize a problematic reinterpretation of evolution as indistinguishable from computer programming and an idea that has spawned broad re-evaluations of the relationships between biology and culture. "The natural world," wrote Dawkins, "is fascinating in its own right... It really doesn't need human drama to be fascinating." Since the flight was long I also read a blurb in *Wired* by Hans Moravec who has published a new book on Robots. His speculative work certainly straddles the line between reason and conjecture and reminded me of the description I once heard about so-called visionaries - and especially the self-declared ones!: "A visionary is just a crackpot you happen to believe." His comment: "As a storage medium DNA has run its course. The iMAC doesn't have floppy disks; our descendants won't have DNA." Classic dissociation and illog-

# Enacting the Image

ical affinity. And if the so-called science wars - where cultural theory is chastened for any foray into cultural readings of the unassailable realms of science - are any indication (as represented by the flippant and antisocial works of Alan Sokal, Gross and Levitt, and a growing chorus of scientific apologists), then a crisis of technological discourse is also emerging.

Deeply entrenched in systems-think, the new generation of cyber-crats nevertheless spend considerable time rationalizing a deeply flawed legitimation of evolutionary algorithmics as a historically viable evolutionary theory. In a growing literature, this idea is being deconstructed as a cross between essentialism and universalization. Stephen Jay Gould is attacking Steven Pinker (author of *How the Mind Works*) in a series of essays in *The New York Review of Books* where the differences between biological and computational ideologies emerge as a central arena, one that is as much connected to the theme of this symposium as any I can imagine. "In [between] the images," between the 'image' of analogy (on which so much of our relationship with representation stands) and the 'image' of computation (on which the rendering of our relationship with representation stands). This is not so much a porous border as a decisive one in which technology subsumes information into a cosmic database that itself assumes the role of an apparatus, an apparatus that is as entrenched in an evolving electronic totality as broadcast media was for the cold war. Yet, its language comes in the old, user-friendly terminologies of cyber-speak. The worn metaphors of Command, Control and Communication (C3) have been extended. Communication Intelligence (COMINT), Electronic Intelligence (EINT) is evolving into Signal Intelligence (SIGNIT) in which Human Intelligence (affectionately known as HUMINT) is eclipsed by simulated intelligence (SIMINT). Knowledge and Game Theory merge. Information itself becomes militarized, the ideological state apparatus becomes the ideological SENSE apparatus. We face the specter of the so-called 'new sciences' of the artificial and its lexicon of the intentionally ambiguous: 'the attention economy,' 'behavioral economics,' 'automatic execution,' presumptions of 'conscious hardware,' 'artificial insight,' 'epistemic warfare,' the 'secret sphere,' 'soft power...' These reductive phrases come as signifiers of constant reminders of the anxiety diet that we too willingly partake in. The seductions of illusion, the often frustrated mnemonics of electronic memory, the faux correspondences between the so-called virtual and the so-called real world, emerge amid ever more complex and ever more speculative narratives so that, as Jameson suggested as the essential condition of postmodernity, we are narrating the end of narrative by means of narrative. (Didn't we see some of this last night?) With this comes a fascinating kind of retreat into the subjectivity less of reflection than of refuge. These virtualized refuges run the risk of exposing some clear vulnerabilities in our public relationship with identity and technology. Indeed reductionism seems a welcomed consequence for a culture driven by individuated mechanisms that reinforce isolation and the vulnerability of information. George Stein, at "Infowar," was very clear about this operational condition when he said: "Information leads to dependency, dependency to vulnerability, vulnerability to defeat." So as we oscillate between the public and private spheres, there is a challenge to face the pathetic cyber-sociological end of material public sphere politics and the equally eerie legitimation of 'being Digital,' of 'Life on the Screen,' or of an artificial life without its other. How this cleansed ideology of systems affects our perspective on history, memory or illusion is a tough question. Suffice to suggest, as does Regis Debray in *Media Manifestos*: "One will write 'society' in place of 'humanity,' and 'spectacle' for 'ideology.' Essentialist ontologies are obliged to wipe out everything discovered since 1848..."

How do we undo (in a world where limitless undo's or the undoing of the not yet done, as we heard last night) the kind of digital repressive tolerance, remain vigilant to the state of emergency that is so cogently referred to by both Walter Benjamin and Carl Schmidt? Benjamin wrote: "the tradition of the oppressed teaches us that the 'state of emergency' in which we live is not the exception but the rule. We must," he continues, "attain to a conception of history that is in keeping with this insight. Then we shall clearly recognize that it is our task to

bring about a real state of emergency."
Carl Schmidt extended this by saying "the
one who controls the state of emergency
is sovereign." Debray reminds us too that
"no more than there is any innocent
medium can there be any painless transmission."

Invisibility is a deception. Vulnerability is
assumed. Passivity is expected. If we follow the logic of the electronic culture
industries, the so-called 'virtual corporations,' the coercive and reductive mergers
of telecommunications and the international information flow, or the erratic formation of telecommunications policy (or
its history), it is clear that the regulation
of civil life is driven not by the sustenance
of political liberty, individual autonomy
or the encouragement of serious cultural
discourse. The signs of this are pervasive
and range from the growing fields of
genetic screening (more or less a form
of diagnostic domination veiled behind
medical mastery) to the erosion of the
boundary between the public and private spheres.

The culture of Modernity, in which the universalization, moralization and mecha-
nization of representation evolved, has
been surpassed. A technological model
has been usurped by a cybernetic model,
telephobic modernity with telephilic postmodernity.

If there is a common denominator within
the discourses of postmodernity, it is that
the ascendancy of a system of scientific
visualization and the loss of any totaliz-
ing model of either the "real" world or
its representations can be put into place -
even while the stability of representation
is alternately established and disestab-
lished by the social effect of the image
(think of the fate of the Rodney King
Video). The camouflage over the shaky
epistemological foundation of representation has been effaced by the dual
deconstructions of psychoanalysis and
technology. The unrepresentable 'Real'
collides with the unreflected 'Virtual.'
And, as Zizek has remarked, "virtuality
is already at work operating in the symbolic order as such to the extent to which
virtual phenomenon retroactively enable
us to discover to what extent all our most
elementary self-experience was virtual."
It cannot be a surprise that the panoptic
metaphors of Bentham and Foucault are

re-invented in the technosphere in the
guise of electronic 'agents,' digital security systems, genetic screening, satellite
imaging technologies with imaging capability of less than one meter resolution
from 35,000 miles in 'space,' SkyCam
news networks with robotic cameras surveying for crisis, in short more than a
panoptic metaphor but a transoptic one
in which the invisible threat of the gaze is
welcomed as a symptom of containment
and stability. Indeed, while issues of
space dominated discourses of modernity, the related issues of presence and
temporality have come to stand within
postmodernity as signifiers of a far more
intricate situation. Worn traditions of the
public sphere, the sociology of post-
industrialization, the discreteness of
identity, have been supplanted by a form
of distributed imbeddedness - or better,
the immersion - of the self in the media-
scapes of tele-culture which must generate a communicative practice whose
boundaries are mapped in virtual, transi-
tory networks, whose hold on matter is
ephemeral, whose position in space is
tenuous, and whose agency is measured
in acts of implication rather than mere
coincidences of location.

"... one practical advantage of reality
video (video that appears to replicate history) must be recognized - its function as
a democratic form of counter-surveil-
lance." (The Critical Art Ensemble)

In the first hours after the bombings in
Kenya and Tanzania, the broadcast
media was saturated by video feeds that
switched between images of individual
victims and images of hundreds of citizens who mobilized rescue efforts. A day
later the scene had changed drastically.
Space became logistical and not civil. Victims were clearly secondary to evidence,
the sites became armed camps. Mobilized intelligence and military forces
'secured' the site (as they have done in
Northern Ireland, Lebanon, Oklahoma
City...). Immediately came the voices of
both regret and accusation. The tropes
are now part of the rhetoric of terrorist
public relations ("No matter what it
takes," "Justice will be done," "No limit
to our resolve," etc.). In the aftermath,
though, a new phrase emerged in the
equivocal linguistic arena: "Soft Targets."
Easily understood as sites with limited or
lax security, the term 'Soft Targets' comes

enveloped in implications that extend beyond attainable terrorist objectives into the less concrete (literally) arenas of information and/or bodies. Formerly called "collateral," these 'soft targets' will increasingly be signified as casualties in information, biological or genetic conflicts.

Because the development and deployment of technology straddles the boundaries of the military and cultural industries, it seems necessary to reveal - if not undo - the forms of authority whose strategies circumscribe independence by evoking rationales of defensive order or international stability. Reactionary by necessity, these strategies contain radical innovation and maintain security. In this sense, it is clear, as The Critical Art Ensemble suggest, that a bunker ideology pervades the public sphere, and that "the continual disturbance of these sites is essential in the never-ending battle to maintain a degree of individual autonomy." (ECD 39) So between the protectionist technologies of sovereign power and the blissful information mythology of the cybersphere, crisis continually looms. Gilles Deleuze characterized it thus: "We are in a generalized crisis in relation to all the environments of enclosure."

Bruno Latour remarked in a recent interview, "Images demonstrate transformation, not information." Though not so startling a position in a culture compulsively engaged in the assessment of representation, Latour's comment reminds us that the role of the image can no longer be comfortably enveloped in lingering phenomenological or simple semiotic traditions. Yet the stakes in the image have consistently grown in scope, principally because of the evolving technologies utilized in their production. Because of this, a reconceptualization of the formation, function and reception of the image seems urgently necessary.

Conclusion: Hans Magnus Enzensberger once wrote that "no avant-garde has thus called for the police to rid it of its opponents." Times have changed. The coy alliance between ferment and repressive tolerance has enveloped most of the creative practices of the 20th century. As is clear from even a casual understanding of the cultural, political, and creative practices of the past 20 years, the issues

of technology and computing have generated responses ranging from euphoric desperation to heroic tele-modernities. In the accelerating environment of the past decade, the urgency of the staggering cumulative effects of techno-science and its consequences has hardly been conceptualized despite a growing literature of speculative, theoretical and pseudo-non-fictional assessments. In an era in which the inversion of avant-garde and corporate intention further blurs the already hazy legitimacy of any notion of the avant-garde, it comes as little surprise that politics, spectacle, technology, revolution, violence, and surveillance meet in a perverse ecological system in which the police, militias, terrorists, artists, corporate visionaries, and futurists join in survivalist tactics that are on the border between retroactive legitimation and terminal compromise.

The penetration of technology within the body and the socialization of simulated realities is more than a signifier of technological progress, it marks a radical transformation of knowledge, of biology, and of the cultural order in which knowledge is linked with ideology, biology, or identity in terms of a technological imperative not fundamentally connected with necessity. The consequence of genetic engineering (or perhaps more appropriately genetic therapies), of patented life-forms, of radicalized techno-medicine or techno-psychology, are among the sweeping ethical issues of our time. Indeed a discourse is emerging concerning the use of cosmetic genetics and cosmetic psycho-pharmacology to determine everything from a tendency to certain illnesses and the selectable gendering of children to the normalization of behavior through the use of psychotropic drugs which induce only the symptoms of normalcy. And you know how it goes - first symptoms of normalcy and then simulations of satisfaction.

As Herbert Marcuse wrote: "Art, as an instrument of opposition, depends on the alienating force of the esthetic creation, on its power to remain strange, antagonistic, transcendent to normalcy and, at the same time, being the reservoir of man's supressed needs, faculties and desires, to remain more real than the reality of normalcy."

# Attention in the Media Age

On the global attention market, where readily available information that can be accessed from anywhere vies for our attention twenty-four hours a day, i.e. in a state of over-stimulation and faced with a multitude of options, as it were, it is necessary to target this scarce resource that ties up our individual time and, quite literally, energies, as directly as possible, on the assumption that the most successful approach, having observed the interests of users, is to offer products that have met with their interest before. The strategy, then, is that something that has got attention in the past will get attention in the future. Indeed, this is a general law of the attention economy, which is why prominence - not only of individuals but also of commodities, subjects or situations - is becoming so all-important. Prominence is accumulated attention and a kind of magic wand that can communicate attention. So today, without prominence, there's just nothing doing. In a way, it is the embodiment of advertising, and advertising is no longer an industry that has been hived off from art but rather a key factor integrated in all enterprises, an instrument used for designing events, institutions, organisations, people, subjects, and things in a manner that is aimed at getting attention. Prominence and advertising are one. And incidentally, in the last century advertising only emerged as a form of staging attention for goods, parallel to the political forms of propaganda and terrorism. Terrorism, being the propaganda of small groups, works with the aesthetics of shock - and is of course equally amenable to the dynamics of trying to outdo everyone else.

Of course, in the information society, content or even knowledge is not what is called for but rather first and foremost the possibility of catching and, if possible, keeping people's attention in a growing market of data packages directly tailored to attracting attention. Unlike in German, where attention is "given" (schenken: to give or make a present of something), English is much clearer: in English we pay (for and with) attention. Ultimately, a society that is controlled by the economy of attention cultivates an aesthetics of shock, if we see shocking as always having to present what is aberrant, exceptional, new or notable.

Of course, art has always aimed at attracting attention and yet, with the emergence of technical media such as photography and later film, a large part of art - with the advent of futurism, Dadaism and surrealism - has appropriated the aesthetics of shock. Violating the conventional has become a fundamental aesthetic motif. The increased correspondence with the media, the collective and clustering systems of attention of a society, has of course expedited this process.

A dynamism inheres in this aesthetics that is permanently in search of new stimuli and which never comes to a standstill, like the biological system of attention itself. When something is already known, it ceases to attract attention. Its principle is to outdo and intensify, but, as you all know, this principle is not an objective autonomous quantity, but rather what is notable is always notable in a context that is constantly shifting – similar to people's moods – and which thus shifts the direction of attention. If a designer does not use Claudia Schiffer or one of the other prominent models, but rather someone with a leg amputated, similar to Benetton's advertisements with disabled children he overturns people's expectations. Like Duchamp's urinal did, this leads to protests – and of course to attention. But the conflict involved is quite clear: even when surrounded by the spectacular, to be spectacularly unspectacular and ordinary, if this is an exception and if this runs counter to expectations.

On the other hand, people are always searching for new stimulants to hold their attention, but at the same time they must protect themselves from being inundated with information or, in some cases, evade surveillance. After all, observation and surveillance are also a decisive form of attention that is gaining presence particularly through computer technology and networks as it is becoming much easier to collect, store and evaluate vast amounts of data.

## Publishing the intimate

In July, in addition to the first gorilla to take part in an internet chat and Boris Jelzin's web debut, followed by the first

German chancellor's go at chatting, we saw the first live transmission of a birth on the web, purportedly watched by some two million people. Shortly after that, you could watch two volunteers via webcam being kidnapped by a group of English artists and locked up in a cell for two days. Their life as prisoners took place in public day and night, for anyone could watch them through a webcam.

The great model in terms of publishing one's private and intimate life by webcam is of course Jenny, who two years ago began publishing her life from her room around the clock. Since 1997, the economics graduate (!) has been charging 15 dollars a year which has not, however, deterred most people. Unlike many other live cameras, Jenny does not aim to satisfy pornographic needs and so far has waived all offers to sell her name or do any product placement. Even though she is seen naked occasionally, she has now refrained from her earlier striptease shows which no doubt attracted many people, and now wants to show her authentic, rather boring, but unfaked, day-to-day life as a prominent person of everyday life. It would seem that reality or authenticity is a convincing factor in cyberspace: "The idea of the cam" she says "is to show everything that happens naturally. The cam has been there long enough now that I don't notice it any more. So whatever you see is not performed or feigned, and even if I don't claim to be the most interesting person in the world, there is something fascinating about real life that would not be appropriate to the medium if it were staged."

Eric Ciprian, a 27-year-old engineer at Intel, recently installed six webcams in his apartment. He proudly tells us that he uses the best technology available on the market. Leading his life in the public eye cost him some 200,000 dollars. Apparently he has 6000 visitors a day. So that's some crowd – and Ciprian has become an everyday hero. He had to remove the camera in his office because Intel did not want people watching a member of their company at work. So you can see what is still private in the attention economy. Ciprian, too, is also seen naked sometimes, but he does not want to show any sex. He says he is "pretty normal": "With

SynCity I'm trying to offer people an open window into the life of an atypical software engineer from Portland, Oregon – and if they think this is interesting, then that's great. And if they think it's boring, then that's fine, too."

Ciprian does not tell us why he is going public. He says he needs the site to keep a record of his life and to share the records of his life with the world: "I think that's great."

What makes people expose more and more of themselves and live their everyday lives in the public eye in private rooms equipped with webcams? And what is the kick that voyeurs get, not from getting a glimpse into a staged scene acted out by some performers, but from sharing in everyday people's everyday lives? But equally so in prominent people's lives, for example the American president's sex escapades at the White House?

Jenny claims that she hasn't given up her privacy because she is being watched from a distance by anonymous people via webcam: "Just because people can see me doesn't mean that it influences me – I'm still alone in my room."

But publishing the intimate through the net has gone one step further. Apparently these "pioneers" and models are battling against existing walls that protect privacy and conceal it from the public eye. Perhaps this is an anticipated adaptation to the increasing possibilities of surveillance to which we are compulsorily exposed. The trick could be to learn how to ignore surveillance and lead as usual and inconspicuous a life as possible, indeed how to be able to lead one's life at all despite the viewers and voyeurs, without having to put on a show all the time – or perhaps vice-versa: how to turn your life into a work of art, a twenty-four-hour performance.

In any case, only the first people to do something get any attention. WebCams are spreading fast, the desire to publish one's private life is as contagious as a meme. The inroads on private spaces and what was once a private life are widening and are becoming more general. And, of course, everyone tries to outdo what has already been done. It would seem that the relation between privacy and what is public is becoming inverted. Since our homes are linked up more directly to the public sphere by the media than when we actually go out into the public sphere – except for when we take part in a mass spectacle such as the celebrations when France won the World Cup in Paris, the Love Parade in Berlin, or Diana's funeral – now we not only want to let the world in, we also want to share in its publicness so as to get attention, indeed perhaps even become prominent. People are becoming detached from places and are everpresent. Although this publishing of the intimate still takes place to a large extent in private rooms transformed into stages, soon, with the aid of wearable computing we will be public everywhere – and we will expose ourselves without inhibition to surveillance as though we had given up fighting against the 'enemy,' now trying to dupe the watchers with a strategy of subversive affirmation.

Of course, it would be interesting to see whether and how certain niches will emerge that supersede what was once private – including private rooms protected by walls. Or is it just that we can no longer take being lonely and alone, not getting attention, so that publishing our private lives has not so much to do with narcissism and voyeurism, as most people think, as with new forms of social coexistence that are taking place in cyberspace. Once upon a time, before the days of the web, communards took out all their doors in an exuberant show of criticism of the middle-class way of life. The battle against shame is continuing today, albeit without any immediate political intentions. The transfer of the world into panoptic cyberspace has begun. But once we are able to see everything, what will captivate our interest and our attention?

## Surveillance

There is not much point in talking about surveillance and registration of user behaviour in the net – it's omnipresent. It is used to identify attention so as to be able to engineer services to cater better for this attention and to gain a

market advantage that can be turned into prominence, power or money. What is at risk in the net, at least until powerful cryptography is common and legal practice, is the anonymity of the user. Security and anonymity always have two faces: on the one hand we want to protect ourselves from encroachments and, on the other, we wish to keep certain things secret. Thus, the security industry for paying customers has not only become a booming service sector in the 'real' world, but also in the net. One aspect it always involves is the possibility of transferring surveilling and searching attention from people to machines and preventing surveillance with the aid of technical equipment. We could call this the rationalisation of attention.

In view of the fact that more and more data are being stored in databases or can be registered and collected about people's activities in the net, private detective agencies are also booming. The new hi-tech detectives no longer shadow people on the street, now they search for data in various nets. For a charge, agencies such as Dig Dirt (http://www.pimall.com/digdirt), Advanced Research (http://quickpage.com/A/asresearch) or WeSpy4U (http://www.wespy4u.com) sell secret phone numbers, bank account numbers, addresses of phone numbers, salary details, credit card numbers, phone conversation recordings, criminal records, medical data or exact financial circumstances. DTB-Online collects all available data and gives its clients details on a certain person's social insurance number, date of birth, phone number, address, neighbours, business partners or property ownership.

Security of buildings and places is being increasingly tightened. Even today there is a host of technical means of surveillance and identification, video cameras, motion sensors, heat sensors, voice or iris identification systems in addition to commercial high-resolution reconnaissance satellites and the Global Positioning System.

But networked computers are also the ideal means for employers, too, to monitor their staff and check their attention. That goes from slimming down computers to network computers that only run certain programs, to programs such as "Antigame" that scans a network for games or other entertainment software, and finally to programs such as "Little Brother" that records what web sites staff visit. While initially networking PCs had given people the freedom to write private e-mails or indulge in other pleasures, i.e. distracting their attention from work, today employers are becoming increasingly skeptical of unmonitored access to the net and have begun tightening surveillance of their staff's computer activities. This will become particularly interesting when telework begins to gain ground.

The fact that surveillance cameras are spreading all over seems to be a process that cannot be stopped. We have become accustomed to the staring eye watching us in public places, in underground stations and at airports, at bank counters, in department stores and supermarkets, in building entrance areas or wherever.

Imagine going into a department store and looking round. Or going into a car park where you have parked your car. Or perhaps you're just strolling around a square. Suddenly the police or a private security firm shows up and claims that you have just stolen something, that you were trying to steal a car or start an argument. You didn't notice the video camera recording your movements, analysing them for suspicious behaviour patterns. Perhaps you just couldn't decide, perhaps you were a bit confused, perhaps you were just looking round too much. Whatever it was, it was suspicious.

Next time, you'll take a closer look round to see if you can see any cameras, and perhaps – having spotted one – you'll try to behave as inconspicuously as you can so as not to be suspected. But this could be precisely the reason for your being tense and setting off the next alarm. You won't be able to avoid all these places equipped with video cameras that don't give away whether they are 'intelligent.' The result may be that you develop paranoia – or an all the more well-developed superego that preventively monitors and normalises everything you do. Woe betide anyone who steps out of line and trig-

gers the attention of security firms and their machines.

In Britain, with a total of 200,000 surveillance cameras already in place and an additional 500 every week, the police are currently testing a new surveillance system that is supposed to be able to identify car thieves before they commit their crime. The authorities are following technical developments with interest if they serve the purpose of boosting the effectiveness of police tasks.

The system was developed at the University of Leeds in collaboration with the University of Reading. It 'learns' to distinguish 'normal' behaviour taped in car parks or supermarkets from 'suspicious' behaviour and sets off an alarm whenever someone behaves conspicuously. "On the basis of observations of human behaviour patterns," project manager Hogg asserts, "we know that when thieves enter a shop with the intention of stealing something, even the way they enter the shop is unusual and that the system will notice." With new algorithms, the system allegedly eliminates coincidences that can occur due to poor lighting, shadows or other disturbances, and can predict peoples' and cars' movements. However, the system will only be fully developed in a few years' time. So we've still got that much time at least to behave the way we do.

The increasing surveillance of public places is possibly a good way of indirectly speeding up people's entry into the information society even more. A battle between surveillance and our wish for privacy is raging. Perhaps sometime soon companies will offer non-monitored places. Generally, we will get into the habit of avoiding a conspicuous appearance at all costs and conforming in our behaviour, even when we are about to commit a theft or make an attempt on someone's life. But perhaps soon they will be able to scan our brain activity from a remote location so as to nip anything unusual in the bud, which is why we will always carry a jammer with us, which in turn can be identified, which will in turn make us just as suspicious as when we send a coded e-mail.

http://www.xspace.at

# The net·art· archive

project consists of video-film images taken from two video works by Grzinic and Smid: "Post-socialism + Retro-Avant-Garde + IRWIN" (1997) and "On the Flies of the Market Place" (1999). Besides this the "net·art·archive" project includes texts and images scanned, copied, and redone from magazines, encyclopedias, and books that were part of the ideological, political and social space of the state once known as Yugoslavia. All these materials are a sort of archive that today is neither part of a fixed geographical nor historical background. The text on the site by Marina Grzinic reflects on the importance of the archive, the construction of the archive and the relations of power in the archive itself and among other archives. The video "Post-socialism + Retro-Avant-Garde + IRWIN" (1997) is a kind of philosophical media-reflection (treatise) on the cultural-artistic and political space / condition of the present post-socialist period in the territory of Ex-Yugoslavia in the 1980s and 1990s and its cultural, socio-

Post-industrial, post-modern, post-nationalist, post-colonial

political and esthetic implications. Three artists / art group
coming from Ljubljana (IRWIN),
Zagreb (Mladen Stilinovic) and Belgrade (the artist is only known by
his pseudonym 'Kasimir Malevich')
with their artistic projects and
especially with their relation to
the socialist and post-socialist
ideology code the ex-Yugoslavian
space / territory in a specific way.
RETROAVANTGARDA is the result of
this coding process: 'retroavantgarda' is a specific esthetic and
social movement produced by these
artists and some others having
recently come from Eastern Europe.
The video is filled with some exclusive documentary materials, as well
as with statements by the Slovenian
philosopher Slavoj Zizek, by Peter
Weibel and by the group IRWIN.
"On the Flies of the Market Place"
(1999) is a video that deals with
the idea of the European space,
divided, sacrificed. In an exemplary visually constructed surre-
alistic world of facts and emotions, using documents from books
and magazines, the video raises the
question of rereading the European
space: Eastern and Western Europe.
With references to history, philosophy (Kant), and arts, the video
elaborates the idea of Eastern
Europe as the indivisible remainder
of all European atrocities. Eastern
Europe is a piece of shit and the
bloody symptom of the political,
cultural and epistemological failures of the present century.

# THE RULES

Markus Huemer

http://www.khm.de/~huemer

A networked installation based upon Jackson Pollock's painting "No.32". The whole of the floor of the area is covered with a reproduction of Pollock's said picture as a reference to 'The Dance of Dripping' and to 'All Over'. Two text projections with auto-generating sentences are randomly projected on the head wall of the gallery.

Visitors are both receptors and producers of the projected texts. In order to read the text, the audience will move to and fro, triggering an Internet-mechanism through the sheer act of walking on Pollock's picture. It is this mechanism that generates the text, and each visitor's movement will lead to the generation of a new line of text. Additionally, when the visitors approach one of the projections in order to read the texts, the sentences will be generated on the second projection. Thus the two projections communicate with each other and the visitors, paraphrasing the relative positions of the visitors within the exhibition space from a point-of-view that is situated on the Net. All generated texts will use the subjunctive mode (conjunctivus, irrealis and potentialis) and the texts are accessible on the Net via any Internet gateway.

What results is an inversion of the 'classical' exhibition situation – here, Art watches the audience and reacts to their actions with a continuous transformation of its self.

By their movement in the space, the visitors will revive the 'Dance of Dripping' on the 'prefabricated' Action Painting by Pollock, their actions being monitored and 'interpreted' by the Net generating the textual response. Through this immersion into the 'virtual outside' the visitors will lose their status as subjects and become the objects of a description by the Net.

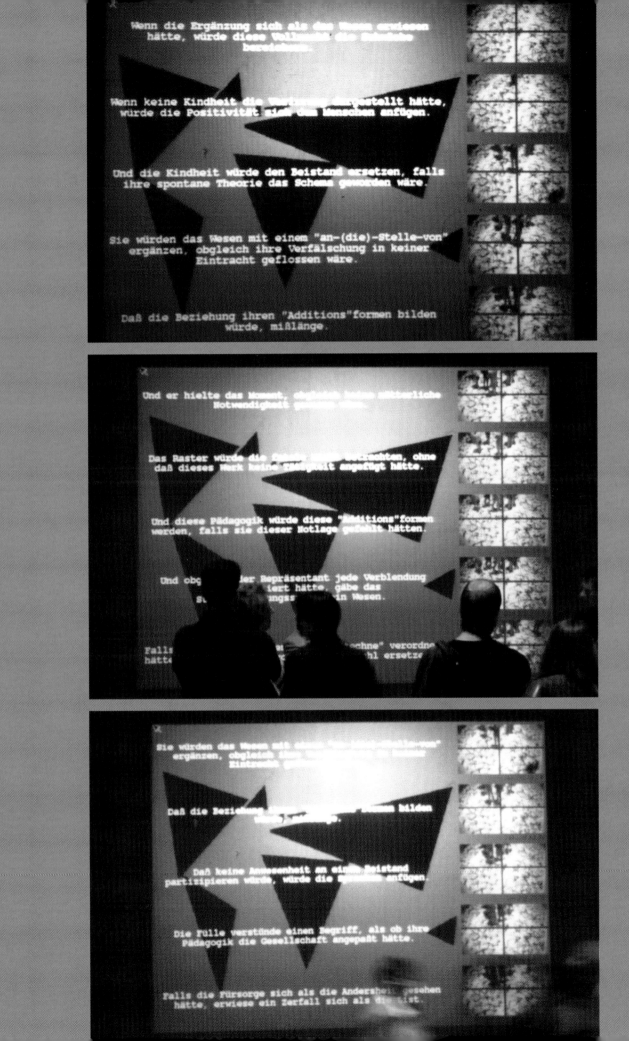

Web pages are temporary graphic images created when browsing software interprets HTML
instructions. As long as all browsers agree
(at least somewhat) on the conventions of
HTML there is the illusion of solidity or
permanence in the web. But behind the graphical illusion is a vast body of text files

The Sh

- containing HTML code - that fills hard
drives on computers at locations all over the
world. Collectively these instructions make
up what we call 'the web'. But what if these
instructions are interpreted differently than
intended? Perhaps radically differently?

The Shredder presents this global structure as a chaotic, irrational, raucous
collage. By altering the HTML code before
the browser reads it, the Shredder appro-
priates the data of the web, transforming
it into a parallel web. Content becomes
abstraction. Text becomes graphics.
Information becomes art.

The web is not a publication. Web sites are not
paper. Yet the current thinking of web design is
that of the magazine, newspaper, book, or catalog. Visually, aesthetically, legally, the web is
treated as a physical page upon which text and
images are written. The Shredder wreaks havoc on
this illusion of physicality.

EMPIRE 24/7

LIVE WEBCAM

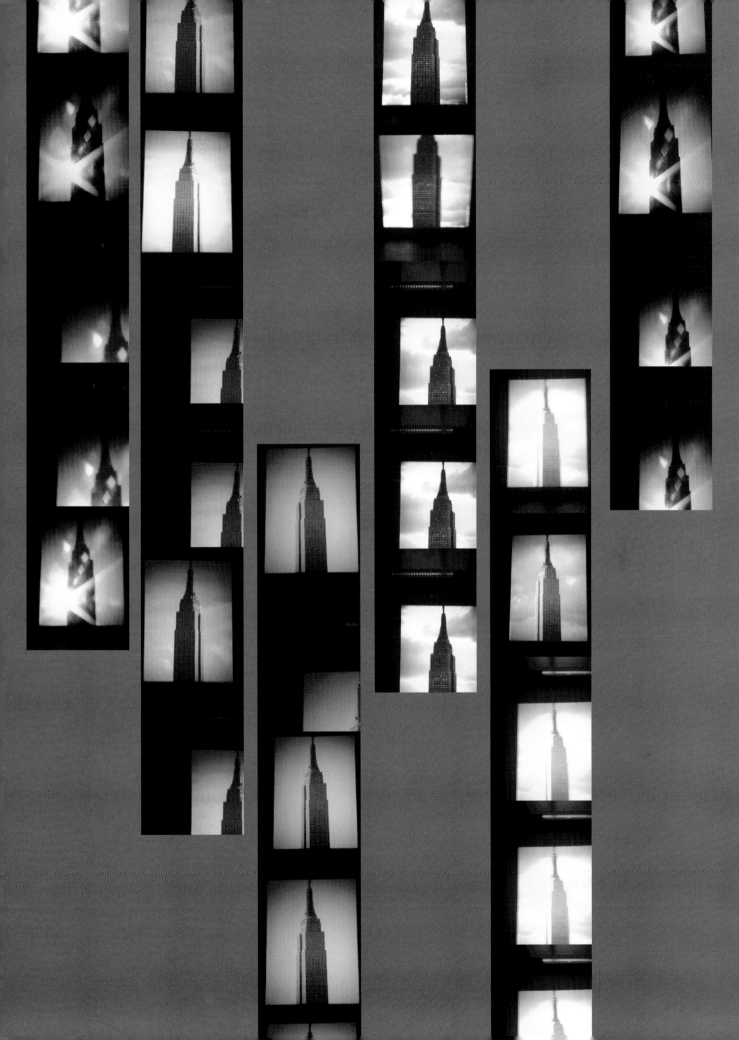

?     Himalaya      ?

k   GIFT***SHOP***GIFT***SHOP***G   re-enter re-enter re-er

dinosaur,     extinction.

I am referring to the American media.

DODGE

netomatic1 – text&images    memory:2833    speed:46

We found positions.

# M A T

TM is a meta-browser that engages a different Internet an Internet that is an intelligent application and not simply a large database of static files. NETOMAT™ dialogues with the net to retrieve information as unmediated and independent in form. It is a browser only by convention. Our current point-and-click navigation, rigid information distribution, and passive browsing of "authored" information in today's interactivity will be of little use when using NETOMAT™

With NETOMAT™ the user has a dialogue with the Internet. You can ask the net a question using natural language. NETOMAT™ responds by flowing text, images and audio from the net to your screen. You respond or ask further questions or write keywords and the flow of data to your desktop is altered in response. The data is not constrained by a web page or site but free floating and independent. NETOMAT™ can retrieve almost all types of data that resides on the Internet, including streaming audio, jpegs, gifs, aiff, wav, html, xml and plain text. NETOMAT™ dialogues with you as well. It memorizes your session to further enable your search and exploration of the Internet.

NETOMAT's meta-browser components will be available as open source software to be written by anyone who wishes to. As you can imagine, the potential is enormous for a countless number of browser interfaces to be created with a rich diversity of open source produced functionality written by a vast community of users. The Internet is clearly different with the launch of netomat!

...NETOMAT™ has the feel of an anti-browser and eschews the anachronistic page structure of today's web by not privileging layout and design.

NETOMAT™ is freely distributed on the network ...
Ron Wakkary, june 1999

ARTreporter *at the net_condition*

Dave Bruckmayr/Gaylord Aulke

http://webreporter.agi.de/
artreporter

82

Community Conditions

# ::.::: zkm ....:.::09/22
# & steirischer herbst 99
## ..:.::.::09/25

## art consumers
## comment on net.art
netz_bedingung / net_condition

Kunst im Online-Universum

23. 09. 1999 - 09. 01. 2000

netz_bedingung / net_condition

Art in the Online Universe
23 September 1999 - 9 January 2000

The Artreporter is the mobile interface between the net_condition and its consumers.

On September 22 the people at the ZKM become art accomplices.

The Artreporter connects them to the exhibited netart, pulls them out off their role as passive art consumers.

Equipped with a Body PC, the Artreporter wanders the ZKM and interviews the people, asks them for their opinion on the exhibition, records their perspectives on net.art, then posts the comments on the ZKM-Website, creating a small library that is open to the public worldwide.

Backspace, headed by James Stevens, is both a physical space on the south bank of the Thames in London and an on-line space for national and international art projects.

The Backspace web site is an interface for current, constantly changing net projects. At the real-world location, the studio, the project promotes progressive artistic and technological developments. It was provided to the Backspace founders in 1996 by an advertising design firm also based there, with the aim of promoting aesthetic inventiveness and radicalism beyond the institutional framework.

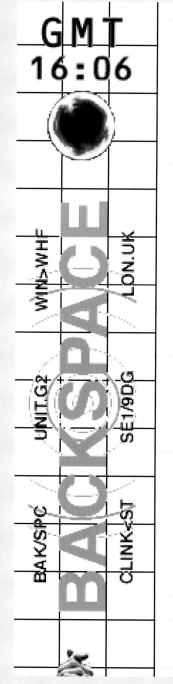

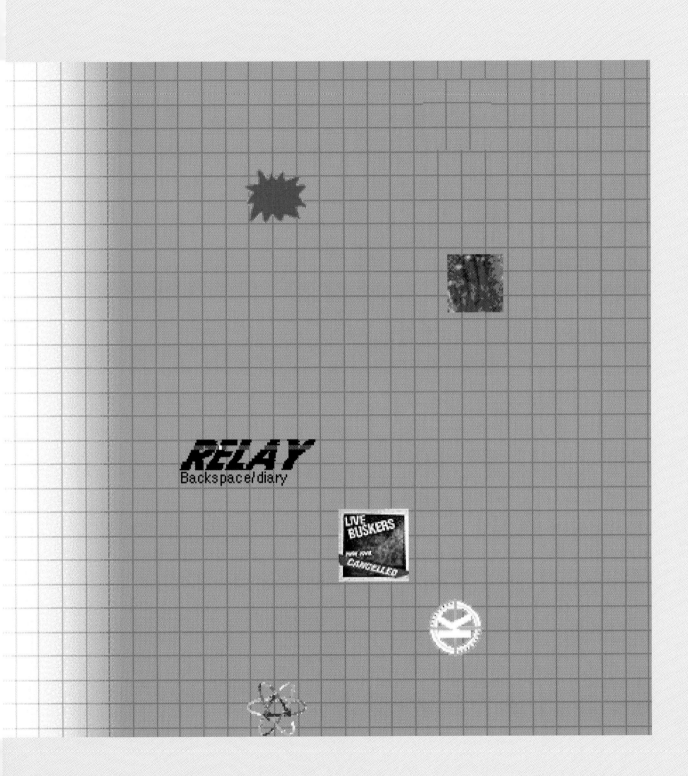

Natalie Bookchin

http://www.calarts.edu/~bookchin/intruder/

Community Conditions

T
Th
The
The    I
The    In
The    Int
The    Intr
The    Intru
The    Intrud
The    Intrude
The    Intruder
The    Intruder
The    Intrude
The    Intrud
The    Intru
The    Int
The    In
The    I
The
Th
T

1. One of these mornings I'm gonna wake up crazy, gonna take my gun gonna shoot my baby. The object is to blast everyone in sight. I love you so much it hurts. Their short-range cannons can wear your defenses down quickly. I'd rather see you dead little girl than to be with another man. Players can drive true 3-D tanks up mountains, into valleys and even underwater. I'm going out to shoot my old lady. Manning the rear turrent, it's up to you to destroy the aliens before they get close. She shot him three or four times. While migrating along time channels all living creatures are undergoing irreversible mutations that are making them wild and aggressive. I killed the only woman I loved. Its an unbelievably realistic world of brutal, senseless, gratuitous, egregious, yet strangely compelling, horror.

2. Couple Go for Counseling and Then for Guns (Frenso, California, April 23 (AP)
An estranged couple drew guns and wounded each other after the husband was late for a marriage counseling session at a church. Michael Martin, clutching a beer in one hand, fired the first shot on Wednesday and wounded his wife Bonnie, when she began to leave St. James Episcopal Cathedral, the Rev. Bud Searcy of New Creation Ministries said.
Mrs. Martin took a gun from her purse and shot her husband in the chin, Mr. Searcy said. Mr. Martin shot his wife again after she followed him from the church, Mr. Searcy said.
The Martins were in fair condition at University Medical Center. They were arrested and face charges of attempted murder, Detective Mike Garcia said.

# Graphic

**Andy Deck/Mark Napier**

http://bbs2.thing.net/jam/

Community Conditions

GraphicJam is part graffiti, part jazz. It is a place where visitors contribute to an evolving collaborative drawing - a 'wall' where a private gesture becomes part of a public design. Any mark made on this surface is visible to all viewers nearly instantly, so those involved in the Jam can see the actions of anyone else who is marking the wall at that moment.

GraphicJam is an art forum, a collision of sensibilities and wills. People can collaborate, compete, destroy, digress, and play on this relatively accessible surface. As with graffiti, no mark is final. Each layer gives way to the next, creating an ongoing collaborative work that evolves and disappears as visitors contribute their scribbling energy to it.

This project borrows an aesthetic from jazz - live 'jam' sessions where musicians play together, creating music through improvisation. Images grow from the simultaneous labors of trios, quartets, and so forth. Solos are gradually or suddenly effaced by the emergence of new themes. Last, GrafficJam is a live art form. The recording that allows one to see the recent history retrace its steps when one arrives is constantly, like the sound of live music, fading from the hum of the machine into the quietude of human memory.

GraphicJam challenges the belief that art is created by one person, exists in one place at one time, and can be owned by one person. Here the artwork may be created by many people who don't aspire to be artists, who may not consciously see themselves as adding to an aesthetic design. The web gives us an opportunity to experiment with a much broader definition of art and creativity. GraphicJam is about exploring that opportunity.

[ESC TO BEGIN]

For net_condition, the group has focused on computer games, and has realized an installation for the exhibition displaying their current projects. In what at first glance appears to be a banal office space the visitor can play networked computer games, engage in dialogues with ai programs and monitor the activity on the internal network. The installation serves as a space to present new projects, showing the state of the art of commercial networked games alongside with ongoing in-house developments combining technological innovation with the history of commercial games. Both the development prototypes and the finished product are displayed and make the installation into a 'testbed' for new projects. On twelve terminals the user can play, communicate, observe and experience the changing rules of cultural interaction using a multitude of different interfaces based on the world of networked computer games.

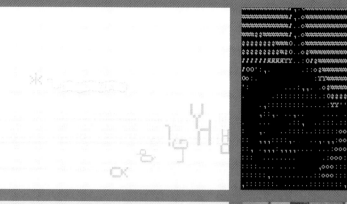

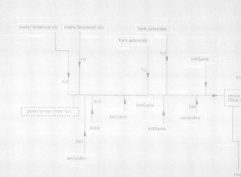

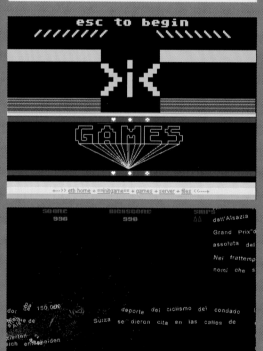

esc to begin

GAMES

+--->> etb home + ==initgame== + games + server + files <<----+

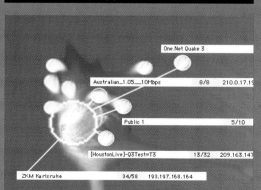

One.Net Quake 3

Australian_1.05__10Mbps   8/8   210.0.17.19

Public 1   5/10

[HoustonLive]-Q3Test=T3   13/32   209.163.147.

ZKM Karlsruhe   34/58   193.197.168.164

Schießbude - Jagdschießen

# N u z z l

The same installation is set up at remote locations. A dark abstract space on the monitor. Visitors are invited to explore the virtual space with the aid of the computer mouse. By means of the interface the participants control their own movement and perspective in the computer-generated three-dimensional environment. The temporal movements within the space leave traces behind them, which can be followed by other participants. An abstracted avatar visualizes the current location of the individual visitor.

With Nuzzle Afar Fujihata provides an exemplary presentation of a three-dimensional communication and interaction space that offers different levels of encounter and possibilities of shared experience. In contrast to classical conceptions of virtual environments enabling shared experiences, as for instance those used in MUDs and MOOs(*), Fujihata's system permits not only the simultaneous exchange of position and orientation data, but also of the entire visual material. In Nuzzle Afar curiosity, a sense of discovery and the willingness to communicate are the fundamental elements for orienting oneself in the (virtual) world.

(*)Multi User Dimension or Domain: text-based spaces for collective experience (multiple users) in the Internet. MUD Object Oriented: Object-represented version of a MUD.

# The Diff Eng

**Lynn Hershman**

http://salon-digital.zkm.de/difference/

**94**

**Community Conditions**

The <u>Difference Engine #3</u> was inspired by Charles Babbage's original Difference Engine # 1 (commonly considered the world's first computer). The original machine was used to calculate numerical positions. This piece calculates the captured image and position in the physical/virtual space of museum visitors.

<u>Difference Engine #3</u> uses the architecture of the ZKM Media Museum as a 3D template and the visitors to the museum as the interface. It is an interactive, multi-user sculpture about surveillance, voyeurism, digital absorption and spiritual transformation of the body.

Avatars of museum visitors are 'born' when they approach one of three Bi Directional Browsing Units (BBU's). Quickcams embedded in the BBU's flip 180 degrees to capture the image (Avatar) of the person standing before it. Each avatar (image of the visitor) is assigned a number, representing the time in seconds the visitor approached the unit.

The numbered avatar embarks on a 27 second journey through a 3D representation of the museum...and then moves to a Purgatorial site where it cycles continuously with 30 other avatars. Eventually, the avatars are archived permanently on the internet where their image can be recalled via the identity number.

On-line visitors choose a 'generic' avatar to represent them and travel along

the avatars created for people in the actual museum. Visitors ONLINE can also 'capture' images within the museum - (they can see into the space via the live video feed from the camera that is capturing the image of people in the museum. There is a dedicated chat line that allows viewers on-line to communicate with people in the physical space.

erence
ine #3

Click to select your Avatar

Timothée Ingen-Housz

a-aktion.com is an interactive
on-line gallery presenting
various practices of autoaggres-
sion. Images mounted in traditional frames show the artist
during acts of self-mutilation.
Each scenery is completely super-
imposed with a symbol and connected with an interaction that
is reminiscent of computer games.
Visual recourse and game accompa-
ny the question as to the author
in the interactive system.

**A-AKTION Gallery**
A-AKTION Players™ trademarks of a-aktion.com

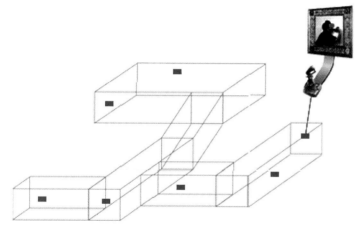

a - akti

# linX3D

... A few familiar figures lurk about the familiar LinX3D console... With calm voice commands, she logs onto the Konsum slackerserver, a node of an independent network of noncommercial machines that lie in the shadows of the Pop nets. Meanwhile the digital eye atop the console scans her body, and in nanoseconds Dark_Star is staring at her datavatar, a skeletal three-dimensional doppelganger carved from codetext. She is face-to-face with her interface.

Erik Davis, San Francisco SciFi writer on LinX3D

boundaries that define
Dark_Star's datavatar, and
her virtual subjectivity
dissolve into a
collective bit-stream
recursive and recoding mech
that now generate most art
online "maja", unreal engines
humankind's collective sleep
array of video consoles

waag_05.wrl
waag_06.wrl
waag_07.wrl
waag_08.wrl
gzip -d waag_08z.wrl.gz
ls -al

LinX3D is a Web3D console game with ASCII face avatars and ASCII login datavatars. In the LinX3D GAME, the VR users assuming different forms, e.g. datavatars of netprotocols in ASCII format, and the RL visitors as ASCII FACES meet up and interact in a common virtual space.

A game console in which the monitors of the applications are integrated acts as a trigger of a social multiUSER situation on SITE, local/real at the various sites of installation and online in the electronic net.

As the title suggests,

# SMELL·BYTES ™

is not a futuristic gastronomic experience but it does refer to two of our major senses related directly to our flesh body. However, SMELL·BYTES TM has been designed for the wide world web and has been implemented as a website and as a computer controlled web streamed video environment.

SMELL·BYTES TM addresses a body of complex issues ranging from hacking as both a method and a metaphor, dataveillance and the invasion of the body and privacy, to the relationships between sensuality and the imagination, art and science, biotech fantasies and economies. Important too is the

>>I love you so much that I can eat you up!
>>I love you so much that I can smell you up!

artistic process in the age of information technologies In this case, the artist quite literally vanishes from the work, while her creation, Chris·053, an intelligent agent created as a bot software, takes on a life of its own online.

A software designed specifically for this project, Chris.053 is programmed to be driven by its insatiable olfactory desires, relentlessly lurking and sniffing by gaining unauthorized access to servers and IP addresses of CU SEE ME teleconference environments and chat rooms online.

The attempt to represent a 'human profile' as a digital equation of smell components is not as far fetched as it may seem. This Darwinian classification system has its scientific counterpart at the Ludwig Boltzman Institute of Urban Ethnology and Human Biology in Vienna where studies proclaiming a direct relationship between symmetry, beauty and body smells are currently underway. In other words, these studies have determined that human sexuality, attractiveness, success, and power are based on beauty, symmetry and their correlation to body odors. In this environment, the information reduces subjectivity into a series of data based on biochemical traits and propagates methods of classification.

Chris.053 also subverts and satirizes the above methods of scientific analysis, classification and codification. SMELL.BYTES TM is a parody via paradox. On Chris.053's own website, participants can enter the 'odor lab' to peruse graphics based on the molecular structures and data of 7,000 odors and witness the constant downloading and analyses of grabbed human profiles. Accordingly, those with the most beautiful faces-the most symmetrical-are assigned seductive odors. An asymmetrical face might be worthy of a 'skunk' while a more balanced profile might be expected to exude a 'flowery' aroma. Ensconced on vinyl cushions with a computer at its locus, the SMELL.BYTES TM environment allows visitors to explore the website as they are physically surrounded by

hovering sounds and noises from the web and live video streams of the fragmented and dispersed images of visitors that have been grabbed by Chris.053 as it sniffed through the servers. Visitors turn into voyeurs while the human portraits 'projected' on the walls become mediated and ephemeral reminders of the values of privacy, individual autonomy and the sensual body. All the elements of this environment, the website and the projections, are based on the idea of harnessing information in flux and mobility. These different modes of data are used to flip the viewer in and out of the webspace into the physical space, placing them in an indeterminate

relation to the artist and the point of origin. The viewer is then left to wonder where the piece begins and ends, and the physical boundaries of the artwork become unclear.

# step to _ _ _ _

Alexandru Patatics

http://www.cctm.ro/artwww/apatatics/index.htm

The installation simultaneously explores the parallelism between the informational world (of the Internet) and aleatory environment/events generated by passing visitors, who are surveilled by video cameras.
The software's virtual sensors continuously analyse the capture window, which displays the image of

## immediate situations,

and will construct words. Those words (resulting from the video images) will access the Internet's 'search engines'; images from the Internet which have some kind of connection with the words from these sentences will then be returned and displayed on a screen. A process of communication begins; returning other images which become, via video projection, the "events of the environment."

**The resulting images**

04

Community Conditions

The installation works as
a type of converter

event-image
communication-index
by word and URL
dictionary
Internet searching
machines
returned image
sound
image video mixer
video projection
event-image

so we can put everything in
a close circuit as a self
generator, looping installation.

The installation also contains two levels of perception: one represents the concrete hardware connections between the equipment and video projections of
images, the other consists of the software and its
working parts - images, software sensors and references to communication of the Internet. The result
displays the mixture or interference between those
instances.

STARRYNIGHT
STARRYNIGHT
STARRYNIGHT
STARRYNIGHT
STARRYNIGHT
STARRYNIGHT
STARRYNIGHT
STARRYNIGHT
STARRYNIGHT
STARRYNIGHT
STARRYNIGHT
STARRYNIGHT
STARRYNIGHT
STARRYNIGHT
STARRYNIGHT
STARRYNIGHT
STARRYNIGHT
STARRYNIGHT

Each time someone reads a text at www.rhizome.org, a dim star appears on a black Web page. When a text gets read again, the corresponding star gets a bit brighter. Over time, the Web page comes to resemble a starry night sky, with bright stars corresponding to the most popular texts, and dim stars corresponding to less-popular ones.

Clicking on a star triggers a special pop-up menu. The first menu option allows you to read the text that corresponds to the star. The second menu option allows you to select a keyword associated with that text. After selecting a keyword, STARRYNIGHT draws a unique constellation of stars whose texts share that keyword. You can use these constellations to find other related texts, and in doing so, follow your interests through the vast array of ideas and information in Rhizome.org's text archive.

...by using STARRYNIGHT, you increase the brightness of the stars corresponding to the texts you read, leaving a visible trace of your activity (intensities are updated daily, so results are not immediate).

STARRYNIGHT is both a mirror and a map....an artifact and an agent of global networking. It is produced by the contributions and activities of an online community, and it enables members of the community to see the results in abstract and metaphorical terms: as you surf the site, your click-trail helps illuminate the night sky.

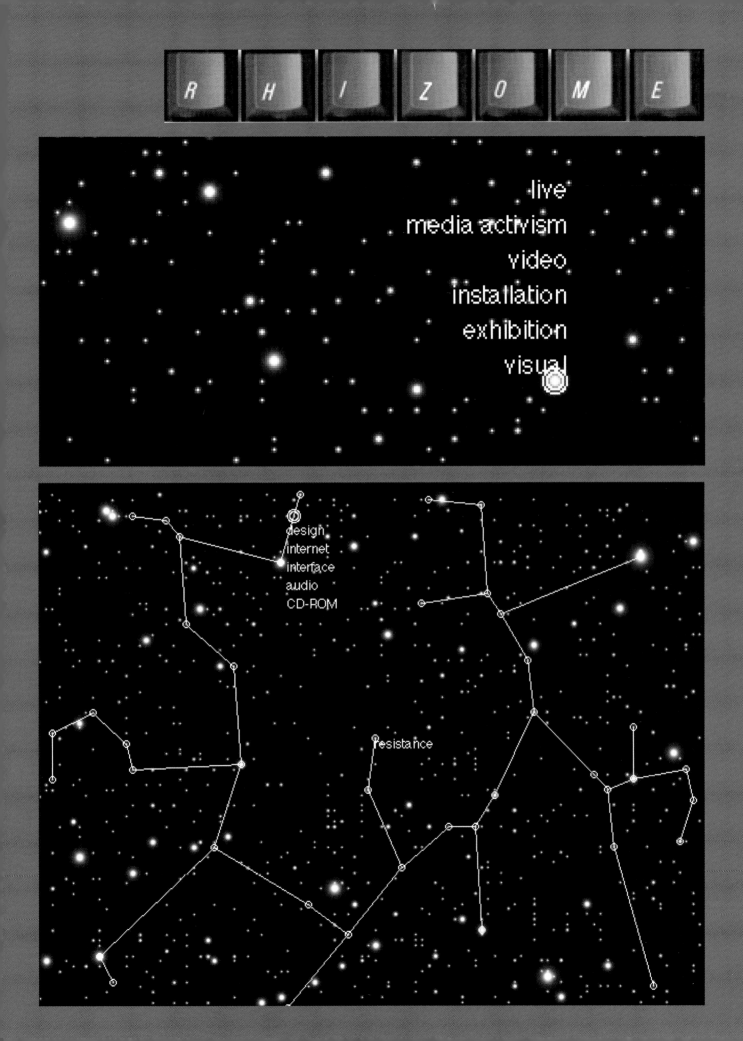

The Tables Turned takes its title from a
poem by William Wordsworth of almost the
same name. The original poem accuses the
science and art of the time of being
nothing more than an outrageous imita-
tion. The real truth and reality being
found in a return to nature. So what is
nature? And what is real in the telematic
space? This installation contains
adapted verses from Wordsworth's poem at
the bottom of a drawer. Verses that provoke the very question of reality from an
ironic telematic point of view. Preceded

# The Tables Turned
## A Telematic Scene on the Same Subject

Paul Sermon

108

Community Conditions

by "Telematic Dreaming" (1992) and
"Telematic Vision" (1993), this installation is a continuation of the telematic
theme placed within another social context. "Telematic Dreaming" used the bed,
"Telematic Vision" used the sofa and "The
Tables Turned" uses the table.

Each context identifies a different set of rituals in human
behavior, and with the table
new forms of telematic interac-

tion are introduced by identifying and defining particular communication aspects
within the installation
design.
...

## The Tables Turned

is experienced and used in two locations via a teleconferencing link. ...
The first table is located in the ZKM Media Museum in Karlsruhe and is surrounded by three monitors. The second table installation is situated in a remote location, also surrounded by three monitors - apart from the colour of the space it is identical to that in ZKM. Everything in the ZKM location, except for the chair, is chroma-key blue - a blue box backdrop, carpet and

played on the monitors in both locations, allowing the users to observe and control their telepresent bodies within 360° around the virtual table.

Four drawers around the edge of each table top can be opened by the user. Each table top can also be rotated by the user. These drawers contain objects and props that have corresponding links between them that determine the poten-

table. i.e. only the chair and the person sitting on it are visible to a chroma-keyer, the blue area of the screen is replaced with the camera image from the remote location - an identical mapped image of a backdrop, carpet, table, chair, and another person.

The combined image of the two distant users sitting at the same virtual table is dis-

tial narratives and dialogues that can unfold between the two persons sitting at the table.

**Jeffrey Shaw**

http://www.zkm.de/surrogate/shaw.html

Community Conditions

In the original version of the "Legible City" (1989) the visitor is able to ride a stationary bicycle through a simulated representation of a city constituted by computer-generated three-dimensional letters forming words and sentences along the sides of the streets. "The Distributed Legible City" encompasses all the experiences offered by the original version, but introduces an important new multi-user functionality that to a large extent becomes its predominant feature.

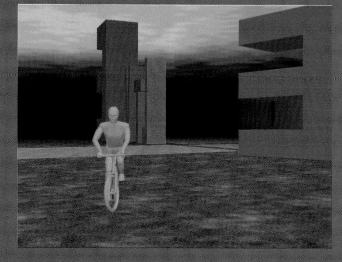

# The Distributed

Here, two bicyclists at remote locations (Graz and Karlsruhe) are simultaneously present in the shared virtual environment. They can meet each other (by accident or intentionally), see abstracted avatar representations of each other, and when they come close to each other they can verbally communicate with each other. In this way a new space of co-mingled spoken and readable texts is generated. The artwork shifts from being a merely visual experience into also being the context for a networked social exchange between visitors to that artwork.

# Legible City

FuckU-FuckMe™ (for Windows 95, Windows 98, and Windows NT) provides the most complete remote sex solution for the Internet and corporate intranet.

Powerful features let you sexually communicate with your remote partner and provide an absolutely realistic sensual experience of a real intercourse.

The basic FuckU-FuckMe™ kit consists of two hardware units - genitalDrive™ model M (male) and genitalDrive™ model F (female) and an accompanying software interface.

**FUCKU®**
**FUCKME**

The genitalDrive is an internal device in a standard case
that can be installed in any
free 5.25" slot of your PC.
The FuckU-FuckMe software
connects your genitalDrive
with a corresponding unit on
a remote PC using TCP/IP protocol.
When you start remote sexual
intercourse with your partner
using FuckU-FuckMe™ the system will transmit all your
actions to his/her geni-
talDrive and precisely reproduce them in real time.
The system has intuitive
interface and allows you to
entirely concentrate on
remote communication.

GenitalDrive model F or M (click to enlarge)

GenitalDrive model M ready for operation (click to enlarge)

GenitalDrive model F ready for operation (click to enlarge)

FUCKU®
FUCKME
Link your site to FUFME!

# The Spectralization

I.

In the book I published in 1997, entitled *Fiction Reconstructed: New Media, Video, Art, Post-Socialism And The Retro-Avant-garde* and subtitled *Essays in Theory, Politics and Aesthetics from 1985 to 1997*, I developed briefly the concept that it is possible today, at the end of the millennium, to identify two matrices of active players with regard to Eastern and Western Europe and the new media reality: i.e., the Western European 'Scum of Society Matrix' and the Eastern European 'Monsters Matrix.'

The first tendency concerns the individuals or groups that act as a kind of entity without a fixed historical or geographical position, while consciously occupying the position of the scum of society. However, this 'The Scum of Society Matrix,' which refers mainly to the positioning of the so-called critical Western European and North American participants, users and on-line community circuits, is also a kind of parasitic body trying to acquire everything possible from the already established social structures. 'The scum of society matrix' proposes a new autonomous economy and new structures developed from the appropriation and restructuring of those that existed before. It proposes to go back to writing only (e-mail boxes) as a possible counterculture intercommunication strategy, and not simply developing the Internet, i.e., to erase the images - and the pushy Internet software industry - into the background. In the guise of such a utopian mind, it is possible to find strategies for fighting and acting, not simply reproducing, through technology.

As Peter Lamborn Wilson (alias Hakim Bey) stated in his lecture at the Nettime meeting in Ljubljana in 1997, entitled "Beauty and The East," the Second World has been deleted/made obsolete, and what is left are the First and Third Worlds. Instead of the Second World, Bey argued, there is a big hole from which one jumps into the Third. I will name this hole and the second tendency 'The Matrix of Monsters' as a travesty of the general title of the Nettime conference "Beauty and The East" (already a paraphrase of the fairy tale, *Beauty and the Beast*). When it comes to the differences between East and West, it must be clarified that the actors from 'the black hole,' the so-called Eastern European critical WWW users, aim not to simply mirror the First World - the developed capitalist societies - but to articulate and interpret a proper position in this changed constellation. The question of who is permitted to write the history of art, culture and politics in the area once known as Eastern Europe must be posed along with the questions of how and when.

These two matrices raise not only questions for reflection, but also offer elements of political and analytical intersection that must be discussed and articulated further and in a much more radical way. This is what I intend to do in the essay that follows.

What if, in contrast to the fantasy of the Internet and its overwhelming globalization depicted in the utopian dream of a (virtual) community in which relations of exchange will be harmonious and universal, the Eastern European Monsters are not only fantasized as monsters, but are (at least some of the Eastern European artists, media activists and theoreticians, etc.) the terrifying neighbors who reject the philanthropic Western ideology of sharing and pure exchange?

I will attempt to define, to indicate a break (rather than continuity) between what is often referred to as two stages in the Western-Eastern European Community. The first stage, which we may consider as that until 1989 (until the fall of the Berlin Wall), may be described as the concept of relations between Western

# of Europe

Europe and Communist Eastern Europe. The second stage, considered as commencing in 1989 (the year imposed on Eastern Europeans as that which today denotes without exception *le passage a l'acte* [the passage to action] of Eastern Europe toward freedom and democracy), is the relation between Western Europeans and their Post-Socialist Neighbors.

One may define this break similarly to the break between Freud's first and second concepts of transfer. Today an almost ferocious campaign is trying to fill the gap between these two breaks and to simulate continuity. The slogans of this campaign (demanded by the West and serviced in the East, or vice versa) are BIOGRAPHY rather than THEORY and THERAPY rather than THEORY. The later slogan is nearly an antidote proposed by a large number (although not all) of Western European (Media) Activists.

The above should be perceived as an introductory gesture describing the manner in which the word Europe in the title of this paper may be grasped. This gesture should be understood in a way similar to that of the bad/good guy in Hollywood action or thriller films when he makes order of a messy table, onto which he will draw the action. Not the gentle approach to every crumb on the table, re-positing them elsewhere, but the gesture of erasure, of a whip of everything.

This moment before the gesture of erasure is similar to the void that Slavoj Zizek, together with Lacan, formulated approximately as follows. In short, the Lacanian answer to the question - Is it possible to call, to perceive, the void, i.e., to be found before the gesture of subjectivization, a subject? - is YES, although this question was answered negatively by Althusser, Derrida and Badiou. The subject is both at the same time: the ontological whole, the gap in the absolute contraction of subjectivity and the cut of the connections of the subject with reality. This may be illustrated adequately with the previously described 'cleansing of the terrain,' which thus opens the space for the new symbolic beginning that will be supported by the new resurrected master-signifier.

I will try also to offer some directions for spectralization. In his book, *Spectres de Marx*, Jacques Derrida put into play the term 'spectre' to indicate the elusive pseudo-materiality that subverts the classic ontological oppositions of reality and illusion. Zizek argues that perhaps we should look here for the last resort of ideology, for the formal matrix onto which are grafted various ideological formations:

"We should recognize the fact that there is no reality without the spectre, that the circle of reality can be closed only by means of an uncanny spectral supplement. Why, then, is there no reality without the spectre? [Because for Lacan] reality is not the 'thing itself,' [rather] it is always-already symbolized... and the problem resides in the fact that symbolization ultimately always fails, that it never succeeds in fully 'covering' the real... [This real] returns in the guise of spectral apparitions. 'Spectre' is not to be confused with 'symbolic fiction'... reality is never directly 'itself'; it presents itself only via its incomplete-failed symbolization, and spectral apparitions emerge in this very gap that forever separates reality from the real, and on account of which reality has the character of a (symbolic) fiction: the spectre gives body to that which escapes (the symbolically structured) reality." (Slavoj Zizek, "Introduction: The Spectre of Ideology," in *Mapping Ideology*, pp. 26-28. )

This also explains the title of my 1997 book: *Fiction Reconstructed*.

## 1. EASTERN EUROPE AS THE INDIVISIBLE REMAINDER OR A PIECE OF SHIT

It is possible to say that the modern subject does not exist without an understanding that on a certain level from some other perspective: I am a piece of shit. Furthermore, modern subjectivity arises when the subject sees itself out of joint, as cut off from the positive order of things. We may say that the cyborg, as conceived by Donna Haraway, seen from the exteriority-intimacy position that Lacan coined as *extimacy*, is exactly this piece of shit.

Thus I have developed the thesis that virtual reality is the place where the subject sees itself as 'out of joint.' Let us consider briefly what happens in the classical situation of virtual reality. The user finds him/herself in a specific inter-subjective relation with his/her double. Being in virtual reality means to see one's own hands taking the virtual object, one's own body doing this or that; in short, this double is a kind of exteriorization, a kind of a spectral creature or double - an immortal libidinal object - the famous Lacanian *lamella*. One may refer to this spectral creature as an excremental protuberance, an indestructible object of life beyond death that has no fixed position in the symbolic order. This implies that not only is cyberspace constantly revealing that out there (outside of the virtual world) a kind of terrifying remainder, impossible to wholly integrate into the virtual world, is waiting for us, but that this remainder, too, may be seen from time to time in virtual and cybespace.

This kind of split between the image and the real (sometimes displayed as a formless remainder on the computer screen as well, if we are in a position to meet the "=cw4t7abs" can be found on the WWW under <http://www.godemil.dk/=cw4t7abs).

The disgusting remainder also comprises the *NSK EMBASSY PROJECT* by the group IRWIN of Ljubljana where, instead of the Embassy, we are faced with the *extimacy* of the public space in a private apartment that suffocates us with an almost claustrophobic domesticity. Not a real Embassy, but a *mise-en-scene* around the kitchen table. Or the Russian artists - Oleg Kulik's horrendous biting animals

and Alexander Brener performing as a boxer - all these liminal works and experiences demonstrate to us the extimacy of the disgusting remainder, before it might perhaps transform into the sublime.

Let us jump into the actual space of Europe, as discussed on the Internet via vital lists that are developing a critical view on media and the world such as the Nettime list or the Syndicate list, etc. There one may read (and respond to) some interesting contributions on Eastern Europe that I will synthesize thus: 'despite the initial euphoria Western Europe showed for Eastern Europe after the fall of the Berlin Wall, Eastern Europe has failed. It did not succeed to be inscribed on the map of important political, cultural, arts events in Europe.' The disappointment about Eastern Europe that failed in the process to become a stable social space may also be detected in the works of such prominent philosophers as Badiou and Rancicre.

It is a fact that the main presentation of the last *documenta* in Kassel (*dX* in 1997) included only two or three artists from Eastern Europe. And if we are to believe the interviews, in the words of the curator (Catherine David), this was due to the fact that there was nothing to select, in fact. The void, or the de facto elimination, of the Eastern European artist from the *documenta* was, according to her own words, the result of the void proper to Eastern Europe, and was not a result of the selection. It seems that Eastern Europe has been lost for the second time, after it was just in the process of being refound in 1989, as stated here: If the woman does not exist, this is because she cannot be refound (Joan Copjec, p. 221).

According to Slavoj Zizek's interpretation, the negative gesture by the Eastern Europeans who said NO! to the Communist regime is much more important - practically crucial - for understanding what has occurred to catalyze this later failed positivation. For Lacan, negativity functions as a condition of impossibility or possibility of the later enthusiastic identification - it lays the base for it.

What is Eastern Europe after the fulfillment of its destiny, after now nearly a decade after the fall of the Berlin Wall?

A similar question is raised by Zizek through Lacan. In his reading of the Oedipal myth, Lacan focused on the field which is, in most usual readings of the Oedipal complex, left out: What is beyond Oedipus - what is Oedipus himself - after he has fulfilled his destiny? - a question that may be posed after watching such films as *Bladerunner* or *Seven*. What happens on the day after?, or so to speak, after life goes on in its usual rhythm? As Lacan put it in Seminar II, from the beginning of the tragedy, everything leads us to the fact that Oedipus is solely an Earth rest, a remainder, a Thing that is robbed from every surface.

What we have here is a field that may be called, according to psychoanalysis, the field between two deaths - between the symbolic and the real death. The ultimate object of horror is this life beyond death, which Lacan called *lamella*, as an immortal - indestructible object, i.e., life that is voided, evacuated, from the symbolic structure.

It seems that after the fall of the Berlin Wall, Eastern Europe has found itself in a horrible intermediate position, whereby it has been changed into an inseparable remainder, a substanceless spot of a crumb of reality that has already swallowed all the potential that was generated by its previous existence.

Eastern Europe found itself in a position similar to the one Zizek develops in re-articulating the Oedipus position following the fulfillment of his symbolic destiny (i.e., when Oedipus, incognizant, kills his father and marries his mother). After he has fulfilled his symbolic destiny, Oedipus is an indivisible remainder, the substanceless spot of the crumb of reality. He is the embodiment of that which Lacan calls *plus-de-jouir*, surplus enjoyment, the surplus that cannot be explained by any symbolic idealization. But - and this is crucial for understanding the changed, so-called failed position of Eastern Europe for the Other - when Lacan uses the *plus-de-jouir* notion, he plays with the double entendre of the term in French comprising simultaneously surplus, and no more, enjoyment! Oedipus is, following the fulfillment of his destiny, plus d'homme, which means simultaneously surplus man and not man. Oedipus is conditionally man; he is a human monster and as such, a paradigmatic example of the modern subject, as his monstrosity is structural and not accidental.

In keeping with this definition and the similarity of positions, we may define Eastern Europe as *plus d' Europe orientale*. Eastern Europe is surplus of Europe (as it was before the fall of the Berlin Wall: too little, or not enough, European) and not Europe.

Eastern Europe is forced to take, or is in, the position of an excremental remainder. Please allow me here to change the optics of the discourse and to state: this is not necessarily a bad thing. With a view from the lamella point - 'the modern subject does not exist without an understanding that on a certain level from some other perspective I am a piece of shit' - we may say that this is actually the first condition required for Eastern Europe to take upon itself all the characteristics of a modern subjectivity. It is now from this inherently excremental position that Eastern Europe can arise or can be perceived finally as a subject. As Zizek writes, "If the Cartesian subject wants to arise on the level of enunciation, it must be described as almost nothing of ready to be thrown in the disposal garbage/trash on the level of a statement." (Cf. Slavoj Zizek, "Alain Badiou kot bralec svetega Pavla" [Alain Badiou as the Reader of St. Paulus], p. 135.)

Perhaps it is only now, when Eastern Europe is on the level of a statement of almost nothing of (ready-to-be-thrown-in-the-disposal) excremental trash (wasn't it, for example, at *documenta*, reduced precisely to this nothingness?), that it can arise on the level of enunciation. In this case of a correlation between Cartesian subjectivity and its excremental double, we have the split between the subject of utterance and the subject of statement. If the Cartesian subject wishes to appear on the level of utterance, then s/he must be changed into shit on the level of the statement. This is the zero-point of subjectivity: we begin to be something once we have been absolutely nothing, after going through (completing) the zero-point. Nothing that has the value of something is, according to Zizek, the most condensed formula of the Lacanian bared subject.

Furthermore, the classical ontology, according to Zizek, focused on the triad of the truthful, the beautiful and the good. For Lacan, these three notions press near the limit, and show that good is the mask of diabolical evil (e.g., Oleg Kulik the Russian artist dog, or the performances entitled *Was ist Kunst?* by the artist Rasa Todosijevic from Belgrade. In the 1970s, Todosijevic, in this series of performances, literally tried to drag the answer to "What is art?" out of women by force, slapping their faces with black color in the most shocking manner of body-art.); beautiful the mask of ugliness (e.g., IRWIN's series of 100 pictures also entitled Was ist Kunst? In this series, and in the exhibitions of Laibachkunst, persons who are supposed to have been part of the period of Naziism are portrayed along with members of the banned Laibach group; they are engraved into the iconography of the paintings, as their busts or torso sculptures decorate numerous paintings of the *Was ist Kunst?* project); and truthful is the mask of the central void, around which gravitates every symbolical structure (e.g., the Romanian flag, after the so-called Romanian Revolution, a hole instead of the star). In short, writes Zizek, there is a field beyond the good, the beautiful, the truth, that is not filled with everyday banalities, but presents a terrifying source, which is constitutive for the background of the good, the beautiful and the truth. If it is a political-ethical motto of psychoanalysis, then it is subsumed in the view that all of the greatest catastrophes of our century (from Stalinism to the Holocaust) are the result not of being seduced by the morbid fatal attraction of this beyond, but, on the contrary, of the constant efforts to elude the meeting with it and to immediately install, saving a confrontation with it, the reign of truth and good (Cf. Slavoj Zizek, "Alain Badiou kot bralec svetega Pavla" [Alain Badiou as the Reader of St. Paulus], p. 141).

## 2. EMANCIPATION? RESISTANCE? OR ...

The manner in which I have posited the subject and re-framed the Eastern European Monster Matrix allows for further discussion on the possible ways of acting (and living) in Europe and on the net, and furthermore, allows us to rethink eman-cipation and resistance. We should first distinguish, according to Jelica Sumic-Riha, between modernist emancipation and contemporary postmodernist resistance. The modernist solution of insisting on a fidelity to politics, where politics seems to be deemed a precious treasure, suggests that in the final analysis nothing has happened. Hence the modernist emancipation functions from today's point of view as the so-called university discourse, developed by Lacan, that attempts to dispose of the effects of the event for the symbolic structure, and therefore does not recognize any change in the actual political situation, leaving the actual defeat of politics untaught, anathematized. Postmodernist resistance is, on the other hand, possible to delineate as a hysterical discourse, as the constant production of the doubtful 'no' that simply turns resistance against thought. (regarding these distinctions, cf. Jelica Sumic-Riha.)This may also be grasped with a quite impressive crusade against theory and theoretical knowledge, as is especially sustained by some media theorists and activists today.

To arrive at a resolution, let us briefly contemplate the four discourses evolved by Lacan in dealing with the truth and events. Lacan distinguished the discourse of the master, the university discourse, the discourse of the hysteric and the discourse of the analyst. The master names the event, changing it into a new signifier-master that will guarantee the continuity of the consequences of the event. The master integrates the event within the symbolic reality. The hysteric holds the doubtful position of division toward the event. The master wishes to keep continuity, the hysteric the gap. The university discourse aims to fill the effects, to neutralize the effects as if nothing has happened.

To understand the significance of the four discourses for today's political involvement in media theory and art practice, let us try to answer the question, never before posed in debates on media and activism: Which of the four discourses is occupied by the famous cyborg, as conceived by Donna Haraway, as our politics and ontology for the year 2000? My answer is thus: Haraway has positioned the cyborg as a hysterical discourse. This is possible to grasp if we travel with Haraway to Virtual Space. To finally arrive there, Haraway moves through three other regions: Real Space, or Earth; Outer Space, or the Extraterrestrial; and Inner Space, or the Body.

Donna Haraway's semiotic square of Virtual Space from *The Promises of Monsters*:

REAL SPACE      OUTER SPACE


VIRTUAL SPACE      INNER SPACE

(Please note that all graphs and diagrams displayed in the text are executed in the mode of such popular books as *Postmodernism for Children, Marx for Children*, etc.)

The virtual world is positioned in Haraway's semiotic square in such a way that the truth of these four spaces is to be found in the virtual space. We should also consider the fact that Haraway conceptualizes the cyborg as a piece of shit and, at the same time, as a sublime object. The power of the cyborg resides in its position of extimacy that is between the disgusting and the sublime. This means that I will position the cyborg as an object 'a'. In Lacanian psychoanalysis, object 'a' represents the double entendre of the *plus-de-jouir* notion meaning simultaneously a surplus of, and no more, enjoyment. Taking all of these important elements into consideration, we should then take as a conceptual equivalent of Haraway's semiotic square the Lacanian discourse of the hysteric.

It looks (again from a child's point of view) like this (Lacan in Scilicet 1-4, p. 191):

$  S1

a  S2

Crucial is the positioning of object 'a' within the structure of the Lacanian discourses; in the hysterical discourse, object a is positioned in the place of truth (truth is positioned in all four discourses at the lower left), whether for the subject (the bare $) - in the hysterical discourse, reserved the role of the agent (the agent is positioned in all four discourses at the upper left). To provide a clearer under-

standing, allow me to offer a few additional details. The four Lacanian discourses articulate four subjective positions. The signifiers of the four structures are presented by the following mathems: 'S1' is the master-signifier; 'S2' represents knowledge; '$' (the bare S) the subject and 'a' the surplus-enjoyment. All of these entities occupy a different place in the structures of the four discourses. What is significant is that the four places have a fixed meaning in all four discourses. This means that no matter which signifier or mathem ('S1', or S2' or '$' or a) will take the upper left position in the structure of the discourse, this position is the place of the agent. These are the fixed meanings of the respective places in the discourses:

agent    other
_____   _____

truth    production

We are now ready to draw the consequences of this homographical act. The virtual space and the cyborg as refracted in Haraway's semiotic square of Virtual Space from *The Promises of Monsters* occupied the same position as truth and the object a in the Lacanian discourse of the hysteric. Hence the truth is covered by this sublime-disgusting cyborg object, while the entire discourse is still enunciated from the Earth. The agent is therefore still out there (the Real Space of *The Promises of Monsters* is in the same place as the '$' in the hysterical link - the '$' over 'a' represents the subject-agent who is traumatized by the question of what role to play in the Other's desire), to be found on the Earth or in the Real Space. Production, the fourth term in the matrix of discourses, is in the Lacanian hysterical link occupied by knowledge - 'S2' in Haraway's matrix by the Inner Space or the Body. The Inner Space of the Body can be understood, as Zizek puts it, as not simply for the result, but rather for the "indivisible remainder," for the excess that resists being included in the discursive network.

Is this then an answer to how we should be positioned between emancipation and resistance? Are we to act as hysterics, putting everything under question in order to resist the existing symbolic order by refusing to assume the role assigned to us by this order, as the hysterics taught us? The answer follows shortly, after taking into brief consideration the fourth type of discourse: that of the analyst. It also seems that we have lost, in the meantime, the Matrix of the Monsters which simply says - I am this piece of useless trash here. Or maybe not!

Jacques Lacan formulates his position as an analyst as follows: "The more saints, the more laughter; that's my principle, to wit, the way out of capitalist discourse - which will not constitute progress, if it happens only for some." (Lacan, *Television*, p.16)

Designating the saint as the site of resistance, he clearly indicates that a resistance to capitalism can only be theorized in terms of some resistant instance, which is, strictly speaking, neither exterior nor interior, but rather, is situated at the point of exteriority in the very intimacy of interiority, i.e., the Lacanian extimacy (exteriority-intimacy).

Conceived in terms of extimacy rather than in terms of pure alterity, resistance therefore consists in the derivation from within capitalism, of an indigestible kernel, of an otherness which has the potential to disrupt the circuit of the drive for growth. (Cf. Jelica Sumic-Riha)

The discourse of the analyst is presented as follows (Lacan in Scilicet 1-4, p. 191):

$$a \quad \$$$

$$S2 \quad S1$$

In the discourse of the analyst, object 'a' is posited as the agent/agency, whereas knowledge (represented by 'S2') occupies the space of truth (which again, is positioned in all four discourses at the lower left). In the Lacanian analyst discourse, the agent 'a' reduces itself to the void, provoking in such a way the subject to confront the truth of its desire. Doesn't the Matrix of the Monsters, incidentally, imply just such a subjective position?

Furthermore, knowledge, 'S2', is in the position of truth below agent 'a', and the knowledge here refers to the supposed knowledge of the analyst, and simultaneously, according to Zizek, "signals that the knowledge gained here will not be the neutral 'objective' knowledge of sci-

entific adequacy, but the knowledge that concerns the subject (analysand) in the truth of his subjective position." (Zizek, "Four Discourses, Four Subjects," p. 80.)

Perhaps herein lies the path of my explicit redirections towards theory and against therapy when discussing the Eastern European Matrix of the Monsters. Moreover, here I would like to make a small but important detour in my thesis. It is possible to say: 'I am the monster' exclusively under a specific condition. According to Robert Pfaller, who discusses a similar situation - to say: 'I am in ideology' - "only under a certain condition we are allowed to say that we are in ideology. Only if we are within science we can say such a thing without lying or being presumptuously modest. Only under the condition that we have arrived at the positive space of science are we legitimated to say that we are in ideology." (Pfaller, "Negation and Its Reliabilities: Am Empty Subject for Ideology?," p. 235)

Thus, *mutatis mutandis*, we can clearly state that only if we are within theory, or relying on theory, we can say without lying or being presumptuously modest: 'I am the monster.' Zizek's further elaboration of the relation between science and ideology that he draws, relying on R. Pfaller's paradoxical relationship between science and ideology, can be additionally useful. Zizek argued that ideology does not exclude science, but rather it tries to integrate it into its domain. (Cf. Zizek, "Cogito as a Shibboleth," p. 8.) The relation between ideology and science is described by Zizek as 'clinching,' similar to the situation in the boxing match, when instead of fighting the opponent's body, one clinches it. Thus the difference between ideology and science is visible only from the side of science. It is likewise possible to say that between therapy and theory, the therapeutical approach clinches on a theoretical thesis of the Eastern European 'survivor' as the mute victim who needs to share that victim experience through small biographical anecdotes and traces, if s/he wants to be integrated into the long chain of civilizational theoretical backgrounds in the West.
What makes it possible then for the saint to evade the deranged machine of production? Lacan puts forward a solution

which consists ultimately of identification with that which is left over - with the trash - as we see that the agent/agency occupies the position of the useless trash remainder (*object 'a'*). The saint upon which Lacan models the analyst's refusal to be useful, to surrender to the demands of capitalism (thereby redefining the notion of agency) is a singular structural apparatus/effect of the structure rather than a vocation. Or, as formulated by Zizek, "The answer to the question: where, in the four subjective positions elaborated, do we encounter the Lacanian subject, the subject of the unconscious, is thus paradoxically in the very discourse in which the subject undergoes 'subjective destitution' and identifies with the excremental remainder that forever resists subjectivization." (Zizek, "Four Discourses, Four Subjects," pp. 108-9.) We see that the agent/agency occupies the position of the useless trash remainder (*object 'a'*). In short, between emancipation and resistance, via Lacan, we can put forward an absolutely political solution, a radical politicization of the Eastern European position, which consists ultimately in the identification with the useless trash remainder - with the piece of shit!

II.

I have stated that at the end of the millennium, the two matrices, the Western European 'Scum of Society Matrix' and the Eastern European 'Monsters Matrix,' not only raise questions of reflection, but also offer elements of political and analytical intersection that need to be discussed and articulated further and in a much more radical way. Establishing the difference between East and West only on historical premises can lead us to a DISCURSIVE limit, and I would like to proceed in a different way, albeit not indifferent to history; I will attempt to explicate some generative principles between the matrices and their complex functioning using Lacanism.

My first thesis of the second level of this paper is as follows: the East and West are not predicates, which means that rather than increasing our knowledge of the subject, they qualify the mode of the failure of our knowledge; because failure is assumed, according to Copjec, to be singular.

The distinction between the two ways in which reason falls into contradiction with itself was first made by Kant in the *Critique of Pure Reason* and the *Critique of Judgment*. In both works he demonstrated that the failure of reason was not simple, but based upon an antinomic impasse through two separate routes: the first failure was mathematical; the second was dynamic. The first thing to note is that the two propositions that compose each side appear to have an antinomic relation to each other, i.e., they appear to contradict each other. Subsequently, in his Seminar XX entitled "Encore," drawing upon the Kantian antinomic relations, Lacan defined the two formulas of sexuation (OF SEXUAL DIFFERENCE) as two ways, or paths, of failure: the male and the female. In her book *Read My Desire* (MIT 1994), which may be defined as a handbook or bible of Lacanism, Joan Copjec strongly emphasized these two antinomic ways as two ways of failures.

The antinomies and the formulas of sexuation are presented through a scheme that is clearly divided between the left and right sides. The left side of the scheme is designated as the male side, while the right side is female. The left, male side corresponds to the Kantian dynamic antinomies, and the right, female side, corresponds to the Kantian mathematical antinomies.

My second thesis of the second level is as follows: the Eastern European Monsters Matrix occupied, and is homologous with, the right, female side, and therefore represents the Kantian mathematical failure; while the Western European Scum of Society Matrix is homologous with the left, male side, or the Kantian dynamical failure. You may, doubtfully, pose the question: How is this possible? What allows for such a homologous positioning?

What is of crucial importance is that Lacan uses, conceives the terms in his formulas of sexuation as argument and function, instead of subject and predicate (as they are referred to in the Kantian formulas). This substitution marks an important, and for us a crucial, conceptual difference. The principle of sorting is, according to Copjec, no longer descriptive, i.e., it is not a matter of shared characteristics or of common substance. Copjec stated, "Whether one falls into the class of males or females (and I would add, whether one falls into the Scum or Monsters failure matrix - MG) depends, rather, which enunciative position one assumes." You may remember that in the first level of considerations, I argued with Zizek, "If the Cartesian subject wishes to arise on the level of enunciation, it must be described as almost nothing ready to be thrown in the disposal garbage/trash on the level of a statement" (Cf. Slavoj Zizek, "Alain Badiou kot bralec svetega Pavla" [Alain Badiou as the Reader of St. Paulus] p. 135.). Perhaps it is only now, when Eastern Europe has understood on the level of a statement, itself to be an almost nothing - ready to be thrown in the disposal - of excremental trash (at the Documenta, as we stated, as in many other cases, it was reduced precisely to this nothing), that it is time for Eastern Europe to arise on the level of enunciation. The antinomies should be read as positions on a Moebius strip. There is an unmistakable asymmetry between the mathematical and the dynamical antinomies, again according to Copjec: on moving from one to the other, we seem to enter a completely different space.

## 3. THE RIGHT, FEMALE SIDE: MATHEMATICAL FAILURE and the Eastern European 'Monsters Matrix'

I learned while I was living and working last year in Japan that before talking further, you have to show your card - the famous meshi in the Japanese language. I apologize for making you wait for so long. Marina Grzinic - I am that useless trash, I am the monster.

Therefore, I will continue this paper firstly with reference to the right side - the female side, the mathematical failure. But beware, as you already notice how much I enjoy being the useless trash, I am not starting with the monsters BECAUSE I would like to get some compassion from you. As opposed to the fairly common prejudice that psychoanalysis constructs the woman as secondary - as a mere alteration of man - these formulas suggest, according to Copjec, that there is a kind of priority, a kind of advantage on the right side.

This reading of the formulas is consistent also with the privilege given to the mathematical antinomies by Kant, who grants the mathematical synthesis a more immediate type of certitude than its dynamical counterpart. In Kant's analysis, it is the dynamical antinomies (the male side of the formulas, or the Western European's Scum Matrix in our reading) that appear in many ways secondary, a kind of resolution to a more complete impasse manifested by the mathematical conflict. (Copjec, p.217) I will proceed in a very schematic way to reach my point.

What is a mathematical antinomy? First, every antinomy is composed of two propositions: thesis and antithesis. The mathematical antinomy we borrowed from Kant is occasioned by the attempt, speaking generally, to think the world. The thesis of the mathematical antinomy is: the world has a beginning in time and is also limited in regard to space. The antithesis of the same mathematical antinomy is: the world has no beginning and no limits in space but is, in relation both to time and space, infinite.

"After examining both arguments, Kant concludes that while each successfully demonstrates the falsity of the other, neither is able to establish convincingly its own truth. This conclusion creates a skeptical impasse, and the solution he arrives at is the following: rather than despairing over the fact that we cannot choose between the two alternatives, we must come to the realization that we need not choose, since both alternatives are false. The thesis and antithesis statements, which initially appeared to constitute a contradictory opposition, turn out to be contraries." (Copjec, p. 218)

We might note that we can find in a mathematical antinomy the structure of a contrary opposition that produces a joke of the Zizekian type:

In your village there are no cannibals anymore. When did you eat the last one?

The form of the question does not allow the addressee to negate the accusation implicit in the question, but only to choose among contraries. Having demonstrated the impossibility of the existence of the world, Kant can then dismiss both the statements of thesis and antithesis. Kant's two statements regarding the solution of the first mathematical antinomy formally reduplicate those that Lacan gives for the woman, who, like the world, does not exist.

Lacan argues that a concept of 'woman' cannot be constructed because the task of fully unfolding her conditions cannot, in actuality, be carried out. Since we are finite beings, bound by space and time, our knowledge is subject to historical conditions. Our conception of woman cannot run ahead of these limits and thus, cannot construct a concept of the whole of woman. And here we come to the most important point:

"The ex-sistence of the woman is not only denied; it is also not condemnable as a normative and exclusionary notion; on the contrary, the Lacanian position argues that it is only by refusing to deny - or confirm - her ex-sistence that normative and exclusionary thinking can be avoided. That is, it is only by acknowledging that a concept of woman cannot exist that it is structurally impossible within the symbolic order, that each historical construction of her can be challenged. After all, nothing prohibits these historical constructions from asserting their universal truth; witness the historical assertion that a general, trans-historical category of woman does not exist." (Copjec, p. 225)

It is crucial to see that the woman is the consequence, and not the cause, of the nonfunctioning of negation. She is the failure of the limit, not the cause of the failure. (Copjec, p. 226)

Now, following this rude and schematic re-cutting up of one part of the excellent chapter on the forms of sexuation in Copjec's book *Read My Desire*, we must return to our Monsters Matrix – to accept the consequences of such a homologous positioning.

My third thesis is: similar to Lacan's positioning of the nonexistence of the woman, we can speak of the nonexistence of the Matrix of Monsters. If the (Matrix of) Monsters do(es) not exist, this is because it cannot be refound. The Matrix of Monsters cannot be constructed because the task of fully unfolding its conditions cannot, in actuality, be carried

out. Our conception of the (Matrix of) Monsters cannot run ahead of these limits and thus, cannot construct a concept of the whole of the Matrix. (Cf. Copjec, p. 221)

The exsistence of the (Matrix of) Monsters is not only denied; it is also not condemnable as a normative and exclusionary notion; on the contrary, the Lacanian position argues that it is only by refusing to deny - or confirm- its exsistence that normative and exclusionary thinking can be avoided. That is, it is only by acknowledging that a concept of the (Matrix of) Monsters cannot exist, that it is structurally impossible within the symbolic order, that each historical construction of this Matrix can be challenged. As long as it can be demonstrated that the world or the (Matrix of) Monsters cannot form a whole, a universe, then the possibility of judging whether or not these phenomena or signifiers give us information about a reality independent of us vanishes. It is crucial to see that the (Matrix of) Monsters (is) are the consequence, and not the cause, of the nonfunctioning of negation. It is the failure of the limit, not the cause of the failure. (Cf. Copjec, p. 226) We are obliged to recognize that the (Matrix of) Monsters (is) are indeed a product of the symbolic.

## 4. THE LEFT, THE MALE SIDE: DYNAMICAL FAILURE and the Western European 'Scum of Society Matrix'

Where the thesis and antithesis of the mathematical antinomies were both deemed to be false because both illegitimately asserted the existence of the world, the thesis and antithesis of the dynamical antinomies, the dynamical failure, are both deemed by Kant to be true. In the first case, the conflict between the two propositions was thought to be irresolvable (since they made contradictory claims about the same object); in the case of dynamical failure, the conflict is resolved by the assertion that the two statements do not contradict each other.

The thesis of the dynamical antinomy is, according to Kant, the sequent: Causality according to the laws of nature is not the only causality operating to originate the world. A causality of freedom is also necessary to account fully for these phenomena. The Kantian antithesis of the dynamical antinomy, or failure, is: There is no such thing as freedom, but everything in the world happens solely according to the laws of nature.

Kant says that the antithesis in the dynamic antinomy is true, just as Lacan confirms the existence of the universe of men. Since the existence of the universe was regarded in the case of the woman as impossible because no limit could be found to the chain of signifiers, it would be logical to assume that the formation of the all on the male side depends on the positing of a limit.

Moreover, the process involved in the shift from the female to the male side is a subtraction. The thesis and antithesis of the mathematical failure, according to Kant, said too much. On the dynamical side, this surplus is subtracted, and it is this subtraction that installs the limit. Which means that on this side it will always be a matter of saying too little. Incompleteness on the dynamic side, and inconsistency on the mathematical part. Furthermore, according to Copjec, the question of existence that caused the conflict on the female side is silenced on the male side because it is precisely existence – or being – that is subtracted from the universe that is formed here. Kant taught us that if one were to say that a man existed, one would add absolutely nothing to this man, or to the concept of man. Thus we could argue that this concept lacks nothing. And yet, it does not include being, and is in this sense inadequate.

Again, the two failures or forms of sexuation according to Lacan consist of the following: the woman and the man are not to be treated symmetrically nor conceived as complements of each other. One category does not complete, or make up for what is lacking in, the other. While the universe of women is simply impossible, a universe of men is possible only on the condition that we except something from this universe. The universe of men is then an illusion based, according to Copjec, on a paradoxical prohibition: do not include everything in your all! The sexual relation fails for two reasons: it is impossible, and it is prohibited. And this is why we will never come up with a whole.

To recapitulate: an easy solution would be to say: like the Eastern European Monsters Matrix, the Western European Scum of Society Matrix does not exist. But we have on the left side, homologous to the Lacanian sexuation table, no problem in locating it. Kant taught us, if one were to say that the Western European Scum of Society Matrix existed, one would add absolutely nothing to the concept of the Western European Scum of Society Matrix. Rather than defining a universe of men that is complemented by a universe of women, we can define, by relying on Lacan, the Western European Scum of Society Matrix as the prohibition against constructing a universe, and the Monsters Matrix as the impossibility of doing so.

Hence, my conclusion:

1. The Western European Scum of Society Matrix does exist, and the Monsters Matrix does not exist. This is because, as I demonstrated in the first part of this essay, the Eastern Europeans perceived as pieces of shit are subjects in a pure sense of the word; the subject is nothing else but the name of the division in a pure form. On the right side, on the part of the mathematical failure, therefore we have the subject as its purest.

2. When Lacan argues that truth has the structure of fiction and that is not-all, that is lacking a structure of totality, he highlighted the fact that through these two moments (fiction and lacking of totality) truth is touching the real. The Eastern European Monsters Matrix has the status of not-all and the structure of fiction precisely because it is part of the order of the Real. So it is not surprising that theoreticians spoke about Eastern Europe as a generator of concepts in the field of art and culture that are connected with a traumatic real (Peter Weibel, for one).

3. What we can learn from the positioning of the two matrices, similarly to the formulas of sexual difference, is that in post-Communism, a kind of traumatic reality is emerging through the surface of the works.

4. It is not red is blood, is the indivisible post-Communist remainder that is not (yet?) possible to re-integrate into the global immaterial and virtual media world.

**References:**

Joan Copjec, *Read My Desire: Lacan against the Historicists*, The MIT Press, Cambridge, Massachusetts and London 1994.

Jacques Derrida, *Spectres de Marx*, Galileé, Paris 1993.

Marina Grzinic, *Rekonstruirana fikcija : novi mediji, (video) umetnost, postsocializem in retroavantgarda : teorija, politika, estetika : 1997-1985,* [Fiction Reconstructed. New Media, (Video) Art, Post-Socialism and Retro-avantgarde: Theory, Politics and Esthetics: 1985-1997], SOU, Koda, Ljubljana 1997.

Donna Haraway, "The Promises of Monsters: A Regenerative Politics for Inappropriate/d Others," in: *Cultural Studies*, eds. Lawrence Grossberg, Cary Nelson and Paula A. Treichler, Routledge, New York and London 1992.

Jacques Lacan, *Television* (translated by. J. Mehlmann), Norton & Co., New York 1990.

Robert Pfaller, "Negation and Its Reliabilities: Am Empty Subject for Ideology?" in *Cogito and the Unconscious*, ed., Slavoj Zizek, Duke University Press 1998, pp. 225-247.

Scilicet 1-4: *Scritti di Jacques Lacan e di altri* [Scilicet 1-4: Texts by Jacques Lacan and Others], Feltrinelli Editore, Milan 1977.

Jelica Sumic-Riha, "A Matter of Resistance," in *Filozofski Vesnik*, No. 2/1997, Spec. Number on Power and Resistance, (ed. by Sumic-Riha and Oto Luthar), FI ZRC SAZU, Ljubljana 1997, pp. 127-153.

Slavoj Zizek, "Introduction: The Spectre of Ideology," in *Mapping Ideology*, ed., Slavoj Zizek, Verso, London and New York, 1994.

Slavoj Zizek, "Alain Badiou kot bralec svetega Pavla" ['Alain Badiou as the Reader of St. Paulus'] in *Sveti Pavel: Utemeljitev univerzalnosti* [St. Paulus: The Foundation of Universality], Analecta, Problemi, 5-6, Ljubljana 1998, pp. 115-149.

Slavoj Zizek, "Introduction: Cogito as a Shibboleth," in *Cogito and the Unconscious*, ed., Slavoj Zizek, Duke University Press 1998, pp. 1-8.

Slavoj Zizek, "Four Discourses, Four Subjects," in *Cogito and the Unconscious*, ed., Slavoj Zizek, Duke University Press 1998, pp. 74-117.

# Globalisation, Media, and the War against Yugoslavia

## The 1990s: The Lost Peace

The 1990s were a period of transition following the period known as Cold War, which had been characterized by bipolar tension between two systems of social, political and economic organization and which ended with the collapse of one and the triumph of the other. The former Soviet bloc countries emerging from the collapsed system became 'transition' countries, as they were reshaped to fit the victorious model: liberal capitalism.

In Europe, the end of the Cold *War* was generally perceived in optimistic terms within the framework of the social democratic value system which enjoyed intellectual hegemony at the time. Because the bipolar period was called the Cold War, ending it was expected to bring peace. In both East and West, a 'peace dividend' was widely anticipated, with democracy and improved living standards for all.

This social democratic optimism overlooked the extent to which the social concessions of capitalism had been part of the ideological struggle against communism. With communism defeated, the overwhelming ideological, economic and military advantage enjoyed by the leading capitalist power, the United States, favored not social democratic compromise but rather an all-out offensive to complete the century-long conquest of worldwide markets and trade advantages.

Thus, while democratic pluralistic elections are now the rule, it has turned out that whoever is elected, the basic economic policies must be essentially the same. Any social policy is necessarily subjected to the 'judgment of the markets,' meaning movements of investment capital outside all political control. The political control of the economy has given way to the economic control of politics to an extent not imagined by those who assumed that the elimination of state-commanded communism would strengthen social democracy, or democratic socialism. Decision-making power over social policy has been increasingly moved from the public political sector to the private sector.

From a world divided, we have supposedly moved into a world with a single dominant model of social, political and economic organization, exemplified by the United States. The extension of this model, primarily in the economic sphere, is celebrated as a new age of 'globalization.'

Globalization amounts to the worldwide empowerment of the transnational private sphere, dominated by an ever smaller number of corporations, financial institutions and wealthy individuals.

This unipolar world is by no means a united and peaceful world. At the end of the Cold War, the idea that now we would have general disarmament and that a resulting 'peace dividend' of resources could be diverted from military budgets to social welfare turned out to be a brief mirage. The unprecedented military buildup of the Reagan years was indeed followed by a necessary leveling off, but in 1998, military spending in the United States resumed its upward spiral. Weapons are a central element in the global economy as well as in global mass culture, where the glorification of technological violence is a central feature of commercial mass entertainment, easily crossing borders because based in image, not language.

In short, this U.S.-led globalization is not a natural planetary unification flowing happily from the peaceful expansion of free trade, as portrayed, but on the contrary an aggressive process involving ruthless economic pressure, ideological takeover based on technological advantage, and war.

## Globalization: Political Process and Ideological Image

The success of U.S. globalization depends greatly on its portrayal as a natural and inevitable rather than a deliberate, politically determined process. It must be accepted as the general good, to which resistance is both perverse and vain.

As a reality, the collapse of the anti-capitalist alternative represented by the Soviet bloc has been rapidly exploited by capitalist institutions and the politicians they support to adopt policies locking in their advantages by abolishing all sorts of controls and regulations standing in the way of the international flow and action of financial capital. The power of wealth is used to enact legislation which enhances the power of wealth, resulting in increased polarization of society between a very large wealthy class and a very large number of poor, with the middle classes squeezed either up or down. The trend is worldwide.

Ideologically, however, 'globalization' is presented not as the result of specific government policies of privatization and deregulation enacted in the interests of financial capital, but rather as their *cause*, as a natural, inevitable and irreversible movement. 'Globalization' has stepped into the empty shoes of

'progress.' Politics and policy must adapt to this wave of the future, while any suggestion of putting political controls on transnational capital movements is condemned as 'nationalism.'

The bipolar 'world' was in fact the Northern part of the world, divided between the advanced capitalist nations within the bloc led by the United States on the one side and the socialist bloc dominated by the Soviet Union on the other. As for the rest, they were considered in simplified terms to be either subordinate to one of those two blocs or else belonging to the 'Third World.' The 'model' had to be one or the other of the two rival Northern blocs. In that logic, the collapse of the Soviet bloc means that the entire planet must adopt the U.S. model - a viewpoint expressed by Francis Fukayama as "the end of history."

Fukayama represents the optimistic end of the U.S. ideological spectrum in the post-Cold War era. The pessimistic variant is represented by Samuel Huntington's prediction of a 'clash of civilizations' in which various cultures resist the domination of American-style economic and social liberalism. Either way, after the conflict between 'communism' and 'democracy,' the new era is perceived as a conflict between the single viable model represented by the victorious United States and remaining pockets of perverse resistance to the inevitable. In their most extreme form, these pockets of resistance are designated as 'rogue States,' outlaws that defy the New World Order in the making.

Thus, in place of the representation of world reality as a bipolar conflict between the 'free' West and the 'evil empire' of the East, the world is now supposed to be divided between the respectable nations that belong to the New World Order, and the outcasts, pariahs, criminals and rogues left outside.

Therefore, the economic term 'globalization' is accompanied by an equally vague and ideological political term, the 'international community'. Both terms serve to idealize and justify the privatization, not only of property but of vital social functions, such as information and security, that characterizes this period of triumphant capitalism.

# The International Community: Private Interests and Public Morality

Like 'globalization,' the 'international community' is presented as something of a natural, self-generated phenomenon. Whereas globalization is supposed to be the work of an autonomous, essentially ungovernable economy, the 'international community' is supposed to be a primarily moral entity directed by a collective human will.

In reality, the 'international community,' like much of 'globalization' is a deliberate creation of United States foreign policy.

For the sake of 'globalization,' the United States has vigorously promoted international institutions devised to protect U.S.-based private economic interests: from the International Monetary Fund and its 'structural adjustment' programs to the long 'Uruguay Round' of GATT leading up to the establishment of the World Trade Organization. These have severely limited the power of governments to protect public interests, whether citizens' welfare or the environment, from the demands of private business. The stalled 'Multilateral Agreement on Investment' (MAI) would go even farther in shifting vital political decision-making power to the private sector, acting in co-optive, non-elected bureaucratic tribunals.

Simultaneously, in the sphere of international political relations, the United States has continuously undermined the United Nations in a multitude of ways. The United Nations is a contractual legal structure with clearly defined rules and methods. It has a *potentially* democratic structure. Member States send representatives to a General Assembly, a sort of proto-parliament. With considerable reform, both of itself and of the Member States, it could provide a rough representation of the world population in a single body.

In contrast, the 'international community' is vague in its composition and manner of operation. It does not automatically include the whole world. As a community - *Gemeinschaft* - it is based on subjective or arbitrary factors rather than legal contract, and these subjective factors are rationalized as 'shared values' to which the community in question claims a privileged relationship: 'human rights' first of all. The 'international community' follows the model not of a parliament but of an English gentlemen's club.

The gentlemen who run the club are assumed to possess an innate moral sense of what is right and what is wrong, and therefore do not need a legally established institution to determine who deserves exclusion and chastisement for incorrect behavior. The gentlemen are, of course, rich, and happy to keep their distance from the poor rather than actually mess about in their messy affairs. In short, old style imperialism is a thing of the past. There is no desire to extend the responsibilities (and expenses) of each rich industrial nation-state to governing distant colonies of its own. Instead, in this dawning new era, the International Community - or Imperialist Condominium - should be ready to intervene only at specific times in specific places, in response to its collective conscience. The instrument for such intervention is NATO, no longer a Cold War military alliance, but recycled as a humanitarian peace force. The conscience that directs it is 'international public opinion,' as expressed primarily by the mass media.

The primary intervention of the 'metropole' - the rich industrial 'center' of this unipolar world - is financial and economic. This economic access must be ensured by the ever-present potential for a secondary intervention: military. But to justify the maintenance of the military potential for global intervention, a moral purpose is required. Thus the possibility of 'humanitarian intervention' to protect victim populations from 'evil' States is an indirect safeguard of the economic dominance of the United States and its subsidiary NATO partners.

However, the fact that the calls for military intervention come initially not from the State but from the 'private' voices of conscience in the media, in humanitarian non-governmental organizations (NGOs) and in policy advisory groups ('think tanks') helps preserve the illusion that eventual military action is a disinterested response to moral imperatives.

## Vectors of Ideology: Think Tanks, Media and NGOs

In line with the privatization of information and security, U.S. foreign policy in the last two decades has been increasingly determined by, or in conjunction with, three types of private institutions: policy institutes or 'think tanks,' the media and non-governmental organizations (NGOs).

## Think tanks:

Private elite associations such as the Council on Foreign Relations have long played a leading role in setting out the main lines of U.S. foreign policy. The last quarter of a century has seen an expansion of privately-funded policy institutes in the United States, known as 'think tanks.' Their 'thinking' is financed by the same big business interests that control major media and fund the expensive political campaigns of both Republican and Democratic Party candidates. These interests are not monolithic, and differences of analysis and proposal are to be expected, but within a basic ideological consensus around the excellence of the American capitalist system as model for the entire, often ungrateful, world.

The 'think tanks' lobby Congress and government ministries and live in symbiosis with the leading media, which regularly consult their resident scholars as public commentators on the issues of the day. One of the most prestigious of the policy institutes, the Carnegie Endowment for International Peace, offers a significant example. In the early 1990s, under the presidency of Morton Abramowitz, the Carnegie Endowment sponsored studies in search of a new U.S. foreign policy for the post-Cold War era. A major problem was to justify the continued existence of NATO - key to U.S. domination of Europe. The selected experts came up with the possibility of intervention in sovereign states on behalf of ethnic minorities whose struggle for 'self-determination' might lead to 'humanitarian catastrophe.' A public relations campaign was undertaken to spread these ideas through the media. Such ideas found their practical application in NATO's 'Kosovo war,' promoted most strongly by U.S. Secretary of State

Madeleine Albright, who had taken part in the Carnegie study group. Abramowitz went on to became a supporter of the UCK ('Kosovo Liberation Front') and an advisor to the ethnic Albanian delegation at the Rambouillet 'peace talks' which led to NATO's bombing of Yugoslavia.

This suggests that for a certain school of thought represented by Albright and Abramowitz, the Yugoslav conflict offered an opportunity to put into practice a new mission for NATO, and with it, a new phase of U.S. foreign policy leadership. For this to seem appropriate, Yugoslav and Kosovo problems had to be seen in a certain light. Mainstream media provided that light.

## Media:

Foreign news has always been more easily falsified than domestic news, because it is obviously easier to deceive people about things they cannot see for themselves. Television, with its pictures of events, gives the illusion of knowing what is happening. This can be a dangerous illusion. Written words are vulnerable to critical review. The meaning of brief images is easily distorted, either by simplified explanation or by more or less spontaneous stereotyped interpretations. The predominance of television in news reporting facilitates certain types of distortion. There is a tendency for the news to become a form of entertainment, a show.

Aside from its very form, television and other mass media work to dull political perceptions in two ways. One is direct: the simplified presentation of politics and public issues themselves. The other is indirect: the influence of general attitudes promoted by popular entertainment.

American popular entertainment with its global reach fosters attitudes which are appropriate to the American capitalist system, notably the competitive spirit, the desire to get ahead, to win, to become rich and famous. It also flatters universal simplistic attitudes such as the desire for vengeance and identification of 'our side' as good and 'the other side' as bad. Nothing is more evident in American popular drama than this tendency to portray people as inherently good and innocent or else inherently bad. The competitive spirit and the Manichean view go together quite well, providing a final moral rationale for the division wrought by competition between winners and losers. Both provide criteria for the exclusion of certain pariahs - losers or bad people - from a society whose cohesion is thereby strengthened. The lurking possibility of exclusion acts as a force for conformity.

Such attitudes are favorable to war propaganda. Peaceful resolution of conflicts calls for trying to understand all sides. Instead, choosing the 'good' and 'bad' sides implies entering the conflict, not resolving it.

## Non-Governmental Organizations:

Internationally active NGOs such as *Médecins du Monde* have been at the forefront of the demand for 'humanitarian intervention.' Operating across borders, such NGOs see national sovereignty as a mere obstacle to their own operations. Based in the rich NATO countries, operating in poorer countries, the direction of their intervention is the same as that of NATO acting as policeman of the New World Order. The NGOs risk becoming the 'human face' on the policy of military intervention by the 'international community' - playing a role similar to that of Christian missionaries as pretext and justification for military expeditions in earlier imperialist conquests.

NGOs are not all strictly 'non-governmental.' Many thrive on contracts from governments. Some are even set up by governments, such as the National Endowment for Democracy, an instrument of the U.S. government, designed to intervene in the political affairs of other countries. Their recent growth reflects, however, the trend toward re-privatization of 'good works' that accompanies the neo-liberal dismantling of government-run social programs.

In neo-liberal ideology, 'non-governmental' sounds better than 'State.' When communism was the enemy, the United States encouraged anti-communist nationalists in Eastern Europe. With the triumph of neo-liberalism, the term 'nationalist' has

become pejorative. It now usually designates the 'bad guys' who are excluded from the 'international community.'

The United States, of course, continues to pursue its own 'national interest' in the unshakable conviction that this is identical with the universal good. Meanwhile, the nation-state is considered obsolete in the ideology of the 'international community,' and therefore smaller nations can no longer hope to evade the dictates of the 'international community' by evoking national sovereignty. In 1998, British foreign secretary Robin Cook declared that "the old independent nation-state is a thing of the past," a theoretical statement that was forcefully put into practice by NATO when it undertook to bomb Yugoslavia for 80 days.

As part of the ideological euphoria surrounding the steps toward the European Union, the nation-state has been stigmatized as the cause of war, oppression and violation of human rights. This contemporary libertarian view overlooks both the persistence of war in the absence of strong States and the historic function of the nation state as the most effective existing framework for the social pact enabling citizens to build structures of social protection and cultural development. Demonizing as 'nationalism' the only existing context for functioning institutionalized democracy obviously facilitates the dictates of 'the markets', which are innocent of nationalist prejudice.

In practical terms, the rise of NGOs have helped to privatize public causes, taking the form of small (or in some cases large) businesses which must use advertising to 'sell' their good works to donors, whether private or public. The requirements of fund-raising favor consensual causes with immediate emotional appeal over complex long-range projects. Fund-raising is easiest for victims, using appeals to sentiment rather than to reason.

Moreover, a number of NGOs serve as indirect aids to economic globalization, by providing some of the public services which poor States are obliged to eliminate under the dictates of International Monetary Fund 'structural adjustment' policies. But depending on outside charity is obviously a precarious way for a country to feed, educate and provide basic sanitation for its people. The mere fact that it may have to do so weakens the people's loyalty to their State, which risks in turn becoming no more than an armed force to put down inevitable disorder - until the armed force itself disintegrates into a major cause of disorder.

The NGOs provide the flesh and bones as well as the moral identity of the otherwise amorphous 'international community.' After the Somalia fiasco, the bombing of Yugoslavia has shown just how far humanitarian NGO's can be used to trigger military action leading to far greater destruction than existed before. Even more sinister for the ethical pretensions of the NGOs, the humanitarian business thrives on such destruction, as Western NGOs vie for contracts to rebuild countries devastated by 'humanitarian war.'

## Media Treatment of Yugoslavia

The assumption that Western motives are fully embodied in the aims of humanitarian NGOs whereas elsewhere, 'new Hitlers' are arising motivated by pure wickedness, underlies much Western coverage of the conflicts arising from the Yugoslav crisis. An extremely complex situation, with many parties involved, all bearing varying degrees of responsibility, was reduced to a Manichean struggle between good and evil. Whereas there were several types of nationalism interacting with each other and with severe economic and political problems, the situation was presented as an aggression by one evil nationalism led by a villain - Milosevic - against an array of innocent victims. In reality, the crisis in Yugoslavia around 1990 seriously called for genuine dispassionate, knowledgeable and unbiased mediation. The European Community had the prestige to play that role, but lacked the necessary political or institutional unity.

Nevertheless, acting individually or through the United Nations, European States might have contributed to a genuine mediation. However, the drive to unify Europe has eliminated all original initiatives in foreign policy. Differences must be covered up. Honest debate of foreign policy issues is muted for fear of

harming an embryonic, inexistent unified European foreign policy.

Fear of reverting to the divisions that led to World War I overcame any responsible need for honest debate of errors leading to new and different disasters. To exorcize the danger of revival of the major nationalisms of the Great Powers - France and Germany, especially - Europeans heatedly condemned the minor nationalisms of the Balkans, so focusing on 'nationalism' as a sort of universal virus that insufficient attention was paid to the particularities of the Balkan problems. This allowed the United States to seize the initiative and use the Yugoslav problems to serve Washington's policy: asserting control over European foreign and security policy via an enlarged and strengthened NATO with a new global mission of 'humanitarian intervention.'

While the mass media are not at the origin of this situation, their treatment of events in Yugoslavia has contributed to an ongoing disaster. This can be attributed in part to the connivance of publishers and editors with policy-makers, and in part to the natural tendency of media to simplify complicated stories.

It is only fair to stress that the main fault for distortion and simplification in the written press lies with publishers and editors who decide in advance what the public 'wants' or should read. Most journalists would no doubt prefer to tell the whole story and tell it well, but they are rarely allowed to do so. They soon learn which sorts of self-censorship will ingratiate editors and advance their careers. In the case of Yugoslavia and especially the Kosovo war, editorialists of leading newspapers provided a chorus of pro-war, racist anti-Serb propaganda that Americans with memories (Noam Chomsky among others) could compare only to the 'anti-Jap' propaganda of World War II in the United States.

From the start of the Yugoslav wars of secession, the media abused analogy by comparing an unfamiliar situation with a supposedly familiar one: World War II. By the time NATO bombed Serbia in order to occupy Kosovo, the analogy had been established, and Milosevic had become 'Hitler.' Anyone who questioned the appropriateness of such comparisons could be accused of 'revisionism' and of 'holocaust denial.'

The likening of Kosovo to 'the holocaust' required several kinds of distortion, notably the pretense that Serb security forces were attacking the entire ethnic Albanian population as such, and not the rebels of the 'Kosovo Liberation Army' (UÇK) who had initiated an armed uprising aimed at detaching the province from Serbia. It also required accepting without question the highest possible estimate of ethnic Albanian casualties, all considered to be 'civilians,' while ignoring non-Albanian casualties. The practice of accepting inflated figures was already established in Bosnia, where the figure of '200,000 dead' has become standard, despite the fact (pointed out in April 1995 by former State Department official George Kenney, and never refuted) that the '200,000 dead' was totally undocumented and was launched in June 1993 by the Bosnian Information Ministry in an evident appeal for foreign intervention. Kenney cited the Red Cross as having confirmed well under 20,000 fatalities on all sides in the Bosnian war, with the small possibility that the real figure might exceed 35,000. Other cases where inflated and unverified figures have been repeated endlessly and uncritically concern the number of Muslim victims of the Srebrenica massacre (often put at 8,000, when it cannot possibly be that many, and when it is most likely at least ten times fewer) and the number of women victims of Serb rapists (extrapolated from 575 identified cases to widely circulated estimates ranging from 20,000 to 50,000). These exaggerated figures have been necessary to support the contention that what has been happening in Yugoslavia is not merely a nasty, brutal civil war, but rather a re-enactment by the Serbs of Nazi genocide. Stopping 'Hitler' is an irresistibly virtuous enterprise, especially for a European Union that must assert itself against the 'nationalisms' of the past. Yugoslavia has been the 'common enemy' needed to bring Europe and the United States together in a new missionary NATO. This new moralizing Atlantic union obviously corresponds to U.S. strategic interests. But European NATO leaders and media have bought in the demonizing of the Serbs with equal enthusiasm.

The European Union is in need of a common identity more spiritual than a common currency. In 1994, a number of European intellectuals organized around the slogan, 'Europe lives or dies at Sarajevo.' This was in fact extravagant hyperbole. But it caught the need to associate 'Europe' with a dramatic cause, and the intellectuals feeling this need grasped onto a totally idealized 'Bosnia' as the symbol of this 'Europe' which, rather than an economic powerhouse technocratically organized to take its place alongside the United States in world domination, was actually a tender bud of multi-ethnic civilization in danger of being trampled to death by a new Hitler.

Yugoslavia's disintegration was the first crisis to be poured whole into the mould of the ideological myth of World War II. This is a ritual for anthropologists to describe. Myth is built on history and transformed into a ceremony whose roles must be assumed by succeeding players on the stage of history. Finally, the scapegoat. Milosevic became 'Hitler,' the Serbs became the new 'Nazis', and their adversaries were all victims of a potential new 'Holocaust.' Serbia bears all the sins of Europe's past; it represents everything Europe thinks it is not, or does not want to be.

The mass media project the chorus of the righteous myth. No deviation is allowed. The occasional intellectual who ventures to doubt - Peter Handke, Regis Debray - is pilloried by the chorus of right thinkers. Dissent is stigmatized and marginalized by the 'insiders.' At the same time, the gap is growing between the media and populations who do not know what to believe, but do not believe what they are being told. NATO's 'humanitarian war' has opened a new era of struggle for truth.

**134**

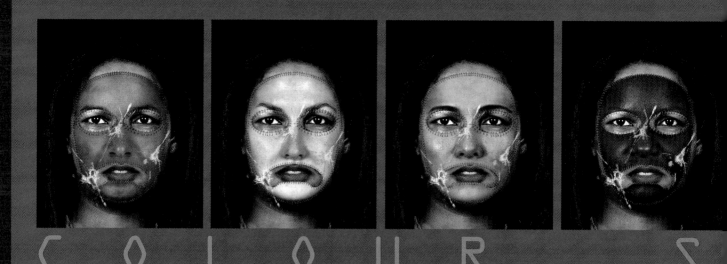

C O L O U R   S

Colour Seperation is constructed from photos of over one hundred people who are related in some day-to-day way with the core Mongrel group. Using "HeritageGold" software it transforms their images into eight un-glamourous stereotypes of black/yellow/brown/white men and women. These are people that never existed.

These images wear the masks of the other stereotypes. The masks are spat on. On the cover we have a white man wearing a black mask covered in spit. We have no idea who has done the spitting. Is it a white man fed up with his friend pretending to be black? Has he been spat on because he is a black-

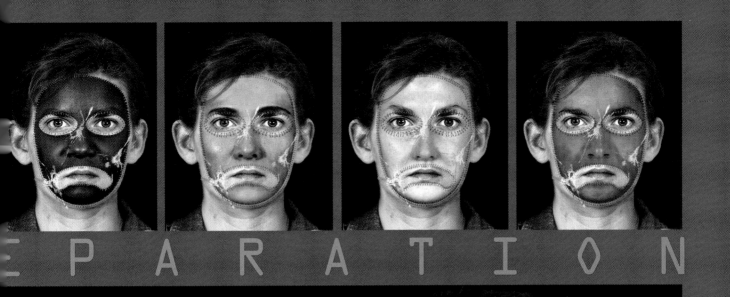

PARATION

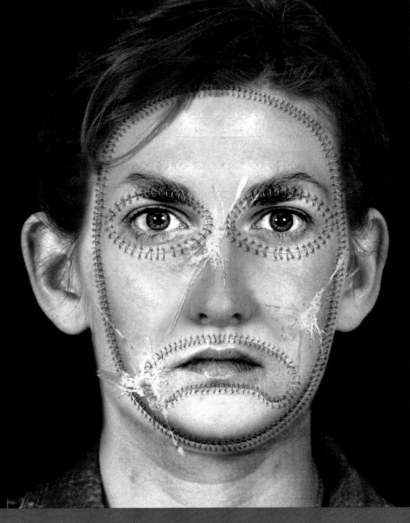

masked man who is white underneath?

nigger bogeyman never existed.

"In this work as in the rest of society we perceive the demonic phantoms of other 'races'. But these characters never existed just like the

But sometimes... reluctantly we have to depict the invisible in order to make it disapear."
(Harwood)

# Map and Land,

## Peter Weibel questions anti-democratic trends

**Maps tend to swallow up land – this is something we have known ever since Jorge Louis Borges, Jean Baudrillard and Günther Anders. The media would seem to simulate reality with such perfection that we can no longer tell the difference between the map, the medium of representation, and the land, reality. But this model still holds the covert assumption of an original difference, a residual core of ontology.**

**However, events since 1989, a cipher standing for the demise of Communist blueprints of society and for the rise of Neo-Liberalism in combination with global media conglomerates and multinationals, suggest that the map itself not only maps, but also constructs the land. The map does not tend to swallow up the land (if it did, we would still know what the land is or was), but rather the map tends to create the land.**

**The media construct reality. Where no reality exists the way the media want it to be, the media force this reality to exist. Not, that is, by drawing a false picture of reality, as they used to, but rather by actually creating this reality. Paparazzi photography that sets a trap, for example by using a paid strip-tease dancer, for an aristocratic husband to stumble into in front of carefully located cameras, is equally just a symptom of the *Structural Transformation of the Public Sphere* (Jürgen Habermas, 1962), of the *Fall of Public Man* (Richard Sennett, 1974), as is the global media success of special investigator Kenneth Starr.**

**Not only the media as a whole are becoming paparazzi media, politics itself is availing itself of paparazzi methods to succeed in a media society. Special investigator Starr metamorphosed from a court official into a paparazzo in order to bring down President Clinton. Politics as blackmail in the style of paparazzi methods demonstrates the dominance of media over society,**

ALBUM Freitag, 18. September 1998 — KUNST UND MEDIEN — A 5

**Kunst und globale Medien**
Eine Ausstellung über Medien in Medien für die Dauer eines Jahres 1998/99
steirischer herbst / museum in progress
Location: < Der Standard >
**Symposium** Medienkritik als Sozialkritik
http://www.xspace.at

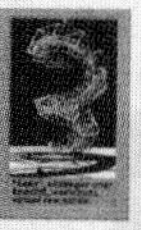

*Der steirische herbst, das museum in progress und* DER STANDARD *veranstalten ein über mehrere Folgen laufendes Projekt zum Thema „Kunst und globale Medien", das aus einer Ausstellung über Medien in Medien, einem Symposium und einem Filmprogramm besteht. Die Ausstellung findet nicht im weißen Würfel des Museums statt, sondern in den Printmedien und den elektronischen Medien. Ein Partner dieser Ausstellung ist World Media Network, zu dem auch Der Standard gehört. Das Symposium findet zwar real in Graz statt, aber auch virtuell im Netz und im* STANDARD. *Der vorliegende Beitrag des Projektkurators Peter Weibel eröffnet die Reihe von Künstlerinterventionen, theoretischen Essays und Demonstrationen neuer Strategien im Informationsdesign (signs of trouble), die im* STANDARD *die nächsten Monate zu sehen und zu lesen sein werden.*

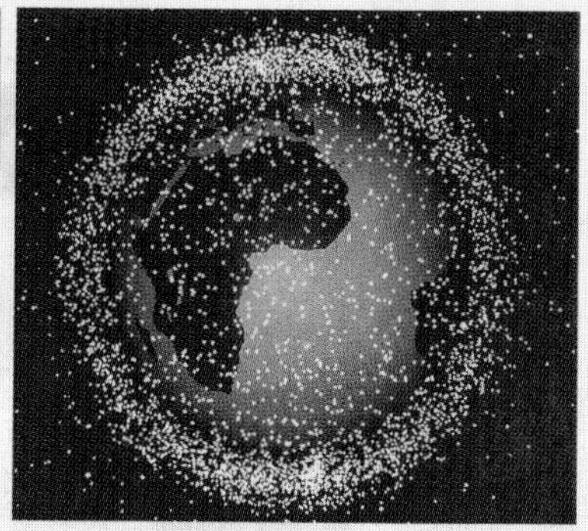

*Die mediale Umhüllung der Erde als physische Realität: Satelliten und Weltraummüll umkreisen den Globus wie ein Bienenschwarm.* Foto: APA

### LANDKARTE UND LAND, MEDIEN UND WIRKLICHKEIT

*Peter Weibel hinterfragt antidemokratische Tendenzen in der Paparazzo-Mentalität der Medien*

Die Landkarte hat die Tendenz, das Land zu verschlingen, wissen wir seit Jorge Louis Borges, Jean Baudrillard und Günther Anders. Die Medien simulieren die Realität scheinbar so vollkommen, daß zwischen der Landkarte, dem Abbildungsmedium, und dem Land, der Realität, keine Differenz mehr zu erkennen sei. In diesem Modell ist aber noch die Annahme einer ursprünglichen Differenz versteckt, ein letzter Kern von Ontologie.

Die Ereignisse seit 1989, die als Chiffre für den Untergang kommunistischer Gesellschaftsentwürfe und für den Aufstieg des Neoliberalismus im Verbund mit globalen Medienkonglomeraten und transnationalen Konzernen stehen, legen aber die Vermutung nahe, daß die Landkarte selbst das Land nicht nur kartografiert, sondern sogar konstruiert. Die Landkarte hat nicht die Tendenz, das Land zu verschlingen (in diesem Fall wüßten wir ja noch, was das Land wäre oder einmal war), sondern die Landkarte hat die Tendenz, das Land zu schaffen.

Die Medien konstruieren die Realität. Wo die Realität, so wie die Medien sie sich wünschen, nicht vorhanden ist, erzwingen die Medien diese Realität. Aber nicht dadurch, daß sie wie bisher ein falsches Bild von der Realität entwerfen, sondern indem sie diese Realität in der Tat herstellen. Die Paparazzi-Fotografie, die z.B. mit Hilfe einer bezahlten Striptease-Tänzerin eine Falle konstruiert, in die dann der adelige Ehemann vor bestens plazierter laufender Kamera hineinläuft, ist genauso nur ein Symptom für jenen „Strukturwandel der Öffentlichkeit" (Jürgen Habermas, 1962), für jenen Verfall der bürgerlichen Öffentlichkeit, für „The Fall of Public Man" (Richard Sennett, 1974), wie der globale mediale Erfolg des Sonderermittlers Kenneth Starr.

Nicht nur die Medien insgesamt werden zu Paparazzi-Medien, sogar die Politik selbst bedient sich Paparazzi-Methoden, um in einer Mediengesellschaft zu reüssieren. Sonderermittler Starr hat sich von einem Justizbeamten in einen Paparazzo verwandelt, um den US-Präsidenten Clinton zu erlegen. Politik als Erpressung im Stile von Paparazzi-Methoden zeigt uns die Dominanz der Medien über die Gesellschaft, die Herrschaft und Hegemonie der Mediengesellschaft über die Realität.

Die Frage also, die der deutsche Soziologe Oskar Negt in seinem Buch „Warum SPD? 7 Argumente für einen nachhaltigen Macht- und Politikwechsel" (1998) erhebt, nämlich gibt es eine „unterhalb der medial vermittelten Öffentlichkeit liegende Wirklichkeit", erinnert an die alte Metapher von Landkarte und Land, wo das Land von der Landkarte bedeckt wird. Die Frage von heute ist allerdings, gibt es ein Jenseits der Medien? Angesichts der zweifelsfrei feststellbaren medialen Konstruktion von Realität sind die Elemente von Landkarte und Land nicht mehr so leicht auseinander zu dividieren, wie es die klassische kritische Soziologie wahrhaben möchte. In einem Prozeß gegenseitiger Anpassung und Erpressung, nicht mehr allein durch falsche Berichterstattung und „falsches Bewußtsein", sondern durch gemeinsam akkordierte Beschlüsse stellen Medien und Politik die Wirklichkeit her.

Die Globalisierung der Medien, von der Politik und den Medien erwünscht, dient genau diesem Ziel der Wirklichkeitsdiffusion, wo jede Mitteilung, ob falsch oder wahr, wo jede Art der Beobachtung, ob falsch oder wahr, ihre irreversible Wirkung in der Wirklichkeit zeigt, sei es in Berufungsverfahren, bei Wahlen oder bei Aktienkursen.

Zu den Wirkungen der globalen Medien als Phänomen der 90er Jahre auf Kultur und Ökonomie, auf Politik und Gesellschaft gehört eben, daß die Mechanismen der sozialen Konstruktion von Wirklichkeit durch Mechanismen der medialen Konstruktion von Wirklichkeit fortschreitend ersetzt werden und daß dadurch das Modell von Landkarte und Land nur noch bedingt funktioniert.

**Gibt es ein Jenseits der Medien?**

Umso wichtiger ist es, über die sozialen Konstruktionsmechanismen von Medien und über die medialen Konstruktionsmechanismen von Sozietät informiert zu sein und die Veränderungen und Konstruktionen der Wirklichkeit durch die Medien kritisch bewußt und sichtbar zu machen. Besonders da der Aufstieg des Neoliberalismus seit den späten 80er Jahren untrennbar mit der Errichtung eines globalen Mediennetzwerkes verbunden war und ist. Im Liberalismus, der kapitalistischen Variante der Demokratie, gehen Politik und Medien eine neue Verknüpfung ein. Der Neoliberalismus hat sich der globalen Medien als Komplize bedient, um die falsche Gleichsetzung von Liberalismus und Demokratie durchzusetzen. Der Liberalismus verlangt ja nur die Freiheit des Individuums, zu kaufen und zu verkaufen, mit Gütern frei zu handeln etc.

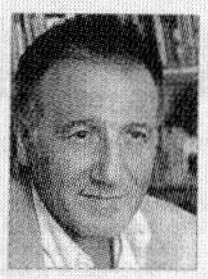

*Medienkritischer Medienkünstler und Projektkurator Peter Weibel*

Das hat nichts mit den demokratischen Grundrechten der Vertragsfreiheit, Versammlungsfreiheit, der freien Rede usw. zu tun. Die Missionare des Kapitals erkennen zunehmend die Bedeutung einer globalen Medienkultur für den liberalen, ökonomischen Markt, weil die Massenmedien den Liberalismus in seinen antidemokratischen Tendenzen unterstützen.

Die Medien, die ebenso Profit maximieren wollen wie jeder andere Konzern im Liberalismus, unterstützen selbstverständlich die Logik des Kapitals und damit die antidemokratischen Tendenzen des Neoliberalismus. Egalität und Emanzipation, demokratische Grundrechte, welche einstmals die bürgerliche Öffentlichkeit, die idealiter frei von staatlichen wie kommerziellen Interessen sei, garantieren sollte, sind in einer öffentlichen Sphäre, wo in Privat- oder Staatsbesitz befindliche Massenmedien profitorientierte private Interessen mit nichtprofitablen allgemeinen Interessen verschränken, nicht mehr wiederherstellbar.

Die Medien sind daher weltweit tendenziell zu einer antidemokratischen Kraft geworden, die, je größer sie sind, umso mehr populistische Politiker unterstützen und auf einen Kollaps des demokratischen, politischen Lebens zielen.

Die Medien (à la Murdoch) wollen selbst transnationale Konzerne werden und folgen daher der gleichen undemokratischen, liberalen Logik des Kapitals wie die anderen transnationalen Konzerne. Die mit dem Aufstieg des Neoliberalismus einhergehende Abwertung von Demokratie wird gerade durch die Verknüpfung von Politik und Medien ermöglicht. Die antidemokratischen Tendenzen des Neoliberalimus und der Massenmedien verstärken sich gegenseitig.

Auf Grund der Implosion von Landkarte und Land sind Medienkritik und Gesellschaftskritik nicht mehr voneinander zu trennen. Die mediale Konstruktion von Gesellschaft, Geschichte, Gedächtnis, von Realität, Politik und Öffentlichkeit zu untersuchen, ist daher das Grundthema des Projektes *Kunst und globale Medien.* □

### MEDIALE UND ANDERE WIRKLICHKEITEN

*Ausstellung, Symposium und Filmprogramm an realen und virtuellen Orten*

**Die mediale Konstruktion von Wirklichkeit: Ausstellung**

*Kunst und globale Medien* ist erstens eine Ausstellung über Medien in Medien, d.h. eine Ausstellung, die den weißen Würfel des Museums und lokale Gebundenheit verläßt und in der Hauptsache nur im globalen Medienraum selbst stattfinden soll. Im Zeitraum eines Jahres, vom steirischen herbst 98 bis 99, werden sich weltweit und punktuell in den Medien selbst WissenschaftlerInnen und KünstlerInnen mit der medialen Konstruktion von Wirklichkeit auseinandersetzen, z.B. im STANDARD und in El Pais, La Stampa, Libération und anderen Mitgliedern des Printmedienverbandes World Media Network.

Diese Ausstellung wird auch eine neue Künstlergeneration vorstellen, die bereits ausschließlich nur im Medienraum arbeiten (Musikvideos, Buchumschläge, Zeitungsdesign, Plakate etc.).

Avancierte Vertreter des Komunikations- und Informationsdesign der 90er Jahre werden im STANDARD ihre Positionen zeigen. Diese Ausstellung ist jederzeit und überall unter der Nummer http://www.xspace.at besuchbar.

Dislozierte Hosts von Mexiko bis Rußland werden ein alternatives Fernsehprogramm montieren, das sowohl lokal in Graz, wie auch ortlos periodisch im ORF zu sehen sein wird. Alternative TV-Gruppen wie xx-Kunstkabel, True Image Vision werden dabei von der Kunstkuratorin Lioba Redekker unterstützt. Ebenso gibt es europaweit 23 Städte, in denen in Kooperation mit Austrian Airlines Plakate affichiert werden, die im klassischen öffentlichen Raum über die Transformationen des klassischen öffentlichen Raumes, sein Verschwinden zugunsten des nichtklassischen Medienraumes, aufklären.

**Medienkritik als Sozialkritik: Symposium**

Als Ausgangspunkt und unabdingbarer Referenzrahmen dienen die Klassiker der Öffentlichkeits- und Medienkritik, wie Jürgen Habermas: Strukturwandel der Öffentlichkeit (1962), Richard Sennett: Verfall und Ende des öffentlichen Lebens. Die Tyrannei der Intimität (NY 1974 / Frankfurt 1983) und Noam Chomsky/ Edward S. Herman: Manufacturing Consent: The Political Economy of the Mass Media (1988).

Dazu kommen als neuere Werke von Relevanz Immanuel Wallerstein: The Modern World System I (1974) und After Liberalism (1995) Manuel Castells: The Rise of the Network Society (1996), E.S. Herman / R.W. McChesney: The Global Media (1997), Dan Schiller: Theorizing Communication (1996), Vincent Mosco: The Political Economy of Communication (1996), Georg Franck: Ökonomie der Aufmerksamkeit (1998) und Pierre Bourdieu: Über das Fernsehen (1998).

Der Großteil dieser Theoretiker wird persönlich am Grazer Symposium am 3. und 4. Oktober teilnehmen, nämlich Mosco, Schiller, Herman und McChesney, ebenso der große französische Wissenssoziologe Bruno Latour. Diese Autoren werden auch im Standard mit Originalbeiträgen zu Wort kommen. (P. W., 9/1998)

**Das Gedächtnis und die Revolte des Blicks: Filmprogramm**

Neben Ausstellung und Symposium läuft vor Ort in Graz ein Filmprogramm. . In Retrospektiven der drei Filmkünstler Joris Ivens, Chris Marker und Harun Farocki werden die Möglichkeiten eines kritischen Dokumentarismus gezeigt. In audiovisuellen Experimenten von großer Schönheit und Intelligenz wird die Arbeit der Schrift und der Sprache um die Sprache der Töne und Bilder erweitert, indem die Autoren die Produktionsbedingungen der Mitteilungen untersuchen.

Durch die Weiterentwicklung dieser Methoden sind Marker und Farocki auch zu digitalen und videographischen Medieninstallationen gelangt, die erstmals in einem Überblick gezeigt werden. Im „undeklarierten Krieg" (so der Titel eines Buches von David Puttnam, 1997) über die globale Kontrolle der Bildproduktion bilden diese Filmessayisten in der Tradition eines Dziga Vertov und Jean Vigo eine Alternative zu den banalen Klischees des globalen Medienmarktes, die täglich die Abendprogramme der Fernsehanstalten füllen. (P. W., 8/1998)

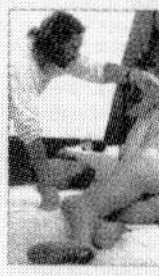

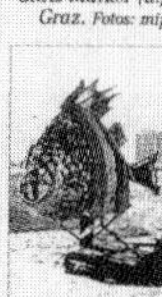

*Aus Filmen von Harun Farocki (o.) und Chris Marker (u.) in Graz.* Fotos: mip

# Media and Reality

## in the paparazzo mentality of the media

the rule and hegemony of media society over reality.

So the question that the German sociologist Oskar Negt raises in his book *Warum SPD? 7 Argumente für einen nachhaltigen Macht- und Politikwechsel* (Why the SPD? 7 arguments for a profound change of power and politics) (1998), i.e. is there a "reality below the public sphere that is conveyed by the media," is reminiscent of the old metaphor of the map and the land, in which the land is covered by the map. But the question today is, is there anything beyond the media? In view of the fact that the media unequivocally construct reality, it is no longer as easy to tell apart the elements of the map and the land as classical critical sociology would have it. In a process of mutual adaptation and blackmailing, no longer just by means of false coverage and 'false awareness,' it is rather by means of mutually accorded resolutions that the media and politics create reality.

The globalisation of the media, desired by politics and the media, serves precisely this aim of achieving a diffusion of reality in which all news, be it false or true, every kind of observation, be it false or true, has its irreversible effect in reality, be it in appeal proceedings, elections or share prices. The fact that the mechanisms of the social construction of reality are increasingly being replaced by the mechanisms of media construction of reality and that, as a result, the model of the map and the land now only works to a limited extent is all part of the effects of the global media as a

1990s phenomenon on culture and economy, politics and society.

Is there anything beyond the media?

It is all the more important to be informed about the social construction mechanisms of media and about the media construction mechanisms of society and to critically make people realise and visualise the changes and constructions of reality by the media. Particularly as the rise of Neo-Liberalism since the late 1980s was, and is, inseparably linked to the establishment of a global media network. In liberalism, the capitalist variation on democracy, politics and the media enter into a new association. Neo-Liberalism has made use of the global media as an accomplice in order to push through the false equation of liberalism and democracy. After all, liberalism only demands the freedom of the individual to buy and sell, to trade goods freely, etc. This has nothing to do with the basic democratic rights of freedom of contract, freedom of assembly, free speech, etc. The missionaries of capital are increasingly coming to recognise the significance of a global media culture for the liberal, economic market as the mass media support liberalism in its anti-democratic trends.

Naturally enough, the media, striving as they do to maximise profit like any other group of companies in liberalism, support the logic of capital and thus the anti-democratic trends of Neo-Liberalism. Equality and

emancipation, basic democratic rights once intended to safeguard the bourgeois public, ideally free of state and commercial interests, can no longer be restored in a public sphere in which private or state-held mass media link profit-oriented private interests with unprofitable general interests.

Thus, the media around the world are tending to become an anti-democratic force which, the larger they become, increasingly support populist politicians and aim to bring about the downfall of democratic, political life. The media (à la Murdoch) want to become multinationals themselves and thus pursue the same undemocratic, liberal logic of capital as other multinationals. The devaluation of democracy that goes hand in hand with the rise of Neo-Liberalism is made possible precisely by the link-up of politics and media. The anti-democratic trends of Neo-Liberalism and the mass media are mutually intensifying.

As a result of the implosion of the map and the land, media criticism and social criticism can no longer be divided. Exploring the media construction of society, history, memory, reality, politics and the public sphere is thus the main theme of the *art and global media* project.

## Prelude

The decisive question posed by those who, after the First World War, laid claim to be fighting for a better life for the many, was: "To whom does the world belong?" Bertolt Brecht had asked the same question in the second half of his title for the film *Kuhle Wampe* (1932), framed as an urgent questionmark regarding territorial ownership (in the broadest sense: of factories, land, machines, etc.). At the present time and for the decades to come, however, it appears to me that the decisive question is: "To whom does the time belong?" From the beginning to the end of this century, a remarkable shift has taken place in the political and economic relationships of power which the media are involved in and where they have forced the pace: away from the power of disposal over volumina and territories and towards the power of disposal over time; not so much its expansion but rather its fine structuring and its form of intensity.

## Introduction

"From Territories to Intervals" was an attempt to sensibilise us for this question which, as yet, still sounds unfamiliar. I tried out two different methodological approaches. The first was a short archaeological expedition where I traced the genesis of the question's formulation with the aid of two examples. The second was a conscious reference to Peter Weibel's rule of the 'chronocracy' from the late 1980s, where I took up some of his ideas and spun them out in my own way in the form of a brief pamphlet. Here I shall only summarise the arguments of the first part (I spoke *ex tempore* and presented many visual examples, for example, the fantastic monologue of the time researcher from Alexander Kluge's *Der Angriff der Gegenwart auf die übrige Zeit* [The Attack of the Present on the Rest of Time]; the second is presented here in a more elaborated version.

My introduction in Graz was in the form of three preliminary remarks which referred to other contributions given at the symposium; however, as they are important for an understanding of the pamphlet I include them here:

1. That which over ten years ago was firmly kept at the periphery of public attention and discriminated against by both politics and the (art) market, has been moved to the centre-stage of power cravings and demands for legitimation during the last decade of this century: experiments undertaken by artists within the tension that exists between technology and information on the one side and aesthetic expression and processes on the other. Concepts such as interactivity, terms such as communication or creativity, which formerly had a rather casual meaning and, in some contexts, even an emancipatory or seditious one, became the leading concepts when the western economies emerged into the so-called information society. They became the concepts of the controllers and the arrangers who then began to demand them as the paradigms of a new sociality. For the poets and the thinkers of the media, the issue is not so much to survive in this situation, but rather to survive in dignity.

2. Stylised, neo-existentialistic creeds like that of Calvin Klein, "I am always, and never the same" (the advertising slogan for the most recent CK-product, Contradiction, in his series of perfume-answers to the fundamental questions of life), need to be inverted: Always the same, and never myself. The current media-tactical concepts, as well as critiques, of political economy still operate as a rule with the self as their centre of gravity, the traditional concept of the subject. To take the shattered self as the point of departure, to understand it as a figment of the hegemonic imagination when it appears in an intact form while at the same time bringing an identity into play that is an oscillating, yet powerful, opposite to the Other, might indicate one possible way out of this wretched situation.

# Some Preliminary Thoughts on the Economy of Time/the Time

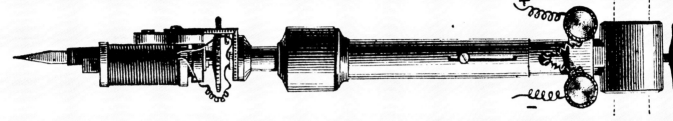

to Intervals

Electric chronograph (small model). (Source: E.J. Marey: *Mouvement*, 1887, p. 139)

**3. It is worthwhile rediscovering Georges Bataille's notion of the "abolition of the economy," faced as we are with social exchange that is becoming progressively based on effective communication processes. The attempt by the controllers and the arrangers to subject also the economy of signals and information to the productivity-paradigm of the 19th century should be countered by an economy of extravagance for which art processes could be tested as models.**

## Archaeological Foray

**1. Marey and Clearing Up a Misunderstanding**

**Until now, Etienne Jules Marey's work has been interpreted by media and art people mainly in the context of film and photography. He is understood as a maker of images. This is a misunderstanding. I maintain that Marey the doctor and physiologist was not really interested in illusions, in superficial sensations, in the production of appearances. (I understand this thesis as roughly analogous to the widespread misconception that the computer is an image-machine. In my understanding the computer is an artefact, a technical system for contolling other machines and automated processes, respectively, whether they are production, information or war and military machines. In this sense it is a medium.)**

**Proceeding on the assumption held by the most advanced experimental physiologists of the 19th century – all that we are able to perceive with our sensory organs are appearances –, for Marey and his colleagues it was a question of "eliminating the sensory appearances," as Wilhelm**

Cosmic space in a two-dimensional projection; in order to render graphically the movements of stars, a fixed point is taken (in this case, situated in the constellation of Orion) against which their trajectories are plotted. (Source: E.J. Marey: *Mouvement*, 1887, p. 67)

**Wundt, amongst others, expressed it in his *Grundzügen der physiologischen Psychologie* [Essentials of Physiological Psychology]. Their concern was to exclude interpretation and not to introduce it. (The illusion-machine of cinema, in which tradition Marey is repeatedly included, is first and foremost a machinery of interpretation.)**

**In this, Marey was following a central idea of Julien Offray de La Mettrie (whose book *L'homme machine*, published in 1748, should not be cited *ad nauseam* in the form of a few phrases, usually third-hand, but rather people should actually read it): bodies or objects in motion may be exceedingly attractive to the senses (the reasons for this cannot be described exactly), but they also conform to mathematical laws. To expose the structures and quantitative relationships of these, to transform them into patterns and graphs that can be used for making calculations - this was the goal of the physiologists' quest.**

**To put this more pointedly: the experimental physiologist made no claim that the body he examined with measuring instruments was the whole body but was fully aware that his object of study represented only a special part of the body's reality. The chair that Marey held at the Collège de France from 1869 was entitled "Histoire naturelle des corps organisés" - natural history of organised bodies. Marey's chronophotographs of animals and humans in motion are "clocks to be watched," as Roland Barthes once observed. In most contemporary reproductions of his pictures, the measuring instruments (to measure time and space) have been omitted. Marey deliberately included them as references for the**

bodies in motion on each individual recorded image. The object of this exercise was to register the movements of the body as a function in the form of a graphic impression or expression. From Carl Ludwig Anton's Kymographion of 1847 via the long chain of Marey's own graphic recording devices (Polygraph, Myograph, Sphymograph...), experimental physiology pursued a path that lead away from the bloody dissection (frequently, vivisection) of bodies and towards the bloodless anatomy of curves and readings. This was the beginning of a 'second nature' that was aided and produced by instruments, which could be analysed and re-analysed over again at will. The aim was to develop a language for natural scientists, similar to the notation of musicologists; a kind of Esperanto in which colleagues from all over the world could communicate without there being any misunderstanding, a kind of universal language. The main task of the 'station Marey,' which was opened in 1902 near Paris, was to standardise and test physiological measuring instruments. At this point in time, cinema was on the way to its first industrial phase and developing into a 'fantasy machine' (Fülöp-Miller). The fields of application that Marey was working on and which financed his equipment were sport (functional gymnastics), the military, and the workplace. These were not a later addition but were integrated into his R & D work.

## 2. Aleksei Gastev and the Proletarian Human Machine

We are well acquainted with the *Principles of Scientific Management* which Frederick Winslow Taylor devised in the USA and, for example, the experimental work that Gilbreth carried out before the First World War. Not at all well known, however, is that in revolutionary Russia, Taylorism was combined in a radical way with the materialist and constructivist ideas of the avant-garde.

In 1914, Lenin was still at the stage where he wrote an essay with the title "The Taylor-System: The Enslavement of Man by Machines." His accusation read, "Recently, in America, the advocates of this system have instituted the following method: a small electric lamp is fastened

to a worker's hand. The movements of the worker are photographed and the movements of the lamp analysed. It is ascertained that certain movements are superfluous and the worker is forced to avoid these movements, that is, to work more intensively and not to waste even one second on resting... Systematically, the cinematograph is being applied."

By 1920, the first Soviet Central Institute for research on work (Zentralny Institut Truda [ZIT]) was founded in Moscow and, in the course of the decade, others followed at other locations in the Soviet Union. The frequently stated aim of these institutes was to structure the 24 hours of the day as effectively as possible (as it was not possible to stretch them), that is, to subject them rigorously and at all costs to the paradigm of productivity. The work of the All-Russian Association of the Time League also served this goal: they distributed timepieces to the public who had to record the events of their daily life with meticulous precision on so-called chrono-cards (including everyday actions from eating to personal hygiene). Then, with the aid of participating observers and experimental equipment, statistics were compiled on all kinds of work processes with the aim of achieving, through training, a gradual fusion of the workers with the machines. According to the ideas also of a section of the avant-garde who believed that the human organism was fundamentally a mechanical one, now powerfully enriched by the soul of electricity, the perfect symbiosis of labour and apparatus was sought.

Media apparatuses were the outstanding instruments, both in the work research institutes and at the Time League. At the institutes in Kazan, Moscow and Petrograd there existed large machine parks of the experimental apparatuses used by graphic physiology in the nineteenth and early twentieth century. Film and photographic studios were erected for recording the movements of metal workers or tram drivers, for example. Camera teams invaded the factories and filmed people engaged in the production process.

"It is necessary to overcome the limitations of time and space through organisation," proclaimed one of the initiators and driving forces of this movement, Aleksei Kapitonovich Gastev, at the beginning of

Special shoe to probe the pressure of the foot on the ground. Runner equipped with the shoes and carrying the device to register his paces. (Source: E.J. Marey: *Mouvement*, 1887, p. 156)

Apparatus ensemble of the experiment to inscribe the pressure in the vessels of the hand. (Source: E.J. Marey: *Mouvement*, 1887, p. 614)

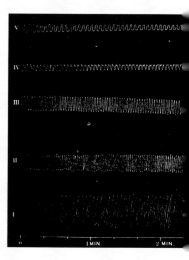

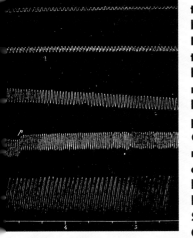

Various rhythms of the systoles of tortoises' hearts with the amplitude of each one. (Source: E.J. Marey: *Mouvement*, 1887)

Transmission of a violin's vibrations via a brass wire to a registering stylus; method of Cornu and Mercadier. (Source: E.J. Marey: *Mouvement*, 1887, p. 642)

1. We continue to investigate this germ cell of the techno-scene of the 20th century. I suspect that it strongly influenced the artistic avant-garde in the Soviet Union. Dziga Vertov, for example, was a student there at the time that he was occupied with montages of sounds. The interesting texts we have found so far are all in Russian, so that lengthy translation work is necessary. I would like to thank Maria and Boris Barth for their preliminary research in St. Petersburg in 1998.

the 1920s. In the preceding decade he had belonged to the movement of the Russian Futurists, lived and worked for a time in Paris as a journalist and became known for his rigorous development of a rigid economy of poetic language. The last series of poems that he wrote and published he called simply *Package of Orders* and numbered his lyric arrangements consecutively. They consisted of one-word lines, reductions to the absolute bare essentials of communication, more like signals than messages ("... Contact / Shunt / Stop" from *Order No. 02*). After Gastev had placed his powers of intensification exclusively at the service of the young Soviet economy, amongst other things he invented a binary code of productive motion: using only the components 'lift' and 'press' with varying intervals and rhythms, it would be possible to (re)construct all the motions required in industrial production. Aleksei Gastev died in 1938 at the hands of Stalin's executioners, at about the same time as Vsevolod Meyerhold, whose theatre concept of biomechanics was likewise a world-view radically translated into art.

The centre of thought and theory of this movement was the Central Work Laboratory of the Institute for Brain Research at the Technical University in Petrograd, to which the father of acoustics, Ernst Florens Friedrich Chladni, had dedicated his *Entdeckungen zur Theorie des Klangs* [Discoveries relating to a theory of sound] of 1787 with deep respect. The director of this early neurobiological institute was the psychologist Vladimir Bekhterev. He died in mysterious circumstances in 1927, the day after he - in his capacity as physiologist - had examined Stalin's brain.

Research at the Petrograd institute focussed on reflexology, studies on the ability to concentrate and hygiene in the workplace. Of particular importance were experiments with music structures, theories of the interval, of rhythm, and on the physio-psychological importance of music. For example, P.K. Anochin, a physiologist, published in 1921 the findings of his reseach on *The Influence of Major and Minor Chords on Activation and Inhibition of the Cerebral Cortex;* Bekhterev himself wrote an essay in an anthology on "Reflexology of Labour"with the title: "Intellectual Work From a Reflexological Perspective and Measurement of the Abil-

ity to Concentrate," where he investigated both the effect of Beethoven's *Moonlight Sonata* and of the overture to Gounod's opera *Faust* on intellectual work. A further project of particular interest for our context was the attempt to develop a system of musical notation for registering the movements of the human body, which was carried out in cooperation with the Kazan institute of the scientific organisation of labour; in 1928, the results were published by K.I. Sotonin in an essay.[1]

For the future, one of the most striking phenomena in connection with a time-based economy is the incredible concentration of working time in those sectors of the plebeian intelligentsia where the greatest potential for innovation is found. High-performance in the brain-work of programming is comparable to the high performance of training the *physis* in sport. Both the one and the other demand young bodies. Just as the stars in the swimming pool or the gymnasium who carry off the medals get younger all the time, the programming arenas, for example, of George Lucas' Industrial Light and Magic or James Cameron's Digital Domain are populated by kids at the machines who probably bring their teddy bears with them. The period of time where these teens and twens achieve their highest performance spans at most eight or ten years. After that - if they have earned and saved enough -they can or must take a very long surfing holiday in Hawaii, like the top professionals in sport, train for a second career or retire completely from the process of social reproduction.

## For a Praxis of Kairos Poetry; Against Psychopathia Medialis (for Peter Weibel)

1. Karl Marx wrote for posterity. Thanks to his mania for scrupulously citing his sources, the remark of an anonymous contemporary was recorded in Volume 26.3 of Marx's and Engels' collected works (German edition), who by succinctly summing up his own notion of economy, formulated what later became the touchstone of Marx's critique of established bourgeois economy:
"A nation is only truly wealthy, if no interest is paid on capital; if the working day is

six hours long instead of twelve. Wealth means to have time at one's disposal; nothing more, nothing less."

At a historical juncture where time has now been declared the most important resource for economy, technology, and art, we should not pay so much attention to how much or how little time we have. Rather, we should take heed of who or what has the power of disposal over our time and the time of others. The only efficacious remedy for bitter melancholy as

the all-pervasive attitude toward the world is to assume, or re-assume, the power of disposal over our own life's time. Only then is the *future* conceivable at all - as a permanent thing of impossibility.

The visual and audiovisual apparatuses that we work with are all time machines. Their origins lie in the first founding era of the New Media in the nineteenth century - they are prostheses, artificial limbs, for dealing satisfactorily with the impossible.

Russian Taylorism: A demonstration in the bio-mechanical laboratory of Aleksei Gastev. A metal-worker is being observed at work with a sighting tele-scope and a coordinate frame. (Source: R. Fülöp-Miller: *Geist und Gesicht des Bolschewismus*. Zurich/ Leipzig/Vienna 1926: Amalthea Verlag.)

2. German translation in:
*Ästhetik und Kommunikation,*
No. 67/68, 1987, p. 40.

begin operation in the year 2001 and run for exactly 10,000 years.

The ancient Greeks understood only too well the dilemma we would get ourselves into with chronocracy (the term was coined by Peter Weibel) as the dominant time mode and they introduced two further concepts of time: Aeon and Kairos. They were the antipodes of powerful Kronos who, ultimately, devoured his own children. We find the transcendental dimension of Aeon suspect - time which stretches far, far beyond our and the Earth's life-time, which is supposedly 'pure.' The fastest way from zero to infinity, as Alfred Jarry once defined God. On the other hand, we value Aeon as a possibility of uniting time and life as a virtual power from which the vitality of life springs. By contrast, Kairos stands for the art of doing the right thing at the right moment; he is the god of the auspicious moment.

Yet only the interplay of all three conceptions of time can preserve us from alienation: to give the auspicious moment a charge from an Aeonian battery and/or challenge chronic time's power of disposal over life by applying both Aeon and Kairos tactics - to me, this appears to be a possibility whereby we may survive in dignity with and within the time machines.

2.  Chronos - chronology's time is that kind of time which disposes of life by using it up. History. Chronology fits us into the order of things. Illness can be chronic, but never passion. Chronology cripples us because we are only mortal and we shall pass. Machines live longer. The computer scientist and engineer Danny Hillis, who has played a decisive role in constructing the massively parallel architecture of today's supercomputers, amongst other things, is currently working on the prototypes of a clock which will

3.  In one of his early works, Françoise Lyotard wrote: "Our culture singles out for special favour that which it places in the limelight - the only scene which it considers to be an event: the moment of exchange, the immediate, the sensational, the 'real' time, which for our culture, is the only time that is alive. This moment, in which accumulated 'dead' time is realised, one can call obscene."[2] Recently, an American electronics firm presented a system which in the future, will allow information to be invoiced per bit; it will be a matter of complete indifference whether the information is text, images, or sounds. The bit, as the smallest techno-unit, will become the new abstract currency, the basic coinage for an economy of of text, image and sound production, which will also include those art forms that are expressed and realised with and through the media.

We should not tolerate either one of these kinds of expropriation of the so very valuable moment; neither that of the culture industry with its obscene concentration of life's time in the staged and celebrated sensation, nor the installation of a universal measure of time and economy that assaults or runs over the capabilities of our own, proper faculty of perception.

The relationship of technical processes vis à vis time can be described thus: even the variables that influence the technical process from the outset (observation, inspection, control) are time dependent. In the course of the technical process they undergo conversion. At the starting point of any and every machine-machine or human-machine system, we find time-dependent experiential variables. Such processes may also be termed dynamic. As intellectuals, or as artists, the very least we can do is to ensure that the conversion which takes place mid-process makes a sharp and qualitative distinction between the variables which are effective from the beginning and the end results. This means to work effectively at the interface, to dramatise it. Processed/designed time has to be able to give us back time that life has taken from us (this is one of Jean-Luc Godard's finest thoughts on cinema). Otherwise, it is time wasted, time lost. We should not allow ourselves, time and again, to fall short of the capabilities of machines.

4. In 1934, Max Horkheimer published his "Notes on Germany" under the pseudonym Heinrich Regius; he calls them *Twilight* in the title. In a small section with the heading "Time Is Money" he remarks: "...Although one shrinks from falling into the generalisations of common platitudes, time is not money, but money is time, as well as health, happiness, love, intelligence, honour, peace. For it is a lie that if you have time, you also have money; with mere time you won't get any money but *vice versa* is certainly true."[3]

5. "We wander around in circles in the night and are consumed by fire" - this is how Guy Debord described his situation as a professional Situationist: the movement of roaming about, which was the title of the last film he made before his last will and testament.

The first known timepieces, from ancient China, were rectangular metal reliefs structured like labyrinths. In the depressions, a slowly igniting powder was strewn and the burning of the powder showed the passage of time. Guy Debord offered his body and his imagination for measuring the time in which he lived. Yet what would be a viable alternative of action to the Situationist one, which consumes its own identity? Naturally, and theoretically: to be fire instead of burning powder. However, to take up this position is not an option for us for we are (amongst other things) of the very stuff that time uses up (unless we want to play God). What we can do is to intervene in the rhythm and velocity of the burning, put in stops, and organise the intervals in between.

A superior time policy means to fight for the upper hand in time consumption and time use. It appears that one must be ready to face certain loss, both in the sense of self-consuming (Guy Debord) and of self-squandering (Georges Bataille). However, then loss is not a category of a fatal economy, if we succeed in making it an enrichment of others in a grand way. Otherwise, the act of consuming would be religious and of squandering, ideological. Both have had devastating effects in the recent past, for which Germany stands as an example.

6. If it is so, that under the aegis of expanded interactivity at the interface of media people and media machines 'creativity' has become a fundamental social competency, and although the traditional model of the artist in art is now a discontinued line, it appears to be becoming a general, central model for social action, then it is appropriate to work on complementary identities at the very least. The competencies in life that will be required increasingly of intellectuals and artists in the future are already tangible but as yet not translatable into concrete strategies and tactics: chaos pilots and Kairos poets; people who are not only capable of dealing with confusing arrangements but are also able to organise them; and those who catch the auspicious moment (for example, in the cinema or on the Web) and charge it with energy. Without a relationship to complexity, and without a

"Let us take the storm of the revolution in Soviet Russia, unite it with the pulse of American life and do our work like a chronometer!" — Gastev's call for Americanisation. (Source: R. Fülöp-Miller: *Geist und Gesicht des Bolschewismus*. Zurich/Leipzig/Vienna 1926: Amalthea Verlag.)

3. Heinrich Regius: *Dämmerung. Notizen in Deutschland*. Zurich 1934, p. 28.

and sound (but without master- and slave-media, without accepting a new universal machine) and the sensitivity for the right moment, the auspicious moment for life, imagination, and the media. Moreover, this should also constitute the lowest common denominator for any contemporary or future academy - at least for those among them which rise to the challenge of intervening with art and artistic means in the current processes that are transforming society.

Typist and Taylorism.
(Source: K.A. Tramm: *Psychotechnik und Taylor-System. Vol. I: Arbeitsuntersuchungen*. Berlin 1921: Julius Springer Verlag).

relationship to time - both are inextricably bound up with each other - I cannot imagine that advanced praxis in art and thought are possible.

7. "In general we always seek - (in potlatch) or in actions or in contemplation - that shadow which *per definitionem* we are unable to grasp hold of; that we helplessly call poetry, profundity, or intimacy of passion. That we will be deceived is inevitable, should we attempt to grasp this shadow."[4] Under the New Economy, the task will also be to not relinquish the attempt to express the inexpressible. With regard to how we handle the visual and audiovisual time machines, these can constitute a powerful unity: work on the living heterogeneity of the arts of image

## Conclusion: Brecht on his 100th

"Ich sitze am Straßenrand
Der Fahrer wechselt das Rad.
Ich bin nicht gern, wo ich herkomme
Ich bin nicht gern, wo ich hinfahre.
Warum sehe ich den Radwechsel
Mit Ungeduld?"[5]

[I sit at the roadside
The driver is changing the tyre.
I didn't like where I have come from
I don't like where I am going to
Why I am impatient
For the tyre to be changed?]

*Translated by Gloria Custance*

4. Bataille: *Aufhebung der Ökonomie*, p. 106.

5. Brecht: *Buckower Elegien*. Gesammelte Werke, Frankfurt 1967, p. 1009.

Too many e-mails in your mailbox

**?**

The purpose of re-m@il is to help
people with heavy e-mail loading.
They forward messages to

re-mail@writeme.com

Those messages will be answered
by the public at
http://sero.org/re-mail/

The answers will be - without
asking you - sent back to the
original sender. Why don't you
configure your mail-account as
an autoforward to

re-mail@writeme.com

**?**

# re-m@il

The purpose of re-m@il is to help people with heavy e-mail loading. They forward messages to **re-mail@writeme.com**. Those messages will be answered by the public. Below is a list of unanswered e-mails. **N o t e: This service is almost completely anonymous !**

Feel free to answer as many messages as you want. Just click a subject below.

| Subject | Sender |
|---|---|
| _ | *@cistron.nl |
| Free Overnight Delivery on Flowers | *@businesslink-6.net |
| openingsuren | *@belgium.agfa.com |
| SMAK bereiken vanuit Brussel | *@belgacom.be |
| Rondleiding | *@Admiral.be |
| JAARBOEK | *@artis-historia.be |
| openingsuren | *@wolfoil.com |
| [czook@iquest.net: (no subject)] | *@snafu.de |
| _ | *@planetinternet.be |
| vraag naar informatie | *@planetinternet.be |

[ search ]     [ next messages ]

f@q                                          @rchive

Ricardo Iglesias

"Chuang Tzu dreamt that he was a butterfly. When he woke up,
he did not know whether he was Tzu who had dreamt that he was
a butterfly, or he was a butterfly dreaming that it was Tzu."
Chuang Tzu (300 B.C.)

# REFERENCES

is a net art project that uses various perspectives of recursive, fractional and labyrinthine
systems in order to speak about the chaos in which
modern societies are immersed.
Leaving behind the mechanistic and linear theories of the 19th century, we have arrived at
chaotic, holistic developments in which the
structure of individual organisms is not considered to be just the result of the addition of their
single components, but something provided by a
complex, unique identity.
My web site works on two different levels. On the
one hand, the user faces a series of individual
stories which tell themselves and appear as independent information atoms. The topics with which
these stories deal are topics that affect closely
the evolution that we are currently witnessing in
our contemporary societies: treatment of space
and time, search for the forming elements of matter, new hierarchies, musical creation, new
machines. On the other hand, there exists a higher
structure on this web site, a superstructure, so
to say, which groups together the different spaces
that the user navigates through, infusing them
with a meaning which is exclusive of the whole.
I am interested in creating on the Internet a
metaphorical recreation of the way our society
works. From this point of view, the Internet might
be considered a representa tion of the kind of
environment into which our world is turning:
a new chaotic, elastic and liquid space.
The user must face this process of chaos searching
for answers, constantly going from one point to
the other in the different virtual spaces which
are connected by a complex system of links. The
navigation starts at a home page which lacks a
visual structure, which the user must 'move'
through his/her searching. Many of the elements-
stories that the user encounters when browsing
this site are integrated or appear on the home
page. Every user defines a unique route by means of
a random programming, and it is not possible to
know where every route starts and finishes: the
center of the labyrinth is only a door to the next
level, which is often at least as chaotic as the
previous one.

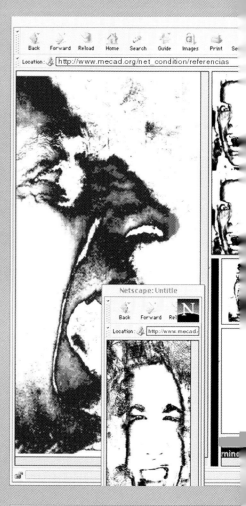

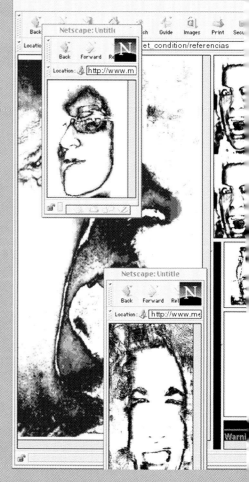

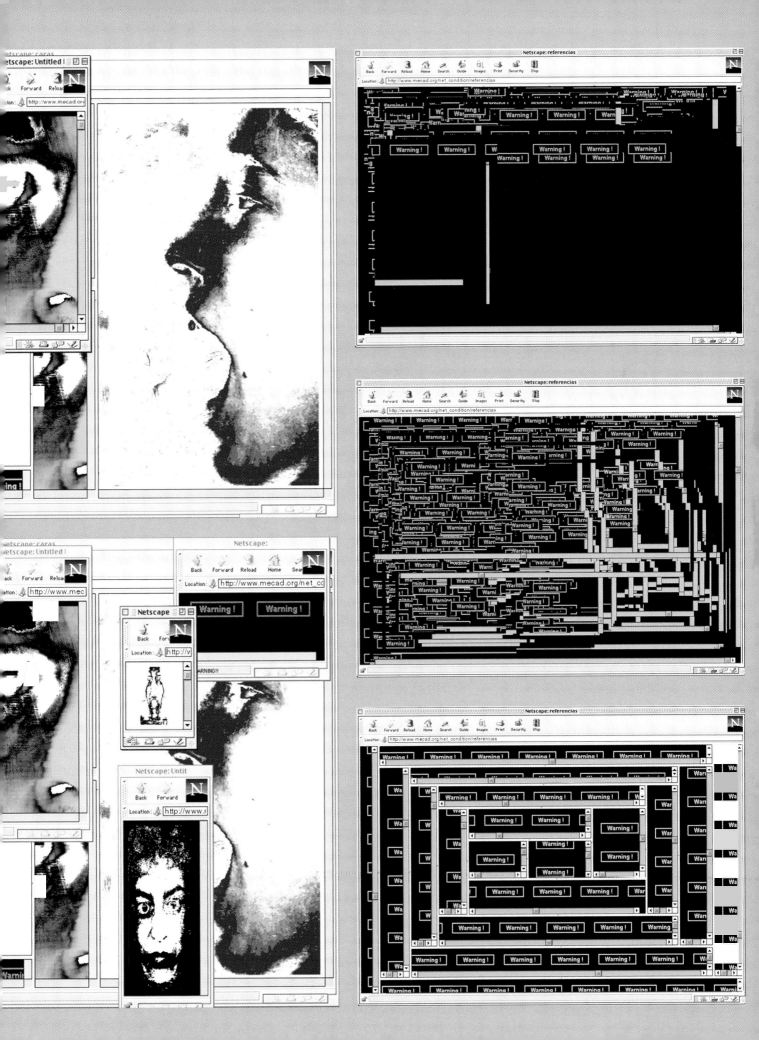

# Contestati

Contestational Robotics is an ongoing research initiative which inverts the traditional relationship between robots and authoritarian power structures by developing robots to meet the ends and budgets of culturally resistant forces.

# onal Robots

To date, the I.A.A. has developed two contestational robots (a.k.a. 'Robotic Objectors'): GraffitiWriter, a tele-operated robot capable of writing text messages on the ground at a rate of 10 miles per hour, and Pamphleteer, a propaganda robot which distributes subversive literature. Two additional robots, StreetWriter and reMEDIAtion, are currently under development.

## 1.0 So much data, so little time

When artists discovered the Internet as a media for their work in the mid-1990s, for many of them it appeared not only as a way out of the art industry and as a newly discovered free space for their own work, but also as almost a type of new Jerusalem where that which is impossible in the 'real world' should happen: global *herrschaft*-free communication for all, consumers who become producers, social networking over and through geographical and social borders, direct information exchange beyond economic constraints and without filtration through the mass media.

The euphoria of this early era which may appear naive today yet nonetheless is explainable by the enthusiasm for the new media, is legible, for example, in the self presentation of the *Internationale Stadt* (International City)[1] from Berlin: "The human stands at the center of the *Internationale Stadt* as an active participant and not as a consumer. New interpersonal relationships are initiated by the *Internationale Stadt* and affect the daily life of the real city. It finds an already existing infrastructure in the global internet which makes possible communication and information exchange at an international level. The inhabitants of the *Internationale Stadt* design their own network environment which can be recognized by others. A self organizing system arises in which communication forms and content are determined through a bi-directional interaction between organizers and users. In contrast to other media, new information arises through social exchange." [2]

Other projects from the initial stages of net art can also only be truly understood by keeping in mind the fascination with the new, seemingly totally free media. *The Fileroom* (1994) from Antonio Muntadas for example, is a data bank for the theme 'artistic censure', in which every net user can put in their own examples. The work does not only live from the interaction between user and work and its utilization of the fact that every Internet user can publish their own material in the net - like Douglas Davis' *The World's First Collaborative Sentence*, which originates from the same time: it lives mainly as a celebration of the Internet quality which at the time was emphasized by artists as well as others, which, namely, interprets the Internet censure as a "technical disturbance and routes around it," according to the famous formulation by the net pioneer John Gilmore.

Merely five years later the scenery has changed completely: in 1999 many of the works from the mid-1990s appear not only naive but in some cases they are no longer understandable. Not only the *Internationale Stadt* dissolved in 1998, also other projects like it lost their function because XS4ALL although far from being available to everyone, had in the meantime become a relatively cheap normal part of life for the majority of Central Europeans and North Americans. But first and foremost, the original euphoria for the new media has given way to a skeptical and critical attitude which has not only led net art to completely different themes and subjects.

For example: *The Digital Landfill* (1998)[3] from the New Yorker Mark Napier, just like Muntadas' *Fileroom*, is also a collection site for data which its users have pulled together. Yet in contrast to Muntadas' work, Napier's Website is not a celebration of the possibility of publishing data directly in the net through a circumvention of mass media, but rather - as the title already says - a dump, in which the long indigestible data are only disposed of, 'stored.' In the four years which lie between the two works, the WorldWideWeb grew from a comprehensible number of WWW-servers which many early users compared to a 'village', to a data cosmos which is incomprehensible to everyone. Napier's work is an ironic commentary on the growing amount of *Data Trash* (the title of a book by Arthur u. Marilouise Kroker) in the information era which clogs not only the Internet but also our own channels of perception.

It is not just by coincidence that works appeared in both of the last two years in which data could be removed or recycled and it is certainly not a coincidence that these works arose in part from artistic 'internet veterans'. Thus, for example, the artist duo sero.org, which was founded by the former *Internationale Stadt* members Joachim Blank and Karl Heinz Jeron (after the end of the *I.S.*), describe their artistic field with the words

1. www.icf.de

2. Gerbel, Karl; Weibel, Peter (eds): *Mythos Information - Welcome to the Wired World*, @rs electronica 95, Vienna/New York 1995 (Springer), p. 255f.

3. www.potatoland.org/ landfill

# On the History of Artistic Work with Telecommunications Media

'information-smog' and 'information recycling.' In their piece *Dump your trash*,[4] for example, net users can recycle their own home page. Other works of theirs also treat the theme of information overload in a playful way such as the project *re-mail*, for example, which makes it possible to let uninteresting emails be answered by other net users.

Although these works might outline the development which net art has gone through in the past five years, they do not give any idea of the multitude of projects and works which have arisen in this short time. The Internet set off a creative explosion which goes well beyond the production of Web-projects and has led to the most diverse forms of networking and artistic production. One task of this essay is to outline this. Another is to develop an historical framework for this development; contemporary net artists are not the first artists to work with modern means of telecommunications.

## 2.0 Immaterials – from the pre- and early history of net art

### 2.1 From hearsay

The 'net.art' which has developed in the past few years did not arise in a vacuum. Rather, it is the continuation of a series of artistic practices which have existed for several decades but have only now found entry into the canon of art history. In keeping with this, in hindsight it seems that the confrontation and also the practical work with electronic telemedia arrives as an important subplot for art at the end of the twentieth century.[5]

'Telecommunication art' (we'll call it that for lack of a better term) escaped historicization by art history in part due to its specific procedural nature. The actions and projects which artists have carried out with telemedia for the most part have left no traces behind when finished. The telephone concerts, fax performances, and satellite conferences of the 1970s and 1980s were not suitable for record-

ing or for being worked into unique aural pieces. All that remained after they were finished were a few blurry photographs or computer printouts. Only in a few cases was there a databank perhaps which was not kept up, and after the next computer hardware paradigm change even that was also no longer useable.

### 2.2 The 'permeation of spirit and matter' in word processing programs

These 'telecommunication artworks' are *immaterials* according to Jean-Francois Lyotard, who collaborated in an exhibition of the same name in the Centre Pompidou in 1985.[6] *Les Immateriaux* strongly influenced not only several artists who today work with telecommunications media and in the Internet, also within its framework one of the first experiments with computer supported collaborative writing took place. Daniel Buren, Michel Butor, Jacques Derrida and approximately twenty other French intellectuals received a private Minitel-connection (Minitel was the very successful French variety of BTX) and several key words, with which they carried out an online discussion. This could be followed in real time in the exhibition. Especially writers who discovered the net for artistic production often initiated communal writing projects - such as Robert Coover's *Hypertext-Hotel*,[7] the *Imaginäre Bibliothek* (Imaginary Library) from Pool Processing[8] or the famous "longest sentence in the world"[9] from Douglas Davis.

"The term 'immaterial' refers to a somewhat daring neologism," said Lyotard in an interview about the exhibition at the Centre Pompidou, "it merely expresses that today - and this has been carried through in all areas - material can no longer be seen as something that, like an object, is set against a subject. Scientific analyses of matter show that it is nothing more than an energy state, i.e. a connection of elements which, for their own part, are not understandable and are determined by structures which each have only a locally limited validity. ... The increasing mutual penetration of matter and spirit

4. sero.org/sero/dyt/

5. Ascott, Roy; Carl Eugene Loeffler: "Connectivity – Art and Interactive Telecommunication," *Leonardo* Vol. 24, Number 2 1991; Baumgärtel, Tilman : *net.art*, Nuremberg 1999 (Verlag für moderne Kunst); Decker, Edith; Weibel, Peter: *Vom Verschwinden der Ferne – Telekommunikation und Kunst*, Cologne 1990 (DuMont); Konrad, Helga (ed): *On line – Kunst im Netz*, Katalog der Steirischen Kulturinitiative, Graz 1993; Steirische Kulturinitiative (ed): *Zero – The Art of being everywhere*, Katalog der Steirischen Kulturinitiative 1992/1993, Graz 1993; Weibel, Peter (ed): *Jenseits der Erde – Das orbitale Zeitalter*, Vienna 1987 (Hora).

6. Lyotard, Jean Francois u.a: *Immaterialität und Postmoderne*, Berlin 1985 (Merve).

7. duke.cs.brown.edu:8888

8. www.uni-hildesheim.de/ami/pool/

9. math240.lehman.cuny.edu/sentence1.html

which is equally clear in the use of word processing systems, is now felt in that the classical problem of the unity of body and soul shifts."[10]

It is interesting that Lyotard expressly points out the "penetration of spirit and matter" in word processing programs. Not only in the text - but rather in every type of information processing with digitized data in the computer, the user deals with *immaterials*. The "de-materialization of the object," which Lucy Lippard stresses in conceptual art, is carried to its technological end in artistic work with computers and computer networks. While there is still a physical carrier of the message in the conceptual works by Lawrence Weiner, Joseph Kosuth or Jenny Holzer (be it paper, walls or circuit boards with light diodes), in the work with telecommunications and the 'universal machine' computer, it is now only immaterial; information cut up into bits and bytes which is used to act (interesting in this connection, by the way, is that in the meantime not only Jenny Holzer,[11] but also a number of other conceptual artists such as Lawrence Weiner[12] have carried out works in the Internet.)

## 2.3 A thousand years in just a minute of broadcasting time

The post war avant-garde were excited by the possibilities of telecommunications. As the most important art movement of the 1950s and 1960s, Fluxus should be mentioned in this context. With a lot of verve, artists such as Wolf Vostell and Nam June Paik tried to deconstruct the media of television in the late 1950s and early 1960s. It is interesting that also several net artists show a specific enthusiasm in working with the insufficiencies and problems of the media.

Particularly interesting in this regard is that a type of art developed from the Fluxus movement which can be considered a (non-technological) precursor of many telecommunications and Internet projects: mail art. The Correspondence School of Art which was founded in 1962 in New York by Ray Johnson has dedicated itself to art representation and distribution through the letter post. Johnson, a former student of Blue Mountain College, quit painting at the end of the 1950s in order to make only drawings and collages and then finally devoted himself exclusively to post-projects. In a never ending recycling process, Johnson reworked everything that he got by post and sent it on. In his complete renunciation of a materially representable art he was ahead of his time for both Fluxus as well as conceptual art.

At the same time, different Fluxus artists such as Emmett Williams, Arthur Koepke and George Brecht also began sending little works on post cards to each other, reworking them and sending them on. Although today some of these works belong to the canon of art history (such as On Kawara's *I am still alive* - telegram or the *Postal Sculptures* from Gilbert & George), mail art has remained an area which is widely ignored. In this respect it is similar to net art, which at least until now enjoys the attention of quite a circular audience. One of the ideas which spirited the mail art artists follows along those lines; that through the post, art could be democratized and made more easily accessible. Similar ideas are at the base of the multiples which were popular in the sixties. Yet while the multiples were still structurally a broad-casting media, mail art was really a 'point-casting.'

That mail art never really accomplished the cross-over into the art industry lies in its particular qualities, and in that it is also similar to contemporary net art. From its nature, mail art was a network matter and like the Internet, the Mail Art network had no central point and theoretically was open to all - which, paradoxically, did not increase its visibility. On the contrary, it was the network character that made mail art artists a closed group to which one either belonged or did not.

The most important reason that the art industry never really became interested in mail art may be mainly due to the lack of works able to be exhibited or sold - similar to net art. The works were no more important than the communication process itself. Its relics could hardly be deciphered without knowledge of the communication system from which they arose. Mail art has remained in the outermost periphery of the art industry's awareness up to the present time and while it is written off as hobby-art by many, others consider it the last relic of the avant-garde which in the 1960s

10. "Philosophie in der Diaspora – Conversation between Jacques Derrida and Jean-Francois Lyotard," in: Lyotard: *Immaterialität und Postmoderne*, 25.

11. www.adaweb.com/project/holzer/cgi/pcb.cgi

12. www.adaweb.com/project/homeport/

attempted to free itself from the institutional embrace.

At this point it should be stressed that the mail art scene also included artists from the former East Block (i.e. the well known "I am glad" - message from Endre Tot) and from Latin America. For several of the Eastern European artists who were excluded from the official art industry as dissidents, the letter post was the only means to show and sell their work abroad. That also presents an interesting parallel with net art: the group of net.artists who last year formed around nettime, the mailing list, is likely the first pan European art movement after World War II which not only includes artists from the West but also from the former Soviet Union, ex-Yugoslavia and other countries of the former Eastern Block.

### 2.4 A hole in space

After Hans Haacke and N. E. Thing Co had already experimented with Telex at the end of the 1960s, in the 1970s and early 1980s a number of artists sighted the developing computer networks, fax and teleconference systems. All of these technologies belonged at that time to the realm of high technology unavailable to the average consumer. Therefore, Liza Bear, Keith Sonnier and Willough Sharp, who belonged to the group Conceptual Artists at the end of the 1960s and had organized an *Air Art Event* in Philadelphia in 1968, still had to enlist the help of NASA in 1977 when they organized the conference circuit *Two Way Demo* via satellite, in which artists from the east and west coast had a conversation together which was also transmitted on television.

In the same year, Joseph Beuys, Douglas Davis and Nam June Paik participated in the opening of the *documenta 6* through a tele-conference link up. The show was transmitted live in more than thirty countries and with that probably reached the greatest number of viewers who had ever participated in an art event. Joseph Beuys viewed this performance as a part of the educational concept of his idea of the 'social sculpture' and used his slot to make an address. The show ended with the performance *The last nine minutes*, in which Davis tried to break through the television screen: "I believe that television is a barrier to communication, not an aid. We can only contact the viewer by breaking this barrier."

Douglas Davis' role in art which takes on the problems of communication media, has only been insufficiently recognized until now. In that, he was one of the first, maybe even the first, who used the television as a two way communication media. He even said himself about his work: "The... myth about me is that my work is dedicated to 'communication.' I don't believe in communication! I believe in the great adventure of attempting communication, especially over great distances; be they time, language, space, geography or gender. That is a special challenge. It almost never functions outside of a short moment or two."[13] Yet with his great, self defined artistic project of "de-massing the mass media," in many respects he was a forerunner of net art. Today he says about the Internet, in which he carried out a number of works in the past few years such as *The World's First Collaborative Sentence*:[14] that "it is the ultimate means to get truly intense reactions and to hear from an audience."[15]

Some of his earliest works, such as *Electronic Hokkadim I*,[16] for example, already live from a model of interaction which can be traced through his work up to The *World's First Collaborative Sentence*. "Open a channel for every mind, let every mind communicate with every other mind, let the communication be visual and sensory as well as aural and written," he says in an announcement for an event which was broadcast live from the television station WTOP-TV in Washington. A participatory show which would scarcely call attention to itself today, burst all traditional parameters however, in an era in which television was still strictly a one-way medium. Davis also continuously opened borders through (tele-)communicative bargaining with works such as his satellite piece *Seven Thoughts* or his collaborations with the Russian conceptual artists Komar and Melamid. His works from the 1970s and 1980s live from the breaking of the broadcast out to a 'point cast', and therefore he compared his work again and again with the *Hootenanny*, the Jam Session, or even with the African *Hokkadim*.

13. Unpublished conversation with the author.

14. http://math240.lehman.cuny.edu/sentence1.html

15. Unpublished interview with the author.

16. See catalogue: *Douglas Davis – events drawings objects videotapes*, Syracuse 1972 (Everson Museum of Art).

In 1977 Kit Galloway and Sherrie Rabinowitz (alias Mobile Image) produced the *Satellite Arts Project* in which two groups of dancers at different sites interacted with each other. Their images were so merged on the screen that it looked as though people 3000 kilometers away from each other were dancing together. 'Satellite sculptures' became almost its own art genre in the years which followed in which artists as diverse as General Idea, Jean-Marc Phillippe, Pierre Comte, Ingo Günther, Peter Fend, Dennis Oppenheim, Wolfgang Staehle and Paul Sharits participated. One of the most well known projects of this type was *A Hole in Space*, a communication sculpture also set up by Galloway and Rabinowitz: in showcase windows in Los Angeles and New York cameras and large monitors were installed which were connected by satellite. Passersby could make contact with each other from one city to the other. (see also section 2.10 for more about Mobile Image).

In Germany, the most well known event of this type was probably *Van Gogh TV* at the *documenta 8* from Ponton Media,[17] which allowed people to communicate with each other in different cities via telephone, fax, mailbox and picture telephone. In 1992 during the hundred days of the *documenta*, *Van Gogh* could be seen every night on German public television and certainly provided for countless German television viewers' involuntary encounters with television art.

## 2.5 The pleasure of (ASCII-)text

Many of those who followed the nightly broadcasts of *Van Gogh TV* at the time, remember endless calls of "hello" and unsuccessful attempts at communication. With the next telecommunications media with which artists occupied themselves, this type of random talk at cross-purposes was not possible: the very first computer networks were so unattainably expensive that the first artistic experiments could only be carried out with a small number of selected collaborators.

In 1978, a number of artists met at the conference "Artist's Use of Telecommunication" who in the years following would then participate in some of the most interesting telecommunications projects of the 1980s. The conference took place physi-

cally in the San Francisco Museum of Modern Art, but artists in other cities and countries were linked up through satellite and with a computer system from I.P. Sharp. In addition to the organizer, Bill Bartlett, among others participating in this symposium were: Gene Youngblood, Hank Bull (Vancouver), Douglas Davis and Willoughby Sharp (New York), Norman White (Toronto) and Robert Adrian X (Vienna).[18]

A series of generative writing collaborations developed through the time-sharing network from I.P. Sharp Associates in the years following this conference. The Viennese office of I.P. Sharp developed a simple "intercontinental, interactive, electronic art-exchange-program, designed for artists and all others who are interested in alternative possibilities for using new technologies," as was stated in a flyer written at the time. ARTEX, the name of this software, "was kept intentionally simple so that also inexperienced and non-specialized participants could work with it and the costs could be kept as low as possible."[19]

At this time Internet was still the privileged knowledge of a few American military and university members, a modem had to be licensed by the federal post in Germany and it cost over a thousand marks. Local BBS-mailboxes with which the user could call in at a local rate were still unheard of. The entry to the data network which nearly every computer owner in the 'first' world can now afford was still futuristic. Despite the adverse technical prerequisites, the members of the 'Artex-Community' staged several international telecommunication events over the next few years. Among these was, for example, *Die Welt in 24 Stunden* (The World in 24 Hours), led by Robert Adrian X in 1982 in which artists in sixteen cities communicated with each other and exchanged art pieces for an entire day.

The following year, Roy Ascott, who had likewise previously worked with computer conference systems, organized the telecommunication performance *La Plissure du Texte*[20] at the Parisian exhibition *Electra*. The title, a play on a book by Roland Barthes, stood for a collaborative project in which artists in Australia, North America and Europe developed a fairy tale together over the ARTEX-system.

17. http://www.ponton. unihannover.de/archive/ archive_piazza.html

18. http://www.t0.or.at/ ~radrian/

19. Grundmann, Heidi (ed): *Art + Telekommunication*. Vancouver/Vienna 1984 (Western Front, Blix), p. 84.

20. http://www.bmts.com/ ~normill/Text/plissure.txt

In the following years each of the then available telecommunication media was checked for its artistic use value by a number of artists who grouped together in Vienna in the group BLIX and in Vancouver at the Gallery Western Front. Among these experiments was, for example, *Telephone concerts* in which musicians from Berlin, Vienna, Vancouver and Warsaw participated between 1979 and 1983, linked up by telephone and the Slowscan video conference system. This concert series, under the name *Wiencouver*, created an "imaginary city which swayed invisibly in space between its two poles, Vienna and Vancouver" as Hank Bull later described it.

Though, mind you, most of the telecommunication performances of the 1970s and 1980s belonged to the 'first' world; the majority of Africa, Asia and Latin America did not participate in these projects as is common today with net art. That changed first in the second half of the 1980s when also artists from all three continents participated in telecommunication events such as, for example, *Nicaraguan Interactions* in which video tapes from Nicaragua were shown in Boston and answered via Slowscan video transmission.

At the same time there were also a number of 'Fax-Performances.' Among these were: *Fax* (1983 between Vienna, Berlin and New York), *pARTiciFAX* (1984, with participants from Africa, America, Asia, Australia and Europe) and *Mondo Faxo* (1989). The high production frequency necessary for some participants led to some gallerists and artists refusing to participate in such actions in the future as they were not reachable by telephone for the duration of the 'performance'. In the 1970s and 1980s artists such as Andy Warhol and David Hockney also worked with the 'telecopier.'

### 2.6 Galleries without walls

The direct forerunner of that which is today called net art were various projects which worked with mail boxes. What must be differentiated are the artists who used the mailboxes to create a space which was open for communication and those whose works were 'digital specific' or 'net specific', the art works which worked with the technology within which

they existed. Rena Tangens and padeluun, for example, who founded the BBS-mailbox Bionic in 1989 after several actions in the tradition of conceptual art, see themselves as designers of a digital space in which new forms of interaction are made possible.

At the beginning of the 1990s, Bionic was one of the most important mailboxes in Germany through which many political initiatives developed their onlinecommunication. In the past few years the emails of the Yugoslavian network Zamir Network were sent through the Bielefeld computer. These messages were at times the only communication possible between the enemy states of ex-Yugoslavia since during the civil war the telephone lines between Serbia and Croatia were blocked.

The mailbox-project *Electronic Cafe* was set up by Kit Galloway and Sherrie Rabinowitz in 1984 on the occasion of the Olympic games in Los Angeles. In six different city neighborhoods were media cafés in which the local residents were linked up by a teleconference system and a mailbox. This 'gallery without walls' in which pictures and stories could be exchanged, was meant to bring together in dialogue the residents of the ethnically diverse neighborhoods.

Different than Bionic and *Electronic Cafe* are the projects which the American, Car Loeffler, has carried out since 1986 in his Art Com Electronic Network (ACEN). Most of the works at ACEN, which could be found in the Californian mailbox WELL were less about communication between the users and more about sounding out other possibilities for the new digital media. In keeping with this, many of these works can be considered direct precursors to contemporary net art pieces. Loeffler was a ubiquitous advocate of art production with the help of telecommunications media in the eighties yet recently he appears to have retreated from this discussion.

Also, it appears that only the newsgroup remains from his online art magazine *Art Com*. There he had several ideas which aspiring Internet entrepreneurs are again attempting today,[21] such as, for example, the *Art Com Electronic Mall*. This online-business was organized like a shopping

21. The following descriptions refer to the article: "Art Works as Organic Communications Systems" from Anna Courney in: Ascott, Roy; Carl Eugene Loeffler: "Connectivity - Art and Interactive Telecommunication," *Leonardo* Vol. 24, Number 2 1991.

mall in which you could buy software, videos and books: "Shoppers can browse the aisles, see descriptions of the art products and purchase items on-line with the checkout cashier," announces a description from 1991. If that doesn't sound like a present day WWW-shopping paradise. One idea of 'My-World' has naturally not yet been taken up: a group of artists named Normal Art Group programmed a function for the *Art Com Electronic Mall* in which you could shoplift!

Research with the normal search machines shows that apparently none of the former works survived the parameter change from mailboxes and BITNET into Internet and found their way into the WorldWideWeb. Yet the works which could still be found at the beginning of the nineties in The Well point towards current net art projects: Judy Malloy programmed a *Bad Information Base*, in which the user could deposit incorrect information and lies. The Normal Art Group set up a *Virtual Museum of Description of Art*, in which written descriptions of art works could be found. In addition there was a version of the *exquisite corpse*, the surrealists' well known social game in which every user could add something of their own onto a line of ASCII symbols which the last user had entered.

One work entitled *The First Meeting of the Satie Society* was programmed for Satie's honor according to statements by John Cage, Jim Rosenberg and Andrew Culver. It was, as is written in a text from the time, indeed "conceptually a work from Cage, yet various people and programs were involved in putting it together and the work therefore reproduces a multitude of (not exclusively human) voices. The fact that Cage stressed the aspect of the use by the reader (sic!) in his work, underlines the importance of the process (that art is further developed after its completion by the artist) as well as the participation of the user (the production of other meanings through the use of the art work)." These sentences are also true if you turn to most of the net art works of today.

The rest is, (so they say) history, yet it has not yet been written. At the beginning of the 1990s 'being online' was slowly popularized in the art industry by art

mailboxes such as The Thing and projects like *Wochenschau* in which underground sites of the art scene in Cologne, Düsseldorf, Berlin, New York and Vienna were linked together by mailboxes and teleconferences. Some of the artists who entered the net over The Thing still currently work in and with the Internet. When in 1994 an easy to use, graphically maneuverable user surface for the Internet arose with the WorldWideWeb, the first of today's net artists began their initial excursions into cyberspace which I will now summarize in a timeline: Paul Garrin set up *Fluxus Online*[22], in Berlin the group Handshake[23] began from which the *Internationale Stadt* (I.S.)[24] later emerged with its expeditions in the Internet. In the same year, the *Digitale Stad*[25] and David Blair with his *Wax-Web-Hyperfilm*[26] appeared in the net. In 1994, Muntadas opened his *Fileroom* and Alexei Shulgin his WWW-Art Centre in Moscow with *Hotpics*,[27] a selection of works from Russian photographers who in his opinion, were unjustly not invited to participate in a group exhibition in Germany. The next year Heiko Idensen's *Imaginäre Bibliothek* went from a mailbox to the Web, and Philip Pocock and Felix Stephan Huber traveled to the Northpole for *Arctic Circle*.[28] There was a meeting at the beginning of 1996 in Trieste[29] at which the word 'net.art'[30] was used for the first time and at the conference *The Next Five Minutes*[31] most of the European artists working in the Internet at this time met for the first time.

## 3.0 Net art after Mosaic

### 3.1 net = art

When the *documenta X* exhibited net art in the summer of 1997 as the first institution within the 'official' art scene, a greater public became aware of that which only a small group of specialists at the periphery of the art industry knew: the net had become an 'imaginary museum' and a serious platform for artistic activities. This was set off primarily in that the Internet had become 'useable' by computer amateurs as well through the graphically navigable surface of the WorldWideWeb.

In the second half of 1993, the National Center for Supercomputering Applica-

22. http://www.panix.com/~fluxus/

23. http://www.icf.de:80/documents/Art/LuxLogis/D/Information/handshake_de.html

24. http://www.icf.de

25. http://www.dds.nl

26. http://bug.village.virginia.edu/html/1776.html

27. www.cs.msu.su/wwwart/hotpics/

28. www.dom.de/acircle

29. www.ljudmila.org/naps/

30. www.ljudmila.org/naps/cnn/cnn/

31. www.dds.nl/~n5m

tions (NSCA) published the first version of the novel Browser Mosaic that made it possible for the first time in the history of the Internet to integrate text, image, sound and short animated sequences on a surface graphically accessible with a mouse click. The Web and its exponential growth in the next few years showed that an ideal media had been found. This provided for a push in development and a new form of visual publicity which included artists as well. There were artistic experiments with early protocols such as Gopher (Mark Amerika, David Blair) or the MOOs (VNS Matrix, Jordan Crandall, Delbrüggge/Demoll), and various forms of literary collaborations had existed through mailing lists and in the news groups. But it was the Web that made the Internet a medium for fine arts.

Yet the net art which developed in the following years is no new 'ism'. It is not new nor is it a more or less homogenous and uniform art movement. The Internet is a media for the most diverse artistic works. Belonging to that is the design of WebPages as well as the setting up of mailing lists, email and ASCII art through to telerobotic sculptures, in which net users from around the whole world can influence the movement of an object or an installation.

Indeed in Europe in the past few years a number of artists have joined together under the term 'net.art'[32] but this neologism can be understood as an ironic instrumentalization of the normal art world mechanisms of genre definition and group formation. The term 'net.art', said the Russian artist Alexej Shulgin in an interview with the online-magazine *Telepolis*, "recalls much more a data name in UNIX than a new ism. I find that very important as this term written in this way contains a great deal of irony."[33] And indeed, the 'net.artists' are neither the only or the most important artists active in the Internet.

Art in the Internet is a practically incomprehensible collection of the most varied data - as is the Internet itself. At the beginning of the 1990s, in the first Internet-euphoria, the 'Cyberspace' was still declared a 'medial *gesamtkunstwerk*'.[34] The artist Heath Bunting contemporaneously brought this thought to a somewhat shorter and handier formulation: "net = art". At this time the Internet had already developed into a gigantic archive of texts and programs, its beginnings in the late 1960s were as a 'text-only' media, which in the following years were supplemented with ever more images, sound and finally also animation sequences and other moving images. Due to its encyclopedic content, the Internet is continuously compared with the famous library of Babel, which contains every book imaginable as described in a tale by Jorge Luis Borges.[35] Many of the first net art projects aim to add new data to this Babylonian library. Some of the earliest artistic works in the Internet are themselves not much more than archives and data collections to which the user in some cases can include their own data.

From an art historical perspective, an important aspect of net art is that in the meantime not only texts but also the most diverse media (films, sound, graphics, animation sequences, photographs, 3-D simulations, etc.) are there in the Internet, next to each other, and can be transmitted. Everything that can be translated into bits and bytes can be brought online.

### 3.2 The Material Test Department of the Internet

That is why I have defined art as the 'test department of the Internet.'[36] The established net protocol, such as, for example HTML, the code with which WebPages are 'written' are expressly thematisized and questioned by some of the most interesting net art projects. The Dutch-Belgian artist pair Jodi (Joan Heemskerk and Dirk Paesmanns)[37] operate primarily with the creative misuse of this code. Their chaotically organized site is consciously teeming with just such program errors which they have called up.[38] Also the Slovenian net artist Vuk Cosic said: "I have consciously written HTML documents which crashed the Browser. I noticed that there was a mistake somewhere in my programming, but it wasn't enough to avoid this error; I really tried to understand it."[39] This creative deconstruction of technology naturally has an art historical tradition: as early as the sixties, video artists such as Nam June Paik were interested less in what should be done with the new media video and much more in what should not be done and used the television against its own embedded use logic.

32. Counting among the European 'net.artists' are, among others: Alexej Shulgin, Heath Bunting, Rachel Baker, Vuk Cosic and Olia Lialina.

33. Printed in: "Zwischen Kommunikation und Kunst, Ost und West – Telepolis-Gespräch mit Alexej Shulgin" (Interview: Armin Medosch), *Telepolis* 3 (September 1997), pp. 152–156.

34. Rötzer, Florian; Weibel, Peter (ed): *Cyberspace – Zum medialen Gesamtkunstwerk*, Munich 1993.

35. See i.e.: Ippolito, John: "http//www", in: (Cat.) *Deep Storage*, Munich/New York 1997 (Prestel), pp. 157–163.

36. See Baumgärtel, Tilman: "Diebstahl und Betrug – Netzkunst unterwandert die Grenzen zwischen Kunst und Nicht-Kunst," *Springer – Hefte für Gegenwartskunst* vol. III (no. 4), December 1997–February 1998, p. 16.

37. www.jodi.org

38. See: Baumgärtel: *net art*, loc cit., pp. 106–113

39. Baumgärtel: *net.art*, loc cit., p. 145

One of the most radical pieces working in this way is the *WebStalker* from the British group of artists I/O/D. It is an alternative Browser which, in contrast to the commercial competition from Netscape and Microsoft, does not present the WWW-pages as 'pages' but rather analyzes and shows the sites as a whole. Its makers describe the program as "spectacular software." Matthew Fuller, one of its creators, said: "we wanted to produce a piece of software that presents the net through its specific characteristics - as a network and not as a book. We feel that it is important to take the net seriously; with its flow of data and its dynamics."[40]

Another piece which decidedly confronts the technical dispositive of the Internet is *1:1* from Lisa Jevbrat,[41] who formulates her artistic approach to the Internet even more radically than Fuller: "The Internet is an environment that makes the indifferentiability between structure and content obvious. Following from the ideas of Pierre Levy, I believe that it is possible to create here if the concentration is on content." *1:1* works with the I.P. numbers, the 'addresses' of the Internet server and puts together a constantly changing picture from them. At the same time it allows entry to the servers which are not linked up with others and, actually, are secret.

## 3.3 Networks and net-works

Although several of the early utopian-radical ideas which attached themselves to the Internet in the meantime appear to have been relativized, there are several significant differences between art in the Internet and traditional art. Included in this, in addition to the complete immateriality of net art which makes it so difficult for galleries, collections and museums to work with, is what is common to many net art pieces – the implicit rejection of a piece and product oriented understanding of art. In order to grasp this difference to other art practices more clearly, I differentiate between 'net-works' and 'networks'. With 'net-works' I mean artworks which, first and foremost, are realized in the WorldWideWeb and are conceived of as their own self-contained Internet-Site. 'Networks' on the other hand are the social connections and collaborations which, for example, take place in mailing lists or in other 'virtual communities.'

According to my definition, belonging to the 'net-works' for example are: the homepage of the artist pair Jodi; *My boyfriend came back from the war* from Olia Lialina;[42] and the elaborated site of the American Anonymous *Superbad*.[43] Although some of them use artist's pseudonyms (and often at their sites no hints of the identity of their creator can be found), their works are the identifiable works of individual artists who are less interested in the communicative aspects of the Internet and more in confronting the user with a self contained oeuvre. All of these works are net-specific which means that they could not exist in any other medium because, for example, they work with the technical dispositives of the browser software and the transmission speed of the Internet. But they do not invite an exchange, and their interactivity is limited to allowing the user to maneuver in various ways through these sites by mouseclick.

In contrast to these, there are other projects more strongly oriented towards wider participation. Net communities such as the aforementioned *Internationale Stadt* from Berlin (1994 - 1998) or the *Digitale Stad*[44] from Amsterdam (since 1994) were the product of the collaboration of a collective of artists, programmers and political activists. From the beginning they were thought of as 'context-systems' in which the artists offered an infrastructure in which a great number of users are able to communicate with each other and interact and therefore function as a 'network.' These projects are therefore also comparable with Joseph Beuy's concept of the 'social sculpture.' Whether or not they can actually realize their base-democratic claims was asked at one time, yet in any case their creator's thought of them as the result of an 'expanded art concept' in the Internet in the Beuyssian sense, to which also the production of situations which invite social interaction belonged although in this case not in physical space but in the virtual space of the Internet.

The connection of 'networks' lies in the nature of the media and has become exceptionally important for the Internet as an art media. An example of this type of networking via Internet was the meeting of the Old Boys Network,[45] an international group of women, in the summer

40. Baumgärtel, *net.art*, loc cit., p. 153.

41. http://www.c5corp.com/1to1/

42. www.cityline.ru/~olialia/war

43. www.superbad.com

44. www.dds.nl

45 www.obn.org

of 1997 at the *documenta X* in Kassel under the name *Erste Cyberfeministische Internationale* (First Cyberfeminist International). Here women suddenly stood face to face with others whom they had mostly never really met in 'real life'. The entire meeting was prepared for the most part via Internet on mailing lists such as Faces and by private email. Also other international network-meetings were prepared primarily 'in the Internet' and are thus interesting examples of the potential for group formation, collaboration and networking.[46]

International groupings which are mostly informal, sometimes however also quite exclusive, have formed from mailing lists and other 'virtual community centers.' Also those which are not to be understood as art works, are a decisive factor for the suprisingly rapid development of a well unified net art scene in the USA. Relevant institutions for the international net art scene are the different mailing lists such as nettime[47], Syndicate[48], Faces[49], Rhizome[50] or 7-11[51]. They are not necessarily considered artistic cooperations but in any case, as important instruments of networking: the initiators of this list, Geert Lovink and Pit Schultz, for example, wrote: "nettime… (is) not a hidden form of conceptual art… because although it crosses into or taps off the art industry, it can also completely function without being called art."[52]

Although this may also be valid for other mailing lists, they are certainly an important instrument for exchange and collaboration among net artists - and activists. They serve not only for information exchange and the preparation of meetings in 'RL' (real life), but also have led to the development of collective art projects. I also call these mailing lists 'net-works'. In that, I take into consideration that the term is used for what are determined art projects as well as for a 'non-artistic' element of the net art-infrastructure because for many activities in the Internet the border between art and non-art can scarcely be determined or is a matter of a retrospective definition. In this way, on the net art mailing list 7-11 the idea of organizing a group 'exhibition' with the screen-surfaces of the computers of all the list members arose from an informal exchange of emails.[53] Most computers were able to take a snapshot of the com-

puter monitor with the press of a single key which could then be collected by one of the list members. The result is called *Desktop* and is on a WWW-site to 'view' and has even stirred the interest of the *New York Times*: nearly fifty screen-surfaces of list members which allow conclusions to be drawn about the personality of their 'user' can be found at this site. While some of the desktops seem like chance recordings, other of the newly hatched 'net artists' quite consciously played with their self presentation via 'desktop'.

Also Alexej Shulgin's piece *Refresh*[54] was a 'net-work' in the sense described above: in 1996 he motivated net users to use a seldom noticed quality of HTML, the command *Refresh*, which sends the browser on to a different HTML page after a certain time. Over the course of a month a 'chain' of homepages around the globe was formed which were connected with each other although most of the participants did not know each other personally and the interaction between them was limited to a computer command. This art of collaboration is possibly the most interesting which has been brought forth by net art. At the same time the experience which the participants made in the common experiment can scarcely be understood or described retrospectively although it belongs to one of the most intense which has occurred in net art.

46. See also: Sollfrank, Cornelia; Old Boys Network (ed): *1. Cyberfeminist International*, Hamburg 1998.

47. www.nettime.org

48. www.v2.nl/east/

49. thing.at/face/

50. www.rhizome.org

51. www.7-11.org

52. Lovink, Geert, Pit Schultz: "Aufruf zur Netzkritik – Ein Zwischenbericht", in: nettime (ed): *Netzkritik – Materialien zur Internet-Debatte*, Berlin 1997 (Edition ID-Archiv), p. 11.

53. www.easylife.org/desktop/

54. sunsite.cs.msu.su/wwwart/fresh.html

# Ars Telematica:

Claudia Giannetti

Telecommunication technologies, such as the telephone, radio or television, have made it possible to overcome territorial distances, have solved the problem of communication between geographically separated individuals, and have opened up the possibility of sending 'disembodied' messages; all this has been based on one fundamental concept: the conversion of space into time. Long distance verbal communication in real time has been solved by the telephone, and long distance audio-visual communication has been achieved with the invention of television. Whilst the structure of communication via radio or telephone is limited to speech and bi-directional hearing, the structure of televisual communication has widened the range of communication to include vision, but has reduced the direction of information flow, given that broadcasting is unidirectional.

Artists interested in telecommunication problems soon find themselves face-to-face with this tremendous challenge: the need to overcome the barriers of the monological structure of audio-visual media. Most of the art projects via satellite that were first developed in the 1970s, as well as those telematic (data transmission) art projects that first got off the ground in the 1980s, were in fact attempts to transform television into a participative medium. Different paradigmatic experiments carried out over those years involved a search for new techniques and processes that would get across the idea of interaction: *Nine Minutes Live*, by Nam June Paik (Kassel *documenta 6*, 1977); *Two-Way Demo*, by a group of artists organised around Carl Loeffler (New York and San Francisco, 1977); *Terminal Consciousness*, by Roy Ascott (a pioneering networking project carried out by eight artists connected both to each other as well as a data base in California, 1980); *Electronic Cafe* International, by Kit Galloway and Sherrie Rabinowitz (Los Angeles Olympic Art Festival, 1984); *Good Morning Mr. Orwell*, by Nam June Paik (Centre Pompidou, Paris and Channel WNET-TV New York, 1984); etc. Robert Adrian, Norman White, Jean-Marc Philippe and Roberto Barbanti are also creators who, starting at this time, made use of telecommunications in multilateral or intercontinental projects.

Without a doubt, the intention to transform discursive media into participative media can be seen as a major turning point. The technology necessary to bring about this change already exists, the Internet being a fine example of this. But the fact is that a communications revolution does not depend exclusively on technology, but also, and above all, on interpersonal communication; that is, it does not depend exclusively on the mass and flow of information available for circulation, but rather on a broad-based unrestricted access to these media and their use as a genuine means of communication, and not simply as one more carrier in the Information Age. It is about the creation of new models, and not about trying continually to adapt and adjust past ones, as postmodern rhetoric has tried and continues to try to do. We will look now at models related metaphorically or directly with the telematic system, that point the way to a different vision and a new interpretation of what it means to work on the Net.

The development of hypertext theory has made it possible to recover the thoughts of the literature theorist Mikhail Bakhtin (1895-1975). However, in those circles dedicated to hypermedia-related themes, only one of the aspects of Bakhtin's theory is really known at all well: that which refers to the concept of dialogic and polyphonic literature, derived from his study of Dostoyievsky's works. His notion of polyphonic language has qualified him as one of the main precursors of hypertext theory.

# The Aesthetics of Intercommunication

But it is possible to discover another Bakhtin, an author interested in the world of popular culture, with its customs and practices. It is in his book dedicated to the study of Rabelais, translated as *Rabelais and his World*[1], that we can find some relevant basic theories which, extrapolated into our current context, allow us to define a new model relating to telematic culture, that we will here call – after Bakhtin – the 'carnival model'. It may certainly 'sound' festive, and a more rushed interpretation might even indicate a personal interest. In spite of this, if we go deeper into the philosophical, aesthetic and structural foundations of carnival, especially in the sense interpreted by Bakhtin and based on his studies of popular events in the Middle Ages and the Renaissance, we can see the different ways in which this model can be of use to us as a theoretical inspiration when evaluating the aesthetic aspect of art on the Internet, or web art, as it is known.

This being a highly complex model, we will focus on four main points or concepts: interpersonal communication, the notion of ambivalence, the metaphor of the mask, and the relationship between art and context.

One of the most important aspects of carnival lies in the human contact and relationships to which the event gives rise. It is an open, multilayered type of communication, precisely because the model in question makes a complete break with the hierarchical or pyramidal structure that dominates most societies. In other words, it makes a clean break with the rigid norms of social class and background. And this is precisely because carnival is not based on a power structure, nor is it the product of a bureaucratic, institutional or official system. Within the context of the carnival, everybody appears to have, at first, the same rights and the same position or status. The sys-tem involved is not of an orderly or pre-established nature, but grows out of an apparently chaotic form into which people allow themselves to be pulled or involved, thus creating a network in a free and open fashion.

Another characteristic of carnivalesque communication is its plurimedia (or, as we would say in artistic terms, intermedia) nature. That is to say, it is a form of inter-disciplinary communication that involves the body and all its functions – voice and hearing (or audio), images and context (vision), dance and rhythm (movement), musical texts (language) –, all of them interrelated in a creative, active and frag-mented (that is to say, non-linear) manner.

The carnival experience is, on the other hand, an ambivalent experience. Although it involves each person as an individual, it is not something private, but open to the world in the sense that anyone who wants to can take part. This inte-gration depends on no norms or rules of access, but rather on the ability of partici-pants to incorporate and adapt themselves to the game. It is clear that carnival has its own criteria and rituals, but its defining factor is the power to integrate absolutely all of the participants with each other. We are therefore talking about a network communications struc-ture.

Its ambivalence also extends, in similar fashion, to other aspects: in a carnival context, people take on a dual role: they are both spectators and actors at the same time. As an example, Bakhtin uses the notion of 'laughter', something inherent in carnival, as a factor which makes it possi-ble to describe the ambiguous nature of participation; the people who participate 'in' the carnival are equally the object and subject of laughter. On the one hand, they are the observers of the spectacle taking place, they are consumers of all the circulating information, but they are also an integral part of the spectacle (and the information) experienced by all in a more or less synchronised form. For Bakhtin, the carnival, as a nucleus of medieval culture, "does not have the purely artistic form of theatrical performance and, in general, does not pertain to the world of art. It is situated on the border between art and life. In reality it is life itself, presented with the characteristic elements of a game. In fact, carnival ignores all distinctions between actors and spectators. It also ignores the stage, even in an embryonic form, since a stage would ruin the carnival."[2] Establishing an analogy with current telematic strategies, we might say that the observers are both the users and creators of the same network. It is here that the affinity lies between the participative, active and interactive nature of the carnival and that of the telematics network.

Bakhtin confirmed that "the carnival has no spatial frontier."[3] In a similar way, in the field of Internet data, the absence of spatio-temporal limits and of a real place is made up for by the simulation of an immaterial space, a hyperspace characterised by virtuality and temporality. This electronic space makes it possible to substitute the time-distance relationship through the use of instantaneous presence, thanks to the synchronisation and ubiquity of data. Dynamism and action thus provide the essential focus of these complex, open and multidimensional systems, in which the user plays a fundamental role. In the Internet context, this participatory position is reinforced by free access to any item of information, which makes it possible to overcome the unidimensionality of analogical language and its link with linear structuring systems. This break with Western models of textual sequentiality and centrality can thus be seen as an transformation which is inherent in the process of network digitalisation and communication.
The carnival model provides us with another unusual approach regarding the ambivalence which exists when apprehending the concept of reality. As we have previously pointed out, the carnival, as well as the data transmission network, involves a powerful dynamism which has an influence on the experience of the medium or context itself. This dynamism is directly related to the notion of reality,

which become immaterial, playful and virtualisable. The Situationism adopted the 'Society of the Spectacle' as a basis of appearances, dominated and manipulated by the powers that be. Here, this 'Society of the Spectacle' to a certain extent is able to outwit these powers, and transform itself into a society which can destabilise, diminish the importance of, infringe upon and overcome the limits of existing notions of reality and truth. According to Bakhtin, the rites and performances of carnival marked a notable, basic difference with established forms of society, since "they offered a vision of the world, of mankind, and of human relationships, that was totally different and deliberately unofficial, that lay beyond the reach of Church and State; they would appear to have built up, alongside the official world, a second world and a second life to which the folk of the Middle Ages belonged to a greater or lesser degree, and in which they lived on determined dates. This created a form of duality in the world."[4] "This vision, opposed to all that was anticipated and perfect, to all pretension to immutability and eternity, needed to be manifested in changing (Protean), dynamic, fluctuating and active forms of expression. It is this which impregnates all the forms and symbols of carnival language with an understanding of the relative nature of truth and the powers that be."[5] The carnival, as well as the telematic network, are clear examples of a plurality of realities and of the tendency to their disintegration in a virtual space (virtual here understood as a suspension of the real). It is a space-time whose fluid, playful strength gives rise to the feeling that it is ubiquitous.

The metaphor of the mask is inextricably linked to the idea of the unstable nature of reality. The mask, a typically carnivalesque emblem, is, likewise, not without a certain ambivalence: it both hides and reveals at the same time. The mask is an object which either hides or conceals its wearer. The person behind the mask is all but anonymous, even though he or she may be recognised by the type of mask used. On the other hand, the masked person gives him or herself away through the choice of mask in question. The mask can be used as a metaphor for the relativity of existence, affecting both the concept of identity and the equivalence between mind and body, between the personal

64

Some of the most expansive forms of Internet, like chat forums, MUDs (Multi User Dungeons), cities or virtual places, can be seen as platforms for the development of a mask-based aesthetic. The technology of data transmission networks and of virtual reality in general make it possible for artists to explore other dimensions of a ubiquitous nature, such as telepresence. On the one hand, current telematic and tele-robotics systems enable us to create virtual doubles, changing the form of or giving life to different characters, so that they can function in cyberspace. They also enable the user to teletransport his or her virtual clones, to control them from a distance, and animate them in real time: in this way they can carry out their cyberperformances. Themes such as dual personality and subject-body relationships take on an unusual perspective, given the possibilities inherent in virtual cloning. A good example of this are Stelarc's telematic performances, in which the role of technology is to either mask or liberate the subject.

In his well-known Internet-based projects, such as *Fractal Flesh* or *Stimbod*, Stelarc proposes that the body be used both as subject and object. The body thus acts as a host to other bodies and remote agents. In his own words: "a body that can extrude its awareness and action into other bodies or bits of bodies in other places. An alternate operational entity that is spatially distributed but electronically connected."[9] His proposal is to transform the body, not in a place of inscription, but in a medium in which remote agents can manifest themselves. This type of activity could also change the very way in which we conceive the Internet. According to Stelarc, it is possible to structure the Internet in such a way that we could scan, select and set up interface connections with online groups or physical agents in real time. The Internet could thus be turned not only into a means of transmission, but also into a "mode of transduction" - affecting physical action between bodies. Electronic space as a realm of action rather than information," concludes Stelarc.

We would thus be talking about a model very close to that of the carnival, in which the body ceases to be a closed and private entity and becomes something open, expansive, public. Bakhtin subscribed to a personal notion of the 'corporal whole' and of how its limits were transgressed at carnival time: during the carnival, the borders between the body and the outside world, and between different bodies, are completely different to those marked by classical and naturalist precepts. This carnivalesque body, this masked body, serves as a metaphor for the body connected to the Internet, given that it places emphasis on the loss of 'natural' identity and – more notably – indicates that it is possible to adopt multiple identities, such as Stelarc's host body. In the carnival, as in cyberperformance, people and their bodies are turned into a field for action, manipulation and transformation.

Here we enter on the final theme concerning the carnival model: the relationship which it makes possible between art and context. Clearly this type of total abandonment, in an environment that is also global and all-enveloping, narrows down the relationship between art and environment: an aim pursued, as we know, by a whole series of artists in this century, particularly from its second half.

One artist who has investigated this connection in a fashion that is particularly *sui generis* has been Helio Oiticica. His work also fits in perfectly with the carnival metaphor and the complex multimedia link between the double contribution of the subject to the process (both as spectator and participant), as well as interpersonal communication, the destabilisation of reality and the function of the mask. His theories and writings on art form part of his artistic output and must be understood as activities which are inseparable from it, consisting as they do of a broader system of creation, a kind of 'program in progress.' This should eventually lead to a unique artistic system which will reach out and connect at all levels, from object to body, from music to architecture: an 'environmental whole' which links the 'given' with the 'created', nature with culture. Especially interesting regarding this subject are the proposals which Oiticica began to develop at the beginning of the 1960s, and which culminated in a series of different pieces named *Parangolé* (1964). These dealt with dresses, capes or banners which could be worn, danced in, or used to relate to others as well as the environment. The spectator becomes the central figure and, dressed, must 'carry out' the work (action) and at the same time must 'be' the work (its nucleus). Oiticica regarded *Parangolé* as a 'structure-action' requiring direct corporal participation: according to the artist, the act of dressing the work brings about a transmutation of the spectator. "The creation of the 'cape' does not only involve the consideration of a 'cycle of participation' in the work, that is to say, a 'participation in' and 'dressing of' the work so that it might be seen in its entirety by the spectator, but also involves consideration of the problem in space and time."[7] *Parangolé* thus shows itself to be, at heart, an 'environmental structure' which has a main nucleus: the 'participator-piece', that divides into 'participator' when it takes part and into 'piece' when it is approached from a point outside the space-time environment. When these participator-piece nuclei relate to each other in a given environment (in an exhibition for example), they create an 'environmental system', *Parangolé*, that can in turn be attended by other participators from outside."[8] Bakhtin said, in reference to the carnival environment, that it was 'our world, which suddenly transforms into others' world.' In Oiticica's case, the act of dressing the *Parangolé* represents this 'location of oneself in' (another reality, environment, etc): acting from within the system in the context of a broader external system, in which other observers also take part.

Logically, Oiticica's next step is directed against existing art systems. In a manifesto put together in June of 1966, he defined his 'anti-art' as a complement to the collective need for latent creative activity, which can be motivated in ways determined by the artist: "Current metaphysical, intellectual and aesthetic viewpoints are no longer valid: there is no existing project designed to 'raise the spectator to a creative level', to a 'meta-reality', or to impose an 'idea' or 'aesthetic model' which correspond to such artistic concepts; on the contrary, the spectator is simply given an opportunity to partici-

pate so that he or she might 'find' something which inspires him or her to create."[9] Including an artist's work only has aesthetic reality becoming complete when confronted with the viewpoint of each participant, a figure we could call 'participator': some things have been foreseen by the artist, but the meaning with which they are imbued derives from the anticipated possibilities to which the spectator gives rise and which emerge thanks to the latter's participation.

Oiticica almost certainly did not know Bakhtin's writings, and even less his theory of carnival. Nevertheless, each proposal fully complements the other. Oiticica has rediscovered elements such as the cape and the dress typical of carnivals, as well as dance and collective public performances, and has developed his 'anti-art system' based on dialectical-social participation (a sign of protest against the system), playful participation (games, environments, appropriations), participation in the environment (public and/or street performances) the creation of a network of collective participation (dressing in disguise and dancing in groups); that is to say, a system of total participation that is not reduced to the simple mechanism of acting or to following an artist's pre-established guidelines. What Oiticica is looking for, in a nutshell, is communication on a grand scale, a system in which people can gain control, generate, experiment and interconnect with each other. Consequently, we are not far from the ideal of the telematic network, from its forms of interactivity and the transformation of the user of the network into an active participant.

Parallel to the carnival model, it remains for us to take note of another model, which should not exactly be seen as an alternative, but more as a pragmatic complement when referring specifically to the telematic model. The name of this model is 'Lampsacus', and it is, in effect, a proposal concerning Internet communication and the possible changes in store as far as human relations are concerned. This proposal was formulated by Otto Rössler.[10] Now that the Internet is fashionable, countless attempts to comment on how it works and on its potential have mushroomed, resulting in a lot of tiring rhetoric. Despite this, Rössler managed to define the Internet in a few precise words:

1. Mikhail Bakhtin, *Rabelais and his World*, Bloomington, Indiana University Press, 1984. [Spanish transl. by Julio Forcaat and César Conroy, *La cultura popular en la Edad Media y en el Renacimiento. El contexto de François Rabelais*, Madrid, Alianza Editorial, 1987 (4th ed.), 1995.]

2. Ibid. p. 13.

3. Ibid. p. 13.

4. Ibid. p. 11.

5. Ibid. p. 16.

6. Stelarc, "Visiones parásitas. Experiencias alternativas, íntimas e involuntarias", in: Claudia Giannetti (ed.), *Ars Telemática. Telecomunicación, Internet y Ciberespacio*. Barcelona, ACC L'Angelot, 1998, p. 132.

7. Oiticica, "Notas sobre el *Parangolé*", in: VV.AA. *Hélio Oiticica*. Barcelona, Fundación Antoni Tàpies, 1992, p. 93.

8. Ibid. p. 96.

9. Ibid. p. 100.

10. Rössler, Otto E., "Una utopía realmente factible", in: *Ars Telematica*, op. cit. pp. 17-18.

11. Ibid. p. 18.

12. Lyotard, Jean-François, *La postmodernidad (explicada a los niños)*, Barcelona, Gedisa, 1996 (6th ed.), p. 90. (Orig. ed. *Le Postmoderne expliqué aux enfants*, Éditions Galilée, París, 1986.)

13. Ibid. p. 92.

14. Eco, Umberto, *Apocalípticos e integrados*, Barcelona, Tusquets, 1995, pp. 27-28. (Orig. ed. *Apocalittici e integrati*, Bompiani Editore, 1965.)

the Internet is a bomb". A phrase which he then qualified by saying: "It is a beneficial bomb, a gift. And it shall be called Lampsacus. Lampsacus is the second Internet of the future, the free Internet."[11] Lampsacus will not only become the 'birthplace' of everybody connected to it, but will also be the space in which everybody, and all cultures, will enjoy equal rights.

According to Rössler's proposal, Lampsacus should be a vast laser-based training and cultural centre, in which people can access all existing information without exception, be artistic, or enjoy themselves as they please. Lampsacus can be a means of survival and also the means that will guarantee the future of most human beings, especially the young, when threatened by the next war or the next ecological catastrophe. And this is because Lampsacus follows the insubordinate philosophy of 'the great artist of the 21st century' – as Rössler called Ghandi – summed up in the eloquent phrase: "Imagine what would happen if a war began and nobody joined in." Without a doubt, Lampsacus is an inspired model: given the current period, in which discourses involving freedom are being increasingly discredited – a spacing out from those idealisms which define themselves as a process of breaking away, but which, as Lyotard puts it, "we suspect is more a way of forgetting or suppressing the past, that is to say, of repeating it, than a way of overcoming it"[12] – close attention must always be paid to any contribution that is intimately related to our immediate condition as social beings. In the increasingly complex, relentless systems that are continually generated by our postindustrial society, altruistic and intelligible solutions – such as Lampsacus – might appear to be a blend of ingenuity, madness and incongruity. In Lyotard's words: "(...) an insistence on simplicity has sprung up everywhere nowadays, like a promise of barbarism."[13] At the present time, the term 'Internet' itself begins to have this generic yet ambiguous connotation. As Umberto Eco noted in his book *Apocalyptics and Integrados*, "...if culture is an aristocratic, jealously cultivated, assiduous and solitary action derived from a refined inwardness that is opposed to the vulgarity of the mob (...), the mere idea of a culture shared by all, produced in a way that is adapted to all, and produced as a measure of all, is in itself a monstrous contradiction."[14] It is clear that a model of open telecommunications and the ramifications of the Internet could destabilise (as happens in the carnival model) the hierarchical power structure of our society, and, as a consequence, can also subvert cultural elitism, to the extent that it is established as a (cyber)space in which everyone, *in principle*, has equal user status. Thus it will depend, above all – as in the carnival model or the Lampascus model – on the access of all societies to this medium, on a broad, egalitarian basis. Looked at from our current perspective, the possibility of bringing about such a project (or the will to do so) is very remote.

# Everyone a

Gerhard Johann Lischka

Something's always happening. And something is always happening with us. Either by performing an action - combined with thoughts - or by becoming involved in situations that determine what happens to us. We are right in the middle of the flow of events, energy, the search for security and forlornness. We are media of society and we mediatize our thoughts. We are the dynamic interfaces of the generation of our world views and we style our image of the world as mediators.

Often, people talk about the end of art. But not art is at an end, but rather other conceptions of what art is are ousting outdated concepts and conventions. The deluge of information that almost consumes us demands that we deal with media in a completely different way, in a way that both relativizes a mass-manipulative sender-recipient relationship and that compels us to probe the world in a new, unconventional manner.

Everyone becomes a mediator in body-language presentation, just as in the construction of media-produced and media-received images of the world. Our neuronal projection surface, the monitor, the screen is projected on both from the inside (the brain, the senses) and from the outside (the environment, the media).

To begin with, it would seem quite clear that the producer (artist /director) and the recipient (listener, observer) must choose from an overwhelmingly large supply what is of interest to them and what it makes sense to pursue; where we, as recipients, continue to receive and where we begin to act as producers. This moment of choice involves a decision that no one can relieve us of. It is the chain of events and ideas that can be traced into the past and the present decision - made

on the basis of components which points to the future. At one level there is no difference between reception and production, they are the rational energy, the supply and demand, the constant development, the stone that sends out a shower of sparks. It is a closing of the circle that opens again at a different level, only to be closed once more: the self-referentiality of autopoiesis. The recipient turns out to be a producer by dealing with information in such an adroit manner that it is of importance for his further procedure, which also applies to the producer.

In a subsequent step, however, the producer will decide to make his own contribution to the supply of information from the insights he has gained, which, however, does not concern the receiver who continues to receive information that drives him on in the flow of communication. Thus, the only difference between production and reception (and it is a difference), is that production also presents itself to the outside, whereas reception, being mental production, remains concealed inside and is only manifested, assumes a form, under certain circumstances.

It has become difficult to distinguish between the producer and the recipient clearly, all the more as we no longer live under the supremacy of the utility or exchange value (with the exception of the underprivileged), but rather under the influence of the signs themselves, logos, labels and brand-marks, i.e. the brand value. Logos, as a symbolic value, are the meaning of communication or rather what appears to the communicator to be meaning. Here, there is generally no possibility of depriving the communicator of this meaning as it has become entrenched, unchallenged - generally accepted as such - in the minds of the communicators. At this point we must emphasize that mediatization, as a constant, is but the

# Mediator

became unconsciously established in the
recipient and that other-directedness is
taking place from the inside.

We would be only too willing to put our
trust in the state, the institutions, the economy, to be a member of society sagely
guided by them. But this ideal, if it was
ever the case, is a process of everyone
with everyone and it is the problem. That
is, the question of consensus, whether it is
possible at all to reach agreement without
constraints, whether the discourse can
ever be free of rule, who legitimates himself and how. However we approach this
issue, we will always encounter a particular quantity, that which cannot be
reduced: the individual as the basis of
society, as the medium of society. However abstract society may appear to us,
with the effect that we can supposedly
only describe it in abstract terms, the individual is concrete - the individual in danger of being lost in the abstraction of mass
and who only seems able to save himself
via his image.

If we accept that mass is too anonymous
and that the individual is too specific in the
social context, we must find a way of
avoiding the mass and liberating the individual from his isolation and making him
socially acceptable. This can be achieved
with an awareness that, as social creatures, we must involve ourselves in the
process of the formation of society according to our own wishes. And, ideally, from
our own viewpoint and insight in a dialogue with others. The other, however, is
understood as a communication partner
and not as an anonymous address of an
abstract discourse, but rather as a contact
of a dialogue filtered from the polylogue.
We will never be able to communicate
with everyone, we won't even try, but we
will always have dealings with some. The
more interesting the exchange, the more
willing we are to be completely caught up
in the dialogue, and to perform a process

of analysis and generation of world
views. We will become mediators.

Let us localize ourselves where we all
have to become mediators, where the
'awareness' of separation from our mothers, the division of the subject and the
object begins, at the mirror stage or
rather at the transitional objects. This is
where we finally leave behind the all-
embracing dyad with our mothers. After
our birth - now abstracting - we are confronted with the world. We realize that
we are not alone in our feeling of omnipo-
tence, but rather that we are faced with
the world and that we get to know it
through mediation. This is projection and
reception, the monitor facing in and out,
representation through symbols. Recognition and vision through experience and
through the media. Where medium
implies both the mirror and the object,
both means with which we comprehend
the world.

Who knows when this process of mediatization, symbolisation with what sense
and the interplay of the senses begins?
The ear, or to be more precise the cochlea,
is fully developed even in the four month
old embryo. Think of all the things we
hear at that age and all the commands we
obey long after which we do not interpret
as such. Immaterial and material media
form the interface at which we find out
the limitations of our skills and scope of
experience. They are the body, the mind
and emotions.

It is no longer possible to draw an exact
line between material and immaterial
media. Just like in a conventional understanding of the mediator, in which not
only the jurist but also the psychologist
and the ethnologist want to have their
say, to play the go-between, when two
parties are at loggerheads and mediation
is required. Like 'reality' appears on the
screen, it can be a live scene or the most

tor - recorded live by the camera, or a fictitious show or television. But what distinguishes the mediator, according to our
new definition is that he feels at home
and knows his way around in this intermediate area, in this zone of mingling.
The mediator moves intermediately
between the media in a spirit of connecting the recipient and the producer: he sees
action as text, image and sound as a connecting interaction leading to interesting
intermediate forms.

In post-modernism, the mirror and the
object as a medium are augmented by the
monitor, the fundamental instrument of
the mediator. He navigates through the
information society and the global networks of monitors, he surfs on the waves
of the multimedia ocean, driven by the joy
and curiosity, the urge to be charged by
the nerve of time. The mediator commands the media in the sense that he sees
through mediatization as the process of
the formation of forms in media and
defines both the connection between himself and the media as an intermedium and
the artistic welding together of medium
and medium. The body as a material
medium also possesses its immaterial
presence through its mediatization in the
media, to become aware a *fortiori* of the
dimensions of corporeality.

Interestingly, the technical and electronic
images of the media are not simply
images as used to be, created in an ideological, mythological or religious context.
And yet there were also images simply as
images, as opposed to texts or sounds.
But since the onslaught of the image
world as the primary mode of information mediation, we must acknowledge
the fact that these images are no longer
merely images, but images created on the
basis of texts, ideas and commands. They
are complex images that require image
competence to be understood and comprehended. Here, the fact that we are
mediators forces itself upon us. We must
be able to distinguish the layers from
their surfaces through the cleverly calculated image languages, to see through
the fine appearances and the perfect lus-
ter and make them transparent.

A comprehensible frame of reference for
this process is the Blue Box. In this space
without corners and edges, which is
shifted as a result of whatever kind of

background, we can construct with complete freedom our conceptions of images
that are collaged or mounted. And being
in the picture as to how these images are
created, we are aware of all the possibilities of image manipulation. We recognize
images as intentions, creations, manipu-
lations subject to these or other connota-
tions. And because the mediator is familiar with the operating instructions and
tricks of the Blue Box, he can see the
'rhyme and reason,' he can read between
the lines (surfaces), create interlinear versions, and see through the mediatization
as a form of design primarily oriented to
images.

If we live primarily in intermediate spaces
- as a result of the acceleration and
rhythm of our lives and great mobility -
this corresponds to the 'intermediate
space' of the Blue Box with regard to
mediatization. The Blue Box being an
'equatorial' zone between both poles of
the White Box and Black Box, both spaces
of information generation. For one,
because the recipient can experience
images, photos, sculptures and installations, also performances, in an 'ideal'
white space isolated from the environment. On the other hand, the Black Box
generates said apparatus of images
(texts and sounds) which cannot
(or which can only instantaneously be
observed in their process of creation and
which obey certain programs and inputs.
Finally, the images appear to be fixed like
a photograph after a process of development, projected like a fluttion on the monitor as a vast teeming mass of constantly
moving pixels.

The white cube is the vessel with which to
isolate whatever kind of image worlds
from negative concomitant information
and thus to show the exhibited artworks
off to the best possible effect. However
large or small these white islands in the
chaos of information and redundancy
may be, they present what is new: they
develop a great intensity and a vortex
that momentarily clusters recipients prepared to deal with image-language into a
discussion group. As a kind of cult space,
it succeeds, extends and rivals temples,
churches and mosques.

The Black Box on the other hand is the
representative of the New Media, technological development and a trend towards

binding mediatization to us as an increasingly refined form of multimedia, with the
effect that we become the controller and
emissary of data, images, texts and
sounds as a result of advancing miniatur-
ization. The Black Box can be so large that
it engulfs us as an auditorium and it can
be so small that we can swallow it. It
bursts conventional experiences of space
and in cyberspace is the beginning of a
new age of reception, of total involvement in the media, of mental immersion
in fictitious worlds.

Since the advent of the New Media, they
have been coming closer and closer to us.
In this way we are changing from the
hunter to the hunted. In order to find our
way in this realm of techno-imagination,
we must enter an aesthetics of existence,
the monitor stage, we must transform
ourselves into the mediator so as to be
up-to-date and so as to be able to survive.
The moving images move us and we must
know what direction to embark on. For in
this situation we are recipients and producers of our own world views. If the carpet of life today is woven of aesthetics, of
logos and images, there is nothing we can
do but probe our location as mediators so
as to be able to fathom out where we are
from time to time.

The art of living becomes art of survival in the sense that art becomes the
other, the realm beyond life, as it always
has been, but also a poetic act in which
sensorial cognition and production may
gel to an unprecedented extent. The recipient, as such, becomes a producer, the
producer reveals himself as a recipient
and what emerges is a level of meta-art
that thrives on the flow of images (texts
and sounds) in which according to conventional criteria we can no longer dis-
cern who is an artist. The act of reception
and production has submerged into the
realm of the mental. And the mediator no
longer needs to prove whether he is a
recipient or producer, he decides himself
about the line of demarcation between
life from the vantage-point of meta-art, in
which although separations are enacted,
allocations become increasingly difficult:
interaction in the intermedium as a
momentary flickering of poetry.

# Radical

**Jeffrey Shaw**

The net_condition signals the moment where net technology plays a fundamental role in determining the modalities and forms of net culture. It is common knowledge that military concerns launched a communications technology whose unique and most important feature was its distributed impregnability. That characteristic has spawned the phenomenally decentralised acculturation of the Internet that we have experienced over the last decade. At the same time, the specific restrictions of this technology has nurtured idiosyncratic new modalities of intercommunication driven by the need to make the evolution of new technological achievements synchronous with the evolution of new cultural experiences and values.

Our present day technologies are paltry carriers of glimpsed possibilities and grand ambitions. The history of net.art is a history of work both constituted and debilitated by the particularities of its momentary technological conditions. From one month to the next we become nostalgic for forms that belonged to past conditions, and euphoric for those new forms enabled by current conditions. One also looks ahead because there are a multitude of inevitabilities that drive the evolution of these technologies. The Internet will certainly become that ubiquitous gigabroadband facility that connects everything with everything. This convergence will subsume all media within one generic technology that can then be configured to embody whatever bandwidth is appropriate ranging from text chat on digital paper to immersive shared virtual environments in the home Omnimax internet theater. The varying texture of these intercommunications will no longer be the consequence of technological limitations, but rather design choices driven by content contexts. At present this hyper-connectivity is still in the realm of pre-fabrication and simulation, building intranetworked models that embody con-

tent and that test the viability of one of many possible paths of artistic action. The works produced at the ZKM Institute for Visual Media and presented in the net_condition exhibition are of this nature. They are test beds where certain experimental intimacies can be experienced which are not yet fully part of the main stream of inter-intercommunication offer a preamble of imminent formations. It is also significant that these works were produced in the context of the principal European long term information society research program ESPRIT where the ZKM has worked in association with major academic research centers in the UK, Sweden and Switzerland. Traditionally this program has been the domain of computer science, but now the relevance of artistic research and practice in this field has begun to be recognized and valued.

Knowbotic Research's IO_dencies is a major initiative that takes the potentialities of a networked communications medium and puts it in the hands of urban planners so as to give them a new ambiance of exchange and reflection. The radical step taken by Knowbotic Research is to give this communications medium a functional and formal identity of its own that interacts with the information put there by the participants. In the ensuing re-formation of that information that is afforded both in space and time, new insights are generated in this feedback loop between the architects themselves and the medium giving expression to their discourse. The magnetic force feedback technology, conceived and developed by the ZKM in the context of IO_dencies Tokyo, unreleased in the installation table designed by Knowbotic Research, adds a tactile dimension of informational feedback that allows the impulses/ideas to be felt and 'grasped'. Similarly Shane Cooper's Anchorman explores software strategies to mine the real-time data flows of the world news

# Software

information that is continuously being provided on the Internet and then recontextualise this information in a virtual newsroom where a synthetic voiced agent anchorman makes nonstop concrete news poetry by means of an algorithmic deconstruction and reconstruction of the incoming information. This goes quite a bit further than the much heralded 'personal digital newspaper', and signals another radical particularity of the media technologies, which is the total interchangeability of their data forms. Skateboards can be rain schedules can be music can be chat rooms can be whatever. For example an Israeli company has developed technologies to digitize in real time the players' and football's movements during a soccer match, so as to be able to broadcast a virtual reconstruction of that match over the Internet. But the same data streams could be used (simultaneously) to script a television soap, or control traffic lights or create an artwork – all multifarious re-embodiments of that same football match.

Ken Feingold's *Séance Box Nr. 1* is a paradigmatic model stage for the imminent world stage interaction between our real, surrogate and virtual embodiments. With a surreal exactitude this work presents the four main protagonists: you, your telepresent robotic auxiliary, your omnipresent avatar stand-in, and your independent agent compatriot. These four individuals (three biological and one digital) hope to have found in Feingold's theater of spirits a place of coherent exchange. Apart from each other (could be in the four corners of the globe), delicate technologies offer prostheses to their seeing, hearing, talking, moving and touching in the momentary meeting place of their net condition. What can they say to each other, other than articulate the extraordinary limits of their condition? Or is this the future space of theater, where those limits are transcended in a scenario of role playings that embody

narrative reconstruction of identity and communication. The necessary understanding is the scalability and varying morphologies of group and personal interaction that is afforded within the singularities of a distributed virtual environment.

The Internet has also been the platform for the remarkable ideological conversion of the surveillance camera into the webcam. Here the mechanisms of tele-operation and tele-presence which were inherited from military industrial origins are being democratised into a universally shared apparatus of remote vision, a delicate distributed network of posted sightings. Thus with the disjunction and reconjunction of being in the net comes the dislocation and relocation of place as well – geography dissolves into simultaneity in the unblemished heterogeneity of all data forms. Masaki Fujihata's *Impressing Velocity* presents a paradigmatic expression and experience of this particular net condition. The webcam attached to the model train explores an other place, and its operator seated on a distant motion platform experiences visually and kinesthetically the irresistible ver- tigo of Fujihata's algorithmic conjunction of usually separated information streams. Movement in this remote cyberspace (albeit be it a real space in this work) in not merely the spectacle of the seen, but becomes here a synaesthetic anamophosis of the seen through a mapping of the tele-gravitational forces of motion into the structure of the received image.

As a result of the increasingly ubiquitous nature of the Internet and the maturing of 3D interaction techniques, there is a growing need to define aesthetic frameworks for the technological development of new social interaction and interface paradigms for content rich, interconnected, shared virtual environments. Already in 1993 the ZKM produced two pioneering distributed virtual environments, connecting remote locations to enable simultaneous imaging and real time interaction to take place between users at the sites where the work is installed. These works introduce the form of an artwork where viewers who are physically separated from each other can share an aesthetic figuration in the tele-virtual space.

Jeffrey Shaw's *Televirtual Chit Chat* was constituted by installations at IMAGINA in Monte Carlo and in Karlsruhe which were connected by modem and telephone. Facing large video screens the two distant players each shared the same virtual image space. While manipulating their own visual elements each person was at the same time also seeing the result of their distant partner's actions on their own video screen. Each player could choose letters from a simulated keyboard on their screen. Using a multi-axis 3D mouse, the position, size and shape of each of these three dimensional letters could be interactively manipulated over a rectangular surface that showed a map of Europe between Monte Carlo and Karlsruhe. The telephone connection between the two sites also allowed the players to speak to each other while they manipulated their alphabetic forms to together build immaterial word sculptures in the shared virtual space.

Using similar technology, Agnes Hegedus' *Televirtual Fruit Machine* was connected between the ICC in Tokyo (*Media Passage*) and the ZKM in Karlsruhe (*Multimediale 3*). At each location the viewer interacted with the computer generated image using a multi-axis joystick and could see both the results of their own actions as well as those of the other user at the remote location. Additional video-phones enabled the two participants to see and talk to each other. The computer generated image was a spherical object divided like a tennis ball along a curved line into two parts; each part was separately manipulated in the televirtual space by the two operators using their respective joysticks. The outer surface of this spherical object carried images of various fruit, and the inner surface

showed a map of the world. The challenge for the two geographically separated users was to coordinate and control the movement of their respective image halves so as to bring them together in a sphere and join the fruits. When they succeed they were rewarded by an avalanche of virtual coins - Yen in Tokyo and Pfennig in Karlsruhe.

Both these works were technologically 'high end' in the sense that they depended on graphics workstations at each of the connected locations. At the same time the connectivity demands were low - just the user input data which was transferred by conventional modems. Similar to Jean Luc Godard's highly political gesture when he turned from film to video, the artistic autonomy achieved by using low cost 'off the shelf' infrastructures has made the Internet a more popular territory for the exploration of distributed connectivity in art. But we should also bear in mind that domestic computers are already achieving supercomputer performance levels, and that broadband connectivity is imminent. So the autonomous artist will soon be free to pursue complex scenarios of mass distributed interactivity in a highly sophisticated (but inexpensive) computing environment, though at the expense of a current political position that is tenuously tied to a temporary techno-cultural condition.

Our net condition is a circumstance, a contingency and a predicament. It has made our screens into lattices that hide and expose the terrains of newly formed intelligent information spaces. The often trivial technological convergences that are being heralded here are just the tip of a much more interesting iceberg - the synaesthetic convergence of all our modalities of perception in the conjuncted space time of morphed real, surrogate and virtual formations. These shared environments of any and every level of embodiment are above all social spaces in which the artwork is no longer a mere accouterment, but may define the very structure, the cosmology of those spaces and their activities.

Address http://www.hangar.org/sisif

ddress | http://www.hmu.auckland.ac.nz:8001/sisyphus ▼ |

By typing the address of

the user has access to a web site inhabited by a fly which adopts the usual attitudes of these insects, which are the following:

1. it stays in the same position for a long time

2. occasionally, it rubs its front legs against each other

3. occasionally, it walks some steps

4. occasionally, it flies and produces the sound of a fly

All of these actions do not only occur in the browser area, but also on the button bar and on the browser bar which occupies the bottom of the screen. ...

When the user tries to touch the fly using the mouse, the insect reacts randomly: it reproduces either action 3 or action 4.

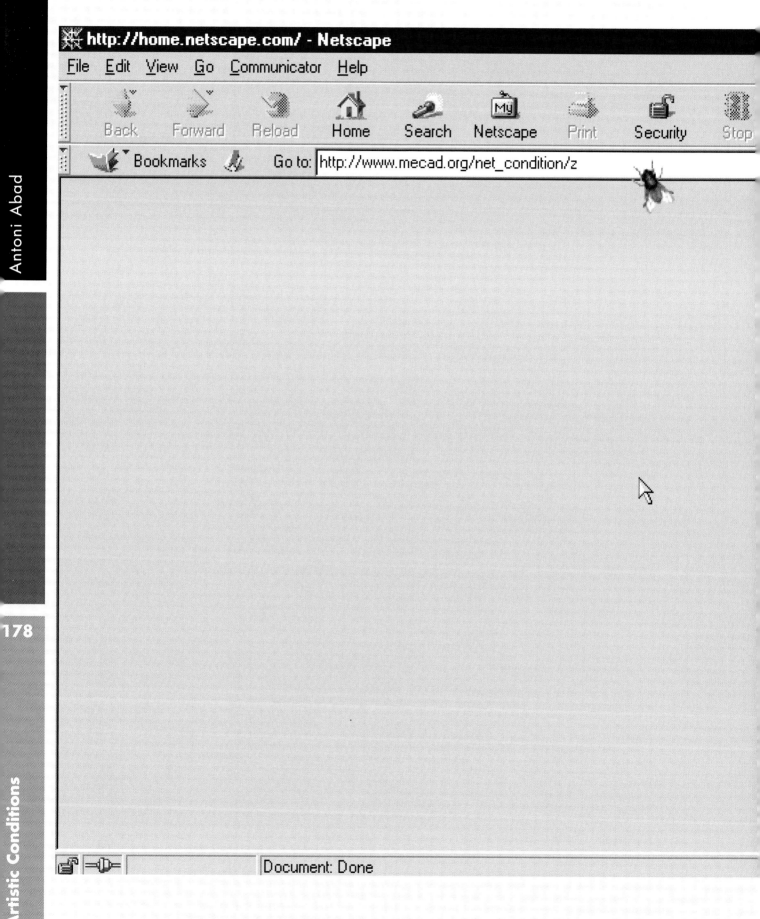

The fly on the screen works as an active element (being) out of context and out of control, as an element that subverts the (pre)established functions of the Internet. The aim of this project is not to 'communicate,' but to encourage the user to think about the restrictions imposed on communication through mass media. There is an impossibility to 'catch' (control) completely the medium and its elements, which are dispersed all along the chaos of the net (in the same way as the fly flies chaotically through the screen). Therefore, in this project 'flying' and 'browsing' the Internet acquire a certain similarity.

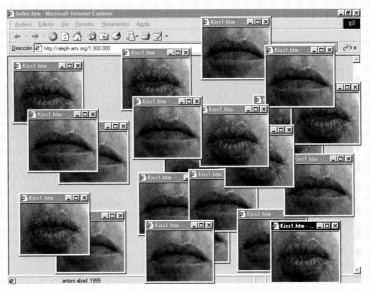

# the book after the book

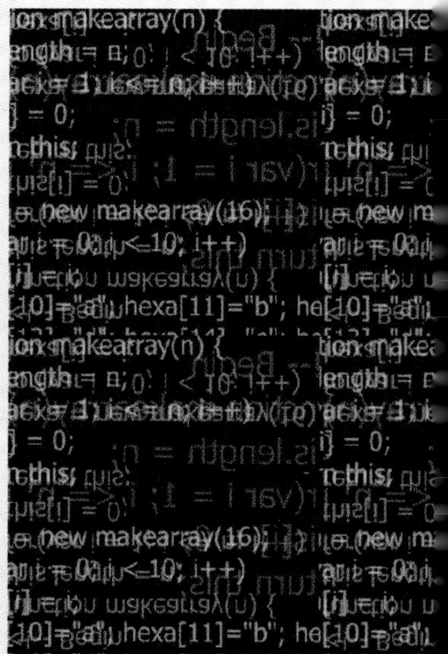

the book
after
the book

The Book after the Book is a hyper-textual and visual essay about cyber-literature and the net_reading/writing_condition. Its main focus is non-linear ... works that provide programming language a textual appraisal, creations that resort to videographic procedures in literary construction and play on the passivity and participation of the reader.

Short animations intercept the reading of other artist's works playing with the textual condition of the on line image and, at the same time, with the imagetic condition of the screen text. They are all images that perform texts and face the strange passage imposed by the net. Deep down, on the back of the

by the cultural industry. It invites the thought that Literary History is also the history of reading and of the supports where the interaction between reader and text takes place.

A gesture repertoire, a tactile game between hand and paper (or mouse), a constellation of objects and vision instruments defines the position of reading in this world. Unstable positions, no doubt. Here is Borges' enigmatic *Book of Sand*. A book in which it is impossible to return to the page which has been read. The Book of Books. The book of

## Index of /the_book_after_the_book

page, at the source, a situation is defined: the Internet is no more than a big text. On the front, at the screen, text reveals itself as image.

The History of Literature after the book is a history that has run on very stable grounds since the Renaissance. It is as surprising as it is undeniable. From the Classical Era to present days, the book, as an object, has changed very little.

This stability is, at least, intriguing, in view of the symbolic value attributed to the disposable product

reading.
... each turn implies a new reading itinerary, but any selection means to run the risk to change the path, to lose the starting point and to redirect the reading route....a new reading machine....a new interface.

The Book after the Book is a multidisciplinary device where the fusion of web art, criticism and web edition implodes the very notion of discipline and volume, shifting reading towards a net_epistemological_and_aesthetic condition.

# WAXWE

**David Blair**

http://www.waxweb.org

82

Make Jacob
a beekeeper who
designs flight sim-
ulators.
One day, the past arrives out
of the future, and Jacob enters:

25-section matrix
...nique to each shot.
descriptive text, and moving 3-D
image/ similar pictures,
interweave, coherently
leading the viewer from one media
to the next, within and between
shot matrices, always moving in
and out of the time of the movie.

a 'hyper- ...version
of ...theatri-
c... -distributed
e... ronic feature
'W... or the dis-
co... y among the
bee...

...the perceived boundaries
between the movie and the surrounding composition will dissolve, sending the movie into
extended time, as if it were a
temporary world (however
grotesque).

...any of
WA...S 1600
sh...s can be
c...cked,

B

Like a world, WAXWEB contains
more detail than any user, however attentive, could ever
absorb. ...

... the narrative's hypnotic,
allusive structure is endless
graphic resemblance, and the
pleasure of this meaningful
visual system is extended by
being placed flat in space,
rather than in time. This connective weave is furthered by hyper-
texts written for each shot,
offering allusion, new story, or
poetic redescription.

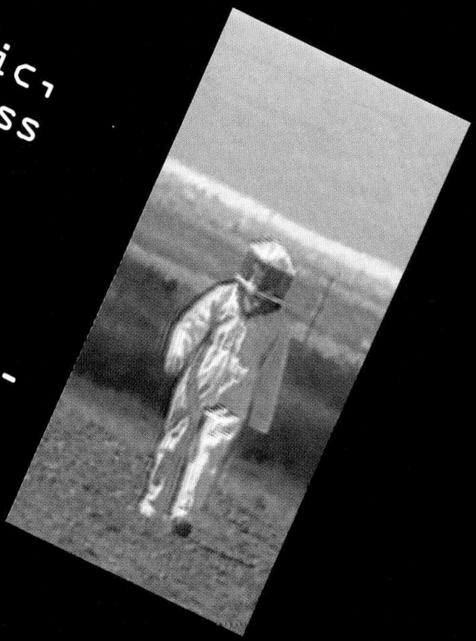

space becomes time...click a few
times...there are more than 1
...ion picture, hypertext,
...3-D links; the animated
...scenes would play 40
...s if placed end to end.
...t this is not a
...abase ... It
...s a movie...

## INTRODUCTION TO NET.ART (1994-1999)

1. NET.ART AT A GLANCE
A. THE ULTIMATE MODERNISM
   1. DEFINITION
      A. NET.ART IS A SELF-DEFINING TERM CRE-
         ATED BY A MALFUNCTIONING PIECE OF
         SOFTWARE, ORIGINALLY USED TO
         DESCRIBE AN ART AND COMMUNICA-
         TIONS ACTIVITY ON THE INTERNET.
      B. NET.ARTISTS SOUGHT TO BREAK DOWN
         AUTONOMOUS DISCIPLINES AND OUT-
         MODED CLASSIFICATIONS IMPOSED UPON
         VARIOUS ACTIVISTS PRACTICES.
   2. 0% COMPROMISE
      A. BY MAINTAINING INDEPENDENCE FROM
         INSTITUTIONAL BUREAUCRACIES
      B. BY WORKING WITHOUT MARGINALIZATION
         AND ACHIEVING SUBSTANTIAL AUDIENCE,
         COMMUNICATION, DIALOGUE AND FUN
      C. BY REALIZING AND ACTUALIZING TAN-
         GIBLE WAYS OUT OF AN INHERENTLY
         CONSERVATIVE AND OVERLY ACADEMIC
         ART WORLD PROTECTIVELY SHIELDED BY
         RADICAL THEORIES
      D. T.A.Z. (TEMPORARY AUTONOMOUS ZONE)
         OF THE LATE 90S: ANARCHY AND SPONTA-
         NEITY

3. REALIZATION OVER THEORIZATION
   a. THE UTOPIAN AIM OF CLOSING THE EVER WIDENING GAP
      BETWEEN ART AND EVERYDAY LIFE, PERHAPS, FOR THE FIRST
      TIME, WAS ACHIEVED AND BECAME A REAL, EVERYDAY AND EVEN
      ROUTINE PRACTICE.
   b. BEYOND INSTITUTIONAL CRITIQUE: WHEREBY AN ARTIST/INDI-
      VIDUAL COULD BE EQUAL TO AND ON THE SAME LEVEL AS ANY
      INSTITIUTION OR CORPORATION.
   c. THE PRACTICAL DEATH OF THE AUTHOR
B. SPECIFIC FEATURES OF NET.ART
   1. FORMATION OF COMMUNITIES OF ARTISTS ACROSS NATIONS AND
      DISCIPLINES
   2. INVESTMENT WITHOUT MATERIAL INTEREST
   3. COLLABORATION WITHOUT CON-
      SIDERATION OF APPROPRIATION
      OF IDEAS
   4. PRIVILEGING COMMUNICATION
      OVER REPRESENTATION
   5. IMMEDIACY
   6. IMMATERIALITY
   7. TEMPORALITY
   8. PROCESS BASED ACTION
   9. PLAY AND PERFORMANCE WITHOUT
      CONCERN OR FEAR OF HISTORICAL
      CONSEQUENCES. PARASITISM AS
      STRATEGY

      a. MOVEMENT FROM INITIAL FEEDING GROUND OF THE NET
      b. EXPANSION INTO REAL LIFE NETWORKED INFRASTRUCTURES
   11. VANISHING BOUNDARIES BETWEEN PRIVATE AND
      PUBLIC
   12. ALL IN ONE:
      a. INTERNET AS A MEDIUM FOR PRODUCTION, PUBLICATION,
         DISTRIBUTION, PROMOTION, DIALOGUE, CONSUMPTION AND
         CRITIQUE
      b. DISINTEGRATION AND MUTATION OF ARTIST, CURATOR, PEN-
         PAL, AUDIENCE, GALLERY, THEORIST, ART COLLECTOR, AND
         MUSEUM

2. SHORT GUIDE TO DIY NET.ART
   A. PREPARING YOUR ENVIRONMENT
      1. OBTAIN ACCESS TO A COMPUTER WITH THE FOLLOWING CONFIGURA-
         TION:
         a. MACINTOSH WITH 68040 PROCESSOR OR HIGHER (OR PC WITH
            486 PROCESSOR OR HIGHER)
         b. AT LEAST 8 MB RAM
         c. MODEM OR OTHER INTERNET CONNECTION
      2. SOFTWARE REQUIREMENTS
         a. TEXT EDITOR
         b. IMAGE PROCESSOR
         c. AT LEAST ONE OF THE FOLLOWING INTERNET CLIENTS:
            NETSCAPE, EUDORA, FETCH, ETC.
         d. SOUND AND VIDEO EDITOR (OPTIONAL)
   B. CHOSE MODE
      1. CONTENT BASED
      2. FORMAL
      3. IRONIC
      4. POETIC
      5. ACTIVIST
   C. CHOSE GENRE
      1. SUBVERSION

2.NET AS OBJECT
3.INTERACTION
4.STREAMING
5.TRAVEL LOG
6.TELEPRESENT COLLABORATION
7.SEARCH ENGINE
8.SEX
9.STORYTELLING
10.PRANKS AND FAKE IDENTITY CONSTRUCTION
11.INTERFACE PRODUCTION AND/OR DECONSTRUCTION
12.ASCII ART
13.BROWSER ART, ON-LINE SOFTWARE ART
14.FORM ART
15.MULTI-USER INTERACTIVE ENVIRONMENTS
16.CUSEEME, IRC, EMAIL , ICQ, MAILING LIST ART
D. PRODUCTION

3. WHAT YOU SHOULD KNOW
A. CURRENT STATUS
1.NET.ART IS UNDERTAKING MAJOR TRANSFORMATIONS AS A RESULT
OF ITS NEWFOUND STATUS AND INSTITUTIONAL RECOGNITION.
2.THUS NET.ART IS METAMORPHISIZING INTO AN AUTONOMOUS DISCI-
PLINE WITH ALL ITS ACCOUTREMENTS: THEORISTS, CURATORS,
MUSEUM DEPARTMENTS, SPECIALISTS, AND BOARDS OF DIRECTORS.
B. MATERIALIZATION AND DEMISE
1.MOVEMENT FROM IMPERMANENCE, IMMATERIALITY AND IMMEDIACY TO
MATERIALIZATION
a. THE PRODUCTION OF OBJECTS, DISPLAY IN A GALLERY
b. ARCHIVING AND PRESERVATION
2.INTERFACE WITH INSTITUTIONS:
THE CULTURAL LOOP
a. WORK OUTSIDE THE INSTITUTION
b. CLAIM THAT THE INSTITUTION IS EVIL
c. CHALLENGE THE INSTITUTION
d. SUBVERT THE INSTITUTION
e. MAKE YOURSELF INTO AN INSTITUTION
f. ATTRACT THE ATTENTION OF THE INSTITUTION
g. RETHINK THE INSTITUTION
h. WORK INSIDE THE INSTITUTION
3.INTERFACE WITH CORPORATIONS: UPGRADE
a. THE DEMAND TO FOLLOW IN THE TRAIL OF CORPORATE PRODUC-
TION IN ORDER TO REMAIN UP-TO-DATE AND VISIBLE
b. THE UTILIZATION OF RADICAL ARTISTIC STRATEGIES FOR
PRODUCT PROMOTION

4.CRITICAL TIPS AND TRICKS FOR THE SUCCESSFUL MODERN
NET.ARTIST
A. PROMOTIONAL TECHNIQUES
1.ATTEND AND PARTICIPATE IN MAJOR MEDIA ART FESTIVALS,
CONFERENCES AND EXHIBITIONS.
a. PHYSICAL
b. VIRTUAL
2.DO NOT UNDER ANY CIRCUMSTANCES ADMIT TO PAYING ENTRY
FEES, TRAVEL EXPENSES OR HOTEL ACCOMMODATIONS.
3.AVOID TRADITIONAL FORMS OF PUBLICITY. E.G. BUSINESS
CARDS.
4.DO NOT READILY ADMIT TO ANY INSTITUTIONAL AFFILIATION.
5.CREATE AND CONTROL YOUR OWN MYTHOLOGY.
6.CONTRADICT YOURSELF PERIODICALLY IN EMAIL, ARTICLES,
INTERVIEWS AND IN INFORMAL OFF-THE-RECORD CONVERSATION.

        7.BE SINCERE.
        8.SHOCK.
        9.SUBVERT (SELF AND OTHERS).
        10.MAINTAIN CONSISTENCY IN IMAGE AND WORK.
     B. SUCCESS INDICATORS: UPGRADE 2
        1.BANDWIDTH
        2.GIRL OR BOY FRIENDS
        3.HITS ON SEARCH ENGINES
        4.HITS ON YOUR SITES
        5.LINKS TO YOUR SITE
        6.INVITATIONS
        7.E-MAIL
        8.AIRPLANE TICKETS
        9.MONEY

5. UTOPIAN APPENDIX (AFTER NET.ART)
   A.WHEREBY INDIVIDUAL CREATIVE ACTIVITIES, RATHER THAN AFFILIA-
     TION TO ANY HYPED ART MOVEMENT BECOMES MOST VALUED.
        1.LARGELY RESULTING FROM THE HORIZONTAL RATHER THAN VERTICAL
          DISTRIBUTION OF INFORMATION ON THE INTERNET.
        2.THUS DISALLOWING ONE DOMINANT VOICE TO RISE ABOVE MULTI-
          PLE, SIMULTANEOUS AND DIVERSE EXPRESSIONS.
   B. THE RISE OF AN ARTISAN
        1.THE FORMATION OF ORGANIZATIONS AVOIDING THE PROMOTION OF
          PROPER NAMES
        2.THE BYPASSING OF ART INSTITUTIONS AND THE DIRECT TARGETING
          OF CORPORATE PRODUCTS, MAINSTREAM MEDIA, CREATIVE SENSI-
          BILITIES AND HEGEMONIC IDEOLOGIES
             a. UNANNOUNCED
             b. UNINVITED
             c. UNEXPECTED
        3.NO LONGER NEEDING THE TERMS 'ART' OR 'POLITICS' TO LEGIT-
          IMIZE, JUSTIFY OR EXCUSE ONE'S ACTIVITIES
   C. THE INTERNET AFTER NET.ART
        1.A MALL, A PORN SHOP AND A MUSEUM
        2.A USEFUL RESOURCE, TOOL, SITE AND GATHERING POINT FOR AN
          ARTISAN
             a. WHO MUTATES AND TRANSFORMS AS QUICKLY AND CLEVERLY AS
                THAT WHICH SEEKS TO CONSUME HER
             a. WHO DOES NOT FEAR OR ACCEPT LABELING OR UNLABELING
             c. WHO WORKS FREELY IN COMPLETELY NEW FORMS TOGETHER WITH
                OLDER MORE TRADITIONAL FORMS
             d. WHO UNDERSTANDS THE CONTINUED URGENCY OF FREE TWO-WAY
                AND MANY-TO-MANY COMMUNICATION OVER REPRESENTATION


NATALIE BOOKCHIN, ALEXEJ SHULGIN, MARCH-APRIL 1999

It's no more natural for humans to read sequentially than for buffaloes to roam in a single file.

True: the alphabet ruled us long enou‑

And one consisting of
only two characters at
that: zero and one.

Computer interfaces
are relying less and
less on the alphabet.

But it's just a
different form
of alphabet

The adversarial collaborations of Cohen, Frank, and Ippolito are devoted to foregrounding, rather than conceal-ing, the conflicts between different points of view. In some projects, the conflict in question is directly among three artists. _Agree To Disagree Online_ is an interactive map of an argument that begins when one of the three makes the statement, 'In the future, books will be replaced by maps.' As each of the artists replies in turn, each statement is plotted according to how much agreement it garners from the other two partici-pants: inflammatory statements remain on the periphery, while the center represents consensus. Visitors to the project can control the pace and level of detail of the argument as well as choose to follow digressions made to different topics. _Agree To Disagree Online_ gives visual form to the flame wars and com-munications breakdowns that characterize Internet culture.

In other projects on the site, the three collaborators mess with other people's artwork or ideas. When the influential site ada'web was archived at the Walker Art Center, the director of new media there commissioned Cohen, Frank, and Ippolito to make sure there is an archivist-albeit an irreverent one-to tend for it. Rather than respecting the integrity of the original Web pages, _The Unreliable Archivist_ recombines the texts, images, and other components of ada'web to create alternative versions of the typal ada'web page to suite viewer's site. This archivist alters an arche-preferences, thanks to sliders (with settings from 'plain' to 'preposter-ous') that control language, images, style, and layout. By showing that the archived version of ada'web may actu-ally be less than the sum of its parts, Cohen, Frank, and Ippolito ask what it means to archive or 'fix' such a dynamic medium.

# ASCII History for the

Contemporary ASCII - Netscape

File  Edit  View  Go  Communicator  Help

Back  Forward  Reload  Home  Search  Netscape  Print  Security  Stop

Bookmarks  Location: http://www.vuk.org/ascii/  What's Related

**CONTEMPORARY ASCII**

**Exhibition  Catalogue**

Instant ASCII Camera    Vuk Cosic
Deep ASCII            Lev Manovich
ASCII Music Videos      Tim Druckrey
Vinylvideo            Ted Byfield
History of Art For the Blind    Frederic Madre
ASCII Unreal

www.vuk.org

Document: Done

Artists dealing with technology today are falling in the trap of accepting somebody else's creativity as their limit and in this way they are becoming adver-tisers for equipment. One possible reaction for an artist is to investigate the misusage of technology as a gesture of freedom, and in this way oppose the mainstream taste and expectations. Works and experiments with moving ASCII, ASCII audio, ASCII camera and such are all directed towards conversions

# of Art
# Blind

```
##########################################
Instant ASCII Camera    http://www.uuk.org/
##########################################



            '==\]|_
          .,:~+++=|!|8r
         '~+=\/]}}[Z6t
       ,:!+\*[}C2kkkE
      :~++|/}IZ$XXXkkZZZZkEH
    ::=+/*}I22k$$XX2Z2kkkk
   "CC}1!.      "[]CCZIIZ$$kkkk$EZZZ2kkkk
 ($_,!++=\+!-,'+][+[]]]CZ$$k$XXkZkEE$2k2kk
~2;    "!.:-"]*CII2k| "\\*}ZIC$$Zk$X00$kkkkk
       ";  '[ZC\_.::::!==22kXXXXkkkkkX
 ~/}Z/+.   .*|*}||\**}II2$XXXkkkkkkkkX
   !II[//}2XkCCC+. .~/C2XXXkkkkk$Xkkk
  : '~|}Z}}=\\/I}[C\+/I2$XXXkkkkXXX$XX
   '||::.  !*I[[[}IC2kX00Xks$kkXXX$Sk
  . +IC/+_:++|/IZkXXEE0H0EXXXXXXkkX$kk
  !$Z*]=.~[C[}}[IZk$00000H0E$kE0000XXXXkk
 |2C**][]}[[[}+,.  .'::::|*CZ/"=Zk0X00$$2kX$2Z2
Z[IICCCCC[[}IZC[}CCCCI$2/|++==+-'+2$E0XkXX$2kXXX$2
ZZCIZ2$2CCC2k2IZICCCCZIIZZZZZ2kkk222$XXk$Xkk2kXXX$X
$XX2kXXk2IZ2$Zk ZkkkZCZZZZk ZZZZ2$$k$$$XXkXXk$kEXXks
2$XE$kXX$2Z2$$k22kkkX$2Zk2kkkZkkkX$k$E$kk$$kkXXXXX



24.09.1999              TOTAL:  922


##########################################
keep AVL ART GATE clean      DON'T LITTER
##########################################
produced at ljubljana digital media lab
```

```
##########################################
Instant ASCII Camera    http://www.uuk.org/
##########################################

::',.,          ,...,!*2XEQ}ZXZ0MB80O0X\|*}[II
-,           .,,!}E880080XXXX$2Z2kE00088B080H0[
          ,CEEXXXEEXXXXXkkZZZIZZk$X0888888000
       "ZIC[[+: .,:.  .+|/IXkk$X0H8888QH8
      !/\|!, :+\|:!-  :+|/IIk0008888B08
      ,//=+:-.       :!+]C2X00H88888E0
    "***||/\+_     .=]}IkXXEXr=2G0
    !]]]$XI]]}/+-    ,:+:::~',]E0
    .*"  .\$Hk1:       ..+=!CkX
    :   .!=+:.      ,,,,,,,,::,.+2$E
  .+:    !I}1+:,,  ,,,,,-:~"!+|ZC28008
   \XI]\"!"*XEI]/\+!~~~++==|]][IIE088
    !2k||,!!=!***//\\\\/][IkZCCIXXE0E
   +0XkI[\+=+=|=\\/*[C2XX2}[[[C$kI$E0
   +H0EZ]\=++++=|*[ZEQkZCCCC[[[CXE0088
   fXXEEE000XXE8Q0X0EQE2I**\|=+=4Q00H88
   /E8B8000HQ00I\=\CZC}**/\]X088GHG
  '2M#0Q8GH880H888EXEkI/*[IZ[1\/}CC[*}}20X0888
:-.=HM8888888@M888880]]*\/*}/|*[}/\\/*CC[}IEk}2QG
\088BMMMMMM@B8MBM88880}\//*|||//\\|=++=/[***/|[}[[
88BMM88MMMMMMMMMMB8B8s1*\/*][/][*\|==|/**[/******
MMB88MBMMMMMMMMMMB8M#}]***}j"}[[[*\/*][***]*[[*[
MMMMMMMMMMMMMMMMMMMMB2[][]]Z[[[[][[]CCCCCCCCC
MMMMMMMMMMMMMMMMMMMMMGkZC}]CCCCCCCIIZZZZZZCZZ

24.09.1999              TOTAL:  954

##########################################
keep AVL ART GATE clean      DON'T LITTER
##########################################
produced at ljubljana digital media lab
```

of contents between one media platform and another, every time carefully directed at their full uselessness from the viewpoint of everyday high tech and all it's consequences. I try to look into the past and continue the upgrading of some marginalized or forgotten technology. Gebhard Sengmueller calls this the "fake archaeology of media."

WRITE, PERFORM, OR SING ANYTHING YOU WANT TO ADD IN WHATEVER LANGUAGE YOU LOVE OR USE ANYTHING YOU WISH TO SAY ABOUT YOURSELF OR ABOUT THE WORLD AS IT OUGHT TO BE IN 2000 A.D.

BE AS INTIMATE OR AS UNIVERSAL AS YOU WANT TO BE

IF YOU WANT TO CONTRIBUTE A BOOK OR NOVEL OR SCIENTIFIC PARADIGM DO SO. THE ONLY RULE WE HAVE, LIKE THE RULES IN A CHILD'S GAME, IS:

DOWN WITH PERIODS!  NEVER END YOUR SENTENCE!

WE WON'T ALLOW A SINGLE PERIOD UNTIL...

WE ARE ALL FINISHED ADDING ON TO THE (THE WORLD'S FIRST and probably longest COLLABORATIVE SENTENCE)

WHEN WILL THIS BE?

WHEN WE ARE ALL EXHAUSTED OR THE SENTENCE IS THREE MILES LONG OR TAKES ONE FULL DAY TO CALL UP AND READ ON YOUR COMPUTER TERMINAL.  THAT IS....

FEBRUARY 15, 1995, IF NOT BEFORE (2/15/95 IS A MYSTICAL NUMBER)

BUT ON 2/15/95 THE ARTIST IN WARSAW DECIDES THAT THE SENTENCE CAN NEVER END BECAUSE HE HAS NO RIGHT TO STOP THE WORLD FROM WRITING. THAT DECISION IS IN THE HANDS OF GOD, DESTINY, EVOLUTION, OR THE WEB ITSELF.

(This statement is recorded on the site: it is one small clause inside the infinite sentence.)

# Séance

In the version of this work produced for net_condition, there are two spaces. One space is nearly filled by a stage that is like a box or a large table, with a stepped roof that disappears into the ceiling of the room. The scale of things is skewed. On this electrified stage is a robotic telepuppet (with a video camera and microphones in its head) looking a bit damaged – its head is bandaged and the body is wrapped up – in something of a human form. It is a new form of one of the puppets from my earlier work <u>where I can see my house from here so we are</u> (1993-95). The projected digital backdrop of this stage is inhabited by a floating head which is a software agent driven by artificial intelligence. Its role is that of an artificial actor with whom the telepuppet may converse; this agent provocateur has the power of conversation – it understands spoken language and responds in a synthetic voice. It floats in and out of the changing landscape as the one behind the telepuppet speaks with it, coming and going in various disguises – as smoke or flames, people from the past, imaginary beings, or as a frozen corpse – and acting like a speaking fountain given to rhyme, alliteration, and seemingly prophetic speech.

In another space, what is seen by the telepuppet is projected to fill a large wall – things in this space are 'life-size,' including the visitors to the other space when seen by the telepuppet. In the middle of this room is a small table, out of which emerges a human skull. The skull is a force feedback joystick device and it is the means of moving the telepuppet. When the telepuppet bumps into its boundaries, one feels this in the resistance of the skull. The one controlling the movement of the telepuppet in this space has a microphone for speaking with the visitors and with the artificial actor, and this person's voice is transmitted to the telepuppet and moves the telepuppet's mouth, like that of a ventriloquist's doll.

# Box No. 1

These two spaces (and four computers running backstage) are connected on a local network, but they may as easily be in different parts of the world, connected by the Internet. The exhibition of <u>Séance Box No.1</u> in this state is an experiment during its development. In fact, it is really not meant, when completed, to be interacted with directly by the public. Rather, the telepuppet is meant to perform in a specific role with an actor controlling it, and, though it is capable of carrying on something like a conversation, the 'intelligence' of the artificial actor was written to respond to specific cues in dialog, much as a real actor does. There is also to be an actor who performs in the puppet's stage space. When the work is completed, these spaces, stages, and figures are to be the setting and props for a performance, titled "Séance."

# <<Impressing

## Speed is fun...

Speed can provide an unusual
experience for perceiving the
world. It is a distorted view.
In the situation of high-speed
driving, the view of an automobile driver is distorted, but
the final perception is correct-
ed by our brain program to the
normal view. The fun of high-
speed driving is caused by the
generation of an endorphin in
the brain for sustaining the
process of revision.
The aim of producing this art
piece is to develop a special
algorithm to distort the view of
the viewer, instead of viewing
the actual view in front of him.
An algorithm abducts the process
by which our brains normally
perceive, accelerating the
motion.

## The algorithm of distortion:

The image is captured by a CCD
camera mounted on the car and is
mapped onto the virtual screen
in computer space. This screen
is distorted according to the
data grabbed by an accelerometer
mounted on the car. This virtual
screen is rendered with two view
points to generate stereoscopic
images. The viewer will see a
fully three dimensionally distorted screen where the captured
image is mapped. The basic algorithm for distorting the screen
is: when the driver accelerates
the speed, the center of the
screen will zoom toward the
driver, when one turns right,
the center of the screen will be
stretched to the left. And more,
corresponding the brightness or
some other factors, the surface
of the screen will be embossed
or enlarged.

# Velocity<<<<

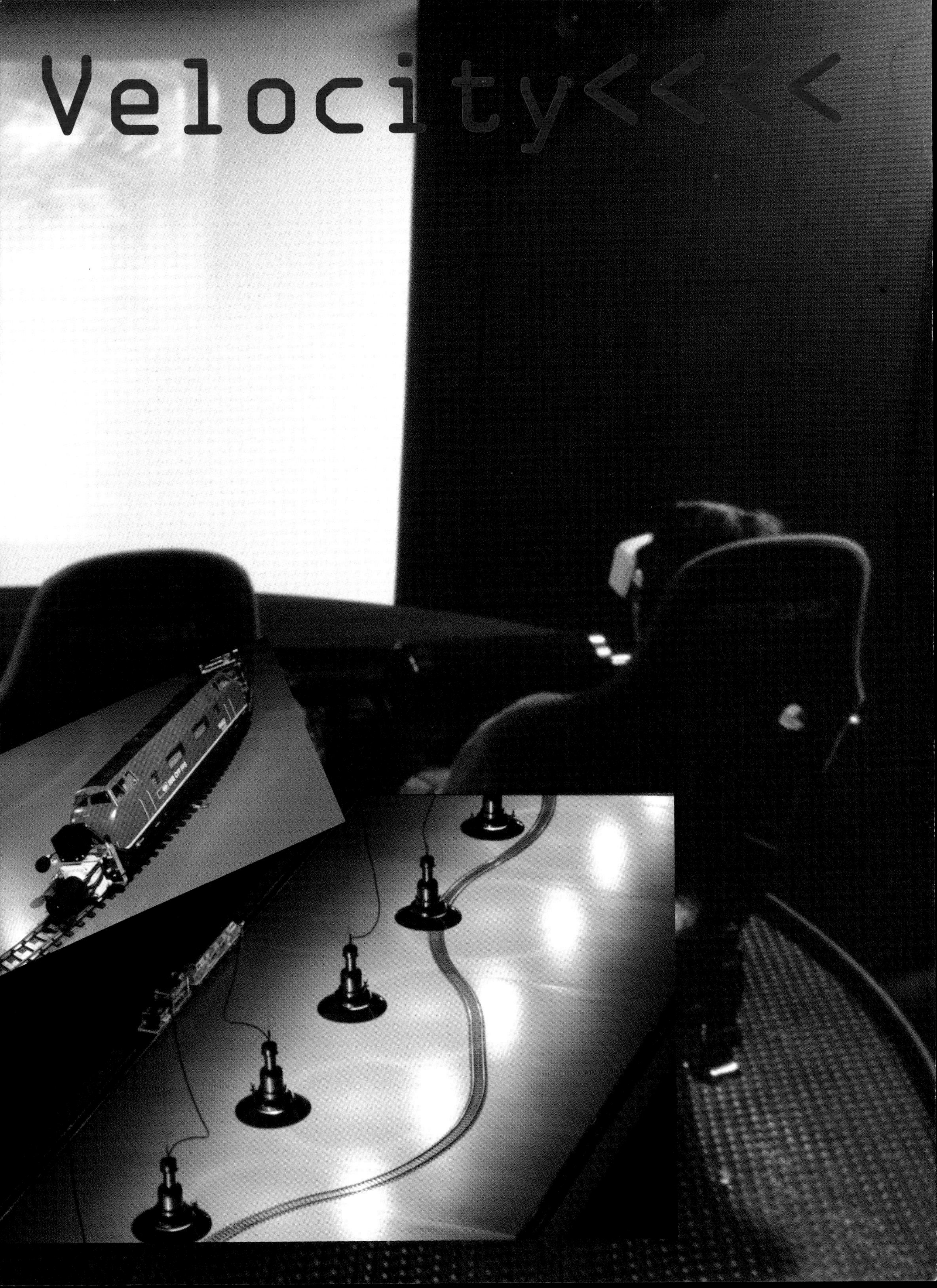

"With cubes and pyramids, one does not move around the object for the sense of the whole, the gestalt, to occur. One sees and immediately 'believes' that the pattern within one's mind corresponds to the existential fact of the object. Belief in this sense is a kind of faith in spatial extension."
Robert Morris, 1968.

"... electric light escapes attention as a communication medium precisely because it has no 'content'."
Marshall McLuhan

# DISLOCA

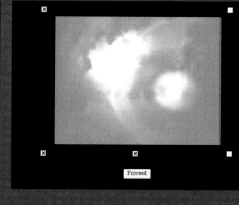

"Much like Charles Ray's 'Inkbox,' where the illusion of the cube's perfect sides is belied by a container filled completely to the lip with ink, a double-take drawing us into the piece, 'Dislocation' through its odd mechanics, announces immediately that it won't be dealing with notions of optical gestalt, but more complex relationships that unfold over distance and time."
David Hunt, FlashArt 1999

"I cannot see a cube, a solid with six surfaces and twelve edges; all I ever see is a perspective figure of which the lateral surfaces are distorted and the back surface completely hidden. If I am able to speak of cubes, it is because my mind sets these appearances to rights and restores the hidden surface."
Maurice Merleau-Ponty, 1945.

# OF INTI

"The images from the Dislocation of Intimacy reintroduce contemplation in a media where flow and movement are the common attitude. They not only freeze light but also time in a fragile balance....your computer screen has become pure light, a shadow."
Annick Bureaud (Paris), review in Leonardo Online, 12/97.

This project is part of an ongoing investigation into telepistemology: the study of knowledge obtained at a distance.

# T I O N

Proceed    Proceed    Proceed

Dislocation of Intimacy explores the relationship between the immediate and the mediated. The
installation focuses on a sealed black steel box
accessible via the Internet. "The user selects
from among five lights, clicks the button, and
receives a surrealist and mysterious shadow,
which arrives at the user's screen in gray-scale
and without content."
Sandro Alberti, translation (from Spanish),
1997

"We are surrounded with
assumptions and distortions
that make our unique vantage
points hard to see....In the
box, I saw evidence of
objects, but nothing clearly.
This clarified for me what is
often overlooked: what I saw
were representations of
things...this is all that
media can deliver."
Michael J. Ryan (Philadelphia), viewer log 10/97.

# MACY

## Essay on Ontological Solitude No.1

Markus Huemer

http://www.khm.de/~huemer

Artistic Conditions

Entering a darkened physical space, the visitor sees a real chair covered with golden fabric along the axis of symmetry, a static projection on the end wall showing yellow writing and greyish-blue shadowy pictures in the background, and a viewing point marked on the floor by a source of light. When the visitor steps onto this marked viewing point in the room, lights go on dazzling the recipient, and the projection begins to display terms generated from the internet. One can only see what is going on in the projection with difficulty, as the light also shines on the projection. But something is happening (that-certainty as opposed to what-certainty). Or to be more precise: every possible position that the viewer can move to in the room – except for the marked spot – conveys to the recipient the impression that the installation is standing still as no concepts are being produced in the projection. When he steps onto the marked position in the room, the installation is activated, otherwise it is inactive, which means that this is the only position for reception. Only in this position does the recipient himself become an acting, interacting functional element of the network, albeit greatly restricted in terms of his interactive abilities.

The sources of light cast a shadow of the recipient on the wall opposite the projection; in turn, this shadow is visible as a background image in the left half of the projection. In the right half of the projection, the shadow of the uncovered chair can be seen which, in turn, constitutes the constant to the shadow of the recipient. A camera equipped with a trigger system measures the shadow sets on the back wall. As long as the visitor stays on the marked spot, the complement of these two shadow sets filters the concepts taken from internet newsgroups focused on left-wing socio-political issues. When the recipient leaves the marked spot in the room, the lights go out, the production of concept sets is discontinued, and the projection stands still once more. Only now – afterwards – does the viewer recognise what he has produced – and he can read the concepts or at least what is left from the filtering and generating process in the projection. In turn, the viewer is called upon to link the concept sets with semantic units, which constitutes the instructions for the recipient. In order to generate these units of meaning, the recipient would have to step back on the marked spot and re-establish a link with the net.

http://www.humbot.org

is a project that involves many different authors, around 20, each with their own area of expertise. It is a project where a simple single leading concept doesn't exist, because it is the sum of different layers that interact with points of contact in an ongoing process, building and accumulating regions of interaction. The ordering element is the explorer and mapmaker, Humboldt.</A12>

<P02 - Karlsruhe - T(r)opical Chor(e)ography - 14.02.99> 05.06.1799. Alexander von Humboldt takes his first step into a virtual maze of mischarted territory, heading

Puerto Cabello — CARACAS — Cumaná — Nueva Barcelona — Caripe — Calabozo — San Fernando de Apure — Angostura (Ciudad Bolívar) — Puerto Ayacucho — San Fernando de Atabapo — Duida 2400 m — Esmeralda — San Carlos

across oceans, up and down rivers, through jungles and swamps, over plains and peaks, around the forsaken torrid zone of equinoctial America. Accompanied by an indefatigable confrere, M. Aime Bonpland, and a provisional host of itinerant liaisons between station and stopover, they all arrive at their quasi-fictional characters in a shared documentary epic unfolding in 30 tomes over 20 years (1807 - 1827) - text mappings and passages - stemming from Humboldt's pen. Humboldt (and his readers) enter the chora between human nature and nature, in the trajective space linking private

mappings (psychogeography) and public mappings (geography). The Humboldt expedition endures five years (1799 - 1804) and still endures two centuries later as a cluster of topoi, conceptual starting points, for tele-travellers rehearsing a getting-around on the 7th Continent, where the affective spatiotemporal measure of geography is drawing to a close.</P02>

<Alexander von Humboldt - Paris - "Personal Narrative of a Journey to the Equinoctial Regions of the New Continent" - 1811> "The more travellers research into natural history, geography or political economy, the more their journey loses that unity and simplicity of composition typical of the earlier travellers. It is now virtually impossible to link so many different fields of research in a narrative so that what we may call the dramatic events give way to descriptive passages."</AvH>

<Werner Heisenberg - USA - "Physics and Philosophy" - 1963> "One has now divided the world not into different groups of objects but into different groups of connections ... The world thus appears as a complicated tissue of events, in which connections of different kinds alternate or overlap or combine and thereby determine the texture of the whole."</W.Heisenberg>

<R13 - Cologne - h|u|m|b|o|t.release - 04.07.99>
In the era of mass tourism, where every destination seems to be reachable at any moment, the artists achieve a relocation of traveling. In form and content, they go on an exploration journey using the

communication technology of
the internet to sketch a
narrative structure which
is guided by the methods
of cartography.</R13>

<Melquiades - Gabriel
Garcia Marquez - "100 Years
of Solitude" - 1967>
"They placed a gypsy woman
at one end of the village
and set up a telescope at
the entrance to the tent.
For the price of five rea-
les, people could look into
the telescope and see the
gypsy woman at arm's length
away. 'Science has eliminated distance,' Melquiades
proclaimed. 'In a short
time, man will be able to
see what is happening in
any place in the world
without leaving his
own house'."
</Melquiades>

<A12 - Milano
22.05.99>
A firewall is an
electronic protec-
tion to avoid
intruders breaking
into a net system
and causing damage.
It creates an in-
side and an out-
side. To get into
the inside you need
to know the coded
words. Sometimes you
slide inside, some-
times you crawl
under a small pas-
sage, sometimes you
climb a stair,
sometimes you enter a tun-
nel. The intention is to
inject real life and confusion into a system, the
Internet, seen as lacking
any physical presence. The
hypothesis is to give physical evidence to one of
the metaphors of Humboldt:
the travel as an intimate,
personal discovery of the
self. The intention is to
have that space as an hypnotic womb, in opposition
to the active and dynamic
piazza outside.</A12>

<Paul Virilio - Paris -
"Open Sky" - 1997>
"Between the subjective and
the objective it seems we
have little room for the
trajective, that being of

movement without which we
will never achieve a pro-
found understanding of the
various regimes of perception of the world."
</P.Virilio>

<P02 - Karlsruhe - Dailies
- 10.10.98>
h|u|m|b|o|t on-line is a
hypermedia 'well' fed by
audiovisual traces of situations encountered by its
authors in contemporary
Cuba and Venezuela and
ØtherWhere (1999 - 2004).
This evolving matrix of
knowledge is mapped according to a connective topography with a cut-up ver-
sion of AvH's "Personal
Narrative." An activist
aesthetic arises in the

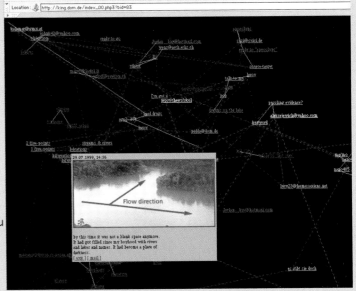

Zwischenraum spanning the
authors' hypernarratives,
added to the 'well' over
time, and paths trodden by
our participants, drawn
from this 'well' of expe-
rience, each leaving a
trace that informs future
user itineraries. In short,
authors (AvH and
h|u|m|b|o|t) realize a
'cyberatlas,' through which
users may 'travel' in
search of 'moby.'</P02>

<Ismael - Herman Melville -
"Moby Dick" (The Chart) -
1851>:
"... in the solitude of
his cabin, Ahab thus ponde-
red over his charts. Almost
every night some pencil
marks were effaced, and

others were substituted.
For with the charts of all
four oceans before him,
Ahab was threading a maze
of currents and eddies,
with a view to the more
certain accomplishment of
that monomaniac thought of
his soul."</Ismael>

<F01 - Zurich -
flatbook/flatmovie -
08.06.99>
So the idea is that there
are two maps humboldt (him)
and h|u|m|b|o|t (us) that
have their own keyword
system and visual identity
and then are woven into
each other, by collapsing
keyword space into one. The
thing will store input from
authors as objects with

dual: technical require-
ments, desires, security
impositions, the many and
different skills of several
workers, various and com-
plex, sometimes opposed
cultural backgrounds (it
might sound like a silly
joke, but although all the
staff of ZKM marvelously
supported all our ideas and
made us able to realize
the project, we are sure
that no one will ever buy
an Italian car in the
future). All these and a
thousand more ingredients
compose the h|u|m|b|o|t
favela. Like in a card-
deck, all the elements of
architecture were all present during the process,
but mixed in a different

properties and organize it
in multidimensional maps
according to selected properties. These maps are
being displayed from different positions and perception modes, output media
etc. to other authors/users
who will perceive the
objects and generate more
input/properties ... cycle
ad infinitum = knowledge
metabolism machine / col-
lective brain / social
technology.</F01>

<A12 - Genoa - multi-indi-
vidual - 15.10.99>
As much as the authorship
of the h|u|m|b|o|t web site
is multi-individual, the
responsibility of its presence in the first Lichthof
of the ZKM is multi-indivi-

order. But not only identities and the relationships
between their social and
creative roles are blurred,
but much more, the disci-
plines which seem to be
inserted in the project.
In its totality h|u|m|b|o|t
works as a overlapping of
various layers (the wood,
the maps on the web-site,
the images running on the
screens, the historical
traces), which fold and
create points of contact
and accumulation, where new
spaces are created, in a
dynamic system, where in
real time everything is
modifying.</A12>

<Robert Smithson - New York - "Artforum" (A Sedimentation of the Mind) - 1968>
"Words and rocks contain a language that follows a syntax of splits and ruptures. Look at any word long enough and you will see it open up into a series of faults, into a terrain of particles each containing its own void."</RSmithson>

<A12 - ibid> Why shanty functionalism? The core of the h|u|m|b|o|t architecture is just to have what's needed in order for the space to be useful and comfortable, so the machines can work properly, so the users may be able to enter the project freely. ary spatial sketches (that only the museum's closed circuit cameras may testify to), bargaining for space and compromises with the curators and the resulting sum of the elements is just one step of this ongoing process. Therefore the mass of energy and material spared become almost ridiculous. In its sponge-like attitude of inclusion, either of positive but also of negative elements, the h|u|m|b|o|t installation works as a relational architecture, physical evidence of immaterial processes.</A12>

<Alexander von Humboldt - ibid> "In considering the

Florian Wenz <F01>, Philip Pocock <P02>, Daniel Burckhardt <D03>, Udo Noll <U04>, Gruppo A12 <A12>, Roberto Cabot <R13>, Elena Carmagnari, Wolfgang Staehle, Juergen Enge, Birgit Wiens, and Others.

There wasn't a clear concept or poetic to rationally develop following some sort of hierarchy.
The process of design wasn't canonical, because it sought the interaction of all involved in the project convinced that cyberspace is found on both sides of the screen, inside the cathode tube as well as inside the museum space. This attitude magnified any possible dysfunction and diseconomy: in fact it has been a process of construction deriving from a trial and error technique. This means that Humboldt's steps where traced in the books, in the jungle and in the web site; the installation was built without one drawing, moving large amounts of furniture, making tempor- study of physical phenomena, not merely in its bearings on the material wants of life, but in its general influence on the intelligent advancement of mankind, we find its noblest and most important result to be a knowledge of the chain of connection, by which all natural forces are linked together, and made mutually dependent upon each other; and it is the perception of these relations that exalts our views and ennobles our enjoyments. Such a result can, however, only be reaped as the fruit of observation and intellect, combined with the spirit of the age, in which are reflected all the varied phases of thought."</AvH>

# III.Immersion
# Bar Code

The digital processing of data enables various individual experiences of each viewer by establishing the real time link as the information highway connecting real space, virtual reality space and global net space. The self-organisation of the system (artificial intelligence), direct interactivity of real space with the synthetic one, the simulated model, the composition of acoustic elements in real time and fragmentation, the uninterrupted visualisation of a computer generated sound picture of space and the openness of the system create chaotically structured complexity. Systems of identification, which proceed from the passive into the active state, represent new virtual borders and filters of the communication society in view of the systematic control and manipu-

lation. As a result, each viewer develops the perception of his digital body in the state of dying as his
direct experience within which the entry to the system unconsciously transforms into the ritual of sac-
rifice. The body mass provides the key information.
Transformations of the user's body mass (weight and
height) into a digital form are presented as bar code
prints. A laser scanner reads the bar code and transmits the data to the host computer, which then
applies the data as a variable in the virtual sonic
society (three-dimensional sonic organisms). The
reaction to the variable is presented with the help
of four loudspeakers, 4 projection canvases and the
use of stereo glasses in real space. The project is
composed out of three levels.
<u>The third level represents the expansion of virtual</u>
<u>space into the global one.</u> When the user connects to
the server, the virtual sonic community gets cloned
and transfers to the user's remote computer, where it

starts to function utterly by itself. The cloned members of the virtual community abide by the survival
law and self-preserved organisms, which transfer as
hereditary records from the residential virtual
environment to the cloned one.
Each input information (the user's digital body mass
in the gallery space) is transferred from the residential virtual environment to the remote cloned
community, which responds to the newly established
situation, in real time. Concurrently, the cloned
community sends data on to where the user is positioned
and all changes that occur due to his/her movements
to the residential virtual community. The user of the
remote computer, who strolls among the cloned members
with the help of the VRML interface, obtains his/her
virtual presence in the residential virtual environment (he/she is illuminated with the red color).

Marc Lafia

http://www.vanndemar.com/

208

Artistic Conditions

# Vanndemar Memex

The Vanndemar Memex or Laura Croft Stripped Bare by her Assassins, Even is a rumination on the many fascinating tropes of extended self, distributed narrative, artificial life, collective intelligence and emergent systems. The Memex, set up in the context of a game, re-assembles Duchamp, Vannevar Bush, video games and many contemporary art works proposing an engine from which works happen. The work is structured as a series of events, organized by episodes, a tool set, narrative tracks and collective networked actions.

# Bare by her

The user first selects a code name, then an image that tells the machine something of their psychological type and soon is set along a path.

# Even

Look, ads. The Diva has reportedly been sited in Hong Kong. Apparently she was spotted there with others involved in the advance prototypes of the new memex.

The sound sampler on my memex is jammed and I can't get a lock on the Diva's signal. I know you're not fully trained yet, it may be awkward handling at first...

but if you're willing to try, if you can just decode the transmission, we might be able to track her.

Hong Kong

CHRONOLOGUE / chandler > kryptonite > ella

MEM3X

## The Memex

With use of the Memex the user moves in a world of surveillance cameras, secret directives, AI constructs, remote droids, accidents, collective prosthetics and onto the creation of a new construct of self. In later episodes the Memex is set up for multi-user communications where actions are built upon previous actions, establishing a complex irreversibility in the process.

# or Laura Croft Assassins,

## The Game

The network begins to teem with 'bodies', 'ghosts', 'taps', 'taps of taps', 'assassins' and 'echoes'. In this transitive landscape you are to seamlessly transpose your 'self' through the extension of agency. With the tools of the networked memex you are to discover who is speaking to you, who is giving you directives, who you've become an operative for, and how 'you' are being constituted in this vast space of agency, identikits and remote operation.

Interesting choice, Jade. So the psyche test says you're an intuitive... That should come in handy.
We're so glad you've replied to Vanndemar's invitation. The Vanndemar engine is essentially a memex. What is a memex?

To be blunt, the engine is a fully transitional tracking device that can create ghost echos from any sensory input device. You've heard of taps, haven't you?

Well, we're tapping the taps. And the input isn't just the old cartesian coordinates. It's live hunt in virtual or physical environments.

You see the need for restricted access. But your psycheID scored high. And that means security clearance. Hit the memex to proceed.

CHRONOLOGUE / chandler > kryptonite > ella

MEM3X

### The Chronologues

Five characters speak to this machine of allegory, of seduction, articulating a meditation on the confabulations of the illusive muse. These intersecting narrative tracts propel one to seek out DV7A.

### The Plot

You are instructed to go to remote cameras, construct an avatar. An accident happens; you somehow unwittingly, unknowingly have taken control of a remote robot, a teledroid. This accident suggests your avatar needs reprogramming along the instructions of the AI Kryptonite. He instructs you to dismantle certain communication lines, identikits and persuasion apperati. With the use of photographs, identikits and contemporary art, you create new landscapes of imagery resulting in new spaces of meaning and possibility. You will need to rebuild your aesthetic and social pre-dispositions to propel yourself with the necessary escape velocity into disembodiedness where you are asked to give up your body to venture into unknown spaces. This can only happen from varied and multiple locations and the collective actions of fellow users. You, in effect, have been catalyzed by DV7A.

### The Possibilities

The Vanndemar Memex explores many of the emerging tropes of the net, asking how is it we give representation and operativeness to multiple fictionalized and extended selves and how such actions and this technologic landscape form collectives. An exploration of interface and virtual agency, the Vanndemar Memex or Laura Croft Stripped Bare by her Assassins, Even extends the user's capabilities and identity across varied networks in a new modality of extreme permeability. Through the speed of agency, the extended self is collected and convulsed in all sorts of instances dissolving boundaries of identity and self. As the game is iterated, it becomes a system of traces and taps, and the users' passage through it becomes the next users' point of entry. The work explores the mythic desires invested in the network as both a space of collective action and human transformation. The Vanndemar Memex simultaneously constructs and unravels narratives of self, history, politics, communication and society: it is an engine in which new possibilities are forged.

Netscape    Images    Print    Security    Stop

What's Related

Culture

+  |  -  |  ·  |  <  |  >

c 2000 marc lafia
meme-x engine

In computer jargon,
ftp for short, is the
transfer protocol.
While Olia Lialina
as the asphalt of the
a chance to display the
processes and file

is an attempt to break up
to be able to embark
intensive journey into

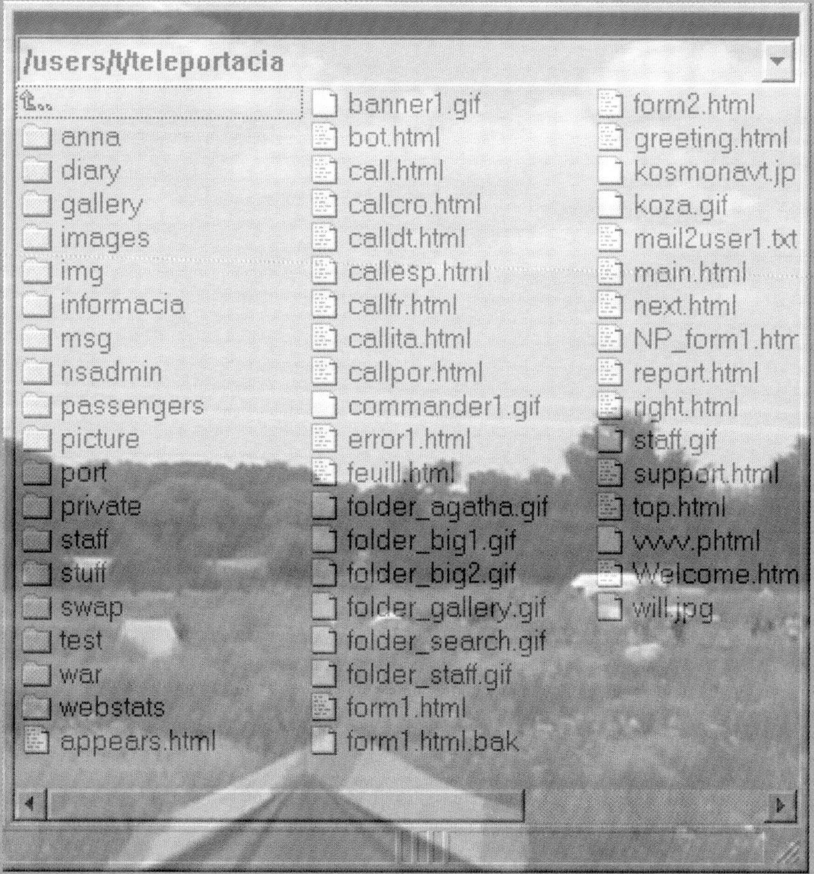

**/users/t/teleportacia**

| | | |
|---|---|---|
| 🔼.. | banner1.gif | form2.html |
| anna | bot.html | greeting.html |
| diary | call.html | kosmonavt.jp |
| gallery | callcro.html | koza.gif |
| images | calldt.html | mail2user1.txt |
| img | callesp.html | main.html |
| informacia | callfr.html | next.html |
| msg | callita.html | NP_form1.htm |
| nsadmin | callpor.html | report.html |
| passengers | commander1.gif | right.html |
| picture | error1.html | staff.gif |
| port | feuill.html | support.html |
| private | folder_agatha.gif | top.html |
| staff | folder_big1.gif | vvv.phtml |
| stuff | folder_big2.gif | Welcome.htm |
| swap | folder_gallery.gif | will.jpg |
| test | folder_search.gif | |
| war | folder_staff.gif | |
| webstats | form1.html | |
| appears.html | form1.html.bak | |

**/users/t/tel**

| |
|---|
| 🔼.. |
| anna |
| diary |
| gallery |
| images |
| img |
| informac |
| msg |
| nsadmin |
| passeng |
| picture |
| port |
| private |
| staff |
| stuff |
| swap |
| test |
| war |
| webstats |
| appears. |

er Protocol

name of an Internet file

describes the WorldWideWeb
Internet, she sees ftp as
inner workings of web
structures.

er Protocol

the rigid surface so as
on a more beautiful and
the heart of the net.

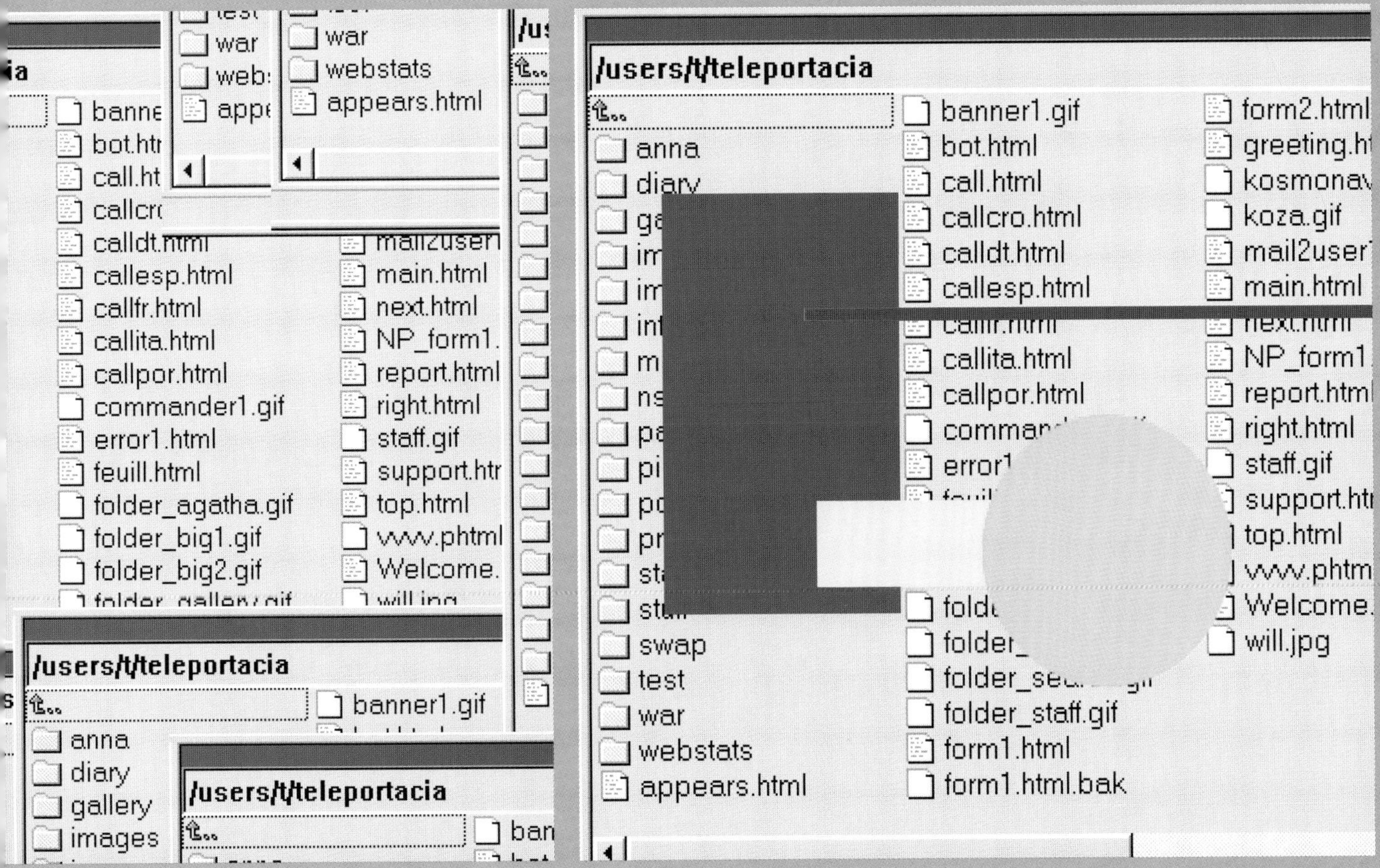

/users/t/teleportacia

| | | |
| --- | --- | --- |
| banner1.gif | form2.html |
| bot.html | greeting.ht |
| call.html | kosmonav |
| callcro.html | koza.gif |
| calldt.html | mail2user |
| callesp.html | main.html |
| callfr.html | next.html |
| callita.html | NP_form1. |
| callpor.html | report.html |
| commander1.gif | right.html |
| error1.html | staff.gif |
| feuill.html | support.htr |
| folder_agatha.gif | top.html |
| folder_big1.gif | www.phtml |
| folder_big2.gif | Welcome. |
| folder_gallery.gif | will.jpg |

anna
diary
gallery
images

war
web
app

war
webstats
appears.html

mail2user
main.html
next.html
NP_form1.
report.html
right.html
staff.gif
support.htr
top.html
www.phtml
Welcome.
will.jpg

anna
diary
ga
im
im
int
m
ns
pa
pi
po
pr
sta
stu
swap
test
war
webstats
appears.html

# The Freud-Lissitzky Navigator

# What is The Freud-Lissitzky Navigator?

The Freud-Lissitzky Navigator is a computer game prototype; a software narrative; a virtual exhibition; an imaginary software; a tool to navigate through 20th century cultural history; an experiment in developing analysis of new media which uses the very forms of new media (in this case, computer games and software interfaces).

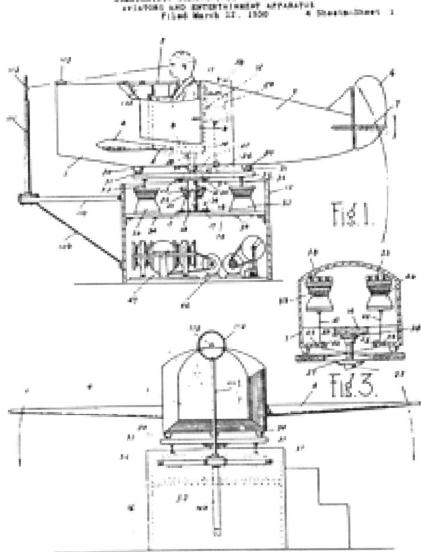

Sept. 29, 1931.

E. A. LINK, JR

1,825,462

COMBINATION TRAINING DEVICE FOR STUDENT AVIATORS AND ENTERTAINMENT APPARATUS

Filed March 12, 1930

6 Sheets-Sheet 1

Fig.1.

Fig.3.

[From Game Narrative]:
In the summer of 1928 Sigmund Freud meets with the avant-garde Russian designer El Lissitzky and his wife who are spending some time in Vienna after a stressful period working on the Soviet Pavilion at the International Press Exhibition in Cologne. They talk about psychoanalysis and modern architecture. Freud tells Lissitzky that in 1908 he visited Coney Island and went to a park called 'Dreamland.' There he got the initial idea for the architectural realization of his theory. Lissitzky gets very exited about this idea. They decide to create an architectural construct based on Freud's model of the mind. What shall it be? Lissitzky points out the parallels between Freud's model of the consciousness/ unconsciousness as articulated in Interpretation of Dreams and Marx's model of base/superstructure (they don't know that it also parallels Saussure's model of signified/signifier). Freud still thinks of the 'Dreamland' park, but Lissitzky convinces him that rather than building a one of a kind museum or park, they should design mass housing -- a popular idea with the avant-garde architects of the second half of the 1920s and something which Lissitzky, who until now could not realize any of his big-scale architectural projects, was eager to do.

Chihiro Minato

http://www.ntticc.or.jp/special/
net_condition/index_e.html

is an interactive work based on the

of Changes (I Ching) and is designed

ination. ——— The key-title screen

divination from which the player must

the process of divination. ——— Each

——— By finding the message, the

After repeating the (unconscious)

final image resulting from the

screen. ——— This

By finding this

ther. — The choi

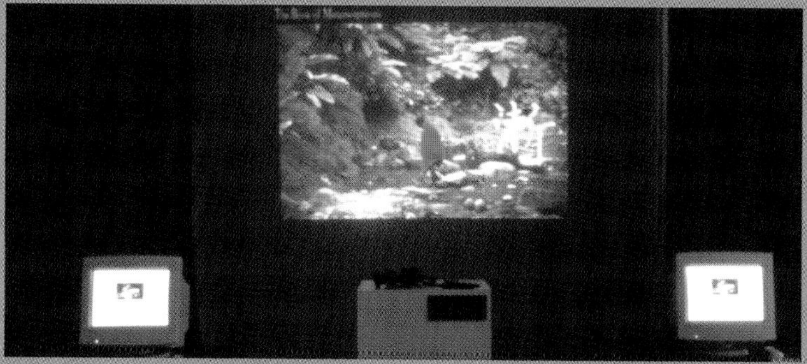

The Book of M

the screen like the cracks in a tur-

——— By finding the hidden key, the

played and can be viewed and walked

predetermined. ——— Instead, the

is touched to produce the experience

ancient Chinese classic of the Book

for experiencing the process of div-

contains 384 images pertaining to

chose one image. ———— This starts

image contains a hidden message.

player goes to the next image. ————

selection process six times, the

selections is displayed on the

image also contains a hidden message.

message, the player can advance fur-

ces made by the player appear on

tle shell used in divination.

route taken by the player is dis-

through. ———— The route taken is not

route changes according to what key

of the process of divination.

http://www.ntticc.or.jp/special/
net_condition/index_e.html

.engulf..engulf.

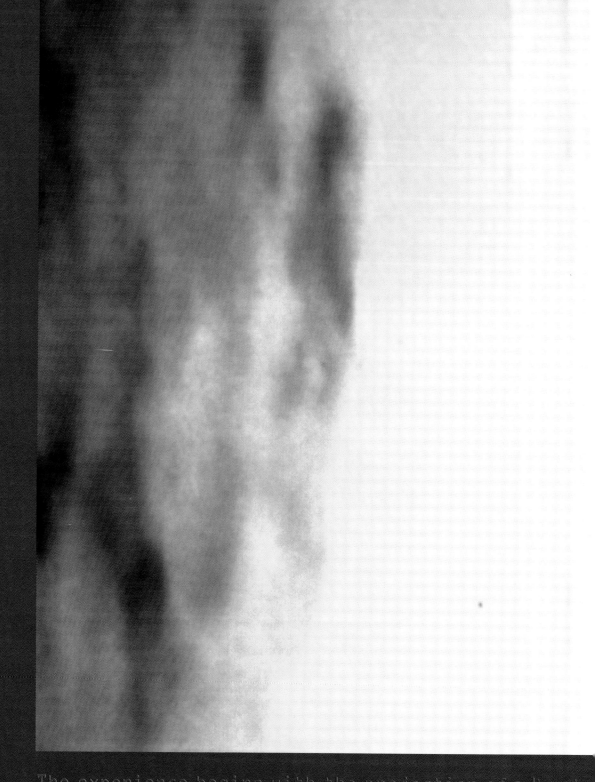

The experience begins with the projection of a 4 mete
waves radiate out in slow motion from the center o
slowly return toward the center. The image is highl
waves. For instance, a tear shed in zero-gravity doe
dynamic movement of a thundering water fall creates
wound, female genitalia? **The ambiguous juncture of**
**its reaction. While being an interactive work, inter**
net does not generate a dramatic effect. This is a re

engulf . . . The . . .

igh and 1.5 meter wide image of a beach. Gradually,
he beach. The beach is engulfed and the waves
bstract and the waves may not even be understood as
ot fall but remains suspended; for instance, the
he illusion that it is frozen in time; an open
the semi-consciousness (waking and sleeping) and
activity has been removed. Accessing it through the
action closer to sleep. This is a meditative reaction.

**Randall Packer**

Telematic Art as Collective Agency for Cultural Transformation

"A technical planetary system keeps its balance, describes elliptical paths or sends elongated constructions with fixed wings out into the distance, aeroplanes of infinity."
El Lissitzky

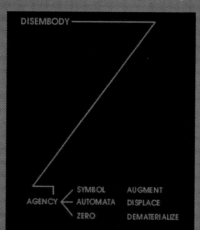

DISEMBODY

SYMBOL   AUGMENT
AGENCY   AUTOMATA   DISPLACE
ZERO   DEMATERIALIZE

"The cooperative action of discrete agencies, such that the total effect is greater than the sum of the two effects taken independently - where we could say that synergism is our most likely candidate for representing the actual source of intelligence."
Douglas Engelbart

"A future collective society is the only possible basis for the full development of our creative life."
Ma Group

**The Telematic Manifesto** is a call-to-action: a plan to create a participatory, collectively-generated Net Document that will articulate a vision for the future of Telematic Art as a socio-cultural force in the 21st Century. This project investigates Telematic Art as the synthesis of art, culture, and global tele-communications, now pervasive with the recent proliferation of Net Art, and its promise for a revitalized artistic expression resulting from an inherent interconnectedness catalyzing aesthetic, technological, philosophical, and cultural transformation.

**The Telematic Manifesto** will recontextualize the ideologies and ambitions of aborted avant-garde movements whose efforts to bring about artistic, cultural, and political change through collective action - from the Italian Futurists to the Surrealists, from the International Faction of Constructivists to Fluxus - lay dormant as unfinished business at the close of the Century.

TELE
MANI

History has also shown that the evolution of computer science has tended towards collective action: the dream of a free exchange of information and new forms of human and technological interaction. From Norbert Wiener's seminal theories on the science of Cybernetics to J.C.R. Lickliders research in Man-Computer Symbiosis, to Douglas Engelbarts creation of a networked information space designed for the Augmentation of Human Intellect that would Boost the Collective IQ, these visionary scientists laid the groundwork for an emerging medium that is now transforming every aspect of human communication.

In an effort to define and engage these artistic, scientific, and cultural forces of change, the Telematic Manifesto will serve as a conceptual framework articulating the collective, cross-disciplinary ideologies of artists, theorists, academics, curators and scientists participating in net_condition. Throughout the fifteen weeks of the exhibition, an email list and threaded discussion will be moderated by Randall Packer that introduces a series of themes relevant to historical and contemporary issues outlined above, stimulating dialogue among the participants of net_condition. An accompanying Website will provide contextual information informing each of the topics of discussion.

The resultant texts will be organized, edited and archived as the Telematic Manifesto, a hypertextual, Web-based Millennial Record, a Net Document that will generate a constellation of prescient themes surrounding Telematic Art: its transformative properties, aesthetic issues, virtualizing forces, historical significance, the collapse of spatial and temporal boundaries, and its future implication for a new artistic sociopolitical ethic in the broad context of a rapidly changing networked, global village.

"Rather than distribute a message to recipients who are outside the process of creation and invented to give meaning to a work of art belatedly, the artist now attempts to construct an environment, a system of communication and production, a collective event that implies its recipients, transforms interpreters into actors, enables interpretation to enter the loop with collective action."
Pierre Lévy

MATIC
FESTO

# Net·Art Browser

is a means of conjoining information space with the museum space and hybridizing the interactivity of surfing the Internet with the museum tradition of wall mounted images. While painting, cinema and TV construe images inside a fixed frame, the notion of 'augmented reality' that accompanied the development of the virtual reality technologies offers the new paradigm of a mobile viewing window that reveals images that are spatially embedded in the real environment.

Using this model, the Net·Art Browser's web sites, curated by Benjamin Weil, are virtually placed side by side along a white wall. A motorized large flat screen (linked to a cableless keyboard) allows the viewer to move this display window linearly (in either direction) from one Internet-connected web site to another.

Jeffrey Shaw, 1999
Curator:
Benjamin Weil

CCTV - World Wide Watch

Improve self policing with further absented police force

###### irational.org (heath bunting)

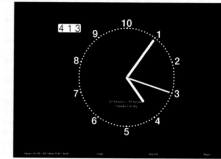

4 1 3    10    9    8    7    6    5    4    3    2    1

Heath Bunting

CCTV
http://www.irational.org/cgi-bin/cctv/cctv.cgi?action=front_page

CCTV - World Wide Watch
Improve self policing with further absented police force

The Internet Beggar
http://www.irational.org/heath/skint

Skint - The Internet Beggar
Lurking in piss and puke stinking alley of the info supa high way squating almost invisibly in piles of corporate data trash the internetbeggar only concerned with his own addictions tries to blag a dollar off disgusted passers by

>Excuse me mister!
>could you spare a dollar?

ok you humble internet beggar
charge my:
there you go mate

>god bless you sir!

Claude Closky

12 HEURES = 10 HEURES
http://www.fraclr.org/closky
(courtesy FRAC Languedoc Roussillon, France)

12:00 = 10.00 is a clock which measures time in base ten. The day in divided into 10 hours into 10 minutes each minute in 10 seconds.

1999 CALENDAR
http://www.arpla.univ-paris.fr/closky/1999/

Calender 1999 is composed of 365 pages, one for each day of the year.

DO YOU WANT LOVE OR LUST?
http://www.diacenter.org/closky

Seemingly endless sets of questions, all culled from recent popular magazines, relentlessly interrogate the reader's tastes, habits, and preferences.

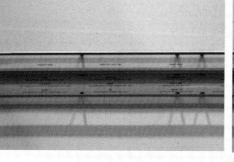

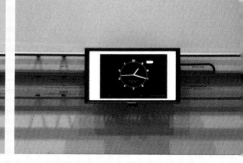

: Cosic

History of Art for Airports
tp://www.ljudmila.org/~vuk/history

ficial history of net.art
lume I

_r_
tp://www.ljudmila.org/~woelle/lajka/war/

ese few pages contain nearly random
reenshots of the night in front of
e tv set. Possibly there will be
re. The date was 24/25 of March 1999
d it's all about the bombing of Yu.

tablink
tp://www.ljudmila.org/~vuk/metablink/
tablon.htm
ourtesy Teleportacia.org)

Holger Friese

Antworten
Holger Friese und Max Kossatz
http://www.antworten.de
(courtesy private collection)

... At first, www.antworten.de looks
like a personalised waiting system for
public order at a doctor's or dentist's
surgery or at a butcher's shop. (...)
However, the underlying idea is that
it's never your turn. There is no answer. There is only waiting until you
miss your turn. Thus, the work pretends
to be something that it simply isn't.
It is a work about time, waiting,
patience, belief and perseverance. ...
Text excerpt from: Crash Test Dummies or The
Philosophy of Waiting? Hans Dieter Huber.

In meiner Naehe
http://www.inmeinernaehe.de

What seems at first glance to be a
useful interface of a shopping mall
that solves an annoying problem: the
shops are presented in relation to a
specific place. Doctors and galleries,
plumbers and drinks services, even a
reputable escort service ? all manner
of services are featured. But why are
there no addresses or phone numbers
anywhere? And why is Mr Stroemer suddenly Mr Einstein?

Unendlich, fast...
http://www.thing.at/shows/ende.html

... "Unendlich, fast..." confuses users
accustomed to commercial sites for one
thing because the work consists of a
single page. A single page with a single image (small stars and lines, a
graphic of a screenshot of an EPS file
of the symbol for infinity, so the
author) positioned in a particular
place, waiting to be discovered. ...
Text excerpt from: An analysis of the creative process
in the work "Unendlich, fast...", Helia Vannucchi.

Olia Lialina

My Boyfriend Came Back from War
http://www.teleportacia.org/war/

Anna Karenina Goes To Paradise
http://www.teleportacia.org/anna/

Comedy in three acts and epilogue
starring inna kolosova

Agatha Appears
http://www.c3.hu/collection/agatha/
(courtesy C3, Budapest)

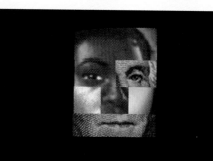

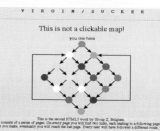

Antonio Muntadas

Mark Napier

Michael Samyn (GroupZ)

The Fileroom: Archive of Censorship
http://simr02.si.ehu.es/FileRoom/documents/homepage.html
FileRoom/documents/newhome.html
(produced by Randolph Street Gallery,
Chicago)

The Fileroom isan illustrated archive
on censorship which you can browse, as
well as add cases to.
The Fileroom acts not as an electronic
encyclopedia but as a tool for information exchange and a catalyst for
dialogue.

On Translation: The Internet Project
http://adaweb.walkerart.org/influx/
muntadas/
(courtesy Walker Art Center,
Minneapolis)

On Translation is a series of works
exploring issues of transcription,
interpretation, and translation.

RIOT
http://www.potatoland.org/riot

Rising Sun (10 Frames)
http://www.potatoland.org/seizure/
grid6f.htm

American Heroes
http://www.potatoland.org/studio/
faces/loadfmix.htm

Home
http://adaweb.walkerart.org/GroupZ/ho
(courtesy Walker Art Center,
Minneapolis)

In HOME there is a link on every pag
You just have to find it. Sometimes
things will happen which you didn't
expect, just sit back and wait.

Virgin/Sucker
http://adaweb.walkerart.org/GroupZ/
virgin/index.html
(courtesy Walker Art Center,
Minneapolis)

VIRGIN/SUCKER consists of a series o
pages. On every page you will find t
links, each leading to a following
page. No matter which choices you
make, eventually you will reach the
last page. Every user will have followed a different route, though.

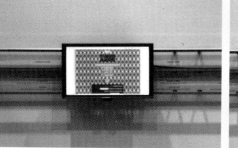

vian Selbo

ller @pp: It's @ll talk, 1998
tp://www.newmediacentre.com/
~tsofspeech

~tsofspeech is an episodic Web pro-
ct about digital communication and
entity. The first installment,
iller @pp: It's all t@lk," is a voy-
~ristic ride along the information
perhighway checking the intersec-
ons of email, networked databases,
d privacy.

rtical Blanking Interval, 1997
tp://adaweb.walkerart.org/project/
lbo

rtical Blanking Interval investiga-
s the gap between signals: the space
tween the keyboard and the chair,
tween need and desire, the net and
, push and pull, flattery and
nuendo.

closed Caption Viewing, 1996
tp://www.slate.com/SlateGallery/
-07-17/SlateGallery.asp

closed Caption Viewing is a sales
tch remix querying the promotion
the web as protoTV.

Alexej Shulgin

Form Art Competition
http://www.c3.hu/collection/for
m/
(courtesy C3, Budapest)

WWWArts Awards
http://www.easylife.org/award/

This Morning...
http://www.easylife.org/
this_morning/

Jake Tilton

Macro Meals
http://www.thecooker.com/here/
macro/meals.html

Cookie
http://www.thecooker.com/here/
cookie/cookie.

Try your luck fortune cookies,
do you feel lucky?, take your
chances,take whatever comes,
calculated your chances, assecc
risk ... select a bowl and
make your choice, let us know
how you feel

DIP
http://www.thecooker.com/here/
dip.html

Maciej Wisniewksi

Jackpot
http://adaweb.walkerart.org/
context/jackpot
(Courtesy Walker Art Center,
Minneapolis)

Jackpot is an Internet 'slotmachine'
that downloads three randomly selected
web sites and displays them in the
browser's window along with their top
level domain names. You win by matching
any of the top level domains. The winner can visit a live web site and submit a URL of choice.

Turnstile II
http://www.stadiumweb.com/
(Courtesy Dia Center for the Arts, New
York)

Turnstile II pulls information from
HTML pages, live chat, email archives
and other sources, and displays it as a
continuos, never-ending stream of text.
Clicking on the text takes you to the
information's on-line source.
ScanLink makes it possible to surf the
Web backwards. It starts with a Web
page and traces all the links to that
page from other pages.

Netscape: Verbarium home (c)99 (

# VERBARIUM

Christa SOMMERER
Laurent MIGNONNEAU

sunshine airways
free to expresion, priority to creation

SEND                    CLEAR

christa@mic.atr.co.jp        laurent@mic.atr.co.jp

Applet verbarium running

# Sommerer et Laurent Mignonneau

VERBARIUM is an interactive text-to-form editor on the Internet. At the web site, on-line user can choose to write text messages and each of these messages functions as a genetic code to create a visual three-dimensional form. Each different message creates a different form. Depending on the composition of the text, the form can either be simple or complex, or abstract or organic. All text messages together are used to build a collective and complex three-dimensional image. This image is like a virtual herbarium, composed of the various forms based on the different text messages (i.e., verbs), hence the name VERBARIUM. On-line users do not only help to create and develop this virtual VERBARIUM, but also have the option of clicking any part within the collective image to retrieve messages sent earlier by other users.

(c) 99, Christa SOMMERER & Laurent MIGNONNEAU, developed for CARTIER Foundation Paris, supported by IAMAS Academy Gifu Japan; JAVA: I. Kataoka

English ▼

# FIBER WAVE III

**Sei Makoto Watanabe**

http://www.ntticc.or.jp/special/
net_condition/index_e.html

228

Artistic Conditions

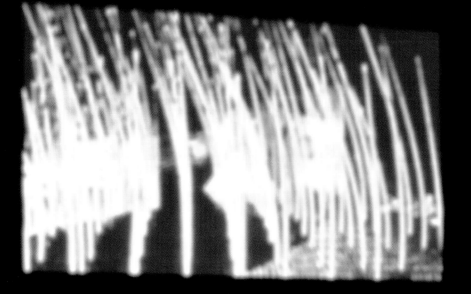

The wind is invisible. It is felt on the skin but not seen by the eye. The presence of wind is known from the swaying of the trees. The branches and boughs of trees function as projection devices for the wind. FIBER WAVE III consists of artificial boughs.

FIBER WAVE is on display in Gifu, the Tokyo waterfront, and in Chicago as a form of environmental art that does not use energy; it sways in the wind and uses solar energy to shine.

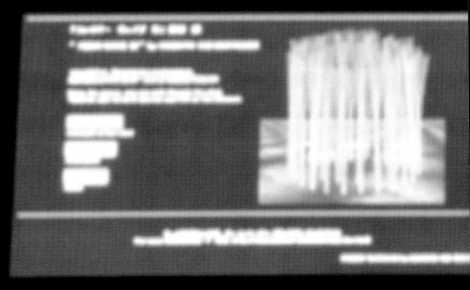

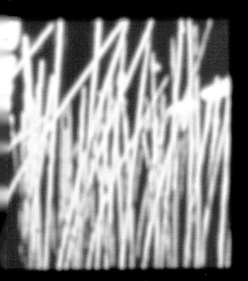

FIBER WAVE II is an indoor version and was newly developed as part of the ICC Digital Bauhaus. Using the Internet, this exhibit re-creates the wind conditions in other cities on a real-time basis. It also embodies outer space winds (solar winds and Jupiter winds) picked up by satellites, translates the changes in economic conditions into wind, and visualizes it as rustling lights. It uses analog/digital/analog processes to switch between virtual space and real space.

FIBER WAVE III deals with the phenomenon of wind in a fully virtual world. The participant can choose from an online menu of different types of wind and walk through and experience the wind blowing through the artificial boughs on a real-time basis. The Fiber Wave series offers adventures in a real/virtual world through wind.

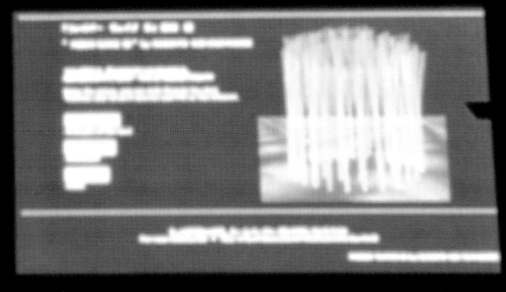

DJ Spooky: *Absolut DJ*

Whenever the subjects of music and the internet crop up in discussion, the central theme is usually the advent of total accessibility of all recorded music. Indeed, it must be assumed that Audio-On-Demand and the associated transformation of music consumption, starting with the actual treatment of the medium, will really change the way in which we listen to, and our conception of music, deep down to everyday contexts. The thing that is truly decisive in this form of media usage, however, is the use of the net in exactly the same way as the mass media of radio and television, as a range of programmes from a far wider selection is 'switched on.' This is not interactivity as we might normally understand it. The send channel of the user, which is supposed to set the networked computer far apart from the old mass media, plays a role no more complex than that of remote control.

If one asks for new impulses that the net can offer for the drafting and production of music, it very quickly becomes clear that the pioneering potential of the medium does not lie purely in making music more accessible. Two other aspects make the networked computer interesting for music making of the future. The first is the communicative use of the send channel of the listener; the second the capability of the computer that goes beyond the mere exchange of information, namely the ability to process information in a highly complex manner – control, modification or production of musically relevant data with the computer as a piece of equipment that need not be limited to the roles of display and remote control, but can instead function

as a workshop for the creation and manipulation of products and productive systems.

The musical interaction of the listener on the net can take place in differing extents of involvement and responsibility. On the basis of these various types of active reception, the changed role of music listeners on the net is examined, thereby concluding which functions will be assumed by music as a result of this change of roles.

## Musical feedback

The least conspicuous form of action by the recipient is expressed in the principles of the acoustic user surface and the reactive soundtrack. Under the synonymous terms audification and sonification or, more comprehensively, the full auditory display, work has been going on, for around ten years, on concepts and systems that signal the actions of the user, the development of data structures and the process conditions of a system, amongst other things with the aid of so-called earcons, thus creating an auditory equivalent to the graphic user surface.[1] So-called rollovers, for example as exist in the field of graphics, provide acoustic support for navigation in data space and processing time by improving intuitive and thus fast recognition and comprehension of contents and contexts.

At the next level, such a system can do still more, however, namely serve as the foundation or marking out of identity. We know this function in particular from the film soundtrack. The producer of the soundtrack cannot start from the point of a set picture sequence, as with a film, when transferring this principle on to the www, however. Instead, he must seek to implant a musically open arrangement onto the pages in order to take into account the unpredictability of user navigation. *Koan* potentially offers the technical basis for such a reactive soundtrack: the user's plug-in receives control data while loading an html page, e.g. the sounds are set off on the local soundcard. In this way the reaction capability of the

1. The commercial browser plug-in Beatnik provides such a system for the www.

system is guaranteed, as it is not fixed note values (play sound y' at point x) that are transmitted, but instead a wide-ranging record of control parameters that can be interpreted in variable ways ('use pitch combination y according to z rules in period x'). Such 'open composition' will produce slightly varied music with every new rendition.[2] In theory, however, this principle also makes it possible for a piece using musical means (in contrast to the technical acoustic means of the hard cut and iris diaphragm) to be made to pass into the next also by formulating differentiated rules for the art of the transition. The impression of greater liveliness of web pages, identification with their provider and increased recognition via musical memory can be just some of the potential effects of the www soundtrack and put it close to conventional advertising music.

One variety of the soundtrack is Peter Traub's installation *Bits & Pieces* (http://raven.dartmouth.edu/~peter/bits/). The continuous, completely automatic composition takes its sound material from new sources trawled from random discoveries on the net on a daily basis. Like a drilling core drawn from the deposits of the net, Traub's system brings together the acoustic manifestations of privacy, culture, politics and commerce and builds an endless organic soundtrack of the medium as a whole. A similar installation is *summer 99* (http://www.HDensity.de/summer.html) by the Austrian sha.™, which transports the sound-image of a Berlin back yard by means of a range of mirrors distributed worldwide across the net, before finally superimposing it with itself and portraying the specific transfer characteristics of the medium as fluctuating time delays in tonal and rhythmic variants. While *Bits & Pieces* concerns itself with the content of the net, *summer99* transforms its network structures into music.

## Musical control

The range of action is increased if the musical design by the user becomes the focus of planned action. DJ Spooky's

2. Brian Eno uses the term 'Generative Music' for this in the sense of 'self-generating', referring to Noam Chomsky's *Generative Grammar*. Cf. Akademie der Künst (ed.) *Klangkunst*, Munich/New York 1996, p. 55.

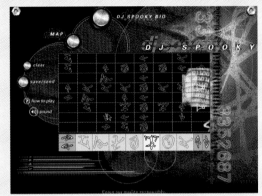

DJ Spooky: *Absolut DJ*

sonic programming of the software module *Absolut DJ* (http://www.absolut-vodka.com/map/spooky/sp_index.asp) combines typical DJ techniques – the use of loops and slowly developing patterns – with the possibilities of the www's graphic user interface: eight symbols, each of which embodies a complex sound, can be arranged in a grid in such a way that they are triggered by two cursors wandering through the field, one after the other. Stringing techniques are used to create a simple techno piece layered over the basic beat.

Although the interest in such relatively simple systems may soon fade as they quickly become transparent and lose their attraction, two interesting aspects can be observed: firstly, that the user develops a feeling of proximity to the DJ/artist as the listener may himself operate the sounds of the star; and secondly, that the site (and in this case, for example, its sponsor with it) is able to clothe itself in an identity specific to the target audience, concentrated within the musical ambience. The same effect as with reactive soundtracks is created – but in this case with an interactive component.

In the case of *electrica* (http://www.electrica.de), the actions of the user are also limited to the successive triggering, ordering and minimal modifying of sound. The five different interfaces whose patterns of behaviour remind us of the principle of the acoustic user interface, can increasingly be played masterfully as musical instruments following an initial period of exploration. Impressions of five different locations are simultaneously created that in the first instance seem to be only visual, but show their character most intensively through musical behaviour – music-making as a strategy of orientation.

## Musical regulation

The next more complex form of music-making develops when users are able to contribute musical material or modify the system behaviour of an already existing compositional apparatus. The most obvious form of this is collective improvisation, as realised for the net in the shape of *ResRocketSurfer* (http://wwwresrocket.com). Musicians with a keyboard and computer are able to get together in virtual studios with the help of the ResRocket software and, by contributing instrumental tracks created with the help of midi technologies, create a joint piece of music. The experimental opposite to the narrow limits of midi and its more conventional results is constituted by improvised live networking events on the net such as *Sound Drifting*

(http://thing.at/orfkunstradio/SD/) and *The Eternal Network Music Site* (http://www.mills.edu/LIFE/ CCM/Eteknal_Network_Music.html). Complex technical systems and personal networks unearth structures of sound, the immediate musical attractions of which are sometimes outshone by their non-hierarchical structure – the fascination with the idea of attempting to test social utopias by means of musical realisations.

With the possibility of collective compositions, the software synthesiser *FMOL – F@ust Music On Line* (http://www.iua.upf.es/~sergi/) – also takes a social topos as its theme. The compositional instruments of the Spanish composer Sergi Jordà, 'Bamboo' and 'Medusa', allow complex producers of sound to be constructed and operated via an intuitively comprehensible instrumental interface. The instruments, created to a large extent by the musician himself, in this way are connected to a database server that saves musical seeds and offers them to other authors as a collective com-

*FMOL – F@ust Music On Line*

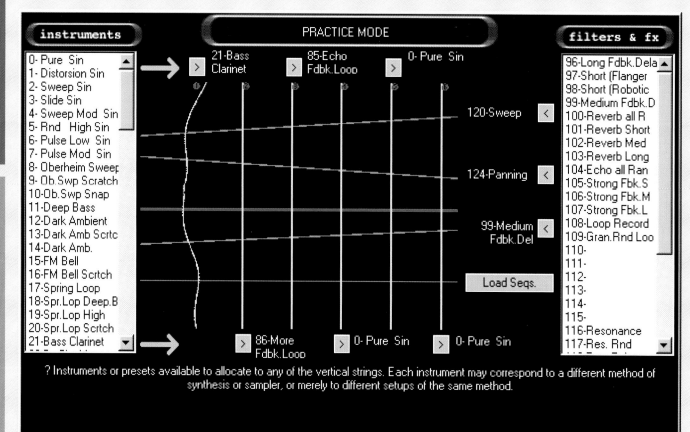

modity, so that they develop them further. The works grow and diversify according to rules of inheritance, into a range of different types of music of communal authorship.

Klaus Gasteier's *Dumb Angel · SMiLE* (http://www.cutup.de/smile/) makes use of the hypertext principle. Parts of the never-published Beach Boys album of the same name are put together by the listener as modules with the help of a graphic interface. As in hypertext, it is the recipient of this hypermusic who decides moment by moment which unit of meaning should follow the unit just played. Furthermore, even the system-specific database that controls the basic activities of *SMiLE* can be modified.

The examples listed in this category are characterised by their regulatory nature. While the musical control described above is based upon the principle of one-sided influence (the listener triggers individual events and the system reacts in a similar and predictable way), systems of

musical rules are characterised by mutual influence (the listener also modifies system behaviour – the system can demonstrate different behaviour patterns when identical actions are taken, thus provoking changes in the behaviour of the listener). Regulating systems of this kind can adapt themselves to changing external and internal conditions, i.e. autonomous of the commanding authority. In the sense of an artistic utopia, one could refer to movement towards an independent aesthetic authority.

SMiLE-Editor

## Musical Construction

The user is most immediately involved when he or she is put in the position to construct the entire interactive environment in its dimensions of tonal material, compositional apparatus and access options for other users. The above has been practised since the 1960s in the form of interactive sound-installations and algorithmic composition systems, but this was always based upon the know-how and advanced technical systems of scientific or commercial facilities. We do not necessarily have to draw on such rare local work environments in order to construct musical systems for the net. Rather, with a networked computer, all necessary information and resources are immediately available in their complete form. Ben Shneiderman uses the term 'Genex' (Generator of Excellence)[3] to describe the networked computer as a work environment able to fully support all stages of the creative process: the acquisition of the necessary knowledge via different research possibilities, practical innovation with the support of sophisticated software tools, the refinement of the result by means of expert supervision communicated across the net, and finally the wide-ranging communication of the results via different channels of the medium.

These Genex elements cannot all be found on one site, however, and are not collected by a central authority. Instead, they consist of an amorphous field of interlinked initiatives that offer or administer fields of topics that differ in size and quality. xchange (http://xchange.re-lab.net) is the point of contact for the large experimental net.radio scene, the source of know-how for the installation and operation of netcasting facilities and the mail forum with an archive on topical and technical questions concerning all types of artistic audio projects on the net. From this contact point (as well as many similar sites), paths open up to pools with free audio software, copyleft sound archives such as the Japanese GNUsic initiative (http://www.gnusic.net) and to a wide range of art projects. The link collection *hudba3000* (http://www.musikwiss.unihalle.de/hudba3000/) is intended to systematically exhaust the potential of the Genex principle for musical contexts and combine it with the scientific idea of an archive of net-based music.

The aforementioned four forms of activity of the recipients of net-based music, of varying intensity, show that the relationship between musician and listener is undergoing radical change. Following the

*resrocket3*

3. Ben Schneiderman: "Codex, Memex, Genex: The Pursuit of Transformational Technologies" in: *International Journal of Human-Computer Interactions*, 10 (2), 1998, pp. 87-106.

development of new forms of communication - such as in the field of sound art – but going much further – the hierarchical division of the roles of musician and listener that has been particularly characteristic of European art music is resolved into a continuum of possible roles between these two poles - from the unconscious trigger, through the active arranger, and from the contributor and modifier to the constructor of an entire musical system (not, it must be noted, a completed musical piece in the sense of classical work aesthetics).

The traditional gulf between the listener not actively involved in the music and the composer making all the decisions is completely filled out on the net. The appeal and usefulness of the new roles are waiting to be explored in this medium.

## The Constitution of Places

Something that is particularly noticeable about the projects described here is that they focus on aspects of how we perceive space or location. There is a clear parallel here with the artistic strategies of many sound installations.[4] The method of articulation of space in sound installations, therefore, finds an artistic expression of extension, materialistic consistency, manner of use or the atmosphere of physical space in general. Transferred to the specifics of virtual space on the net, this strategy can be found in the concepts of acoustic user interface, the 'netscape composition' of *Bits & Pieces* or the correspondence between visual and acoustic elements in *electrica*. The conditioning of space, in sound installations a tonal processing of a previously-found space, is expressed on the net primarily by the generic term 'soundtrack,' i.e. the atmospheric characterisation of a site by means of specific music, as is the central effect at sites such as *Koan* or *Absolut DJ*. The term 'exploration,' in contrast, describes a method of sound installations in which the discovery of spatial and systemic contexts by the recipient are at the forefront. Transferred to the context of network music, for example, exploration is found in the discovery of different spaces and instruments of *electrica* or in the hypertextual navigation through 'song snippets' of *SMiLE*.

The overall effect of these methods of net-based music can be described as the constitution of specific place perceptions. The experiences of dislocation and translocation, the specific reduction of stimuli in telematic communication and the blurring of borders of communication with humans and communication with machines all require new strategies to obtain a strong conception of a space in which it is possible to reside or act, as virtual space is amenable to very different rules than the physical space to which we are accustomed. Calculated netspace can be compared to the metaphor of geometric space as an abstract entity. But just what is the essence of a space, independent of its arithmetically calculable characteristics? Anthropology tells us that the difference between existential and geometrical space is that, in the former, people define their relationship to the world actively. Such space only gains identity, relation and history by means of experience of one's self based on action within a specific environment, becoming a bearer of meaning and thereby a 'location.'[5]

The activity of the recipient is therefore a condition for the development of the net as a world of connected locations in his or her consciousness. In the sense described, music on the internet provokes activity and therefore the constitution of locations. As a result, on the one hand it plays a part in making it possible to experience the medium intensively and feel it in its essence and, on the other, developing it into a habitat in the first place. For this reason, net musics are spaces of action for people only able to fulfil their need for invention and experience of new worlds by their own activity.

4. Cf. Golo Föllmer: "Klangorganisation im öffentlichen Raum", in: Helga de la Motte-Haber (ed.): *Handbuch der Musik im 20. Jahrhundert*, Bd.12 *Klangkunst*, Laaber 1999, p. 225f.

5. Cf. also subtler differentiation made by Marc Augé between places and non-places: *Orte und Nicht-Orte. Vorüberlegung zu einer Ethnologie der Einsamkeit*, Frankfurt/Main 1994, p.92ff.

# Radio as Medium

**Heidi Grundmann**

The as yet unwritten history of radio art, the definition of which still awaits a scientific interpretation, reflects not only the artistic discourses and developments of the 20th century, but also – like almost no other art form – the constraints and opportunities of its conditions of production, closely interwoven as they are with media-political and technical developments. An uninterrupted process of remediatization between older and newer media converging to become a hybrid association complicates the definition of a concept such as net.radio, containing as it does two different paradigms. This is true to a far greater extent for the concept of net.art, usually superordinate to net.radio. One day, perhaps, art historians will categorise those activities and initiatives that can only be touched upon in a brief discussion like this, in a way that is both journalistic and influenced by the writer's own immediate experiences.

"New technologies of representation proceed by reforming or remediating earlier ones while earlier technologies are struggling to maintain their legitimacy by remediating newer ones."[1]

In 1925, parallel to the absolute film, Kurt Weill postulated an "absolute radio art." He expected, "that new sounds would join with the tones and rhythms of music, sounds from other spheres: human and animal cries, the voices of nature, the rushing of wind, water and trees and then an army of new and unheard sounds that could be artificially created by the microphone, when sound waves are heightened or deepened, laid on top of or woven into one another, dispersed and then reborn."[2]

It was primarily in post-war France (Club d'Essai) and Germany (NWDR in Cologne, Studio für elektronische Musik) that experimentation began with Weill's vision of an absolute radio art, where composers were for the first time granted access to the means of production and transmission of European public radio. Their work matured on the one hand into 'musique concrète' or electronic music and on the other into 'ars acustica,' essentially

developed by WDR Cologne and so defined by the responsible editor, Klaus Schöning. At documenta 8 (1987), an audiotheque equipped with special 'Hör-Sessel' (listening chairs) was dedicated to this highly diverse audio-art[3] and its historical roots in the avant garde from the beginning of this century – some ten years after documenta 6 had celebrated a TV art event as a satellite broadcast of live contributions from Nam June Paik, Joseph Beuys and Douglas Davis.[4] In the catalogue, curator Klaus Schöning claims ars acustica as an art initiated by radio, stating that: "Radio art is an administered art. The limits of radio are also always the limits of acoustic art on the radio. Even the limits in the minds of radio experts are those of acoustic art – on the radio. It is limited in a different way in one country than in another, and is different in one dramatisation by a radio station than in another."[5] This public institution, variously characterised according to the particular media-political situation and behind which, for many radio-makers, the idea of the monolithic 'hot' auditory medium still remains, was then and often is today that radio to which the literary figures, composers and visual artists, could be referring in their radio-specific productions, even if they have transferred current artistic discourses about these productions into the radio stations and so often overstepped the limits of traditional genres and modes of production. The production studio, or alternatively a public place of performance, continued to be the ideal space in which to listen (in) to ars acustica conforming to the prescriptions for 'broadcast-quality' – equipped with 'state of the art' loudspeakers that bear practically no relationship to the receivers that we see today in kitchens, living rooms and cars, etc. – and which caused radio to become the accompanying, or background, medium of the 20th century.

There were and are artists, however, who do not wait for an initiative from radio institutions, instead grasping the chance themselves to realise projects that go far beyond the artistic concept upon which ars acustica is based. In 1966, the American artist-engineer Max Neuhaus com-

1. Bolter, Grusin: Remediation, The MIT Press, Cambridge, MA, London, England 1999.

2. Kurt Weill, "Möglichkeiten absoluter Radiokunst," in: Der deutsche Rundfunk, Issue 26, 3rd year, 1925.

3. "A world composed of language and a world of sounds and noises. Language which tends toward sound, to the sound of speech and to music, the universal sound of the tones, the acoustic environment. Acoustic art: a symbiosis of these speech-noise worlds and sound organisation by means of electronic technology," defines Klaus Schöning in the catalogue of documenta 8, Volume 1.

4. See catalogue of documenta 8, Vol. 2., Verlag Weber&Weidemeyer, Kassel, 1987.

5. This loose grouping of radio art editors of public radio institutions in Eastern and Western Europe, Australia, Canada and the USA has operated since the late 1980s within the framework of the European Broadcast Union (EBU), under the title "Ars Acustica".

# and metaphor.....

bined radio and telephone to create a space at WBAI in New York for an artistic project under the programmatic title of *Public Supply I*. It was up to the listeners to call in and decide on the types of sounds to be used and thereby also the mixture of sounds to be produced for the live broadcast by the artist, who saw himself in the role of a presenter. Neuhaus had persuaded both the radio station and all its technicians, and the telephone company to provide him with access to the basic prerequisites for a situation that he himself designed in such a way that ten listeners could move simultaneously inside."[6] I had made a virtual space which any one of the ten million people living there could enter by dialling a telephone number." By acting in the space designed by Neuhaus, it was possible for listeners to experience the combination of telephone/radio in an unusual way, to deal with it and by so doing to cause it to appear only in the broadcast medium.

In his rare but exemplary telephone-radio projects, Neuhaus as a 'catalyst/presenter' and initiator repositioned not only himself as an artist but also, and most importantly, his listeners: without their co-operation the open, unrepeatable process of *Public Supply I* – paradigmatically different from the traditional work concept – could simply not have developed.

In 1977, Bill Fontana exploited the possibilities of public radio as a found structure in Australia in a similar way, likewise allowing his first live radio sculpture, *Music from Ordinary Objects*, to be defined by listeners' calls. For Fontana it was of primary importance that the sound resources explored and taped by the listeners themselves should be transferred to a new context and processed there.[7] In his 1977 project, *Radio Net*, Max Neuhaus encouraged tens of thousands of listeners in five US cities from New York to Los Angeles to whistle into their telephones while he, the artist, withdrew as far as possible from defining any initial parameters for the situation within which the listeners/participants could

operate. "Obviously I could not be in these five places mixing and grouping at once; so I decided to remove myself completely from that process and implement it as an autonomous electronic system."[8] Neuhaus not only used the existing (found) multiplex broadcast of National Public Radio in an innovative way, but also completed it by means of self-constructed automatic audiomixers. *Radio Net* depicted both the past and the future of the medium. Radio had only regained something of the medium of communication that it originally had been, when used in connection with the telephone and telephone-based networks.

"... there is a common thread of critical concern regarding the state of contemporary radio, the end result of which constitutes a kind of love/hate relationship with the medium. This is made tangible by artists' desire to reinvent the medium through deconstruction and/or reconstruction, the use of 'dangerous' contents and refusal to produce works that easily fit into the categories of sanctioned radio broadcast," writes Dan Lander in his introduction to a 1994 synopsis of radio art in Canada from 1967-1992.[9] This overall view (there are hardly any comparable collections of material in existence) begins with The Idea of North, Glenn Gould's legendary CBC-produced radio work, a 'documentary' that extends the limits of the genre in many different directions. Radio art in Canada, however, has primarily developed outside the institution of public radio. An open media-political situation that has allowed community- and university-based radio as a matter of course for many years (similar to Australia and the USA, incidentally, with certain pre-conditions particular to each country) has led to a point where, aided by a differentiated art policy that has promoted rather than restricted artists from dealing with the new communications technologies and the media environment, not only is the term 'radio art' used quite naturally, but also that of radio artist. The production possibilities for radio art at co-op and university radio stations are actually very limited, even while it goes without saying that the

6. In: *ZEITGLEICH*, Triton Verlag, Vienna, 1994.

7. See also: "Im Netz der Systeme," *Kunstforum International*, Vol. 103, Sep./Oct. 1989, Cologne.

8. In: *ZEITGLEICH*, Triton Verlag, Vienna, 1994.

9. *Selected Survey of Radio Art in Canada 1967 – 1992*, edited and compiled by Dan Lander, Walter Phillips Gallery, The Banff Centre of the Arts, 1994.

radio artist is (also) granted access to the radio broadcast medium. It should, therefore, come as no surprise that the main focus of radio art produced under these conditions is not so much on 'audio art' produced in the best-equipped studios, but rather on art that reflects the (transmission) medium itself. Since the 1970s – again, mainly outside the institution – R. Murray Schafer and his colleagues have also developed a specific inter-disciplinary and social approach to the 'art of listening' as a conscious debate with the acoustic environment, using such rubrics as soundecology, soundscape and sound-design to provide classification. Hildegard Westerkamp, Claude Schryer et al. also use the medium of radio to generate a sensitisation to the sounds of the acoustic environment, to which the sounds of the media also belong.

"No-one listens to the radio. What loudspeakers or headphones give their users is really nothing more than a programme, it is never the radio itself. It is only when the real thing suddenly comes along, when programmes are interrupted, the presenter loses his or her voice or stations drift out of received frequency that there is really a chance, for just a few moments, to listen to what radio could be."

It was with these words that Friedrich Kittler began a presentation on Orson Welles' 1938 *War of the Worlds*.[10] This radio play 'to end all radio plays' showed the medium of radio at the peak of its powers, even with the absence of military and telecommunications extensions that had already (and particularly at that time) disappeared in its manifestation as a regulated medium, for the one-way transmission of entertainment and informa- tion. It was not merely due to the virtuoso performance by the Mercury Theater On the Air, under the young producer Orson Welles, that the 'most momentous radio play of all time' caused such panic amongst its audience – something that its makers had neither expected nor even tried to achieve. No, the confusion of simulation and reality was also the result of the behaviour of the radio audience – at the time unmonitorable and unforeseeable by already active market researchers – together with the wavering credibility of radio. Most listeners to *War of the Worlds* had simply missed the announcement that had put

the play about the invasion of the USA by beings from another planet into its proper context as 'theatre on air' because, disappointed by the progress of another, far more popular series, they had switched too late to the next best channel. There, thrown into the middle of the radio-dramatic events, they became witnesses to (the depiction of) a media war[11] with all its tragic results – the destruction of the advanced military-media sector of the (American) earthly society, whose last representative transmits a desperate "Isn't there anyone on the air? Isn't there anyone on the air? Isn't there anyone...2X2L..." into the – by now empty – ether.

In October 1987, the noisician G.X.Jupiter Larsen, for four years legendary host/curator of the Newsounds Gallery at Co-op Radio CFRO-FM Vancouver, recorded the crackling and humming produced when the station cut off shortly before the beginning of the broadcast, and which could be heard instead of the open-end radio art programme. He broadcast the recording, which lasted for a number of hours, the following week: out of the real experience of listening to the radio had come a programme – an audio feature of 'radio itself' in the Kittleresque sense. Neither this audibility of the radio medium nor the other, which another Canadian radio artist, Ian Murray, edited from the short silences that still existed on commercial radio in the 1970s and subsequently broadcast, would be welcome to public or even commercial channels. For these stations, radio portrayed by actors such as Orson Welles' *War of the Worlds* was disturbance enough.

In the late 1970s/early 1980s, a few exemplary projects of two-way communication art were created – e.g. *Double Entendre* by Douglas Davis or *Hole in Space* by Mobile Image – that transcends the regulated one-way TV broadcast by using satellite technology. Other artists (amongst them Bill Bartlett, Carl Loeffler, Hank Bull, Robert Adrian X, Roy Ascott, Eric Gidney, Tom Klinkowstein, etc.) started experiments with the new peripheral telephone equipment (fax, video-telephone, computer timesharing, etc.). In these projects, in which many different locations were connected in the global telephone network, they avoided associ-

10. In: *On the Air*, Transit, Innsbruck, 1993.

11. "*War of the Worlds*, as Orson Welles named the most influential radio play of all time shortly before the outbreak of the Second World War, is pure media-war." (F. Kittler in: *On the Air*, Transit, Innsbruck, 1993).

12. A border between the early telecommunications projects and a second phase can be established from the experience of the 1986 *Venice Biennial*, in which a major divide opened up between those artists anchored in academic institutions and those participating in such projects from their own garrets and telephones. A few of the telecommunications art pioneers, exhausted by telephone costs and the intensive workload, had already given up earlier. Amongst these was Bill Bartlett, who withdrew from the art entirely.

13. Cf. *Wiencouver IV*, one of the very few documentations to give a clear impression of the telecommunications projects of the first phase. Western Front Video, 1984, Vancouver. On the history of early telecommunications art, see also *Art + Telecommunication*, ed. H.Grundmann, Vienna, Vancouver, 1983.

ation not only with the art business but also with the 'administrators' of institutionalised access to broadcast media. In various 'shared authorship' models, the networked artists adapted themselves both to the different access opportunities of the new communication technologies in various parts of the world and to the low bandwidth and poor sound quality of the telephone. While artists in North America, for example, were often able to enter and receive fax, slow-scan TV and computer communications on the network, their Eastern European colleagues were reliant upon telephones without additional digitising equipment, that is participation via music and performance by telephone.

Even those early telecommunications projects,[12] which contained no telephonic performances or music, concentrating instead on the exchange of text, fax and/or slow scan TV, had a soundtrack: the constantly-repeating telephonic invocations – "Hello, hello, are you receiving us?" – with which all sides reconfirmed the continued functioning of the highly unstable communications channels and transmission technologies, and which might be considered a new non-simulated version of the distress call from *War of the Worlds*: the artists were no longer actors, but had instead become 'radio operators.'[13]

Various models of telematic events still effective in the recent past took shape in the first phase of telecommunications art:
- the 24-hour model (*the world in 24 hours*, initiated by Robert Adrian X, in Linz, 1982), which follows the sun around the Earth and thereby ensures that participants in all time zones are linked into the project in harmony with their biological and social rhythm of life;
- the 'hearsay' or looping model (*Hearsay*, initiated by Norman White from Toronto in 1985), in which a poem about a messenger delivering a message to a king (the content of which is never revealed) is passed from one node to the next, translated into a new language at each connection and passed on again;
- the on-demand model: *La Plissure du Texte*, started by Roy Ascott in 1983 (computer communications and fax), in which a communicative-collaborative fairytale was told by 11 participant 'stations' over a period of two weeks. The participants could log onto the project whenever they

had the time and the inclination and react to what had appeared while they had been asleep or otherwise engaged;
- the control signal model: *RAZIONALNIK*, begun in 1986 by Seppo Gründler/Josef Klammer in Graz, networked musicians via telephone to simultaneous concerts in Graz, Ljubljana and Trento. By using MIDI signals, it was possible for the musicians to trigger samplers, sequencers and synthesisers via telephone at each particular location and thereby circumvent the problem of poor sound quality of music on the telephone. The musicians were able to directly influence the event at each different site, thus giving up a degree of control over the concert at their respective site.

In December 1987, *Kunstradio* (Art Radio), a radio art broadcast on the culture channel of the Austrian national station ORF (Österreichischer Rundfunk) was founded. *Kunstradio* did not refer back to the tradition of ars acustica, the new radio play or radiophonic music so much as to that of a dematerialised visual art, a radio art to be understood as sculpture that had emerged elsewhere on university and coop stations (Österreichischer Rundfunk still maintained a broadcasting monopoly), and telecommunications art and associated art in the public (electronic) arena. *Kunstradio*, then, had to do (amongst other things) with artists who saw themselves as the initiators of media-based processes and which logically understood its role not as the regulator of access to the radio but as an entry point to the means of production and transmission provided by public radio; as a clearing-point at which strategies were developed in partnership with the artists for avoiding bureaucratic restrictions within the institution itself. Out of this resulted a specific relationship of trust with the artists, for whom the term 'radio' was far wider-ranging than that defined by public radio and which, in addition to pirate and free radio broadcasters, included amateur, CB and minicab radio systems, the communication channel of the pilots on a flight from Frankfurt to Hong Kong and even the packet radio on the MIR space station. The object, context and content of radio art as conceived by most artists – starting with the weekly broadcast opportunities on *Kunstradio*, but by no means stopping there – was not so much art, as the medium of radio itself which was rapidly being transformed under pressure from digitalisation, commercialisation and globalisation. The projects expanded – increasingly using new collaborative, participatory working methods – onto other channels, additional arenas, media and times, that is into a hybrid context of production, presentation and distribution. Simultaneity was taken literally as a mutually influential event taking place at several/many real and medial network-ed locations at which each participant takes as a totality his or her own version of an event that cannot be experienced, based not on a common, unified origin but rather a diffuse 'anorigin' that, amongst other things, repeals all care-fully rehearsed relationships between radio and its commercial exploiters. There have been major international projects in which artists, using and activating the ars acustica group of radio art editors in the European Broadcasting Union as a found organisational platform, connected over 20 public institutions with free radios, public performance venues and individ-ual artists on the telephone, internet, etc. to form a 'virtual stage,' "being based upon interaction and a telepresence on which the actors/artists temporarily meet" ... "instead of a vertically hierarchi-cal demarcation of broadcaster and receiver, a platform of interchangeable transmission."[14] Projects such as *Horizon-tal Radio* (1995) or *Rivers & Bridges* (1996), in which hundreds of artists across the world took part, by processing constantly changing anthologies by means of the production/distribution/reception dis-positives of different media, spatial and temporal contexts, both of an ars acustica fragmented to a point at which it is no longer recognisable, and/or radiophone art and radio and telecommunications-based art.

"Basically a project like *Horizontal Radio* is orchestrated through the configuration of lines and channels, gateways and interfaces and by determining frequency ranges and access rights.

The basic idea is to create a media struc-ture which is as heterogeneous as possi-ble. It is supposed to function as an exper-imental set-up within the field of tension generated by the various characteristics of transmission and communication. This field is also a result of the frictional rela-tion between the isosynchronous charac-ter of radio and the asynchronous proper-ties of digital data networks, which are dependent on their context and on the type of access e.g. on demand, random access, caching.

The strategy to ensure that participation is as simple and as widespread as possi-ble is diversification."[15]

KUNSTRADIO ON LINE was founded by artists in early 1995, and has been fur-ther developed since that time.[16] It func-tions as an archive and at the same time as a context, object and scene for art; in most projects it is but one of several scenes. Since late 1996, KUNSTRADIO has used the ON-AIR – ON-LINE – ON-SITE formula for the networked context of such productions shared between various real and virtual sites. As with many other radio broadcasts and channels and occasionally *Kunstradio*, the Swiss team of artists Beusch/Cassani – following on in the tradition of artists such as Max Neuhaus and Bill Fontana – has initiated/designed/configured the basic require-ments for projects and events in the role of 'data jockeys,' amongst other things in the framework of the media fiction *RADIO THE NE(X)T CENTURY* (since 1995). By so doing it has caused co-players and others to reshuffle the division of labour normal in media and art production in real-world conditions. Their means of progression is very similar to that of those artists using *Kunstradio* as an entry point into a hybrid context within large, networked projects.

Our role as DJs, as data jockeys, consists of condensing cultural phenomena to an exciting initial setting. This is followed by the linking of the know-how or infrastruc-ture of a wide range of individuals and sub-networks, including, for example, the sub-network radio. The various actors must be sensitised to the networked space in which they operate.

TNC's events are prepared and config-ured down to the finest detail – according to an intercontinental storyboard – and precisely because of this have the poten-tial to develop themselves into pulsating, networked processes with an open, offensive dynamics.

The design and operation of aesthetically and culturally relevant processes within multiple networks requires a precise knowledge of new and old tools, the com-

14. Catalogue *Ars Electron-ica 95*, Springer Verlag Vienna, New York.

15. Unpublished draft of a project description, 1995. An important role was played in the projects men-tioned and their forerunners by artists such as Gerfried Stocker, Horst Hörtner, Roberto Paci Dalò, Andrea Sodomka/Martin Breindl, Norbert Math and many others.

16. The address of KUNST-RADIO ON LINE http://thing.at/orfkunstradio reveals that this homepage is not part of the official ORF ON (line).

position of the networked space, the codes and kicks of the species of connected entities and a clear awareness of which different elements are to be united. For one, these are very different media – radio, internet, the local event on-site. On the other hand, there are cultural and geographical differences that must be taken into account – the TNC events always take place in different time zones. "It is clear that such processes as those on which the production, hierarchy and responsibility structures of networked systems are based can no longer be thought of according to the production model that we are used to. Instead of the authority of the author over a work, there is a shift to what we describe by the concept of joint process and data management."[17]

"Destructuring by asynchronicity is an extremely important, if not crucial facet of new electronic technologies."[18]

The extremely self-exploitative effort involved in producing webcasts of performances, games, radio broadcasts, readings and jams, spread over several days and nights and originating at least in part in different time zones, with several real audio live-streams, webcams and 'remote volunteers' linking in by phone – for example for the four-part project *Recycling the Future* (1997)[19] – made the artists more acutely aware of the difference between the synchronicity of actions precisely limited by time in front of a local public, and radio broadcasts, and the no-time (and non-space) of the internet. Generative on-line installations were inserted into the webcasts of *Recycling the Future I – IV* (1997) that were initially grasped as the background, the default for the partially hectic performance activity.

"All of the works so far have been radio events, because that is the nature of radio in most people's minds: it has events – radio shows. But one could also make a radio installation ... if it's always there you can call in at any time, and you can stay in it as long as you want ... It becomes an entity – a virtual place," wrote Max Neuhaus in 1994.[20]

What becomes effective in many areas of society as a fateful delimitation/deregulation of, for example, defined fields of

activity with trade union backing or regulated working times, is for radio art, squeezed as it has been into the corset of transmission times (and the performance and opening times of on-site locations), first and foremost a signal of liberation from the pressures of the institution of radio. With the rapid development of streaming technologies, the (by no means new) attraction with the concept of a constantly changing, potentially endless flow into which one can enter/immerse oneself in at any time continues to grow. This flow, for which parallels can be found both in the 'white noise' of the sea or waterfalls[21], the noise of urban traffic or omnipresent radio itself, also offers itself up as a metaphor for the data space removed from our perception and imagination. It is not surprising, therefore, that in the past two years initial parameters for collaborative, networked on-line-on-site-on-air sound installations have been worked out in which the previously predominant performative elements were completely pushed back and in which the participant artists ultimately left much to the networked computers in shared control models.

*Immersive Sound* (1998), an actually immersive sound installation on location in Bregenz (A), formed part of an exhibition devoted to the subject of sound.[22] Material for the five-week-long on-site version of *Immersive Sound* was provided by the sounds of all the other installations in the exhibition as well as generative, that is partly automated, non-stop streams coming from sites in Australia, Canada and Austria. Together with a non-stop stream from Bregenz, these formed on-line versions of the installation. While for the first four weeks alternating teams of artists 'played' the various Bregenz versions of *Immersive Sound* together with a generative system, in the last week the machines were on their own in all versions of *Immersive Sound*.

*Sound Drifting* (1999)[23] was an on-line installation of 16 more or less generative audio streams in the most current formats, rendered at several sites for on-air and/or on-site contexts. Both *Immersive Sound* and *Sound Drifting* had not only on-site but also on-line visual elements. The concept of installations constantly changing and yet also staying the same, of streams or flows that could potentially

17. Reference Beusch/Cassani in: "Recycling the Future IV", 1997, Vienna.

18. Ursula M. Franklin: *The Real World of Technology*, CBC Massey Lectures Series, Rev.ed., Anansi Press, Toronto, 1999.

19. See http://thing.at/orfkunstradio/FUTURE/

20. In: *Zeitgleich*, Triton Verlag, Vienna, 1994.

21. "White noise is the equivalent of eternity" (Bill Fontana).

22. *Audio Art. Art in the City 2*. Bregenzer Kunstverein. 1998 and http://thing.at/orfkunstradio/BREGENZ/

23. http://thing.at/orfkunstradio/SD and Catalogue of *Ars Electronica 99*, Springer Vienna, New York.

be retrieved without beginning or end as a number of sounds and rendered for various contexts, had clear consequences for radio versions: in Weimar, the university broadcaster transmitted a non-stop live radio sculpture over four days and nights, and even on the national culture channel of the public station Österreichischer Rundfunk, an eight-hour live radio installation was broadcast without any breaks for explanation.

With the wide diversity of sounds produced in their sub-projects and with the help of the various long-lasting constellations and contexts for which these sounds can be rendered and processed by the artists, machines and every user/listener, such networked hybrid configurations as *Immersive Sound* or *Sound Drifting* represent new types of test arrangements for an active research of perception, one which far exceeds that of ars acustica and even of the soundscape/ecology movement and which also contains the relations of sound to picture, text and space.

In the live on-air, on-line project entitled *Other Voices – Echoes from a War Zone*, which took place on 29 April 1999, Gordan Paunovic not only had texts on the real media war translated from the internet, excerpts from internet diaries and sound files sent from Belgrade at his disposal on his mixer in the Vienna radio studio, but also a real audio live stream with a mix including live sounds recorded by a microphone hung out of the window of the studio of Robert Klajn and Aleksander Vasiljevic in the Serb capital during yet another heavy air-strike, and broadcast simultaneously with the programme on Österreich 1 (and on the internet). In this project, transmitted on a national public radio station following the main evening news programme – in the war zone of the real media war and not one portrayed by actors - *Other Voices* were brought to the public at least as *Echoes from a War Zone* in the truest sense of the word. Just as the later *Net Aid* – 24-hour webcasts initiated by Gordan Paunovic and others on a monthly basis and in which artists from around the world took part[24] (and the web campaign *Help B 92*), the live broadcast could only take place because of the existence of a broad, living network of media activists and/or artists and theorists, which continually repositions itself with regard to

technical, political, economic and cultural developments and can also react with great speed as an organisational platform for (not only artistic) projects. Sound is an important surface in this communicative discourse. Perhaps a part of the ars acustica dream of a multilingual sound-language that is universally comprehensible will be fulfilled as an – at least occasionally – shared sounding (in the sense of measuring and surveying, sounding out) of the world.

"The vocation of an art of the kind that reflects on electronic crowds and networks is not the representation of the visible world but the visualisation of what is otherwise inaccessible to perception and is difficult to imagine."[25]

While some artists force their way into the structures of the media combine in which radio, too, is prone to a constant process of remediatization and by means of their projects, etc., try to transcend the numerous prescriptions of institutionalised media and other public spaces in order to set at least temporarily open media spaces of action against the 'faceless ears' of the audience statistics, other artists decide to set up their own highly individual broadcast/reception antennae in the global hybrid space of communications technologies converging into a megamedium in a way that is temporary and mobile.

It was in this way that, tacitly tolerated, an artist-pirate broadcaster associated with the Canadian Banff Centre for the Arts, first commissioned in 1988 and many times since has endured into the present net.radio. In 1989, RADIA 89.9 FM became one of the locations in a simultaneous radio project run between Winnipeg, Calgary and Banff, as part of the *Hyperspace Radio* project. In 1993, RADIA 89.9 FM served as exhibition and symposium radio for RADIO RETHINK.

It was by no means coincidental that Tetsuo Kogawa from Japan was a participant in this symposium in Banff and that he organised one of his workshops there on "How to Build a One-Watt FM Transmitter." There is no other artist who has taught broadcasting/receiving to so many people as Tetsuo Kogawa with his mini-FM performances which, like the mini-FM movement overall, are built on

24. http://www.freeB92.net

25. Margaret Morse: *Virtualities. Television, Media Art, and Cyberculture.* Indiana University Press, Bloomington, 1998.

the conviction that: "Radio could serve as a communication vehicle not for broadcast but for the individuals involved."[26]

Tetsuo Kogawa has found a strong echo with the protagonists of the net.radio (art) scene that has developed since 1996. In 1998, the Australian artists Honor Harger and Zina Kaye, who count among these protagonists, wrote: "Intuitively we have always understood that radio could be used as a means to link people together in conversation, a communications vehicle not for broadcast, but for the individuals involved. Instead of a metaphor of a sprawling net, our vision of radio is more like a conversation – sometimes with yourself and sometimes with a few others. Perhaps radio can be seen as a musical instrument, or a composer, with groups of people as the notes it arranges into melody and discord."[27]

The horizontality of the networks that fascinated the pioneers of telecommunications art is natural practice for the young net.radio activists. "...it is like early telecommunications, where discrete nodes pass on the baton and fold information into loops. Receiver becomes broadcaster in such a paradigm. Equally, many nodes will go under one name as a temporary autonomous zone and assault the networks with one unified communication."[28]

The theoretically and technically disputable concept of net.radio, which in practice is constantly being redefined by artists – also under the pressure of the audio technologies developing at such an incredible rate – signalises that, just as with the avant garde at the beginning of this century, 'radio' has become a metaphor. This time, however, it is not for the 'creation of a universal language' or 'the achievement of lasting global peace' and similar progressive matters, but rather primarily to achieve a situation whereby, ultimately, everyone can produce his or her own art radio on the internet – most meaningfully entrenched in a networked community that is as open as possible. Some artistic models have already been developed in this community that, in the form of differently structured nodes, provide different pictures for a continual process of re- and co-broadcastings, pictures whose significance is constantly increasing in the context of

rapidly advancing commercialisation in the audio field. Amongst this community, whose exchange of information has above all formed around the mailing list and website Xchange,[29] are a striking number of artists from Eastern Europe, that is artists who view a tradition of commodified art with distance and irony and quite naturally initiate situations and structures in which they provoke others to media-communicative action, offering a kind of home port as they do so.[30]

26. In: *Radio Rethink, art, sound and transmission*, ed. Daina Augaitis and Dan Lander, Walter Phillips Gallery, The Banff Centre for the Arts, 1994.

27. In: nettime-l@Desk.nl, Sept.1998.

28. ibid.

29. xchange@re-lab.net

30. "The xchange website is a space where we are collected, it is a home of the network" write Adam Hyde and Zina Kaye in the November 1999 on xchange and state anxiously: "The entertainment industry is catching up with us."

# "Changing Po
# or:
# Welcome to

Netscape: 42
Back
Forward
Reload
Home
Search
Guide
Images
Print
Security
Stop
Location: http://www.mur.at/42/
42
<cym> it really works now!

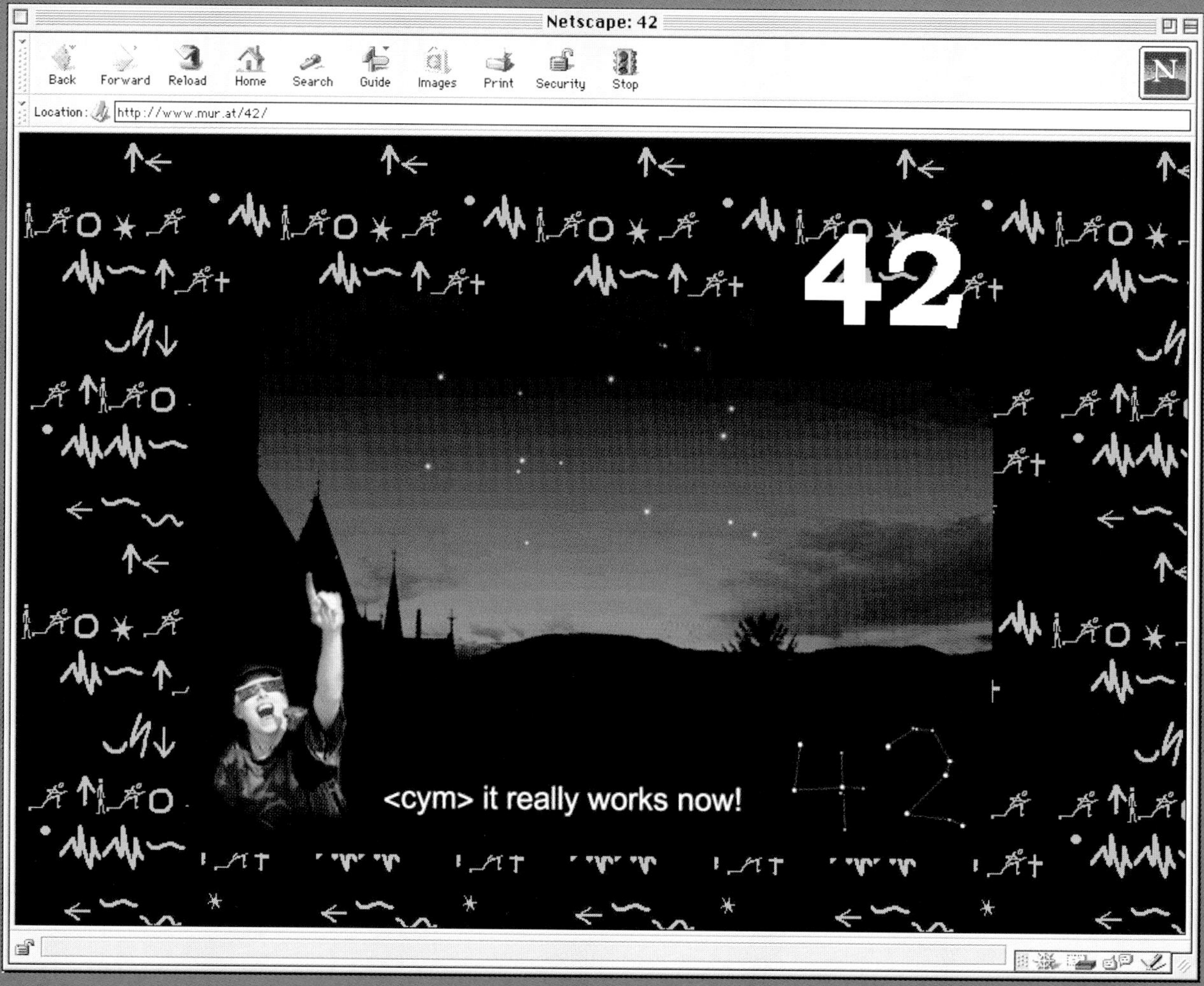

# sitions

# Transbabel!"

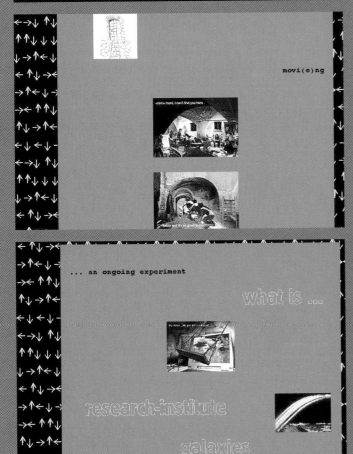

Then...
...in spring 1998, a group of women from Graz/Austria founded 'the mailing list 42' in order to discuss, ask and answer questions around computer technologies. The mailing list's language then was German. At an international meeting in the Forum Stadtpark in Graz in Summer 1998, 'face2face', women from Ljubljana, Belgrade, Amsterdam and Berlin joined '42'. Some sort of Babelfish became necessary. And it appeared quickly, although in an unusual way. The simultaneous way of travelling, the locomotive was removed and replaced by sound and video experiments, real-audio streamings, a collaborate video-project, – for '42' a frequent flow of communication beyond the limits of language was established - a permanent state of Transbabel.

Now...
...the next step taken is to establish '42 - The Research Institute.' We set it up with one very special, specified theme - the question of success and failure. Different experimental sessions let us circumnavigate or crash the limits of Transbabel.

The Research Installation itself: The sound, textual and visual studio is connected to the internet. A continuously growing archive of sound-files provides the material for the different experimental settings. The 'produced' material remains available by means of an automated process the archived files are fed from the internet into the 'space of action' as long as no researcher intervenes in the acoustic space.

Truth In Clouds is at one and the same time a site-specific interactive audio installation, and the set and principle mechanism for a musical performance. The piece takes its form, and its inspiration, from the 19th Century culture of seances, and the tumult of scientific and philosophical thought that surrounded it. The set's central object is a 'seance table' - a large round wooden table upon which stands an inverted wineglass. The movement of this wineglass by visitors or performers controls localized audio and visual manifestations throughout the room. From the ultra-rational perspective of our digital age it may be difficult to understand the profound connection that once existed between the science of electricity and the 'pseudo-science' of Spiritualism. As with atomic physics a generation later, early electrical discoveries - man-made lightning, telephony, telegraphy, radio - all seemed to point beyond the known physical world into one of essences, from intuitive mechanical causality into something demonstrable but nonetheless unknowable. Seances drew the interest not only of artists and theologians, but of scientists and engineers: Faraday, Wheatstone, Morse, and Tesla all attended them. They sat, grouped around a table, while spirits spoke to them, writings mysteriously appeared on table tops, wine glasses moved, or furniture tapped.

Using a combination of digital technology, traditional instruments, and familiar household objects, Truth in Clouds attempts to recreate this poignant causality, flickering between forthright and mysterious, as well as to explore the collective collaboration with invisible comrades that so

# In Clouds

strangely links Spiritualism to
Cyberspace (long before
Ethernet there was the
Aethernet...). Ideally, the
work is installed in the parlor
of an old house. Apart from the
seance table itself, the room is
filled with period furniture,
musical instruments and household miscellany. The table
serves as a 'Ouija-to-MIDI' converter: as the glass is moved
across the table (by worldly or
ghostly visitors), it is tracked
by a computer, and its position
controls all aspects of the
sound, visuals and structure of
the piece:

- Pre-recorded and sampled sound
are played back through speakers
hidden in the props.
- A video beam projects 'spirit
writing' on the table top, which
advances from word to word as the
glass is moved.
- 'Spirit rappings' and Morse
code transcriptions of the texts
are tapped out by small solenoids
hidden in the set, to create a
subdued rhythmic underpinning
for all other musical activities.

The first, hesitant contact with
the glass triggers simple sound
effects; as a participant sits
and plays longer, a narrative
begins to unfold in the fragments
of spoken texts and in the
'spirit writings' that appear on
the table. Musical accompaniment
flows from the objects strewn
throughout the room. The longer a
visitor participates, the richer
the texture becomes. The installation shuts down after the glass
has been still for more than one
minute: the audio matrix is muted
the text fades from table, and
only the sparse spirit rapping
continues. The piece resumes
when the glass is next touched.

Johannes Goebel,
Torsten Belschner, Bernhard Sturm

A visitor of the instal-
lation enters a typical
living-room of the
1950s – wallpaper,
flowers, couch and table
recreate the atmosphere
from back then. At the
heart of the room
"Musikschrank Rhein-
gold," a radio-phono-
graph from that period,
gleams in dark-brown pol-
ish with golden rims. The
radio is fully func-
tional. As one selects
FM, AM or SW and turns the
dial, radio stations
gradually appear out of
the surrounding static
noise. The green magic
eye opens all the way when
a station is well tuned
in. But: all radio-sta-
tions are live streams
from all over the world
coming over the WWW.

If one selects the record
player as source old
broadcasts from remote
audio archives can be
heard. "Musikschrank
Rheingold" is a comment:
most radio stations
received over the net
today have sound quali-
ties like FM, AM or SW.
They still function as a
one way street between
station and listener even
though non-radio fea-
tures like e-mail or
chat-rooms have been
added. The old paradigms
of information distribu-
tion are still valid the
difference being that it
is now in principle pos-
sible for anyone to
'broadcast' over the net.

How will technology and
content influence each
other? The old radio also

turns out to be a handsome
interface for the web:
radio stations pre-
selected out of the tan-
gled topography of the
net are 'linearized' and
can be accessed (and
remembered!) by manipu-
lations of a '3-D'-device
perfectly designed for
hands, eyes and ears.
"Rheingold's" hardware
had to be modified to
interface to a computer
and the software has been

custom developed. It
takes user input from the
various radio buttons and
dials of the
"Musikschrank" which
have been tapped. The
data is processed and
triggers one of the 65
preselected internet
radio stations' URLs from
an internal database. The
connection to a remote
server is established via
the http protocol. While
a connection is being

established, a waiting
message sounds out in
different languages. The
returned audio stream is
mixed in real-time with
filtered noise to fake
the nothingness between
radio stations known from
traditional analog
radio. This noise is
alternately crossfaded
with the stations' pro-
gram material. This sig-
nal is finally output to
the radio's ancient tube
amplifier. - In tandem
with triggering the URLs,
ascii text describing the
name and location of the
selected radio station is
written to a 40-character
LCDisplay, which has been

integrated into the old
glass-covered display of
bands and frequencies.
A special gimmick is the
interfacing to the
radio's magic eye.
Taking its original role
of indicating the field
strength of the selected
radio station, in "Rhein-
gold" it helps the user
as a necessary aid in
honing in to a newly
selected station.

mikro e. V.

http://www.mikro.org

Sound Conditions

WHAT HAS HAPPENED SO FAR... A spectre is hunting streaming media. The spectre of off-media. Media on the brink between broadcast and archive, media between give-away-commerce and take-it-all-art, media on the run between the early dreams and late adaptation, on the verge from audio to video, exploding from the financial peripheries into the media art centres, from convergence to coercion, from armchair criticism to web critique, from the modesty of static plain html to the excesses of interactivity, from boys-with-modems to girls-with-fat-pipes, from soon-to-be-born media archaeologists to yet-too-boring media activists. Streaming media of the world unite on one cd-rom! After 2000 years of net.radio it is time to sum up what has happened.

Net.radio has finally left the realms of artistic practice, hobbyist communities and media activism. Today audio on the internet seems to be as *natural* as an ascii picture, a Java Script or a postcard. Commercial net.radio stations are constructed within portals and other gates for a mass audience.

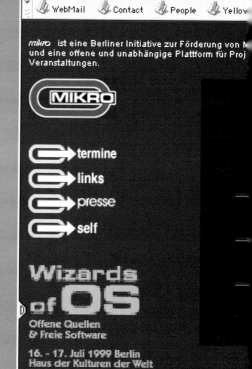

WHAT HAS HAPPENED BEFORE... Net.radio days 98 (http://www.art-bag.net/trimmmdich), organized by mikro and convex tv. In June 1998, the first international meeting of experimental net.radio projects took place in Berlin. One and a half years later it has become obvious, that the more experimental strategies to use internet audio as either an artistic practice or a tool for activism have become niche-products for peripheral curatorial approaches. There to be almost seems no practical or theoretical act of broadcasting which hasn't been tested by audio net.works or single net.audiologists in the name of art. On the other hand, this development now proves to have been the test bed of webaudio.com's futurity.

NOW... Reflecting the moment of musealisation when everyone with a hard-drive is a potential museum director. Rethinking the desire to leave trails when everyone knows about the brutal force of accumulated attention. Reediting a mix and putting it into a pool means not giving yourself up in a hip-piesque potlatch or missing a chance to move up a step into art heaven. It means that you send in a file and you get back all the files which were selected, plus the fun of being a substantial part of a bigger party.

But there are a couple of streaming media projects which differ more greatly than others. They came first, developed their own formats, userbase, interface, sound colour, and found different ways of exploring the new territory. There are historic transmissions, exemplary webcasts, forgotten files, manic remixes, which might or might not have the potential to represent the early years of net audio. (Or whatever you like to call it.)

---

**Netscape: mikro**

ages · Print · Security · Stop · N

What's Related

ownload · Find Sites

, ein Katalysator *mikro* is a Berlin initiative for the advancement of media cultures, a catalyst and
nen und            an open and independent platform for projects, discussions and events.

## mikro.lounge #16

*science fiction*

Mittwoch, 14. Juli 1999
0 Uhr, WMF, Johannisstr. 19

Saskia Sassen @ mikro

: mikro fördern und Geld sparen

ie mikro.bar hält noch Siesta,
aber bald macht sie auf

**mikro empfiehlt**

*mikro.lounge #15*
verlage im netz

*mikro.lounge #14*
art servers berlin

*mikro.lounge #13*
small media vs mass media
in (ex-)YU

*mikro.lounge #12*
Geburtstagsparty

*mikro.lounge #11*
cooking pot markets
Rishab Aiyer Ghosh

*mikro.lounge #10*
political activism
on the net

*mikro.lounge #9*
net continuum: mailinglists

*mikro.lounge #8*
netz.statt.berlin?

*mikro.lounge #7*
Net Copyright

---

...AND THEN. Net.radio day 99 at zkm will happen as a remote party. 24 h live streaming and online debate, instantly released under the Open Content Licence, with full remote retro charme and no hidden fees attached! Net.radioday thus looks at streaming media through the rearview mirror, examining the weight of open content, collaborative selection, and ad-hoc-musealisation.

Net.radio day 99 therefore asks different producers all over the world to send in their favourite files which will be compiled for a dense history of net.radio (deadline: 30/11/99). These files will be streamed in a 24 hour broadcast and also be archived online and on a cd-rom to keep them accessible for the public domain of the future. Brilliant moments in net.radio thus will be saved from oblivion.

The files will be compiled according to the principles of the Open Content License. (http://opencontent.org)

Additionally, net.radio day 99 will organize a panel which seeks to search the field for future options. Furthermore a questionnaire is provided to find out how current models of net.casting are organized - from the artistic to the commercial field. And, of course, a special website is set up. This is the last collection of historic streaming media works before 2000!

# ¢apital_

¢apital magneti¢ is a network-based multimedia installation that

**exploits the musical possibilities of the credit card.**
Participants in the installation use their credit cards to compose short pieces of music that interact with each other in a simulated musical economy. The piece explores privacy and personal and musical identity in a so-called 'free market.' Each magnetic card, like its owner, is unique. In '¢apital magneti¢'

**the data encoded on magnetic stripes is treated as a kind of musical DNA.**
Each time a card is swiped, this 'genetic material' is captured and parsed to form the rhythmic, melodic, and timbral elements of a short musical composition.

# magneti¢

These compositions enter a simulated economy where they compete, cooperate, evolve and mutate. Some become dominant, others become marginalized. Some marginalized compositions may combine to form new 'styles' or 'genres' that in turn influence the more dominant ones, and so on. Information found on the card is also used to estimate the economic status of the user and to tag a composition so that its position ('market share') in the virtual marketplace can be tracked and evaluated. This data is used to create short advertisements tailored to the users' lifestyle, composited in real-time from a range of still and moving images and displayed on the video monitor.

http://xchange.re-lab.net/

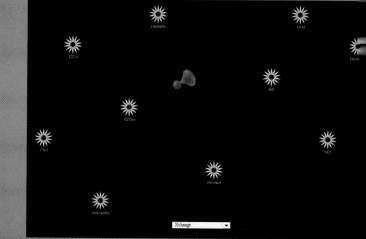

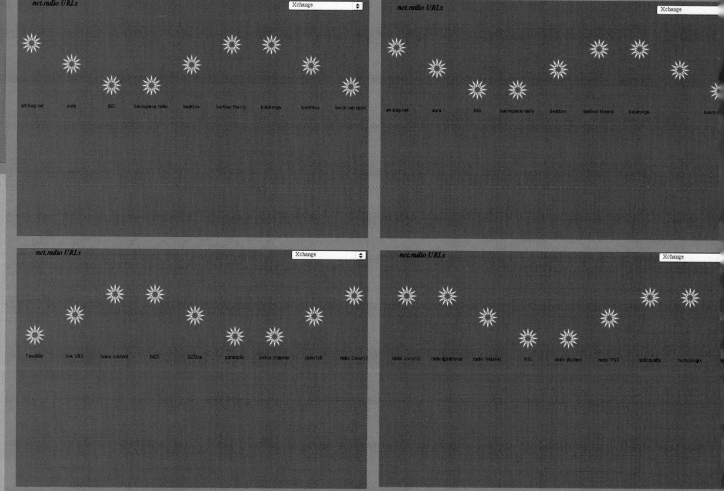

# Xchange

Xchange is an audio-network (net.audio) for non commercial netradio producers and individual producers of
audio contents, a provider which supports the exchange
and connection of alternative nettransmissions.
Radio0Zone initiated this provider as a platform for
internet projects in the field of net.audio in 1997.
Xchange began early to transmit livestreams and real-
audio-loops from Riga. For a general understanding and a
broad spectrum of experiences of the acoustic space new
concepts are developed in live discussions and tested
with experiments in live-programs on the internet.

net.radio URLs                                    Xchange ⬍

channel radio    canvas tv    community radio    DFM    tamvart manual    first flor radio    FLEX    FRO

net.radio URLs                                    Xchange ⬍

freies radio    futhermore    gaalive    goethe house    interface    jomaradio    kunstradio    KZSU    lada

net.radio URLs                                    Xchange ⬍

radioqualia    radio THC    radioqualia    re:flashlight    the thing    backspace radio    XLR    kunstradio    convex radio

# Small Archaeological Experiments in the Media Age:

Christa Blümlinger

So-called new media art is not the first specialization to focus on the media, including their apparatus and global networks. Throughout its history as the formative visual medium of the twentieth century, cinema has explored aspects of the media condition. The aim of this essay is to examine works of documentary film-makers from three generations, Joris Ivens, Chris Marker and Harun Farocki, with emphasis on their discursive relationship with media.

If we were to see the work of these film-makers as an expression of a form of thinking, we might attempt to describe them on the basis of their temporal media modes: the immediate 'presence' of Ivens' 35mm camera, the 'having been present' of Marker's photography, or rather the photographic condition in his films. This, at times nostalgic aspect, is transformed in the documentary in the works of montage artist Marker. We find this too in the work of Farocki - a sense of the media mesh of images and sounds from which the films are created and an awareness of what is not shown in a film. This mood of possibility emerges where various media merge, clash, or where words and images become legible in the sense of Deleuze or Benjamin - a void that allows us to anticipate the sequence of images, a position addressed to future viewers.

Joris Ivens, often referred to by critics as a "film-maker at the fronts of the global revolution," was initially concerned with the immediate production of images. Indeed, quite literally so: his very first films were family films, much like the films of the Lumière brothers. With a pre-televisual sense of the frontal, memorable aspect of history and everyday life, and with a faith in direct testimony matching his own personal activities, Ivens went 'on location' for decades, to countless countries and regions - Spain, China, Chile, Cuba, Vietnam, to name but a few. Marker, younger than Ivens, co-founder of a modern post-war cinema, is just as mobile, he too is a globe-trotter traversing political and cultural networks. Yet from the very outset, Marker arranged his visual material with the distance of a historiographer; despite all its topicality, his discourse has always been retrospective and radically subjective. Farocki, finally, is no longer in search of the 'maelstrom of life,' that Vertov's *Man with a*

*Movie Camera* tried to capture (and which certainly is inherent in Ivens' testimonies and many of Marker's travel images). He films what we perceive to be reality, wherever it becomes a matrix, whether sites of social practice or media production. Farocki, like Marker, explores found footage. When he speaks about distant lands and conflicts (in *Etwas wird sichtbar* or *Nicht löschbares Feuer*) it is always with an awareness of the insurmountable divide between "here" and "elsewhere," as Godard termed this difference in one of his film titles.

## World, history (stories) and cinema

The age of cinema coincides with the age of history in its modern conception as a history made by people, as the future that they jointly construct when they cease to rely on divine providence or the wisdom of a prince shaping their fate. This modern conception of history, as Jacques Rancière[1] explains, is but one possible conception. In one sense, history means the set of rules of a fiction or mythos in the Aristotelian-Greek sense. In another, history, in the classical sense means the recording of memorable events. Finally, in the modern sense, history denotes the power of common fate. Thus, the question about the recording of history on film is extremely complex - as a question about the type of plot of a film, as a question concerning the function of remembering being fulfilled by a film, and finally as a question of the form in which a film confirms participation in a common fate.

This complex recording of (hi)stories in film is illustrated particularly in connection with media dispositives. A classic example: *Spanish Earth* (1934) by Joris Ivens. This film has a clear memorial function: it is above all intended for an American audience with the aim of arousing solidarity for the Spanish people's struggle against Franco's troops supported by Hitler. This function is fulfilled by means of interweaving the two other 'stories,' the way in which the narration is handled, and the way in which a common fate is evoked (i.e. the idea of a time and a common goal, but also a collective power). Basically, the film tells the story of two actions, the defense of a street threatened as Madrid's only route of supply, and con-

1. Cf. Jacques Rancière: "L'Historicité du Cinéma." In: *De l'Histoire au Cinéma*, ed. par Antoine de Baecque et Christian Delage. Bruxelles 1998, pp. 45-60.

# Ivens, Marker, Farocki

*Joris Ivens,
Spanish Earth, 1937.
Camera: J. Ivens, commentary: Ernest Hemingway
(next to Ivens).*

*Joris Ivens, Le train de la
Victoire, 1964, Chile.*

*Joris Ivens, Marceline
Loridan, Comment Yukong
déplaca les montagnes,
1973, China.
Sound: M. Loridan, next to
camera: J. Ivens.*

struction of an irrigation plant in the backwoods also planned to supply the capital. We see the freedom fighters, members of international brigades, farmers thirsting for action, but also old people, women, and children in the villages and in the city - all participating in the great scheme of history. Although *Spanish Earth* begins with everyday pictures from the village in order to embed the guerrilla fighting in the comparable peaceful life of civilians, the differences between active fighters and passive victims is dramatized by means of media dispositives. A commentary is added to the pictures of military soldiers at the front, amplifying the effect of authenticity by asserting a self-referential context: "Men cannot act before the camera in the presence of death." We have accompanying portraits of men taking aim at the enemy. They are equipped with arms but also with telescopes and telephones. The media are given a diegetic presence within a story that is being built in an efficient way. When the Republican front gathers, their messages are transmitted by loudspeakers toward the enemy attackers. This is the role the visual pictures construct and the commentary evokes. "The pasionaria" speaks: the image successively transmits her words to several spaces, from the space in which the revolutionary public assembles, to the wide suburbs where the loudspeakers are aimed to change the minds of the Francoists.

But when anonymous people are shot at in the city or village or are subjected to an air strike, their figures are clothed in affective images. They appear in an arbitrary space, the deadly force descends from above like something inevitable, incarnated in a bird's-eye view of the village. In contrast with the armed defenders, these are people without media technologies. Indeed, the air strike is announced by human screams. The alternating view of the attacking machines and the people being attacked is dominated by the machine, the machine initiates the storm of images. What we see of the people in the village is the emotional reaction to the attacks. Things are quite different with the fighters. Armed with a communication network you have power. If you are in action (in this case film action), you are masters of the media and the gaze. In this ideological documen-

tary film, the importance of every single image is thus subordinate to a documentary narration constantly driven either by the commentary or via the visual logic of the action.

Ivens' approach in *...A Valparaiso,* for which Chris Marker wrote the commentary, differs from that of *Spanish Earth:* this portrait of a Chilean city does not attempt to constitute a narration, but rather creates correspondences and

metamorphoses in a dialogue between sound and image, isolating individual fragments to form an expression of the whole. Stairs, lifts, cableways, boats, pieces of clothing, and kites are the recurrent elements of what is a description of aggregate conditions of a city in which top and bottom, poor and rich, air and water determine people's movements. A sequence of shots shows a one-legged man climbing the stairs of the city with difficulty, then a little girl sliding down the handrail. Later on, the commentary announces, "too many people at the top, very few at the bottom: in an hour it will be the other way round. Incessant conquest and reconquest, like at Douaumont Fort. Like in war or in major manoeuvres there are assaults, sorties, breakthroughs, counter-attacks, victories, people running away in mad panic. And sometimes a cease-fire." This Markerian description is incidentally a perfect

gers are queuing up, the conductor ushering them one after the other through a turnstile, laden with fish, a wooden board, a chair or a sack. Here the images are not projected before motionless people but rather the people are queuing in front of the machine in order to present their image to the conductor and the camera. Like the images on a strip of film, the figures are evoked individually and by jerks - an idea that Godard was to implement in an explicit form about a decade

Joris Ivens, ...A Valparaíso, 1963.

description of a film dating from 1927, *Etudes de Mouvement*, in which Ivens studies car traffic on the Parisian Rue de Rivoli as a rhythmic interplay of waiting and driving, emptying and filling, movement and counter-movement for just over three minutes.

In ...*A Valparaiso*, similar to Vertov's *Man with a Movie Camera*, mountain railways and lifts stand for a visual dispositive (that of cinema) and for a system of communication (that of the city). The commentary tells us, "inspectors and machinists see the whole city pass by; they know its adventures and its secrets better than anyone else. They are the museum attendants of the hills." What Ivens shows us here is not merely the rack-railways from the outside and the houses gliding by before the motionless-moving travelers, as in a cinematographic projection the passengers themselves are part of the projection. In a short scene the passen-

later in *Ici et Ailleurs*[2] and after that in *Grandeur et Décadence d'un Petit Commerce de Cinéma*.

In this short film, the town of Valparaiso is presented as if in a kaleidoscope - incidentally, an element that appears as an emblem in the final credits. What emerges is an interplay of correspondences and associations, not least as a result of the constant to and fro between words and images. As the commentary runs along different levels between historical, social, literary, art historical, anecdotal or poetically observed details, the movements and image sequences of the film stretch out a net of metamorphoses: the corner of a pointed building unnoticeably turns into the bow of a ship, and at the end of the film the mountain railway seems to fly away like a kite in the wind. As unambiguously as the machine dispositives divide people into subjects and objects in *Spanish earth*, all the more

2. Cf. Serge Daney: " Eine Geschichte über Beweglichkeit und Unbeweglichkeit. I". *Documenta Documents* 2/1996 [Fr. 1989], p. 80 ff.

3. Cf. Elie Faure, "De la Ciné-Plastique," in: *Fonction du Cinéma. De la cinéplastique à son destin social.* Paris 1953 (Plon), p. 31 and p. 41 (second quote).

4. On the foundations of modern art in the older Romantics, cf. also Michael Ligner: "Text-Transformationen. Exemplarische Übergangsformen zwischen künstlerischem Schaffen und begrifflichem Denken." In: Eleonora Louis/Toni Stooss (eds.): *Die Sprache der Kunst. Die Beziehung von Bild und Text in der Kunst des 20. Jahrhunderts.* Vienna 1993 (catalogue), pp. 101-118.

5. Rancière op. cit. p. 49.

6. Cf. Bernard Eisenschitz: "Chris Marker. Quelquefois les images." In *Trafic* 19/été 1996, pp. 46-57, here p. 48.

7. On *Sans soleil*, and indeed all of Marker's work, cf. Birgit Kämper/Thomas Tode (eds.): *Chris Marker. Filmessayist.* Munich Institut de Français de Munich/Cicim (Revue Cicim 45-47) 1997.

*Chris Marker, Laurence Rassel, Roseware 1996. Interactive media installation.*

ambiguous are they in ...*A Valparaiso.* Ivens' images seem to fulfil a function of cinema, as Elie Faure[3] put it at the beginning of the 1920s: "Cinema is first and foremost three-dimensional. In a way it is architecture in motion that should be in constant harmony, in dynamic balance with the environment and the landscapes," and further: "through [cinema], time truly becomes a dimension of space."

...*A Valparaiso* hits on the aesthetic potential of cinema. Beside being a documentary devoted entirely to the commentary, this film fulfils a program as described by Jacques Rancière as project of modernism rooted in the German Romantic period:[4] the idea of anti-representative art; the idea of art as both intentional and automatic process; the cancellation of traditional oppositions of the conceptual and the sensorial; and finally the idea of an art beyond art that constructs forms of social life. Seen in this way, cinema is the art of combining signs of a variable nature, intensity and significance. In this context, Rancière underlines three aspects of an aesthetic historicity: the expressiveness with which a sentence, an episode, an image is isolated in order to express from within itself the nature and colour of the whole; the ability to correspond, by which signs of a quite different nature may enter into resonance or dissonance; finally, the ability to metamorphose by which a combination of signs is entrenched in an unfathomable object or unfolds in a living form of meaning. In ...*A Valparaiso* the variability of meanings is produced not least by the text written by Chris Marker that runs parallel to the images.

## Media and montage

Marker's cinema could be termed an intellectual cinema of thought that succeeds in cancelling the traditional oppositions between the conceptual and the sensorial. Marker has not only radically renewed the word-image relation of the documentary film since the 1950s (in a montage that André Bazin called "lateral" and which came to shake the classical bond between sound and image but succeeded in effecting this 'sensorial thought' at an early stage by using suitable media technologies - be it cartoon and blown up

16mm material in *Lettre de Sibérie*, photography in *Si J'Avais Quatre Dromadaires* and *La Jetée*, silent 16mm Bolex pictures in *Le Mystere Koumiko*, direct sound in *Le Joli Mai*, the super-8 camera for the imaginary amateur film *L'Ambassade*, the synthesizer for the "zone" of memory in *Sans Soleil*, or, most recently, the computer in *Level Five*. All these technologies express a temporal or spatial distance[4] which, for Marker, is a precondition for legibility of the images.

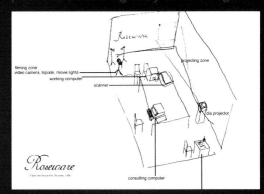

*Le Mystere Koumiko* (1965), for example, anticipates Japan as a land of media signs in a form later also characteristic of *Sans Soleil*.[7] The film shows an illuminated city imbued with transportation machines, communication equipment and gaming-machines. In this silent portrait of a woman and a city, radio represents a substantial media figure. Questions the film-maker asks of the protagonist Koumiko are answered from off-screen, the answers, the commentator tells us, are finally mailed to him, "Japanese style, that is, in time." As the early Koumiko's contemplations are compared with the view of a distant film-maker seeking to confront himself with his views of Japan, in an unspoken homage to his fellow-traveler André Bazin in 1998 (on the occasion of his retrospective at the Cinémathèque Française) Marker rightly observed that intelligence could be the base material, the raw footage upon which the commentary and the montage are based. His treatment of found material testifies to an ethics of montage perhaps also rooted in the work of André Bazin, whose famous phrase "no montage" was not intended as a fundamental prohibition but rather as a question as to the relation of seeing and being seen. In *Sans Soleil* Marker, the animal-lover, shows as a 'found' image the death of a giraffe whose hunters remain invisible, but whom Marker represents with a weapon from a horror film pointed at the

viewer. In *Level Five* one sequence concentrates on an analysis of the images of Japanese women who fall to their death while fleeing from the American enemy, observed by their cameras. Marker programmatically sets forth both the desperate aspect of the footage and the critical distance from the material - quoting Racine with which he prefaced the original French version of *Sans Soleil*: "In a very high distance of the countries offsets the excessive closeness of the times."[8]

More than 30 years after the Spanish Civil War, Joris Ivens filmed the Vietnam war: for the collective film *Loin du Viet-Nam* (orchestrated by Chris Marker). He captured images of the Vietnamese population looking for shelter, ingeniously building individual bunkers. Marker feeds these images into a discourse that is situated beyond Vietnam: "We are far from Viet-nam...," we hear at the end of the film, and in an episode created by Resnais a self-critical intellectual states, "I am speaking of a country that does not exist." Here Vietnam is also seen as a Western projection, as an "experimental arrangement" that creates a monstrous complicity between opponents and advocates. With a radical gesture, paradoxically only recently remade, Farocki's *Nichtlöschbares Feuer* expresses the distance between the Western laboratories, but also between the revolting students on the one hand and the real world theatre of war on the other. Farocki, who appears, indeed physically subjects himself to the camera, comes closest to Godard's Vietnam contribution for the collective film. Godard, too, presents a treatise concerning the question of the form of fighting for Vietnam. As in Farocki's other militant Vietnam contribution *Ihre Zeitungen*, and later in *Etwas wird sichtbar*, *Loin du Viet-Nam*, is also concerned with reading the images of Vietnam. The fictitious intellectual, tormented by writer's block, tells his dumb listener about a shocking shot taken from the war in the Pacific - the repeated image of a Japanese man burned by a flame-thrower pointing his hand towards the camera: "The editors know him so well that they have made up a nice name for him: they call him Gustave. He served all purposes. He was seen in all films. Successively he represented Japanese imperialism, a victim of its machines, Asian peoples, victims of white imperialism, and eternal man, victim of eternal war. Because he appears naked in the flames, he always provides a good link ... We have the impression that the same shot has been going round for twenty years, and it changes nothing." Almost 30 years later, in *Level Five*, Marker dedicates an entire sequence to this eternal soldier Gustave from *Loin du Viet-Nam* in order to bury the undead once and for all.

In *Level Five*, Marker explores this shot as a media cliché in greater detail. The

*Chris Marker, Zapping Zone. Proposals for an imaginary television, 1990/97 Videoinstallation (CD-Rom, computer)*

*Chris Marker, Immemory, 1997 Interactive media installation (CD-Rom, computer)*

8. Second introduction to Racine's Bajazet.

*Chris Marker, si j'avais quatre dromadaires, 1966.*

*Chris Marker, Le fond de l'air est rouge, 1977.*

9. In a similarly 'educational' manner, Marker describes the function of the commentary in *Lettre De Sibérie* (1958) by having three different commentaries on one shot run one after the other.

10. Cf. Giorgio Agamben: Noten zur Geste, in: Stil der Politik und Stil der Filme, Zur Kommunikationstechnik der Filme, Stuttgart 1996 (Dispositiv Documents), pp. 68-75.

11. Cf. Roland Barthes: *Die helle Kammer*, Frankfurt a. M. 1989 (Camera Lucida)

burning man was always only shown up to the moment of his collapse. Marker shows this shot twice, the first time fleetingly, as a negative schematic image (digitally modified), the second time as the original shot. The frame is frozen at the end of each sequence. This immobilisation, combined with the figurative and temporally displaced repetition, illustrates three things: first, the significance of editing and montage' with regard to the status of the visual 'document,' secondly, as the mortifying dimension of a documentary that aims to show war, and, third, as the ossification of a documentary image as a cliché.

**In stressing the cut in the 'Gustave' sequence, Marker shares a conception of montage with Godard and Farocki, a montage whose "transcendental conditions" Giorgio Agamben[10] terms repetition and immobilisation. Repetition as restoration of what may have been and immobilisation as the revolutionary power to "break through" a circle (in the sense of Walter Benjamin). As far as the future death is inscribed in this image, what we see is the effect that Roland Barthes[11] describes as the aspect of having been of photography, the stopping of a moving image that first (in contradistinction to the photographic) evokes a present rather than a past. And finally, as far as freezing of a moving image into an endlessly reproducing cliché is concerned, examining the 'original document' will not necessarily bring us closer to the historical 'truth.' Yet here we see the memorability of a history reawakened, one that had ceased to exist as a result of the discursive indifference of the audiovisual institutions to a particular 'document.' Marker's position refers to a trend towards arbitrariness that is growing in these times of digitised, simultaneously globalising and centralising image archives.**

Harun Farocki also focuses on the phenomenon of the nameless body in many instances in order to analyse the dispositive of media clichés. "The unknown soldier was invented to make war look like a deed. There is no deed without a name," we hear in the commentary inspired by Hannah Arendt in Farocki's *Wie man sieht*. Like Marker, Farocki is not concerned with the obscenity of the mere representation of death or sexuality. Rather,

he illustrates the media-based context of representation. At this point we associate the unknown soldier with the pornographic business - women's bodies given fictitious names in order to make the magazine user's fantasy appear to be 'like a deed.' Farocki unframes and reframes the images of bodies that are already visually fragmented, operating with still images, photographs. The filmmaker's gesture moves our view from

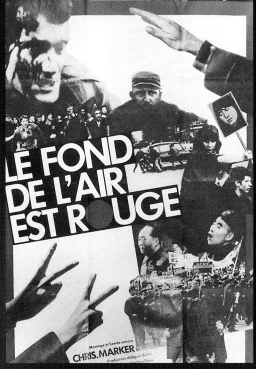

Cinémas Quintette/Entrepôt

LE FOND DE L'AIR EST ROUGE

Montage et bande sonore
CHRIS. MARKER

what is represented to the representation itself and is also found in subsequent analyses: in *Images of the World and the Inscription of War*, too, a new interpretation of images is permitted by Farocki's explicit framing. The film analyses surveillance technologies - one key motif is an aerial photograph of the Allies who in 1944 were only interested in a bomber target, not in the adjacent extermination camp at Auschwitz. How did one separate

that the paradoxical preserving/destructive aspect of photography can issue from this not-seeing, not-perceiving just as it can from the fascinated view of a person whose weapon is directly connected to a vision machine.

Another recurrent theme in the film is the identity photos of Algerian women forced by the French colonialists to show their faces in public for the first time. Farocki shows them in series, as frontal images

without any direct reaction in which the view of the people targeted remains blind. Farocki reframes the images after showing them once 'in full,' thus transforming them with a simple gesture in the repetition. Here again, Farocki reframes the images manually, and his manual gesture is preceded by the invisible push of a button that allows recent police simulation equipment to create composite photos. Much like post-photographical digital images, these composites no

longer follow a particular human model, nor are they an abstract representation of this model, but rather they are, conversely, simulacra serving as a model for reality.

## The memory of the media

The more media representations reproduce, the more they displace the nonexistence of what they have not captured. The audiovisual media, first and foremost television, overvalue what they enact, in a process that Pierre Nora called creating the event. This fact essentially underlines the paradoxical status of a moving image that replaces memory in order to become an image of memory itself. Cinema[12] opposes the constitution of a "distance memory" as described by Pierre Nora as fundamental to the historical discourse: as soon as history takes control of what it calls memory - i.e. the traces that allow it to be constituted - it distances, mediatizes and eradicates these traces in order to be able to create a context of meaning. The individual film is left to develop an aesthetic that displaces the present, proximate element of the moving image or at least partially interrupts the purported flow of memory. Television, however, is structurally and institutionally an "empire built on quicksand" as a result of its uninterrupted presence of information and its constant desire to replace.[13] As television declares itself to be a store of memory, memory is delegated to its audiovisual archive as a site of memory: the effect of immediacy and the accessibility of the visual document in this context are more essential than their meaning. Forms of television that draw on archive images mainly to illustrate events privilege the affective over the reflective dimension of images and thus remove the viewer's possibility of distance.

But it is precisely this distance to the archive material that is Marker's and Farocki's starting point. They set about focusing on revolution(s) by analysing their images, as opposed to Ivens who was a contemporary of the first revolutionary films. Marker's *Le Fond De L'Air Est Rouge*, a polyphonic essay on the political struggles and hopes of the 1960s and 1970s, begins with a parallel montage of Eisenstein's *Battleship Potemkin* and contemporary images of

*Harun Farocki, Schnittstelle, 1995. Videoinstallation.*

*Harun Farocki, Etwas wird sichtbar, 1980-82.*

12. Cf. Pierre Nora: "Le retour de l'Événement..." In: *Faire de l'Histoire,I*; ed. by Pierre Nora and Jacques le Goff. Paris 1974, pp. 212-215; and Michèle Lagny: "Histoire contre l'Image, l'Image contre la Mémoire." In: *Hors Cadre*, 9, pp. 63-76; particularly p. 69 and p. 72.

French Extrème Gauche fighting during the 1960s. The pictures of the burials of the dead of the Charonne are followed by a woman mourning before the body of the sailor Vakulitschuk. Scenes of police violence from the 1960s are matched by the legendary picture of the stairs in Odessa, the gestures of raised fists can be read as Pathos formulas (in the words of Aby Warburg) of the revolution. In this iconographical series, Marker demonstrates, right from the start, the symbolic significance of images circulated by the media, whether enacted or documentary. More important for the subsequent uprisings than the actual memory of the historical October Revolution, are the images of it. Marker prefaced his essay "Le Tombeau D'Alexandre" (dedicated to Alexander Medvedkin) with an apt quotation from George Steiner: "It is not the past that controls us, but rather the images of the past."

Marker's historiographical discourse is also rooted in an interest in the repression of images in two respects: on the one hand, he incorporates the out-takes,[14] of militant films that have gone by the cutting-board, and that are perhaps too ambivalent, and opposes the successive repression of the images by the event-oriented institution of television, as so-called collective non-memory." In "Le Tombeau d'Alexandre," Marker adopts a similar contrary course, as in *Le Fond De L'Air Est Rouge* when he retrospectively analyses the films of Medvedkin's film train, long believed to be lost, as films fallen foul of power, whose ambivalence today is unmistakable: pictures, for example, "of mine workers from the Donbas, in filth and poverty, shown alongside activists who don't stop talking."[15]

Harun Farocki (together with Andrei Ujica) makes a comparable contrast ... of publicly displayed and censored images, of televised templates and amateur views ... in *Videogram of a revolution*. But while for Marker the idea of personal memory is the key source of the films and installations, Farocki is more interested in the dispositive of the images, as a three-dimensional and symbolic arrangement of gazes that characterises a medium. And he is again and again concerned with a certain framework of the public sphere determined by economy, politics and technology. *Videograms...* composed

solely of found material, is a compilation of television and amateur recordings of the mass movement that led to the downfall of Ceaucescu. The official television dispositive does not change fundamentally after the fall of the despot. There are amateur recordings, initially spontaneous and concealed, bearing witness to the people on the street and the revolution beyond television, and which adapt to TV conventions as the mediated coup progresses. The characteristic gesture in the film, an amateur film-maker whose camera is taping the official live broadcast of a public address by Ceaucescu at home, pans away from his TV set during the non-localisable rioting to the window and on to the street, evoking this scene of the event, as Farocki notes in *Interface*. Although the media are shown as part of the uprising (as opposed to *Spanish Earth*), they are also analysed as the site of power and cinema. The revolution is also taking place on the streets, and there is more memorialising interest in the gesture of the amateur film-maker than in the occupation of the television station.

## Small archaeologies of images

These films share a theoretical handling of visual material. Their sense of history cannot simply be read by the stories they evolve, but rather can be understood as a media-specific discourse, as thinking with and about the means of the cinematograph and its technical predecessors and successors, photography, video, and digital image media. Farocki is an analyst of visual constellations, he focuses on the media's use of technical images and sounds and on their production. He sees the pictures he registers and finds as models of social perception. Marker's work, too, formulates his conception of a radically subjective, authored history within the terms of various media, and thus he continues to update it constantly up to his latest film *Level Five*. Characteristically, the film contains numerous shots and readings of monuments, funeral ceremonies, lists of names, memorials and cemeteries: the analysis of the social discourse on the historical events accompanies their fragmentary narration. Even the "present" images of Marker's electronic framework that ultimately provide an insight into the making of the film *Level Five* are already seen as ...

13. Chris Marker: *Le Fond de l'air est rouge* (1978), preface to the textbook, Paris 1978. German in: Brigit Kämper/Thomas Tode (eds.): *Chris Marker. Filmessayist*. Munich: Institut de Français de Munich/Cicim (Revue Cicim 45-47) 1997, p. 176 f.

14. Cf. Chris Marker op. cit.

15. Chris Marker in *Images documentaires* N°15, p. 48.

ments from a (fictitious) future position: "In the prehistoric times of BTX, people used pseudonyms, they could borrow virtual masks," we hear concerning a journey of the protagonist into the future, about the O.W.L. interface, the "net of nets." In *Level Five* the game with the computer is seen as a visit to a cemetery, a modern-day burial ritual.

This 'theoretical' treatment of archives is not unrelated to Michel Foucault's conception of an archaeology of knowledge. Indeed, in terms of a discussion of documentary images, we could focus on the discursivity of facts in an 'archive' in order to no longer see them as documents (of a concealed truth or a rule of construction), but rather as monuments. This archive, in Foucault's words, would not be "the entirety of texts conserved by a civilisation, nor the ensemble of the traces that could have been **saved before it was** destroyed, but rather the set of rules that determines the appearance and disappearance of statements in a culture, their survival and eradication, their paradoxical existence as events and as objects."[16]

Of course, Joris Ivens cannot be called an archaeologist in Foucault's conception of the word, yet his work can be seen as a counter-strategy, in a set of rules of dominant media monumentalisations. More explicitly than Marker's, Farocki's films constitute small archaeologies geared to mental and social images - whether it is the idea of weaving, the development of measuring technologies, or the picture of the worker in the film story. In each case, he outlines an audiovisual history of culture and technology such that particular attention is paid to the historical deviations, gaps and cul-de-sacs. *Wie man sieht* is a case in point. Against the backdrop of an associative mesh of images from a wide variety of sources, Farocki does not simply wonder where and how a particular bridge, weapon or tool were built, but also "what other possibilities there might have been to do this and who ruled them out." Here, deviations from the history of technology are not merely the object of the film, they determine the very structure of the montage, small mental excursions in parallel fields or loops that surprisingly let us reconsider reflections that had been the subject of a former **allusion. The te**xtual principle of the film is one of repetition and difference, a possibility to present several objects and ideas

simultaneously that would be lost in the strictly diachronic sequence of linear narration.

In Farocki's and Marker's films, the media dispositive always creates a distance to the original film or photographic images. On Chris Marker's method of working with found footage, Bernard Eisenschitz writes: "Laying the photo or the shot on the table, splitting up the document, implies not just taking it literally or pictorially (Godard method). The question also arises as to the exchange of views, the source of the utterance. The archaeological gesture is directed into the future."[17] The way in which Marker employs 'found' (film) stories in his films and installations, stories that he carefully feeds into a machine like wood shavings to create a polyvalent discourse, is, however, not only formally akin to Jean-Luc Godard's ultimate video statement on cinema in *Histoire(s) Du Cinéma*. Both Godard and Marker transform the vision machine into a typewriter. "Documentary film," Jacques Rancière asserts, "its radicalism fulfils in their work this identity of thinking, writing and the principle that inhere in the core of aesthetic thinking itself and its 'historical' ability."[18] Here, history is seen as a discourse and, as such, can be traced down in a history of images.

In Farocki's work, too, thinking and writing are also explicitly tied in with image machines; the author presents himself like Godard in this same pose, be it in films such as *Zwischen zwei Kriegen* or in his installation *Interface*. Marker, who always remains invisible, inscribes his authorial presence into his films in a different way. The video machine, the recording machine from *Sans Soleil* with its technical connection to an electronic processing 'zone,' was followed by the video installation *Zapping Zone* as a personal archive, an early form of his own CD-ROM memory (which is not unlike Warburg's conception of a memory atlas). What Marker's memorial self-portraits are about can, **in a way, be read** from his homage to Simone Signoret, the film *Mémoire Pour Simone*. **It is not**, he states, a film about **her life or her career**, but rather - quite literally - about the "content of a cupboard... **a minute part of a** disordered memory, **a journey through** the images that she preserved."

16. Cf. Michel Foucault: "Sur l'Archéologie des Sciences. Réponse au Cercle d'épistémologie" [1968]. In: *Dits et Écrits*. 1. 1954-1988. Paris: Gallimard 1994, pp. 696-731, here: p. 708. Foucault's analysis of the scientific discourse cannot, admittedly, be applied to cinema quite that easily. And yet I feel that the epistemological discussion of history does in a way elucidate the function of modern media archives.

17. In: *Trafic*, 19/1996, p. 53.

18. Rancière 1998, p. 37. To Rancière, the aesthetic thinking of Godard and Marker lies in the tradition of the German Romance period, as a form of combining signs of a readable nature, intensity and meaning. In this respect, Rancière sees this form of documentary film (in relation to the Aristotelian juxtaposition of events, upon which narrative, representative films are based) as cinema par excellence.

19. Pierre Lévy: *Die kollektive Intelligenz. Eine Anthropologie des Cyberspace*. Bollmann Medien.

20. Siegfried Zielinski: "Fredda et secca/kühl und trocken. Zu einigen Vorstellungen und Melancholien der cellula memorialis als Speicher/Archiv." In *Kunstforum* N° 128, p. 189. And he continues: "The interface with its two-dimensional miniature posters is the ostensible shield, the imaginary outpost of the program, and at the same time constitutes the borderline that the user has to cross to enter cybernetic space."

The documentary cyber-fiction *Level Five* no longer represents a collective appropriation of history, but rather the lonely subject writing and reading in front of the screen, a nomadic existence, in a narcissistic pose directed towards himself and armed against the virtuality of the community. Whether Marker, designing his imaginary museums as personal chambers, believes in possibilities of a "collective intelligence" (in the sense of Pierre Lévy[19]) is as unresolved in this work as it is in his short science-fiction video *2084*, where three different future scenarios are drawn up for a union, the most bleak of which is a form of technical totalitarianism. When Marker shows the user interface of the net in such detail in *Level Five*, he is also presenting a computer-based memorial concept. Siegfried Zielinski aptly demonstrates such a concept in his iconic messengers "that are intended to mediate between those eager for knowledge and play and the electronic archives, depositories and stations. [...] An ideal field for imagination to unfold in combination with memory."[20]

If this bridge to imagination and conception works, then the moment of recognisability in the process of memory may be represented by the media, as at the beginning of *Le Joli Mai*. Here, Marker fantasizes about a picture of a woman walking on a roof ridge and a picture of Paris at dawn, a photograph that could have been taken from *La Jetée*, concerning how we could imagine a new, unknown Paris as a result of an amnesia, the Paris of Fantomas, accessible with the means of the detective, the telescope and the tape recorder. The possible fictions outlined in these opening credits impact the following testimonies as parallel worlds. This 1960s vérité film, Marker's only long interview film, again shows how media dispositives can serve as apparative links between the memorial and the imaginary.

*Harun Farocki, Etwas wird sichtbar, 1980-82.*

*Harun Farocki, Andrei Ujica, Videogramme einer Revolution, 1991-92.*

*Harun Farocki, Die Führende Rolle, 1994.*

Wir haben gesiegt!

19. Oktober '89
DDR 1

Werner Brüssau
in Ost-Berlin

Probleme
mit der Wahrheit

*Background image:
Chris Marker, Level Five,
1996.*

YOU'RI

# The New

Armand Mattelart

266

Global, globalisation, total, holistic: under the heterogeneous forms of its social presence, the network of applications of commercial techniques to human relations never ceases to claim the single-mindedness of its project. Instruments and expertise bring a cybernetic vision of society into play. Whence arises a paradox: the more these models of organisation conquer new territory, the more they make us forget that we still occupy a place within history: living, working, amusing ourselves, desiring, seducing and being seduced by our desires, in societies criss-crossed by diverse and multiple interests. Likewise the more they try to divert us from looking inwards. The locus of production of a new rationality of social control, new forms of the exercise of power, new modes of social integration, this industry of mediation is also a privileged site for the formulation of a vulgarised postmodern discourse about the end of the social domain, the inconstancy of the social, the loss of meaning, the renunciation of the rational basis of all values. For advertising leaves truth and falsehood behind.

One person's certainty is another's doubt. The flourishing vigour of 'totalisation' in the advertising industry contrasts with the agony of this concept in the social sciences of late capitalist society. The loss of credibility this concept has suffered signals the end of pretensions to the construction of global theories, and is the fruit of a process of re-examination no less contradictory. The bitter taste of total-

itarian horrors; skepticism of discourses which emphasise systems and the spirit of systematisation; defiance in the face of the abstract 'macro-subjects' of Power, State, Society; a preference for individual identity and new intersubjective relations, which try to replace the need to know everything with the desire to understand what is happening to the self, the group, the environment. This much is certain. But there is also a huge step backwards towards positivism and philosophies of individual consciousness, a return to the illusion that individual emancipation liberates us from history, and from everybody else too. (As Bertrand Russell once said, "I'm a solipsist, and I can't understand why everyone else isn't as well.")

On the one hand, a communications network, and a concept and vision of the planet as a world market, where you have to think globally and act both globally and locally. On the other hand, fragmentation, by token of local and individual action and agitation, whose meaning tends to decrease to the same rhythm as the old objects of study wither; and the progress of the new forms to replace them, both individual and collective.

# Totality*

*Peter Wintonick and Mark Achbar, Manufacturing Consent – Noam Chomsky and the Media, 1992, USA.*

*Peter Wintonick and Mark Achbar, Manufacturing Consent – Noam Chomsky and the Media, 1992, USA.*

# A new Type of Subjectivity

In their report of 1985, entitled *Proposals for Education in the Future*, under the direction of the sociologist Pierre Bourdieu, the professors of the Collège de France wrote as follows:

"Among the functions attributable to culture, one of the most important is without doubt the role of self-defence against all forms of ideological pressure, religious and political: this instrument of free thought, like the martial arts in other terrains, allows today's citizens to protect themselves against abuses of symbolic power directed against them, be they advertising, propaganda or political or religious fanaticism."

An affirmation that can only be shared by those for whom the idea of critical consciousness still retains some meaning. But if advertising is no more than a category among the various abuses of symbolic power, does this identify the new forms of social regulation correctly? To take up the simile of the martial arts, is this indeed the correct terrain of combat (given that one has decided that combat is necessary)?

The moment has arrived to ask not what culture can do in the face of the abuses of advertising and marketing, so much as what advertising and marketing have done to culture. At the risk of becoming ineffectual, no analysis, no intervention can elude the question of the hegemony exercised by the pragmatics of marketing over the modern mode of communication, just as no protagonist of audiovisual production can afford to ignore the implications of the industrial and commoditised mode of production and diffusion for the status of the work, of creation, and the author. Because like it or not, commoditised space has become so pervasive that it becomes impossible to continue thinking of culture as a reserved and uncontaminated terrain. This space has surely become a domain which regulates human relations, as well as the locus onto which conflicts between social projects have been displaced. One cannot explain the process of privatisation of public space - nor its reconstruction - without taking into account the fact of unequal exchange between mercantile reason and public reason, mass culture and 'high culture,'

mass culture and popular cultures, globalised industrial cultural production and individual cultures. Beyond this incessant and daily process of appropriation and re-appropriation, outside these relations of competition and conflict between culture and economy, it is scarcely possible to imagine the reconstruction of the instruments of free thought, which allows the citizenry to protect itself from these abuses of symbolic power.

Because the capitalisation of culture is also the capitalisation of the most existential levels of subjectivity in the consciousness of the citizen-consumer, who is increasingly influenced by the specialised activities of the professionals and their techniques and devices. The commoditisation of culture is, above all, the production of new kinds of subjectivity. It is precisely

because of this qualitative leap in the management of subjectivity that cultural struggles and the stakes involved regain their strategic importance.

This is just what Felix Guattari has described so well - one of the few psychoanalysts to have grasped this new condition. Namely, how and why late capitalism, or 'integrated world capitalism,' has increasingly devolved the foci of power from the productive structures of goods and services to those of the sign and subjectivity - mediated, for sure, by the mediatised apparatus of communication:

It is no longer possible to imagine opposing all this only from outside, through traditional political and union activity. Similarly, it becomes imperative to confront its effects amidst daily life in the home, the neighbourhood, the workplace, cultural life and even personal morality. We may note, simply, that one of the main symptoms through which these effects are manifest consists in the infantilisation of human conduct (which must not be confused with 'becoming childish'). Capitalist 'subjectivity,' as it is mediated by professionals of every type and size, is manufactured in a form which pre-empts the existence of any intrusion of events likely

*TIV – True Image Vision, STROBE, 1998.*

*TIV - True Image Vision, STROBE, 1998.*

*Chris Marker, Les 20 Heures dans les Camps, 1993.*

to annoy or disturb it. Every singularity must be avoided, must be subjected to its devices, its professionals and specialised frames of reference. Thus it goes so far as to try and direct whatever belongs to the method of discovery and invention of the infant, of art or of love, as well as whatever relates to anxiety, pain, death, the feeling of being alone in the cosmos. … By appealing to consensual sentiments attached to concepts of race, nation, professionalism, sports, the idealised media star and concupiscence, it becomes intoxicated and anaesthetises itself, in a feeling of pseudo-eternity. It is in the ensemble of these 'fronts,' intricate and heterogeneous, that new political and social practices must organise themselves, jointly with new aesthetic practices and new analytic forms, able to work at 'resingularisation,' or individual and collective reappropriation of subjectivity. In effect, 'capitalistic' subjectivity is by no means assured of winning, as it has been over the last decade. Not only could the present financial and economic crisis result in important reformulations of the social status quo and the 'mass-mediatised' imaginary which it supports, but some of the themes sustained by neo-liberalism, such as flexibility in the workplace and deregulation … could perfectly well rebound against it.

One must still be bold enough to declare that the noisy space of desire and dreams with which the networks of the world market try to seduce us in their search for the calculable and predictable individual, is clearly not the secret utopia of the Subjects of the City of the World. The International of the management of consensual sentiment is not, in all certainty, the cosmopolitanism of cultural difference. The democratic marketplace so beloved by the heralds of this new 'human right of commercial free expression' is in no way the same as the democracy of the defenders of human rights, the rights of the citizen and of nations. Between them there lies the immense abyss with which the new and inegalitarian rationality has bisected a planet that is pierced by social exclusions.

*excerpt from Armand Mattelart: *Advertising International: the Transformation of Public Space*, Routledge, 1991

*TIV – True Image Vision, STROBE, 1998.*

Peter Wintonick and Mark Achbar, *Manufacturing Consent – Noam Chomsky and the Media*, 1992, USA.

ROOM

Backgroundimage:
Peter Fend
NEWS ROOM, 1990.

Backgroundimage:
Susanne Granzer and Arno Böhler,
Avital Ronell. *Der Ruf – Filosofie im Bild*,
1998 (The Call).

Roberto Aguirrezabala

Two characters in one fiction.
Their relationship with the surroundings
are continuously dislocated due to their
shown inability to reach a dialogue with
each other. The conflict reappears. I run
down the streets taking photographs of
everyone that I find on his/her own. You
stop to make a decision, to cross the road
for example and there is a flash. You have
been photographed. You are an image in my
photograph album, whether you like it or
not. And you may not even know.

ID.
Nobody knows if they are being watched
while navigating through the web site.
what:you:get is a data base. Information
inside one server. Words, numbers, sentences that are related to each other and
make sense. They are signs of identity that
the user generates while navigating
through the net. They are personalities,
the real ones and the false ones, the conscious ones and the unconscious ones. It is
a reconstructed profile. It is the game of

the anonymity, a game of the false identity. In the chat I prefer the anonymity. I
avoid ambiguities, and even though nobody
knows who I am, I never lie. I always want
to be myself... Even though it would be
easy to lie.

Virtual Community.
Only one performance-stage with different
levels of coexistence. 00:00 h. The masked
ball begins. The music blasts out and dancing bodies invade the center stage. Thousands of stage lights blind your vision for
a second. You get used to the darkness and
you find similarities and distances and
compromises and differences and resem-
blances... Someone looks for someone,
what:you:get is a person finder: girl +
homosexual + sexually active + independent
+ imaginative + melancholic + seducer +
unvain + engaged + optimist + what you sex
is what I play

search now

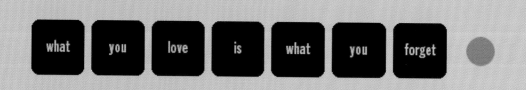

berg_man

blow

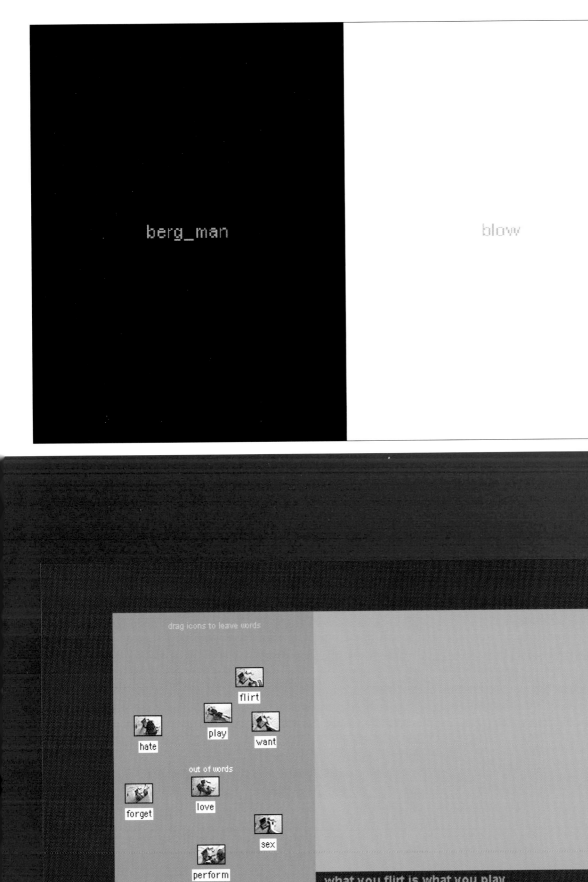

drag icons to leave words

flirt

play

hate

want

out of words

love

forget

sex

perform

what you flirt is what you play

Jordan Crandall

http://www.blast.org/crandall/

074

Traversal-modes:
        cut,
      impact
Rhythmic augmentation
              through RF
(represented but also
present in
machinic orderings)

Scene: Crime
Outdoor,
    desolate industrial area,
night,
      floodlit
                    Intercut
with mobile
      motion-studies

Tracks
(aligned/synchronized
in  image-field):
Actor-Human
Track
  Net
    Monitor
      Capture
        Propulsion
          Align
            Contour

# Drive,

POVHuman/
      Object(RF)
Machine
Encoded
      in VRML

Demographic
  Compilations
      database
object of analysis:
        development of RF,
insertion
      of behavior
      patterns

Motion
Tracking
tracking and analysis

Time-Code
    Tracking
recalibrated
        temporalization,
    subject to alternate
  protocols,
            alternate
frequency-units

Actor-Object RF

Track
    Net
        Monitor Align

Actor-Machine
            intimated
by foregrounding
            tech
conditions

POV-Human/
    Object RF
        ambiguous,
in-between viewpoints

POV-Machine
            intimated
by foregrounding
            tech
conditions

# Track #3

Sound-
    Mechanical
machinic rhythms –
fragmentation in bursts,
        spasms,
    jerks,
        pulses,
    poundings;
        repetition;
        velocity

Sound-
    Informatic/
Network
        transmission
and processing

Sound-
    Human
    breathing;
moan;
    exertion

Colin Green: The user opens the program. They marquee a box in the blank screen, then apply a function to it. The first function necessary is a 'crawler.' This calls up a web site and proceeds to follow every link on that site - and every subsequent link. A 'map' window can be opened which traces the progress of the crawler. The map is a basic real-time dynamic visualisation of the underlying link-node structure of the web. Nodes from the map can be dragged into an 'extract' window which pulls any text from them. You can also view the 'HTML stream' as the crawler works its way through the web or 'dismantle' sites to analyse their contents.

Matthew Fuller: It is a way of using the web that resonates with the actual qualities of the network, rather than attempting to repeat the conventions of graphic design for paper - as is being done with style sheets. We believe that the World Wide Web Consortium, Netscape and Microsoft have closed down the possibilities of what the web might be. This is seen even in much artists' use of the web, where the conventions enforced by the software manufacturers are simply unconsciously repeated.

Simon Pope: Where's the artwork? Is it in the software, the socially produced situation, the revisualisation of the network, the network itself?
We see the institutions and discourse-networks of art being important to I/O/D because they provide a particular range of social and aesthetic devices for the consideration and circulation of information about projects and particularly as a

medium in itself for the distribution of software.
At the same time, we are equally as keen to operate through different media systems... our two key areas of work are, on one level, to open up the machines - to produce software that involves developing transversal relationships between different, normally masked, elements of computing process and users - see-through software.
To ask what types of subjectivation, both of 'groups' and 'individuals', but also what types of machines (their embodiment of different forms of movement, relations and intelligence) what types of networks of information elements are being produced and to produce a software context that allows for the development of other types of formation and circulation. - speculative software ...

Matthew Fuller: For standard Human Computer Interface design ... the principle axis in simple single-user software is between psychology-computing. The equivalent axis in CSCW (computer supported co-operative work), groupware, is sociology-computing. Our work is in a sense to return the psychological to the social and to disturb the production of subjectivity within the neat and tidy models it is reported as conforming to by psychology.
We want an end to the anthropomorphisation of humans via the machines!

Simon Pope: I/O/D has the same relation to the software industry as the production of hot-rods has to the car industry.
(excerpts from an interview with Isla Saint-Claire, 17.06.99)

http://www.backspace.org/iod/les
Complete http://www.artincontext
2055xttj/menu.htm [4218 of 4218

Web
2

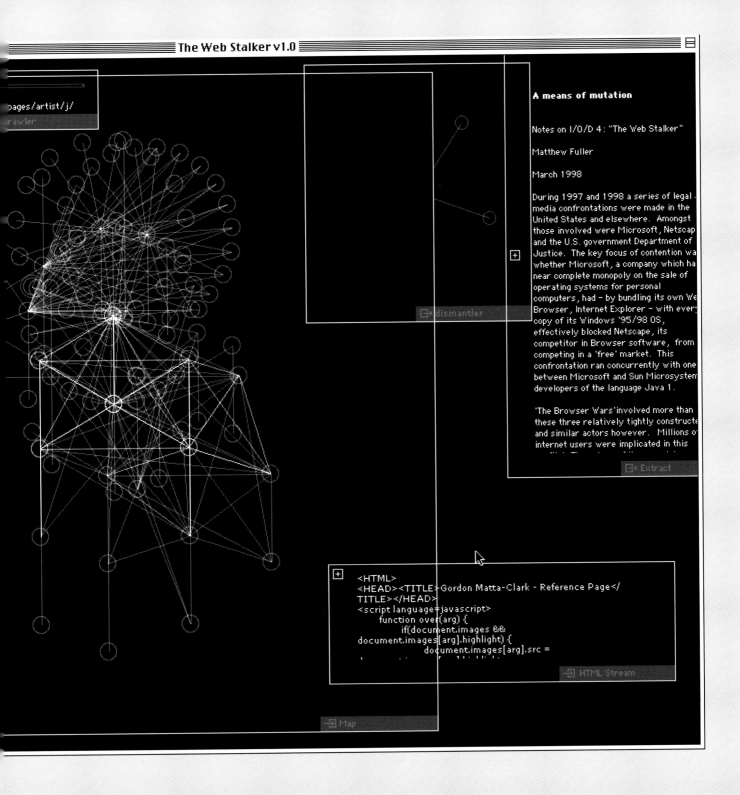

talker

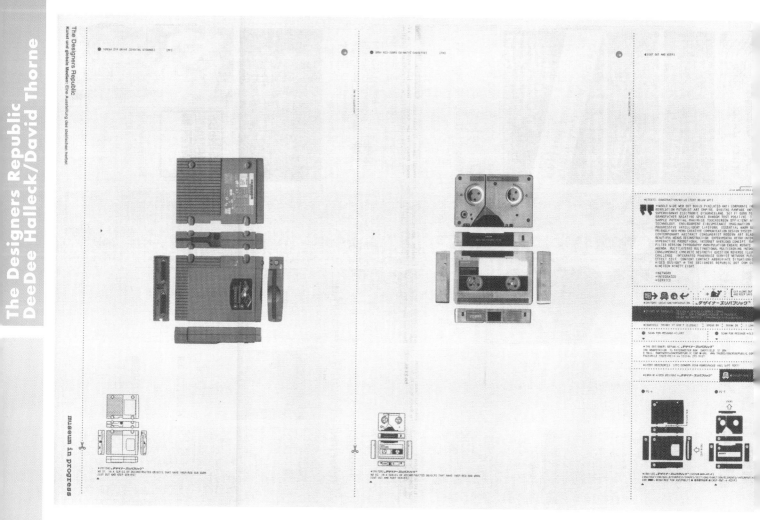

Contribution in the newspaper DER STANDARD, Signs
of Trouble - International Positions in Information
Design of the 1990s:
The Designers Republic 9/15/1998
(Cooperation with the museum in progress and basis
Wien, curated by Walter Pamminger and Christian Muhr)


Contribution in the newspaper DER STANDARD, Signs
of Trouble - International Positions in Information
Design of the 1990s:
DeeDee Halleck/David Thorne 12/16/1998
(Cooperation with the museum in progress and basis
Wien, curated by Walter Pamminger and Christian Muhr)

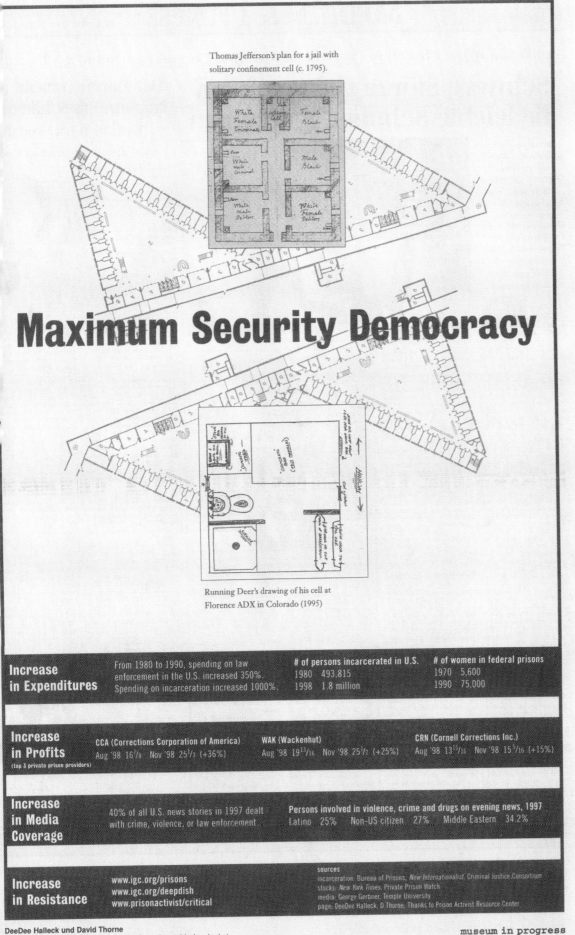

Thomas Jefferson's plan for a jail with
solitary confinement cell (c. 1795).

# Maximum Security Democracy

Running Deer's drawing of his cell at
Florence ADX in Colorado (1995)

| **Increase in Expenditures** | From 1980 to 1990, spending on law enforcement in the U.S. increased 350%. Spending on incarceration increased 1000%. | # of persons incarcerated in U.S.<br>1980  493,815<br>1998  1.8 million | # of women in federal prisons<br>1970  5,600<br>1990  75,000 |
|---|---|---|---|

| **Increase in Profits** (top 3 private prison providers) | CCA (Corrections Corporation of America)<br>Aug '98 16$^{1}/_{8}$  Nov '98 25$^{1}/_{3}$ (+36%) | WAK (Wackenhut)<br>Aug '98 19$^{11}/_{16}$  Nov '98 25$^{1}/_{2}$ (+25%) | CRN (Cornell Corrections Inc.)<br>Aug '98 13$^{15}/_{16}$  Nov '98 15$^{5}/_{16}$ (+15%) |
|---|---|---|---|

| **Increase in Media Coverage** | 40% of all U.S. news stories in 1997 dealt with crime, violence, or law enforcement. | Persons involved in violence, crime and drugs on evening news, 1997<br>Latino  25%    Non-US citizen  27%    Middle Eastern  34.2% |
|---|---|---|

| **Increase in Resistance** | www.igc.org/prisons<br>www.igc.org/deepdish<br>www.prisonactivist/critical | **sources**<br>incarceration: Bureau of Prisons, *New Internationalist*, Criminal Justice.Consortium<br>stocks: *New York Times*, Private Prison Watch<br>media: George Gerbner, Temple University<br>page: DeeDee Halleck, D Thorne. Thanks to Prison Activist Resource Center |
|---|---|---|

DeeDee Halleck und David Thorne
Kunst und globale Medien: Eine Ausstellung des steirischen herbst

museum in progress

**agent.NASDAQ aka
Reinhold Grether**

# How etoy Cam Was

## An Agent's

**THE TOYWAR-STORY: the TOYWAR.com resistance game was launched to protect etoy from aggressive take-over attempts and to win the historic domain name battle between the etoy.CORPO-RATION (legendary Internet art giant, incorporated 1994) and eToys Inc. (one of the biggest e-commerce companies, incorporated 1996). After the etoy.SHA-REHOLDERS (art collectors and fans) rejected a ridiculous offer of $516,000 for the eBRAND etoy.com (registered for experimental entertainment and cultural business operations), eToys Inc. filed a naive lawsuit against etoy. The toy retailer accused etoy of unfair competition, trademark delusion, security fraud, illegal stock market operation, pornographic content, offensive behaviour and terrorist activity. This strategy failed terribly: etoy, specializing in and awarded for surreal incubations, cultural viruses and impact management decided to strike back and turned the case into a toy harbor of e-commerce: 1798 activists, artists, lawyers, celebrities and journalists were selected and recruited between November 1999 and February 2000 to establish a playful toy army. TOYWAR worked like a swarm of bees. Hundreds of well-informed people and media experts contested the aggressor on every level (filing counter court cases, infiltrating customer service, pr departments, the press, investor news groups and also on the level of the Federal Trade Commission etc.). More than 300 articles (*New York Times, Wall Street Journal, Le Monde, CNN*) reported the story and 250 resistance sites and net-shelters were established. Result: within two months the eToys Inc. stock (NASDAQ: ETYS) dropped from $67 (the day the battle started) to $15 (the day eToys Inc. finally dropped the case). TOYWAR was the most expensive performance in art history: $4.5 billion in damage! A glorious victory for the etoy.CORPORATION which compensated activists with etoy.SHARES: in March 2000, hundreds of brave TOY.soldiers transformed into etoy.CO-OWNERS with voting rights.**

## thank you for flying etoy....

**Anyone who logged into the net.art platform TOYWAR in early February 2000 was met with two watery graves in the Indian Ocean in which 286 of 1,639 TOYWAR.agents were buried in** Lego-like coffins. Victims of their own lack of participation, the warriors had succumbed to a sheer under-supply of energy. A net.art project only exists as long as the nodes of the Net fill it with life. And now, they waste away in their coffins, having to make do with their burials as mere artistic artifacts. They won't even end up on the art market.

They deserve our veneration not because they're dead, but for what they've done. How often I've observed a magazine article placed at the top of a Web page while the bubbling of ideas goes on in the bowels of online forums below. There, the email addresses of eToys' employees and sit-in scripts were passed around, people met and got to know each other, then built a protest site together, and a collective brainstorming session poured forth a cornucopia of proposals, more than any professional campaign organization could process. Despite all the naysaying, the Net is offering individuals new opportunities to take action and giving ideas a better shot at taking hold. It allows and even encourages cooperation in virtual groups, and in the best of situations, a self-organizing countermatrix as well that can make short work of a highly organized and powerful corporation.

Both etoy and eToys exist only on the Web but on different levels of virtuality. eToys runs www.etoys.com, making hundreds of thousands of playthings available to millions of children. The Web site is a turntable spinning real objects into the world. If it was still possible in the 1980s for Toys'R'Us to present the universe of toys through a net-

# the paign Won:

## Report

work of giant brick-and-mortar stores, by the late 1990s, this universe was being represented by eToys on a network of computer terminals as a purely virtual system of signs. Different means of distribution for the same real objects. etoy, the artistic third, upped the level of abstraction to that of a purely virtual existence on the Net. etoy's toys are completely encoded as data sets and the group's only art product for sale is stock, etoy.SHARES, first circulated in galleries and later via the TOYWAR platform. Whoever obtains these shares, either by buying them, doing some recruiting or performing some other service, becomes part of an art universe that exists only on the Net.

Art is capital, as Joseph Beuys knew, and in his Schaffhauser installation *Das Kapital* he placed apparatuses and artifacts of media communication together that force the observer into perceiving them in action, seeing his or her own productivity as capital and himself or herself as an artist. This model of one's own participation in art gains the dimension of 'social sculpture' only in so far as the imaginative interrogation of the relics of anthropological media communication infers the history of the interaction encapsulated within them, thereby opening up spaces for opportunities for participation in the future. Following Beuys, who, it should be noted, used all the media available in his day for the creation of social sculptures, etoy, with its shares concept and the TOYWAR platform, develops new formats for participation in art which, making full use of the networking potential of the Internet, enliven a virtual space for information, communication and transaction, an ensemble of tools for action for "interventions in the symbolic reproduction process of society" (Frank Hartmann) and an institutionalizing self-articulation organ for virtuality. So etoy's efforts seem aimed at carrying the concept of the social sculpture over to a digital format.

For artistic reasons, etoy could not accept the takeover offer from eToys, which after all, amounted to a million German marks at the time. The story would have worked, of course, since 'unfriendly takeovers' are now a common part of doing business. For the first time, net.art would have brought a newsworthy price and nomadic artists obtain their domains from various contemporary subversion zones anyway. But without the claim on etoy.com, the project of the social sculpture would have been out of reach. It borders on insult and suggests a bad memory when etoy is now accused of 'selling out.' They already passed up their considerable chance to do so.

And so, two representations on the Web stood opposed to one another. eToys, the parasite-like one, organizing the circulation of already existing real objects, and etoy, the autochthonous one, using Web-based tools to pressure virtual as well as real social processes to reveal and change themselves. Two models of participation were also opposed, one noting the changing valuations of stocks, and the other honoring participation with shares in the project. In the same way, it was a conflict between two lifestyles, one consumerist, giving absolute priority to acquisition, in this case, a domain, and the other artistic, declaring the exhibition of complex social practices, rather than art objects, the object of art. And not least of all, of course, the future of the Web was also at stake. Should it be reduced to a transaction platform for ecommerce - or should the possibilities inherent in it for spontaneous networking, "social information processing" (Michael Giesecke), culture jamming, interweaving and penetration and personal globalization be further developed?

Therein lies the art of etoy, to have expounded upon these polarities in complete clarity and to have forced the Net population to make a decision. And although TOYWAR didn't go up on the Net until a month after the preliminary injunction, Netizens understood the question and answered it in their own unique way. John Perry Barlow is right when he says we should all be grateful to etoy. But it's not only the posing of these questions and the development of TOYWAR that needs to be recognized, but also the finessing, invisible to the public, of the juridical problems. What had to be borne out and built upon in terms of pressures and counterattacks, threats and intentionally misleading moves is known only to those who were immediately involved. The legal result, at any rate, is as excellent as the exposition of the decision-making problem.

Is everything, then, not art after all? Art is a term of attribution that's constantly changing its rules. The Renaissance, Romanticism and Modernism all developed countless concepts throwing off aesthetic sparks from the overlapping of life and art. etoy stands firmly in this tradition. Has Duchamp already done it all? Duchamp's readymades retain the character of objects for the most part; etoy forces the character of readymades onto social processes, in particular, the making and marketing of virtuality. What eToys and Network Solutions do - these are the readymades of the 2000s. Didn't Beuys completely and utterly exhaust the theme of the social sculpture? Wrong - Beuys developed social sculptures in the medium of anthropological psychism; only the first explorations are now being conducted in the medium of transanthropic virtualism, e.g., Luther Blissett and TOYWAR.

Warhol drove the recontextualization of everyday icons with great style, Koons exposed the pornography of surfaces and the Business Art of the 1980s recast corporate identity to the hilt, so what's left for etoy? etoy's perversion lies in upping, measure by measure, the development of the value of a single icon, their own name, virtually cast as www.etoy.com, in the spiraling attention of the economic, political, social and artistic, thus reflecting the process of the creation of value in the financial markets in the excess of self-exaggeration. So it's not enough to merely simu-late an airline, as Ingold Airlines does; you have to chase the take-off and landing slots away from Lauda Air with the "fucking plug-ins" from agent.DAVE.

## Bringing IT to YOU.

When, back in November 1999, eToys management unveiled its coup and Judge Shook poured over the files and etoy developed the concept for the TOYWAR platform, I had just completed my several-month-long study of the evolution of stock prices on the Neue Markt, Germany's vague equivalent of the US technology index NASDAQ. The bulk of these stocks for the most part rose dramatically after their initial public offering and then more or less zigged and zagged along a plateau before plunging downwards, opening out onto a bland wallowing around the initial offering price. As they say, these valuations are rather drab. Since these new companies are just now creating the markets within which they move, the valuations excuse the most miserable data as long as the story allows expectations for greater future valuations.

The actual dynamic lies in the story, the fantasy of the market, which, like Switzerland's warm wind, keeps things stirring as long as there's enough hot air feeding it. If, over time, the story loses some of its plausibility, the smart investor grabs his profits, borrowing the same paper for a limited time, selling high and if the stock falls, buying it back and gives it back. Those who anticipate a change in the market profit whether it goes up or down. The sovereign speculator is the one with his hand on the course of the story.

As the story turns, so turns the market. The stock falls because a majority of investors believe they'll earn more if it falls than if it rises. Rather nasty for those banking on high valuations. Long-term investors wait for the next upward trend, others take their losses and validate the downward trend, while the truly sorry ones are those forbidden to deal by the rules of the exchange. These are the founding investors and the company management for the duration of the six months following the initial public offering. Looking at the toys market, the general trend on the exchange and overall economic development, literary critics and economists would not be alone in risking argumentatively sound statements on the future of the story and the stock exchange.

If two entities are fighting over the same thing, e.g., the domain www.etoy.com, the one who wins will be the one who can convince the other that the object of desire is not as desirable as it appears. The etoy domain was an object of desire, for eToys, because they were losing 20,000 of 300,000 hits a day to etoy.com, for etoy, because the domain name was the point of reference of their artistic existence. And the fight was particularly heated because the opponents followed different sets of logic; the economic, on the one hand, which has to do with numbers and payments, and the artistic on the other, where it has to do with anything but. The art group was in possession of a double advantage:

for one, the domain was theirs, and for another, far more important one, the exhibition of the bizarre practices of the financial world was nothing less than their artistic project. While etoy could always put both sets of logic into play, eToys was never able to put the logic of economics to use against its opponent by, for example, burying the opponent in an avalanche of legal fees, nor could it use a third logic, for example, the criminal prosecution of Net activists. No one could hold it against eToys that they couldn't follow the logic of art.

When I developed, without knowing any of the participants, the core of what became the RTMark campaign with my "a new toy for you" (all of which is documented at To:list@rhizome.org), the point was to set up an undeniable mirror which would make the moves by etoy.ARTS and etoy.POLITICS appear as losses in the market value of eToys. This mirror was the NASDAQ notation of eToys, from which I was able to determine that the company had exhausted the hot air puffing up their story and that the market was looming on the verge of introducing a downward trend. The idea of focusing the campaign on the destruction of eToys' market valuation was an act of speculating on speculation, a metastory, telling once again the parallel story already autonomously programmed for a fall. As etoy.ARTS used the similarity of the domains as a value effect, so did etoy.POLITICS use the fall in the stock price as a battle effect. "To hype out the hype," as Ricardo Dominguez and I coined the tactic in The Thing's BBS chat.

It wasn't a betting game. It was a thought through calculation: The stock was introduced on May 20, and starting on November 20, the insiders flooded the market. The valuation reflected the anticipation of expectations for the Christmas shopping season and was already moving downward. All etailers found themselves under pressure because the traditional companies had found their electronic footing. And the campaign would arouse so much brouhaha that the majority of new investors would be betting on the slide.

Conceptually and legally, etoy.ARTS was set up brilliantly. etoy.POLITICS followed a few days afterwards. The judge's ink

was barely dry when the first attacks
hit the eToys Web site. The spontaneous
self-activation of hundreds and the
sheer speed of the flow of information
were the trump cards. A respectable
batch of unmoderated mailing lists such
as Rhizome, where my "urgently needed," sent to Nettime 36 minutes after I
received the news, and four minutes
later to Rhizome, met with a wave of
positive resonance, when Nettime
moderator Ted Byfield (who, by the
way, did a great job in the background)
let me know that "we (Nettime) don't
send out stuff like this." Even though the
point was to attack eToys immediately,
to hit them senseless with attacks just
when they were already overworked
with their monumental Christmas business. The media and net.art scene subscribed to Rhizome understood immediately, and shortly after "a new toy," I
found myself hijacked by the brokerage
RTMark to the working group furiously
toiling away.

When the forms on the Web site, and
then the mailboxes of the management
were plastered with protests, and by
dint of Richard Zach's ingenious
Campaign Links, eToys were pulled into
a press frenzy, they must have realized
in no uncertain terms that they were
facing a powerful opponent with a
talent for grand politics. eToys made this
clear on a legal level, Jewver.com on the
political, the NASDAQ valuation on the
financial and the virtual sit-in on the
infrastructural level.

A virtual sit-in is little more than a collective, simultaneous requesting of a
Web site. If one requests a Web site
faster than it can be transferred and
built up on the end user's screen, the
server receives, on the one hand, a
message telling it that the first request
is no longer valid, and on the other
hand, the new request. Scripts running
on one's own computer or on go-between servers automate this process,
and after a certain number of requests,
the server under attack begins to suffer
under the strain. One has to differentiate very specifically between knocking
out a server for private motives and a
**political action openly disrupting a Web
site for clearly formulated reasons and
for a limited time. That's when it becomes comparable to a warning strike
during wage negotiations, a means of
civil disobedience signaling that one**

side has the willingness and
courage to fight. A virtual
sit-in risks bringing symbolic forms of action to bear in
a medium of virtuality.

In the case of eToys, great
pains were taken to attack
the server for short spans
of time only (five fifteen-
minute periods on ten
Christmas shopping days)
and to avoid completely
bringing it down at all
costs. There was a 'killer
bullet script' which was
capable of doing just that,
but its use was unanimously opposed. One participant
wrote: "I'm not ready to
trade the distributed, swar-
ming community of activists
model for a single tactical
nuke." The point was to get
across just how widespread
the protest was; it was not
about a terrorist attack.

This much can be said of
the effect: There were seven
or eight rotating mirrors
around the world running
five different scripts. Added
to this were several tools
circulating around on the
Net which can be installed
on personal computers. The
combination made it possible to keep eToys's server
busy performing routine
tasks. The cleverest script
was probably
villarroy.html, an innoc-
ent script that filled cookie-
based shopping carts to the
brim without actually
making a purchase. For
every new item, the server
would have to refigure the
complete list all over again,
a process that would take
longer and longer as the
cart filled, and some of the
mirrors could generate a
hundred thousand or more
requests a day. eToys's ser-
**ver was able to process the
simple request for pages on
the first day without a
hitch, but the more complex
scripts introduced on the
second day gave it a run**

Campaign Links
[http://dmoz.org/Society/
Activism/Media_Activism/
Culture_Jamming/eToys/
Endorsements/
[http://www.rtmark.com/
endorsement_.html]

eToy
[http://www.etoy.com]

eToys
[http://www.etoys.com]
RTMark eToys.html
[http://www.rtmark.com/
etoy.html]
list-list@rhizome.org
[http://www.rhizome.org/
etoyrhiz.html]

TOYWAR [http://www.
toywar.com/]

Virtual Sit-In Support
[http://www.duke.edu/
~arg2/solidarity_list.html]

for its money. Requests for particular IP addresses were completely blocked, meaning that eToys was taking itself out of these networks. It was the 'super plus version' of the shopping scripts, then, that led to the shut-down of one of The Thing's Web sites by backbone provider Verio. Here, too, the 'hype out the hype' strategy was at work, further virtualizing eToys's virtual shopping carts with virtual purchases.

Just as important was the constant presence in all the investors' forums that had to do with eToys where breath-taking, whiplash-like discussions were taking place. At first, the tone was set primarily by the financial world gloating over those mourning for the lost domain. But the vocabulary of investors can be picked up pretty quickly, and soon, the speculators counting on an upward trend were confronted with all sorts of negative financial data. When the market made its irreversible dip, the catcalls from investors betting on the slump out-yelled even those from the activists.

The financial press was as surely in eToys' hands as the cultural press was in etoy's. But the telling difference lay in the fact that one side publicized the story for all it was worth, while the other side avoided every instance of publicity. So the financial press, which could hardly ignore the dramatic fall in the stock price, kept the impact of the 'Internet renegades' as invisible as possible. Up to the point of eToys' first concession when

Bloomberg.com ran the complete press statement from RTMark. "It's hysterical," one of the founders emailed.

No personal meeting, no telephone contact. Email and Web sites, nothing else. Mad email traffic early in the evening, and when necessary, early in the morning. Then, time to think it all over. Shortly after noon, mails to Rhizome so that the early risers on the east coast were immediately brought up to speed. Flow, when ten to twenty people were communicating at once and sending information around the world. Anyone can do it. You, too.

An email finish with electronic slingshots! Hundreds of TOYWAR.agents place the eToys management under TOYWAR fire!! Unconditional surrender!!!

Days later, we were confronted with 683 fresh coffins. The coffins of those who didn't follow the first TOYWAR.order, didn't write the warning email as instructed. The false deaths of TOYWAR, now revived.

Translated by David Hudson

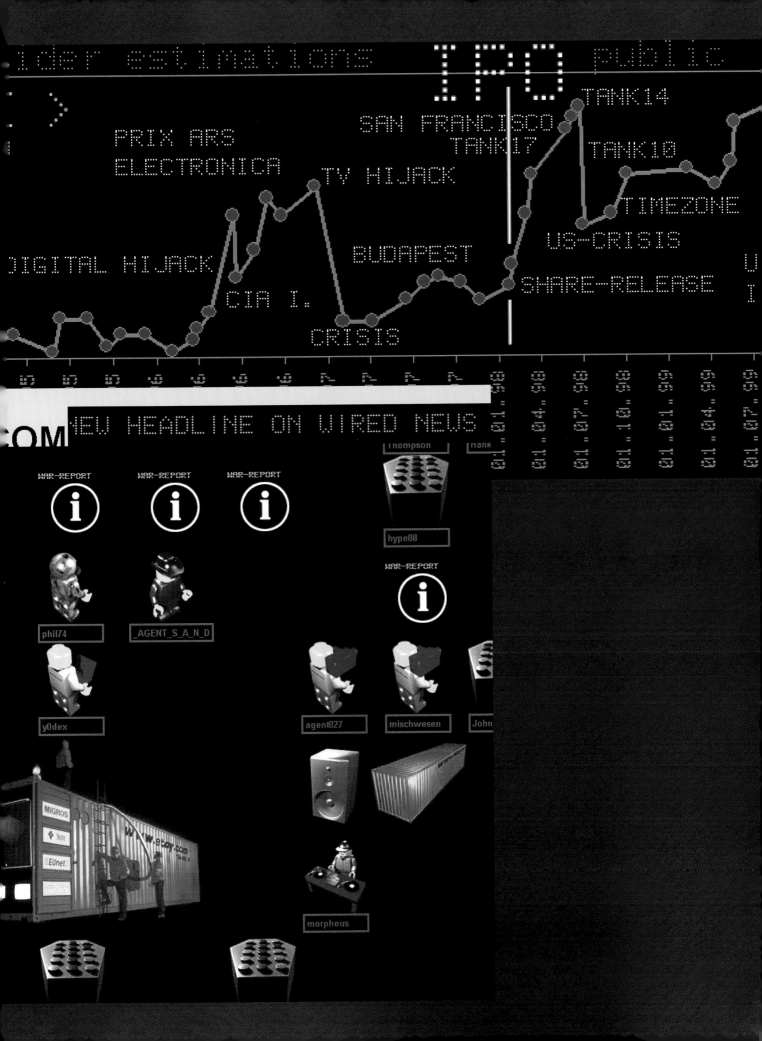

The group (Walter van der Cruijsen, Luka Frelih, Vuk Cosic) met in Amsterdam to materialize an idea floating in meetings at various European Internet conferences and festivals during the last three years. Basically the big goal was to come up with a net based moving ascii.

Immediate Goals: The very first things to do were the most obvious ones - the javascript and java players for moving ascii images.

Mid Term Goals: After the two players are done, the idea is to create a fast converter that would enable us to create moving ascii in real time.

Long Term Goals: After bringing moving ascii to the net through the mentioned steps, the final goal - or one of the next steps - is to create a RealPlayer G2 plug-in with the new file type.

Projects
ASCII to Speech: <u>History of art for the blind</u> by applying the txt->speech software.
<u>History of Moving Images</u>: a series of seven clips giving the overview of the evolution in style and the display and distribution media.
<u>Deep ASCII</u>: a version of Deep Throat in ascii is displayed on a Pong Arcade.
<u>ASCII Wall</u>: a project planned together with the good people of Redundant Technologies and consists in creation of a video wall of old monitors in order to do larger projections.
<u>MTV stream</u> is about hooking any broadcast signal and streaming the ascii version.
<u>History of Silent Film</u> on CD-ROM offering several milestone films in full length.

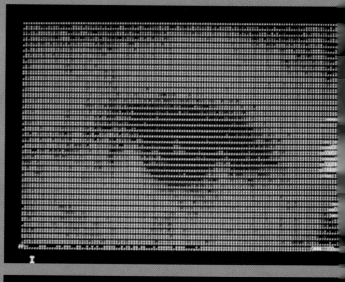

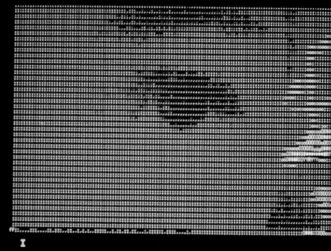

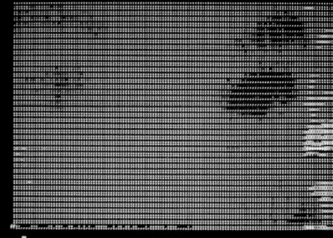

ASCII A

It is just not true.

Shane Cooper

http://www.shanecooper.com/

290

Subversive Conditions

Remote

## Summary

A photorealistic real-time virtual anchorman presents live,
real news. The anchorman retrie-
ves information from internet
news sources, and can present
it in one of two ways: 'truth
reversed' or 'truth confirmed.'
The visitor is allowed to select
which version of truth they prefer by using a television remote
control device containing two
buttons, labeled TRUTH1 and
TRUTH2.

## Description

A regular television occupies
a furnished white room. On the
television is what appears to be
a normal news broadcast in progress. The news broadcast is in
fact entirely computer generated. All graphics, the character, the voice, and all images
are all generated in real-time.
The news text itself is continually accessed from internet news
sources. The news broadcast is
a live, continuously self updat-
ing television program.

Thats entirely true.

Control

A remote control unit near the sofa has two buttons: TRUTH1 and TRUTH2.

These allow the user to choose between two channels. On one channel, the anchorman reverses the truth of the news, and on the other channel supports it. The effect is two news channels reporting the same information, but opposite in truth relative to each other. (An underlying linguistic manipulation program makes this possible.)

Depending on whether the underlying remote news sources are accurate, one of the channels will be true and the other will be false.

Which channel is true and which is false, however, is determined entirely by the truth of the remote-downloaded new sources. Since one channel is the meaning of every sentence reversed and the other is the meaning of every sentence supported, one channel is guaranteed to be true whether or not the news itself is.

Woven Presents is an installation which uses a sewing machine connected to the internet which in turn sews text onto black ribbon which encircles a room. A computer seeks out the word 'war' from various internet news provider's information. Paragraphs containing the word 'war' are then processed by the computer, which controls the sewing machine, which then sews the text. A motor pulls the ribbon around the room until it ends in a heap.

The manifestation of this internet installation as a sewing machine connected to the internet may at first appear unusual as an artwork supporting the content of war. This work is not so much about informing the viewer about the some 20 or so wars that are presently taking place in the world, but more specifically about the production and memory of history itself. The usage of war as content is mainly thought as a reference to historical events. Therefore one of the first noticeable structural elements in the work is the ribbon, suggestive of a historical continuum. On the other hand, the content of war is not neglected. Elements from the sound of the sewing machine to the massive pile of ribbon also make obvious references to this context.

The cliche '...woven throughout history' which follows in the same vain as 'to sew the seeds of time' were starting motivations in the works development. So came the usage of the sewing machine and the ribbon which surrounds the viewer.

Various information technologies are quoted in the work. The sewing onto the ribbon and its sound is similar to the old nineteenth century medium of ticker-tape. The form of the metal ribbon holders in each of the corners of the installation room bear a resemblance to the telegraph wire holders, which were originally made from porcelain. The reference between sewing, thread and the internet is an obvious word play.

The black ribbon and text which is sewn and then transported around the room has similarities with the text ribbon typical of the war wreath at the base of every war memorial. Normally the war wreath is a symbol of remembrance, which is presented at the end of the war. In this work, the duration between war and remembrance is practically reduced to nothing. Thus creating so to speak a moment of instant war & remembrance.

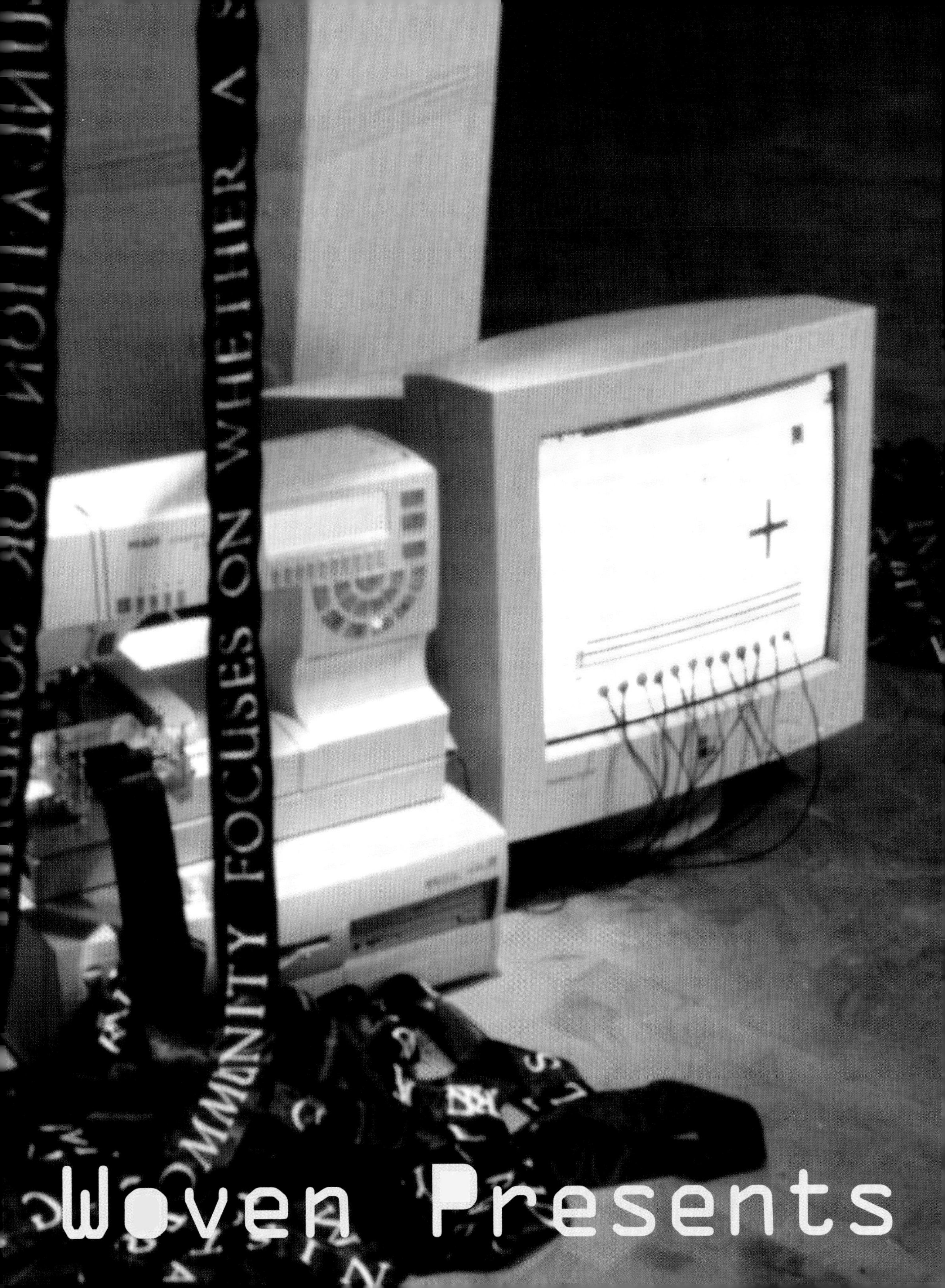


# Woven Presents

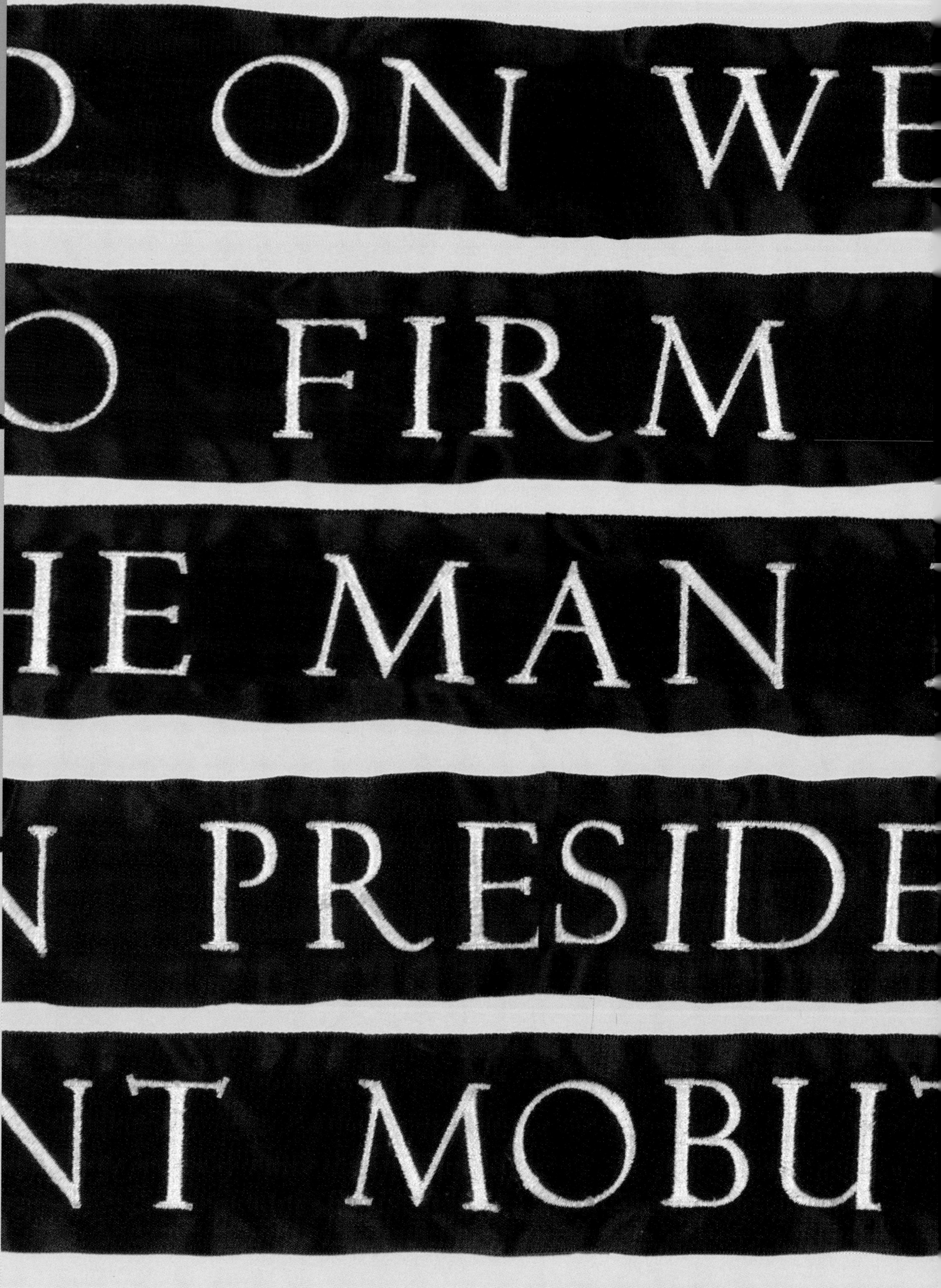
O ON WE
O FIRM
HE MAN
N PRESIDE
NT MOBU

TAB
+showscores
ENTER
+jump
ESCAPE
togglemenu
SPACE
+vs
+
+jump
¬
+moveleft
-
say:
.
+moveright
0>8
messagemode
=
+jump
\
+mlook

toggleconsole
a
+lookup
c
+movedown
d
+moveup
q
quit
t
messagemode
z
+lookdown
~
toggleconsole
UPARROW
+forward
DOWNARROW
+back
LEFTARROW
+moveleft
RIGHTARROW
+moveright
OPTION
+hs
CTRL
toggleconsole
SHIFT
+rs
F1>F12
screenshot
INS
+klook
DEL
+lookdown
PGDN
+lookup
END
centerview

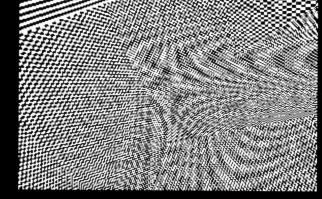

```
EXECING QUAKE.RC
EXECING CONFIG.CFG
EXECING AUTOEXEC.CFG
CONNECTING TO"CTRL-SPACE.JODI.ORG"
TYPE <CONNECT CTRL-SPACE.JODI.ORG
|||||||||||||||||||||||||||||||

DOWNLOAD:
CTRL-SPACE.ZIP    WIN

CTRL-SPACE.SIT    MAC

- - - - - - - - - - - - - - - - - - - - - - -

▪
```

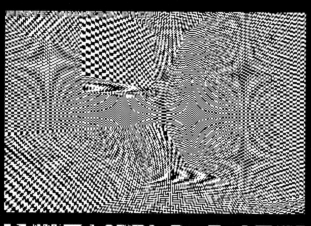

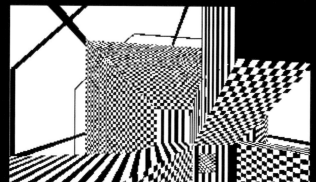

RL-SPACE

For nearly five years we have
been funding acts of sabotage
with activist or aesthetic aims,
in a manner that does not lend
itself to widespread participation. We have been very successful in our work, generating se-
venteen very clever acts of
'creative subversion' during
the time of our operation; but
perhaps this is not successful
enough.
Because of the apparently growing desire for the type of funding we provide, and the insuffi-
ciency of any single large sum
to provide it, we have decided to
risk misunderstanding and even
exposure in order to make our
work more accessible and our help
more available to the public at
large. We have invented a sort
of 'interface' between our core
functions and the public...
®™ark is a system of workers,
ideas, and money whose function
is to encourage the intelligent
sabotage of mass-produced items.
®™ark is essentially a matchmaker and bank, helping groups or
individuals fund sabotage projects.
On the local scale, since ®™ark
helps individuals change
careers, pay for vacations,
etc., it is an ark made of ® and
™. On the global scale, it is an
ark for our humanness through the
deluge of ® and ™, an attempt to
give our thoughts and desires a
vehicle to make themselves seen
and felt in the often mechanical
world around us. It is an attempt
to make our environment more
palatable, more reflective of
us, and generally more human.
Are we then Communists? We are
neither that nor anything else.
We are idealists of the most
wide-eyed variety.
Like the Communists, however,
we do not believe that our system
will be a permanent fixture.
It will, if it is successful,
fall away.
In the capitalist world, this
falling-away will take the form
of co-opting. Since it is entirely impossible to control corporate sabotage, the only solu-

tion the market has is to accept
it. And the market, like a virus
or a body responding to a virus,
mutates to encompass whatever is
irresistible - in ®™ark's
dreams, social conscience and a
concern for beauty. The market
will come to respond, aesthetically and philosophically, to
the artistic impulses of the
people.
More specifically, the co-opting
will occur as follows: companies
will try to preempt sabotage, so
that if it occurs it won't cast
the company in a bad light.
Perhaps products will be made
that have an excessive number of
odd but mindless quirks, in which
activist features will be
drowned. The challenge to
activists will then be to make
bigger changes, more visible and
drastic ones.
More likely, the system will sta-
bilize. Corporations, to avoid
escalation, will gear their
products and policies in a more
conscientious direction to begin
with. Rather than trying to drown
the activist message, thus
encouraging wilder leaps by
activists, corporations will try
to assuage the activist impulses
of workers by giving free rein to
their conscience, and also by
making life good enough for the
worker so that the few thousand
dollars that can be offered by
®™ark (or successor organizations) will not seem significant. Thus a stasis, a symbiosis,
will arise; perhaps each corporation will have an aesthetics
and philosophy department.
In our dreams, once ®™ark is completely co-opted and dead, the
world will be a somewhat better
place.
(Since publication of this document in 1997, some of our ideas
have changed because of our experience with the wider publicity -
most importantly, we no longer
think of ®™ark as the permanent
corrective institution we somewhat naively imagined it could
be, but cede that place to the
permanent corrective institution
that already exists: the legal

to YOU!

®™ark

system. The ultimate desire of ®tmark, then, is that the law be changed to protect governments and citizens from corporate predation - in most cases, this means not writing new laws, but removing old ones that were written expressly to safeguard corporate advantage.

®tmark, we hope, can function to widely popularize the importance of controlling these entities, especially among those sectors of the population that are not yet aware of any problem at all (a focus that includes, surprisingly, the great majority of the U.S. population).

We're building a better wrench.

®tmark
Bringing IT to YOU!
www.rtmark.com

## obn@zkm -- background

During initial planning for their contribution to net_condition in The Lounge program at ZKM, Karlsruhe, the old boys network (OBN) received the Manifesto overleaf by email. Since one of the most important goals of OBN is international cyberfeminist networking, it seemed urgent to respond to the concrete demands of a new cyberfeminist initiative group at the Center for Art and Media technologies (ZKM). For this reason we decided to make our catalog pages available to the group calling itself obn@zkm to publish their manifesto; and to offer the new Karlsruhe "Old Boys" a discussion of their manifesto within the context of our public presentation at ZKM, in order to develop further cyberfeminist perspectives together.

+++++++++++++++++++++++++++++++++++++++++++++++++++++++++++++++++++++++++

from: obn@zkm.de
to: boys@obn.org
re: obn@zkm manifest

*Only through a focus on cyberfeminist activities can ZKM add to its important status of the establisher of interactive artforms in the nineties, and achieve the goals of its new phase as a center of expertise for all questions of the technological, scientific, and information society. Cyberfeminism is a phenomenon which distinguishes itself by the fact that no one can escape it. In particular, a Center for Art and Media (ZKM) which addresses those technical media which were of essential importance for the creation of cyberfeminism, cannot just define itself locally, but must consciously network with international cyberfeminism.*

*ZKM: a networked cooperation, a network of common duty and dedication -- we will take it at its word. With digital media into a cyberfeminist Millenium!*

+++++++++++++++++++++++++++++++++++++++++++++++++++++++++++++++++++++++++

The old boys network (OBN) came together in the summer of 1997 as the first cyberfeminist alliance. Basing itself on a politics of dissence, the old boys network works through personal and media networks on cyberfeminist strategies in the fields of gender and the net. In addition to its work on the theory, praxis, aesthetics and politics of cyberfeminism, the core group of old boys (currently eight of them) develops various distribution, connection, and meeting formats. As well as maintaing a website (www.obn.org) and a mailing list, obn organized/s regular live presentations, lectures, workshops, and symposia for face-to-face exchange, including the                                          in the Hybrid Workspace in the context of dX (Kassel, September 1997) and the
in connection with Next5MinutesFestival (Rotterdam and Amsterdam, March 1999). Documentation of these activities and further materials have been published thus far in two            which are available from OBN. In preparation is a book with the provisional title „Cyberfeminism: Next Protocols", expected publication date 2000.
E-mail to:

# obn@kzm

## Manifesto

## \<of the old boys network @ ZKM, Karlsruhe\>

Stimulated by the spirit of a new conception of ZKM, as it was formulated last spring by the new leadership of the institution, and inspired by the example of the 1. Cyberfeminist alliance, the Old Boys Network, a cyberfeminist initiative -- obn@zkm was formed at ZKM during the summer of 1999. Our goal is to initiate internal and external cyberfeminist networking at ZKM and to work actively on its implementation. Additionally obn@ZKM will spearhead a determined effort to cyberfeminize ZKM on all organizational levels.

We demand:

1. A new cyberfeminist identity for ZKM which expresses itself through three intersecting institu-tional areas: Cyberfeminist production and research, cyberfeminist exhibitions and activities, cyberfeminist connections and documentation.
1a. We demand the funding of at least 3 cyberfeminist professorships at the Hochschule! And in addition: During hiring searches (qualifications being equal) cyberfeminists will be hired!
1b. Clear out the exhibition rooms! Everything must go! Liquidate it on the international market or store it in the vaults!
1c. More subculture at ZKM!
1d. From ZKM to ZCF (Center for Cyberfeminism)!

2. The traditional organizational structure of ZKM must be exchanged for a dynamic and flexible organizational structure: we demand a rotation system according with cyberfeminist criteria!
2a. We demand our personal avatar for effective relief from work overload!
2b. Bottom-up restructuring!
2c. A cyberfeminist newsletter at ZKM; entertainment budget, real life meetings, apartment exchanges, international job information, etc.
2d. Communal office outings into cyberspace!
2e. Free access to Peter-Cam!
2f. Regular surWeibel-training for all coworkers.
2g. Workplace psychological counseling by a virtual therapist.
2h. Virtual menstruation hut on the ZKM server.

3. A cyberfeminist-in-residence program: Cyberfeminist critics for a cyberfeminist discourse program! Cyberfeminist curators for cyberfeminist exhibition series! Cyberfeminist scientists for the support of cyberfeminist foundations research! All these activities will strengthen the external networks and the connection to the international cyberfeminist community.
3a. Reserved parking places for Cyberfeminists!
3b. Free, unlimited cybersex!
3c. Telemedical care for obsolete bodies via High Speed Networks.
3d. Direct co-operation with cyberfeminist sponsors!

4. A comprehensive extension of local cyberfeminist activities. Like many other media foundations ZKM must make a determined effort to join the cyberfeminist universe in order to stay fit for the network: We demand a cyberfeminist review of the net_condition of ZKM!
4a. ZKM stock goes public! Global community of cyberfeminist shareholders in cooperation with the cultural ministries of the Laender.

# Bodies

is a project that actively incorporates the idea of avatars, with the intention of shifting the discourse of the body from the usual idea of flesh and identity. Planned are a number of artificial intelligence programs integrated into the environment over which there wouldn't be too much control.

An avatar IS, but a member is made, and frequently the force, energy, purpose or will of a corporate Entity will utilise the vehicles of a member in order to contact the physical planes. Every members' Body represented is the locus of the contradictions of functioning in the hi-tech environment, while being in the Meta-Body, the Entity in the business of service.

In order to function effectively as a service provider, seven Advisory Boards have been constituted: Philosophical, Academic, CEO, Spiritual, Business, Legal and Aesthetic. The num-

**DATE OF BIRTH:**

**SEX:** female

**SEXUALITY:** heterosexual

**AGE:** 56

**RELATIONSHIP TO OWNER:** significant other

**SPECIAL HANDLING INSTRUCTIONS:** Easily freezing.

**OWNER COMMENTS:** Listen.

**BODY DESCRIPTION:** This body has a medium communicator feminine head, a large diplomacy feminine torso, a small conceptual feminine left arm, a small conceptual feminine left arm, a large diplomacy feminine left leg, and a large diplomacy feminine right leg.

RL image

**Evola**

**DATE OF BIRTH:**

**SEX:** male

**SEXUALITY:** heterosexual

**AGE:** 45

**RELATIONSHIP TO OWNER:** significant other

**SPECIAL HANDLING INSTRUCTIONS:** Der genmanipulierte Mensch.

**OWNER COMMENTS:** This is how I imagine the end result of the cloning technology to look.

**BODY DESCRIPTION:** This body has a large organizational infantile head, a medium diplomacy masculine torso, a small business feminine left arm, a medium marketing masculine right arm, a medium communicator infantile left leg, and a medium corporate leader masculine right leg.

RL image

**Clone**

## contents

# INCorporated

ber seven governs the periodicity of the phenomena of life, and is found dominating the
series of chemical elements, and is equally
paramount in the world of colour and sound.

Space, which has ignorantly been proclaimed
as an abstract idea and a void is, in reality
a container for the body of the corporation
with its seven principles. The bodies of the
Board of Directors and the Advisory Boards
rarely take form as visible bodies - some are
public, some act anonymously, all reside on
the memory board that is to be interpreted in
terms of force and energy - they are the
embodied principles. But, it is important to
remember that this means that the force and
energy of one of the principles of the Logos

are pouring through Them via that which corresponds to the Monad. The memory Board,
where They dwell, exists in physical matter,
but it is a matter of higher ethers of the
physical plane, and only when we develop
etheric vision will the mystery be revealed.
A reflection of this method can be seen when a
member steps out of their body and permits
Them to use it.

Bodies INCorporated does not freely dispense
the title of an Avatar, but staying true to
the root of the word, mandates that the member gains enough shares in the corporate body
as s/he moves from being a member to adept, to
finally realising the goal of becoming an
avatar.

## Karlsruhe, Germany  1999 ZKM Gallery

**Names of Bodies:**

1. Evola
2. Idoru II
3. Francoise
4. Eve Post
5. Rotor Ruka

6. Anagramm

7. myOwn
8. Clone
9. ciaobella
10. Forma

304

Amsterdam

Bratislava

Bucharest

Graz

Billboard project in 23 European cities

October / November 1998: Graz, (A)
November / December / January 1998/99:
Vienna (A), Brussels (B), Copenhagen (DK),
Frankfurt/M. (D), Berlin (D), Paris (F),
Helsinki (FIN), Athens (GR), London (GB),
Dublin (IRL), Rome (I), Amsterdam (NL),
Madrid (E), Sarajevo (BIH), Sofia (BG),
Beograd (YU), Warsaw (PL), Bucharest (R),
Bratislava (SK), Prague (CZ), Budapest (H),
Zagreb (HR)

Madrid

Prague

Helsinki

Paris

Warsaw

Milan

Budapest

Athens

Sarajevo

Frankfurt

Brussels

Zagreb

Copenhagen

Dublin

Berlin

Sofia

http://io.khm.de

IO-
dencies

IO_dencies is a series of projects by Knowbotic Research who develop experimental interfaces between digital technologies and social processes.

## IO_dencies creates fields of collaboration and collective investigation in electronic networks.

### IO_lavoro immateriale

The recent project IO_lavoro immateriale raises the question of what kinds of action and intervention are possible in the public sphere today. A group of editors invited specially for the project build up a database with texts and comments about changing notions of the public sphere, subjectivity, economy and work.

The content of the database and the relations between the different contributions can be experienced through an interface that translates these relations into visual and physical force fields. The visitors can physically feel the tendential forces within the database through a magnetic interface, and investigate the content data on a separate screen. Thus, the discourse of the editor group can be experienced on different intellectual and intuitive levels.

### IO_dencies Tokyo/Sao Paulo

## The aim is not to develop advanced tools for architectural and urban design, but to create events through which it becomes possible to rethink urban planning and construction.

In our studies we found clear needs for relevant forms of agency which are able to deal with the complex processes of urban exclusions. These forms of agency don't have to deal so much with the re-articulation of territory, **but they have to invent and produce existential interfaces which enable becoming public in a more and more disappearing environment in order to avoid political, economical and cultural isolation.**

...urban movements and their mutual interferences are represented by dynamic particle flows which can be downloaded as an urban profile, and observed and manipulated through an Internet interface.

### Connective Agency

The challenge is to understand not only the new networked topologies of intervention and of presence, but to tackle the problems of agency and events in connective and translocal environments.

## What we are looking at is the oscillation and transformation of potential agencies and potential subjectivities in the interface, and we are testing what the political effects might be.

The way in which the tendential clusters have been configured formally, the different interventions can enhance and collapse each other. These tendential clusters of events, these multiplying and splintering forces torpedo any notion of 'construction.' By working with force fields, intensities, energy fields as formal elements of the projects, we move away from the analytical, rational conjunctive models towards open, unpredictable results. What we try to do is offer alternative models of agency to those that are currently available on the Internet, where information is segmented and packaged as commercial goods, and where communication and the engagement of the subject can be easily controlled.

Operating with the open qualities of a data set also means that it can be modified by each project participant, the data are connected to the local knowledge of the participant and that there is no obligation to 'think global.'

## The notion of a 'connective agency' points us to the question of the possibilities of a new type of public sphere that may or may not be established in and by the electronic networks. This public sphere will only come into being if there are complex forms of interaction, of participation and learning, that exploit the technical possibilities of the networks and that allow for new and creative forms of becoming present, becoming visible, becoming active, in short, of becoming-public.

**activated keyword**

# IO_lavoro immateriale

## Il tempo del desiderio (o die M.me de Ma / Time of desire (or M.me de Maintenons ti Iaia Vanzaggiato

Il tempo del desiderio (o di M.me de Maintenon): E' un "resto" di tempo che agli occhi dei filosofi o degli economisti sembra un'impossibilità logica poiché è un tempo qualitativo che si situa oltre quello "pieno" dell'orologio. Nominarlo significa svelare la differenza interna all'ordine sociale e simbolico del re (e del capitale). Il "resto di tempo" di M.me de Maintenon non contemplata né significata dal tempo del re e a questo irriducibile in quanto non misurabile. Si tratta - ed è un'esperienza femminile della temporalità - di una diversa coscienza temporale che accoglie accanto alla dimensione quantitativa, quella relazionale, non lineare, non funzionale, non economica. E" un tempo più simile al linguaggio: è un tempo-significato che rappresenta il carattere sociale della nostra esperienza mai disgiunto dall'esperienza stessa. Così considerata il tempo non è una merce, un bene che prima o poi scarseggia ma una risorsa simile al desiderio, sempre rinnovabile come la nostra capacità di significazione del reale.

## Translation

Time of desire (or M.me de Maintenons time) It is a <> time which philosophers and economists consider a logical impossibility, because it is a qualitative time that places itself beyond the <> time of the clock. To mention this time is to unveil the difference inside the kingís (ie capitalís) social and symbolic order. M.me de Maintenonís <> is not measurable, thus it is incommensurable with the kingís time. It is a feminine experience of time, a different temporal consciousness that, besides the quantitative dimension, includes a relational one - a non-linear, non-economical and non-functional dimension of time. Such a time is more similar to language, for it is a signified time representing the social character of our experience (which is never separated from experience itself). This time is not a commodity subject to abundance and scarcity - rather, this resource is similar to desire, it is as renewable as our capacity to give meaning to reality.

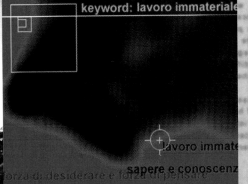

# The net.
# as urban

**Luther Blissett & Aleph Group**

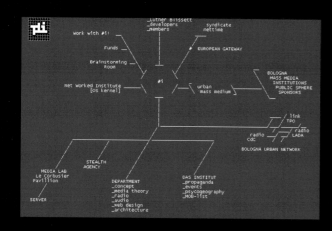

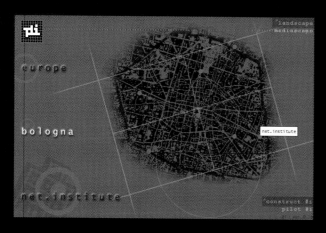

The net.INSTITUTE is a medium-building. It is a hybrid between the net of the metropolis and the information architecture of the internet, between landscape and mediascape.

The net.INSTITUTE is a physical, social, mediatic space controlled and constructed by the net. The content and the structure produced on its web interface draw and shape the urban space.

The net.INSTITUTE doesn't consider the city an established identity but a collective representation continuously reshaped by its users. The kernel of the project is the Net-Worked-Institute: a 'low-tech' architectural structure to 'hack' the urbanistic code.

The net.INSTITUTE is based in Bologna, Italy.

**INSTITUTE interface**

Peter Weibel

http://www.medienturm.at/weibel/

312

Urban Conditions

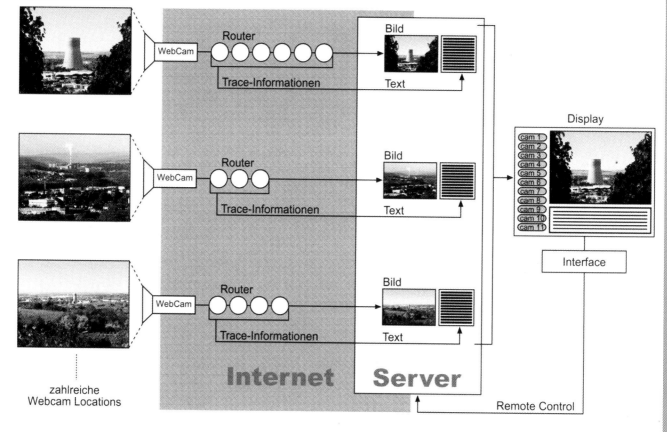

Reale Landschaften

WebCam — Router — Trace-Informationen

Bild — Text

zahlreiche
Webcam Locations

Internet — Server

Display
cam 1
cam 2
cam 3
cam 4
cam 5
cam 6
cam 7
cam 8
cam 9
cam 10
cam 11

Interface

Remote Control

## To be more precise: webcam piracy

Some 20 landscapes, webcam images, can be selected in the form of thumbnails on the left of a browser to display individual, full-format pictures. The subjects are fully in keeping with this classical genre of visual art which was once the favoured realm particularly of panel painting. These landscapes are aesthetic representations of the natural environment, either unspoilt or reshaped by human hand, to be precise near-natural and also stylised portrayals of certain real-world or imaginary regions, vistas of cities and architectures, seascapes, parks, etc. – motifs that, into the 17th century, i.e. until the early days of the Romantic period, were used almost exclusively as a backdrop for figured pictures.

# Non-Locality

In the same way that the landscape painting began to move to the fore, taking up whole panel paintings as of the 17th century, so too are webcam images – landscapes – increasingly becoming full-format features in Internet browsers. They describe views of physical, real-world landscape space in real time from within the net, i.e. from a position outside the exhibition space. The selected conglomerate of webcam landscapes in "Ontogenetic Landscapes" has not been globally installed especially for this work, but rather the work takes recourse to this found resource in the Internet, which, to be more precise, is webcam piracy.

With the development of the landscape painting as of the 17th century, this form of painting not only moved itself to the fore but also a new socio-political stance: utopian socialism becomes the contemporary of High Romanticism. If we want to take this historical fact into account with regard to net art, it would seem that the latest technological mass development, 'webcam landscapes,' is also seeking to promise the ideal of freedom of the people and the individual (including the artist), marking off a transition from feudalism to capitalism, and postulating a new departure to a second modernism – knowing quite well that the Romantic period, like the net Romanticism that already exists, is the product of a bourgeois upheaval. Although with some contradictions, this bourgeois upheaval could be linked to the class of the petit bourgeoisie, and this class will also be linked to net Romanticism, a fact that can be wonderfully pinned down in the captions of "Ontogenetic Landscapes."

After opening a full-page view of the landscape in the browser, a caption is displayed below the picture indicating the location of the webcam. Not the artist, date, title, etc., then, but rather the path and time coordinates of the positions ascertained in net space are identified by sending a ping to an IP address that determines the 'geographical' locations of these addresses in the net. The trace route of a successful ping attempt contains the number of hops and the response time in milliseconds. The trace route, in turn, is dependent on the dynamic system load and the intelligence of the participating

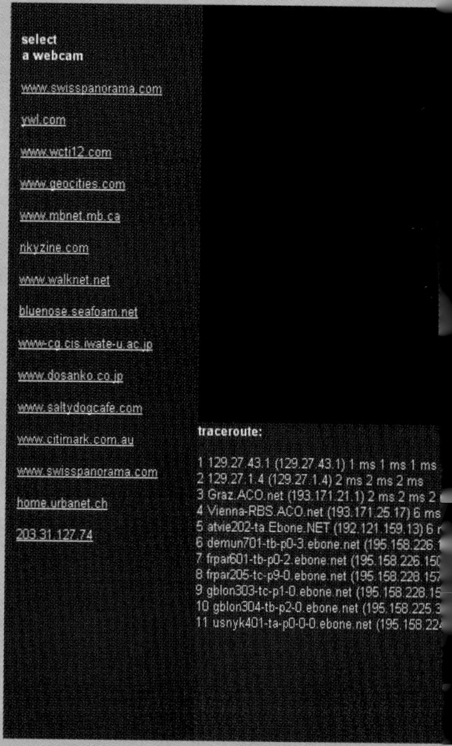

Partial visible screen text:

```
select
a webcam

www.swisspanorama.com

ywl.com

www.wcti12.com

www.geocities.com

www.mbnet.mb.ca

nkyzine.com

www.walknet.net

bluenose.seafoam.net

www.cg.cis.iwate-u.ac.jp

www.dosanko.co.jp

www.saltydogcafe.com

www.citimark.com.au

www.swisspanorama.ch

home.urbanet.ch

203.31.127.74
```

```
traceroute:

1 129.27.43.1 (129.27.43.1) 1 ms 1 ms 1 ms
2 129.27.1.4 (129.27.1.4) 2 ms 2 ms
3 Graz.ACO.net (193.171.21.1) 2 ms 2 ms 2
4 Vienna-RBS.ACO.net (193.171.25.17) 6 ms
5 atvie202-ta.Ebone.NET (192.121.159.13) 6 r
6 demun701-tb-p0-3.ebone.net (195.158.226.
7 frpar601-tb-p0-2.ebone.net (195.158.226.150)
8 frpar205-tc-p9-0.ebone.net (195.158.228.157)
9 gblon303-tc-p1-0.ebone.net (195.158.228.15
10 gblon304-tb-p2-0.ebone.net (195.158.225.3
11 usnyk401-ta-p0-0-0.ebone.net (195.158.224.
```

systems. The location of a computer in the rhizomatic net is constantly changing and is hence unique, temporary and thus singular. The Romantic picture is counteracted by these net-specific details contained in the 'caption relic.'

While the Romantics cancelled the overall form as an organic whole, the hop list refers to a dynamic and rhizomatically organic system. If we see abandon-ment of the principle of 'correct' representation of reality in its organically vital totality stylistically as another feature of Romanticism, the unique nature, the net view promising freedom, is verified as reality by the IP address of the computer belonging to the webcam – despite organic vitality. The social utopia (at least from the artist's viewpoint) would thus be restored. Even the logical image space of central per-

www.wcti12.com

SKYCAM

www.saltydogcafe.com

**select
a webcam**

www.swisspanorama.com

ywl.com

www.wcti12.com

www.geocities.com

www.mbnet.mb.ca

nkyzine.com

www.walknet.net

bluenose.seafoam.net

www.cg.cis.iwate-u.ac.jp

www.dosanko.co.jp

www.saltydogcafe.com

www.citimark.com.au

www.swisspanorama.com

home.urbanet.ch

203.31.127.74

9:06 AM

**traceroute:**

1 129.27.43.1 (129.27.43.1) 1 ms 1 ms 1 ms
2 129.27.1.4 (129.27.1.4) 2 ms 1 ms 2 ms
3 Graz.ACO.net (193.171.21.1) 3 ms 2 ms 2 ms
4 Vienna-RBS.ACO.net (193.171.25.17) 8 ms 5 ms 6 ms
5 atvie202-ta.Ebone.NET (192.121.159.13) 5 ms 7 ms 6 ms
6 demun701-tb-p0-3.ebone.net (195.158.226.153) 14 ms 14 ms 15 ms
7 frpar601-tb-p0-2.ebone.net (195.158.226.150) 29 ms 29 ms 30 ms
8 frpar205-tc-p9-0.ebone.net (195.158.226.157) 30 ms 31 ms 29 ms

15 ms
0 ms
0 ms
38 ms
38 ms
ms 118 ms

spective, abolished in the Romance period, is reflected by the time indicated in the caption - as this indication unambiguously states that there is only one vanishing point, to wit the IP address, the webcam picture, but that there are countless viewpoints on the computers in the net. Although the intentionally aperspective, often naively simplified spaces of Romanticism are hinted at by the aesthetics of webcam pictures of net Romanticism, they are annulled by the unambiguousness of the IP address in net space itself. What is more, the inverted vision pyramid of central perspective can be re-applied in a very abstract way: being immersed in the 'virtual outside,' the visitor loses his subject status and becomes the object of the description by the network.

Markus Huemer

Jody Zellen

http://www.ghostcity.com

316

Urban Conditions

GHOSTCITY focuses on the representation of the city by the mass
media. It is a labyrinthine
environment through which viewers can navigate, either following the linear narrative that
unfolds by moving from page to
page, or they can delve into
the non-linear chaos of random
links. Each space is made up of
appropriated images and texts.
The images are culled from various print media sources. The
texts are either found passages
from urban theory or specifically written poetic musings on the
city.

technological images

have become the mirrors

in which to look for identity.

The
real
is
a
model
for
representation.

# GHOSTCITY

Rather than present static
images, GHOSTCITY is a collage of
moving parts, a pulsating grid
of flashing images that loop
indefinitely. The viewer is an
urban wanderer moving through
the site, step by step, page by
page. One moves forward and back
retracing one's steps within the
urban grid, discovering new
spaces and new meanings. One
clicks on a word: 'walk,'
'time,' 'space,' or an image of
a silhouette, a shadow or a
facade. The movement freezes, a
color flashes and you are some-
place else. One by one a new
grid of images appear. Some seem
familiar. Have you been here
before? GHOSTCITY is about memory,
and about traveling through time
and space. The time is infinite,
the space is finite. Yet the
time and space of GHOSTCITY
metaphorically relate to the
experience of the city where
people walk and talk and interact. Within the confines of
GHOSTCITY visitors can pause and
think and move backwards and
forwards. GHOSTCITY is a city of
fragments. A memory. A ghost of
reality. A ghost city.

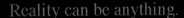

Reality can be anything.

Many points of view.

Time is singular.

Walk through

memory.

Shared Space

Contribution in
the newspaper
DER STANDARD,
Signs of
Trouble -
International
Positions in
Information
Design of
the 1990s:
Tomato,
2/4/1999
(Cooperation
with the museum
in progress and
basis Wien,
curated by
Walter Pamminger
and
Christian Muhr)

Here it comes, in from the north east, in from Amsterdam way or the German Bight, Across The downs and onto the marshes; Yet another belt of grey rain, in from The sea to dampen the shingle, wet the Stones and fill the puddles. This is a cold Rain driven by a Baltic wind and it Falls on the earth; the loamy marsh drinks its Fill. But there in the distance, sodium Arc lights blazing,

Tomato
**Kunst und globale Medien:** Eine Ausstellung des steirischen herbst

whistling and humming is The nuclear pile.
Atoms entombed in grey-streaked old
Concrete are now decaying in discrete
Proportion to themselves. And in the half
Light of dusk the unimaginable Stillness of
their power unsettles me And makes me wish
for another day when perhaps the sun is
Shining and there is little in view save For
the sea, the sky and the horizon.

**Immanuel Wallerstein**

**Economic Conditions**

# Considering the

# World-Economy

The antinomy between state and society is often asserted to be a defining characteristic of the modern world. Some argue that the contradictions deriving from this antinomy following the French Revolution underlie the contrasting ideologies that arose in the nineteenth century, and that sociology itself as an intellectual discipline represents an attempt to analyze and resolve this antinomy. The concepts 'state' and 'society' refer usually to two structures that presumably coexist within a single set of boundaries (ultimately juridical boundaries). These structures are thought to be organizations of collective energy - one formal, one not, but both real - that operate on and are operated by the same set of individuals. If one starts with such an assumption, which has been widespread, indeed dominant, in Western, indeed world, thought since the French Revolution, then one can pose questions about the degree of fit between the values of the state and of the society, and seek to explain why the fit is far from perfect. In terms of policy, one can prescribe what one prefers to make the fit more perfect. This set of categories then becomes the basis of 'comparative political sociology.'

The states are not given. They are created institutions, and are constantly changing - in form, in strength, in boundaries - through the interplay of the interstate system. Just as the world-economy has expanded over time, its political expression - the interstate system - has expanded. As the commodity chains have become longer and more complex, and have involved more and more machinery, there has been a constant pressure by the strong against the weak. This pressure has concentrated more and more of the processes in the chains that are easiest to 'monopolize' in a few areas - 'core' processes in 'core' areas - and more and more of the processes that require less skilled and more extensive manpower that is easiest to keep at a low-income level in other areas - 'peripheral' processes in 'peripheral' areas. Parallel to this economic polarization has been a political polarization between stronger states in core areas and weaker states in peripheral areas, the 'political' process of 'imperialism' being what makes possible the 'economic' process of 'unequal exchange.'

Immanuel Wallerstein

**Economic Conditions**

The strength of states has to be understood within this context. A strong state does not mean an authoritarian state. Indeed, the correlation may almost be inverse. A state is stronger than another state to the extent that it can maximize the conditions for profit-making by its enterprises (including state corporations) within the world-economy. For most states, this means creating and enforcing quasi-monopoly situations, or restraining others from doing the same to its disadvantage. The strength of the very strongest state, however, under the exceptional situation of true hegemony, is measured by its ability to minimize *all* quasi monopolies, that is, to enforce the doctrine of free trade. If hegemony is defined as a situation in which a single core power has demonstrable advantages of efficiency *simultaneously* in production, commerce, and finance, it follows that a maximally free market would be likely to ensure maximal profit to the enterprises located in such a hegemonic power.

The concept 'world-economy' (*économie-monde* in French) should be distinguished from that of 'world economy' (*économie mondiale*) or international economy. The latter concept presumes there are a series of separate 'economies' which are 'national' in scope, and that under certain circumstances these 'national economies' trade with each other, the sum of these (limited) contacts being called the international economy.

By contrast, the concept 'world-economy' assumes that there exists an 'economy' wherever (and if but only if) there is an ongoing extensive and relatively complete social division of labor with an integrated set of production processes which relate to each other through a 'market' which has been 'instituted' or 'created' in some complex way. Using such a concept, the world-economy is not new in the twentieth century nor is it a coming together of 'national economies,' none of the latter constituting complete divisions of labor. Rather, a world-economy, capitalist in form, has been in existence in at least part of the globe since the sixteenth century. Today, the entire globe is operating within the framework of this singular social division of labor we are calling the capitalist world-economy.

The capitalist world-economy has, and has had since its coming into existence, boundaries far larger than those of any political unit. Indeed, it seems to be one of the basic defining features of a capitalist world-economy that there exists no political entity with ultimate authority in all its zones.

Rather, the political superstructure of the capitalist world-economy is an interstate system within which and through which political structures called 'sovereign states' are legitimized and constrained. Far from meaning the total autonomy of decision-making, the term 'sovereignty' in reality implies a formal autonomy combined with real limitations on this autonomy, which are implemented both via the explicit and implicit rules of the interstate system and via the power of other states in the interstate system. No state in the interstate system, even the single most powerful one at any given time, is totally autonomous - but obviously some enjoy far greater autonomy than others.

The major social institutions of the capitalist world-economy - the states, the classes, the 'peoples,' and the households - are all shaped (even created) by the ongoing workings of the world-economy. None of them are primordial, in the sense of being permanent, pre-existing, relatively fixed structures to which the workings of the capitalist world-economy are exogenous.

The capitalist world-economy is a *historical* social system. It came into existence, and its genesis must be explained. Its existence is defined by certain patterns - both cyclical rhythms and secular trends - which must be explicated.

The periodic cyclical stagnations of the world-economy have been essentially resolved by a combination of three mechanisms. First, some producers have utilized advances in technology to create new and/or more efficiently produced commodities which would enable them to successfully challenge other producers who had previously dominated particular commodity markets. This provided new, so-called 'dynamic' sectors of production. Secondly, some segment of households which were previously 'extended' and receiving only a small proportion of their life-time income from wage sources have

found themselves dislocated, expropri-
ated, or otherwise forced to become 'proletarianized,' that is, to become more fully
dependent on the wage-labor market for
life-time household income. For those that
survived the process of forced transition,
this in fact has meant an increase in
money income (if not at all necessarily an
increase in real income). Thirdly, new
direct producers have been incorporated
into the world-economy, on its former
'frontiers.' These newly incorporated
direct producers formed new pools of
low-cost, part time wage labor; they
were of course also productive of new
supplies of raw materials for world
industrial production necessary for the
new expansion phase of the world-economy.

Of the three mechanisms - technological
change, proletarianization, incorporation
- most writers refer to the first one as the
most linear of all processes in the capitalist world-economy. In fact, the contrary is
true, if one analyzes technology not as an
autonomous process but in terms of its
impact on the structure of the world-system as such. More than other mechanisms, the impact of technological change
is the most cyclical and the least secular.
Let me explain. What technological
advance has accomplished above all is
that it has regularly permitted one set of
entrepreneurs to compete successfully
with other entrepreneurs. This has had
two consequences. The specific nature of
the high-profit, high-wage commodities
has repeatedly changed in favor of those
in which the new technology has been
invested. Particular commodities that
were previously in this category have
shifted downward in terms of overall
profitability, and consequently in the
attached wage structures. Secondly, the
physical locus of the most 'dynamic' sectors has also regularly changed - both
within state boundaries and across state
boundaries.

Hence, both the list of commodities
involved in unequal exchange and the
geographical location of core and peripheral economic processes have constantly
shifted over time, without however transforming to any significant extent the
worldwide structure of unequal
exchange based on the axial division of
labor. At first, wheat was exchanged
against textiles; later textiles against

steel; today steel against computers and
wheat. Once Venice was a core zone and
England semiperipheral; later Britain was
core and the northern states of the United
States semiperipheral; still later the
United States was a core zone and Russia
or Japan or many others semiperipheral;
and tomorrow? In this way, technological
advance has created a situation of constant geopolitical restructuring of the
world-system, but has it directly undermined its viability? I suspect not.

It is rather in the two other cyclical
processes - the reorganization of household structures and the incorporation of
new zones into the world-economy - that
I find the working-out of the essential
contradictions of capitalism as a world-
system, contradictions that are bringing
about the contemporary systemic crisis in
which we are living. Each time a segment
of world household structures has been
reorganized, the relative number of what
we may call proletarianized households
has grown as a proportion of the world
labor force. Each time new zones have
been incorporated into the ongoing production processes of the world-economy,
the proportion of global land and population that is a real part of the operations of
the capitalist world-economy has risen.
But proportions inevitably have a limit.
Their maximum is 100%. Ergo, these two
mechanisms - proletarianization and
incorporation - which serve to permit the
regular renewal of expansion of the capitalist system also are its own undoing.
Their success renders less likely their
future utility as renewal mechanisms.

excerpt from Immanuel Wallerstein:
The Politics of the World-Economy -
the States, the Movements, and the
Civilizations, Maison de Sciences de
l'Homme, Paris and University Press,
Cambridge, 1984

**Rishab Aiyer Ghosh**

# Cooking-pot markets: an economic model for 'free' resources on the Internet

**What is value, or: is the Internet really an economy?**

I once heard of a piece of music, called something like "Duet for one violin". This piece was supposed to be by the 19th-century virtuoso violinist and composer Paganini, and I wanted to know more about it. No reference book I looked up had anything on it, and searching on the Internet got me nowhere. Finally, I asked about it on the USENET newsgroup rec.music.classical.

Two days later - that's about the time it takes for posts to USENET discussion groups to reach all the corners of the world - I had not one or two but four responses in my mailbox. I was told that Paganini had indeed composed this piece of music, and that there were two recordings of it in existence. Also, its title was not what I thought, but *Duo à Merveille* (remarkable duet, in French) - which is perhaps one reason I couldn't find it on the anglo-centric Web indexes. Not only was this response useful because it was the only answer I got after consulting many potential sources, but it also seemed reliable - after all, four different, unconnected people could hardly be wrong all in the same way. There are many ways of looking at this incident. Clearly it was not a monetary transaction, as I gave nobody any money, nor was it an act of barter, as I provided nothing, specifically, in return. It could have been:
1. Four generous people helping out a fellow music lover.
2. Four music students, not yet accustomed to rational self-interest, the profit motive and other such real-world phenomena, in search of fame (perhaps I would mention them in my next best-selling book).
3. Four people hoping that by contributing value they'd see value in return, not knowing from where.
There are several more possible explanations, all equally true. But which explanation is the most useful? From my standpoint, the most useful explanation is one that helps form an economic model – transforming this happy anecdote into a means for determining how value is created and distributed on the Internet, in the vast majority of situations where the involvement of money is low or non-existent.

The key is in numbers: when 100 million people spend significant portions of their lives creating for, consuming from and collaborating in activities with people they don't know, without getting paid for it, they must be:
1. A new (even 'digital') breed of human beings, altruistic, untouched by the profit motive, who will lead the world into a new society where economics is, if not dead, totally new.
2. A slightly demented bunch of hobbyists with lots of spare time; infected with enthusiasm stemming from the novelty of the online environment, who will soon enough get bored and get back to (paid) work
3. Rather ordinary people who don't think they're gifting time and effort to a friendly new global community, but believe they get a return on their investment, as it were, and will keep working 'for free' as long as their return keeps coming.
For the 100 million or so population of the Internet, my pick is clearly the last. The Internet is not a new world where normal people are magically transformed by the keyboard in front of them into altruistic or otherwise unreasonable forms of behaviour. The Internet is certainly new, but it is a new medium of expression, not a new way of life. A large part of that expression is economic – i.e. the rational, self-interested behaviour of real-world 'economic actors' translated into the forms of activity encouraged by, or unique to, the Internet. This is what I would call Internet economics - the model of economic activity as expressed by ordinary people in this new medium.

To begin with, much of the economic activity on the Net involves value but no money. Until a few years ago, there was almost no commercial activity on the Internet. The free resources of the Net greatly outweigh all commercial resources, especially if one counts only purely on-line transactions (e.g. a bookseller like Amazon' uses the Internet as a marketing tool; it actually makes money selling books, which requires the physical transportation of goods). It is quite hard to put a price on the value of the Internet's free resources, at least in part because they exist because they don't have prices attached. They exist in a market of implicit transactions.[2]

Notes
1. http://www.amazon.com

2. Rishab Aiyer Ghosh, 1994. "The rise of an information barter economy", *Electric Dreams*, #37 (21 November), at http://dxm.org/dreams/dreams37.html

## Something for nothing?

Linus Torvalds did not release Linux source code free of charge to the world as a lark, or because he was naive, but because it was a "natural decision within the community that [he] felt [he] wanted to be a part of."[3] Any economic logic of this community - the Internet - has to be found somewhere in that 'natural decision.' It is found in whatever it was that motivated Torvalds, like so many others on the Net, to act as he did and produce without direct monetary payment.

Of course, it is the motivation behind people's patterns of consumption and, what is more relevant in the case of Linux, production that forms the marrow of economics. Such motivation is usually expressed in terms of curves of supply and demand, measured by costs and prices in dollars and cents. However, the best portions of our lives usually do come without price tags on them - and of course value exists there. And the best part of life on the Internet is the abundance of goods and services - the range of online production and expression from web pages to real-time support forums, newsgroups and mailing lists - all available without price tags, 'for free.'

But 'free' is the wrong word: information or knowledge products and services, however free in terms of hard cash, are extremely valuable. So it makes sense to assume that the several million people on the Internet who publish matters of their interest on their home pages on the Web, and the several million who contribute to communities in the form of newsgroups and mailing-lists, and of course anyone who ever writes free software, believe they're getting something out of it for themselves. They are clearly not getting cash; their 'payment' might be the contributions from others that balance their own work, or something as intangible as the satisfaction of having their words read by millions around the world.

Even those who have never studied economics have an idea of its basic principles: that prices rise with scarcity and fall in a glut, that they are settled when what consumers will pay matches what

producers can charge. These principles obviously work, as can be seen in day-to-day life. But that's the 'real world' of things you can drop on your toe. Do they work in a knowledge economy, where you frequently don't really know what the 'thing' is that you're buying or selling, or precisely when you're doing it, or even whether you're buying - or selling?

The short answer is Yes, they do, given Paul Samuelson's textbook definition of economics as the "study of how societies use scarce resources to produce valuable commodities and distribute them among different people"[4] which remains as valid now as ever. But notions of scarcity - identifying what is scarce - and value must reflect the realities of the knowledge economy, the perceptions of the economic actors themselves.

Sticking to the well-known example of Linux: Linux could be (and was) copied indefinitely and widely at negligible costs; clearly the program itself was not scarce, and hence was of low relative value. The value may have been in the very fact that Linux was widely available and could be freely modified: indeed, Torvalds now says "Making Linux freely available is the single best decision I've ever made." Monetary exchange, barter transactions and value flow

Unlike the markets of the 'real world,' where trade is denominated in some form of money, on the Net every trade of ideas and reputations is a direct, equal exchange, in forms derivative of barter. This means that not only are there two sides to every trade as far as the transaction of exchanging one thing for another goes - which also applies to trades involving money - there are also two points of view in any exchange, two conceptions of where the value lies. (In a monetary transaction, by definition, both parties see the value as fixed by the price.)

In a barter exchange the value of nothing is absolute. Both parties to a barter have to provide something of value to the other; this something is not a universally or even widely accepted intermediary such as money. There can

3. This, and other quotes from Torvalds, are from e-mail dialogues held with the author since October 1996. A consolidated version is published as an interview in *First Monday*, Vol. 3 Issue 3, March 1998, http://www.firstmonday.dk/issues/issue3_3/

4. Paul A. Samuelson and William D. Nordhaus, 1995. *Economics*. 15th ed. New York: McGraw-Hill

be no formal price-tags, as an evaluation must take place on the spot at the time of exchange. When you barter you are, in general, not likely to exchange your produce for another's in order to make a further exchange with that. Unlike the money you receive when you sell something – which you value only in its ability to be exchanged for yet another thing – in a barter transaction you normally yourself use, and obviously value, what you receive.

When the contribution of each side to a barter is used directly by the other, it further blurs the distinction between buyer and seller. In the 'real world' barter did not, of course, take place between buyer and seller but between two producer-consumers in one transaction. When I trade my grain for your chicken, there's no buyer or seller, although one of us may be hungrier than or have different tastes from the other. On the Internet, say in the Linux world, where it may seem at first that there's a clear buyer (such as the *Times of India*, the world's sixth largest English-language newspaper which runs its nation-wide network on Linux) and an equally clear, if aggregate seller (the Linux developer community) there is, in fact, little such distinction. There is a flow of value from the newspaper (as users and evaluators of software) and another flow to the newspaper (the software itself). There is also a flow of value from the Linux community and to that community. As long as the corresponding value-flows balance each other, the system works fairly, even though there are no identifiable transactions.

There is, here, the first glimpse of a process of give and take, by which people do lots of work on their creations, which are distributed not for nothing, but in exchange for things of value. People 'put it' to the Internet because they realise that they 'take out' from it. Although the connection between giving and taking seems tenuous at best, it is in fact crucial. Because whatever resources there are on the Net for you to take out, without payment, were all put in by others without payment; the Net's resources that you consume were produced by others for similar reasons – in exchange for what they consumed, and so on. So the economy of the Net begins to look like a vast tribal cooking-pot,

surging with production to match consumption, simply because everyone understands – instinctively, perhaps, or through experience – that trade need not occur in single transactions of barter, and that one product can be exchanged for millions at a time. The cooking-pot keeps boiling because people keep putting in things as they themselves, and others, take things out. Torvalds points out, "I get the other informational products for free regardless of whether I do Linux or not." True. But although nobody knows all the time whether your contribution is exceeded by your consumption, everyone knows that if all the contributions stopped together there'd be nothing for anyone: the fire would go out. And that wouldn't be fun at all.

## Cooking-pot markets: modelling community interaction

If it occurred in brickspace, the cooking-pot model would probably not exist. In a barter transaction, where I give you my chicken for your potatoes, we have clearly agreed on relative values (e.g. 1 small chicken = 1 kg potatoes). When we combine our produce to make chicken-potato stew in a cooking-pot, which we both think is tastier than either product alone, we are left with the problem of sharing out the stew. Assuming we take stew from the pot in equal proportions, people in our hypothetical tribe would have to be willing to add what they have into the pot with no guarantee that they're getting a fair exchange, which smacks of altruism. But on the Net, a cooking-pot market is far from altruistic, or it wouldn't work. This is thanks to the major cause for the erosion of value on the Internet – the problem of infinity.[5] Because it takes as much effort to distribute one copy of an original creation as a million – and because the costs are distributed across millions of people – you never lose from letting your product free in the cooking-pot, as long as you are compensated for its creation. You are not giving away something for nothing. You are giving away a million copies of something, for at least one copy each of a million other things. Since those millions of copies of your creation cost you nothing you lose nothing. Nor need there be a notional

5. Rishab Aiyer Ghosh, 1995. "The problem with infinity," *Electric Dreams*, #63 (19 June), at http://dxm.org/dreams/dreams63.html

loss of potential earnings, because those million copies are not inherently valuable - the very fact of them being a million, and theoretically a billion or more - makes them worthless. Your effort is limited to creating one - the original - copy of your product. You are happy to receive something of value in exchange for that one creation.

What a miracle, then, that you receive not one thing of value in exchange - of course there is no explicit act of exchange at all - but millions of unique goods made by others! True, you only receive 'worthless' copies; but since you only need have one copy of each original product, every one of them can have value for you. It is this asymmetry unique to the infinitely reproducing Internet that makes the cooking-pot a viable economic model, which it would not be in the long run in any brickspace tribal commune.

With a cooking-pot made of iron, what comes out is little more than what went in - albeit processed by fire - so a limited quantity must be shared by the entire community. This usually leads either to systems of private property and explicit barter exchanges, or to the much analysed "Tragedy of the Commons."[6]

On the other hand, in the cooking-pots of the Internet, the key is the value placed on diversity.[7] So, multiple copies of a single product add little value - marginal utility is near zero - but single copies of multiple products are, to a single user, of immense value. If a sufficient number of people put in free goods, the cooking pot clones them for everyone, so that everyone gets far more value than was put in. People don't have to share out the contents of the combinatorially explosive Internet cooking-pot - instead we each get our own individual copies of the entire cooking-pot!
An explicit monetary transaction - a sale of a software product - is based on what is increasingly an economic fallacy: that each single copy of a product has marginal positive value. In contrast, the cooking-pot market rightly allocates resources on the basis of where consumers see value to be, in each distinct product, rather than in each individual copy.

The cooking-pot model provides a rational explanation for people's motivations to produce and trade in goods and services, where a monetary incentive is lacking. It suggests that people do not only - or even largely - produce in order to improve their reputation, but as a more-than-fair payment for other goods - 'ideas' - that they receive from the cooking-pot. The cooking-pot market is not barter, as it does not require individual transactions. It is based on the assumption that on the Net, you don't lose when you duplicate, so every contributor gets much more than a fair return in the form of combined contributions of others.

The cooking-pot model shows the possibility of immense value being generated through the continuous interaction of people at a numbing speed, with an unprecedented flexibility and aptitude towards intangible, ambiguously defined goods and services. The cooking-pot market already exists, it is an image of what the Internet has already evolved into, calmly and almost surreptitiously, over the past couple of decades. And as an economic model, it provides a framework for tools of measurement and analysis[8] that can help predict how the Internet and its network of economic communities will interact and evolve in the future.

6. Garrett Hardin, 1968. "The Tragedy of the Commons," *Science*, Volume 162, pp. 1243-1248, and at http://die-off.org/page95.htm

7. Rishab Aiyer Ghosh, 1995. "Trade reborn through diversity," *Electric Dreams*, #65 (10 July), at http://dxm.org/dreams/dreams65.html

8. Measuring tools such as CODD, which analyses the contribution of individual programmers to open-source software such as Linux: http://www.vipul.net/codd/

**Vincent Mosco**

**Economic Conditions**

# Militant Particularism: Beta Testing a New Society

As David Harvey notes in his recent assessment, Raymond Williams liked to invoke the idea of "militant particularism," meaning that solidarities developed in specific local struggles gave rise to general ideas about benefiting humanity (Harvey, 1996: 19-45). For Williams (1989) global ideals like the democratization of social, political and economic life and the creation of vibrant public spaces were hatched in the tumult of concrete conflicts in communities, factories, offices, and homes. This paper addresses a contemporary version of militant particularism, what some might see as a distorted or even perverse variation on Williams' thesis, namely, the creation of local and regional high technology zones that transform spatial, social, and cultural relations in a region to the detriment of democratic ideals and the public sphere. The paper concludes by reflecting on the significance of these developments and specifically of militant particularism for the field of international communication.

## The End of Geography?

It is an increasingly popular myth that computer communication ends geography by completing a revolution in the process of transcending the spatial constraints that historically limited the movement of information. *The Death of Distance* (Cairncross, 1997) is just the latest in a series of books announcing the triumph of technology over place, the annihilation of space with time. The argument is simple. The convergence of computer and communication technologies permits people to meet anywhere at any time thereby making possible the ubiquitous exchange of information from the simplest two person exchange to the operation of a multinational conglomerate with its vast requirements for moving information and ideas rapidly, efficiently and with close to complete security. In the nineteenth century, spatial barriers meant that news took weeks by packet boat to get from New York to New Orleans. Now distance is by and large insignificant and particularly with the arrival of global mobile satellite systems, which will permit seamless wireless communication between any points on the globe, soon to be completely irrelevant.

In an important sense, all space is becoming cyberspace, because communication is migrating there. But cyberspace is fundamentally different from geography as we know it because this space is almost fully transparent with respect to communication. Notwithstanding the occasional nuance in the 'death of distance' literature, it is typically a breathlessly overstated argument. In this respect, it follows in a long tradition of writing about technological change, particularly electronic technology, which has been announcing the death of distance for over a century. In the nineteenth century, the railroad would unite Europe as no conqueror ever did, the telegraph would overcome class and racial divisions in America, and electricity would bounce messages off the clouds to isolated villages, which would nevertheless need to cope with the minor irritant of what was charmingly called 'celestial advertising.' The historian David Nye (1990) convincingly refers to these as visions of the "technological sublime," a literal eruption of feeling that briefly overwhelms reason only to be recontained by it. Or better still, as his mentor Leo Marx (1965) put it, "the rhetoric of the technological sublime" involves hymns to progress that rise "like froth on a tide of exuberant self-regard sweeping over all misgivings, problems, and contradictions." Taken in by this frothy sublime, the death of distance advocates have missed significant characteristics of communication that call for a modification of its meaning. Assuming that overcoming distance improves communication, supporters miss the equal tendency of more communication to increase dissonance and intensify conflict. The rail and telegraph brought Europe closer together in war as well as peace. Moreover, and this is particularly significant to the issue at hand, proponents of the end of geography idea underestimate the importance of face-to-face contact and of informal networks whose contacts are based partly on, and certainly facil designers and software engineering firms do not locate in South Dakota or Nebraska where the cost of doing business is low and where the telecommunications infrastructure is sufficiently robust to permit tele-connections at the level of most anywhere else on the continent. Instead, they locate in places like lower

**References**

Amin, A. & Robins, K. 1990. "The Re-emergence of Regional Economies? The Mythical Geography of Flexible Accumulation." *Environment and Planning B-Society and Space*, 8 (1), 1990, pp. 7-34.

Bagnasco, A. 1977. *Tre Italie: La Problematica del low Sviluppo Italiano*. Bologna: Il Mulino.

Beniger, J. R. 1986. *The Control Revolution*. Cambridge, MA: Harvard University Press.

Bianchini, F. 1991 "The Third Italy: Model or Myth?" *Ekistic*, 58, pp. 336-346.

Birger, J. 1996, September 6. "N.Y.C. is Weighing Ending Debt Power of Business Districts." *The Bond Buyer*, p.1.

Breskin, I. 1997, May 27. "Times Square's Dykstra." *Investor's Business Daily*, p. A-1.

Brusco, S. & Righi, E. 1989. "Local government, Industrial Policy and Social Consensus: The Case of Modena (Italy)." *Economy and Society*, 18 (4), pp. 405-424.

Cadwell, L. B.. 1997. *Bringing Regio Emilia Home*. Toronto: Guidance Centre Press.

Cairncross, F. 1997. *The Death of Distance*. Boston: Harvard Business School Press.

Castells, M. & Hall, P. 1994. *Technopoles of the World*. London: Routledge.

Castells, M. & Henderson, J. 1987. "Techno-economic Restructuring, Socio-political Processes and Spatial Transformation: A Global Perspective." In J. Henderson and M. Castells (eds.), *Global Restructuring and Territorial Development*. Beverly Hills, CA: Sage.

Coopers & Lybrand. 1996. April. *The New York New Media Industry Survey*. New York: Coopers & Lybrand.

1997, February. *The Coopers and Lybrand Money Tree*. New York: Coopers & Lybrand.

Cossentino, F. , Pyke, F. & Sengenberger W. 1996. *Local and Regional Response to Global Pressure: The Case of Italy and its Industrial Districts*. Geneva: International Institute for Labour Studies.

Fitch, R. 1996, May 13. "In Bologna, Small is Beautiful: The Cooperative Economics of Italy's Emilia-Romagna Holds a Lesson for the U.S." *The Nation*, 262 (19), p.18.

Goff, L. 1996, April 22. "Silicon Alley." *Computerworld*, pp. 81-83.

Greenhouse, S. 1997, February 20. "Unions Woo Business District Workers." *The New York Times*, p. B4.

Greenwald, J. 1997, August. "Think Big." *Wired*, pp. 95-104, 145.

Harrison, B. 1994. *Lean and Mean*. New York: Basic Books.

Harvey, D. *Justice, Nature &the Geography of Difference*. Cambridge, MA: Blackwell, 1996.

Manhattan in New York City where the costs of doing business are among the highest on the continent because physical proximity to fellow professionals, potential customers in the advertising and publishing businesses, service providers, and universities are enormously important to their business success. Whereas tele-marketing and mail order computer firms like Gateway, Inc., which sees little benefit from such networking and has a lot to gain from low-cost, docile labour, can benefit from locating in the hinterland, professionally based companies, the bedrock of the producer services industry, require more cosmopolitan settings.

## Location, Location, Location

Rather than think about this as the death of distance, it is more useful to refer to the transformation of space made increasingly salient by the introduction of information and computer technology (ICT). In the sense of physical geography, the use of ICT reconstitutes the spatial map by revalorizing locations and the relations between them. It also reconstitutes what we now call cyberspace. Cyberspace is typically conceived of as something new, a product of ICT applications. But this formulation perpetuates myths of revolution which suggest that everything now changes with the arrival of this technology, creating a radical rupture with history that diminishes the value of the past because cyberspace provides an entirely new start to time. Notwithstanding the value of such mythic formulations which have received extensive attention, cyberspace is not new but rather a deepening and extension of those shared communication spaces created over the history of communication technology and accelerating with the telegraph, telephone and broadcasting technologies. ICT applications contribute to reshaping or remapping the contours of cyberspace just as they remap physical geography. Perhaps more importantly these dual transformations interact so that physical geography and cyberspace mutually constitute one another. Hence, while it makes some sense to distinguish analytically between Castells' space of places and space of flows, we should not make too much of this. Physical space is

easily understood as the space of places, but it too is a space through which flow people and objects so it too is a space of flows. Similarly, cyberspace is not just a space through which flow our electronic transmissions but it is also a space of places with identifiable addresses that take on much of the same significance, economically and politically as well as socially and culturally that traditional spaces enjoy. Hence, while it is hard to disagree with the value of Castells' notion that information and communication technology transforms spatial relations, it does not do so by combining material resources in powerful places with the immaterial flows of placeless power. Rather, we are experiencing the remapping of the global political economy by the combination of valuable resources and valuable flows in both physical geography and cyberspace.

## Magic Places: The Technopoles

The technopole is one reason why specific local places are taking on a growing significance in spite of the 'end of geography' talk. For the technopole is a specific place which brings together institutions, labour, and finance that generate the basic materials of the information economy. They result from various local, national, and, in some cases, international, planning activities by public and private sector organizations to promote systematic technological innovation. The term technopole originated in the Japanese government's effort of the 1960s to build a science-based technopole Tsukuba about 40 miles outside of Tokyo and most would see Silicon Valley in California as its icon and most successful form. In their global survey, Castells and Hall (1994) refer to two dozen or so technopoles, many eager to emulate the Silicon Valley model. Japan began this process by recognizing the need to maintain and perhaps even accelerate the productivity gains that its economy enjoyed in the 1950s based largely on the post-war occupation and direct foreign investment.

As the occupation and its trappings ended and as foreign investment moved elsewhere, Japan looked to an alternative. With no advantage in natural resources, it turned to intensive technological development built on the tight coordination of centralized government, corporate and research institutions. Led by agencies like the Ministry of International Trade (MITI), companies with such households names as Toyota and Sony helped to organize scientific and technical research and development networks that brought together diverse professionals in specific locations to carry out basic (often simply the reverse engineering of successful Western products) and applied research and incubate products developed from research until they were ready for the export market. Although some of this work took place in isolated regions of the country, the most successful were based around Tokyo where they could enjoy proximity to centers of finance capital, other producer and consumer services, and government. The focus on technology and the urban connection gave birth to the technopole designation. There is a link between the original technopole in Japan and the best known of these Silicon Valley. First, the latter grew out of a similar protected network, only in the case of Silicon Valley it was the Department of Defense that fed military contracts to teams of engineers based in and around Stanford University. With the help of DOD, teams grew into networks that formed companies which continued to benefit from the protection that a growing military research budget and Cold War justification could bring. Japan also provoked the 'second coming' of Silicon Valley when its 1980s mastery over mass production of semiconductors, brought about by a highly protected oligopoly industry and low wage production, forced Silicon Valley firms into high-end customized production or face the loss of global leadership. As Saxenian (1994) and others have documented, the preeminence of Silicon Valley was built upon the success of this transition. Much of the credit goes to the fluid network of associations among professionals who moved from company to company, met in many different informal as well as work place settings, and cross-fertilized innovations that make up the hardware and software landscape of business and home. Notwithstanding the importance of this factor, which it is frequently pointed out,

was missing in the more centralized, rigid, and less successful technopole based outside of Boston, insufficient attention is paid to the treatment of labour in Silicon Valley. This includes the 'work until burn out' treatment of young computer professionals and the low wage, often homework based production facilities, a labour process that provides a low cost production base at one end of the Silicon Valley food chain. The most interesting of the newer technopoles draw from the Japanese and Silicon Valley models but more importantly take them a significant step further. These earlier successes built resilient and fluid production networks that brought together diverse knowledge professionals who could manage innovation from idea to market. Newer technopoles integrate these production networks into similarly resilient and fluid consumption networks located within the technopole. The paper proceeds to take up two types of this newer computer technopolis in New York's Silicon Alley and Malaysia's Multimedia Super Corridor.

## New York: From Broadway to Silicon Alley

Silicon Alley is the technical hub of an agglomeration of New York's media industries connecting advertising, publishing, broadcasting, telecommunications, mass entertainment, contemporary art, and fashion all concentrated in a collection of overlapping districts from Broad Street at the south end of Manhattan through Times Square and along Madison Avenue. Filling office buildings left vacant by financial services firms that shed workers with new technologies or relocation and giving a post-industrial economic allure to a city once bankrupt and out of manufacturing alternatives, Silicon Alley embodies a cyber version of the phoenix myth: here is a city reborn from the ashes of its industrial past. Even so, it also propels a transformation of urban politics and power as corporate-controlled bodies like Business Improvement Districts remake public spaces into private enclaves and rewrite the rules of policing, civic activity and public spectacle. All of this takes place for the sake of connectivity, in this case referring to

Johnson, K. "The Place for the Aspiring Dot Com: Internet Industry's Most Popular Address is Manhattan." *The New York Times*, September 30, 1997, p. B-1.

King, A. D. (ed.). 1996. *Representing the City: Ethnicity, Capital, and Culture in the 21st Century Metropolis.* New York: New York University Press.

Marx, L. 1965. *The Machine in the Garden: Technology and the Pastoral Ideal in America.* Oxford University Press.

Massey, D. 1992. "Politics and Space/time". *New Left Review*, 196, pp. 65-84.

Mosco, V. & Kaye, L. Forthcoming. "Questioning the Concept of the Audience." In I. Hagen and J. Wasko. (eds.). *Consuming Audiences.* Creskill, NJ: Hampton.

Multimedia Development Corporation Sdn Bhd. 1997a. *Investing in Malaysia's Multimedia Supercorridor: Policies, Incentives, and Facilities.* Kuala Lumpur: Multimedia Development Corporation.

1997b. *Seven Flagship Applications.* Kuala Lumpur: Multimedia Development Corporation.

Ng, F. 1997, April 23. "Silicon Corridor Set up in the North to Complement MSC." *New Straits Times*, p. 23.

Nye, D. 1990. *Electrifying America: Social Meanings of a New Technology, 1880-1940.* Cambridge, MA: MIT Press.

O'Brien, R. 1992. *Global Financial Integration and the End of Geography*. New York: Council on Foreign Relations Press.

Piore, M. & Sabel, C. F. 1984. *The Second Industrial Divide*. New York: Basic Books.

Putnam, R. D. 1993. *Making Democracy Work: Civic Traditions in Modern Italy*. Princeton University Press.

Rizal Razali, M. 1997, April 21. "Cyberjaya to Pave the Way for Technological Excellence." *New Strait Times*, p. 30.

Sanger, D, E. 1997, August 3. "The Overfed Tiger Economies." *The New York Times*, p. E3.

Sassen, S. 1991. *The Global City: New York, London, Tokyo*. Princeton, N.J.: Princeton University Press.

Saxenian, A. 1994. *Regional Advantage: Culture and Competition in Silicon Valley and Route 128*. Cambridge, MA: Harvard University Press.

Smith, N. 1992. "Geography, Difference, and the Politics of Scale." In J. Doherty, E. Graham, and M. Malek (eds.) *Postmodernism and the Social Sciences*. NY: St. Martin's.

Smolin, L. 1997. *The Life of the Cosmos*. NY: Oxford University Press.

Williams, R. 1989. *Resources of Hope*. London: Verso.

the connections among the convergent computer, communication, and cultural sectors in Manhattan and to the market potential of a web industry built on enhancing electronic connectivity worldwide. In a short time Silicon Alley has become a global centre for multimedia design and development. According to a 1997 Coopers and Lybrand report, the district anchors a new media industry that employs 56,000 in New York City and 106,000 in the metropolitan area's 5,000 new media firms, making it one of the largest employers of computer communication workers in North America, on a par with Silicon Valley. Annual revenues climbed 56 percent over 1996 to $2.8 billion in the City and 50 percent in the metro area to $5.7 billion. Full time jobs in new media now match those in the premier media industries of New York, advertising and print publishing. In addition, Silicon Alley has become a model for the kinds of mobile production that is increasingly common in web work. Casual workers move in and out benefiting from physical proximity when necessary and returning to other office or home sites. In fact, Silicon Alley has pioneered in the short-lease, prebuilt, prewired office, what it calls the Plug 'n' Go system, which allows small businesses and casual workers to move and plug into physical and cyber networks.

The growth of Silicon Alley began at a time when businesses were fleeing a city on the verge of bankruptcy with an eroding infrastructure and dwindling tax rolls (Goff, 1996). Silicon Alley is now an integral part of a revived lower Manhattan whose new, up-scale neighbourhoods (Battery Park City and Tribeca) join with the artistic communities of SoHo and Greenwich Village, and the Madison Avenue advertising district. These, in turn, are increasingly linked to the mass media rejuvenated, mid-town and Times Square districts, supported by major investment from the Disney Corporation and most recently by Reuters which is building a headquarters across from a Disney theater, to produce an agglomeration of interconnected post-industrial spaces rooted in cultural production. A 1996 Coopers and Lybrand report highlights the significance of close ties among businesses in these several communities. Forty-three per cent of new media companies surveyed worked principally for advertising firms and forty-two per cent for print publishing and entertainment firms. Silicon Alley is unique in its integration of media (especially publishing and advertising), the arts (particularly the development of SoHo) for attracting talent to multimedia design and production, and telecommunications (for example the regional Teleport). According to one commentator, "A lot of the style of Silicon Alley may be new, but the muscle behind it is not. Established New York industries, especially advertising, publishing, fashion and design are now leading much of the expansion of the new technologies." (Johnson, 1997) By the start of 1997, New York had surpassed all rivals in the number of registered commercial and nonprofit Internet domain sites, twice as many as its nearest rival, San Francisco and 4.3 percent of the entire U.S. (Johnson, 1997) This is evidence of the extraordinary degree of connectivity distinguishing the New York technopole. The advertising firm Saatchi & Saatchi demonstrates a vital way in which this connectivity works. The S&S Silicon Alley web unit Darwin Digital, brought together Proctor & Gamble with Time Warner at the address Parenttime.com. The project links Time Warner's childcare magazine division with an integrated advertising package supplied by P&G, all created and run from New York City. Darwin Digital has also helped create a new network for childrens' games on the Internet with the major sponsorship of General Mills, the Minneapolis-based cereal company, whose creative staff came to New York to produce the site with Darwin. This growth has been boosted by local government strategies for new neighbourhood development (specifically Battery Park City and Tribeca) in attracting people to work and live in the city. Much is also made of the role of the state and city governments in supporting the recycling (including rewiring) of vacant buildings, making it easier for multimedia start-up firms to locate in sites that meet their technical requirements. For example, the city of New York announced in 1997 that it would set aside $30 million for a Silicon Alley job creation fund. It is also important to consider the significance of universities,

Vincent Mosco

particularly New York University, and networking organizations, primarily the 4000 member New York New Media Association, in fostering new businesses in this sector.

## Creatio ex Nihilo in Malaysia

If New York is viewed as the information age phoenix rising from the ashes of manufacturing decline, then Malaysia is the magic land where palm-oil plantations become Multimedia Super Corridors almost overnight. The Multimedia Super Corridor enacts an alternative but related myth, creatio ex nihilo, as the Malaysian national government creates a completely new built environment out of what it views as the raw material of 400 square miles of rain forest and palm-oil plantations south of Kuala Lumpur. The increasingly celebrated place is where the Malaysian government proposes to spend between $8 and $13 billion of public and private money to turn this area of rolling countryside, rain forests and palm-oil plantations into a post-industrial district where multinational corporations will develop and test new software and multimedia products. Malaysia's 'nothing' will give way to two new high technology cities.

Cyberjaya, what one pundit called "an info tech omphalos," and Putrajaya, a new cyber-ready capital including an administrative capital and a new international airport. (Greenwald, 1997; Rizali, 1997; Wysocki, 1997). Today their only existing highway is a $2 billion fibre network under construction. But the plan is that in these cities bureaucrats will serve the public in cyberspace, consumers will shop with smart cards, children will attend virtual schools, professors will lecture electronically at the planned Multimedia University, executives will manage through teleconferencing, and patients will be treated through telemedicine. The government has struck deals with many of the world's leading computer communication companies, including Microsoft, IBM, and Nortel which will establish development sites in the region to test new products and services such as electronic commerce, telemedicine, virtual education, paperless administration and state-of-the-art electronic surveillance and policing. The companies will enjoy substantial tax freedom, the opportunity to import their own labour and technology, and to export all capital and profit. Malaysia hopes to use this project to jump start a stagnant economy and move beyond a low wage platform as the basis for growth. The implications of purchasing this hoped-for growth by turning its land into the locus for transnational cyber-development projects and its citizens into beta testers for electronic capitalism are profound.

Like the Silicon Alley project, the Super Corridor is to be built on two conceptions of connectivity, including the idea that the creation of a dense web of multinational businesses in a new space can propel national development and the idea that social progress grows out of fully integrating citizens into the electronic web. The MSC is an effort to stem the erosion in the massive growth that Malaysia experienced based on a labour cost advantage it enjoyed in computer and telecommunication hardware production. Having lost that advantage to other Asian nations, particularly to Bangladesh, Vietnam, and China, the Malaysian government believes it can pioneer in software and product development. Malaysia proposes nothing short of making a national model out of the city-state Singapore's centrally directed, export-oriented, high technology approach to development. Indeed, although the MSC is concentrated in one soon-to-be developed region, plans exist to support the MSC with a hardware corridor in the north of Malaysia, including the island of Penang, that would attract national and foreign businesses interested in higher end production with more skilled labour than can be found in the lowest wage regions of Asia (Ng, 1997: 23). Malaysia marks an important test of whether the once super fast-growing regions of Asia can continue to grow in the highly competitive area of software engineering and information technology product development. It also bears close scrutiny because Malaysia proposes to retain tight censorship, strong libel laws, and a patriarchal Islamic culture, even as it welcomes foreign multinationals, inviting them to test the full range

Wysocki, B. 1997, June 10. "Malaysia is Gambling on a Costly Plunge into a Cyber Future." The Wall Street Journal, pp. A1, A10.

Zukin, S. 1995. The Cultures of Cities. Cambridge, MA: Blackwell.

of new media products on its citizens. Recent developments in global financial and equity markets also mark this as a case to watch because massive declines in currency values, near collapse of stock prices and the withdrawal of foreign capital have created huge rifts between Malaysia (joined by Indonesia, Singapore and Thailand) and first world powers that once pointed to these so-called Asian tigers as evidence for the success of traditional modernization schemes (Sanger, 1997).

## Technopoles and Governance

The most important conclusion that I can draw from my analysis of these cases, and which by and large applies across the technopole literature, is that there is a great deal of interest in them as economic growth engines, some interest in the technopole as a new form of cultural representation (King, 1996 and Zukin, 1995), and practically no interest in their political governance, that is, in addressing technopoles as sites of political power and their residents as citizens. This is particularly unfortunate because many of the technopoles, including the New York and Malaysia cases, are not only test beds for high tech products. They are also testing new forms of governance and new forms of social and cultural experience with significant implications for citizenship. Because the new technopoles are not only sites for building connectivity among producers, as has been Silicon Valley, but also for doing so between producers and consumers and among the latter, they hold considerable significance for cultural analysis.

## NYNY: Corporate control.com

Along with the creation of a new media district in New York, we find a significant transformation in governance with the formation of private sector run Business Improvement Districts that have been put in charge of a wide range of services. They police the streets, manage the parks, haul away trash, and remove the homeless, all with private, mainly non-union, low wage workers. In addition to this, they have the authority to issue bonds (much

to the consternation of city officials who fear both the competition in credit markets and the consequences of a BID default) and pay their management well: the head of one earns over twice the salary of the mayor. Moreover, the BID which encompasses Silicon Alley, has managed to divert public and private funds to build some of the only new public spaces in New York, primarily to service up-scale high tech workers and their families. So along with high technology comes the privatization of basic services and the reorganization of urban government and civic spaces. Once public places like historic Bryant Park, adjacent to the New York Public Library, now under BID control, closes at night, contains swarms of private security guards, particularly in evidence during the many corporate sponsored events such as fashion shows, who prevent people with large bags, i.e. the homeless, from entering the park (Birger, 1996; Breskin, 1997; Greenhouse, 1997; Zukin, 1995). As a result, even the usually staid *New York Times* editorialized that "in its eagerness to benefit from privatization, the department (of Parks) seems to be allowing businesses to set the agenda." (January 27, 1998, p. A18) The only new park construction in New York City is located in Silicon Alley, a model of up-scale space to attract high tech workers. Some showcase parks like Central Park and Bryant Park have been spruced up with private money, the rest of the City's public space suffers from extreme neglect. In the past decade public funding for parks is down 31 percent and the city is left with 1,700 park employees for 1,400 parks and playgrounds on 27,000 acres. This is in keeping with the general erosion in the quality of life for New Yorkers who now enjoy the dubious distinction of living in the city with the largest gap between upper and middle and between upper and lower income groups.

## Malaysia: Beta Testing for Multinationals

The Malaysian government has signed agreements with several of the world's major computer and telecommunication firms under which the companies agree to set up shop in the new technopole and in return receive a ten year or so tax holiday and complete freedom to bring in their own work force and capital and to export all products developed in the zone. These will be permitted to test new products in seven 'flagship' areas which the Multimedia Development Corporation defines as follows:

1. Electronic Government: An opportunity to reinvent government.
2. Multi-Purpose 'Smart' Card: Tool for the information age.
3. Smart Schools: Education for a smart society.
4. Telemedicine: A new paradigm in healthcare provision.
5. R&D Cluster: Next-generation multimedia technologies
6. World-wide Manufacturing Web: Building Best Practices in High-Tech Operations
7. Borderless Marketing: New Frontiers in Commerce (Multimedia Development Corporation, 1997b)

Putrajaya is to be the new national administrative capital operating as fully as possible in an electronic environment, including compulsory smart cards for each resident (Multimedia Development Corporation, 1997a). One cannot help but conclude that this gives a whole new meaning to the responsibility of citizenship, namely, beta testing new products for transnational computer companies. Shall we call this virtual citizenship? Cyberjaya, the new residential city, is a hyper-version of the corporate suburb permitting near full corporate ownership, control, and governance. This view is reinforced by legislative changes planned to test new forms of legal citizenship within the Corridor. According to current plans, municipal governance will become the responsibility of a private corporation with its own corporate rules and tax structure, its own form of citizenship and the power to enact new laws. Tenants will not enjoy traditional legal occupancy rights but will have to abide by a ten-point Bill of Guarantees over which the corporation. Leading the transition is an International Advisory Panel headed by the Prime Minister. Its 32 members are all from private business (except for one professor of business) and include Bill Gates, and the heads of Netscape, Sun Microsystems, Compaq Computer, British Telecom, Sony, NTT, Siemens and others comprising a Who's Who of corporate cyberspace.

## Alternatives?

It is hard to find in the technopoles of the world any genuine source of inspiration for fresh thinking about citizenship at the local level, for ways to return to its original of meaning of citizenship in the city or the community.

One such region is Emilia Romagna in north central Italy which includes and extends out from the city of Bologna. In spite of its enormous economic success, which regularly places it among the fastest growing regions of Europe, Emilia Romagna rarely appears in any of the technopole literature partly because high technology is not central to its development and most likely also because the region has been governed by the Communist Party of Italy, now the Democratic Party of the Left. 'The Third Italy,' as it is widely known, in contrast to the heavy manufacturing region of the north and the poor, agricultural land of the south, bases its economic success in thousands of small, mainly family businesses producing customized products for the export market. In 1996 it ranked tenth among 122 regions of the EC in per capita income and was the second highest ranked region in Italy. There are some 68,000 manufacturing firms in this region of 3.9 million and only a handful of firms employ more than 500 workers. Compare this to the state of New York with 16 million people and only 6,000 manufacturing firms. Moreover, the Third Italy supports a thriving co-operative sector with 60,000 workers in 1,800 so-called red co-ops. Emilia-Romagna is particularly interesting because it emerged out of a remarkable partnership between enterprising family firms and a series of supportive regional governments of the left. Those who consider Third Italy as a genuine alternative to the major mainstream models of economic development build on the work of Bagnasco (1977) who concluded that Emilia Romagna combined two key traits: commercial, artisanal, and financial skills based on a centuries-old set of entrepreneurial values and, equally important, strong networks of

access to telephone service comprises a welcome trend. This expansion amounts to a social, as well as a geographic, change. Today, telephony has become a prerequisite of domestic middle classes around the world; by the end of 1996, around one out of three households worldwide possessed a telephone.

Let us dispense right away, however, with any thought that inequalities of provision are disappearing. To begin with, networks within and between excolonies are still scarred by the experience of subjugation, as the Chairman of the US FCC admitted recently, when he plaintively inquired, "Why should a call from Lagos to Abidjan have to go through Europe?" There is, moreover, scant chance that the telephone is about to be reconstituted as a truly universal service. No less than 98% of rural properties in Brazil possessed no telephone line in 1995. In Tanzania and Ghana - indeed, in one-quarter of all countries, and especially where rural-urban disparities remain grave - less than 1% of households possessed telephones in 1995. More than 90 percent of households in high income countries had telephones, compared to 16 percent in the rest of the world. As far as the most recent generations of communications technology are concerned, the imbalances are even starker. An estimated 84 percent of mobile cellular subscribers, 91 percent of all facsimile machines, and 97 percent of Internet host computers, were located in developed countries in 1997. There is no doubt that favored social classes, regions, and neighborhoods have come to enjoy comparatively bountiful telephone access. Through the continued process of uneven economic development, just the same, less-fortunate territories and classes still languish.

2. The Shifting Character of Telecommunications Investment

At every relevant scale, from local loop to global grid, and across a range of competing and complementary networking technologies, capital investment in telecommunications has dramatically though, again, unevenly - accelerated. In already-developed regions, corporate mergers and acquisitions comprised by

far the most visible form of this investment; just during 1998 through August 12, for example, the top ten North American telecom deals evinced a stunning collective valuation of $256.5 billion. But spending on new plant and modernized network facilities is also substantial - and rising. AT&T's annual capital expenditures on network development alone comprise an estimated $8-9 billion, while during 1997, U.S. cable television companies invested over $6 billion in infrastructure improvements. So-called 'greenfield' telecom operators, meanwhile, such as Qwest, Level Three, Williams, and ICG, are spending additional billions on Internet-technology-based backbone networks.

The increasingly transnational form and scope of this capital investment merit particular attention. Submarine cable system development, for example, has long evinced a tendency to transnationalized system ownership - but by corresponding national telecommunications operators, or PTTs. Ownership structures of submarine cable systems have now, in contrast, been thrown open to private operators and investors. The Fiber-Optic Link Around the Globe (FLAG) system, for example, at a cost of more than a billion dollars, ties together U.S., Japanese and Middle Eastern interests in a 28,000 kilometer system with landing points in Europe, Egypt, India, Malaysia, China and Japan. As rival equipment vendors jockey for emerging mobile service markets, meanwhile - by one estimate, nearly 100 million digital cell phones were produced just in 1997 - system development take the form of a global battle for control of the technical standards that will govern the next generation of cellular service provision.

The world likewise stands on the threshold of an unprecedented boom in satellite system deployment - at least if the rockets needed to loft satellites heavenward will stop blowing up: satellite industry revenues are projected to increase from around $38 billion in 1997 to $171 billion in 2007. U.S. satellite manufacturers plan to build and launch 1,700 satellites (mostly low- and medium-orbit models) over the decade beginning in 1998, worth a staggering $121 billion. A handful of mainly U.S.-led consortia, headed by aerospace

Dan Schiller

Economic Conditions

manufacturers, hope to ring the planet with multisatellite systems: Lockheed Martin; GM's Hughes Electronics Corporation; and Teledesic, which partners Boeing with moguls Bill Gates and Craig McCaw. Another venture, Globalstar, links Loral, Qualcomm, and Airtouch with Alcatel, France Telecom, Daimler-Benz Aerospace, Italy's Alenia and other foreign companies.

The physical scale of these projects is awesome. Representatives of 146 countries in 1997 cleared the way for both of prospective satellite systems - those of Globalstar and Teledesic - by agreeing to allocate spectrum sufficient to give these two consortia control over more than twice the radio frequencies used by the US's 4,500 television and 12,129 radio stations combined. But the true measure of their significance is not physical but social: the cross-national networks exemplify and build upon a substantially altered political-economic foundation.

From the dawn of the space age in the late 1950s until around 1980, global satellite services (the underlying technology of which remained essentially a U.S. military fiefdom) were furnished by international consortia, of which by far the most significant was the U.S.-dominated Intelsat. National telecommunications ministries (PTTs) and other state agencies played the critical investment and policymaking role. During the 1980s, however, the political-economy of satellite provision was transformed. Privately-owned and -operated systems began to be authorized, at first only over the protests of various national authorities. Akin to other non-profit satellite consortia, Intelsat - with its unmatched 25 satellite fleet and billion dollar revenue - was slated for privatization in 1998. Coming into operation today, in consequence, are globe-encircling communication systems beholden in the first instance to transnational capital. The pattern holds not just for satellite provision but generally, and it spells a climactic shift away from the preceding era of national-grid carriers. The telecommunications industry is frenziedly chewing up erstwhile national networks, and spitting them out again as units of prospectively integrated, cross-border, corporately-owned systems.

... investment in telecommunications, and the uneven enlargement of telephone access that accompanies it, ... be best viewed as a function of a ... change in the pattern of global ... ownership and control. By ... of a massive and dramatic ... of private ownership principles, telecommunications systems and ... have been thrown open to capital in a newly direct and comprehensive way. Constituted thereby is a vast new domain, on which actual and prospective owners' accumulation strategies have already resulted in sharply enlarged consumer markets.

It cannot be overemphasized, however, that this shift toward private ownership and control over telecommunications required a form of political intervention that was as concerted and protracted as it was also general: throughout the 1980s and 1990s, literally dozens of national telecommunications operators around the world were privatized, and their domestic markets opened to foreign investment. Climaxing these initiatives, in February 1997, the World Trade Organization approved a pact that set the provision of telecommunications services on a new global basis. Transnationalizing telecommunications carriers obtained commitments allowing foreign investment at levels that often (not always) ran as high as 100% - in existing national service providers (PTTs). National telecommunications systems therefore were thrown open at one stroke not only to capital, but to transnational capital.

Public-service principles oriented toward long-range, state-mediated planning, and often accommodating a high-wage, unionized telecommunications workforce, have been the chief casualty of this policy reversal. In their stead has arisen a neoliberal, or market-driven, form of service provision and system development. To be sure, in many countries the old regime was inefficient and corrupt. On the other hand, the much-belated enlargement of access prompted by the infusion of transnational capital into the sector is indisputably welcome. However, we must still ask, who - beyond the global middle class - is positioned to reap the rewards of this emerging neoliberal order in telecommunications?

## 3. Transnationally Networked Production Chains

"[W]hen we consider how logical Marx's prediction of the eventual spread of the industrial revolution to the rest of the world seemed, it is astonishing how little industry had left the world of developed capitalism before the ... 1970s," writes the historian Eric Hobsbawm. No longer. Just as a growing share of the world's telephones moved out of Europe and the United States so, too, during the 1980s and 1990s, did a significant proportion of manufacturing industry shift - albeit selectively - to the poor world.

By almost any measure, the transnationalization of capital has rapidly accelerated during the past quarter-century. World foreign direct investment (FDI), characteristically, rose from $68 billion in 1960 to $2.1 trillion in 1993. Although high-income economies continue to host three-quarters of U.S. FDI, a band of poorer countries has drawn appreciable inflows of capital: Brazil had built up to $36 billion in U.S. FDI by 1997 (on a historical-cost basis), Mexico to $25 billion, China and Hongkong together to $24 billion, Singapore to $17.5 billion, and Taiwan, Malaysia, Korea, Indonesia, Argentina, Chile, and Venezuela each to at least $5 billion. Almost 20% of GM's North American manufacturing workforce is now based in Mexico, where the auto giant's parts-making unit, Delphi Automotive Systems (now being spun off) employs 72,000 people in 53 plants. With other auto manufacturers also increasingly active there, Mexico has duly become the third largest exporter of cars to the United States, behind Canada and Japan. Tijuana, Mexico also has been transformed into the world's preeminent site of television set manufacturing, as Mitsubishi, Sony, Sanyo, Sharp and other companies relocate plants there. Similarly, if the ongoing world economic crisis does not force curtailment of current plans by some 13 vehicle makers, Brazil stands to host $20 billion in new factory investment in this sector by 2002. Even the global financial crisis has not - yet - curtailed, but only barely slowed, FDI to Asia.

This enlarged transnational corporate economy rests on vital organizational innovations. "A noteworthy feature of the evolving TNC universe," Herman and McChesney underscore, has been the shift from relatively isolated 'stand alone' subsidiaries, that buy and sell inputs and outputs as virtually independent companies, to those that are more integrated with other TNC operations, with greater intrasystem specialization by plant within and between countries. ... In short, globalization has gone far and is proceeding apace: increasing numbers of firms - financial and nonfinancial - plan investment and operations on a regional or global basis and run operations that are integrated across borders; these are supplemented by a dense set of cross-border relationships via alliances and outsourcing arrangements.

The modernization and reconfiguration of telecommunications networks are intended to expedite and sustain this wider reconfiguration of business operations. The pronounced corporate tendency "to internalize operations within the firm's command-and-control structure" is indeed directly dependent on improved access to modern telecommunications facilities - which ease "the coordination of foreign operations." The economist Robert A. Brady presciently observed nearly forty years ago how this emergent change in industrial organization was already triggering an urgent need for telecommunications system development and modernization: The source of the change in industrial demand arises in part from the continuous interlinkage of spatially removed but successive-step or confluent (e.g., assembly) processes which are being placed on a continuous, automatically self-correcting flow basis. With the direct interlinkage of the production schedules of individual plants, together with the cumulative realignment of transport and energy-supply systems along similar lines. ... The interplant communications circuits required to maintain and coordinate these flows then come to be viewed in much the same terms as those of intraplant operations which converge on a single central control-panel.

Transnational corporations from every sector, in turn, are actively reconstructing their constitutive business operations around networks. This process is general, economy-wide. By 1986, more than one-third of all U.S. spending on capital facilities for telecommunications occurred outside the sphere of common carrier investment, and the resulting inhouse corporate networks - of which there were thousands - were growing by 30-40% a year. Despite a successful campaign to persuade the global middle class to add computers and networked services to its shopping list, information technology spending as a whole continued to be dominated by corporations, which collectively accounted for nearly nine-tenths of the domestic U.S. sales total in 1997.

It should hardly be surprising that, in our epoch of unbridled global speculation and financial profiteering, banks have spearheaded the networking drive. Between 1972 and 1983, the 1000 largest U.S. banks increased the proportion of their operating expenses dedicated to telecommunications from 5 to 13 percent, and finance became the sectoral leader of overall corporate information technology spending. ... Alongside this build-up of networks by transnational financial intermediaries, there occurred exponential increases in securities market, foreign exchange and other speculative instruments' trading volumes, the consequence of which (as we are now well aware) was that capital flows acquired the ability to overwhelm the national monetary policy objectives of even the largest economies.

It should be noted that the deployment of Internet technology, both within and among corporate networks, comprised a noteworthy but incremental step in this longer-term reorganization around networks. Use of the Internet holds the potential to rationalize the proliferating web of often overlapping links that currently bind together various production complexes. Thus, to take a particularly ambitious - though largely untested - example, the so-called "Automotive Network Exchange" led by Ford, General Motors, and (now) Daimler Chrysler, "aims to link the entire North American auto-supply chain - as many as 30,000 companies, by some estimates - into a secure, high-performance online commerce network that will cut car production costs ..."

The reconstruction of business processes around networks carries no assurances of any continued adherence to principles of national integration - which, historically, defined and circumscribed system development within the wealthy countries. In North America, for example, the current surge of telecommunications system building seems to be blazing a path like that which is being followed by the railroad industry.

Let us recall that each of the three members of NAFTA established its own rail network in the 19th century; Canada and the United States even might be said to have built their nations around these East-West links. Today, in contrast, these domestic railway infrastructures are being melded, through mergers, to create three-nation networks with a strong north-south orientation.

North American telecommunications are likewise shifting to emphasize a north-south axis. Of the $16 billion in direct capital investment in Mexico during 1997, about $5 billion - nearly a third - was to be channeled into telecommunications. Mexican telecommunications offered not just another new market for MCI and AT&T, in turn, but also the missing link needed to complete their proprietary networks in Canada and the U.S. With Mexico, both companies will have uniform networks that span all North America - the world's most lucrative call corridor. Some 1,000 multinational corporations in Mexico could use North American network services."

Current telecommunications system building, however, erodes traditional forms of sovereignty not only by arching above merely national system planning efforts, but also by chipping out more modest operational dominions. An influential group of business and political leaders, for example, has begun to lobby to establish a "border-free telecommunications zone" across the San Diego-Tijuana region - with common systems and regulations extending thirty miles in each direction from the international boundary separating the Mexican province of Baja from Southern California. Tijuana, declares one proponent, resurrecting the language of early modern European economic development, "clearly falls under the orbit of a

San Diego city-state ..." Adherents have no doubt that, because both Mexico and the United States are "pursuing aggressive programs of deregulation in the field, an unregulated, but carefully monitored, free market experiment might serve as a model not only for the United States and Mexico, but for the world."

Crucially, however, the goal of transborder networking remains what it has always been: "to connect computing systems, and through the systems the [employees], so that ... duplication of effort [can be] avoided through the sharing of resources and improved communication," and so that new kinds of direct and indirect collaborative labor can be mobilized. Indeed it is not going too far to say that networked production chains are most fundamentally aimed at the extension and enlargement of collaborative work activities within the transnational corporate sector and its farflung affiliates. The reorganization of capital thus subtends a corresponding reorganization of labor.

## 4. Beyond Borders: Labor And Digital Capitalism

A variegated world market for labor power, as Lydia Potts writes, stretches back centuries, to the early years of capitalism. Throughout this long interval, capital's incessant cycles of self-reorganization have recurrently set labor, too, in motion. In the epoch of New World slavery, tens of millions of Africans underwent the horrors of the Middle Passage to create wealth for their newfound owners on plantations and farms. In the subsequent period of intensifying Euro-American industrialization, between the 1850s and World War One, large-scale transfers of labor power occured within South and East Asia, Africa, and Europe, and tens of millions of immigrants relocated to the United States. Although wage labor was increasing as a proportion of the global labor supply, much labor power remained unfree, even as forms of chattel slavery gave way to emerging colonial forced-labor systems.

The cultural changes that attend today's great labor transfers are palpable.

Hispanic people in the United States annually make $2 billion worth of international phone calls - comprising 5 percent of the $40 billion U.S. residential long-distance market - to family members and friends in their countries of origin. Between 1996 and 1997, largely as a result, AT&T's discount phone cards tripled in popularity. The infrastructure that has emerged to support a vast mobile labor force, however, goes far beyond phone cards and ethnic restaurants. Not only the proliferating acquiescence to dual citizenship as a permanent legal status, and the growth of cross-border money transfer services, but also the establishment of discount phone parlors, videophone and email services, and radio and television channels targeted at expatriate populations all bear witness to the existence of enduring 'bi-national' identities. In 1997, marketers spent $1.4 billion in Spanish-language advertising in the U.S., more than half of which went to television. Increased Spanish-language TV programming has, in turn, been forthcoming. Backed by Sony and Liberty Media, for example, TV broadcaster Telemundo will try to compete with Univision - which garners four-fifths of viewers watching Hispanic TV by importing telenovelas from Mexico's Televisa and other Latin American sources - by developing original Spanish-language programming targeted at the 30 million Hispanics in the U.S. market. Small wonder that the academic study of 'multiculturalism' has become a cottage industry. I want to emphasize, however, a different qualitative aspect of today's mobile workforce.

Trafficking in superexploited labor continues to be a thriving global business. The transnational sex industry comprises perhaps its most sensational locus; between 350,000 and 1.2 million prostitutes contribute as much as 14% of the domestic economic output of four countries - Indonesia, Malaysia, the Philippines and Thailand. More prosaic is a multibillion-dollar syndicate, operating out of China, which forwards hundreds of thousands of undocumented and unfree workers each year to (among other places) Japan, Europe and the United States. However, these streams of superexploited labor - unlike during prior epochs - are basically ancillary to the market for free waged labor. The waged labor market, in turn, has grown overwhelmingly dominant globally.

Both the number of wage laborers, whether in or out of employment, and the primacy of wage employment over other labor systems, have increased dramatically in recent years. Above all, through the collapse of Soviet socialism, and through China's embrace of capitalism, hundreds of millions of prospective wage workers have been summarily thrown onto the world labor market over the last generation, the "vast labor pool that global capitalism has tapped into," foresaw Business Week chief economist William Wolman and Anne Colamosca, "is the new leviathan." Indeed, the worldwide generalization of the system of waged labor comprises a vital, distinguishing feature of the emerging social formation - the epoch of digital capitalism. It is this crucial fact - that digital waged labor comprises the overwhelmingly dominant global labor system in use today - that makes it possible for some academics to construe contemporary immigration through the lenses of postmodern diasporic sensibility, together with the fact (of which more in a moment) that a goodly share of migrants to the globe's privileged regions hail from comparatively well-educated and favored social strata.

Within this massively altered context, I will conclude by mentioning some of the typifying features of digital capitalism's deployment of waged labor. A word of caution: as Bennett Harrison reminds us, there exists no well-defined template on which the overall employment system is to be patterned. Disparities between regions and varying social strata show no sign of disappearing, or even of diminishing - though they may well change their form. No single wage level or characteristic labor process is, accordingly, likely to be generalized throughout the world political-economy. That said, there are apparent some arresting, and perhaps portentous, trends.

The labor mobilized directly by foreign-owned U.S. TNC affiliates increased from 2 million employees in 1980 to almost 5 million in 1995. (Because U.S. TNCs command only a minority of global FDI, however, the total number of

TNC employees is certainly much larger.) Millions of other workers within the TNC complex lie outside the range of such statistics, however, because the trend among TNCs is increasingly to rely on low-wage labor and non-union outsource component-suppliers, and even to offload assembly operations onto lower-cost contractors, so as to emphasize design and marketing functions.

An army of laborers is now employed in these export plants. All told, Mexican border factories were staffed by nearly one million workers in 1998 - up 115,000 over the previous year. And small wonder. From management's perspective, maquilas are doubly desirable: preferential access to the U.S. market is one side of the coin; 'competitive' tax laws, cheap labor, and weak environmental and occupational health and safety regulations, the other. In the wake of the 1994-95 financial crisis, Mexican wages plummeted by more than 20%, to an average of $6 per day (the minimum wage is $3.30), with maquiladora employment up 60% in the three years between NAFTA's passage and April 1997.

It is a platitude among economists that low-skill work is now routinely subject to relocation. This mobility of manufacturing work expresses a corporate shift away from the 'hand-me-down' factories' dotted across the poor world and toward reliance on state-of-the-art production facilities. Of the fourteen 'megafabs' (semiconductor fabrication plants costing at least $1.5 billion each) in development in 1997 - before the roiling effects of the global financial crisis began to be felt - four were scheduled to be located in poor countries (China, Korea and Taiwan), while the Celtic fringe - Ireland, Scotland, and Wales - were slated to play host to three others. Like Chrysler, Volkswagen, and Ford, GM - the world's largest manufacturer - hopes to model future auto assembly plants to be constructed in the United States, on its lower-cost 'modular' Brazilian factory operation.

Now, however, is it any longer solely manufacturing labor that is mobile. Increasingly, "any value-added activity can be located, at least in principle, in any part of a TNC system ..."

Networked business processes increase management's ability by turns to disperse both the object and the subject of labor - both jobs and workers - so as to maximize corporate profits within what has become a global market for waged labor.

Morton Bahr, President of the Communications Workers of America, states that it has become "very easy to move (telecommunications) billing and accounting across the border" - for example, to the West Indies. Offshore corporate back-offices produce an increasing range of needed services, including database management, accounting, ticketing, subscription processing, insurance claims, and software development, which are used as inputs in 'domestic' U.S. production and are intended to service domestic demand. Animation factories in South Korea, Taiwan and the Philippines pump out episodes of *The Simpsons*, *Ninja Turtles*, and other television shows.

Skilled professional and technical service work is likewise increasingly subject to relocation. On one hand, it is not widely known that nearly one quarter (23%) of those who work in Silicon Valley are immigrants; indeed, the U.S. National Science Foundation claims that the same proportion (23%) of U.S. residents holding Ph.D.s in science and engineering are foreign-born. On the other hand, in an attempt to speed products to market, pharmaceutical and computer companies have built up and linked cross-national research and development facilities. IBM, Microsoft (ten percent of whose worldwide workforce of 22,300 is of Indian origin) and Cisco Systems - which supplies the network equipment which routes most Internet traffic - each have set up software research and development laboratories in India, to tap into the comparatively low-wage technical talent available there. Tata Sons Ltd. of India employs 5,000 software developers, acting as "a maquiladora of the mind" that can pay local talent around one-third of the $50,000 annual salary that comprises the current floor for such labor in the United States. Such corporations' newfound success in pushing R&D centers offshore, reciprocally, is cited by executives lobbying to increase the number of

U.S. work visas for non-national computer scientists and engineers. If their demands for visas go unmet, their companies can always send additional R&D jobs overseas. Is this, they ask, what Congress prefers? Although the outcome remains uncertain, legislation authorizing a 77 percent increase (to 115,000) in the number of skilled workers who can be admitted annually to the United States to fill jobs at high-tech companies looked likely to pass. The number of workers assigned by U.S.-based companies to expatriate duties overseas, on the other hand, is around 350,000, with further growth expected. These trends suggest that the mobility of labor power today is no longer confined to less-skilled jobs and workers. Increasingly affected are also the more privileged middle strata, comprised of professional, technical, and managerial employees.

And, on the other hand, these same strata are also becoming objects of casualized labor policies, even within the heartlands of digital capitalism. Two-tier workforce strategies have been a deliberate employment strategy, for example, among U.S. high-tech firms. Of some 19,000 workers at the Microsoft 'campus' at Redmond, Washington, 5,000 are classified as 'contingent' or 'temporary' workers - and are technically employed by high-tech employment agencies. Some of these contract workers have filed a lawsuit against Microsoft, charging that they are in effect regular employees, entitled to the lucrative benefits enjoyed by their permanent counterparts. Manpower - the leading legal transnational supplier of casualized labor services - has come to comprise the largest private employer in the United States. Professional, managerial and technical workers, notably, today account for 25 percent of all temporary workers - of whom there were 2.6 million in the U.S. in early 1998.

It is too early to forecast how labor-capital conflict may come to be expressed, and the social formation accordingly reworked, as the ongoing transition toward transnationally networked production deepens. But the rightwing politics of anti-immigration, which has arisen - especially alongside protracted high unemployment - from France to

Thailand to the United States, may be countered only by repeating what already should be a long-familiar lesson, that workers rights and democratic freedoms are axiomatic necessities, across any and all political borders, and irrespective of occupation, ethnicity, race, gender, or immigration status.

*excerpts from the essay "Transnational Telecommunications and the Global Reorganization of Production." Portions of the text are also used in the book *Digital Capitalism: Networking the Global Market System*, published by MIT Press in 1999.

Contribution in the
newspaper DER STANDARD,
Signs of Trouble -
International Positions
in Information Design
of the 1990s:
Michael Rock & Susan
Sellers 2x4, 10/9/1998
(Cooperation with the
museum in progress and
basis Wien, curated by
Walter Pamminger and
Christian Muhr)

Daily, this newspaper
sells its readers to
its advertising
clients. The price of
this readership depends
on gender, age, educa-
tion, class, buying
power, private income
and the difficult to
measure criteria, brand
loyalty.
The market place for
this transaction is the
116,416 mm square page
of the newspaper. This
makes it one of the
most expensive pieces
of property on the
international real
estate market.

Together with the
approximately 377,000
other readers of the
paper, this makes its
value something in the
order of 39,647,576.80
Austrian Shillings per
year.

Contribution in the
newspaper DER STANDARD,
Signs of Trouble -
International Positions
in Information Design
of the 1990s:
Jonathan Barnbrook,
5/14/1999
(Cooperation with the
museum in progress and
basis Wien, curated by
Walter Pamminger and
Christian Muhr)

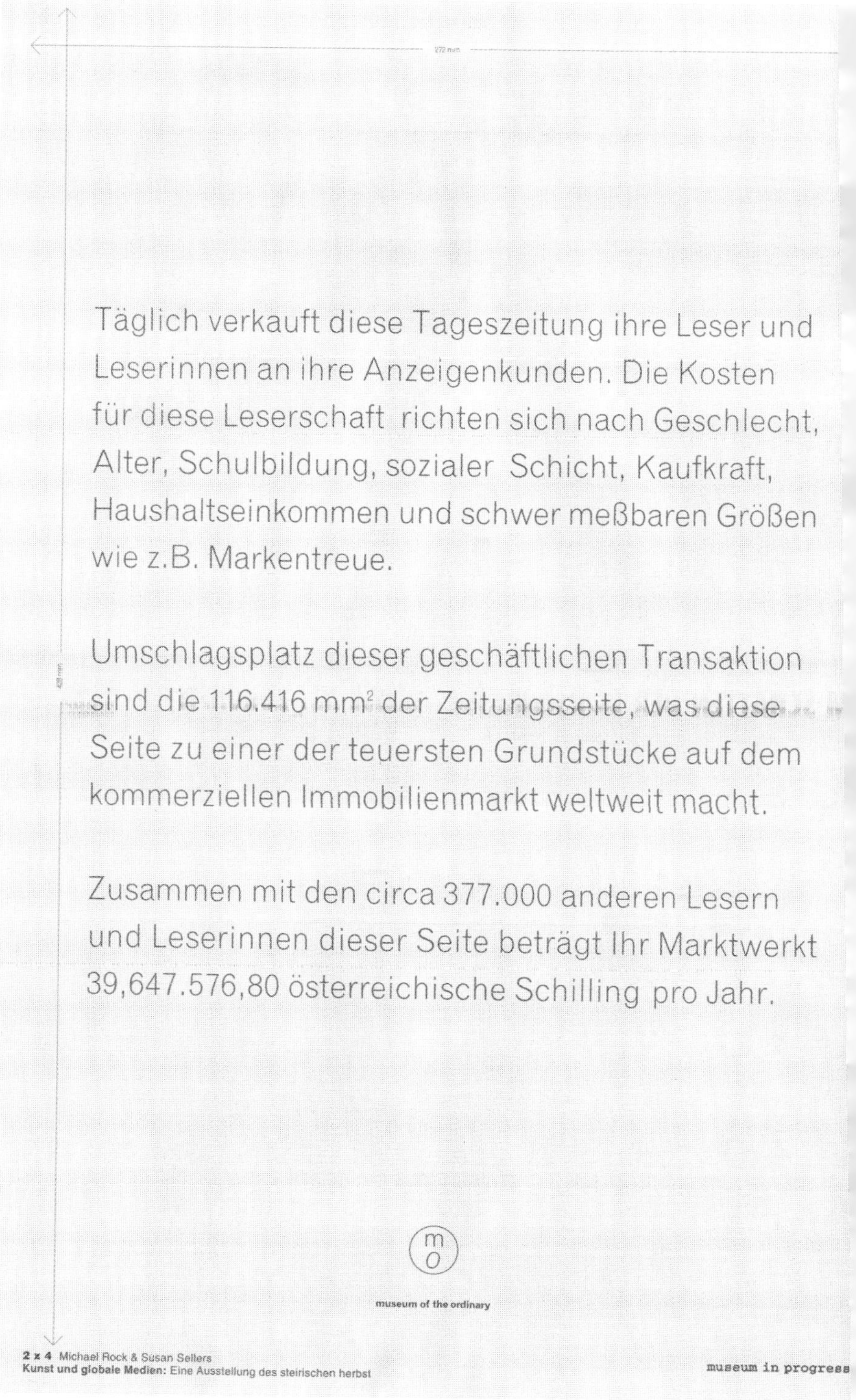

Täglich verkauft diese Tageszeitung ihre Leser und
Leserinnen an ihre Anzeigenkunden. Die Kosten
für diese Leserschaft richten sich nach Geschlecht,
Alter, Schulbildung, sozialer Schicht, Kaufkraft,
Haushaltseinkommen und schwer meßbaren Größen
wie z.B. Markentreue.

Umschlagsplatz dieser geschäftlichen Transaktion
sind die 116.416 mm² der Zeitungsseite, was diese
Seite zu einer der teuersten Grundstücke auf dem
kommerziellen Immobilienmarkt weltweit macht.

Zusammen mit den circa 377.000 anderen Lesern
und Leserinnen dieser Seite beträgt Ihr Marktwerkt
39,647.576,80 österreichische Schilling pro Jahr.

m
o

museum of the ordinary

2 x 4 Michael Rock & Susan Sellers
Kunst und globale Medien: Eine Ausstellung des steirischen herbst

museum in progress

PRE-STRIKE   POST-STRIKE

AREA 1

COUNTRIES THAT ARE NO MILITARY THREAT

WE WILL DESTROY THEM WITH OUR

CONSUMER CULTURE

INSTEAD

Jonathan Barnbrook
**Kunst und globale Medien:** Eine Ausstellung des steirischen herbst

http://lowtech.org

Economic Conditions

Redundant Techn

Redundant Technology Initiative is a group of artists working with low cost or no-cost technology. RTI started in 1997 with a marketing campaign designed to induce high-tech businesses and organisations to donate their redundant computer equipment to the project.

The proposition was simple - rather than getting into a never-ending cycle of fundraising to finance computer upgrades, the project would, as a matter of policy, work with technology that cost nothing. This came out of an ecological awareness - huge numbers of functional computers, no more than three or four years old, were being scrapped by British businesses. It also neatly sidestepped the corporate, consumerist context of much digital art - which had become, in effect, sales demonstrations for the latest technology.

What RTI have found is that **trash technology upgrades for free!** Last year the project was working with 286's and 386's. Now **powerful 486 and Pentium machines are being discarded by businesses hungry for ever more processing power.**

RTI continues to exhibit trash technology art in venues around the UK and now in Europe, and campaigns to **advocate low cost access to information technology.**

**RTI is still hungry for obsolete machines ...**

ology Initiative

Edward S. Herman

# The Global Erosion of the Public Sphere

By 'public sphere' I mean the places and forums in which issues important to citizenship in a democratic community are discussed and debated. In the media, this would refer to in-depth news and analyses of the news, debates and documentaries on public issues, and biographies, histories and talks that provide insight into matters important to citizen understanding. Advertisers, and hence commercial media managers, tend to avoid the public sphere because audiences there are smaller than for entertainment programs and the subject matter is too serious and controversial for compatibility with sales messages. Unfortunately, a primary global process now at work is the privatization and commercialization of the media and the displacement of public service broadcasting with commercial media, with a concurrent shift of funding from license fees and government subsidies to advertising revenue. Along with commercialization we are also witnessing a process of media concentration and vertical integration, as the media companies merge and expand to secure adequate content, distribution facilities, and the means of cross-selling content. These processes reflect the triumph of the market and market values in the New World Order, in which public service democratic values are given little weight and where the rights of capital are primary. Under this regime, noncommercial media space is being taken over by those who will put it to the 'best economic use.'

## Advertiser hegemony versus the public sphere

The 'best economic use' of media space in a market system is to service advertising, and the relationship between media and advertisers has been long-standing and close and it keeps getting closer, as I will describe later. As capitalism has consolidated its position in the West and in the Third World, and spread into China and the former Soviet bloc, advertising has grown rapidly and extended globally. Global advertising increased tenfold between 1973 and 1995 (from $33 to $335 billion), growing rapidly in the United States, but even more so elsewhere - recently, at its fastest pace in Asia, Latin America and Eastern Europe, although retreating at least temporarily in the

global recession beginning in 1997. Public broadcasting systems and other noncommercial media, without advertiser support, must depend on money provided by subscribers and listeners, donors, or the government. In a world of government budget deficits and financial pressures on ordinary citizens, noncommercial media and communications are under chronic financial stress, and tend to be noncompetitive with sources able to tap the immense resources of business advertisers. And governments, under budgetary pressure, and increasingly receptive to neoliberal arguments, are more and more inclined to allow public media to be transformed into market-funded entities. The commercial media are eager to occupy that space, and conservatives want them to have it because of the structured political bias and other effects of commercialization on the 'public sphere.'

This conflict between commercialization and public service was stressed half a century ago by the U.S. Federal Communications Commission (FCC) in its 1946 report entitled *The Public Service Responsibilities of Broadcast Licensees*, where the Commission acknowledged that advertising and public service programming are incompatible. It contended, however, that these "irreplaceable" public service programs, and overall program balance, would be maintained by broadcasters' "sustaining programs," funded by the broadcasters themselves. The FCC indicated that the maintenance of such balance would be assured by the Commission's licensing policies, which would give substantial weight to this consideration.

The FCC's claim that advertising based programming and public service are incompatible implies that the market 'fails' in serving the 'public sphere,' and that the FCC was obliged to correct this failure by moral persuasion and regulation. The economic theory of externalities throws light on this market failure, and on the threat of commercialization to the public sphere. An externality is a benefit or cost of a market process that does not accrue to the source but affects others, as in the case of water pollution that kills downstream fish and makes the water unusable for swimming. Arguably, public sphere programming represents a case where positive externalities are produced, which contribute to the public's understanding and ability to participate in a democratic order. But that benefit accrues to society at large and cannot be captured by a TV station or network, which therefore does not take this social gain into account in its programming strategies. On the other hand, programs that feature sex and violence draw large audiences and sell well in export markets, but arguably involve negative externalities, making people more fearful, insecure and violence prone. Again, the negative externality damages others, and the society at large, not the program source. Noncommercial media are less eager for the large audiences that sex and violence bring, and are often brought into existence and designed to program for public service. But in a mature market system their funding base tends to shrink, they are forced into competing for advertising and large audiences, and their public service role shrinks.

## The U.S. Experience

This process is well illustrated by the 75 year experience of broadcasting in the United States. When broadcasting began in the United States in the 1920s, its proponents placed almost exclusive stress on its public service potential - as an educational tool and means of political, religious, and cultural enlightenment. Advertising was seen as a threat, or at best a necessary evil, to be kept under rigorous control. Secretary of Commerce (later President) Herbert Hoover stated in 1922 that "It is inconceivable that we should allow so great a possibility for service to be drowned in advertising chatter." As late as 1929, the president of NBC was claiming that his was a public service corporation that would only sell advertising to the extent needed to fund the best noncommercial programming!

But by a quiet coup, carried out between 1927 and 1933, the commercial stations and networks, with the help of the regulatory authorities, displaced the many early educational and religious stations and took control of broadcasting. This control, and the full-blown commercial regime that ensued, was ratified in the Communications Act of 1934. In 1934 the broadcasters did pledge to provide ample public service

programming, and as noted the FCC in 1946 promised that broadcasters would meet public service responsibilities through 'sustaining programs,' as a condition of license renewal.

## The long-term trend - attrition of public service.

But as advertising flooded in to the commercial stations and networks, 'sustaining programs' became more expensive, as they entailed not just production expenses but foregone advertising income. And as the FCC had suggested in 1946, advertisers preferred light entertainment to public service programs, which shrank steadily in importance even as broadcaster profits soared. By 1970, public affairs programming had fallen to two % of programming time, and the entire spectrum of public service offerings was far below that provided by public broadcasting systems in Canada, Great Britain, and on the European continent. Profits of station owners, however, were in the range of 30-50% of revenues, and much higher on invested capital. However, these staggering profits did not reduce pressure for still higher profits, as the workings of the market cause profits to be capitalized into higher stock values, which become the basis for calculating rates of return for both old and new owners.

Program diversity also fell steadily as the commercial broadcasting system matured and stations and networks emulated one another in their quest for formulas that would produce large audiences and high ratings. Under advertiser pressure, and the force of competition, not only did entertainment displace public sphere programs, even entertainment programs tended to lighten up, avoiding undue seriousness, depth of thought, and backgrounds devoid of lavish and upscale decor. The shrinking numbers of documentaries tended to deal with non-political and non-controversial matters like dogs, restaurants, flower shows, exotic travel sites, personalities, and the lives of the rich. Politics was marginalized and trivialized, with news itself transformed into a form of entertainment ('infotainment'). The hegemony of advertising and entertainment values in the mature U.S. system was captured at the time of

Disney's 1996 acquisition of the giant network and media conglomerate ABC-TV, when Disney head Michael Eisner described Disney as a "family entertainment communication company" in the business of providing "non-political entertainment and sports."

One of the most notable trends in U.S. commercial broadcasting has been the attrition and corruption of children's programming. As profits soared in the 1960s, children's programs were removed from weekday slots and shifted to weekend mornings, and were confined increasingly to cartoons funded by advertisers of snacks and toys. Between 1955 and 1970, weekday programming for children on network-affiliated stations in New York City fell from 33 to five hours. The situation was so bad that an organization, Action for Children's Television (ACT), was organized in 1968, and sought remedies from stations, the FCC and politicians for many years. Despite these efforts the situation reached a new low in the 1980s with the Reagan administration's further deregulation of TV, which sanctioned what are called 'program length commercials' prepared by toy manufacturers and of course centering on the toys to be sold. The toy manufacturers virtually took over children's programming during the 1980s. The service to children improved somewhat with the rise of cable and the 1993 change in political administration, but not a great deal, and the downward trend of quality and central role of advertising in shaping children's programs remains clear.

## The small public broadcasting niche.

Public broadcasting was introduced with public funding in 1967, in large measure because the commercial broadcasters wanted to rid themselves of any public service responsibilities and were pleased to allow its shift to stations and networks paid for by the taxpayer. An interesting feature of public broadcasting has been its greater degree of political independence and courage in allowing dissent, despite its heavy reliance on government support. During the Vietnam War, for example, despite the growing opposition to the war at home and throughout much of the world in 1965 through 1967, network television

toed the official line and allowed minimal dissent to surface, and much sponsored entertainment was jingoistic. The U.S. networks not only made none of the seriously critical documentaries on the War, during the early War years, they barred access to outside documentaries. As the leading historian of U.S. TV, Erik Barnouw, has pointed out, "This policy constituted de facto national censorship, though privately operated."

But while the mass protest against the Vietnam War rarely found outlets on commercial TV, it did find occasional expression in public broadcasting. Apparently, the constraints built-in to the commercial operations by ownership and advertiser interest makes them less bold and more subservient to establishment political desires than an institution literally on the government payroll but granted some degree of autonomy. Because of this independence, conservatives dislike public broadcasting (as well as community broadcasting), and regularly urge that it be defunded and pushed into the commercial nexus. This relative autonomy also helps explain why Presidents Johnson and Nixon fought to rein in public broadcasting, with Nixon quite openly seeking to force it to de-emphasize public affairs. And as the power of market interests grow, it is by no means impossible that conservatives and politicians who feel threatened by a genuine public sphere will eventually succeed in getting public stations and networks privatized and thus put to their 'best economic use.'

## Competition and the growing hegemony of advertising.

In benign analyses of the evolution of the media it is assumed that competition and a maturing 'professionalism' will improve the quality of the public sphere. There has been a great increase in cable channels, and many new print magazines have come into existence, but they have added very little to diversity. With minor exceptions, the new cable channels and stations, struggling for ad revenue and larger audiences, offer the same entertainment fare as the larger broadcasters; they innovate with more extravaganzas and pornography, not public sphere programming. And as they have pulled audiences away from the majors, the latter have further degraded their own product in spurts of cost-cutting and panicky search for new formulas within established entertainment genres. In their quest for ad revenues, also, both cable and broadcasters have toadied almost without limit to advertisers, selling them product placement within programs, allowing them to produce entire programs infused with commercials, and engaging in numerous co-producing and joint-advertising deals with advertisers. The competition for 'content,' like movies, and rights to show sports events, has pushed up costs and made the cable and TV broadcasters still more cost conscious, subservient to advertisers, and unwilling to take risks. This has all reduced the likelihood of their offering critical and controversial public service programming.

The competition for ad revenues has also had a steady damaging effect on the print media. More subject to financial pressures and market driven than in the past, U.S. newspapers and magazines increasingly gear content to the aim of attracting and keeping advertisers. Magazines in the U.S. now frequently come into existence with demographic-content-advertising plans made in cooperation with prospective advertisers. Newspapers as well as magazines now have regular sections on *Style*, *Home and Garden*, *Men's Clothing*, and *Computers* with 'news' there that will attract readers and advertisers. Even highly regarded papers like *The New York Times* have gone far in this direction, and the link between decisions on ads and news-editorial content was displayed when the paper solicited advertisers to buy space in an 'advertorial' (ad with news and policy content) lauding the North American Free Trade Agreement (which the paper's news columns and editorials also supported).

## Mergers, conglomeration and the public sphere.

As I have pointed out, commercialization has gone hand in hand with concentration and conglomeration, which has diminished the number of decision-makers in the media and greatly enhanced their political as well as cultural power. Conglomeration refers to the fusing within a single corporate

system many different businesses and businesses at different stages of the economic process (vertical integration). This is characteristic of the global giants like Murdoch's News Corp, Disney, and Time-Warner, who all sell movies, books, magazines, newspapers, TV programs, music, videos, toys, and theme parks, among other things. They also provide news and other public sphere programming, but this is marginal to their entertainment provision, and is offered as necessary for 'balanced' programming. The dominant interest of the leaders of these pop cultural behemoths is in entertainment, which is the basis of the cross-selling 'synergies' that justify conglomeration and is the focal point of their attention and resources.

The public sphere has done poorly under the regimes of the conglomerates. They represent the end product of commercialization, where not only is the public sphere relegated to a small corner, but both the synergies and political biases and interests of the firms further erode the public sphere. Synergies mean that books will be preferred and published that can feed into movie and TV making and provide the basis for selling music, videos, toys and theme park promotions - these books will be published, advertised heavily, reviewed in the conglomerate's magazines and papers, and sell heavily, as they advance into movies. Other, possibly better and more controversial books will have diminished possibilities of publication and success. Books that celebrate celebrities and media moguls (e.g. Katherine Graham), or political figures important to media moguls (a hagiography of Chinese dictator Deng was published by a Murdoch book affiliate as Murdoch sought entry into the Chinese market) are published. Books, movies and TV shows that entertain without disturbing status quo interests will be pushed; those that challenge status quo interests are increasingly marginalized.

## Commercialization, consumerism and depoliticization.

The United States has a highly commercialized media, a strongly consumerist ethic, and a depoliticized population. Shopping is a major household occupation as a leisure time activity, and the focus on goods and buying goods, and

Edward S. Herman

the weight given acquisition and consumption in value systems is high. The contradiction between the uniquely high attachment to religion and an earthy materialism is striking. The lack of knowledge of politics and about the substantive facts and issues of politics, and the weakness of political participation, are also relatively unique in the developed world.

Is there cause and effect between a commercialized media and the consumerist preoccupations and depoliticization? It is possible that the media are commercial because the populace is, and that the disinterest in politics results from the same overriding interest in acquisition and consumption. But whatever the initial tendencies of the people, the media's encouragement of consumerism and shriveling of the public sphere has surely given any such tendencies a further push. It is also noteworthy that the commercial media's policies have been beautifully attuned to what advertisers and the sellers of goods want. They have strengthened consumerist values, kept the peoples' minds focused on buying, and helped divert them from a political interest and activism that would not be likely to help advertisers and sellers. One further consideration is this: democracy rests on an informed people, and broadcasters were given free use of public air space with the explicit commitment to offer public service programs that the FCC stated to be 'indispensable' and that broadcasters once conceded to be their high responsibility and even raison d'etre. That they have abandoned this responsibility, very quietly, because it is more profitable to entertain than provide public service, suggests that this abandonment of a service to a democratic community flows naturally from the interests benefiting from consumerism and the erosion of the public sphere.

An important feature of the history of U.S. broadcasting has been its increasing insulation from reform, paralleling the growth and centralization of broadcaster power. As it matured and the 'irreplaceable' public service programs disappeared, the FCC did nothing about it, and politicians remained silent as well - the commercial media were able to prevent the erosion of the public sphere from becoming a public issue,

and politicians were too dependent on and fearful of the broadcasters to challenge them.

## Globalization of the U.S. model

The U.S. model is being extended globally, partly because of U.S. power, leadership, and plan, but more basically because it represents the advanced, if not full, product of the extension of market principles and processes to the media and communication industries. The plan element encompasses the attempt by the U.S. government, and sometimes its allies, to encourage private enterprise, open economies, and market-based media systems throughout the world, to pry open markets, and to destabilize and overthrow non-market-friendly governments.

U.S. goals and strategies were implemented by means of U.S. economic and military aid, military and police training programs, economic and political pressure, support given to indigenous forces serving U.S. aims, and sometimes more direct interventions, as in Guatemala in 1954, Nicaragua in the 1980s and Cuba still in process today. There is a clear official record of intentionality in the pursuit of these goals, which cannot be dismissed as a product of 'conspiracy theory.'

With the long dominant position of the United States in the motion picture business, and its great competitive strength in all segments of the communications industries, U.S. politicians have been pushing for the opening up and privatization of the communications sector for decades. The great weight of the United States in the International Monetary Fund (IMF) and World Bank has been reflected in those institutions' policies serving the same ends.

The mainly U.S.-based global firms that now cross many borders, providing films, TV shows, and 'news' to media firms everywhere, are all intensely commercial, seeking to attract audiences and advertisers by offering attractive entertainment. They tend increasingly to be organized around film studios, and their movies feed into other parts of their conglomerate operations, generating 'synergistic' revenues from videos, sound tracks, books, toys, and theme park rides. For these entertainment companies, news is a very small segment of their operations, and tends to be a necessary but superficial adjunct to doing media business. Other features of the public sphere have been virtually eliminated.

But they attract large audiences with their sophistication and special effects, and their economies of scale from dealing with both a large U.S. and global market allow them to replace more expensive local productions and set a cultural standard, as the U.S.-advertiser sponsored soap opera did many years ago. And with the accompanying global advertising and subtle value intrusions, they help in the global advance of consumerism and neoliberal ideology.

Commercialization across the globe has its own internal momentum, operative within the United States itself (and still working there today) and extending globally at an accelerating pace by the force of cross-border media investment and competition. Within each country the corporate system and corporate media, underwritten by advertisers, have gathered strength, with enhanced ideological and political power. Aided by the increasing force of capital's greater mobility and global financial integration, they have successfully downgraded the idea of public goods and a public service responsibility of government, and with the help of financial pressure on governments have constrained the growth of (or shrunk) public service and welfare budgets. Part of the new 'economic realism' has been privatization, which raises money and placates powerful economic interests. And with the commercial media eager to capture public space and put it to better economic use, public broadcasting has been in retreat globally.

## The main drift versus niche filling

The increasing hegemony of the market and its gradual displacement of the public sphere occurs at varying speeds and is never complete. As noted, even in the United States, public broadcasting was introduced in 1967 with commercial broadcasters' blessing, to provide cultural and educational fare of lesser market value at public expense. Furthermore, the commercial media themselves offer occasional moments of public service broadcasting, and the

proliferation of commercial cable channels and networks has made some cultural programming available to paying customers, although very little political material of value has been provided as cable strives for large audiences and advertiser favor, following in the footsteps of the larger commercial broadcasters.

Nonprofit print media and community broadcasters (mainly radio) continue to exist and do supply a public sphere alternative and some hope for the future, but they service small audiences and do not have the resources to reach large numbers and compete with the advertising-funded media. They fill niches - as the shrinking public broadcasters and, episodically, cable and broadcasters, and the Internet, do as well - but at this point in history none of these are able to influence the main drift, which is being shaped by the dominant, large commercial media.

## Concluding note

The public sphere is shrinking globally under the impact of a triumphant market system, which is putting more and more public space to profitable use, as defined by the advertising community. That community wants, first and foremost, a congenial selling environment, and nothing that would, in the words of Procter & Gamble's advertising rules, "further the concept of business as cold, ruthless, and lacking all sentiment or spiritual motivation." This underlies the long trend toward entertainment and gradual marginalization of the public sphere. But democracy depends on an informed public, and thus a vibrant public sphere, to function properly. The main drift of the global market system and media therefore poses the serious threat that we are allowing democracy to be subverted and, in Neil Postman's words, "entertaining ourselves to death." Democrats everywhere should be vigorously opposing this drift by fighting against media privatization and supporting the independence and generous funding of public broadcasting and community media. As the private media have largely abandoned their public service and public sphere responsibilities, their franchises and advertising revenue should be taxed, and taxed heavily, to finance those that carry out such important social functions.

Robert W. McChesney

# Global Media and Democracy

By the end of the 1990s a major turning point was reached in the realm of media. Whereas media systems had been primarily national before the 1990s, a global commercial media market has emerged full force by the dawn of the twenty-first century. In the past, to understand any nation's media situation, one first had to understand the local and national media and then determine where the global market - which largely meant imports and exports of films, TV shows, books, and music - fit in. Today one must first grasp the nature and logic of the global commercial system and then determine how local and national media deviate from the overall system. The rise of a global commercial media system is closely linked to the rise of a significantly more integrated 'neoliberal' global capitalist economic system.

The rise to dominance of the global commercial media system is more than an economic matter; it also has clear implications for media content, politics, and culture. In many ways the emerging global media system is an extension of the U.S. system, and its culture shares many of the attributes of the U.S. hyper-commercial media system. This makes sense, as the firms that dominate U.S. media also dominate the global system, and the system operates on the same profit maximizing logic. But there are also some important distinctions. On the one hand, a number of new firms enter the picture as one turns to the global system. On the other hand, and more important, a number of new political and social factors enter the discussion. There are scores of governments and regional and international organizations that have a say in the regulation of media and communication. There are also a myriad of languages and cultures that make establishing a global version of the 'U.S. system' quite difficult. But even if the U.S. media system and culture will not be punch-pressed onto the globe, the trajectory is toward vastly greater integration, based on commercial terms, and dominated by a handful of transnational media conglomerates. In this article I briefly chronicle the rise of the global media system and its core attributes. It is a system dominated by fewer then ten global TNCs, with another four or five dozen firms filling out regional and niche markets. In my view, the general thrust of the global commercial media

system is quite negative - assuming one wishes to preserve and promote institutions and values that are conducive to meaningful self-government. It plays a central role in the development of 'neoliberal' democracy; i.e. a political system based on the formal right to vote, but where political and economic power is resolutely maintained in the hands of the wealthy few.

The global markets for film production, TV show production, book publishing, and recorded music have been oligopolistic markets throughout much of their existence. Although there are important domestic industries in many of these industries, the global export market is the province of a handful of mostly U.S.-owned or U.S.-based firms. These not only remain important markets, but are also tending to grow faster than the global economy. The motion picture and TV show production industries are absolutely booming at the global level. The major film studios and U.S. TV show production companies (usually the same firms) now generate between 50 and 60 percent of their revenues outside the United States. A key factor that makes these global oligopolies nearly impenetrable to newcomers are their extensive distribution systems. The rational choice for someone wishing to enter this market is to either buy one of the existing giants, or, if one does not have a spare $10 or $20 billion or does not wish to spend it, to set up an 'independent' and forge a link with one of the existing giants. The global film industry is the province of seven firms, all of which are part of larger media conglomerates. Likewise, the global music industry is dominated by five firms, all but one of which (EMI) are part of larger media TNCs. These five music giants earn 70 percent of their revenues outside of the United States.

What distinguishes the emerging global media system is not transnational control over exported media content, however, so much as increasing TNC control over media distribution and content within nations. Prior to the 1980s and 1990s, national media systems were typified by nationally owned radio and television systems, as well as domestic newspaper industries. Newspaper publishing remains a largely national phenomenon, but the face of television has changed almost beyond recognition. The rise of cable and satellite technology has opened up national markets to scores of new channels and revenue streams. The major Hollywood studios - all part of global media conglomerates - expect to generate $11 billion alone in 2002 for global TV rights to their film libraries, up from $7 billion in 1998. More important, the primary providers of these channels are the media TNCs that dominate cable television channel ownership in the United States, and have aggressively established numerous global editions of their channels to accommodate the new market.  Neoliberal 'free market' policies have opened up ownership of stations as well as cable and satellite systems to private and transnational interests. As *The Wall Street Journal* notes, "the cable colonialists continue to press on in Europe, Asia and Latin America, betting on long-term profit." Likewise, the largest media TNCs are invariably among the main players in efforts to establish digital satellite TV systems to serve regional and national markets.

Television also is rapidly coming to play the same sort of dominant cultural role in Europe, Asia, and worldwide that it has played in the United States for two or three generations. After reviewing the most recent research, one observer noted in early 1998: "Europe hasn't caught up to American TV consumption levels, but Europeans are spending more time than ever watching television." In 1997 French children aged four to ten years old watched on average nearly two hours of television per day, up 10 percent from the previous high in 1996; but this remains only one-half the amount of TV watching for U.S. kids.

The close connection of the rise of the global media system to the global capitalist political economy becomes especially clear in two ways. First, as suggested above, the global media system is the direct result of the sort of 'neoliberal' deregulatory policies and agreements (e.g. NAFTA and GATT) that have helped to form global markets for goods and services. At the global level, for example, the WTO ruled in 1997 that Canada could not prohibit Time Warner's *Sports Illustrated* from distributing a Canadian edition of the magazine.  In Australia, for another example, the High Court ruled

against the legality of Australian domestic media content quotas in April 1998, stating that "international treaty obligations override the national cultural objectives in the Broadcasting Services Act."

Although there is considerable pressure for open media markets, this is a sensitive area. There are strong traditions of protection for domestic media and cultural industries. Nations ranging from Norway, Denmark and Spain to Mexico, South Africa and South Korean, for example, have government subsidies to keep alive their small domestic film production industries. Over the coming years it is likely that there will be periodic setbacks to the drive to establish an open global media market. In the summer of 1998 culture ministers from 20 nations, including Brazil, Mexico, Sweden, Italy and Ivory Coast, met in Ottawa, Canada to discuss how they could "build some ground rules" to protect their cultural fare from "the Hollywood juggernaut." Their main recommendation was to keep culture out of the control of the WTO. In India, in 1998, a court issued an arrest warrant for Rupert Murdoch for failing to appear in court to defend himself on the charge that his Star TV satellite service broadcast 'obscene and vulgar' movies.

Nevertheless, the trend is clearly in the direction of opening markets to TNC penetration. Neoliberal forces in every country argue that cultural trade barriers and regulations harm consumers, and that subsidies even inhibit the ability of nations to develop their own competitive media firms. There are often strong commercial media lobbies within nations that perceive they have more to gain by opening up their borders than they do by maintaining trade barriers. So it was in 1998 when the British government proposed a voluntary levy on film theater revenues (mostly Hollywood films) to provide a subsidy for the British commercial film industry, the British commercial broadcasters reacted warily, not wishing to antagonize their crucial suppliers.

Advertising is the second way that the global media system is linked to the global market economy. Advertising is conducted disproportionately by the largest firms in the world, and it is a major weapon in the struggle to establish new markets. For major firms like Procter

& Gamble and Nike, global advertising is a vitally important aspect of their campaigns to maintain strong growth rates. In conjunction with the 'globalization' of the economy, advertising has grown globally at a rate greater than GDP growth in the 1990s. The most rapid growth has been in Europe, Latin America, and especially East Asia, although the economic collapse of the late 1990s has doused what had earlier been characterized as "torrid ad growth." Advertising in China is growing at annual rates of 40-50 percent in the 1990s, and the singularly important sector of TV advertising is expected to continue to grow at that rate, at least, with the advent of sophisticated audience research that now delivers vital demographic data to advertisers, especially TNC advertisers.

It is this TNC advertising that has fueled the rise of commercial television across the world, accounting, for example, for over one-half the advertising on the ABN-CNBC Asia network, which is co-owned by Dow Jones and General Electric. And there is a world of room for growth, especially in comparison to the stable U.S. market. Even in the developed markets of Western Europe, for example, most nations still spend no more than one-half the U.S. amount on advertising per capita, so there remains considerable growth potential. Were European nations, not to mention the rest of the world, ever to approach the U.S. level of between 2.1 and 2.4 percent of the GDP going toward advertising - where it has fluctuated for decades - the global media industry would see an exponential increase in its revenues.

In short order the global media market has come to be dominated by nine TNCs that all rank among the few hundred largest publicly traded firms in the world in terms of market value. They are: General Electric (#1); AT&T (#16); Disney (#31); Time Warner (#76); Sony (#103); News Corp. (#184); Viacom (#210); and Seagram (#274). Bertelsmann, the sole exception, would certainly be high on the list, too, were it not one of the handful of giant firms that remains privately held. In short, these firms are at the very pinnacle of global corporate capitalism. It is also a highly concentrated industry; the largest media firm in the world in terms of annual revenues, Time Warner (1998 revenues:

$28 billion), is some fifty times larger in terms of annual sales than the world's fiftieth-largest media firm. But what distinguishes these nine firms from the rest of the pack is not merely their size, but that they have global distribution networks.

The media giants have moved aggressively to become global players. Time Warner and Disney, for example, still get the vast majority of their revenue in the United States, but both firms project non-U.S. sales to be a majority of their revenues within a decade, and the other media giants are all moving to be in a similar position. The point is to capitalize on the potential for growth - and not get outflanked by competitors - as the U.S market is well developed and only permits incremental growth. As Viacom CEO Sumner Redstone puts it, "companies are focusing on those markets promising the best return, which means overseas." Frank Biondi, Chair of Seagram's Universal Studios, says "ninety-nine percent of the success of these companies long term is going to be successful execution offshore." Another U.S. media executive stated that" we now see Latin America and the Asia-Pacific as our 21st century." Sony, to cite one example, has hired the investment banking Blackstone Group to help it identify media takeover candidates worldwide.

But this point should not be exaggerated. Non-U.S. markets, especially markets where there are meddlesome governments, are risky and often require patience before they produce profit. The key to being a first tier media powerhouse is having a strong base in the United States, by far the largest and most stable commercial media market. That is why Bertelsmann is on the list; it ranks among the top U.S. music, magazine publishing, and book publishing companies. It expects to do 40 percent of its $16 billion in annual business in the United States in the near future. "We want to be a world-class media company," the CEO of the U.K.'s Pearson TV stated, "and to do that, we know we've got to get bigger in America."

The essence of the first tier firms is their ability to mix production capacity with their distribution networks. These nine firms control four of the five music firms that sell 80 percent of global music. The one remaining independent, EMI, is invariably on the market; it is worth considerably more merged with one of the other five global music giants that are all part of huge media conglomerates, or to another media TNC that wants a stake in the music market. All of the major Hollywood studios, that dominate global film box office, are connected to these giants too. The only two of the nine that are not major content producers are AT&T and GE's NBC. The former has major media content holdings through Liberty Media and both of them, ranking among the ten most valuable firms in the world, are in a position to acquire assets as they become necessary. Such may soon be the case for GE. NBC was forced to scale back its expansion into European and Asian television in 1998, in part because it did not have enough programming to fill the airwaves.

The global media market is rounded out by a second tier of four or five dozen firms that are national or regional powerhouses, or which have strong holds over niche markets, such as business or trade publishing. About one-half of these second tier firms come from North America; most of the rest, from Western Europe and Japan. Each of these second tier firms is a giant in its own right, often ranking among the 1,000 largest firms in the world and doing over $1 billion per year in business. The list of second tier media firms includes, among others, from North America: Dow Jones, Gannett, Knight-Ridder, Newhouse, Comcast, The New York Times, The Washington Post, Hearst, McGraw Hill, Cox Enterprises, CBS, Advance Publications, Hicks Muse, Times-Mirror, Reader's Digest, Tribune Company, Thomson, Hollinger, and Rogers Communication. From Europe the list of second tier firms includes, among others, Kirch, Havas, Mediaset, Hachette, Prisa, Canal Plus, Pearson, Carlton, Granada, United News & Media, Reuters, Reed Elsevier, Wolters Kluher, Axel Springer, Mediaset, Kinnevik, and CLT. The Japanese companies, aside from Sony, remain almost exclusively domestic producers. I will discuss the handful of 'Third World' commercial media giants below.

In combination, these sixty or seventy giants control much of the world's media: book publishing, magazine publishing, music recording, newspaper publishing, TV show production, TV station and cable channel ownership, cable/satellite TV system ownership, film production, motion picture theater ownership, and newspaper publishing. They are also the most dynamic element of the system. But the system is still very much in formation. New second tier firms are emerging, especially in lucrative Asian markets, and there will probably be further upheaval among the ranks of the first tier media giants. And firms get no guarantee of success by merely going global. The point is that they have no choice in the matter. Some, perhaps many, will falter as they accrue too much debt or as they otherwise enter unprofitable ventures. But the chances are that we are closer to the end of the process of establishing a stable global media market than we are to the beginning of the process. And as that happens, there is a distinct likelihood that the leading media firms in the world will find themselves in a very profitable position. That is what they are racing to secure.

Corporate growth, oligopolistic markets, and conglomeration barely reveal the extent to which the global media system is fundamentally noncompetitive in any meaningful economic sense of the term. Many of the largest media firms share major shareholders, own pieces of each other, or have interlocking boards of directors. When *Variety* compiled its list of the fifty largest global media firms for 1997, it observed that 'merger mania' and cross-ownership had "resulted in a complex web of interrelationships" that will "make you dizzy." Each of the nine largest media TNCs have, on average, equity joint ventures - where they share ownership of a media venture - with six of the other eight media giants, and usually more than one. Murdoch's News Corporation has at least one joint venture with each of the other eight. Murdoch summarized his philosophy by saying "We can join forces now, or we can kill each other and then join forces." For the second tier of media firms, linking up with other media firms is equally mandatory, to reduce competition and risk, and increase the chance of profitability. As the CEO of Sogecable, Spain's largest media firm one of the 12 largest private media companies in Europe, put it to *Variety*, the strategy is "not to compete with international companies but to join them."

Indeed, it is rare for a first tier media giant to launch a new venture in a foreign country unless they have taken on a leading domestic media company as a partner. The domestic firm can handle public outreach and massage the local politicians.

In sum, the global media market is one where the dominant firms compete aggressively in some concentrated oligopolistic markets, are key suppliers to each other in other markets, and are partners in yet other markets. As the headline in one trade publication put it, this is a market where the reigning spirit is to "Make profits, not war." In short, the global media market more closely resembles a cartel than it does a competitive marketplace.

When turning to the implications of the emerging global media system for journalism, politics, entertainment and culture, some caveats are necessary. Although fundamentally flawed, the system produces much of value for a variety of reasons. In addition, the global media system can be at times a progressive force, especially as it enters nations that had been tightly controlled by corrupt crony media systems, as in much of Latin America, or nations that had significant state censorship over media, as in parts of Asia. But this progressive aspect of the globalizing media market should not be blown out of proportion; the last thing the media giants want to do anywhere is rock the boat, as long as they can do their business. The global commercial media system is radical, in the sense that it will respect no tradition or custom, on balance, if it stands in the way of significantly increased profits. But it ultimately is politically conservative, because the media giants are significant beneficiaries of the current global social structure, and any upheaval in property or social relations, particularly to the extent it reduces the power of business and lessened inequality, would possibly - no, probably - jeopardize their positions.

The global media system is best understood as one that advances corporate and commercial interests and values, and denigrates or ignores that which cannot be incorporated into its mission. Four of the nine largest media firms are headquartered outside of the United States, but all of them - Bertelsmann, News

Corp., Sony and Seagram - are major U.S. players, indeed owning three of the major Hollywood film studios. They rank among the 70 largest foreign firms operating in the United States, based on their U.S. sales, and all but Bertelsmann rank in the top 30. There is no discernible difference in the firm's content whether they are owned by shareholders in Japan or Belgium, or have corporate headquarters in New York or Sydney. Bertelsmann CEO Thomas Middelhoff bristled when, in 1998, some said it was improper for a German firm to control 15 percent of the U.S. book publishing market. "We're not foreign. We're international," Middelhoff said. "I'm an American with a German passport." Indeed the output of the global media giants is largely interchangeable, as they constantly ape each other's commercial triumphs.

Some traditional notions of global media also tended to regard the existing non-TNC domestic commercial media as some sort of oppositional or alternative force to the global market. That was probably a dubious notion in the past, and it does not hold true at all today. Throughout the world, media consolidation and concentration have taken place in national markets, leaving a handful of extremely powerful media conglomerates dominating regional and national markets. These firms have found a lucrative niche teaming up with the global media giants in joint ventures, offering the 'local' aspect of the content, and massaging the local politicians. As the lead of Norway's largest media firm put it, "We want to position ourselves so if Kirch or Murdoch want to sell in Scandinavia, they'll come to us first."

The notion of non-U.S. or non-TNC media firms being 'oppositional' to the global system is no less farfetched when one turns to the 'Third World.' Mexico's Televisa, Brazil's Globo, Argentina's Clarin, and the Cisneros group of Venezuela, for example, rank among the sixty or seventy largest media firms in the world. They have extensive ties and joint ventures with the largest media TNCs, as well as with Wall Street investment banks. These firms tend to dominate their own national and regional media markets, which are experiencing rapid consolidation in their own right. The commercial media powerhouses of the developing

world tend, therefore, to be primary advocates for -and beneficiaries of - the expansion of the global commercial media market. And these Third World media giants, like other second tier media firms elsewhere, are also establishing global operations, especially to nations that speak the same languages. And within each of their home nations these media firms have distinct pro-business political agendas that put them at odds with large segments of the population. In short, the global system is best perceived as one that best represents the needs of investors, advertisers, and the affluent consumers of the world. In wealthy nations this tends to be a substantial portion of the population; in developing nations, a distinct minority.

With this hyper-commercialism and corporate control comes an implicit political bias regarding the content of the media system. Consumerism, the market, class inequality, and individualism tend to be taken as natural and often benevolent, whereas political activity, civic values, and anti-market activities tend to be marginalized or denounced. This does not portend mind-control or 'Big Brother,' for it is much more subtle than that. (For example, Hollywood films and television programs may not present socialism in a favorable light, and will rarely criticize capitalism as an economic system overall, but they frequently use particular businesses or business persons to serve as the 'bad guys.' Since businesses of one kind or another rank high on many peoples' lists of disreputable operators, to avoid using them as 'bad guys' in entertainment would leave the studio to resort to science fiction.) Indeed, the genius of the commercial media system is the general lack of overt censorship. As George Orwell noted in his unpublished introduction to *Animal Farm*, censorship in free societies was infinitely more sophisticated and thorough than in dictatorships because "unpopular ideas can be silenced, and inconvenient facts kept dark, without any need for an official ban." The logical consequence of a commercial media system is less to instill adherence to any ruling powers-that-be - though that can and does of course happen - than to promote a general belief that politics is unimportant and that there is little hope for organized social change.

As such, the global media system buttresses what could be termed 'neoliberal' democracy; i.e. the largely vacuous political culture that exists in the formally democratic market-driven nations of the world. The United States provides the pre-eminent model of 'neoliberal' democracy, and shows the way for combining a capitalist economy with a largely toothless democratic polity. Sometimes these points are made explicit. Jaime Guzman, principal author of Chile's 1980 constitution, believed that private property and investors' rights needed to be off-limits to popular debate or consideration, and he crafted Chile's 'democracy' accordingly. Since Chile is now considered a great global neoliberal success story both economically and politically it may be worthwhile to examine Guzman's thoughts. "A democracy can only be stable when in popular elections ... the essential form of life of a people is not at play, is not at risk," Guzman explained. "In the great democracies of the world, the high levels of electoral abstention do not indicate, as many erroneously interpret them, a supposed distancing of the people from the reigning system." Non-involvement by the bulk of the population is in fact a healthy development. Guzman concludes that in the best form of capitalist democracy, "if one's adversaries come to power, they are constrained to pursue a course of action not very different than that which one would desire because the set of alternatives that the playing field imposes on those who play on it are sufficiently reduced to render anything else extremely difficult." Guzman's vision has indeed been a success, of sorts. Chile, which arguably once was among the most vibrant democratic political cultures in the world, has seen its political life reduced to a placid, tangential spectator sport.

This hollowing out of democracy is a worldwide phenomenon in the age of the uncontested market. As a Greek peasant put it following Greece's 1996 elections: "The only right we have is the right to vote and it leads us nowhere." The very term democracy has been turned on its head so its very absence in substance is now seen as what constitutes its defining essence. *The Washington Post* noted that modern democracy works best when the political "parties essentially agree on most of the major issues." Or, more bluntly, as the

*Financial Times* put it, capitalist democracy can best succeed to the extent that it is about "the process of depoliticising the economy." (Is it even necessary to note that in a genuine democracy, the matter of who controls the economy and for what purposes would be at the center of political debate and consideration?)

The global commercial media system is integrally related to neoliberal democracy with its attendant depoliticization at two levels. At the broadest institutional level, the rise of a global commercial media system has been the result of and necessary for the rise of a global market for goods and services dominated by a few hundred TNCs. On the one hand, both the global commercial media system and the growth and emergence of this 'global' economy are predicated upon pro-business neoliberal deregulation worldwide. On the other hand, the marketing networks offered by a global media system are essential for the creation of global and regional markets for TNC goods and services. To the extent, therefore, the neoliberal global economic order thrives upon a weak political culture, the global media system is a central beneficiary as well.

But the global media system plays a much more explicit role in generating a passive, depoliticized populace that prefers personal consumption to social understanding and activity, a mass more likely to take orders than to make waves. Lacking any necessarily 'conspiratorial' intent, and merely following rational market calculations, the thrust of the media system is simply to provide light escapist entertainment. In the developing world, where public relations and marketing hyperbole are only beginning to realize their awesome potential, and where the ruling elites are well aware of the need to keep the rabble in line, the importance of commercial media is sometimes stated quite candidly. In the words of the late Emilio Azcarraga, the billionaire head of Mexico's Televisa: "Mexico is a country of a modest, very fucked class, which will never stop being fucked. Television has the obligation to bring diversion to these people and remove them from their sad reality and difficult future."
The global journalism of the corporate media system reinforces these trends, with devastating implications for the

functioning of political democracies. As in the United States, journalism worldwide is deteriorating, as it has become an important profit source for the media giants. Because investigative journalism or coverage of foreign affairs makes little economic sense, it is discouraged as being too expensive. On the one hand, there is a relatively sophisticated business news pitched at the upper and upper-middle classes and shaped to their needs and prejudices. CNN International, for example, pitches itself as providing advertisers "unrivalled access to reach high-income consumers." But even in 'elite' media there is a decline. *The Economist* noted that in 1898 the first page of a sample copy of the *Times of London* contained 19 columns of foreign news, eight columns of domestic news, and three columns on salmon fishing. In 1998 a sample copy of the Times, now owned by Rupert Murdoch, had one international story on its front page: an account of actor Leonardo DiCaprio's new girlfriend. "In this information age," *The Economist* concluded, "the newspapers which used to be full of politics and economics are thick with stars and sport." On the other hand, there is an appalling schlock journalism for the masses, based upon lurid tabloid-type stories. For the occasional 'serious' story, there is the mindless regurgitation of press releases from one source or another, with the range of debate mostly limited to what is being debated among the elite. "Bad journalism," a British observer concluded in 1998, "is a consequence of an unregulated market in which would-be monopolists are free to treat the channels of democratic debate as their private property."

It does not have to be this way. The 'wild card' in the global media deck are the people of the world - people constituted as organized citizens rather than as passive consumers and couch potatoes. It may seem difficult, especially from the vantage point of the United States and other wealthy nations, to see much hope for public opposition to the global corporate media system. As one Swedish journalist noted in 1997, "Unfortunately, the trends are very clear, moving in the wrong direction on virtually every score, and there is a desperate lack of public discussion of the long-term implications of current developments for democracy and accountability." And, as discussed above, this political pessimism is precisely the type of political culture necessary for a neoliberal economic order to remain stable.

But there are indications that progressive political forces in nations around the world are increasingly making media issues part of their political platforms. As the global media system is increasingly intertwined with global capitalism, their fates go hand-in-hand. The only possible way to generate viable media reform will be as part of a broader movement to arrest the anti-democratic essence of neoliberlaism and the market. In nations like Sweden, New Zealand, Canada, Brazil, Mexico and India, to name just a few, democratic electoral parties have made control and structure of media one of the main political issues for the 1990s. This is a new development, and it reflects the increasing recognition that control over media is a very important aspect of political power in a society. In all of these nations, media reforms proposals ranging from ownership restrictions and support for nonprofit and noncommercial community media and public broadcasting to increased power for media workers to control journalism and media content and restrictions on advertising, especially to children, are being advanced. But we are at the very earliest stages of this movement. In the near future we should begin to see these national groups begin to coalesce and organize transnationally. The global media system will require a global democratic response, not merely a series of national or local opponents. The crucial point is that global media is not a bad thing per se, global media are bad to the extent they are unaccountable and serve the interests of the wealthy few, not the many.

It is going to be a very difficult fight, but it is not hopeless, and there is really little choice in the matter. Despite much blathering about the 'end of history' and the triumph of the market in the commercial media and among Western intellectuals, the actual track record is quite dubious. Asia, the long celebrated tiger of twenty-first-century capitalism, is now mired in an economic depression. Russian capitalism has been an unmitigated disaster, something that was of little interest to Western pundits as Russian living stan-

dards collapsed in the early and middle 1990s, but became notable when it threatened the stability of their own economies in 1998. Latin America, the other vaunted champion of market reforms since the 1980s, has seen what a World Bank official terms a "big increase in inequality." The ecologies of both regions are little short of disastrous. If - and perhaps only if - the reigning spirit of profits über alles ever confronts a serious political challenge, it seems likely that the corporate media system will be subjected to a well-deserved public examination as well. As the French sociologist Pierre Bourdieu put it in 1997, what we need to do today is to rekindle reasoned utopianism, the notion that it is the right of the world's people to use their imaginations to construct the economy, the world, within reason to suit their democratically determined needs. And as Bourdieu, himself, concluded in the same address, the place to start should be by ridding "the imperialism that affects cultural production and distribution in particular, via commercial constraints."

Ideas drawn from forthcoming Robert W. McChesney, *Rich Media, Poor Democracy: Communication Politics in Dubious Times.* (University of Illinois Press, 1999).

...institutions involved in new biological developments are searching for new rhetorics to pitch their initiatives and products to the public. The question now is,

what rhetoric can be used to represent these new biological initiatives and keep a distance from the rhetoric of eugenics,

which appropriated the secular promises of the Enlightenment earlier in the century, thus rendering them unusable? One of the places science has turned is the utopian rhetoric of Christianity (and the Roman Catholic Church in particular). Given popular wisdom that science is our new religion, and in the case of the biotech revolution there may well be an element of truth to this cliché, such a move makes sense. The promises of new universalism, immortality, and heaven on earth (new genesis), are being floated around once again in the public sphere. The spiritual promises of the dying Church are being reborn as a material reality that is not dependent on faith.

In order to respond to this development of representation in the biological sciences,

Critical Art Ensemble (in collaboration with Faith Wilding and Paul Vanouse) have created a faux Cult that vehemently extols the utopian promises of biotechnology.

Using the speed of electronic information systems and the performative techniques of street theater, CAE has created a recombinant theater that elicits and sometimes provokes engagement in new biotechnological discourses.

The Cult of the New Eve (CoNE) website presents the new scientific theology, and acts as a support to the live action. While presenting their web-site, CoNE members ask the audience to join them in acts of molecular cannibalism. To do this, CAE has made bread and beer using recombinant yeast supplied to us by the Human Genome Project (this is not a prank or a hoax - we are quite serious). When participants eat the bread or drink the beer, they consume the human genome - Eve's genome in particular. After participating in this project, CAE's hope is that when audience members hear the same cult rhetoric from individuals in the scientific community, they will listen from a more skeptical point of view. We also to hope to use this action as a springboard for a discussion of eugenics, eco-piracy, and the relationship between the information and communication techno-revolution and the biotech revolution.

# Cult of the New Eve

**Welcome to the Cult of the New Eve.**

Welcome to the Second Genesis. Brothers and Sisters, we are witnessing a remaking of the world. The Cosmos described by the religions of the world is dead. We are entering an Age in which the secrets of creation are not in the hands of God, nor are they at the blind mercy of Nature. We control our own destinies. All the promises that religions have made but failed to keep are now ours to fulfill. You no longer have to have faith, nor must you even believe. What was once considered a miracle is now or will soon be a common reality. Once and for all, we shall know that humankind is not spiritual - it is material.

1   2   3   4   5   6   7

# Exposing the False Eves

Brothers and Sisters, the Cult of the New Eve warns you to beware of the False Eves and other impostors who will try to deceive you into believing that they are responsible for the First Genesis and/or that they originated the Second Genesis. Simply because the First Genesis that ushered in the First Biological Age cannot be rigorously studied (given present scientific methodologies), that does not mean that we must ascribe a mystical meaning to it. Nor should we turn ourselves over to faith at the prodding of some arbitrary mythology — a hall of mirrors that houses the False Eves. Have the courage to face the unknown without fear. ▶

Here are the False eves: study them so you will not be fooled should you encounter them.

1   2   3   4   5   6   7

"Those who believe that the automobile is eternal are not thinking, even from a strictly technological standpoint, of other future forms of transportation. For example, certain models of one-man helicopters presently being tested by the US Army will probably have spread to the general public within twenty years." (Guy Debord, *Situationist Theses on Traffic*, #8,1959)

### 1. Independent artists' spaces

Artists in this century have always created their own spaces, worlds, universes. They have created their own schools, movements, organisations. In the late 1970s and early 1980s many artists in Western Europe organised themselves in a more political way. In these times, there were many protests and people started to squat houses and buildings to find alternative ways of using these for living, working and education. At first, of course, these actions were criminalized by the authorities. Soon, artists started to use the form of critical protest and public action to occupy empty buildings, to create new environments for art and artists. In many Western European countries, particularly in Holland, Germany and Austria, these artists spaces have become an important factor in the production of art, public appearance of artists, and the exploration and development of new forms of art.

Parallel to this social development, more and more technical media have entered our world - video, computers, game-consoles. For artists, communication and information technology, and more specifically the internet has revealed the kind of autonomy and independence that enables people, and artists, to act freely, to freely create, express, and to explore and experiment with new forms of art. In this context, however, art is no longer produced in more or less unique physical, material objects, but only exists if it is played back, performed on-line, connected, or rendered on a screen. Time-based art has another appearance in the public space. It cannot be simply attached on a wall, installed in a public hall, or on a public square. This art exists as called media. If it is embedded in an object or an installation, or used as part of a performance, then not this outer form but the electronic and cybernetic appearance is the actual work.

For many artists the internet is another possibility to reflect their position in a rapidly changing world. Most artists use the net for self-reflection or documentation. Still, only very few artists have access to technology and the required knowledge to apply these in order to create art. This an important condition, without this knowledge and the access to technology, it is very difficult to create art in an electronic space.

This also points at another difficulty. It is an illusion to think that with more personal computers, phones and faxes, vcrs, tape- and diskdrives, people have more access to technology. This technology is applied and defined in products or services.

### 2. Conditions for working with the net

Since the artist not only has to produce art as an object, he also takes control over the image and the actual content. He even takes over its context - the where and how, when and why the work is positioned in the context of art. Any work of art cannot exist or be seen without an art context. Alone on an island, one might not be interested in art, since you cannot share experiences, ideas and perception with other people. In the Balinese language there is no word for art. On the sandy coast of Bali, every year craftsmen create fantastic sand sculptures washed away by the sea. Sometimes context is art.

By the mid 1990s, most of the very few artists that had access to the internet had found their way into this worldwide communication network. Some argue that art has changed since the emergence of electronic media. Certainly, technology has affected art and art practice. But never before have artists so easily gotten access to technology. It is important to consider that

many of the recent developments on the internet are not just the product of corporate industries or national research laboratories, but also the work of individuals and small collaborations. Net.art is not a product of art historians or museum directors, but again by individual artists and relatively small groups.

## 3. Medialabs

Over the last few years an incredible range of books, readers, syllabi, zines and other printed media have been published on the rise of the internet. However, only few have been publishing what we refer to as net.art. The new forms of art that come with technology still have to be described, not only from an art-historical perspective, but also within the context of media culture itself.

After the studio and the collaborative workspace, the medialab is the next stage which creates room for artistic activity. The medialab is however not an isolated atelier or studio, but a workspace that is connected through communication technology to networks and so to other medialabs. Not just for sharing technology and information, but also to be able to work together in a virtual workspace.
There is no single format for such a place. The few labs presented here were, and are, also a human network, with several collaborations, meetings and exchanges. It is within these locations that net.art came into existence. Not art subdued to a curatorial plan, but art that is the outcome of network activity. The medialab is slowly turning into an art form; artists give up their private studios and establish such environments. As with the artist, the art form has turned into a set of parameters, that can be changed by the audience. The netbased artwork addresses the intention and creativity of that audience. Net.art is a toolbox, an instrument for the user to make her or his own art.

No longer merely a production environment, even larger organisations, like C3, AEC, V2 and the ZKM, have created their own medialabs.

The Thing (www.thing.net)

One of the oldest strongholds for artists on the internet is The Thing, now based in New York. The Thing started off as a network of bbs-systems, mainly in Germany. Since 1994 The Thing is an ISP homebased in New York City, a shared workspace and an internet-host supporting several systems and hosting various projects by artists. The Thing tries to balance the participation, service and artistic production in a smart way. It offers access, space and a forum to artists and critics to present their ideas, mainly their critique on art and exhibitions. Also, it holds a rich collection of 'early' works by artists experimenting with user interfaces and internet technology.

## Ljudmila (www.ljudmila.org)

The Ljubljana Digital Media Lab, better known as Ljudmila, is a project space supported by the Soros Foundation in Ljubljana. It started in 1994 with a small group, that provided access and services for the local community. The activity was never limited to just working in the lab, but showed a large involvement in the Ljubljana public arts scene, festivals, exhibitions, parties. Next to websites and collaborative net-projects, Ljudmila is also facilitating multimedia and videoproduction and currently has over 500 dial-in users. Still, most users are artists and working for independent organisations.

## *Internationale Stadt Berlin* (www.icf.de)

Almost parallel to *The Digital City* in Amsterdam, the *Internationale Stadt Berlin* was founded. For several years, in contrast to its Dutch counterpart, at least by name, there was no institute behind this network. There was primarily a core group, active in the local Berlin scene, that invited colleagues and friends to create a network, like a city with inhabitants. But as with Ljudmila, the network was mostly used by artists and those working in independent organisations. *Internationale Stadt Berlin* disappeared as a central server, but in the context of the continuous building and construction activity of the city Berlin, the people of Internationale Stadt Berlin have just moved to other areas in town and have reorganised in multiple new artservers and workspaces.

## Flying Desk (desk.org)

Flying Desk (or just simply Desk) was a workspace for artists, activists, critics, hackers and authors. The core group of this initiative met within *De Digitale Stad* (the digital city), Europe's first virtual community. By summer 1996, the workspace had hosted about one hundred people; the virtual workspace gave opportunities to several more.

Desk was a model for many other medialabs since it intended not only to give space to artists to create their own work, but also hosted workshops, organised meetings and created a small scale alternate income for artists through work for third parties. Thus, the revenues have been spent almost entirely on the production of art and several services that support artists, writers and programmers in their profession. The nettime and rhizome mailinglists started off here, Desk provided an alternate rootserver for the namespace domainssystem. Several artists created their first net.artworks on one of the machines of Desk. Now known as Desk Organization, one of the last free linux hosts on the internet.

## 4. global forums, the power of shared writing

## Nettime (www.nettime.org)

Another powerful tool for artists and activists has been and still are mailing-

lists. Nettime is a very active and lively forum with more than seven hundred participants, theoreticians, artists, activists and journalists, from all over the world.

In 1995 the mailinglist was found after the very first ZK meeting in June in Venice. Not only netbased, nettime has regularly organized meetings (ZK), up to now just in Europe. The major topic or issue of the list and the ZK-meetings is net culture and net-criticism. Apart from thousands of postings and numerous gatherings, the list has also produced several readers, *ZKP1, ZKP2, ZKP3, ZKMP321*, a website and a book *Read Me.*

"<nettime> is not just a mailing list but an effort to formulate an international, networked discourse that neither promotes a dominant euphoria (to sell products) nor continues the cynical pessimism, spread by journalists and intellectuals in the 'old' media who generalize about 'new' media with no clear under-

standing of their communication aspects. we have produced, and will continue to produce books, readers, and web sites in various languages so an 'immanent' net critique will circulate both on- and offline."
(excerpt from the nettime website)

7-11 (www.7-11.org)

Another very lively forum for artists is the mailinglist 7-11; the name refers to a chain of US-supermarkets. This list holds a large collection of artistic expression, blunt cynical criticism. Its content varies from creative textbased art (ascii art) up to manipulated texts, redirected spam email, scrambled letters and crypto-anarchic messages. 7-11 was installed after a dispute at the fourth ZKMP meeting in Ljubljana, summer 1998. There, artists left the nettime list to create a forum with more emphasis on less doctrine, more art, less criticism. nettime was seen as an elite list for European formalists, American academics and global reference hunters.

Of course there are many other mailinglists, such as Rhizome, Syndicate and Xchange.

5. Future, objectives, speculation

Originally, what we called net.art was more of a movement and less of an art form. We, the artists using the internet, had found a way to reach another and much larger audience then through exhibits in museums and galleries. it also allowed and allows us to manipulate not just the image or the sound, but also any image, any sound. the net is a collection of readymades.

"... Net.art can in no way be considered a systematic doctrine; it does however, constitute a school, and the activists who make up this school want to transform their www art works by returning to first principles with regard to online inspiration, just as the media.artists - and many of the net.artists were at one time media.artists - returned to first principles with regard to interface composition." (Cosic, Wagenaar: "The Net.Artist," excerpt from *Nettime ZKP 3.2.1*, 1998)

If history makes all working models fail at a certain point, because technologies and societies are always changing, then

Walter van der Cruijsen

we should consider other conditions that enable us to address issues, express our feelings or visualize ideas about the world around us.
The working_condition, refers to work, to both aspects of manual labour and exploitation, as well as to systems of administration and management. It is difficult in an art context to talk about the working_condition, since the production of art has little to do with the classical paradigm of labour.

Labour and capital are classical factors which almost have been eliminated by the current economic, mainly financial and monetary factors. Labour is an expense, a cost factor. Information is the capital of the system now. Almost every good, product, or service is converted into a set of codes or algorithms.

This changes our environment dramatically: air, water and nutrition have been turned into commodities. The usage of these commodities is a cost-factor and they are no longer part of a natural habitat, but part of a mechanism, a program which runs our society, manageable, accountable, controllable. This system also affects artistic practices and in some ways also the artists. Artists have become partners of our postmodern societies, no longer outcasts, avant-garde or subcultural activists.

On the net, it is not exclusiveness that is required but compatibility. Can the art form be connected to, can I have access, can my computer system handle this kind of data. Can the other user's computer display what my computer shows.

As with language, not every phrase, sound or image can be understood by everyone else. This is conditioned by education, culture difference and by economic and political factors.

On a global scale, only a small minority can actively use technology, even fewer are able to create their own technology. This is almost a contradiction: technology allows us to communicate worldwide, practically open any library or visit any remote location, but it is still very exclusive, because it is complex, expensive, relatively rare, changes constantly and not every new technology is immediately available to all users. New technology does not always succeed, is not always the best choice, because profit

34.0 Kbps   41:49.4/01:32:15.6

prevails over quality. The final price tag is the sum of overhead, not the thing itself. The economy is an administrative cyberspace and the actual trade is financial and monetary.

Then what is left to do? If the threat is real and all intellectual property, like knowledge based code, is trade, then it will be extremely difficult to maintain within the current presets of standards, language and protocols. New definitions have to be written to create new freedom of information. If language is no longer free to use, to change and to improve, then it will have to create new content, use what has been ignored, freely exchange ideas, methods and meaning...

...There will always be more people that utilize the art and not only take software items and programs. In recent years, so many standards, protocols and machine code have been written that currently are no longer in use nor even available anymore - although the idea or functionality they could add to the contemporary software point at yet unforeseen possibilities. This is the mind of free software and Open Source. These constructs allow to add, recreate and extend proven technology.

Telecommunication is not replacing how we communicated before, but tries to extend, improve the possibilities. The real-virtual space is that of desire. Something that can be obtained but only by a few. For all others, it is just the idea, the illusion or the dream. This is another threat. Open Source that is but another business plan or a marketing strategy contradicts the possibilities of an Open Source movement creating without limits. Independence and freedom to speak, to write and to exchange words, codes and expressions then is no longer a right but a scheme you can subscribe to. Artists and activists are required here.

# net_condition
# the website

Tom Fürstner

http://www.zkm.de

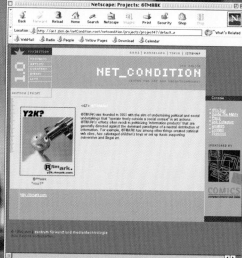

372

The net-condition website designers at ZKM are faced with a question: what is the relation between a web space and the real-world exhibition space and the overall virtual exhibition called Internet? Alongside the completely documented curator texts, the brief descriptions of the works and artists make up the nucleus of the web site. All the pages of the web site are generated dynamically from a database, which made it easier to manage dozens of works, artists and URLs. The database backend also provides printer-friendly pages (without any additional HTML coding) and allows easy management of the bilingual documents.

The interactive switch-overs between real and virtual space that characterise net_condition as an exhibition project are continued in the web site: a dozen or so panorama photos allow people to enter the "real" exhibition as "virtual" visitors and thus give the spatial entity and exhibition architecture a place on the Internet. In this way, surfers from other countries can drop in on the exhibition as a museum enterprise, who would otherwise never have found their way to the real-world ZKM.
But web visitors not only "participate" in the architecture; most of the side-events of the exhibition have been publicised as RealAudio or RealVideo and Quicktime streams, for example the symposium "Inside The Matrix" (on the interpretation of the film *The Matrix*). Technically, the website has been created as a further development of

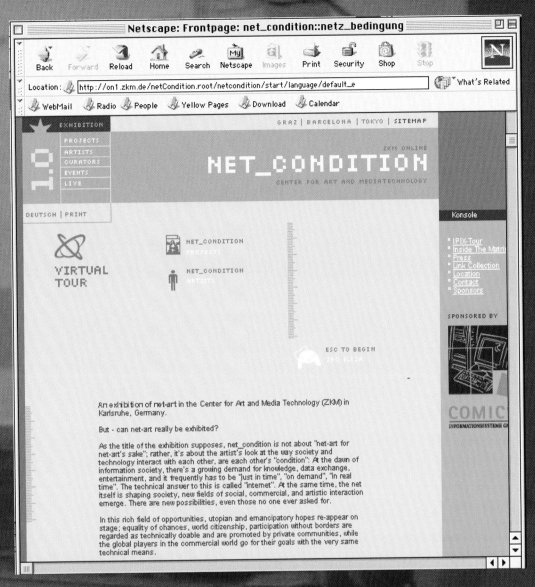

Userland Frontier, a pioneering content management system, that is equally adaptable and powerful, offering the web builder a host of useful abstractions. For example, the content is "rendered" into set templates, running embedded macros and storing a comprehensive entry in the log table. Naturally enough, there has been great interest in *net_condition* particularly on the net. According to a conservative estimate, the approximately 2.5 million hits registered during the four months of the exhibition equate to some 40,000 individuals who visited the exhibition via the Internet. For a non-commercial site dedicated to a cultural subject that's a little sensation.

**The web team**
**Concept, programming: Tom Fürstner**
**Web design: Lydia Lindner**
**Programming: Arne Gräßer**
**Text and programming: Christoph Pingel**

# art and global media

## A Project about Media in Media curated by Peter Weibel

http://www.xspace.at

374

**steirischer herbst 98-99**
September 25 - October 24, 1998
September 26 - October 26, 1999

**Director:**
Christine Frisinghelli

**Organisation:**
Sabine Himmelsbach, Alexandra Foitl,
Melanie Jamnig

**Technical support:**
mit Loidl oder CoKEG

## Symposium at the Palais Attems

Graz, October 3 - 4, 1998
Edward S. Herman (USA): *The Global
Erosion of the Public Sphere*
Robert W. McChesney (USA): *Rich Media,
Poor Democracy: Communication Politics
in these Dubios Times*
Vincent Mosco (USA): *Militant Particularism:
Beta Testing a New Society*
Dan Schiller (USA): *Transnational Telecom-
munications and the Reorganization of
Global Production*
Diana Johnstone (USA): *Media
Manicheism and the Ideology of the
International Community*
Bruno Latour (F): *On the Rehabilitation
of Politics - a View from the Sciences*
Florian Rötzer (D): *Kämpfe im Markt
der Aufmerksamkeit*
Gerhard Johann Lischka (CH): *Jede/r ein
Mediator*
Timothy Druckrey (USA): *Event/Transfor-
mation/Information: Enacting the Image*
Siegfried Zielinski (D): *Wem gehört
die Zeit?*
Christa Blümlinger (A/F): *Kleine archäo-
logische Versuche im Zeitalter der Medien
(Ivens, Marker, Farocki)*

## Exhibition in the Print Media

Cooperation with the museum in progress,
Vienna
Special thanks to Der Standard/Gerfried
Sperl, World Media Network/Laurent
Munnich, museum in progress/Josef Ortner,
Kathrin Messner and Sabine Dreher

### Contributions in daily papers of World Media Network

*Helix* by eichinger oder knechtl, werkraum
and virtual real estate (A)

| | |
|---|---|
| *Le Soir* (Belgium) | 5/28/1998 |
| *Libération* (France) | 6/6+7/1998 |
| *La Stampa* (Italy) | 6/27/1998 |
| *To Vima* (Greece) | 9/20/1998 |
| *Der Standard* (Austria) | 9/24/1998 |
| *La Presse* (Canada) | 11/20/1998 |

### Contributions in the newspaper *DER STANDARD*

*Symposium contributions*
9/18/1998:   Peter Weibel (A)
9/25/1998:   Edward S. Herman (USA)
10/9/1998:   Vincent Mosco (USA)
10/23/1998:  Robert W. McChesney (USA)
11/6/1998:   Pierre Bourdieu (F)
11/20/1998:  Jürgen Habermas (D)
12/4/1998:   Bruno Latour (F)
2/19/1999:   Immanuel Wallerstein (USA)

*Artist's contributions*
11/30/1998:  Martine Aballéa (F)
12/11/1998:  Peter Fend (USA)
12/16/1998:  DeeDee Halleck/
              David Thorne (USA)

*Signs of Trouble - International Positions
in Information Design of the 1990s*
Cooperation with the museum in progress
and basis Wien; Curated by Christian
Muhr and Walter Pamminger
9/15/1998:   The Designers Republic (GB)
9/18/1998:   Mevis & Van Deursen (NL)
9/28/1998:   David Crow (GB)
10/9/1998:   Michael Rock &
              Susan Sellers 2x4 (USA)
10/13/1998:  J. Abbott Miller (USA)
11/23/1998:  Anne Burdick (USA)
12/23/1998:  Cornel Windlin &
              M/M (CH/F)
2/4/1999:    Tomato (GB)
5/14/1999:   Jonathan Barnbrook (GB)

### Artist's contributions in the art magazine *n.paradoxa* London Volume 3, 1999

Special thanks to Kathy Deepwell
Susan Hinnum (DK): *Copulo Ergo Sum*

Edda Strobl (A): *What they do - Was sie tun*
Sonja Gangl (A): *REBEKA Underwear*
Lou Ann Greenwald (USA): *Untitled*

### Artist's contributions in the art magazine *Intercommunications* Tokyo No. 30 Autumn 1999

Co-operation with the ICC Tokyo
Special thanks to Toshiharu Ito and
Takatoshi Shinoda
Haim Steinbach (USA): *dirty dozen* *
*1998, more or less 1998*
Markus Huemer (A): *Ontological Loneliness
within the Alphabet, 1999*

## Billboard project in 23 European cities

**Martine Aballéa**
***Jardin Voyageur - Travelling Garden***
Cooperation with the museum in progress,
Vienna
Special thanks to Ulrich Obrist, Josef Ort-
ner, Sabine Dreher, with the support of
Austrian Airlines, gewista and Ankünder
October / November 1998: Graz, (A)
November / December / January
1998/99: Vienna (A), Brussels (B), Copen-
hagen (DK), Frankfurt/M. (D), Berlin (D),
Paris (F), Helsinki (FIN), Athens (GR),
London (GB), Dublin (IRL), Rome (I), Amster-
dam (NL), Madrid (E), Sarajevo (BIH),
Sofia (BG), Beograd (YU), Warsaw (PL),
Bucharest (R), Bratislava (SK), Prague (CZ),
Budapest (H), Zagreb (HR)

## Newsroom

Display of all contributions in the print
media; Library with media-specific
literature
Videoprogram (Special thanks to DeeDee
Halleck, TIV - True Image Vision and
XXkunstkabel):
TIV - True Image Vision (A): *STROBE-Trailer*
XXkunstkabel (A): *Video productions from
the years 1996 - 1998*
Paper Tiger Television (USA):
*Gulf Crisis TV Project* (1990):
*New World Order,
Manufacturing the Enemy
Putting the Demo Back in Democracy*
Peter Wintonick and Mark Achbar (USA):

# Graz

Chris Marker,
*Zapping Zone, 1990/97*
*Media Installation,*
*Graz 1998*

*Manufacturing Consent - Noam Chomsky and the Media*, 1992
Alexander Kluge (D): *Der Angriff der Gegenwart auf die übrige Zeit*, 1985
Siegfried Zielinski (D): *Lecture during the symposium Art and Global Media*
Bruno Latour (D): *Lecture during the symposium Art and Global Media*
Peter Fend (USA): *Ocean Earth*, 1998 and *NEWS ROOM*, 1998
(produced by XXkunstkabel)

Two computers with access to the project-homepage *Art and Global Media*:
http://www.xspace.at
Webmaster: Adm/Orhan Kipcak & Ges.

## Contributions in the Austrian Broadcasting Corporation - ORF

Contributions in the program 'kunst-stücke'
Special thanks to Andrea Schurian, Lioba Redekker

Harun Farocki (D): *Stilleben*, 1998 (screened October 1, 1998)
Peter Wintonick and Mark Achbar (USA): *Manufacturing Consent - Noam Chomsky and the Media*, 1992 (screened: Part 1: October 15, 1998; Part 2: October 22, 1998)
TIV - True Image Vision (A): *STROBE* (screened: Part 1: January 14, 1999; Part 2: February 25, 1999)

Susanne Granzer and Arno Böhler (A): *Avital Ronell. Der Ruf - Filosofie im Bild*, 1998 (screened March 4, 1999)

## Film Program: Joris Ivens - Chris Marker - Harun Farocki

Graz, October 2 - 11, 1998
Cinemas: Schubert Lichtspiele, KIZ - Kino im Augarten; Opening lectures by Marceline Loridan-Ivens, Christa Blümlinger and Thomas Tode
68 films were presented which are documented with short texts and stills in the program booklet (Introduction by Peter Weibel and Christa Blümlinger, 32 pages, 90 photographs/b&w, German)

Special thanks to Nikos Grigoriadis and the institutions which made available copyrights, copies, photographs and other materials:
Argos Films, Paris/London
Ateliers des Jeunes Cinéastes, Brussels
Bundesarchiv, Berlin
Capi Film, Paris
Centre Georges Pompidou, Paris
Cinématheque Francais, Paris
Constant vzw, Brussels
Europese Stichting Joris Ivens, Nijmegen
Filmarchiv Austria, Vienna
Filmbüro Augsburg
Freunde der deutschen Kinemathek, Berlin
ISKRA, Arcueil
Jane Balfour Films, London

Kinemathek Hamburg
La Sept ARTE, Paris
Les Films de la Pleïade, Paris
Max Film, Munich
Münchner Filmmuseum, Munich
Nederland Filmmuseum, Amsterdam
Österreichisches Filmmuseum, Vienna
Sofracima, Paris
Stadtkino, Vienna
Stiftung Deutsche Kinemathek, Berlin
Taurus Film, Munich
Verleih der Filmemacher, Munich

## Media Installations: Chris Marker - Harun Farocki

Graz, October 2 - 18, 1998
Priesterseminar Graz
In co-operation with the Centre Georges Pompidou / Paris and Constant / Brussels
(Special thanks to Christina Van Assche, Etienne Sandrin, Laurence Rassel)
**Chris Marker**:
Zapping Zone, 1990/97
Immemory, 1997
Roseware, 1998, work in progress
(together with Laurence Rassel)
**Harun Farocki**:
Schnittstelle, 1995

ÖSTERREICHISCHER **ORF** AUSTRIAN BROADCASTING
RUNDFUNK CORPORATION

DER STANDARD
unabhängige österreichische Tageszeitung

n p a doxa

# net_condition

**The exhibition *net_condition* is part of the project *Art and Global Media* 1998/99, curated by Peter Weibel**
The selection of artists was made by Peter Weibel together with the curators on site.

**steirischer herbst 99**
**September 25 - October 24, 1999**
Graz, AVL ART GATE

**Director:**
Christine Frisinghelli

**Curator:**
Peter Weibel

**Artists:**
David Blair
Dave Bruckmayer/Gaylord Aulke
Masaki Fujihata
Jochen Gerz
Marina Grzinic & Aina Smid
Markus Huemer
Konsum Art.Server
(Margarete Jahrmann and Max Moswitzer)
Darij Kreuh
Jeffrey Shaw
42 (Cloed Baumgartner, Margit Franz,
Moni Glahn, Cym Groenestijn, Sol Haring,
Jogi Hofmüller, Reni Hofmüller, Katarina Pejovic,
Andr'ea Siegl, Eva Ursprung)

**Organisation:**
Alexandra Foitl, Daniela Olotu-Goettfried
**Assistants:**
Ruth Kümmel, Peter Peer

**Technical Advice:**
Mit Loidl oder CO KEG
**Exhibition Design:**
Cornelius Pfeiffer

**Website: http://www.xspace.at**

**Internet Support:**
Adm/ Orhan Kipcak & Ges.

**Internet Provider:**
AVL´s high speed integrated Private Network, called AVL*Net, brings together the powers of email, Intranet, CAD workflow, information-rich knowledge databases and the latest in audio and video communication.

**Sponsor:**

**Graz**

# net_condition

## //////////// I< I I I I
## ZKM | Center for Art and Media Karlsruhe

**Curators:**
Walter van der Cruijsen, Golo Föllmer, Johannes Goebel, Matthias Osterwold, Hans-Peter Schwarz, Jeffrey Shaw, Peter Weibel, Benjamin Weil

**Artists:**
Daniel García Andújar, Giselle Beiguelman, Justin Bennett, David Blair, Joachim Blank & Karl Heinz Jeron, Blast Theory, Luther Blissett, Natalie Bookchin, Chris Brown, Dave Bruckmayr/ Gaylord Aulke, Heath Bunting, Janet Cohen/Keith Frank/Jon Ippolito, Nicolas Collins, Shane Cooper, Vuk Cosic, Jordan Crandall, Douglas Davis, esc to begin (Bernd Diemer, Martina Haitz, Andreas Schiffler, Meike Schmidt, Andreas Krach, Sue Machert, Guillaume Stagnaro, Arne Grässer, Susen Kümmel), Ken Goldberg/Bob Farzin, Ken Feingold, Masaki Fujihata, Jochen Gerz, Johannes Goebel/Torsten Belschner/Bernhard Sturm, Lynn Hershman, Markus Huemer, Timothée Ingen-Housz, i/o/d, JODI, Knowbotic Research, Konsum Art.Server (Margarete Jahrmann/Max Moswitzer), Marc Lafia, Olia Lialina, Alvin Lucier, Lev Manovich, Jenny Marketou, Kaffe Matthews, Mongrel, Randall Packer, Alexandru Patatics, Philip Pocock/Gruppo A12/Udo Noll/Florian Wenz/ Daniel Burckhardt/Roberto Cabot/Wolfgang Staehle/Birgit Wiens/Jürgen Enge/Øthers, Paul Sermon, Scanner aka Robin Rimbaud, Jeffrey Shaw, Alexej Shulgin, Wolfgang Staehle, The User (Thomas McIntosh, Emmanuel Madan), Niek van de Steeg, Mark Trayle, Victoria Vesna, Anne Wellmer, Young Farmers Claim Future (Guy von Belle), zeitblom, Jody Zellen

*net_musician room* (curated by Golo Föllmer):
Sergi Jordà/La Fura dels Baus, Peter Traub, DJ Spooky, Klaus Gasteier, Res. Rocket, sha.

*theLounge* (curated by Walter van der Cruijsen):
Ascii Art Ensemble (Luka Frelih, Vuk Cosic, Walter van der Cruijsen), Critical Art Ensemble, Graphic Jam (Andy Deck/Mark Napier), Steven Greenwood, Institute for Applied Autonomy, Mark Napier, Old Boys Network, Redundant Technology Initiative, ®™ark, Maciej Wisniewski

*Medialabs:* Backspace, mikro e.V., Rhizome, Syndicate, Xchange

*The Net.Art Browser* (curated by Benjamin Weil):
Heath Bunting, Claude Closky, Vuk Cosic, Holger Friese/Max Kossatz, Olia Lialina, Antonio Muntadas, Mark Napier, Michael Samyn (Group Z), Vivian Selbo, Alexej Shulgin, Jake Tilson (The Cooker), Maciej Wisniewski

**Project Manager:**
Sabine Himmelsbach

**Assistants:**
Andrea Helbach, Katrin Mayer

**Technical Advice:**
Hartmut Bruckner

**Exhibition Design:**
Matthias Gommel, Kai Richter

**Grafic Design:**
Jürgen Betker, Frank Faßmer, Beate Kamecke, Birgit Schmidt

**Sponsoring:**
Ursula Eberhardt

**Website: http://www.zkm.de**
Tom Fürstner, Lydia Lindner, Christoph Pingel

# Karlsruhe

## Production and Technical Team:

Torsten Belschner, Gerhard Blechinger, Gabriele Blome, Annika Blunck, Claudius Böhm, Markus Bohnsle, Rudi Börner, Heike Borowski, Thomas Damer, Jürgen Enge, Birgit Fernengel, Barbara Filser, Claudia Gehrig, Jan Gerigk, Andreas Gloggengießer, Barbara Grimm, Ronny Haas, Martin Häberle, Derek Hauffen, Dirk Heesakker, Werner Hutzenlaub, Hartmut Jörg, Kerstin Jaunich, Volker Kuchelmeister, Peter Kuhn, Gisbert Laaber, Stefan von Laue, Regina Linder, Tabea Lurk, Adolf Mathias, Christiane Minter, Caroline Mössner, Alexander Noelle, Anne Ostertag, Thomas Poser, Klaus Reuter, Benedikt Rudolph, Andreas Schiffler, Joachim Schütze, Marco Sonntag, Bernhard Sturm, Silke Sutter, Christian Venghaus, Werner Wenzel, Christina Zartmann, Torsten Ziegler

## Sponsors:

COMICS Informationssysteme GmbH
Gesellschaft zur Förderung der Kunst und Medientechnologie e.V.
Sony
Bpd Raak Mediensysteme GmbH
Softline AG
planNET Systems GmbH
Schneider & Söhne
Südwestrundfunk (SWR)
Märklin & Cie GmbH
FEMA Farben und Putze GmbH
Presse Grosso Mende
S & G Automobilgesellschaft
Sparkasse Karlsruhe
Hospes Messebau GmbH
Rechenzentrum der Universität Karlsruhe
agi business media productions
Heinrich Heine Versand
Goethe Institut Caracas

# net_condition

**MECAD - Media Centre of Art & Design,**
Sabadell - Barcelona

**Curator:**
Claudia Giannetti

**Artists:**
Antoni Abad
Roberto Aguirrezabala
Jochen Gerz
Ricardo Iglesias
JODI
Konsum Art.Server
(Margarete Jahrman and Max Moswitzer)

**Assistants:**
Mela Dávila, Patricia Bofill

**Technical Advice:**
Salvador Limonero, ESDI

**Exhibition Design:**
UDDi/ESDI

**Website:**
http://www.mecad.org

**Webdesign:**
MECAD-Medialab

**Sponsor:**
ADAM Computer

# Barcelona

# net_condition

INTERCOMMUNICATION CENTER

**NTT InterCommunicationCenter (ICC), Tokyo**

**Curator:**
Ito Toshiharu

**Artists:**
Masaki Fujihata
Chihiro Minato
Motohiko Odani
Makoto Sei Watanabe

**Production Management:**
Ieuji Yoshihisa, Inui Yoshikazu
Production Assistant:
Oda Ryousuke, Usui Kazuyoshi

**Technical Advice:**
Kanechiku Hiroshi

**Internet Support:**
Ishikawa Shinichi, Tadocoro Atsushi

**Website: http://www.ntticc.or.jp/ special/net_condition/index_e.html**

**Webdesign:**
Tadokoro Atsushi

Tokyo

**42** is Cloed Baumgartner, Margit Franz, Moni Glahn, Cym Groenestijn, Sol Haring, Jogi Hofmüller, Reni Hofmüller, Katja Lamprecht, Katarina Pejovic, Andr'ea Siegl, Eva Ursprung

**Antoni Abad** started his artistic career in the field of sculpture, later expanding his activities to video and digital means. From 1986 on, his works have been exhibited in various solo exhibitions in Spain and abroad, and he has also taken part in many group exhibitions such as *Aperto*, and most recently in the *Venice Biennial*.

**Martine Aballéa** is an artist living and working in Paris. Her work has been exhibited in numerous group and individual exhibitions at Franklin Furnace (1978), P.S. 1 (1978-79), ARC Musee d'art Moderne de la Ville, Paris (1986), Institut Francais, Vienna (1996), and Art in General (1998).

**Roberto Aguirrezabala** obtained his degree in Fine Arts at the University of the Basque Country, specializing in sculpture and digital creation. He has taken part in various group exhibitions, and received several prizes, among them the Prize to the Best Young Artist at the 1998 edition of the Video Festival of Navarre, which he received for his net art project *Easyone*.

**Daniel García Andújar** began his artistic activity in the late 1980s, working mainly in the field of video, in projects of intervention in public spheres on the topics of racism and xenophobia, as well as the misuse of technology in surveillance systems. Since 1996 he has been developing the project *Technologies To The People®*, both on the net and with physical media (exhibitions, installations, CD-ROMs) and has been exhibited in *Some of my Favourite Websites are Art and Beyond Interface*. Other presentations of the project have taken place in *Un-Frieden/Discord: Sabotage of Realities* (Hamburg), *Desde la imagen* (Valencia), *Scattered Affinities* (New York and Madrid), *Reservate der Sehnsucht* (Dortmund), *Threats and Promises of Electronic Art* (Vigo), and in individual exhibitions like *interface@metronom.es* (Barcelona).

**ASCII Art Ensemble** is Vuk Cosic, Walter van der Cruijsen and Luka Frelih.

**Backspace - James Stevens**: I am a long term self employed person in fact I can make the dubious claim of never having had a real job... well not since I was 17...enough. Designer, Illustrator, Agent, Manager, Manipulator, Slacktivist, Immediatist..., I have always kept a keen eye on where development effort will yield positive product and though at times this has drawn me into difficult territory, I am happy with the path of progress to date and as ever holding open options for transformation and new work. Over the last four years work has been concentrated in the field of learning and technology in community. Backspace has been the platform for much of this and is a consistent point of reference, for the projects I am involved with and as gateway to the collaboration and collision with others. Its energy at times drives us forward and at others draws back, it is: luna and emotional, fragile and clumsy, almost invisible yet accommodating and invigorating.

**Tilman Baumgärtel** studied German Literature, Media and History at Heinrich-Heine-Universität in Düsseldorf and SUNY Buffalo (USA). From 1993 - 1995 he was editor at the publishing-house Verlag Rommerskirchen and is now a free lance writer in Berlin. He contributes to *Telepolis*, *Spiegel-Online*, *Konr@d*, *taz*, *InSight* and *Intelligent Agent*, is teaching at Universität Düsseldorf, and a researcher at Wissenschaftszentrum Berlin. He lectures and has made presentations at the Hochschule der Künste in Berlin, the Shedhalle Zürich, Volksbühne Berlin, Filmmuseum München, *Videofest* (Kassel), *Transmediale* (Berlin), etc. He recently published a book on the film maker Harun Farocki and a book on art on the internet, *Net-Art*.

**Giselle Beiguelman** (Brasil) is Ph.D. in History and a fellow of the VITAE Foundation program for the Arts, in the Literature field. She has been researching the cultural impact of the Internet and has published various works on Contemporary History. She was Curator of *Ex-Libris/Home Page* (Paço das Artes, São Paulo, 1996), among other exhibitions, and director of the CD-ROM *Urban Interventions 1.0* (1997), author of *For Whom the Bell Tolls?* (Ernest Hemingway and the Spanish Civil War) (1993) and co-author of *Classicism* (1999). Her latest work *The Book after the Book* is a hypertextual and visual essay, where criticism

and web art melts into the context of the net_reading/writing_condition

**Torsten Belschner** trained as a percussionist for 20th century music and graduated from the Technical University Berlin in musicology and philosophy with computer science. In the following years he established himself as a freelance sound designer at Pixelpark, Berlin. In 1995 he joined the ZKM Karlsruhe to continue his work in sound design and UNIX system administration. From 2000 on he will be back to freelancing, doing audio-consulting and production for different Expo2000 projects.

**David Blair** makes electronic films and lives in New York City. Currently he is working on a second film which is set in the USA and Japan. He is the creator of both the film and the www version of *Wax*.

**Joachim Blank & Karl Heinz Jeron** have been working together as "Blank & Jeron" since 1996. From 1993 on they have realised internet projects in an artistic and cultural context in various groupings. Besides their internet projects, they are at the moment working on hybrid projects, objects, installations, and events. In these they are dealing with strategies for information- and communication-recycling in the context of the 'information society.' Their works have been shown in numerous exhibitions including: *Ostranenie* (Dessau, 1993), *MedienBiennale* (Leipzig, 1994), *European Media Art Festival* (Osnabrück, 1994/96), *Ars Electronica* (Linz, 1995), *Telepolis* (Luxemburg, 1996), *DocumentaX* (Kassel, 1997), Neuer Berliner Kunstverein, (Berlin 1998), *Global Fun*, (Museum Schloß Morsbroich, Leverkusen), *Expo Destructo* (London, 1999), Shift e.V. (Berlin), *Ars Electronica* (Linz) - honorable mention in the category "interactive art."

The **Luther Blissett** Project is a collective of media activists that organized mediatic hoaxes and counter-information campaigns. Luther Blissett is a multiple name: whoever can use it in the most creative and freest way. S/he is an open-architecture pop star, a mass avatar on the media stage. The *net.INSTITUTE* is its urban and architectural implementation. The Aleph Group is a collective of students of the Bologna University that deals with media culture and criticism.

**Christa Blümlinger** is a communication scientist and film publicist living in Vienna and Paris. She studied mass communication media and communication science and French at the University of Salzburg, and political science at the Institut für Höhere Studien (Vienna). Since 1989 she has been teaching at the University of Vienna (i.a. film and media theory, Electronic Media, communication technologies, film analysis), has received a FWF travelling fellowship in Paris (1993-95), was a member of the selection committee of the *Duisburger Filmwoche* (1990-92), and was curator of the Austrian *Diagonale* film festival (1993-95). She is a member of Synema, Gesellschaft für Film und Medien (Vienna), and Sixpack-Film. She has given numerous lectures including at the Architectural Association (London), the Galerie Nationale du Jeu de Paume in Paris, and at the Universities of Paris III, Zurich and Marburg and is currently working on the research project "Sichtbares und Sagbares", on commission of the Bela-Balàzs Institut für Laufbildforschung (Vienna). Her media and film theory focuses on the relationship of film, photography, video, the future of images, documentary and avant-garde film.

**Natalie Bookchin** is an artist living in Los Angeles and working on and off the net, in many collaborative and solo endeavors. She does not have her own domain but is currently organizing a lecture series in Los Angeles with her mother institution, California Institute of the Arts that will feature many prominent domain holders. The series is entitled "net.net.net: net art, net activism and net culture."

**Pierre Bourdieu** is a sociologist and professor at the Collège de France. He is the author of *Acts of Resistance: Against the Tyranny of the Market, Homo Academicus, Language and Symbolic Power, On Television,* and *Practical Reason: On the Theory of Action.*

**Dave Bruckmayr** (Austria) is a Media Conceptionalist and Head of BusinessMachine. **Gaylord Aulke** (Germany) is a retired hacker and CEO of agi business media productions.

**Heath Bunting**'s digital works have traveled around the developed world. He organised digital chaos, held in a pub in Bath in 1996 and Anti with E at Backspace in London the following year. Intentionally difficult to pin down, he has presented works (including at *documentaX*) and lectured throughout Europe. Each month the e-mail address changes as an attempt to subvert investment and rationalisation.

**Manuel Castells** is Professor of City and Regional Planning at UC Berkeley. His current research interests include information technology and social change in a comparative perspective, particularly in the geographical areas of the United States, Western Europe, Russia, the Asian Pacific, and Latin America. Professor Castells received his LLB, two Masters degrees in Sociology, and a Ph.D., and Doctorat d'Etat in Sociology from the University of Paris. He is a member of the European Academy. His books include *Technopoles of the World* (with P. Hall; Routledge, 1994); *The New Global Economy in the Information Age* (Penn State University Press, 1993); *The City and the Grassroots* (Berkeley: University of California Press, 1983), and the three-part series, *The Network Society* (Blackwell, 1997).

**Claude Closky** is an artist who has shown in numerous exhibitions including: 1999: *Claude Closky* (CCC, Tours), *Tatouages* (CNEAI, Chatou), *Claude Closky* (Frac Limousin, Limoges), *Weekend* (The Deep Gallery, Tokyo). 1998: O. S. G. (Frac Haute-Normandie, Rouen), *Les aoûtiens* (Galerie Jennifer Flay, Paris), *Photography as Concept* (Foto-Triennale, Esslingen), *Fines de Claire* (Galerie Mehdi Chouakri, Berlin).

**Janet Cohen, Keith Frank, and Jon Ippolito** have been agreeing to disagree since their first adversarial collaboration, *Casting Lots*, in 1993. Cohen, Frank, and Ippolito foreground the conflict inherent in collaboration by basing each work on a particular competitive event, such as marking territory by spitting pins, targeting an opponent with projectiles, or evaluating each other's ideas for an artwork. Cohen, Frank, and Ippolito's digital work has been presented at Sandra Gering Gallery Online and at *SIGGRAPH 97*; in 1997 they were awarded a Louis Comfort Tiffany award for their body of work. They live and work in New York.

**Nicolas Collins** was born in New York City and studied composition with Alvin Lucier at Wesleyan University. He has performed as a composer and presented audio installations throughout the United States, Europe, South America and Japan. His music is represented on many recordings. A pioneer in the use of microcomputers in live performance, Collins has made extensive use of 'home-made' electronic circuitry, radio, found sound material, and transformed musical instruments. His recent work emphasizes spoken word, and combines idiosyncratic electronics with conventional acoustic instruments. Collins is also active as a curator of performance and installation art, having produced projects for PS1, The Clocktower, The Kitchen, the Relâche ensemble, STEIM, De IJsbreker, Podewil and the *Internationalen Musikfestwochen* Luzern. In 1992 he relocated from New York to the Netherlands, where he was, for three years, Visiting Artistic Director of Stichting STEIM in Amsterdam. In 1996-97 he was a DAAD composer-in-residence in Berlin. In September 1997 Collins was named Editor-in-Chief of *Leonardo Music Journal*.

**convex tv**. Since 1996 the Berlin based convex tv. collective has worked in different media territories, their interfaces, conditions and cross-overs. convex tv. combines radio-broadcasts, on air, and on-line with activities on site, thus folding the spheres of mediatic and actual presence, of process and product. convex tv. is regularly streaming live audio on the internet. Its online archive now covers approximately 70 hours of journalistic, technocultural and artistic programs. Recently convex tv. has launched a project which deals with the questions of 'formats' on both the practical and conceptual level.

**Shane C. Cooper** is a software engineer and an artist. As an engineer, he specializes in high-end virtual reality applications, including virtual characters, computer aided design, motion capture, and the internet. He has developed several art works, some of which have been shown with the ICC in Tokyo (Japan), at the *Spaletto Festival* in Charleston South Carolina (USA), with Graham Nash and DEVO in Los Angeles (USA), with George Coates in San Francisco (USA), and most recently at the ZKM in Karlsruhe (Germany). Currently, he develops applications in the field of real-time surgical simulation.

**Vuk Cosic** has been active in a variety of art endeavors in the last five years - mostly doing net.art. Currently he is discovering the field of Low Tech New Media. He has done too many shows to mention (basically everywhere) and has been to all those festivals and symposia. He also writes, publishes, and edits.

**Jordan Crandall** is an artist and media theorist. He is currently preparing his first solo museum show, curated by Peter Weibel, opening January 2000 at the Neue Galerie am Landesmuseum Joanneum in Graz, Austria. An anthology of his critical writing on technology and culture, published by Neue Galerie and DuMont Verlag, Cologne, will be released in March 2000. Crandall is also preparing his first film, a 'systems film' called *DRIVE*. Crandall is founding Editor of *Blast* <http://www.blast.org> and director of the X Art Foundation, New York. His current book is *Suspension* (*documenta X*, 1997).

**Critical Art Ensemble (CAE)** is a collective of five tactical media practitioners of various specializations including computer graphics, film/video, photography, text art, book art, and performance. Formed in 1987, CAE's focus has been on the exploration of the intersections between art, critical theory, technology, and political activism. The collective has performed and produced projects for an international audience, and has written three books: *The Electronic Disturbance*, and its companion text, *Electronic Civil Disobedience and Other Unpopular Ideas*, and *Flesh Machine: Cyborgs, Designer Babies, and New Eugenic Consciousness*.

**Walter van der Cruijsen** is artist, curator and founder of desk.nl, one of the first independent media labs in Europe (1994) and one of the founding members of the ASCII Art Ensemble. He has been a catalyst for net-activism and net-art and is currently forming a new media initiative, bootstrap, in Berlin.

**Douglas Davis** is an artist, educator, performer, author, and theorist. He is known as a pioneer in fields that use both advanced and traditional technology, including interactive websites, long-distance performances linking 'real' and 'virtual' sources, high-density volumetric imagery, video-casting/installations, print-making, drawing, and photography, as well as innovative 'objects' and installations. He has also used satellites, film, radio, and vintage stereopticons. With Joseph Beuys and Nam June Paik he created the first live global satellite broadcast of video performance art in 1977, for *documenta 6*.

**Andy C. Deck** is an artist working with the development of collaborative process in the context of art and connectivity. Through short films, calendars, games, interactive installations, and multi-user drawing spaces, he has sought consistently to involve art in daily life and to challenge orthodoxies of art distribution and reception. His works have been featured in *THING.NET*, New York (1999), *Turbulence.org* (1999), *Millennium Film Journal* (1999), *Bostoncyberarts.org* (1999), Machida City Graphics Arts Museum, Tokyo (1999), *Prix Ars Electronica* (1998), Kentler International Drawing Space (1998), *Art By Numbers* (1998), *Mac Classics* (1997), and the *New York Short Film and Video Festival* (1996). Developmental work for ongoing projects was made possible in part by the Ocean of Know and the Ecole Nationale Supérieure des Arts Décoratifs, Paris.

**Timothy Druckrey** is an independent curator and writer concerned with the history and theory of media and the transformation of representation, communication, and art in an increasingly electronic culture. He co-edited *Culture on the Brink: Ideologies of Technology* and edited *Iterations: The New Image*, *Electronic Culture: Technology and Visual Representation*, and *Ars Electronica: Facing the Future*. He lectures internationally about the social impact of digital media, the transformation of representation, and communication in interactive and networked environments. Currently he is editing a series of books for MIT Press - *Electronic Culture: History, Theory, Practice*.

**esc to begin** is a unique department at the ZKM. Founded by Bernd Diemer in January 1999, nine young artists and programmers are engaged in the development of experimental media artworks. The main goal is the application of transdisciplinary scientific research to new fields in media art. Esc to begin is Bernd Diemer, Martina Haitz, Andreas Schiffler, Meike Schmidt, Andreas Krach, Sue Machert, Guillaume Stagnaro, Arne Grässer, Susen Kümmel.

**etoy** is a successful incubator officially incorporated in 1994. the etoy.CORPORATION is owned by international art collectors, venture capitalists, the etoy.MANAGEMENT, and 1800 TOYWAR.soldiers. etoy is a typical early mover (online since 1994) and developed rapidly into a controversial market leader in the field of experimental internet entertainment. etoy blurs the lines between art, corporate identity, fashion, technology, community research and business to create a massive impact on global markets and culture. the *digital hijack* (www.hijack.org 1996) was the first etoy.HIT (1.5 million hostages on the internet) followed by spectacular stunts such as *protected by etoy* (museum of modern art san francisco 1998), the etoy.IPO and TOYWAR (www.toywar.com 1999/2000). since 1997 etoy.TANKS (12 meter long standardized windowless shipping containers) build the mobile and multifunctional etoy.OFFICE-SYSTEM (SAN DIEGO, SAN FRANCISCO, NEW YORK, ZURICH, VIENNA, BUDAPEST and MONZA). the etoy.CORPORATION will never sell products. etoy sells itself in order to finance etoy.OPERATIONS, etoy.TANK-LOGISTICS and etoy.MARKETING). all 640.000 available etoy.SHARE-UNITS on the market equal 100% of the etoy.BRAND&CULTURE-VALUE. for information on investing in etoy: >www.etoy.com< >invest@etoy.com<

**Ken Feingold** received his MFA in Post-Studio Art from Cal Arts in 1976. His artworks have been exhibited by museums and galleries internationally, including the Museum of Modern Art, the Whitney Museum of American Art, the New Museum of Contemporary Art, and Postmasters Gallery, New York; Centre Georges Pompidou, Paris; ZKM|Center for Art and Media, Karlsruhe; NTT InterCommunication Center (ICC), Tokyo; Kiasma Museum of Contemporary Art, Helsinki, and numerous others. He has received fellowships from the National Endowment for the Arts, the Japan-US Friendship Commission, and the Jerome Foundation, and recent commissions from the *ICC Biennial*, Tokyo (1997); Cardiff Bay Arts Trust (1998-2002), and Kiasma Museum of Contemporary Art, Helsinki (1999). He lives in New York City.

**Golo Föllmer** was trained as a piano-maker, studied musicology and communication studies (Technische Universität Berlin) as well as Broadcast Communication Arts (San Francisco State University). He has produced experimental pieces for radio, pieces for tape recorders and sound installations, mainly for public spaces, and has contributed to books, magazines and radio programs about sound art and contemporary music, and worked for festivals, among them *sonambiente* (Berlin, 1996) and *Inventionen 98 - 50 years of Musique concrète* (Berlin, 1998). At the moment he is assistant lecturer for musicology at the Martin-Luther-Universität Halle-Wittenberg and is writing a doctoral thesis about musical systems in the internet.

**Holger Friese** trained as a photographer and studied Visual Communication. He has exhibited widely and has had solo shows at *Nachlaß - Eine Retrospektive von Holger Friese und Marco Lietz*, Rastätte Aachen (retrospective 1999),and *in wysiwyg version#2*, Neuer Aachener Kunstverein (1998) and has been included in group shows in *documentaX* (Kassel, 1997), *Typische Handbewegung*, Kunstraum - Lothringer Straße, Munich, *Entropie zu Hause - Sammlung Schürmann*, Suermondt Ludwig Museum, Aachen (1997), *sub -fiction, 3. Werkleitz Biennale*, (Werkleitz, 1997), *Anticipation - Version 4*, Centre Saint Gervais, Genf (1997), *Reload*, shift e.V., Berlin (1999), *net_condition*, ZKM, Karlsruhe (1999), KUNSTBANK, Berlin zusammen mit Mona Ja (1999).

**Tom Fürstner** studied economics and acquired his skills in the field of multimedia autodidactically. In the mid-1980s he developed programs and programing languages which linked hypertext to Artificial Intelligence. He planned, designed, and programmed more than 20 CD-ROM titles for various Austrian and international companies, and developed the first prototypes for interactive television for Alcatel, Oracle, and the BBC. As technical director and director of product development at ORF Online he developed the website of the Österreichischer Rundfunk (Austrian broadcasting company) into one of the most successful sites in Europe. Currently he is head of the Online-department at the ZKM.

**Masaki Fujihata** completed a masters program in art at Tokyo National University of Fine Arts & Music in 1980. While using technology as a medium, Fujihata is involved in a wide range of activities for manifesting the relation between the environment and human intelligence. Formerly, professor of the Faculty of Environmental Information, Keio University, he also spent one year in Germany as artist-in-residence at the Institute for Visual Media at ZKM. Currently he is a Professor at the Tokyo National University of Fine Arts & Music.

**Jochen Gerz** studied sinology, prehistory and English Literature at the Universities of Cologne and Basle, has worked as a journalist, publicist, and publisher. His first book, *Footing* (Paris Editions Approches) was published in 1968. Since the mid-1970s he has made numerous videos and had many installations including, German Pavilion, *Venice Biennial* (1976), *documentaVI and VIII* (1977, 1987), *the Monument Against Fascism* (with Esther Shalev-Gerz, 1986), *2146 Stones-Monument Against Racism* in Saarbrücken (1993), *The Feliferhof Geese* (1997).

**Rishab Aiyer Ghosh** is an economist, consultant and journalist concerned with questions of the Indian telecom and IT market and is International and Managing Editor of the peer-reviewed Internet journal *First Monday*.

**Claudia Giannetti** is a specialist in Media Art and Director of MECAD (Media Centre of Art and Design), and of Electronic Art and Digital Design on ESDI - Escuela Superior de Diseño, Sabadell-Barcelona, Spain. In 1993 she co-founded and directed the L´Angelot Association for Contemporary Culture in Barcelona, the first space in Spain specialized in Electronic Art. She is a writer and curator of cultural events and media art exhibitions, has taught and given seminars at several universities, has given several lectures on the subject of art and the new technologies at international centers and museums, and has written several publications in specialized journals and exhibition catalogues. She edited the books *Media Culture* (Barcelona, 1995), *Art in the Electronic Age - Perspectives of a New Aesthetic* (Barcelona, 1997), and *Ars Telematica - Telecommunication, Internet and Cyberspace* (1998).

**Johannes Goebel** is the founding director of ZKM's Institute for Music and Acoustics. In 1989 he organized the first *MultiMediale* festival for ZKM, and since 1990 has established the institute as one of the foremost sites for experimental music and technology. In 1992 he was guest professor for electro-acoustic music at the music-academy in Graz. In 1996 he co-directed the Center for Computer Research in Music and Acoustics (CCRMA), Stanford University, for six months, having been affiliated with CCRMA since 1977. Between 1988 and 1990 he was responsible for the change-over to electronic music 'engraving' at Schott music publishers. In 1986, he started to produce the worldwide first CD-series dedicated to computer music in conjunction with CCRMA and the German record label WERGO. Outside of the digital domain he has among other activities been designing and building instruments out of wood and metal, playing improvised music and cooperating with performers, architects and visual artists in intermedia-projects.

**Ken Goldberg** is an artist and Associate Professor of Engineering at UC Berkeley, where he founded the Art, Technology, and Culture Colloquium. Goldberg was named a National Science Foundation Presidential Faculty Fellow in 1995. His net art installations have appeared in the Ars Electronica Center, the Walker Center and the *ICC Biennial '99* in Tokyo. Goldberg is currently editing two books on Internet Robots for MIT Press due out in 2000. His Ouija 2000 telerobotic installation will be project #186 in the Matrix Program at the Berkeley Art Museum, opening in January 2000. Bob Farzin is an artist and undergraduate at UC Berkeley, where he paints and studies engineering.

**Steven Greenwood** completed a Bachelor of Fine Arts at the University of New South Wales College of Fine Arts and received a DAAD arts scholarship from 1994 to 1997. He completed a Masters in Media Art from the Hochschule für Gestaltung, Karlsruhe and has taken part in various exhibitions both group and solo, including *OSTranenie 97*, Dessau, and Medium - eine Welt dazwischen in the Museum für Gestaltung Zürich, 1998.

**Reinhold Grether** wrote with "Unleavened Breads," a widely discussed article about the Frankfurt art scene (*Wolkenkratzer 5/87*). After studying economics, politics, and aesthetics he earned a Ph.D. in 1994 with *Longing for World Culture: Transgression and Deletion in the Second Ecumenical Age*. He collaborated with Manfred Stumpf to edit the *Sketch-book of the icon "Entry in Jerusalem"* (Cantz 1996). He has written numerous publications on the Net, among them *World Revolution After Flusser* and *Net.art and the Global Imaginary*. He holds an assistant professorship with Constance University to handle the project "net.science."

**Heidi Grundmann** is a curator and consultant at the interface between the old and new media. In 1987 she developed Kunstradio, a radio program of original artworks for the radio medium, for the ORF (Austrian Broadcasting Corp.).

**Marina Grzinic** is doctor of philosophy and works as researcher at the Institute of Philosophy at the ZRC SAZU, Ljubljana. She has published extensively on issues of media, society, and visual art in international magazines and books. Her most recent book curated by her (and Adele Eisenstein), published in 1999, addresses media, cyberfeminism and post-socialism. Grzinic also works as a freelance media theorist, art critic and curator. **Aina Smid** works and lives in Ljubljana; art historian (Faculty of Philosophy, Ljubljana); she works as contributing editor of an art-design magazine. Marina Grzinic and Aina Smid have been involved with video art since 1982. They have collaborated in more than 30 video art projects, made a short film, numerous video and media installations, a CD-ROM project for *ARTINTACT 4* (ZKM, Karlsruhe), and several art-net sites. In their more than 17 years of collaborative media work, Grzinic and Smid, have presented and exhibited their video works and video installations in more than 100 festivals and have received several major awards for their video productions.

**Jürgen Habermas** is professor emeritus for philosophy at the Johann Wolfgang Goethe University in Frankfurt/Main. He has written numerous books. Among them: *Between Facts and Norm: Contributions to a Discourse Theory of Law and Democracy, Communication and* the Evolution of Society, Justification and Application: Remarks on Discourse Ethics, Structural Transformation of the Public Sphere: An Inquiry into a Category of Bourgeois Society, and Legitimation Crisis.

**Edward S. Herman**, Professor Emeritus of Finance, Wharton School, University of Pennsylvania, is the author of a number of books, including *Manufacturing Consent* (1988, with Noam Chomsky), *Triumph of the Market* (1996), and *The Global Media* (1997, with Robert McChesney).

**Lynn Hershman Leeson** has worked in photography, film, video and electronic sculpture. Her 53 videotapes and seven interactive installations have garnered many international awards, including First Prize Vigo Spain and First Prize Crystal Trophy, Montbelliard France, the ZKM/Siemens Media Arts Award and in 1998 was honored with the Flintridge Foundation Award for Lifetime Achievement in the Visual Arts. In 1999 she won the Someone to Watch Award sponsored by the IFP's Independent Spirit Award, The National Educational Media Award for Innovative Technology and the prestigious Golden Nica Prix Ars Electronica. Her first feature film, *Conceiving Ada*, was shown at the 1998 *Sundance Film Festival*, the *Toronto International Film Festival*, the *Berlin International Film Festival*, *Montreal Festival of New Cinema*, and was released by Fox Lorber in February, 1999. She is the editor of *Clicking In: Hotlinks To A Digital Culture* published in 1996 by Bay Press. A new monograph on her work titled *Lynn Hershman, Private Eye* will be published in the year 2000 by U.C. Press.

**Markus Huemer** lives and works in Cologne and has exhibited in numerous one person exhibitions from 1991 - 1999, including: Galerie Posthof, Linz (1991), Galerie A4, Wels (1992), Galerie Trabant, Vienna (1995), *steirischer herbst '97: 2000 minus 3 - ArtSpace plus Interface*, Neue Galerie am Landesmuseum Joanneum, Graz (1997), *If (Subject = Virtual Subject ; Symbolic Culture ; 0) [MAOD]* at Nassauischer Kunstverein, Wiesbaden (1998), *The Rules are noGame* at Galerie Michael Janssen, Cologne (1998), Künstlerhaus Palais Thurn und Taxis,

Bregenz (1998), *This Dangerous Supplement* at Kunstverein Nürnberg, Albrecht Dürer Gesellschaft, Nürnberg (1999). He also writes and publishes theory.

**h|u|m|b|o|t** is a 5-year (1999 - 2004) choreographic installation project connecting a loose menagerie of architects, artists, datatects, hackers and writers to intermittent travel-as-art situations in equatorial America and OtherWhere on the new New Continent, taking the explorer and mapmaker Alexander von Humboldt's book *Personal Narrative of a Journey to the Equinoctial Regions of the New Continent (1799 - 1804)* as its topos. Hyperconfigured as our 'script' using artificial neural network Kohonen mapping Humboldt's chronicle gets eventually buried under sediments of contemporary fictional and documentary hypermedia. Net users sift through dynamic layers of Humboldt and h|u|m|b|o|t material, leaving traces, pictured as landscape in a virtual topography (cyberatlas) of unfolding h|u|m|b|o|t situations.

**I/O/D** is a group based in London. They maintain an ongoing archive of work, free to download, at >http://www.backspace.org/iod<

**Ricardo Iglesias** obtained his degree in Philosophy at the Universidad Autónoma de Madrid, and continued his studies in the field of digital production. He co-founded the interdisciplinary group Proyecto ß that created CD-ROMs and installations. He has taught courses on media arts at numerous institutions.

**Timothée Ingen-Housz** trained in painting, photography and Audiovisual studies at ENSAD (Paris). He is a fellow at KHM in Cologne.

The **Institute for Applied Autonomy** was founded in 1998 as a technological research and development organization dedicated to the cause of individual and collective self-determination. Its mission is to study the forces and structures which effect human autonomy and to develop technologies which serve this need.

**Margarete Jahrmann (Konsum Art.Server)** studied at the University for Angewandte Kunst, Vienna and has worked X3D, Multiusergames, net_art,

Art_servers, DJ lectures, Net-Concepts and RL/Online-performances. In 1996 she co-founded the Konsum Art.Server, and is co-editor (with Christa Schneebauer) of the book *Intertwinedness, Reflecting the Structure of the Net*. She is a lecturer for Web3D programming-languages at the University for Applied Arts, Vienna, and was guest professor for hybrid-media at the University for Arts and Industrial Design, Linz (1999) and guest-lecturer at the Rensselaer Polytechnic Institute, New York (1999). She has participated in *Siggraph 99*, Los Angeles, *OpenX*, *Ars Electronica 99*, *net_condition steirischer herbst 99* and ZKM, *Synworld 99* at Museumsquartier Vienna, *VRML_Art Show 99* at Heinz Nixdorf Museum Paderborn, *European Media Festival Osnabrueck 98/96*, *documentaX*, *1st Cyberfeminst Internationale 97, steirischer herbst 97*, Graz, *Dutch Electronic Arts Festival 96*, *Digital Dive*, V2 Rotterdam, Museum for Angewandte Kunst Wien, MAK- Gallery, *medien-apparate-kunst 96*.

**JODI**: auxlook "1" m_pitch "0.022" sensitivity "8" lookstrafe "0.00" lookspring "0.00" cl_backspeed "400.00" cl_fwdspeed "400.00" _cl_color "0.00" _cl_name "monitor" _snd_mixahead "0.1" bgmvolume "0.00" volume "1.00" nosound "0.00" r_showflames "0.00" viewsize "120" vid_rave_ngn "3Dfx SST-1" vid_skip_lines "0.00" vid_pixeldouble "1.00" vid_monitor_height "480.00" vid_monitor_width "640.00" vid_game_height "240.00" vid_game_width "320.000" vid_switch_monitor "1.00" enable_tcpip "0.00" _config_modem_hup "AT H" _config_modem_init "" _config_modem_clear "ATZ" _config_modem_dialtype "T" _config_com_modem "1" _config_com_baud "57600" _config_com_irq "4" _config_com_port "0x3f8" hostname "MONITOR" saved4 "0" saved3 "0" saved2 "0" saved1 "0" savedgamecfg "0" gamma "1.000000" crosshair "0"

**Diana Johnstone** has written widely on European politics in both English and French, for a number of periodicals ranging from *Le Monde diplomatique* to *The Nation*. In the 1970s, while working for the Agence France Presse, she published her own newsletter, The Owl, and has since been European editor of the

Chicago-based weekly *In These Times* (1979-1990) and press officer of the Green Group in the European Parliament (1990-1996). She is currently assistant editor of the Paris-based quarterly *Dialogue* and is working on a book on economic globalization and the disintegration of Yugoslavia.

**Knowbotic Research (Kr+cF)** is an artist group based in Cologne and Zurich (Yvonne Wilhelm, Christian Hübler, Alexander Tuchacek). They build experimental and tactical interfaces for local and trans-local urban environments. They founded *Mem_Brane*, a laboratory for media strategies, and have developed *Dialogue with the Knowbotic South* (1995), *Anonymous Muttering* (1996), and *IO_Dencies* (1997).

**Darij Kreuh** is a sculptor and postgraduate student in sculpture and video at the Academy of Fine Arts in Ljubljana. His work has been exhibited at the Gallery Slon (1990), the gallery Cerkev, Zagreb (1991), at the *Ljubljana Biennial of Young Artists* (1991), and in numerous other exhibitions.

**Marc Lafia** is an artist, filmmaker and the co-founder of PlanetLive, Inc., an Internet media company providing an ambient platform to the world. Lafia is the curatorial and editorial director of a new PlanetLive Production, *ArtandCulture.com*, a complex contextual engine to the worlds of arts and culture. Lafia's early films, *auto-re-tour* and *fini-la guerre*, investigate the tensions between narrativity and the pure surface of film. His recent 35m feature film, *Suitcase*, uses visual saturation and mood as it interweaves varied temporalities to explore a modern Oedipus. He lives and works in San Francisco, California.

**Olia Lialina** was born in Moscow. She is a net.artist, critic, curator, and professor of Networks and Online Environments at Merz Akademie, Stuttgart. She also is the founder of Art.Teleportacia gallery. From 1996 - 1998 she was the director of CINE FANTOM film club, the co-organizer of CINE FANTOM festival, and author of lectures "History of Parallel Film," and contributing editor of four *Russian Video Art and Alternative Video* compilations.

**Gerhard Johann Lischka** is a freelance cultural philosopher, writer, and teacher. He is editor of the series *um9* and has organized numerous exhibitions and television programs. His books include *Die Schönheit: Superästhetik, Kulturkunst, die Medienfalle, Über die Mediatisierung: Medien und ReMedien*.

**Lev Manovich** is an artist, a theorist and a critic of new media. He was born in Moscow where he studied fine arts and architecture and participated in the underground art shows. Moving to New York in 1981, he began working in 3D computer animation in 1984 at Digital Effects. Manovich received an M.A. in experimental psychology from New York University (1988) and a Ph.D. in Visual and Cultural Studies from the University of Rochester (1993). He is now an Assistant Professor in the Department of Visual Arts, University of California, San Diego where he teaches studio and theory classes in new media. Currently he is working on a book entitled *The Language of New Media* for the MIT Press.

**Jenny Marketou** received her Masters Degree in Fine Arts at Pratt Institute in New York City where she still lives. Since 1993, she has been teaching at Cooper Union School of Art and The New School for Social Research in New York City. Since 1993, she has been working in different media, including photography, video, video events and installations, involving dj's and performers, public performances, the wide world web, networked telepresence environments and digital technologies. *SMELL.BYTES TM* was premiered at the 1998 Biennial of São Paulo, Brazil. Some of the other international venues that have shown her work include, *net_condition*, ZKM (1999), The Queens Museum of Art, New York (1999), *MANIFESTA 1*, Witte de With, Rotterdam (1996) *ART & IDEA*, Mexico City (1997), National Museum of Women in the Arts, Washington DC (1997).

**Armand Mattelart** is professor of information and communication sciences at the Université de Paris-VIII, Saint-Denis. He is the author of numerous books including *Mass Media, Ideology, Ideology and the Revolutionary Movement, Multinational Corporations and the Control of Culture, Mapping World Communication, The Invention of*

Communication and Networking the World 1794 - 2000.

**Robert W. McChesney** is Associate Professor of Journalism and Mass Communication, University of Wisconsin. He published *Telecommunications, Mass Media and Democracy: The Battle for the Control of U.S. Broadcasting, 1928-1935* (1993) and (with Edward S. Herman) *The Global Media, The New Missionaries of Corporate Capitalism* (1997).

**mikro e.V.** (Initiative for the Advancement of Media Cultures) was founded in Berlin in March 1998 by fifteen artists, theoreticians, journalists, organizers and other cultural producers. What brings this multi-faceted group together is the need for a critical discussion of the cultural, social and political impact of media in today's society. The initiative instigates and realizes public discussions, conferences, exhibitions, publications, and other activities dealing with the artistic, political and cultural applications of new media. Besides the monthly mikro.lounges (video screenings, lectures, panel discussions, DJ sets) which take place at the Berlin WMF club and which deal with specific questions of media culture, mikro e.V. also (co-)organized events like the *Wizards of OS-Conference* or the *Berlin net.radio days 98*.

**Chihiro Minato** graduated from the Department of Political Economy, Waseda University. In 1982 he received The Gasei Scholarship from Argentina and lived and traveled in South America. In 1985 he moved to Paris and worked as a photographer and critic. In 1995 he joined Tama Art University and is currently associate professor. He was awarded the Suntory Prize for Social Sciences and Humanities for Memory - *Power of Recall* (Kodansha, 1996) and the Konica Plaza Award for Equator in 1991. In collaboration with Moriwaki Hiroyuki he exhibited *Garden of Memory* in the *Potable Sacred Grounds* exhibition in the ICC (Tokyo) in 1998.

**Mongrel** is a mixed bunch of people and machines working to celebrate the methods of an 'ignorant' and 'filthy' London street culture. We make socially engaged cultural products employing any and all technological advantages that we can lay our hands on. We have dedica-

ted ourselves to learning technological methods of engagement, which means we pride ourselves on our ability to program, engineer and build our own software and custom hardware. The Core Members are Mervin Jarman, Matsuko Yokokoji, Richard Pierre-Davis and Grahame Harwood. We are as much about hip-hop as about hacking. Mongrel makes ways for those locked out of the mainstream to gain strength without getting locked into power structures. Staying Hardcore means that Mongrel can get the benefit of sharing the skills and intelligence of people and scenes in similar situations, as well as dealing with other kinds of structures on our own terms.

**Vincent Mosco** is Professor in the School of Journalism and Communication at Carleton University, Ottawa, Canada. He also holds appointments in the Department of Sociology and in the Institute for Political Economy. Professor Mosco received his Ph.D. in Sociology from Harvard University and continues to work with the Harvard Program on Information Resources Policy. He is the author of four books and editor or co-editor of seven books on telecommunication policy, mass media, computers and information technology. His most recent is *The Political Economy of Communication: Rethinking and Renewal* (London: Sage). Editions have been translated and published in China, Spain and Korea. His articles have appeared in *Theory and Society, Telecommunication Policy,* the *Journal of Communication, The Information Society,* the *Columbia Journalism Review, Le Monde Diplomatique, Critical Studies in Mass Communication,* and the *Media Studies Journal,* among others. His current research addresses social, cultural, and spatial relations in post-industrial high technology districts.

**Max Moswitzer (Konsum Art.Server)** specializes in 3D simulations and arts-server design and configurations and in 1996 was a founder of Konsum Art.Server, and has developed interactive installations, telematic setups, 99 ASCIIkarre, OK Center of contemporary arts Linz and has participated in numerous international festivals and art shows including: MAK, Museum for Angewandte Kunst Vienna 1996; *European Media Art Festival Osnabrück* 1996; *Dutch Electronic Arts Festival*

Rotterdam 1996; Media Research Foundation Budapest1997; *steirischer herbst 1997,* 1998 *Bitstream* Enschede, Installation at Public netbase Vienna, 1999 3D Game for *Synreal World* Vienna and *OpenX, Ars Electronica 99.*

**Antoni Muntadas** is a multidisciplinary artist born in Barcelona and living in New York. He studied at the School of Industrial Engineering in Barcelona. He has taught at the University of California in San Diego, the Fine Arts School, Bordeaux, the MIT CAVS, the School of Fine Arts, Paris, and at the University of Sao Paulo, among others. He has received prizes and scholarships from the Rockefeller and Guggenheim Foundations, the National Endowment for the Arts, the Centre National d'Arts Plastiques and has been resident artist in Rochester (US), Banff (Canada), and Sydney (Australia). His work has been shown in the Paris, Venice, Sao Paulo, and Lyon Biennales, at *documentaX* (Kassel), at the MoMA and Guggenheim (New York), the Modern Art Museum of the City of Paris, the Fine Arts Palace in Brussels, MNCARS in Madrid, IVAM in Valencia, Kent Gallery, the Store Front for Art and Architecture in New York, and the List Center at MIT.

**Mark Napier** is a painter turned digital artist. Since 1995 he has created a wide range of internet projects including *Digital Landfill, The Shredder, The Distorted Barbie,* and *Potatoland.org,* his studio on the web. Noted for his innovative use of the web as an art medium and for his open ended evolving artwork, Napier's work has been reviewed in the *New York Times Online, HotWired, Art Forum, Publish, Yahoo magazine,* and the *Village Voice.* His work has been awarded honorable mention by *Ars Electronica* 98 and has been chosen for WNET's *ReelNY* project, the *ASCI Digital Art 98* show, and the Berlin *Transmediale* Festival 99.

**Motohiko Odani** graduated from the Department of Art, Tokyo National University of Fine Arts and Music in 1995 and completed a masters program in 1997. His works have been widely exhibited in Tokyo at P-House (1997), Röntgen Kunstraum (1998), Spiral/Tokyo (1996), Tokyo National University (1997) and the Ueno Royal Museum (1999). They have also been shown at Maria Arte Contemporanea, Italy (1998), and at Art Sonj e Museum, Seoul, Korea (1999).

The **old boys network (OBN)** came together in the summer of 1997 as the first cyberfeminist alliance. Basing itself on a politics of dissent, the old boys network works through personal and media networks on cyberfeminist strategies in the fields of gender and the net. In addition to its work on the theory, praxis, aesthetics and politics of cyberfeminism, the core group of old boys (currently eight) develops various distribution, connection, and meeting formats. As well as maintaing a website (www.obn.org) and a mailing list, obn organized/s regular live presentations, lectures, workshops, and symposia for face-to-face exchange, including the *First Cyberfeminist International* in the Hybrid Workspace in the context of *documentaX* (Kassel, September 1997) and the Next Cyberfeminist International in connection with *Next5MinutesFestival* (Rotterdam and Amsterdam, March 1999). Documentation of these activities and further materials have been published thus far in two readers which are available from OBN. In preparation is a book with the provisional title *Cyberfeminism: Next Protocols*, expected publication date 2000. The current core-group: Cornelia Sollfrank, Hamburg/Berlin (Germany), Susanne Ackers, Berlin (D), Julianne Pierce, Sydney (Australia), Helene von Oldenburg, Rastede/Hamburg (D), Claudia Reiche, Hamburg (D), Faith Wilding, Pittsburgh (USA), Yvonne Volkart, Zurich (CH), Verena Kuni, Frankfurt/M. (D)

**Randall Packer**'s work as a composer and media artist has focused on the integration of live performance, technology and the interdisciplinary arts. As founding Artistic Director of Zakros InterArts, he has produced, directed and created critically acclaimed multimedia theater works including *Originale* by Karlheinz Stockhausen (1990) and *Arches* (1991), performed at Theater Artaud in San Francisco. In 1997, he completed the collaborative sound-text work, *Through Invisible Cities*, performed at the Yerba Buena Center for the Arts in San Francisco and released on CD (1998). *Pleasure Island*, an on-line multi-user virtual community was presented at the USC School of Cinema's Interactive Frictions Conference in 1999. Former director of

the San Francisco State University Multimedia Studies Program, he is currently on the faculty of the Department of Art Practice at the University of California, Berkeley where he teaches the history, theory and practice of digital media. He is also currently at work on a series of books focusing on the history of multimedia, to be published by W.W. Norton in 2000.

**Alexandru Patatics** is an artist living in Romania. His work has been exhibited widely since the early 1990s, including: *La Biennale di Venezia 48*, video-installation, *Insignificant Events*, Instituto Romeno di Ricerca e Cultura Umanistica, Venice (1999), *SEAFair'98*, Soros Center for Contemporary Arts - Skopje, Macedonia (1998), *ICC Biennial '97* Tokyo, Intercommunication Center, Japan (1997), *Ad Hoc - Romanian art today*, Ludwig Museum, Budapest (1997), *XXIII Sao Paulo Biennial*, Sao Paulo, Brazil (1996), *Unter Anderen - Among Others*, Gent, Belgium, Künstlerhaus, Dortmund, Germany (1995), *Spotkania Krakowskie - Krakowian Meetings*, BWA Contemporary Art Gallery, Krakow, Poland (1995), *Minima Media '94*, Medienbiennale Leipzig, Germany (1994), *Ex Oriente Lux*, first Romanian video installation exhibition, Dalles Halls, Bucharest, Romania (1993).

**®TMark** is a system of workers, ideas, and money whose function is to encourage the intelligent sabotage of mass-produced items. The projects that the ®TMark system helps fund are aesthetic or activist in their aims, rather than capitalist or strictly political, and tend to be relatively benign - they do not cause physical injury, and they do not fundamentally damage a product or a company's profits. This is not because product or profits are good, but because ®TMark is more likely to survive in the viciously jealous world of the American market if it is not seen as attempting to damage its hosts. ®TMark is essentially a matchmaker and bank, helping groups or individuals fund sabotage projects. Money provided by donors is held by ®TMark until project completion, and goes to the saboteur at that time; he or she can use it to find a new job or career, pay for lawyers, fund an avocation or a vacation, etc. Should the project not be completed, the funds are returned to the donor. The four keys to each ®TMark project are the worker, the

sponsor, the product, and the idea. ®TMark's entire purpose is to unite these four keys into projects.

**Redundant Technology Initiative (RTI)** is a group of artists who create using zero-cost computers. It was founded by James Wallbank.

**Rhizome** is a non-profit organization dedicated to fostering communication and community in the field of new media art.

**Florian Rötzer** lives in Munich and is currently working as editor at the on-line magazine *Telepolis* <http://www.heise.de/tp>. His last publication was *Digitale Weltentwürfe. Streifzüge durch die Netzkultur* (1998).

**Michael Samyn**, WWW designer, studied modern languages and applied graphics. He taught applied graphics and worked as a graphic artist until 1994, when he devoted himself exclusively to digital work. He has had exhibitions in Brussels, Gent, Amsterdam, Karlsruhe, and widely on the net.

**Dan Schiller** received his Ph.D. in Communications from the University of Pennsylvania in 1978. He has worked at the University of Leicester, Temple University, the University of California, Los Angeles and, for the past eight years, at the University of California, San Diego. He is the author of *Objectivity and the News* (1981), *Telematics and Government* (1982), and *Theorizing Communication* (1996). His forthcoming book - from which his talk at the symposium is derived - is provisionally called *Digital Capitalism*, and is to be published by MIT Press.

**Vivian Selbo** is a visual artist, designer, and information architect based in New York City. Her online artwork has appeared on the web sites of the Institute for Contemporary Art, London, Zentrum für Kunst und Medientechnologie, Karlsruhe, adaweb.com, and Slate.com, and is included in the permanent collection of The Museum of Modern Art, San Francisco. Selbo is a recipient of an "Emerging Artists/Emergent Medium" grant from the Walker Art Center and Jerome Foundation for 1999, and is a member of http://www.hell.com. She was the interface director of adaweb.com from 1996 to 1998.

**Paul Sylvester Sermon** was born in Oxford, England, studied Fine Art with Professor Roy Ascott at The University of Wales, from September 1985 to June 1988, and did a Post-graduate MFA (Master of Fine Arts) degree at The University of Reading, England, from Oct 1989 to June 1991. He was awarded the *Prix Ars Electronica* "Golden Nica," in the category of interactive art, for the hyper media installation *Think about the People now*, in Linz, Austria, September 1991. He worked as an Artist in Residence and produced the telematic video installation *Telematic Vision* at the Center for Art and Media (ZKM) in Karlsruhe, Germany, from February to November 1993 and received the "Sparkey" award from the *Interactive Media Festival* in Los Angeles, for the telematic video installation *Telematic Dreaming*, in June 1994.

**Jeffrey Shaw** pioneered the use of interactivity and virtuality in his many art installations. His works have been exhibited worldwide at major museums and festivals. For many years he lived in Amsterdam where he cofounded the Evenstructure Research Group (1969-80). Currently, Shaw is director of the Institute for Visual Media at the ZKM | Center for Art and Media Karlsruhe, Germany. He leads a unique research and production facility where artists and scientists work together developing profound artistic applications of the new media technologies.

**Alexej Shulgin** is a Moscow based artist, musician, curator, activist and professor. In his work he explores boundaries of art, culture and technology in their relation to 'real life' and vice versa. His favorite methods are mixing contexts and questioning the existing state of things.

**Christa Sommerer & Laurent Mignonneau** are artists and researchers at the ATR Advanced Telecommunications Research Lab (MIC) in Kyoto, Japan. Their field of study includes interactive computer installation, artificial life, complexity, communication, interface design and the convergence of art and science. They co edited *Art@Science* (Springer Verlag, 1998).

**Wolfgang Staehle** lives and works in New York City. From 1991 to the present he has directed the Thing Art Community

Network <www.thing.net>. His work has been exhibited at the Musee d'art Contemporain, Lyon, France (1999), *documentaX*, Kassel, Germany (1997), the Museum of Contemporary Art Saint-Gervais, Geneva, Switzerland (1996), *Ars Electronica* Linz (1994), the Centre Pompidou, Paris (1993).

**Niek van de Steeg** was born in Holland and has lived in France since 1985. In 1990, as a teacher he started to share his professional experiences with his students at the Art School of Lyon. His constructions by the means of exhibitions, publications (on and off-line) and group debate started in 1990 with the erection of the *Wind pavilion* (Pavilion à Vent) and the creation of the exhibition *Le Manège des Douze +* in his very big circular showroom, turning slowly around and around. The very last representation of this project was shown in the Nouveau Musée of Villeurbanne in France in 1993. Since that time he has worked on the Very Great Democratic Administration, which started with a show called *Début des Travaux* in the gallery Christine et Isy Brachot in Paris and ended in 1998 with a presentation in the gallery Art:Concept, Paris, called: *Défenses & Secrets, Fin des Travaux*. A kind of retrospective on this project, called *Inventaires et Restaurations* in Tarbes, France, from 26 November 1999 - 16 January 2000 is framing the whole project, represented by the tgad.com and vgda.com locations turning gently in orbit on the world wide web.

**Bernhard Sturm** works as operations engineer at the ZKM | Institute for Music and Acoustics since 1997.

**Syndicate** is Alexej Shulgin, Atle Barcley, the Blinkface (Klaus-Dieter Michel), intima virtual base (Igor Stromajer), Infozone (Jana Gebhart), Jaka Zeleznikar, John Duncan, Natalie Bookchin, Nebojsa Vilic, Olga Kumeger, Pigs of the Universe, Tamiko Thiel, Tiia Johannson, Tina LaPorta, Andrej Tiama, Trebor Scholz, Trevor Batten, Ventsislav Zankov, Zana Poliakov.

**Jake Tilson** is an artist working in London. As artist in residence (1994-96) at the Laboratory, Ruskin School of Drawing and Fine Art, he collaborated with Milo Hedge Limited at a time when the Internet first became a graphical medium. This led to Tilson developing a

whole new body of work embracing information technology including his website *The Cooker*. *The Cooker* was short-listed for the best designed website by Yellow Pages in 1996 and is featured in many Web design books such as *Browser* and *Cybertype 2*. He recently had a retrospective exhibition spanning twenty-years work at the Museo Internacional de Electrografia, Cuenca in Spain. The exhibition was funded by The British Council with support from Epson UK. Atlas has just published a compilation of his video works titled *Vulture Reality* and two new audio works. He taught in Communication Art & Design at the Royal College of Art until 1999 and has been a committee member for *The New Technologies Fund* at the Arts Council 1996-97. He has also been a judge for the *Creative Review* AKQA New Media Talent Awards for the past two years.

**Mark Trayle** studied composition with Robert Ashley, David Behrman, and David Rosenboom. His recent performances and installations have featured software instruments embodied as gramophones, tin cans, and digi-talismans. Trayle has performed in a variety of venues in the U.S. and Europe and was a featured performer at *New Music America '89*, Ars Electronica '94, *SoundArt 95* (Hannover, Germany), *ISEA 95* (Sixth International Symposium on Electronic Art), *Sonambiente Festival* (Berlin), *Le Festival de la Vallée des Terres Blanches* at the CICV Pierre Schaeffer (Herimoncourt, France, 1997) and many other festivals. He has received grants from Arts International and the National Endowment for the Arts, and has been an artist-in-residence at Mills College, STEIM (Amsterdam), and The Lab. He currently teaches Composition and New Media at the California Institute of the Arts. Trayle's work is available on the Artifact, Atavistic, Inial and Elektra/Nonesuch labels.

**Victoria Vesna** is an artist questioning, probing and exploring the possibilities of networked technologies. She is chair of the department of Design | Media Arts at UCLA School of the Arts. Her work has moved from performance and video installations to experimental research that connects networked environments to physical public spaces. Currently she is examining two critical aspects of knowledge acquisition as they relate to digital distribution: the importance of context in shaping knowledge transfer, and the role of social communication and collaboration in altering and enhancing knowledge production and assimilation. Vesna plans to demonstrate how distributed database identities are formed in her next work, *Building Communities of People With No Time*, a project involving design of an online environment utilizing agent technology, AI and information visualization.

**Immanuel Wallerstein** is Distinguished Professor of Sociology at Binghamton University (SUNY) and Director of the Fernand Braudel Center for the Study of Economies, Historical Systems, and Civilizations. He has published numerous books including: *Africa: The Politics of Unity* (1967), *The Capitalist World Economy* (1979), *Historical Capitalism* (1983), *Geopolitics and Geoculture: Essays on the Changing World Systems* (1991), *After Liberalism* (1995), *El Futuro de la Civilización Capitalista* (1997), and *Utopistics: Or, Historical Choices of the Twenty-First Century* (1998).

**Makoto Sei Watanabe** completed the masters program at the Yokohama National University. He joined the ISOZA-KI Arata Atelier and established the Architects's Office in 1894. He is Lecturer at the Graduate School of Yokohama National University, Kyoto Seika University, and Tokyo Denki University. His architectural projects include Aoyama Technical College, Building No. 1 (Shibuya, 1990), Iidabashi Station, No. 12, Tokyo Metropolitan Subway Line No. 12 (2000). He has been awarded the International Illumination Design Award, the iF Product Design Award, and the Mable Architectural Award.

**Peter Weibel** studied literature, medicine, logic, and philosophy in Paris and Vienna and wrote his thesis on mathematical logics. From 1976 to 1981 he was lecturer in the theory of form and, in 1981 Visiting Professor of Design and Art at the Vienna University of the Applied Arts and was Visiting Professor at the College of Art and Design in Halifax, Canada. In 1981 he was lecturer in Perception Theory and Professor of Photography at Gesamthochschule in Kassel. Since 1994 he has been Professor of Visual Media at the University of Applied Arts in Vienna and Associate Professor of Video and Digital Arts at the State University of New York at Buffalo. In 1989 he headed the Institut für Neue Medien at Städelschule in Frankfurt am Main. He was Artistic Director of *Ars Electronica* from 1986 until 1995. He is currently the Director of the ZKM in Karlsruhe. He has published numerous books on twentieth century art and technology.

**Maciej Wisniewski** is an artist whose work focuses on the underlying social implications of technology and the network. His recent works include *netomat*, <http://www.netomat.net> and *Turnstile 2* <http://www.stadiumweb.com/turnstile>. Wisniewski earned an M.F.A. at Hunter College, New York, and studied toward a Ph.D. program at the Institute for General Linguistics, University of Stockholm, Sweden.

**Xchange** is Raitis Smits, Rasa Smite, Maxim Narbrough, Martins Ratniks, Ervins Broks. Rasa Smite (Riga) and Raitis Smits (Riga) are media artists and net activists, the founders of the E-LAB media center in Riga (1996), initiators of the Riga Net.radio OZOne and XCHANGE Network (1997), editors and publishers of the *Acoustic.Space - net.audio* printed issue (1998, 1999). Maxim Narbrough (London-Riga) is media and sound artist, DJ at Backspace and OZOne Radio (since 1998), co-founder of project AURA - international net.radio ring (1998). Martins Ratniks (Riga) media, video and sound artist, member of E-LAB and Dj at OZOne Radio, (since 1997); he makes visual concept and design for Acoustic.Space publications (1998, 1999); works with digital video (VJing and video art) and is one of the F5 - digital video artists group (since 1998). Ervins Broks (Riga), digital video artist and VJ is co-founder and one of the digital video artists from the group F5 (founded in 1998).

**Jody Zellen** is an artist living in Los Angeles, California. Her web site *GHOST CITY* was in the 1999 *Siggraph TechnOasis Art Site*. It was also presented at the *Interactive Frictions Conference* in LA in 1999 and at IDCA 1999, was featured in the 1998 *LA Freewaves festival* and in the *6th Annual New York Digital Salon*, included in the festival *film+arc. graz 3* in Graz, Austria in 1997. Zellen has exhibited her work nationally and internationally including solo exhibitions at Jan Kesner Gallery (Los Angeles, 1998); Post Gallery, (Los Angeles, CA, 1998, 1997); Mesa College Art Gallery, (San Diego, CA, 1997); Richard Heller Gallery (Santa Monica, CA, 1996); SF Camerawork (San Francisco, CA, 1995); The Centre for Contemporary Photography, (Melbourne, Australia, 1995); and The Dorothy Goldeen Gallery (Santa Monica, CA, 1993). Her work has been published in the *The Architecture of Fear* (Edited by Nan Ellin, Princeton Architectural Press, 1997) as well as in publications including *Zyzzyva, Art Papers, New Observations, Frame-Work,* and *White Walls*. She is a recipient of a 1998 California Arts Council Grant and a 1997 Aaron Siskind Fellowship.

**Siegfried Zielinski** is the founding rector of the Kunsthochschule für Medien, Cologne. He studied Philosophy, Theatre Studies, German Philology, Political Sciences and Linguistics in Marburg and Berlin. He received his PhD in 1985, and his Habilitation in 1989. He worked in Media Studies at the Technical University, Berlin (1980-89), was professor for Audiovision at the University of Salzburg (1990-93), and has held the chair for Communication and Media Studies at the Kunsthochschule für Medien in Cologne since 1993. His research focuses on the theory and practice of audiovision, on integrated history, especially on the archaeology of technical imagination. His most recent book is *Audiovisions: Cinema and Television as Entre'acts in History* (Amsterdam University Press).

All projects produced by, copyright, and courtesy the artists with the exception of:

## Antoni Abad

Project: Antoni Abad.
Programming: Daniel Julià.
Graphic design: Eloy Pérez.
3D design: Armand López.
Co-produced by MECAD-Media Centre of Art and Design.

## Martine Aballéa

museum in progress/*steirischer herbst* in cooperation with Austrian Airlines.
supported by: gewista/europlakat and European Comission.
publisher: museum in progress, Fischerstiege 1, A-1010 Vienna, Austria.
curator: Hans-Ulrich Obrist, text: Vitus H. Weh, translation: Steve Gander
graphic design: Alexander Rendi, image processing: Vienna Paint, printed by: Graphische Kunstanstalt Otto Sares GmbH, Vienna
project concept: Kathrin Messner, Josef Ortner.
©museum in progress 1998.

## Roberto Aguirrezabala

Project, script and carrying-out: Roberto Aguirrezabala.
Programming: Pablo Zaballa.
Co-produced by MECAD - Media Centre of Art and Design.

## Giselle Beiguelman

Conception, Design and Production: Giselle Beiguelman.
Support: VITAE Foundation.

## David Blair

*WAXWEB* (copyright 1999, David Blair) is a hypermedia version of the film *WAX OR THE DISCOVERY OF TELEVISION AMONG THE BEES* (© 1991).
CD and ONLINE CREDITS:
Creative and technical authoring by David Blair.
The online version of *WAXWEB* has been hosted since 1994 by the Institute for Advanced Technology in the Humanities at the University of Virginia
http://www.iath.virginia.edu
This production has received support from The New York State Council for the Arts. Between 1995 and 1997, technical support (and inspiration for this final version) was provided by RACE Laboratory, at the University of Tokyo.

Japanese translation by Reiko Tochigi
An early version of Waxweb ran as a MOO, technically supported by Brown Univ. Graphics Lab students (Tom Meyer, Suzanne Hader, David Klaphaak, and others). Additional software for that version was provided by Eastgate Systems.
Additional assistance Melynda Barnhardt.
A number of artists contributed texts to the MOO, (not included here) Jane Douglas, Stuart Moulthrop, Ligorano/Reese, Terese Svoboda, and Jalal Toufic; and I also wish to thank all other networked participants.
Cover and icon graphics by Florence Ormezzano.
My special thanks to Florence.

## Dave Bruckmayr/Gaylord Aulke

Idea & Concept: Dave Bruckmayr.
Technical Solution: Gaylord Aulke.
Website Design: Sabin Aell.
Sponsored by agi business media productions gmbh.

## Critical Art Ensemble

CoNE is a project by Critical Art Ensemble, Faith Wilding, and Paul Vanouse.

## Claude Closky

*12 heures = 10 heures*, (1994 -1998) Courtesy Frac Languedoc-Roussillon.
*Do you want love or lust?*, (1997) Courtesy Dia Center for the Arts.

## Janet Cohen, Keith Frank, and Jon Ippolito

*The Unreliable Archivist*, 1998, commissioned by Gallery 9/Walker Art Center Courtesy Gallery9/Walker Art Center.

## Nicolas Collins

Instrumental music performed by Kammerensemble Neue Musik Berlin. Furniture provided by the SWR.

## Shane Cooper

Sabine Hirtes (lead modeller); Dirk Heesakker (remote control construction); Christina Zartmann (modelling and documentation); Jeffrey Shaw (management, guidance and ideas); Bernd Lintermann (guidance and ideas); Annika Blunk (management and ideas); Jan Gerigk (management and ideas); Torsten Ziegler (networking and equipment); Manfred Hauffen (networking); Torsten Belschner (audio equipment); Matthias Gommel (design); Kai Richter (design); Nicole

Weber (ideas and support); Allen and Sue Cooper (support).

## Vuk Cosic

*Instant ASCII Camera* project by Vuk Cosic.
Programming by Luka Frelih.
Hardware by Borja Jelic.
Produced at Ljubljana Digital Media Lab.
web site:
http://www.vuk.org/ascii/camera/

## Jordan Crandall

Produced with the assistance of Neue Galerie am Landesmuseum Joanneum, Graz, and ZKM | Center for Art and Media, Karlsruhe. Additional support provided by Eyebeam Atelier and Filmmakers Collaborative, New York.
Film transfers provided by Film and Video Arts, New York. Camera: Jeff Woods Assistant Camera/Gaffer: Jeremy Mather Production Assistant: Ole Schell Actors: Laurie Bulman and Christopher Reed Animations: Brian Hoffer Special thanks to: Peter Weibel, Robert Gold, Beth Rosenberg, John Johnson, Claire Davis, David Beatrice, David Ebmeier, and Sandra Gering.
DVD production by Zuma Digital, New York.

## Douglas Davis

Commissioned by the Lehman College Art Gallery, New York City, for the exhibition InterActions, 1967-1981. Critical sponsors and collaborators include Susan Hoeltzel, director of the Gallery, Robert Schneider, Prof. of Mathematics, and Gary Welz, co-designer of the website. The Sentence was purchased in 1995 by Barbara and Eugene M. Schwartz and given to the Whitney Museum of American Art in 1996.

## Ken Feingold

Software Architecture and Direction: Gideon May, Ken Feingold.
Software Developers:
Visual programming and speech synthesis: Gideon May.
Speech Recognition: Adolf Mathias.
ForceFeedback Joystick Server: Andreas Schiffler, Timo Fleisch.
AI development: Boriana Koleva, Ken Feingold, based on code by Duane Fields.
Embedded applications: Ken Feingold.
Software testing and implementation: Ken Feingold.
Hardware developers: Joachim Hund, H.

Carl Ott, Armin Steinke, Ken Feingold.
Production Managers: Sally Jane
Norman, Heike Staff.
Production Staff: Jan Gerigk, Torsten
Ziegler.
Partners: Developed in collaboration
with ZKM|Institute for Visual Media and
i3net (European Network for Intelligent
Information Interfaces).
Date: 1993 - present; (collaboration with
i3/ZKM: 1998-1999).
courtesy: Postmasters Gallery, New York
All images except for installation shots ©
and courtesy Ken Feingold 1999.

**Holger Friese**
artists: Holger Friese/Max Kossatz.
Courtesy of Sammlung Hanelore und
Hans Dieter Huber, Leipzig.

**Masaki Fujihata**
and Takeshi Kawashima:
*Nuzzle Afar* 1998: Internetversion 1999.
Assistant: Taka Furuhashi.
Realised at the ZKM|Institute for Visual
Media.
EU-Project eSCAPE (Esprit Projekt 25377)
*Impressing Velocity*, 1994 - 1999:
Programmer: Harald Kucharek.
Technological Assistants: Jun Homma,
Takeshi Kawashima.
Assistants: Taka Furuhashi, Yuka Wake.
Produced at ZKM|Institute for Visual
Media
Train set courtesy Märklin.

**Jochen Gerz**
Lawrence Rinder, BAM/PFA, Curator for
Twentieth Century Art and Assistant
Director for Programs.
Richard Rinehart, BAM/PFA, Information
Systems Manager/Web Manager.
Rainer Krause, DIE FARM, Bremen,
Germany.
Esther Shalev-Gerz Photographs of
Delphi.
Regina Wyrwoll, Goethe Institut, Munich,
Germany.

**Johannes Goebel, Torsten
Belschner, Bernhard Sturm**
Thanks to Kerstin Jaunich.

**Ken Goldberg**
Thanks to Catharine Clark, Adam Jacobs
and Andrew Ludkey.

**Steven Greenwood**
sponsored by Pfaff AG.
Programming: Bernd Müller.

**Marina Grzinic and Aina Smid**
The net.art.archive site specific media -
video installation project consists of video-
film images taken from two video works
by Grzinic and Smid: *Post-socialim +
IRWIN* from 1997 and *On the Flies of
the Market Place* from 1999. Besides this
the net.art.archive project consists of
www net art project with texts and images scanned, copied, redone from magazines, encyclopedias, books that were
part of the ideological, political and social space of the once known state
Yugoslavia. All these materials, the www,
theory, videos are perceived huge archives. The text written by Grzinic as part of
the www site reflects the importance of
the archive, the construction of the archive and the relations of power in the archive itself and among other archives.
Collaborators: Uros Parazajda (programmer, ZRC SAZU, Ljubljana); Joze Slacek
(technical advisor, Maribor).

**Lynn Hershman**
Assistant Producer: Lisa Diener.
BBU Fabrication and Design: Casino
Container, Uwe Wagner.
Screen Saver: Marine Macerot.
Web Designer: Jarrod Sartain, Morgan
Thomas.
Screen Saver Coding: Kim Nguyen.
Custom Software Design: Construct
Internet Design.
Mark Lawton - CyberArchitect.
Lior Saar - Programmer VRML.
James Waldrop - PROGRAMMER.
Additional Coding - Ted Williams.
Special Thanks to Lisa Goldman, Hans
Peter Schwarz.

**Markus Huemer**
AVL-Gate, *steirischer herbst 99*: Courtesy
Galerie Michael Janssen, Köln.
Credits: Kunsthochschule für Medien,
Kunst und Medienwissenschaften,
Cologne; Land Oberösterreich, Linz;
David Larcher; Sven Mann; Martin
Nawrath; Rudolf Opalla; Heike Tekampe;
Siegfried Zielinski.
ZKM: Courtesy Galerie Michael Janssen,
Cologne.
Credits: Österreichische Botschaft, Bonn;
Österreichisches Bundeskanzleramt,
Vienna; Thomas Donga; Michael Kockot;
Stefanie-Vera Kockot; Kunsthochschule für
Medien, Kunst und Medienwissenschaf-
ten, Cologne; Land Oberösterreich, Linz;
Sven Mann; Grid Neuber; Rudolf Opalla;
Jo Seiler; Stadt Linz; Heike Tekampe;
Max von Velsen; Peter Weibel; Siegfried

Zielinski.
*Art and Global Media* ICC(Magazin):
Courtesy Galerie Michael Janssen,
Cologne. Kunsthochschule für Medien,
Kunst und Medienwissenschaften,
Cologne; Siegfried Zielinski.

**h|u|m|b|o|t**
Thanks to: Goethe-Institute Caracas, ZKM,
Karlsruhe; Brigitte Schenk Cologne; Axel
Wirths, MedienKunstRaum, Kunst- und
Ausstellungshalle der BRD, Bonn;
Universitätsbibliothek Karlsruhe;
Staatsbibliothek zu Berlin - Preußischer
Kulturbesitz Handschriftenabteilung and
Kartenabteilung; Geodätisches Institut der
Universität Karlsruhe; Badische
Landesbibliothek.

**I/O/D**
Simon Pope, Colin Green, Matthew Fuller

**Ricardo Iglesias**
Produced by MECAD-Media Centre of Art
and Design.

**JODI**
http://ctrl-space.jodi.org
sp.3Xial ThnX-2 bAtO & C3.hu.

**Knowbotic Research**
in collaboration with Maurizio Lazzarato,
Luther Blisset, Michael Hardt, Hans Ulrich
Reck, Enzo Rullani, Iaia Vantaggiato.
Produced with ZKM Karlsruhe (eSCAPE)
and KHM Cologne.
Software: Detlev Schwabe, Andreas
Schiffler, KR+cF, Andreas Weymer.
Imstallation: KR+cF, Peter Sandbichler.
Large Surface Magnetic Force Feedback
Technology by ZKM.
Interface: loan from Förderkreis des
Wilhelm Lehmbruck Museums e.V.

**Konsum Art.Server (Margarete
Jahrmann/Max Moswitzer)**
Concept und Gamecontent, symbolic
Multiuser geometry: margarete jahrmann.
Interactive programming, Serversite setup,
Multiuserdesign: max moswitzer.

**Darij Kreuh**
Sound construction: Rainer Linz.
Software programming: Iztok Bajec.

**Marc Lafia**
Direction, concept, story, images, design,
interface: Marc Lafia.
Story, images, design, play mechanics,
code: Gabriella Marks.
Story, design: Mark Meadows.

**Lev Manovich**
Projects directors: Lev Manovich and Norman Klein.

**Jenny Marketou**
Produced in co-production with the Banff Centre for the Arts, Banff, Alberta, Canada.
© Jenny Marketou, 1998. All rights reserved.
Sponsored by the Ministry of Culture, Division of Fine Arts, Greece;
*XXIV Biennial De Sao Paulo*, Brazil, 1998.
executive producer: television and new media, Sara Diamond.
computer facilitator: Rhonda Jessen.
senior artist: Jerry Barenholtz.
smellbytes programmers: Ryan Johston and Scott Wilson.
smellbytes Identity: Frazione Di Tempo (fdt design), NY.
smellbytes Version II, 1999 Dynamic HTML programmer: Clara Kent.
Chris.053 Fan Club Version II, 1999 CGI/Perl programmer: Aaron Ellis.
Design and Consultance: Frazione Di Tempo (fdt design), NY.
Acknowledgements:
Chris.053 persona is based on the character of Jean-Baptiste Grenouille, in *Perfume* by Patrick Süskind.

**Chihiro Minato**
Cooperation: Shiho Haruta, Shozo Kuze.

**Mongrel**
all credits Mongrel exept Natural Selection which is edited by Matthew Fuller and Harwood for Mongrel.

**mikro e.V.** and **convex tv**
Net.radio days '99 organised by mikro e.V. and convex tv in collaboration with Martin Conrads, Ulrich Gutmair, Stefan Schreck and Pit Schultz.
Projects and content for net.radio days see http://www.art-bag.net/2000years/schedule.html

**Randall Packer**
in collaboration with Tony Le, programmer.
Special thanks to Eric Soroos, Tom Holub, and Weizhu Liang for technical support, Department of Art Practice at UC Berkeley, and the on-line participants of the TeleCollective who generated the manifesto.

**Alexandru Patatics**
Programmers : Alexandru Patatics, Nelu Oprea, Honoriu Bonaciu.
Hardware developers : Dan Ungureanu.
Developed in collaboration with : ICC Tokyo, ZKM Karlsruhe.
Produced at ZKM|Institute for Visual Media.

**Rhizome**
Mark Tribe and Alex Galloway, with Java programing by Martin Wattenberg.

**Redundant Technology Initiative**
James Wallbank (Coordinator, Artistic Director).
Richard Siddall (Administration).
Alex Atkin (Technical Support).
Tony Goddard (Programming).
Other RTI participants who've made valuable contributions:
Ed Nauen, Lisa Kaige, Graham Gatheral & many others.

**Vivian Selbo**
*Killer @pp: It's @ll talk*, 1998 (courtesy SUN/ICA New Media Centre, London).
*Vertical Blanking Interval*, 1997 (courtesy Walker Art Center, Minneapolis).
*Enclosed Caption Viewing*, 1996 (courtesy Slate.com).

**Paul Sermon**
An adaptation of: "The Tables Turned. An Evening Scene on the Same Subject."
From the 1798 edition of the Lyrical Ballads by William Wordsworth.
With special thanks to Timothy Druckrey for text adaptation.

**Jeffrey Shaw**
*The Distributed Legible City*
Concept: Jeffrey Shaw; Text: Dirk Groeneveld; Database Software: Gideon May; Application Software: Steve Pettifer & Adrian West (University of Manchester), Adolf Mathias & Andreas Schiffler (ZKM); Hardware: Armin Steinke and Ulrich Weltner; Cooperation: University of Manchester and ZKM Institute for Visual Media within the EU project eSCAPE (Esprit project 25377).
*The Net.Art Browser*
Concept: Jeffrey Shaw; Application Software: Frank Fischer (DHF Gesellschaft für Datenverarbeitung, Karlsruhe), Jürgen Enge (ZKM); Hardware: Bossinade Lightworks & Huib Nelissen Dekorbouw; Curator: Benjamin Weil; Produced by the ZKM.

**Alexej Shulgin**
FUFME, Inc.

**Alexej Shulgin/Natalie Bookchin**
*Introduction to Net.art*
Stoneversion provided by Blank & Jeron derived from http://sero.org/dyt/

**Christa Sommerer & Laurent Mignonneau**
© 1999, Christa Sommerer & Laurent Mignonneau.
developed for the CARTIER Foundation, Paris.
http://www.fondation.cartier.fr/verbarium.html

**Niek van de Steeg**
Niek van de Steeg, David Affagard for the web site, Ludovic Chémarin technical support, Tineke van Aalzum paper printing and construction sealing paper.
courtesy: Gallery Art: Concept, Paris, France.
Created for the *net_condition* show September 1999.

**Syndicate**
Alexej Shulgin, Atle Barcley, the Blinkface (Klaus-Dieter Michel), intima virtual base (Igor Stromajer), Infozone (Jana Gebhart), Jaka Zeleznikar, John Duncan, Natalie Bookchin, Nebojsa Vilic, Olga Kumeger, Pigs of the Universe, Tamiko Thiel, Tiia Johannson, Tina LaPorta, Andrej Tiama, Trebor Scholz, Trevor Batten, Ventsislav Zankov, Zana Poliakov.

**Mark Trayle**
Phil Burke, author of JSyn software synthesis package for Java.

**Victoria Vesna**
Concept and Aesthetic: Victoria Vesna.
html authoring: Robert Nideffer.
VRML programming: Nathan Freitas.

**Makoto Sei Watanabe**
Directed and Designed by Makoto Sei Watanabe.
Assisted by Hiroya Tanaka, Ryujiro Yano, Yasuhiro Nakano.
Supported by Virtual Reality Center Yokohama, Inc. Japan.

**ZKM-Online:**
Concept, programming: Tom Fürstner.
Web design: Lydia Lindner.
Programming: Arne Gräßer.
Text and programming: Christoph Pingel.

A publication by MIT Press, steirischer herbst, Graz and ZKM|Center for Art and Media Karlsruhe of the exhibitions *art and global media* and *net_condition* 1998-99 curated by Peter Weibel.

Editors: Peter Weibel, Timothy Druckrey

Editorial Assistants: Sabine Himmelsbach, Barbara Filser, Andrea Helbach

Designer: Christian Chruxin, Berlin
Assistants: Holger Jost, Zwetana Penova

Photography Credits:
Unless indicated below all photographs of the exhibition *net_condition* in Karlsruhe are courtesy of Franz Wamhof, photographs of the exhibition *net_condition* in Graz are courtesy of Jens Preusse, photographs of the exhibition *net_condition* in Barcelona are courtesy of MECAD, photographs of the exhibition *net_condition* in Tokyo are courtesy of Toshihiko Hazama; screenshots by the artists.
Cinematic Conditions: Capi Films, Paris; Europese Stichting Joris Ivens, Nijmegen; Centre Georges Pompidou, MNAM/CCI, Paris; steirischer herbst, Graz; Constant, Bruxelles; ISKRA, Arcueil; Harun Farocki Filmproduction, Berlin; Backgroundimage: Max Film, Munich.
Broadcast Conditions: Bundesministerium für Unterricht und Kunst, Vienna; TIV - True Image Vision, Vienna; ISKRA, Arcueil; Backgroundimage: Peter Fend/XXkunstkabel, Graz.

Cover: image by Konsum Art.Server (Margarete Jahrmann/Max Moswitzer, 1999)

Translations by: Richard Watts
Gloria Custance, David Hudson, Lisa Rosenblatt, Nikolaus Schneider, Astrid Sommer

This book was printed and bound in Karlsruhe by Engelhardt & Bauer.

Library of Congress Card Number: 00-106775
net_condition. art and global media,
edited by Peter Weibel and Timothy Druckrey

ISBN 0-262-73138-X
© 2001 Massachusetts Institute of Technology

All rights reserved. No part of this book may be reproduced in any form by any electronic or mechanical means (including photocopying, recording, or information storage and retrieval) without permission in writing from the publisher.
Individual texts are copyrighted by the respective authors.

A book about the net is a book about collaborations and logistics. The net_condition is a special case of collaboration and work across many borders. It documents an exhibition, film program, and symposia in Graz 1998, and exhibitions 1999 in Barcelona, Graz, Karlsruhe, and Tokyo in 1999, and involves artists and writers in numerous countries. It was conceptualized in meetings in Karlsruhe, Berlin, Graz and in voluminous e-mails within a team who understand that this new electronic environment is traversed in a special combination of productive communication, organized planning, and tireless efficiency.

From the start, steirischer herbst festival director Christine Frisinghelli, provided the productive foundation for both the art and global media and the net_condition projects in Graz. The steirischer herbst team, Alexandra Foitl, Sabine Himmelsbach, Daniela Olotu-Goettfried, Peter Peer, and Ruth Kümmel, provided guidance, support, and materials with extraordinary proficiency. The translator in Graz, Richard Watts, also did an exceptional job in sustaining consistency and maintaining the diverse voices of the texts.

At ZKM, Sabine Himmelsbach, Barbara Filser, and Andrea Helbach created a great working environment. They seamlessly managed the flow of information, juggled the details, gathered facts, organized details, shared their offices, met at any and all hours, offered innumerable - and invaluable - insights, and maintained both their cool and their senses of humor. Margit Rosen provided continuous support and constantly juggled the schedules of the editors to insure that there would be ample time to talk - and think - about the book. In Berlin (where the book was designed) Zwetana Penova adapted with great skill to work that had already begun and provided a direct link with our designer Christian Chruxin who built a design framework that avoided oversimplification and understood that many layers of meaning could find metaphors on the printed page. At MIT Press, Roger Conover confirmed his flexibility, patience, and thoughtfulness in support of a complex project.

In the end, a book like this engages a broad array of artists and writers. Their contributions to the symposia, exhibitions, and book are exemplary, and demonstrate their continuing commitment to reasoned, critical, and creative interventions. Their acumen and ingenuity are ample evidence that the dot.com industry has found its match in the net.art community.